NEHRU

THE FIRST SIXTY YEARS

Nehru

THE FIRST SIXTY YEARS

Presenting in his own words the
development of the political thought
of Jawaharlal Nehru and the
background against
which it evolved

Including significant passages from
Nehru's writings, speeches, statements
before the court, press conferences,
conversations, interviews and other
documents, up to the founding of
the Republic of India, 1950

*Selected and edited, with introductory, historical
and other interpretative commentary by*
DOROTHY NORMAN

with a foreword by
JAWAHARLAL NEHRU

VOLUME TWO

THE JOHN DAY COMPANY
NEW YORK

O8709

First published 1965 by The Bodley Head Ltd, London
Published by
The John Day Company Inc.
62 West 45th Street, New York, N.Y. 10036
Printed and bound in Great Britain

CONTENTS OF VOLUME TWO

Map of India after Partition, *x–xi*

PART SIX

1940–1941

1. On U.S. Understanding of India—From Five Letters—What of Russia Now? The Russo-German Pact and the Russo-Finnish War, *3*

2. Constituent Assembly—Congress and the War—World War II Developments—Congress and Non-Violence—Related Problems, *18*

3. Resumé of Developments: World War II (Summer, 1940), *27*

4. Fresh Congress Offer—Viceroy's August 8 Statement—Reactions to Statement—Bombay Congress Meetings, 1940, *33*

5. Individual Satyagraha—Eighth Arrest—Letter from Gandhi—Statement at Trial, November, 1940—Letters from Jail—Interruption of Work of National Planning Committee, *42*

6. Eastern Federation—India, China, Asia, *50*

7. World War II Developments, 1941: Atlantic Charter—Evolution of U.S. and British Policy Toward India, *53*

8. Tagore and Gandhi—Letter from Jail—Release from Prison, *55*

9. Statements after Release from Prison, 1941, *62*

PART SEVEN

1942

1. Military Situation and Developments in East—International and Domestic Issues, *71*

2. Visit to India of Madame and General Chiang Kai-shek—U.S. and Chinese Efforts in Behalf of Indian Freedom, *75*

3. The Cripps Mission—Congress Resolution Concerning Mission—Breakdown of Mission—Roosevelt's Efforts to Avert Breakdown—Further Statements, *79*

4. Post-Cripps Mission Period—Congress Resolution on Possible Invasion of India—India's Day of Reckoning—Other Statements of the Period—Press Interview, July, *96*

5. India and China, *112*

a*   v

6. Quit India Movement, Summer, 1942—Comments on Quit India Resolution—Ninth Prison Sentence—Consequences of Movement and Jailing of Congress Leaders—British Statements—Further U.S. Interest in Indian Independence—*The Discovery of India*—Afterthoughts on August, 1942 Struggle—Jinnah and the Muslim League —India's Communists—Letters from Jail, *117*

PART EIGHT

1943–1945

1. The War, 1943—Phillips-Roosevelt Efforts in Behalf of Indian Freedom—Famine, *135*

2. Reveries in Jail, *140*

3. Industrialization in India—Religion, Philosophy and Science— *The Discovery of India*—Letters from Jail, *143*

4. Further Course of World Events, 1944–1945: End of War in Europe —Fresh British Proposals—After Prison, 1945—Pious Platitudes, *161*

5. The Simla Conference, June, 1945—Statements on Other Matters, Summer, 1945, *165*

6. End of World War II—Fresh Examination of "Indian Problem"— For an Undivided, Progressive India—Britain's Decision to Convene Constitution-Making Body for India, and to Create Representative Executive Council, *168*

7. The Indian National Army and Military Disaffection, *173*

8. Dialogue with Gandhi—Message to Youth of Ceylon—Anti-National Policy of Communist Party of India—End of 1945, *177*

9. On Development of Indian Literature as a Uniting Force, Address at P.E.N. Symposium, 1945, *186*

PART NINE

1946: Year of Decision

1. Developments, Early 1946: Cross-Section of Statements, *195*

2. Mounting Tensions: Naval Mutiny—Acts of Violence in Bombay and Related Problems—Announcement of 1946 Cabinet Mission, *201*

3. Reactions to Cabinet Mission Proposals—Colonialism Must Go— India and the Future, *206*

4. Publication of *The Discovery of India*—Trip to South-East Asia— First Meeting with Lord and Lady Mountbatten—Statements on Return to India, April, *217*

5. Clarification of Purpose of Cabinet Mission—Arrival of Mission in India, *223*

6. Simla Conference Proposals—Mission's Further Offer, and Failure of Conference—The Princes: General Congress-League Controversies, *225*

7. Cabinet Mission's Own Plan, May 16—Formation of Interim Government, *230*

8. Cabinet Mission's and Viceroy's June 16 Statement—Journey to Kashmir—Congress and Muslim League Reactions to Britain's Proposals—Speech to Congress, July 7, *232*

9. Muslim League Reactions to Cabinet Mission Plans and Congress Position—July 10 Press Conference—Criticism of Statements at Conference—Speech of July 22, *235*

10. Summer, 1946, *242*

11. The Interim Government—Reactions to Communal Riots, August, *247*

12. Congress-League Controversy, October—Letters to Jinnah—Correspondence with Wavell, *254*

13. Of Subjects other than the Impending Independence of India: Statements at Time of Arrest in Kashmir, on Atomic Bomb, Racial Issues, Foreign Policy, Food Situation, African Aspirations, Communalism (Summer-Autumn, 1946), *263*

14. Congress-Muslim League Tensions, November, *273*

15. London Conference, December—Creation of Constituent Assembly, *275*

16. After Return from London: Resolution Concerning Independent Sovereign Republic, *278*

17. Appointment of Lord Mountbatten as Viceroy, *287*

PART TEN

Year of Independence: 1947

1. Upheaval and Transition—Of Gandhi and Difficulties within Congress, *291*

2. Congress Resolution—Mountbatten Accepts Invitation to Become Viceroy—Constituent Assembly Acceptance of Objectives Resolution, *294*

3. Attlee's February 20 Statement—From Letters to Gandhi—Jinnah's Decision to Cooperate with Congress: Proposal to Divide the Punjab—On the Punjab, *303*

4. Inter-Asian Relations Conference, *309*

5. Mountbatten's Arrival in India and Subsequent Developments, March–April, *316*

6. Developments, May 18–June 2—The Mountbatten Plan, *320*

7. Acceptance of Mountbatten Plan—Commonwealth Relations and Dominion Status, *325*

8. Indian Independence Act—Problem of Princely States and Patel's Role in Integrating Them, *329*

9. On the Eve of Freedom—Independence: Creation of Pakistan, *333*

10. In the Wake of Independence, *341*

11. The Tragedy of Kashmir, *345*

12. Hyderabad—India's Foreign Policy—"The Universities Have Much to Teach", *353*

PART ELEVEN

1948

1. January, 1948, *363*

2. Assassination of Gandhi, *363*

3. Kashmir Developments: January, *375*

4. Economic Policy—Foreign Policy, *379*

5. Launching of S.S. *Jala-Usha* (first ocean-going steamer made in India): March 14, *387*

6. Kashmir Developments—March, April, *389*

7. Current Dilemmas, *398*

8. Economic Freedom for Asia, *402*

9. Kashmir: Further Statement, Summer, 1948, *407*

10. Departure of Lord and Lady Mountbatten—On Partition—Socialism and Communism, *410*

11. Commonwealth Relations—European Trip—Last Lap of Our Journey, *414*

12. Hyderabad—Kashmir, *433*

13. Of the Father of the Nation, *443*

PART TWELVE

1949–1950: To The Founding of the Republic of India—January 26, 1950

1. Eighteen Nations Conference—Emergence of India in World Affairs, *449*

2. Foreign Policy—India and the Commonwealth, *460*
3. Independence Day, 1949, *486*
4. First Visit to United States of America, *490*
5. Miscellany: End of 1949, Early 1950, *516*
6. Indo-Pakistan Relations, *526*
7. Sages of India, *530*
8. 1950—Republic Day, January 26, *536*
9. Postscript: "Changing India", *538*

Appendix, *543*
Glossary, *577*
Bibliography, *583*
Index, *589*

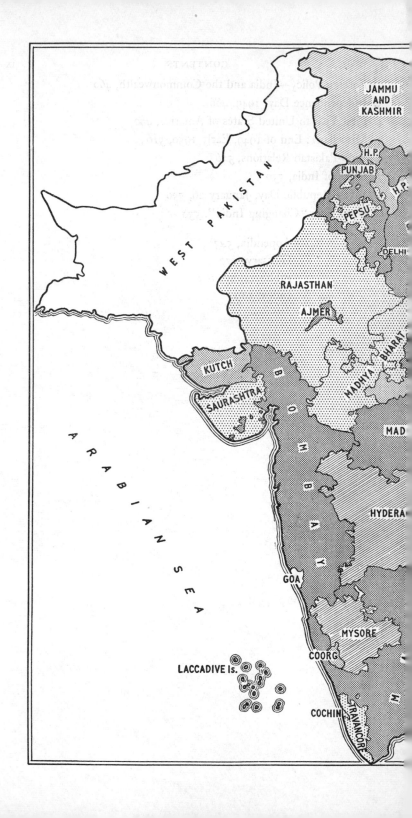

JAMMU
AND
KASHMIR

WEST PAKISTAN

H.P.

PUNJAB

H.P.

PEPSU

DELHI

RAJASTHAN

AJMER

KUTCH

BHARAT

MADHYA

MAD

B
O
M
B
A
Y

SAURASHTRA

ARABIAN SEA

HYDERA

GOA

MYSORE

COORG

LACCADIVE Is.

M

COCHIN

TRAVANCORE

INDIA
AFTER PARTITION

KEY

H.P.	HIMACHAL PRADESH
P.E.P.S.U.	PATIALA AND EAST PUNJAB STATES UNION
	UNIONS OF STATES
	STATES REMAINING AS SEPARATE UNITS
	GOVERNOR'S STATES
	CENTRALLY ADMINISTERED AREAS
	FOREIGN POSSESSIONS

NEPAL

SIKKIM

BHUTAN

ASSAM

RADESH

BIHAR

HYA PRADESH

MANIPUR

E. PAKISTAN

TRIPURA

W. BENGAL

BURMA

DESH

ORISSA

AS

B A Y

O F

B E N G A L

ANDAMAN Is.

NICOBAR Is.

ON

Government of India

[After Fall of Paris—1940.] I think the British Government must be feeling sorry today for having treated India in the manner in which they have. . . . If India were a free country today, it would have made a great difference in the present circumstances. . . . Even if the British Government [wins] the war British Imperialism [will] never live.[1]

*

[October, 1940.] The war has made it clear that smaller nations cannot exist as separate entities. . . . It [is] difficult even for the greater nations to claim a separate existence or to command wide empires.[2]

[1] I.A.A., p. 89.
[2] Ibid., p. 91.

PART SIX
1940–1941

I

On U.S. Understanding of India—From Five Letters—What of Russia Now? The Russo–German Pact and the Russo–Finnish War

[Nehru continued to assert that he would favor joining the war effort if India were to be granted her freedom and thus the right to make her own decisions. He consistently attempted, throughout the war years, to clarify Congress' position concerning international and domestic issues, both for foreign readers and the Indian people. He often found it necessary to indicate that his own views and those of Congress were by no means invariably identical. Nor did his ideas always coincide with those of Gandhi.

It should be noted, however, in conjunction with World War II, that even when the majority of other Congress leaders were moved to back the war effort, they too found it impossible to do so because of Britain's attitude with respect to their own aspirations toward freedom.]

A Note on U.S. Understanding of India—January 6, 1940

It is right and proper . . . that what happens in India should attract attention in the United States of America and that they should seek to understand India's problems in relation to the world, for on them ultimately will fall the burden of the future, whether they will it or not. Their great material resources and dominating position in the world have cast this burden on them today, but even more so has this responsibility been cast upon them because of their leadership of the forces of democracy. If, in the words of President Roosevelt, the American people are going to "keep ablaze the flames of human liberty, reason, democracy, and fair play," they will have to throw their weight on the side of liberty and democracy in other parts of the world also, so that out of present-day chaos and violence, real peace and freedom might emerge. Peace is indivisible, it has been said; so is freedom, and there will be no enduring equilibrium unless it spans the world and is based on peace and freedom.

3

As India has grown in strength and self-reliance and approached the gates of freedom, she has thought of herself more and more as a part of a larger order, and has considered her own problem as a part of the world problem.[1]

From Five Letters

I. [To Edward Thompson[2]—January 5, 1940.] For various reasons I should very much like to go to England and possibly to America. I always feel that I can be of more use to India outside India. The feeling that I do not quite fit in here, pursues me and depresses me.[3]

II. [To J. Holmes Smith[4]—Meerut, January 10, 1940.] I have welcomed your great enthusiasm for the cause of Indian freedom and your desire to do something to advance this cause in the U.S.A. . . . . While we fully realise that the struggle for Indian freedom will have to be carried on and won in India itself, we value very greatly the good opinion and sympathy of the people of America. In the world today they represent the most powerful democracy, and they will no doubt play a dominating part in the re-shaping of world affairs. As we are ourselves devoted and committed to the ideal of a democratic free State in India we naturally look to America in many ways. It seems to me obvious that there can be no proper settlement of the world's problems unless India and China are also included in this settlement and are treated as free nations. Naturally we demand independence for ourselves. But we have made it clear that we stand for a new world order and India will gladly cooperate in such fashioning of the world's affairs. This can only be satisfactorily done on the basis of peace, freedom and democracy. Therefore it becomes essential that India and China should have freedom and democracy. Otherwise there will be no satisfactory political or economic settlement and the present want of equilibrium and conflict will continue. It is obvious that the tremendous resources, both actual and potential, of India and China must play an important part in the world's affairs.

[1] U.I., pp. 357–58.
[2] Edward Thompson, author of many books on Indian history. Scholar, lecturer at Oxford University. Had long career in India as professor.
[3] B.O.L., p. 421.
[4] J. Holmes Smith, Methodist minister. Was asked to leave India in 1940 because of his affiliation with the independence movement. Later returned to India to run an Ashram.

For the present we have to concentrate on India's freedom but we try to view this in the wider perspective of the world, and inevitably in doing so we think of America.

You know the attitude that we have taken up in regard to the European war. We have always been opposed to the Fascist and Nazi doctrine and have condemned all aggression. If we had been sure that the present war was a conflict between freedom on the one side and Nazism on the other, we would gladly have thrown our weight on the side of freedom. But the invitation we issued to the British Government for a statement of war aims and for the treatment of India as a free country met with a rebuff and it was made clear to us that this war was essentially meant for the preservation of British imperialism. For this objective we cannot agree to the utilisation of our men and resources. If we are against Nazism, we are also against imperialism. This war, as it is at present waged, seems to us a conflict between rival imperialisms and we can be no party to it unless it is made clear that the objective is freedom and democracy. That can only be made clear by the treatment accorded to India. Our demand is a simple one, though it raises fundamental issues. We want the declaration of Indian independence and the recognition of the right of the Indian people to frame [their] constitution through a Constituent Assembly without any interference from outside. If this is done, we feel that the whole fabric of British imperialism, as well as other imperialisms, will undergo a vital change and imperialism itself will be liquidated.[1]

III. [To Gandhi—January 24, 1940.] I have no doubt in my own mind that Russia has acted very wrongly in regard to Finland[2] and she will suffer because of this. But what concerns us even more is the fact that behind the Anglo-French-German war, what is really happening is a consolidation of the imperialist and Fascist power to fight Russia. It is clearer now than it was even before that the war is a purely imperialist venture on both sides. Fine phrases are being used by politicians as they were used in 1914. It seems to me highly important and vital that we should not be taken in by these phrases and pious protestations. All this has an intimate bearing on our own position in India and any talks with the British Government. The object of the Government is to gain our goodwill for their war. Under existing circumstances, quite apart even from the question of India, I do not see why we should give our moral support to an imperialist war. Of course if Britain changed her attitude

[1] Ibid., pp. 422–23.
[2] Russia had invaded Finland on November 30, 1939.

radically towards India and acknowledged our independence that in itself would mean that her imperialism has undergone a vital change. But what is more likely to happen is that this imperialism will fundamentally continue and the war will continue to be waged for its sake, though under stress of circumstances some vague declarations are made in regard to India. Even these declarations, it will be said, will be honoured at the end of the war. This seems to me a very dangerous position for us as we shall be involved, whether we want it or not, in supporting British imperialist policy in all manner of nefarious undertakings. I feel, therefore, that we must be very cautious and wary and should make it perfectly clear that we are not going to support these imperialist objectives of the war. . . .

The position is likely to grow much more complicated soon if the Western Powers mobilise against Russia and their intrigue with Italy succeeds. They will call it a holy war against communism and under cover of that not only try to strengthen their own Empire but break up the socialist State of Soviet Russia. That would be a calamity from every point of view, quite apart from our agreement with Russian policy or not. I would beg of you to bear this in mind and to view Indian talks in this perspective.

You will notice that one or two optimistic phrases in your articles as well as some minor occurrences . . . have led to an extraordinary impression everywhere that some kind of a settlement is coming with Britain and that the Congress Ministries will soon be back in office. Jinnah profits by this by making fun of our independence, the Muslim League gets an opportunity to raise its head a little, and as for our newspaper editors, they misbehave as usual. All this creates a wrong impression in the minds of the public in India as well as England. It makes even a possible settlement far less likely. What will happen again is that the Viceroy will complain that he was misled. The *Pioneer* has come out with a heading "Congress Ministries' Resignation Bluff—Called by Viceroy" and so on. Everywhere there is questioning, what is happening behind the scenes? Everywhere there is expectation of some big and sudden development.

All this not only does not square with the facts and with the existing situation, but creates a wrong atmosphere for any kind of mental or other preparations.

Personally I feel sure that there is no real chance of a settlement, although the British Government would no doubt like it. But they are very far from agreeing to what is our minimum. The British Government today is more reactionary and imperialist than it has ever been and to expect it to give in to us is to expect something that cannot happen at this stage. To raise false hopes is unfair and inexpedient and may even weaken our position. I would suggest that it is fairer to lay stress on the other side so that the other party may know exactly how matters are and should adjust itself accordingly.[1]

IV. [To Gandhi—February 4, 1940.] Everything that has happened during the last month or so confirms me in the belief that there is not the slightest ground for hope that the British Government will accept our position. In fact many things have happened which demonstrate that they are following a very definite imperialist policy. You must have seen that the British Parliament has just passed a Bill amending the Government of India Act which limits the powers of Provincial Governments in regard to taxation. This was [done] specially in view of the Property Tax in the U.P. which is thus vetoed. Apart from the demerit of such a decision which reduces the powers of the Provincial Assembly, the time and method chosen for it are eloquent of the imperialist outlook of the British Government and indicate that this has in no way changed.

I wonder if your attention has been drawn to a recent social function in London, organised by the Royal Central Asian Society. Lord Zetland presided and a number of Cabinet Ministers were present. The ostensible object was to establish a centre of Muslim culture and religion in London; the real object was to encourage pan-Islamism and to exploit this sentiment in India and in the Islamic countries to the advantage of the allies in the war. It is extraordinary how the war is developing along true-blue imperialist lines and how events are repeating themselves.

All this does not fit in with the notion that England is preparing to deliver up her Empire. Nor is it at all encouraging to find that we are going to have again a procession of people headed by you to interview the Viceroy. The same old game is played again, the background is the same, the various objectives are the same, the actors are the same, and the results must be the same.

There are, however, some unfortunate indirect results also. An atmosphere of approaching compromise pervades the country when, in effect, there is no ground for it. It is enervating and depressing because it does not come out of strength but, in the case of many individuals, from the excessive desire to avoid conflict at all costs, and to get back to the shreds of power which we had previously. Conflict is undesirable but obviously conflict cannot be avoided at all costs, for sometimes such avoidance itself is a more costly and harmful affair. For the moment, however, there is no

[1] Ibid., pp. 424-25.

immediate question of conflict. The question is of maintaining our position with dignity and not weakening it in any way. I fear that the impression is widely prevalent in England as well as in India that we are going in no event to have any conflict and therefore we are going to accept such terms as we can get. This kind of impression is demoralising. I have noticed during the last fortnight that even our Congress delegates' elections have been influenced by this. Many people who, for fear of possible conflict, were keeping in the background, have now pushed themselves in front again when the possibility of enjoying the plums of office and power seem to dangle again in front of them. The effort of several months to keep undesirables out of the Congress has partly failed because of this sudden change in the Indian atmosphere which led them to believe that the compromise was imminent.

The British Government is also reacting in a way unfavourable to us, though it may use soft language. Of course it wants to come to terms with us because it wants our support in the war. But it is much more certain that it does not wish to give up any shred of real power or change its fundamental imperialist policy in order to come to terms with us. It is carrying on and will carry on its old intrigue on the communal issue, though occasionally it uses a few critical words against the Muslim League in order to soothe the Congress. So far as it is concerned, it will try to win us over, keeping its present position intact. If this is possible, well and good for it. If this does not take place, as seems likely even to it, then to carry on from time to time conversations with Indian leaders, to prolong the issue, to make it appear that we are on the verge of a compromise, and thus to soothe both world opinion and Indian opinion. This second policy has the additional advantage, from their point of view, of exhausting our energy and toning us down, so that, if ultimately a conflict does come, the requisite atmosphere is lacking for it. It is the general belief among official circles in England that their policy of parleys and postponement has had this result and the situation in India, which was threatening when the Congress Ministries resigned, is much easier now and no dangers are to be feared.

It seems to me that while we cannot and must not precipitate a conflict and, while we need not bang the door to a possible and honourable compromise, because your methods are never to bang the door, still we must make it crystal clear that there can be or will be no compromise except on the conditions stated by us previously. As a matter of fact even these conditions have to be slightly reviewed from the point of view of developments in the war. We cannot now say, as we then said, that we want to know whether this war is imperialist or not. The British Government's answer to us as well as their consistent policy in the war and in foreign affairs has been one of full-blooded imperialism. We must therefore necessarily proceed on this admitted fact that it is an imperialist war, any profession to the contrary notwithstanding. The war and British policy grow more and more sinister every day and I would hate to see India entangled in any way in this imperialist adventure from which India can only lose, not only materially but spiritually. This point seems to me of vital importance today.

Thus it seems to me that the most important thing for us to do is to make our position perfectly clear to the world, to the British Government and to the Indian people. There is too much misunderstanding on this issue of compromise and this misunderstanding is entirely to our disadvantage and to the advantage of British imperialism which meanwhile is exploiting our resources for the war and even pretending to have a large amount of our goodwill. An approach by us to the British Government or to the Viceroy increases these misunderstandings and leads the British Government even further away from a right compromise.[1]

V. [To Maulana Azad—February 22, 1940.]

[As already indicated in Nehru's January 24, 1940 letter to Gandhi, the Soviet invasion of Finland was extremely disturbing to him—a point further touched upon in the following letter to Azad. Equally distressing to Nehru was the friendly approach of Russia toward Japan, and the Russo-German Pact of August 24, 1939. "Were there any principles", he inquired, "or any standards of conduct in this world . . . or [is] it all sheer opportunism?"[2]]

There are some points which I should like to place before you for your consideration. . . .

Following an imperialist line . . . the Chamberlain Government was well known [before the War as being] utterly reactionary and on many occasions they encouraged the Fascist and Nazi Powers and crushed democracy in Europe. This was evident in the case of Abyssinia, Spain, Austria, Czechoslovakia and Albania. Their policy in Manchuria was also of the same kind. Mr Chamberlain's Government was known to be the most reactionary and imperialist Government that England has had for more than a hundred years. . . .

[1] Ibid., pp. 426–29.
[2] T.F., p. 370.

I*

Russia has made many mistakes and notably, I think, her invasion of Finland was a very serious error, both from the point of view of principle and expediency. It is true that Finland was being used by England as a place for intrigue against Russia and as a future jumping off platform for an invasion of Russia. Munitions were being accumulated there. Russia was frightened of this development and tried to forestall it by a rapid invasion. This was very foolish and it played into the hands of England and France and at the same time alienated progressive opinion all over the world. It gave the chance which England wanted of posing as the friend of democracy and of making people forget its own sins in the past few years. The League of Nations, which had never even discussed Fascist and Nazi aggressions and invasions, suddenly woke up to condemn Russia. Now there is no doubt in my mind that Russian policy recently has been wrong and must be condemned. But at the same time one must remember how this policy took shape because of the consistent attempts on the part of the British Government to encircle Russia. What is more important now is that we should realise that England is trying to exploit the situation in Finland to its own imperialist advantage and to spread the War to Russia. This is full of danger for us, because if there is war between England and Russia, our own frontiers become involved and it becomes important for us to be clear about our policy. While we must criticise and disapprove of much that Russia has done, it will be dangerous in the extreme if we permit British imperialism to use that to its own advantage.

I think it would be a tragedy if Soviet Russia was crippled and weakened by a war against her, for then the only powerful opponent of imperialism would be removed. But even apart from this, anything that goes to strengthen British imperialism is dangerous for us. Therefore it is very important that we should be clear in our minds about the present British policy towards Russia and that we should declare that we are against it and in no event can we support or approve of British action against Russia. I think a clearly expressed policy on our part will make a difference. If Britain thinks that India will accept everything that she does without much objection, then there is every chance of the War spreading and Russia being involved in it with consequences to our own Indian frontier. On the other hand, if England feels that there is strong objection in India to any attack on Russia by England and that any such policy would be resisted in India, then England might well hesitate before she spreads this war to other regions. The British Government is doubtful at present as to what it should do. It wants to attack Russia but is afraid of the consequences. If it is assured that it will have peace in India, it will go ahead with the attack. Otherwise it will hold its hands. Therefore our attitude in this matter counts, and it is desirable to express it as clearly and as strongly as possible.

What is happening in England and France shows how very reactionary these countries are growing. France today is a military dictatorship with complete suppression of civil liberty. Scores of members of the Parliament there have been arrested because the Government does not like their views. Several hundred municipalities have been suppressed for the same reason. In England matters have not gone quite so far but the tendency is the same. In effect both England and France are becoming more and more Fascist in their Government, though they talk about democracy. They refuse to say anything about war aims and are clearly aiming at, as they did in 1914, entrenching their own empires and weakening [any] rival imperialisms as well as all progressive forces within or outside their empires. The question that the Congress put to the British Government in September has been answered very clearly by British policy as well as French policy. That answer is that we stand for imperialism and we fight to maintain it. Now we condemn Fascism and Nazi-ism and it would be bad if Hitler won in the War. We do not want that. On the other hand a victory of British imperialism means a continuation of Chamberlainism, more strengthened than before. That is equally bad and would lead to constant wars. Hence it would be folly for us, from every point of view, national and international, to help in any way such a victory. Quite apart, therefore, from any internal solution of India's problem as between England and India, it should be clear that we are not going to throw our weight in an imperialist war to preserve the British Empire.

You will have noticed the rebirth of the idea of Pan-Islamism. This is not merely due to the Muslim League here or to other organisations. This is fundamentally due to the desire of the British Government to encourage it. Pan-Islamism in 1914 and later was an anti-imperialist force. It weakened the British people in their war effort and later it coloured the background of the Khilafat movement in India. Today this very idea is being used in support of British imperialism. This breaks, to some extent, the national front in India and helps to influence Muslim opinion in the Near East in favour of England. The fact that Turkey is a friendly power in alliance with England also helps British policy in this regard. I do not know what the effects of the British propaganda have been in the Muslim countries. But what I wish to point out is the definitely imperialist character of the new phase of Pan-Islamism.

All this shows how all our own internal problems, whether it is the communal problem or the larger problem of independence, are intimately connected with the larger war issues and those of British foreign policy. If we consider India apart, we fall into an error. The main difficulties of the communal problem are due to the attitude of the British Government today. It becomes very difficult for us to solve . . . even if the Muslim League . . . were agreeable. Of course the British Government wants a solution of the Indian problem in order to strengthen itself in the war and entrench its own imperialism. . . . [Those] . . . acting entirely on behalf of British policy [want] to do the same. But fundamentally this policy is based on strengthening British imperialism. Our policy on the other hand is based on weakening imperialism. That is the basic difference which prevents compromise and no amount of talks with the Viceroy or with the Muslim League will get over that, till the British Government itself is prepared to renounce its imperialism. The Working Committee's statement of September 14th demanded this renunciation. Far from that having been done, the British Government has affirmed its imperialism. India's attitude is of great importance because it affects America and other neutral countries. America at present is very strongly anti-Hitler, and in that sense, pro-British. At the same time, it is certainly not in favour of British imperialism and, therefore, it hesitates to join the British. If the British could explain to America that they had come to terms with India, it would be a tremendous help to them.

During the last few months there has been so much confusing talk about compromise with the British Government that both our own people and the world at large have been misled and no one knows what is going to happen. It seems . . . that we should make it clear once [and] for all that there can be no compromise with us in the structure of imperialism and the sooner all such attempts are given up the better. There must be a finality about this.

British policy in India during the last few months has progressively been a reversion to autocratic rule and it is surprising to people outside India how we have calmly submitted to it. Not only have the popular Provincial Governments been upset but actually the scope of Provincial autonomy has been limited by Amending Acts in Parliament. This kind of thing shouts louder than all the sweet words of the Viceroy. Ordinarily even a suspension of the Constitution should have led to a severe conflict. But we have calmly put up with it. We have also put up with the Amending Bills. This amendment of the Constitution is not important so far as we are concerned except in so far as it shows the trend of British policy. All this indicates that there is nothing in common between us and the

Britisli Government, and British imperialism is going as strongly as ever. . . .

It seems to me very dangerous to agree to a Constituent Assembly consisting of the present Provincial Legislatures. That is giving up our basic demand of adult franchise which we have made for the last four years. That means also that our Constituent Assembly will be within the framework of British imperialism. This would lead, under present circumstances, to the same communal and other conflicts and thus our own weakness will be shown up and there will be no agreement as regards the Constitution. It would mean, in effect, that we are functioning almost within the framework of the Act of 1935 with some minor changes. If a Constituent Assembly is to succeed, it must be completely outside the framework of this Act as well as of British imperialism. The question of our relations with the British Government can only be considered after the Constituent Assembly has framed our Constitution. The technical difficulty of adult franchise can be got over by having an intermediate step of indirect election. The point is that this Constituent Assembly must be looked upon as the organ of the Indian people functioning completely outside the orbit of British imperialism and the British Parliament. Otherwise it will just become an offshoot of some enactment of the British Parliament.

I think it should be made clear also that there can be no going back by our Provincial Governments under existing conditions of services, control, etc. . . . The whole structure of Government must change from top to bottom.[1]

What of Russia Now? The Russo-German Pact and the Russo–Finnish War—January 19, 1940

The last few months have brought many changes and many disasters and the world sinks deeper into the morass. The future is uncertain and full of gloom and the bright idealism which persisted even through the conflicts and betrayals of the thirties seem to fade away. War and violence, aggression and duplicity, and unadulterated opportunism overshadow the world, and the shape of things to come grows more and more amorphous and shapeless. None pays heed to or believes in the fine phrases of politicians or gives credence to their promises. The new order that was to come, the dream that was to find realisation, where is it now? From whose womb

[1] B.O.L., pp. 429–34.

will it find birth? Will this growing chaos give birth to the bright star of freedom and world cooperation?

Perhaps we grow unduly pessimistic and lack faith and courage and the future is not so dark as the present would lead us to think. But that future must have its roots in the present and must grow out of the soil on which we stand today. It is this today that depresses—not so much the War and all the horrors that [accompany] it, as the weakening of the ideals which have given us strength for so long. Those ideals remain, but doubts creep in and disturb the mind. Is humanity prepared for the realisation of those ideals? Can it achieve them in the near future?

Nothing is more significant today, or more full of sorrow, than the weakening almost everywhere (though not so much in India) of the progressive forces. Shock after shock has shattered them and laid them low, and today they are a disbanded and disgruntled army, not knowing which way to turn. Soviet Russia, their symbol of hope and fulfillment, has descended from the pedestal on which her ardent champions had placed her, and bartered away her moral prestige and the friendship of so many of her friends for seeming political advantage.

It has never been easy for any one to be neutral about Russia; there has been either open-mouthed admiration and enthusiasm or bitter hatred. Both attitudes were inevitably wrong and yet both could be understood. For hatred was natural among those who clung to vested interest and ancient privilege and saw in Russia the uprooter of both; and enthusiasm for a new order based on a juster and more scientific economic system filled the minds of those who were weary of the conflicts and misery of the old order. Joy at this tremendous step made the enthusiasts overlook or excuse many an error that acccompanied it. That was right, for what counted most was the basic change in Russia, and yet it was no good turn to her to accept unthinkingly everything that came out of her. No nation or people prosper if they grow complacent or avoid all criticism.

The prestige of Russia grew with her planning and her wonderful advances in many directions. Then came the batches of trials which cast a gloom on this picture. Those trials, or most of them, may have been justified, but why should so much intrigue and sabotage occur on such a scale even in a country which had passed through a mighty revolution? All was not well internally, and violence and suppression of criticism grew. But the masses were not affected by the conflicts at the top and they continued to progress. The economic order was justifying itself.

Whatsoever doubts there were about internal conditions, there were none about Russia's external policy. Year after year this policy was based on peace, collective security and the aiding and encouragement of those who resisted aggression. While the Nazi and Fascist powers were openly carrying out their programme of unabashed aggression and England and France were aiding them by their foreign policy, Soviet Russia stood as a symbol of a straightforward and integrated policy of international peace. Because she did not fall in line with the tortuous intrigues of the Western European powers, she was ignored, insulted and humiliated.

This was a hard pill to swallow for a great power and resentment grew and the desire to avenge [herself]. The pill was rejected, but in this process Russia overreached herself by adopting a policy of a too facile opportunism even at the cost of what she has stood [for] in the eyes of the world.

The Russo-German Pact was a shock and the manner and the timing of it smacked patently of this opportunism. Yet it could be understood and partly explained. Subsequent policy in the Baltic regions carried us a step further. There was explanation [for] this also, for the Soviet [Union] wanted to protect its northwestern frontier from attack and every one knew that this was the danger zone. Yet our doubts increased.

Then came the attack on Finland. The demands made on Finland had some justification from the point of view of Russia's future security. Yet it must be remembered that every great power tends to extend its frontiers on the plea of security. In war time and with the possible danger of a shift in Europe which might bring about a concerted and joint attack on Russia, the desire to protect these frontiers and the great and vital city of Leningrad, was understandable. But the armed invasion of Finland passed these bounds, and Russia lined herself with aggressor nations and thereby was false to the traditions she had herself nourished for these many years. She has paid heavily for this vital error, and paid in a coin which cannot be counted, for it is made up of the wishes and ideals of innumerable human beings. No individual, no nation can play about with this priceless coinage without suffering grievous loss, much less a nation which has prided itself on its basic principles and ideals.

It is probably true that Soviet Russia never expected any serious resistance from the Finns and believed that they would capitulate rather than risk war, as the other Baltic States had done. It is also probable that the Soviet Government expected the Finnish workers and peasantry to welcome the invasion by the Red Army. In both these beliefs they were wrong. It is an undoubted fact that Finland was and is being assisted by Italy, France and England, and has thus become the nucleus of an anti-Soviet combination. It is also true that the news that comes to us is tainted and one-sided and we cannot place much reliance on it. But there can be little doubt that the Finnish people are resisting the [Soviet] invasion as a united nation, and both the Finnish Trades Union and the peasantry are backing this resistance. A small democratic nation [is] fighting gallantly for its freedom and against aggression and it is inevitable that sympathy should go to it.

To the forces of reaction everywhere this war in Finland has come as a special dispensation from heaven. Under cover of it, they have hidden their own aggressions and betrayals, and [have] presumed to stand up as the champions of the oppressed against aggression. Their hatred of socialism and Soviet Russia as a social state finds a congenial atmosphere [in which] to function. The League of Nations, which had slumbered peacefully throughout the rape of Austria and Czechoslovakia, which had philosophically accepted Munich and connived at the infamous policy of non-intervention in Spain, which had said nothing about the Nazi invasion of Poland, now suddenly wakes up and is used as a weapon to strike Soviet Russia.

But the real tragedy is the effect on progressive opinion everywhere in Europe, America and Asia. Those who are in charge of Russia's government have themselves dealt a [more severe] blow to their cause than any enemy or combination of enemies could have done. They have lost that enormous fund of goodwill that they possessed, and injured, by associating aggression with it, the cause of socialism itself. There is no necessary connection between the two, and it is well that we separate them. But for us to advocate and defend Soviet aggression or even to acquiesce in it passively, is to do grave disservice to socialism. There are those who have made it their creed to defend every activity of the Soviet Government, and who consider it a heresy or *lèse-majesté* for anyone to criticise or condemn any such activity. That is the way of blind faith which has nothing to do with reason. It is not on that basis that we can build up freedom here or elsewhere. Integrity of mind and sincerity of purpose can be given up only at peril to ourselves and our cause. We are not tied down to any decisions made for us elsewhere. We make our own decisions and fashion our own policy.

We have to beware of the spate of propaganda that comes to us from tainted and partial sources against Russia. We have to keep on guard against the atrocity campaigns worked up in foreign countries or in India against the Soviet [Union]. We have to hold to our belief, if we so believe, in socialism and the socialist order as a solvent of the world's ills. We have to remember that Soviet Russia, in spite of her many failings, has gone a long way [toward establishing a socialist] economic system, and it would be [a] tragedy if this mighty scheme of things, so full of promise for the future, [were] ended or crippled. We can be no [party] to this.

But we must also realise that the Soviet Government [have] erred egregiously [on] many matters and [have relied] . . . too much on violence and opportunism and authoritarianism. They have not sought to keep their means above reproach and so their ends are being twisted to fit in with these means. Means are not ends, though they control them. But means must be in keeping with . . . ends or else the end itself becomes a misshapen thing, totally different from the objective aimed at.

We in India, therefore, extend our friendly sympathy to the socialism of Russia, and any attempt to break it will meet with our strong disapproval. But we do not give our sympathy to the political manoeuvres and aggressions of Russia's government. In the war against Finland our sympathies are [with] the people of Finland who have struggled so gallantly to preserve their freedom. If Russia persists in [opposing them], the result will be disastrous for her and for the world.

We have to remember yet again that in this revolutionary age of transition and change, when all our old values are upset and we seek new standards, we must retain our integrity of mind and purpose and hold fast to means and methods which are right and which are in conformity with our ideals and objectives. Those objectives will not be achieved through violence or authoritarianism or the opportunism of the moment. We must adhere to non-violence and right action and evolve through this the free India for which we labour.[1]

[1] N.H., January 19, 1940. (From Ms. copy.)

	Constituent Assembly—Congress and
2	the War—World War II Developments—
	Congress and Non-Violence—Related
	Problems

On Continued Need For Constituent Assembly—
Allahabad, March 8, 1940

I can understand, though I do not appreciate, the criticisms of those who differ from us fundamentally in politics; those whose ideas of Indian freedom are limited by the will and desire of the British Parliament; those who are afraid of revolutionary change; those who are terrified at the prospect of the masses marching along the stage of Indian politics. But it has surprised me greatly to find some—there are not many—among those who claim to be the most ardent champions of Indian independence who have also joined this band of critics.

I am convinced that there is no way out for us, if we aim at real democratic freedom, except through a Constituent Assembly. The alternatives are: (1) continuation, in a greater or less degree, under the control of the British Parliament; (2) some kind of fascist or military dictatorship or dictatorships; (3) Soviet Communism in some parts of India with disruption and chaos in other parts; (4) complete disruption and chaos.

For my part, I would like to have a socialist economy all over India, and I think that the Soviet form of government, with certain variations and adaptations suited to India, may well fit in here. Thereby I do not mean that the Russian system or methods should be introduced here *in toto*. I think the Soviet system can be allied to a great deal of real democracy. But any attempt to introduce Sovietism in India would, I am sure, now and for some time to come, lead to terrible conflicts and disruption.

Therefore, of necessity, I am led to the conclusion that the way of the Constituent Assembly is the only way. But let it be remembered that this way is not the way of advancing step by step to the haven of Dominion status. It means the creation of a new State; it means the walking out and away from the economic foundations and structure of imperialism. This cannot be done by the wisest of lawyers sitting together in conclave; it cannot be done by small committees trying to balance interests and calling that constitution-making; it can never be done under the shadow of an external authority. It can only be done effectively when the political and psychological conditions are present, and the urge and the sanctions come from the masses. Hence the vital importance of adult suffrage.

Are these political and psychological conditions present today? No, obviously not, or else we would have got the Constituent Assembly already. But I cannot say about tomorrow or the day after, for we live in dynamic and swiftly moving times and all manner of forces are at play.

Why do we ask the British Government for a Constituent Assembly? Strictly speaking, we are not asking for any gift. We are stating what we propose to have and are going to have some time or other. We shall have it when we are strong enough for it, no sooner, and probably after a struggle. But, then, are we to refrain from saying what we want and aim at, because for the moment we cannot attain it? Surely that is not even the way of preparation. And then it is never wise to rule out the odd possibility of our gaining it without a major struggle, for our strength and world events may force the pace. To envisage this possibility does us no harm, unless it leads us to complacency and surrender of the idea of struggle.

Why do we ask the British Government to acknowledge the independence of India? Does that make any difference? Of course it does, though it does not mean that we have gained our objective or that the British Government will not go back on their word. The mere fact that they refuse to acknowledge it, itself shows what value they attach to such a declaration. If there was such a clear declaration of Indian independence, of the right of the Indian people to frame their own Constitution through a Constituent Assembly elected by adult franchise and without any external interference, that in itself would create a psychological situation of revolutionary significance. That by itself will not take us to our goal but it will strengthen us enormously and bring the masses into play.

The question of the Constituent Assembly is an acid test for all of us. It shows where each one of us stands. Britain refuses it because she will not give up her imperialism. The Liberals in India, or the Muslim League, or other protestants, oppose it because they do not want real independence, and they have no conception of a new State, or, if they can conceive of it, they dislike it. Howsoever much they might dislike things as they are, they prefer them to that new free State where the people can make or unmake. Hence the objections to adult suffrage, and even to large numbers of people being associated with this undertaking. Small committees

of the elect are suggested whose chief function will be to move warily
within the limits laid down by the British Government and to discuss
interminably communal claims and counter-claims.

That is not our idea of Indian freedom or the State that we seek to
build. [The British Government categorically rejected the demand for a
Constituent Assembly and its basis, self-determination. In a speech
delivered subsequently at Manchester, on November 20, 1941, the
Secretary of State for India said: "Congress has demanded that the
future constitution should be settled by a Constitutional Assembly elected
by universal adult franchise over the whole of India. This is an impossible
demand."][1]

Congress and the War

[From report of interview—Allahabad, May 21, 1940.] I do not wish to
see Nazi domination of Europe. . . . But our attitude toward the British
Government [is] not determined by the war situation, but [rather] by
Britain's attitude towards India and her refusal to recognize Indian
independence.[2]

[Whereas Gandhi continued to assert that Satyagraha in some form or
other should be undertaken at this time, in order to defend India's honor
and dignity, Nehru tended increasingly to differentiate between what
India should do in conjunction with "external", as opposed to "internal"
factors.]

To talk of Satyagraha immediately, chiefly because England stands in
great peril, is wrong. We [can] not time our actions to take advantage of
England's peril. That would not fit in with our policy or with Satyagraha.
I [have] opposed, therefore, the [proposal made at the Congress Session
of March, 1940] to that effect. But I made it clear that this did not mean a
postponement of Satyagraha or making it dependent on war conditions.
. . . Nor could Satyagraha be postponed when we thought the time was
ripe for it in India. This [must] depend on internal factors, not . . .
external.[3]

[1] U.I., pp. 370–72. (Bracketed material based on footnote ibid., p. 372.)
[2] I.A.A., p. 334.
[3] Ibid., p. 334.

World War II Developments

[The Russo-Finnish war ended on March 12, 1940. Within a month German troops had occupied Denmark and attacked Norway. After Luxembourg, Holland and Belgium were invaded and conquered in swift succession, Winston Churchill replaced Neville Chamberlain as Prime Minister of Great Britain. Dunkirk fell to the Germans on June 5. Six days later the French Government fled from Paris. French troops already had been withdrawn when the capital surrendered. France's Vichy regime sued for an armistice with Germany which was signed on June 22. (The Free French, led by Charles de Gaulle, declared war on Japan on December 8, 1941.) In the last weeks of July, 1940, the Baltic states of Estonia, Lithuania and Latvia were absorbed into the U.S.S.R. The Battle of Britain occurred in August. By September, 1940, Japan had become a firmly established member of the Rome-Berlin Axis.]

Congress and Non-Violence

[In view of the continuing deadlock between Congress and Britain, Gandhi, who took command of Congress affairs during early 1940, continued to favor the launching of a civil disobedience campaign. Because of Britain's extraordinarily courageous stand against the threat of invasion—even possible annihilation by the Nazis—Nehru's resistance to Gandhi's attitude increased considerably. A number of other Congress leaders similarly opposed Gandhi's stand, especially at the time of the fall of France.]

[To Rajendra Prasad—May 25, 1940.] Satyagraha is not immediately indicated, even if we were ready for it . . . I think it would be wrong for us at this particular moment, when Britain is in peril, to take advantage of her distress and rush at her throat.[1]

[During the summer of 1940 the Congress Working Committee met in emergency session, announcing its readiness to cooperate in the war effort, if Britain would grant complete independence to India (the only other Congress condition being that a provisional national government should be constituted immediately). Even potential agreement to cooperate in the war effort on the above terms diverged so markedly from the traditional Gandhian position that Nehru once again found himself attempting to calm troubled waters within Congress, while trying simultaneously to remain true to his own ideas.]

[1] Quoted in M.B., p. 267.

The difference between [Gandhi's] approach and that of the Working Committee must be understood and must not lead the people to think ... there is a break between him and the Congress. The Congress of the past twenty years is his creation and child and nothing can break the bond.[1]

[In spite of the truth of Nehru's declaration, a number of Congress members continued vigorously to disagree with the Mahatma's stand. Like Nehru, the Working Committee came to the conclusion that it was legitimate to wage a non-violent struggle for the country's internal freedom, but not for national defence. Nehru again and again attempted to clarify not only Gandhi's position, but that of Congress, and his own attitude. His task in so doing was by no means an easy one. Thus his writings of the period understandably reflect anguish, conflict, torment. Meanwhile, efforts to negotiate with the British continued, despite consistent failure.]

[Further review of Congress policy.] The Congress had long ago accepted the principle and practice of nonviolence in its application to our struggle for freedom and in building up unity in the nation. At no time had it gone beyond that position or applied the principle to defense from external aggression or internal disorder. Indeed it had taken an eager interest in the development of the Indian Army and frequently demanded the Indianization of its officer personnel. The Congress party in the central legislature had often moved or participated in resolutions on this subject. ...

In 1937-38 the Congress party had put forward in the Central Assembly, after consulting all the provincial governments, proposals for the expansion of the Indian Army, its mechanization, the development of the absurdly small and almost nonexistent naval and air arms, and the progressive replacement of the British Army in India by the Indian Army. As the cost of British troops in India was about four times that of Indian troops, the latter could have been mechanized and expanded without much additional cost, if they took the place of British troops. Again during the Munich period the importance of developing the air arm was emphasized, but the government said that expert opinion was not agreed about this. In 1940 the Congress party especially attended the Central Assembly and repeated all this and pointed out how incompetent the government and its military department were in making arrangements for India's defense.

At no time, so far as I am aware, was the question of nonviolence considered in relation to the army, navy, or air forces, or the police. It was taken for granted that its application was confined to our struggle for

[1] Ibid., p. 269.

freedom. It is true that it had a powerful effect on our thinking in many ways and it made the Congress strongly favor world disarmament and a peaceful solution of all international, as well national, disputes.

When the Congress governments were functioning in the provinces, many of them were eager to encourage some form of military training in the universities and colleges. It was the Government of India that disapproved of this and came in the way.

Gandhi no doubt disapproved of these tendencies, but he did not interfere. He did not even like the use of the police as an armed force for the suppression of riots, and he expressed his distress at it. But he put up with it as a lesser evil, and hoped that his teaching would gradually sink into the mind of India. It was his disapproval of such tendencies within the Congress that led him to sever his formal membership connection with the Congress in the early thirties, though even so he continued as the undoubted leader and adviser of the Congress. It was an anomalous and unsatisfactory position for all of us, but perhaps it made him feel that thus he was not personally responsible for all the varied decisions which Congress took from time to time, which did not wholly conform to his principles and convictions. Always there has been that inner conflict within him, and, in our national politics, between Gandhi as a national leader and Gandhi as a man with a prophetic message which was not confined to India but was for humanity and the world. It is never easy to reconcile a strict adherence to truth as one sees it with the exigencies and expediencies of life, and especially of political life. Normally people do not even worry themselves over this problem. They keep truth apart in some corner of their minds, if they keep it at all anywhere, and accept expediency as the measure of action. In politics that has been the universal rule, not only because unfortunately politicians are a peculiar species of opportunists, but because they cannot act purely on the personal plane. They have to make others act, and so they have to consider the limitations of others and their understanding of and receptivity to truth. And because of this they have to make compromises with that truth and adapt it to the prevailing circumstances. That adaptation becomes inevitable, and yet there are always risks attending it, and the tendency to ignore and abandon truth grows and expediency becomes the sole criterion of action.

Gandhi, for all his rocklike adherence to certain principles, has shown a great capacity to adapt himself to others and to changing circumstances, to take into consideration the strength and weakness of those others, and especially of the mass of the people, and how far they were capable of acting up to the truth as he saw it. But from time to time he pulls himself up, as if he were afraid that he had gone too far in his compromising, and returns to his moorings. In the midst of action, he seems to be in tune with the mass mind, responsive to its capacity and therefore adapting himself to it to some extent; at other times he becomes more theoretical and apparently less adaptable. There is also the same difference observable in his action and his writings. This is confusing to his own people; more so to others who are ignorant of the background in India.

How far a single individual can influence a people's thought and ideology it is difficult to say. Some people in history have exerted a powerful influence, and yet it may be that they have emphasized and brought out something that already existed in the mind of the people, or have given clear and pointed expression to the vaguely felt ideas of the age. Gandhi's influence on India's mind has been profound in the present age; how long and in what form it will endure, only the future can show. That influence is not limited to those who agree with him or accept him as a national leader; it extends to those also who disagree with him and criticize him. Very few persons in India accept in its entirety his doctrine of nonviolence or his economic theories, yet very many have been influenced by them in some way or other. Usually speaking in terms of religion, he has emphasized the moral approach to political problems as well as those of everyday life. The religious background has affected those chiefly who were inclined that way, but the moral approach has influenced others also. Many have been appreciably raised to higher levels of moral and ethical action, and many more have been forced to think at least in those terms, and that thought itself has some effect on action and behavior. Politics ceases to be just expediency and opportunism, as it usually has been everywhere, and there is a continuous moral tussle preceding thought and action. Expediency, or what appears to be immediately possible and desirable, can never be ignored, but it is toned down by other considerations and a longer view of more distant consequences.

Gandhi's influence in these various directions has pervaded India and left its mark. But it is not because of his nonviolence or economic theories that he has become the foremost and most outstanding of India's leaders. To the vast majority of [Indians] he is the symbol of India determined to be free, of militant nationalism, of a refusal to submit to arrogant might, of never agreeing to anything involving national dishonor. Though many people in India may disagree with him on a hundred matters, though they may criticize him or even part company from him on some particular issues, at a time of action and struggle when India's freedom is at stake, they flock to him again and look up to him as their inevitable leader.

When Gandhiji raised in 1940 the question of nonviolence in relation to the war and the future of free India, the Congress Working Committee had to face the issue squarely. They made it clear to him that they were unable to go as far as he wanted them to go and could not possibly commit India or the Congress to future applications of this principle in the external domain. This led to a definite and public break with him on this issue. Two months later further discussions led to an agreed formula which was later adopted as part of a resolution by the All-India Congress Committee.[1] That formula did not wholly represent Gandhiji's attitude; it represented what he agreed, perhaps rather unwillingly, for Congress to say on this subject. At that time the British government had already rejected the latest offer made by the Congress for co-operation in the war on the basis of a national government. Some kind of conflict was approaching, and, as was inevitable, both Gandhiji and Congress looked toward each other and were impelled by a desire to find a way out of the deadlock between them. The formula did not refer to the war, as just previously our offer of co-operation had been unceremoniously and utterly rejected. It dealt theoretically with the Congress policy in regard to nonviolence, and for the first time stated how, in the opinion of the Congress, the free India of the future should apply it in its external relations. That part of the resolution ran thus:

The All-India Congress Committee "firmly believes in the policy and practice of non-violence not only in the struggle for Swaraj, but also, in so far as this may be possible of application, in free India. The Committee is convinced, and recent world events have demonstrated, that complete world disarmament is necessary and the establishment of a new and juster political and economic order, if the world is not to destroy itself and revert to barbarism. A free India will, therefore, throw all her weight in favor of world disarmament and should herself be prepared to give a lead in this to the world. Such lead will inevitably depend on external factors and internal conditions, but the State would do its utmost to give effect to this policy of disarmament. Effective disarmament and the establishment of world peace by the ending of national wars, depend ultimately on the removal of the causes of wars and national conflicts. These causes must be rooted out by the ending of the domination of one country over another and the exploitation of one people or group by another. To that end India will peacefully labor, and it is with this objective in view that the people of India desire to attain the status of a free and independent nation. Such freedom will be the prelude to the close association with

[1] See Part Six, Section 4.

other countries within a comity of free nations for the peace and progress of the world." [1]

[From statement to *Hindustan Times* on Congress Working Committee Resolution of July 7—July 10, 1940.] We cannot easily tolerate the methods of compulsion that are being increasingly used by Government officials in regard to the war effort or the thousands of arrests [of Congressmen and others] that have taken place. . . . We do not forget them. . . .

We have made it perfectly clear in the past that we cannot help the war effort of British imperialism or become its recruiting sergeants. That position continues completely unchanged, but to maintain our own independence for our defence and the defence of freedom, we are prepared under our own direction to do our best.

In spite of the terrible violence that is going on in the world, we adhere to our policy of non-violence in our struggle for freedom in all its implications. We are anxious and eager to extend this principle to other fields also and, so far as we can, we shall do so. [2]

[From report of reply in debate on Congress position regarding Gandhi's advice to Britain about non-violence—July, 1940.] Mahatma Gandhi wanted to give his message of non-violence to the world. The Congress [is] a political organization working for the political independence of the country. Therefore it [has] to take its decision bearing this in mind. . . .

It [is] not possible to create a free State and yet protect it without an army. Even though the present army [is] not a national army it [is] composed of Indians. [3]

Related Problems

[Extracts from talk with Punjab Journalists—Lahore, June 12, 1940.] I have great sympathy with the people of France and England in their hour of trial. I do not understand at all the manner in which Italy has declared war after sitting on the fence for such a long time. A more blatant example of sheer opportunism it would be difficult to find. As has been stated before, India's attitude towards the British Government does

[1] D.I., pp. 451–54.
[2] I.A.A., pp. 335–36.
[3] Ibid., p. 338.

not depend on the war situation, but on the British Government's attitude towards the Indian problem.[1]

[British offer to France—Interpretation of Congress Working Committee Statement of June 21, 1940.] It is absurd to think that the revolutionary developments of recent weeks in Europe are due to purely military reasons or to Germany's superiority in armament or numbers. They are essentially due to the fact that the British and French ruling classes have lost [their] grip and do not understand the world we live in. They seek to hold on to something which belongs to a past age, and everything slips from their hands.

We in India must beware of these mental ruts. Let us remember that an age is over and we are witnessing this bloody transition to a new age. I do not know that this age will necessarily be better, but I do know that it will be very different.

The old Empires end, even the old national boundaries fade away. Could a more astonishing proposition have been made than the British Government's suggestion that France and England should become one State?[2]

3 | Resumé of Developments: World War II (Summer, 1940)

[A Crumbling World—July 16, 1940.] It would be worth while . . . for us to consider dispassionately what has happened in Europe, with all its future implications, if we are to understand the curious and changing world that we live in. Wishful thinking is at any time an unhelpful occupation; today it is full of peril. All of us are much too apt to remain in the old ruts, to think the old thoughts, to utter the old slogans, even though everything else may have changed beyond recognition. Fundamental principles and objectives must have a certain stability and continuance, but in other ways reality demands that we adapt ourselves to it.

[1] Ibid., p. 89.
[2] Ibid., p. 336.

What has happened? The map of Europe has changed utterly and many nations have ceased to be. Poland went, Denmark and Norway succumbed, Holland collapsed, Belgium surrendered, France fell suddenly and completely. All these went into the German orbit. The Baltic countries and Bessarabia have been more or less absorbed by Soviet Russia.

These are mighty changes, and yet it is being increasingly realized that they are but the prelude of what is to come. We are not merely witnessing a great and overwhelming war with all its destructive horror. We live today in the midst of a revolutionary epoch of vast significance, more important and far-reaching perhaps than any given in recorded history. Whatever the outcome of this war may be, this revolution will complete its appointed course, and till this takes place there will be no peace or equilibrium in this planet of ours.

We must realize that the old world dies, whether we like it or not. Already those who were most representative of it have become phantom figures, ghosts of a yesterday that is no more.

If the Nazis won through, as they well might, there is little doubt of what they would try to make of Europe and the world. They would create a new type of European Union under German leadership and control, a Nazi Empire of Europe. The small States would go and so would democracy, as understood by us, and the capitalist system as it has prevailed. A form of State capitalism would flourish in Europe and big industry would be concentrated in the Germanic lands, the other countries, including France, being reduced largely to an agricultural status. This system would be based on a collective supernational economy and would be subject to authoritarian control. The Nazi Empire would have its colonies, chiefly in Africa, but it would also try to control the economy of other non-European countries and harness the labour power of their peoples. The economic weight of such a mighty authoritarian Union would be tremendous and the rest of the world would have to adapt itself to it.

Such is the Nazi thesis. What of England if this happens? If there is a complete German victory, England ceases to be a Power that counts. In Europe she has no influence left; she loses her empire. It is almost immaterial whether she joins the Germanic European Union or not. The centre of gravity of the British race shifts elsewhere, most probably to Canada, and [it becomes] closely allied to, or even absorbed in, the United States of America.

Much will depend upon Soviet Russia. There is little doubt that she dislikes intensely the rapid growth of Nazi power which may threaten her later. Nevertheless, she will adapt herself to the change unless the war drags on for a lengthy period and brings exhaustion of the combatants.

A swift German victory would thus lead to a Nazi Empire in Europe with outlying possessions. This may be allied to Japan in the East. Two other great federations will remain—Soviet Russia and the United States of America—both essentially hostile to Germany. The war may have ended, but the seeds of future wars will remain between these mighty groups. . . .

In any event therefore this war will bring about a fundamental political and economic change, a change that will be more in keeping with modern conditions which demand closer intercourse between nations and a breaking down of international barriers. The strength of Germany today lies not so much in her ruthless efficiency and military machine, as in the fact that, perhaps unconsciously, she has become the agent of a historic process. She is trying to turn it in an evil direction; she may even succeed in this for a while. The weakness of France and England was essentially due to their desire to hold on to forms and structures which were doomed to disappear. They represented something that was dying, whether in their empires or in their economic system. They had repeated chances during the past twenty years of putting themselves in step with history, of being the leaders in building up a real international order based on social justice and national freedom. They preferred to hold on to their past gains and vested interests and empire, and now it is too late and everything slips out of their hands.

France passes away for a while. But England still fails to learn the lesson. Still she talks in terms of empire and seeks to preserve her special interests. It is sad to see a great people so blind to everything except the narrow interests of a class, and risking everything but not taking the step which would put them right with the world and with the great historic processes that are marching on with giant strides.[1]

[The Burma–China Road—July 16, 1940.] The news about China is ominous. We were told recently that the British Government had agreed to close the Burma–China Road during the monsoon. We are now informed that this Government is engaged in a peace move in the Far East.

England may be in a perilous condition today and it is easy to understand that she does not want further entanglements. But the betrayal of China will not bring her relief; it will have far-reaching consequences affecting American . . . as well as Indian opinion.

The policy of appeasement of the aggressor has proved to be disastrous

[1] U.I., pp. 318–21.

in the past; it will not succeed now. It will expose still further the pretension that Britain fights for democracy and confirm us in our resolve not to be a party to [that fight].[1]

[What of Us?—July 17, 1940.] Whether Germany wins or loses will obviously make a great difference to the future of Europe and the world. And yet, in either event, certain changes and developments of far-reaching significance are bound to take place. Small States will disappear and give place either to some world Federation or to three, or possibly four, Federations or Empire States. If the latter emerge, there will be continuing hostility and conflict, both internal and external. Internal, because an Empire State necessarily involves the enforced subjugation of other peoples and nations, which will continually attempt to free themselves. External, because there will be rivalry between the different Empire States or Federations. Each may try to develop some kind of autarchy or self-sufficient economy within its territories. But this can bring no equilibrium or stability, and either peacefully or through war, a single world Federation must emerge. It is inevitable that this should be so, for the alternative is continuing mutual destruction on a vast scale and a relapse into barbarism. Such a world Federation must be a real union of free nations. An imposed order means that the so-called Federation is really an Empire State with the seeds of disruption within it.

Whatever is the outcome of the war, it seems clear enough that the British Empire ends. There are inherent reasons why this should be so, but the course of the war has made this obvious. Even if a number of Empire States emerge, the British Empire, as constituted today, will not be one of them. There might conceivably be an Anglo-American Federation, to which some other countries adhere, or an Empire State. In such a Federation or Empire England's part will be a subordinate one. The type of spread-out empire which England possesses today cannot exist in future, except in the remote contingency of a world Empire State being established. Such a far-flung empire necessitates a command of the seas and the world's trade routes as well as an effective command of the air. No country or group of States is likely to have this world predominance. If empires exist, therefore, they must essentially be compact empires, with possibly some distant colonial possessions, which do not make any essential difference.

For a year or so before the war began there was considerable discussion about the possibility of a Union or Federation between various nations.

[1] I.A.A., p. 90.

Clarence Streit's "Union Now" attracted much attention, and there were many other proposals. Nearly all of them suffered from the vital defect of looking at the world as if it consisted of Europe and America only. China, India, and other Eastern countries were almost ignored. These proposals, though much discussed and welcomed, never had a chance of adoption in the pre-war world. No major country had the least intention of countenancing them. And so the time for this passed, when it could have made a difference, and how bitterly must some countries and Governments regret this lost opportunity. As the French Republic lay dying, England's Government, compelled by the peril of the hour, made their remarkable proposal for a Union with France. It was too late then, as so much has been too late in England's story. But it demonstrated, in a flash, how the old ideas of independent countries, and even of the British Empire, no longer applied.

And yet some people talk still of dominion status and the like,[1] not realizing that this idea is dead and cannot be revived. Some people again suggest a partitioning of India, on some strange and fantastic basis, forgetting that the world demands not further splitting-up, but a gathering together and a union of nations. It will tolerate no longer the small State.

What about our independence, then? Is this not a breaking-up of a present grouping of nations, and how does it fit in the future of world Federation? It is perfectly true that we want to end the British Empire because out of imperialism no true federation can emerge. And, in any event, India is not going to remain in this Empire, whatever happens. But the independence that we seek has never been looked at as isolation or the mere addition of a new national State to a crowd of others. We have always realized and looked forward to the world gathering closer together, and functioning through federation or union, which we would gladly join. But to ask us to accept dominion status, or to try to impose a particular union on us against our wishes, is something which, in the world context today, is singularly absurd, and is in any event not going to be tolerated by us, whatever the consequences.

The third inevitable change of the war is likely to be the ending of present-day capitalism and the introduction of far more planning and control in the economic system throughout the world. Together with this, capitalist democracy will also change, for it is a kind of luxury system for well-to-do nations, and it will not survive the hard times that will come. Under stress of war this democracy has already gone in many countries.

It will be unfortunate if democracy itself disappears and gives place to

[1] In relationship to a non-independent India, within the British Empire.

forms of dictatorship. There is that danger and we must try to guard against it. But the democracy that can survive will have to be different in some ways and more efficient than the type we have seen fading away in the West.

In this picture that unrolls itself, where do we come in, where does India stand? That has been made clear enough. We are entirely opposed to Naziism and we think that it would be a tragedy if Nazi Germany dominated the world. But we are sick and tired of being imposed upon by British imperialism, even as it passes away, and we would sooner perish than be the tools of this or that imperialism. It is astonishing that even now the independence of India sticks in the throat of the British Government; it is amazing that they still behave in the old lordly way and expect us to carry out their behests. Still they threaten us with pains and penalties. Still they preach to us their homilies. Still they are blind to what is happening. Do they imagine that they are strengthening themselves for this war by the policy they are adopting in India? Do they think that threats and compulsion are the keys to India's heart and India's help? They may get some money in this way, but they are running up an account against themselves in a currency that counts far more than gold or silver. There is anger today in India at what is happening and at the insufferable ways of numerous underlings.

To us waiting patiently for months and deliberately not trying to embarrass the English people in the hour of their trial and distress, this functioning of British imperialism has come as a revelation. Many of us sympathize with the British people, but we cannot help seeing that one of the war fronts of Britain today is in India and against us. If that is so we shall face it whatever the consequences. One thing may be taken for certain—we are not going to put up with dictation from any authority.[1]

[Britain's expansion of the Executive Council in India on July 22, 1940 to twelve members—of whom eight were Indians—failed to satisfy Congress leaders who continued to have but a single major aim: complete independence. A national Defence Council of thirty-one members, twenty-two from British India (twenty of them Indians), the rest from Indian States, was set up as an advisory body, to make suggestions concerning the war effort. An Indian member of the Executive Council was appointed Agent-General to Washington. The Congress policy of non-cooperation with the war effort nevertheless continued.]

[1] U.I., pp. 322-25.

4 | Fresh Congress Offer—Viceroy's August 8 Statement—Reactions to Statement— Bombay Congress Meetings, 1940

Fresh Congress Offer to British

[A more conciliatory proposal than Congress previously had offered to the British was made by Rajagopalachari[1] during the summer of 1940 (a proposal with which Nehru finally concurred). When the British rejected the offer, the Viceroy made a statement on August 8, 1940, which was instrumental in hardening the position of Congress.]

The development in the war situation posed new questions before the Congress Working Committee. Gandhiji wanted the Committee to extend the principle of nonviolence, to which we had adhered in our struggle for freedom, to the functioning of a free state. A free India must rely on this principle to guard itself against external aggression or internal disorder. This question did not rise for us at the time, but it occupied his own mind, and he felt that the time had come for a clear enunciation. Every one of us was convinced that we must adhere to our policy of nonviolence, as we had so far done, in our own struggle. The war in Europe had strengthened this conviction. But to commit the future state was another and a more difficult matter, and it was not easy to see how anyone moving on the plane of politics could do it.

Mr Gandhi felt, and probably rightly, that he could not give up or tone down a message which he had for the world. He must have freedom to give it as he liked and must not be kept back by political exigencies. So, for the first time, he went one way and the Congress Working Committee another. There was no break with him, for the bond was too strong, and he will no doubt continue to advise in many ways and often to lead. Yet it is perhaps true that by his partial withdrawal, a definite period in the history of our national movement has come to an end. In recent years I have found a certain hardness creeping into him, a lessening of the adaptability that he possessed. Yet the old spell is there, the old charm works,

---

[1] A leading member of Congress, a former Prime Minister of Madras; later to become Governor-General of Independent India before Republic Day, 1950.

and his personality and greatness tower over others. Let no one imagine that his influence over India's millions is any the less. He has been the architect of India's destiny for twenty years and more, and his work is not completed.

During the last few weeks, the Congress, at the instance of C. Rajago-palachari, made yet another offer to Britain. . . . Eager to avoid conflict, he put forward a proposal which was hesitatingly accepted by some of his colleagues. This proposal was the acknowledgment of India's independence by Britain and the immediate formation at the center of a Provisional National Government, which would be responsible to the present Central Assembly. If this were done, this Government would take charge of defense and thus help in the war effort.

This Congress proposal was eminently feasible and could be given effect to immediately without upsetting anything. The National Government was inevitably going to be a composite affair with full representation of minority groups. The proposal was definitely a moderate one. From the point of view of defense and war effort, it is patent that any serious effort involves the confidence and co-operation of the people. Only a national government has the chance to get this. It is not possible through imperialism.

But imperialism thinks otherwise and imagines that it can continue to function and to coerce people to do its will. Even when danger threatens, it is not prepared to get this very substantial help if this involves a giving up of political and economic control over India. It does not care even for the tremendous moral prestige which would come to it if it did the right thing in India, and the rest of the Empire. So the Viceroy gave reply on behalf of the British Government and rejected the Congress proposal. The alternative proposal that he put forward was identical with what he had suggested nine months before. . . .

The Viceroy made it further clear that no major change would take place even after the war unless this was approved of by various groups in India. Thus he gave a power of veto, not only to any minority group, but to the feudal princes and even to British vested interests. This was a complete negation of democracy. It was much worse. For he laid down conditions which were impossible of fulfillment and which made Indian independence even in the future impossible. What came as a peculiar shock to us was the deliberate attempt made by the British Government to encourage every disruptive and reactionary tendency and thus to break the unity of India.[1]

[1] T.F., pp. 370–72.

Viceroy's Statement—August 8, 1940

["1. India's anxiety at the moment of critical importance in the world struggle against tyranny and aggression to contribute to the full to the common cause and to the triumph of our common ideals is manifest. She has already made a mighty contribution. She is anxious to make a greater contribution still. His Majesty's Government are deeply concerned that that unity of national purpose in India which would enable her to do so should be achieved at as early a moment as possible. They feel that some further statement of their intentions may help to promote that unity. In that hope they have authorized me to make the present statement.

2. Last October, His Majesty's Government again made it clear that Dominion Status was their objective for India. They added that they were ready to authorize the expansion of the Governor-General's Council to include a certain number of representatives of the political parties, and they proposed the establishment of a consultative committee. In order to facilitate harmonious co-operation, it was obvious that some measure of agreement in the provinces between the majority parties was a desirable prerequisite to their joint collaboration at the Centre. Such agreement was, unfortunately, not reached, and in the circumstances no progress was then possible.

3. During the earlier part of this year I continued my efforts to bring the political parties together. In these last few weeks I again entered into conversations with prominent political personages in British India and the Chancellor of the Chamber of Princes, the results of which have been reported to His Majesty's Government. His Majesty's Government have seen also the resolutions passed by the Congress Working Committee, the Muslim League and the Hindu Mahasabha.

4. It is clear that earlier differences which had prevented the achievement of national unity remain unbridged. Deeply as His Majesty's Government regret this, they do not feel that they should any longer, because of those differences, postpone the expansion of the Governor-General's Council, and the establishment of a body which will more closely associate Indian public opinion with the conduct of the war by the Central Government. They have authorized me accordingly to invite a certain number of representative Indians to join my Executive Council. They have authorized me, further, to establish a War Advisory Council which would meet at regular intervals and which would contain representatives of the Indian States and other interests in the national life of India as a whole.

5. The conversations which have taken place, and the resolutions of the bodies which I have just mentioned made it clear, however, that there is still, in certain quarters, doubt as to the intentions of His Majesty's Government for the constitutional future of India, and that there is doubt, too, as to whether the position of minorities, whether political or religious, is sufficiently safeguarded in relation to any future constitutional change by assurances already given. There are two main points that have emerged.

On those two points His Majesty's Government now desire me to make their position clear.

6. The first is as to the position of minorities in relation to any future constitutional schemes. It has already been made clear that my declaration of last October does not exclude examination of any part either of the Act of 1935 or of the policy and plans on which it is based. His Majesty's Government's concern that full weight should be given to the views of minorities in any revision has also been brought out. That remains the position of His Majesty's Government.

It goes without saying that they could not contemplate transfer of their present responsibilities for the peace and welfare of India to any system of government whose authority is directly denied by large and powerful elements in India's national life. Nor could they be parties to the coercion of such elements into submission to such a government.

7. The second point of general interest is the machinery for building within the British Commonwealth of Nations the new constitutional scheme when the time comes. There has been very strong insistence that the framing of that scheme should be primarily the responsibility of Indians themselves, and should originate from Indian conceptions of the social, economic and political structure of Indian life. His Majesty's Government are in sympathy with that desire and wish to see it given the fullest practical expression subject to the due fulfilment of the obligations which Great Britain's long connection with India has imposed on her and for which His Majesty's Government cannot divest themselves of responsibility. It is clear that a moment when the Commonwealth is engaged in a struggle for existence is not one in which fundamental constitutional issues can be decisively resolved. But His Majesty's Government authorize me to declare that they will most readily assent to the setting up after the conclusion of the war, with the least possible delay, of a body representative of the principal elements in India's national life in order to devise the framework of the new Constitution. . . . They will lend every aid in their power to hasten decisions on all relevant matters to the utmost degree. Meanwhile they will welcome and promote in any way possible every sincere and practical step that may be taken by representative Indians themselves to reach a basis of friendly agreement, first upon the form which the post-war representative body should take and the methods by which it should arrive at its conclusions, and secondly, upon the principles and outlines of the Constitution itself. They trust, however, that for the period of the war (with the Central Government reconstituted and strengthened in the manner I have described, and with the help of the War Advisory Council) all parties, communities and interests will combine and co-operate in making a notable Indian contribution to the victory of the world cause which is at stake. Moreover, they hope that in this process new bonds of union and understanding will emerge, and thus pave the way towards the attainment by India of that free and equal partnership in the British Commonwealth which remains the proclaimed and accepted goal of the Imperial Crown and of the British Parliament."[1]]

[1] U.I., pp. 417-19.

Reactions to Viceroy's Statement

I. The Viceroy and the British Government have said a final no to us and to India. On the eve of the French collapse, Britain's rulers were unorthodox enough to propose a union of England and France. That was an astonishing proposal. It came too late. But it showed that the British Government had got out of the rut and could take a big step if the situation demanded it. But where their own interests are so vitally concerned, as in India, they still live in the rut, and not all the shock of war and danger has taken them out. Even an obvious advantage in this war cannot make them give up the special position that imperialism has conferred upon them. They talk complacently still of their Empire and of their desire to maintain it, forgetting perhaps that the word, which sounds so good to them, is a symbol to us of our own subjection, degradation, and poverty.

I repeat that it is incorrect to say that there is any new parting of the ways, for our ways never lay together. But this declaration of the British Government means the final breaking of such slender bonds as held our minds together; it means the ending of all hope that we shall ever march together. I am sorry, for in spite of my hostility to British imperialism and all imperialisms, I have loved much that was England, and I should have liked to keep the silken bonds of the spirit between India and England. Those bonds can only exist in freedom. I wanted India's freedom for India's sake, of course; but I also wanted it for England's sake. That hope is shattered, and fate seems to have fashioned a different future for us. The way of co-operation does not lie for us; the hundred-year-old hostility will remain and grow in future conflicts, and the breach, when it comes, as come it must, will also not be in friendship but in hostility.

I am told that the British Government has been led to believe that we shall tamely submit to their decrees because so far we have been quiescent. Our very restraint appears to have made them think that we were incapable of any action. In this world of force, of bombing airplanes, tanks, and armed men, how weak we are! Why trouble about us? But perhaps, even in this world of armed conflict, there is such a thing as the spirit of man, and the spirit of a nation, which is neither ignoble nor weak, and which may not be ignored, save at peril.

To those of us who are intimately connected with Indian politics, the British Government's reply needs no analysis or clarification. To do them justice, it is clear enough, and there is no ambiguity. Yet others perhaps might miss its significance and be misled by the use of resounding

words into thinking that something worthwhile was offered, that the
people of India were getting some power in her government.[1]

II. ["Dominion Status Idea Is Dead As A Door Nail"—August 11,
1940.] There is a big gulf between the Viceroy's statement and the present position of the Congress. . . .

Nationalism and imperialism . . . [are] fundamentally different and
[can] never come to terms because the basis of a national struggle [is] the
removal of imperialism and the establishment of independence.

The whole conception of Dominion Status [is] "as dead as a door nail"
and it [can] not survive because the whole background of the world [has]
changed and there [will] be further changes after the war. . . .

I do not want Indianization of the army. It is absurd. I want a national
army. The basis is different. I may engage British officers but that is a
different matter.[2]

III. [Congress Resolution—August 22, 1940—reply to Viceroy.]
The [Congress] Working Committee . . . passed the following Resolution
on August 22, 1940, in reply to the Viceroy's statement of August 8, and
[the Secretary of State for India] Mr Amery's subsequent statement in
Parliament:

"The Working Committee have read the statement issued by the
Viceroy on the authority of the British Government on August 8, and the
report of the speech of the Secretary of State for India in the House of
Commons, explaining the Viceroy's statement. They note with deep
regret that the British Government have rejected the friendly offer and
practical suggestion contained in the [recent] resolution of the A.I.C.C.
of July 28, framed for a solution of the deadlock and to enable the Indian
National Congress to withdraw its non-co-operation and secure in the
recent crisis the patriotic co-operation of all the people of India in the
governance of India and the organization of national defence.

"The Working Committee have read with pain and indignation the
declarations and assumptions contained in the statements and speeches
made on behalf of the British Government which seek to deny India her
natural right of complete national freedom and reiterate the untenable
claim that Britain should maintain herself in a dominant position in India
in the discharge of the higher functions of the state. These claims render
false and empty even their own promise to recognize India at an early date
as a free and equal unit within the British Commonwealth.

"Such claims and recent events and developments in the world have
confirmed the Committee's conviction that India cannot function within
the orbit of an imperial power and must attain the status of a free and
independent nation. This does not prevent close association with other

[1] T.F., pp. 379-80.
[2] I.A.A., p. 338.

countries within a comity of free nations for the peace and progress of the world.

"The Working Committee are of the opinion that the assertion contained in the statements made on behalf of the British Government that they will not part with power and responsibility in favour of the elected representatives of the people of India and that, therefore, the present autocratic and irresponsible system of government must continue, so long as any group of people or the Princes, as distinguished from the people of the States, or perhaps even foreign vested interests, raise objections to any Constitution framed by the elected representatives of the people of India, is a direct encouragement and incitement to civil discord and strife, and amounts to a fatal blow to all willingness to compromise and adjustment of claims.

"The Committee regret that although the Congress has never thought in terms of coercing any minority, much less of asking the British Government to do so, the demand for a settlement of the Constitution, through a Constituent Assembly of duly elected representatives, has been misrepresented as coercion, and the issue of minorities has been made into an insuperable barrier to India's progress. The Congress has proposed that minority rights should be amply protected by agreement with elected representatives of the minorities concerned. The Working Committee, therefore, cannot but conclude that the attitude and assertions contained in statements made on behalf of the British Government, confirm the prevailing feeling that the British authority has been continually operating so as to create, maintain and aggravate differences in India's national life.

"The Working Committee note with astonishment that the demand for the constitution of a provisional Government, composed of persons commanding the confidence of the various elected groups in the present Central Legislature, formed under the 1919 Constitution of India, has been described by the Secretary of State for India as one that would raise the unsolved constitutional issue, and prejudice it in favour of the majority and against the minorities.

"The Working Committee are of the opinion that the rejection of this proposal unmistakably indicates that there is no willingness on the part of the British Government to part with any power and authority even for the immediate purpose of securing co-operation in the war [effort]. The British Government would gather together and carry on with such dissentient groups and individuals as oppose the wishes of the majority of the people of India and without any co-ordination with the elected Legislature at the centre or in the provinces, rather than concede anything that would work towards the recognition of the rights of the people of India to rule themselves democratically.

"For these reasons the Working Committee have come to the conclusion that the statements referred to are wholly opposed not only to the principle of democracy, as acclaimed by the British Government in the war, but also to the best interests of India, and they cannot be a Party to accepting the proposals contained in the statement or advising the country to accept them.

"The Working Committee consider that these declarations and offers not only fall far short of the Congress demand, but would be impediments to the evolution of a free and united India.

"The Working Committee call upon the people to condemn the attitude adopted by the British Government by means of public meetings and otherwise, as also through their elected representatives in the provincial Legislature."[1]

Bombay Congress Meetings, 1940

[In view of Congress rejection of the Viceroy's August proposal, the All-India Congress Committee passed the following resolution, in pursuance of which Gandhi assumed leadership, ordering civil disobedience. According to the Mahatma the language of the resolution was essentially his own, although it was drafted by Nehru.

Gandhi described what occurred: "The language of this resolution is in the main mine. It appealed to Pandit Jawaharlal Nehru. I used to be the Congress draftsman. Now he has taken my place. He saw it was inevitable if we were to be true to . . . non-violent resistance to the extent to which we wanted to go. The Working Committee has accepted this phraseology deliberately, well knowing its implications. . . .

"I do not want England to be defeated or humiliated."[2]

Nehru was, in fact, by no means satisfied with the Resolution.]

[From Congress Resolution, moved by Nehru—September 15, 1940. Since the Resolution was approved, Gandhi was to assume Congress leadership and order Civil Disobedience.]

"The All-India Congress Committee cannot submit to a policy which is a denial of India's natural right to freedom, which suppresses the free expression of public opinion and which would lead to the degradation of her people and their continued enslavement. By following this policy the British Government have created an intolerable situation, and are imposing upon the Congress a struggle for the preservation of the honour and the elementary rights of the people. The Congress is pledged under Gandhi's leadership to non-violence for the vindication of India's freedom. At this grave crisis in the movement for national freedom, the All-India Congress Committee, therefore, requests him to guide the Congress in the action that should be taken. . . .

"The All-India Congress Committee sympathises with the British people as well as the peoples of all other countries involved in the war.

[1] U.I., pp. 419–21.
[2] T.D.G. (Vol. V), p. 322.

Congressmen cannot withhold their admiration for the bravery and endurance shown by the British nation in the face of danger and peril. They can have no ill will against them, and the spirit of 'Satyagraha' forbids the Congress from doing anything with a view to embarrass them. But this self-imposed restraint cannot be taken to the extent of self-extinction. The Congress must insist on the fullest freedom to pursue its policy, based on non-violence. The Congress has, however, no desire at the present moment to extend non-violent resistance, should this become necessary, beyond what is required for the preservation of the liberties of the people."[1]

[When the Mahatma sought an interview with the Viceroy, and met him on September 27, the Viceroy stated that the course of action proposed in the name of Congress would inhibit India's war effort. In view of the inhibition of the civil liberties of Congress members themselves, however, and the fact that India remained a subject nation, the Viceroy's logic held little appeal. Moreover, personal indignities continued to multiply: During the year since the war had begun, "Over two thousand Congressmen and women had been arrested, and a large number of people had been directed (1) to report themselves at the police stations at regular intervals; (2) not to take part in any subversive movement or indulge in any anti-war campaign; (3) not to converse, communicate or associate with any school or college students; (4) not to attend meetings of any kind; and (5) to notify in person departure from one place to another to the police station at least twenty-four hours before the time of departure."[2]

When the Viceroy "rejected the [Congress] demand for unlimited freedom of speech on the grounds that the war effort would be seriously impaired", Gandhi decided that there was no alternative save to launch a civil disobedience campaign. "Despite the free hand given him by the Congress, he restricted himself to the least effective weapon in his armoury —individual civil disobedience. His primary objectives were to symbolize the Congress protest against 'participation without consultation' and to establish the right of free speech, even in time of war, but not to embarrass the war effort as such. It was a strange campaign indeed. Selected individuals were to recite in public a set formula of an anti-war slogan: 'It is wrong to help the British war effort with men or money. The only worthy effort is to resist all war with non-violent resistance.' No other action was prescribed."[3]

Nehru continued to be agonized by conflicting emotions—concern about opposing the Nazis and Fascists, his desire for Indian independence, his respect for Gandhi's ideals.]

[1] U.I. p. 422.
[2] T.T.N., p. 83.
[3] M.B., p. 271.

2*

| 5 | Individual Satyagraha—Eighth Arrest—Letter from Gandhi—Statement at Trial, November, 1940—Letters from Jail—Interruption of Work of National Planning Committee |

Individual Satyagraha

[On October 17, 1940, the day on which individual satyagraha, or civil disobedience, was initiated.] Mahatma Gandhi's approach to many problems is often a non-political approach. Some of us, including me, view [the same] questions from a political angle only, though all of us, I hope, keep in mind the moral aspect of every question. I have sometimes found it difficult to understand Gandhiji's approach because my mind functions differently. While fully appreciating the political aspects of non-violence in our struggle, I have been unable to appreciate many of its implications. Gandhiji, though he lays emphasis on certain ethical and other aspects, does not ignore political aspects, as everyone knows. It is perhaps a question of emphasis for him. He has developed a certain technique of action which has yielded great results to our movement for freedom.

It is clear that the Congress and the country want that technique to be continued and it is obvious that Gandhiji is best fitted to lead a movement with that technique. In many matters I have ventured to disagree with him and probably I may continue to disagree with him. But at the present moment I have no doubt that we must give full and loyal co-operation to him, so that he may have full [opportunity] of developing this great movement. Any other course would be a foolish one, leading nowhere. Events are likely to develop fast. Let us be prepared for them and not waste our time in theoretical arguments.

This does not mean my accepting all the implications of everything that Gandhiji may put forward, but I do propose to function as a disciplined soldier so long as I can.[1]

[1] I.A.A., p. 339.

Eighth Arrest

[Vinoba Bhave—a devoted disciple of Gandhi, later to become leader of India's Bhoodan, or land-grant movement—was chosen to be the first satyagrahi by the Mahatma. He delivered an anti-war speech on October 17. Nehru, who was to be the second to offer satyagraha on November 7, was arrested on October 31, for three speeches he had made in the district of Gorakhpur on October 6 and 7.[1]

The public reason given for Nehru's arrest was that he had participated in launching individual civil disobedience. A confidential British report admitted a secret motivation: his imprisonment served to terminate "the sort of agrarian discontent" that he was accused of "endeavouring to stir up".

Nehru's eighth jail sentence ended on December 4, 1941. Although his original term was to have been for four years, even Churchill conceded that this was too extreme a punishment, requesting that Nehru "receive specially considerate treatment". [2]]

Letter from Gandhi to Nehru—October 24, 1940

["If you are ready you may now ceremonially declare your civil disobedience. I would suggest your choosing a village for your audience. I do not suppose they will allow you to repeat your speech. They were not ready with their plans so far as Vinoba was concerned. But should they let you free I suggest your following the plan laid down for Vinoba. But if you feel otherwise, you will follow your own course. Only I would like you to give me your programme. You will fix your own date so as to leave me time for announcing the date and place. It may be that they won't let you even fulfil your very first programme. I am prepared for every such step on the part of the Government. Whilst I would make use of every legitimate method seeking publicity for our programme my reliance is on regulated thought producing its own effect. If this is hard for you to believe, I would ask you to suspend judgment and watch results. I know you will yourself be patient and ask our people on your side to do likewise. I know what strain you are bearing in giving me your loyalty. I prize it beyond measure. I hope it will be found to have been well-placed for it is 'do or die'. There is no turning back. Our case is invulnerable. There is no giving in. Only I must be allowed to go my way in demonstrating the power of non-violence when it is unadulterated."[3]]

[1] T.T.N., p. 83.
[2] Quoted in M.B., p. 272.
[3] B.O.L., pp. 453–54.

Statement at Trial—Gorakhpur Prison, November 3, 1940

I have been told that the charge against me is based on the reports of three speeches I delivered in the Gorakhpur district early in October last. Copies of these reports, and in one case their translation into English, have been given to me. I have read these, and I cannot congratulate the persons who were responsible for the reporting. These reports, though presumably taken down in shorthand, are scrappy and incomplete, confusing, and often making little sense.

I am a lover of words and phrases and try to use them appropriately. Whatever my opinions might be, the words I use are meant to express them intelligibly and in ordered sequence. A reader of these reports will find little intelligence or sequence in them, and is likely to obtain an entirely distorted impression of what I actually said.

I make no complaint of this reporting, and I do not suggest that deliberate distortions have been made. But I do want to make it clear that what I said was in many respects entirely different from what the jumble of words in the reports would lead me to imagine. If this is so in the reporting of my speeches, when care is taken and . . . more qualified men are employed, I cease to wonder what happens when the speeches of others are reported by totally unqualified persons and these are made the basis of charges in courts of law.

It is not my intention to give details of the many errors and mistakes in these reports. That would mean rewriting them completely. That would waste your time, sir, and mine and would serve little purpose. I am not here to defend myself, and perhaps what I say in this statement will make your task easier. I do not yet know the exact nature of the charge against me. I gather that it has something to do with the Defence of India Rules and that it relates to my references to war and to the attempts being made to compel the people of India to take part in the war effort. If that is so, I shall gladly admit the charge. It is not necessary to go to garbled reports to find out what I or other Congressmen say in regard to India and the war. The Congress resolutions and statements, carefully and precisely worded, are there for all the world to know. By those resolutions and statements I stand, and I consider it my duty to take the message of the Congress to the people of India.

As a matter of fact, ever since the Congress came to the conclusion that, in order to give effect to the Congress policy, *satyagraha*, or civil disobedience, should be started, I have endeavoured to check myself in my utterances and to avoid what might be termed *satyagraha*. Such was the direction of our chief, Mahatma Gandhi, who desired that the *satyagraha* should be confined to particular persons of his choice.

One such person was selected, and he expressed in public utterances the Congress attitude to the war, laying some emphasis on the Congress policy of non-violence. It was my good fortune to have been selected to follow him and to give expression to the Congress viewpoint, with perhaps greater emphasis on the political aspect. It had been decided that I should do so, after giving due notice to the authorities, from November 7 onwards, in the district of Allahabad. That programme has been varied owing to my arrest and trial, and the opportunity to give frank and full expression to Congress policy in regard to the war has come to me earlier than I anticipated.

If I was chosen, or if before me Shri Vinoba Bhave was chosen for this purpose, it was not to give expression to our individual views. We were symbols who spoke the mind of India in the name of India, or, at any rate, of a vast number of people in India. As individuals we may have counted for little, but as such symbols and representatives of the Indian people we counted for a great deal. In the name of those people we asserted their right to freedom and to decide for themselves what they should do and what they would not do; we challenged the right of any other authority by whomsoever constituted to deprive them of this right and to force its will upon them. No individual or groups of individuals, not deriving authority from the Indian people and not responsible to them in any way, should impose their will upon them and thrust the hundreds of millions of India, without any reference to them or their representatives, into a mighty war which was none of their seeking. It was amazing and full of significance that this should be done in the name of freedom and self-determination and democracy, for which, it was alleged, the war was being waged.

We were slow in coming to our final conclusions; we hesitated and parleyed; we sought a way out honourable to all the parties concerned. We failed, and the inevitable conclusion was forced upon us that, so far as the British Government or their representatives were concerned, we were still looked upon as chattels to do their will and to continue to be exploited in their imperialist structure. That was a position which we could never tolerate, whatever the consequences.

There are very few persons in India, I suppose, whether they are Indians or Englishmen, who have for years past so consistently raised their voices against Fascism and Naziism as I have done. My whole nature rebelled against them, and on many an occasion I vehemently criticized the pro-Fascist and appeasement policy of the British Government. Ever since the invasion of Manchuria, and subsequently in Abyssinia, Central Europe, Spain, and China, I saw with pain and anguish how country after country was betrayed in the name of this appeasement and how the lamps of liberty were being put out. I realized that imperialism could only function in this way; it had to appease its rival imperialism, or else its own ideological foundations were weakened. It had to choose between this and liquidating itself in favour of democratic freedom. There was no middle way.

So long as appeasement applied to Manchuria, Abyssinia, Czecho-Slovakia, Spain, and Albania, to "far-away countries about which few people had ever heard," as the then Prime Minister of England put it, it did not matter much and was faithfully pursued. But when it came nearer home and threatened the British Empire itself, the clash came and war began.

Again there were two alternatives before the British Government and each Government engaged in the war—to continue to function in the old imperialist way or to end this in their own domains and become the leaders of the urge for freedom and revolutionary change the world over. They chose the former, though they still talked in terms of freedom, self-determination, and democracy. But their conception of freedom was, even in words, limited to Europe, and evidently meant freedom to carry on with their Empire in the old way. Not even peril and disaster have weakened their intention to hold on to their Empire and enforce their will upon subject peoples.

In India we have had over a year of war government. The people's elected Legislatures have been suspended and ignored, and a greater and more widespread autocracy prevails here than anywhere else in the world. Recent measures have suppressed completely such limited freedom as the Press possessed to give facts and opinions. If this is the prelude to the freedom that is promised us, or to the "New Order" about which so much is said, then we can well imagine what the later stages will be. . . .

I am convinced that the large majority of people in England are weary of Empire and hunger for a real new order. But we have to deal, not with them, but with their Government, and we have no doubt in our minds as to what that Government aims at. With that we have nothing in common, and we shall resist to the uttermost. We have therefore decided to be no party to this imposed war and to declare this to the world.

This war has led already to widespread destruction and will lead to even greater horror and misery. With those who suffer we sympathize deeply and in all sincerity. But unless the war has a revolutionary aim of ending the present order and substituting something based on freedom and co-operation, it will lead to a continuation of wars and violence and utmost destruction.

That is why we must dissociate ourselves from this war and advise our people to do likewise and not help in any way with money or men. That is our bounden duty. But even apart from this, the treatment accorded the Indian people during the past year by the British authorities, the latter's attempt to encourage every disruptive and reactionary tendency, their forcible realizations of money for the war from even the poor of India, and their repeated affronts to Indian nationalism, are such that we can never forget or ignore.

No self-respecting people can tolerate such behaviour, and the people of India have no intention of tolerating it.

I stand before you, sir, as an individual being tried for certain offences against the State. You are a symbol of that State. But I am something more than an individual also; I, too, am a symbol at the present moment, a symbol of Indian nationalism, resolved to break away from the British Empire and achieve the independence of India. It is not me that you are seeking to judge and condemn, but rather the hundreds of millions of the people of India, and that is a large task even for a proud Empire. Perhaps it may be that, though I am standing before you on my trial, it is the British Empire itself that is on its trial before the bar of the world. There are more powerful forces at work in the world today than courts of law; there are elemental urges for freedom and food and security which are moving vast masses of people, and history is being moulded by them. The future recorder of this history might well say that in the hour of supreme trial the Government of Britain and the people of Britain failed because they could not adapt themselves to a changing world. He may muse over the fate of empires which have always fallen because of this weakness and call it destiny. Certain causes inevitably produce certain results. We know the causes; the results are inexorably in their train.

It is a small matter to me what happens to me in this trial or subsequently. Individuals count for little; they come and go, as I shall go when my time is up. Seven times I have been tried and convicted by British authority in India, and many years of my life lie buried within prison walls. An eighth time or a ninth, and a few more years, make little difference.

But it is no small matter what happens to India and her millions of sons and daughters. That is the issue before me, and that ultimately is the issue before you, sir. If the British Government imagines it can continue to exploit them and play about with them against their will, as it has done for so long in the past, then it is grievously mistaken. It has misjudged their present temper and read history in vain.

I should like to add that I am happy to be tried in Gorakhpur. The peasantry of Gorakhpur are the poorest and the most long-suffering in my Province. I am glad that it was my visit to the Gorakhpur district and my attempt to serve its people that has led to this trial.

I thank you, sir, for your courtesy.[1]

[Sentenced to four years' rigorous imprisonment on November 4, 1940, Nehru was sent to Dehra Dun jail.]

From Letters to Krishna Hutheesing—from District Jail, Dehra Dun

I. [December 2, 1940.] I have gone through nearly six years of prison with relative ease because of the work I have done. I bear prison lightly. And always I am thinking of preparing myself in mind and body for my next job. I store energy so that I might be able to squander it later on.

I have been a month in prison—out of the forty-eight months [to which I am sentenced]. If there [were] any likelihood of . . . forgetting this, the new moon was there to remind me. I came to . . . prison with the new moon—the day after Divali and on the eve of Id. During this month I have read a score of books, spun a good deal of good yarn, taken regular exercise and slept abundantly. And not once, so far as I can recollect have I lost my temper! That in itself is a sure sign of physical and mental health.

I have taken things easily during this month. I wanted to get rid of a feeling of tiredness, and it takes some time to settle down. I have done little hard work intellectually. I wanted to let my mind lie fallow—to busy myself with odd physical activities. It is surprising how many such jobs can be done in prison. Cleaning and washing and generally keeping "my own quarters" in as decent a condition as is possible, absorb quite a deal of time. Then I started digging. I decided to make the most of the digging. It was hard work for the soil is stony. Digging anyhow is not a

U.I., pp. 395–400.

light occupation, and I was annoyed at myself when I found that I got tired easily. I improved with practice. Having done this, I played about with the fresh earth—how delightful it is!—and we put in some seedlings and flower seeds. Like a fond but foolish parent, straightway I started spoiling our work by too much attention. I think I watered them more than was necessary and some of the seeds and seedlings seem to have rolled away. However, I shall get over these minor difficulties.[1]

II. [December 12, 1940.] It is not just superfluous energy that leads me to dabble in . . . various activities. I do it deliberately to have peace of mind and a certain harmonious and well-ordered life. I succeed. I keep physically fit and mentally fit and sane. It is a fact, I think, that every visit to jail has done me good in some way or other; not merely the actual work I have done there, but some kind of development on, I hope, the right lines has taken place. I succeed very largely in cutting myself away from the worries and responsibilities that encumber me outside. I do not forget them but I think about them more calmly and dispassionately and look at them from a larger perspective.

In the world today, torn by war and disaster and possibly on the brink of vast changes, not to do so would lead to mental collapse. Long periods in prison are apt to make one either a mental and physical wreck or a philosopher. I flatter myself that I kept myself very well during all these years. I do not know if they have led me far towards philosophy.[2]

Interruption of Work of National Planning Committee

[While out of jail, Nehru had worked constantly and devotedly with the National Planning Committee (see Part Five, Section 12). Although the Committee's work could have been extremely helpful to the war effort, it was not utilized because of Britain's refusal to liberate India from colonial rule.]

The Planning Committee continued its work and had nearly finished dealing with its subcommittees' reports. We were to finish what little remained of this work and then proceed to the consideration of our own comprehensive report. I was, however, arrested in October 1940 and sentenced to a long term of imprisonment. Several other members of the

[1] N.L.H.S., pp. 66–67.
[2] Ibid., p. 70.

Planning Committee and its subcommittees were also arrested and sentenced. I was anxious that the Planning Committee should continue to function, and requested my colleagues outside to do so. But they were not willing to work in the committee in my absence. I tried to get the Planning Committee's papers and reports in prison so that I might study them and prepare a draft report. The Government of India intervened and stopped this. No such papers were allowed to reach me, nor were interviews on the subject permitted.

So the National Planning Committee languished, while I spent my days in jail. All the work we had done which, though incomplete, could be used to great advantage for war purposes, remained in the pigeonholes of our office. I was released in December 1941 and was out of prison for some months. But this period was a hectic one for me, as it was for others. All manner of new developments had taken place, the Pacific war was on, India was threatened with invasion, and it was not possible then to pick up the old threads and continue the unfinished work of the Planning Committee unless the political situation cleared up. And then I returned to prison.[1]

[The work of the Planning Committee, which was to be taken up again at a later time, will be described in future sections.

Gandhi stated in 1940: "Nehru wants industrialization, because he thinks that if it is socialized, it [will] be free from the evils of capitalism. My own view is that the evils are inherent in industrialism, and no amount of socialization can eradicate them."[2]]

6 | Eastern Federation—India, China, Asia

Everyone who has been following the course of events, and everyone who can at all pierce the veil of the future, must have come to the conclusion that we have come to the end of an age. The old world we have known so

[1] D.I., pp. 407–08.
[2] T.D.G. (Vol. V), p. 336.

long is dead or lies dying before us. That, of course, does not mean that the world will cease to be. That does not even mean that civilization will perish. But it does mean that the many things that we have known— political forms, economic structures, social relationships, and all else connected with these—will undergo a vast transformation. If any person thinks in terms of the continuation of the world as we have known it, he thinks in vain.

It is patent that the day of small countries is past. It is also patent that the day of even big countries standing by themselves is past. Huge countries like the Soviet Union or the United States of America may be capable of standing by themselves, but even they are likely to join themselves with other countries or groups.

The only intelligent solution is a world federation of free countries. Perhaps we are not wise enough to seek that solution or strong enough to realize it.

If there is going to be no world federation in the near future, and if the day of individual nations is past, what, then, is likely to happen? There may be groupings of nations or large federations. There is a grave danger in this, as it is likely to lead to hostile groupings and therefore to the continuation of large-scale wars.

It is possible, also, that these groupings may be the first steps to the larger world grouping of nations.

In Europe people talk of a European federation or union; sometimes they include the United States of America and the British Dominions in this group. They leave out always China and India, imagining that these two great countries can be ignored. There can be no world arrangement which is based on ignoring India or China, nor can we ever tolerate the exploitation of Asia and Africa by the combined European and American Powers.

If there are to be federations, India will not fit into a European federation where it can only be a hanger-on of semi-colonial status. It is obvious that under these circumstances there should be an Eastern federation, not hostile to the West, but nevertheless standing on its own feet, self-reliant and joining with all others to work for world peace and world federation.

Such an Eastern federation must inevitably consist of China and India, Burma and Ceylon, and Nepal and Afghanistan should be included. So should Malaya. There is no reason why Siam and Iran should also not join, as well as some other nations. That would be a powerful combination of free nations joined together for their own good as well as for the world good. Power would not be merely material power, but something else also, which they have represented through these long ages. It is time, therefore, in this fateful period of the breakdown of empires that we thought in terms of this Eastern federation and worked for it deliberately.

With two nations, even more than with others, this Eastern Federation will be intimately connected. These nations or groups will be the Soviet Union and America.

There is a great deal of talk about the downfall of Western civilization. This is probably correct in so far as the finance-imperialism of the West, as well as the capitalist order is concerned. But ultimately much that is best in European civilization should survive. Nevertheless, it is true, I think, that present-day civilization is ending and out of its ashes a new civilization will be built up, continuing, I hope, the best elements of the East and of the West. No country can do without the science of which the West has been the pioneer. That science and the scientific spirit and method are the basis of life today, and there lies in science the search for truth on the one hand, and the betterment of humanity on the other. But the application of that science to evil ends has brought disaster to the West. It is here that India and China, with their restraining influence and long background of culture and restraint, come in.

So let us look forward and labour for an Eastern Federation, never forgetting that it is a step towards the larger world federation.[1]

[India, China, Asia—November, 1940.] China and India have represented throughout the ages two distinct and deep-rooted civilizations and cultures, each very different from the other and yet with numerous common features. Like all ancient countries, they have gathered round them all manner of débris in the form of old custom and tradition which hinder growth, but underneath this mess of useless material there lies the pure gold that has kept them going for all these ages. Not all the degradation and the misfortunes that have befallen both China and India have melted this golden core which made them great in the past and which even today gives stature to them. . . .

For many years now, and more especially for the last three years and more, China has been going through the ordeal of fire. How can we measure the immeasurable suffering of the Chinese people, invaded and attacked by an imperialist aggressor, bombed in their cities night after night and made to face all the horrors of modern war by a first-rate power. London has suffered greatly from bombing during the last two or three

[1] U.I., pp. 326–28.

months. But what of Chungking that has had to face this bombing for years now, and yet lives? We cannot measure this suffering, nor can we measure the determination and epic courage which has faced these disasters and sufferings unmoved and unbent. In the magnificent story of the Chinese people from the dawn of history to today there are many glorious periods and fine deeds. But surely the past three years will stand out even in that great record.

These years have been years of swift transition from the past to the present and preparation for the future that is to come. The dross and the débris are being burned away in the fire of a nation's suffering, and the pure metal comes out. We in India have had our own share of trials and tribulations and are likely to have much more of it in the near future. So nations who are slothful and who have sunk into subjection are made again; so China and India are being rejuvenated.[1]

[From letter, December 17, 1940.] I am firmly convinced that the future of the world depends on the outcome of the united struggle of our Asiatic peoples. In view of the ever increasing Japanese ambition and the momentous world changes, we, in order to safeguard liberty and freedom, must first of all bring the chief perturber of peace to account.[2]

| 7 | World War II Developments, 1941: Atlantic Charter—Evolution of U.S. and British Policy Toward India |

World War II Developments, 1941 : Atlantic Charter

[On March 8, 1941, the U.S. Senate passed a Lend-Lease bill, empowering President Roosevelt to give "all-out" aid to Britain, or any other countries opposing the Axis. On March 11, France ceded territory in Indo-China to Thailand, under a peace protocol arranged by the Japanese. Belgrade was captured by the Nazis on April 13. On the same day Russia and Japan signed a five-year treaty of non-aggression and mutual friendship. On June 22, Germany invaded Russia; on July 24 the Japanese initiated their occupation of Indo-China.

[1] Ibid., pp. 331–32.
[2] Quoted in M.H.I., p. 128.

The Atlantic Charter, promulgated by U.S. President Franklin D. Roosevelt and British Prime Minister Winston Churchill, was made public on August 14, 1941. Among its provisions were the following clauses: that the U.S. and Britain "(1) . . . seek no aggrandizement, territorial or other; (2) . . . desire to see no territorial changes that do not accord with the freely expressed wishes of the peoples concerned; (3) . . . respect the right of all peoples to choose the form of government under which they will live; and . . . wish to see sovereign rights and self-government restored to those who have been forcibly deprived of them."[1]

Louis Fischer recounts that immediately after the signing of the Charter: "I was in the House of Commons in London in September of 1941 when Winston Churchill returned from his rendezvous with President Roosevelt in the Atlantic, where they drew up the Atlantic Charter. A member of Parliament stood up and said to Churchill, 'Mr. Prime Minister, does Article III of the Atlantic Charter which grants all countries the right to choose their own form of government, apply to India?'

"Churchill rose and said, 'No, sir,' and sat down. In other words, the Atlantic Charter which President Roosevelt said applies to the whole world does not in Churchill's word apply to India."[2] "Neither, according to Churchill, did the Charter apply to Burma, but only to the 'European nations under Nazi occupation'."[3]

"Prime Minister Churchill, in his House of Commons statement of September 9, 1941 asserted that the [Atlantic Charter] . . . did not qualify in any way various statements of policy which had been made from time to time about the development of constitutional government in India, notably the declaration of August 1940, and that he and President Roosevelt had primarily in mind the restoration of sovereignty to the peoples of Europe under [the] Nazi yoke. The formal extension of the war to the Far East and the general acceptance by the nations engaged in fighting the Axis Powers of the Declaration by [the] United Nations made these qualifications highly anomalous."[4]

Evolution of U.S. and British Policy Toward India

[Announcement by U.S. Department of State, July 21, 1941: "The Government of the United States and the British Government, in consultation with the Government of India, agreed to an exchange of representatives on a reciprocal basis between the United States and India.

"It is expected that an American Foreign Service officer will be designated to represent the United States in the capacity of Commissioner at Delhi, the capital of India."[5]

[1] T.A.Y. (XII–XIII), p. 45.
[2] T.A.Y. (X–XI), p. 51.
[3] I.N. (Feb. 22, 1963), p. 8.
[4] D.A.F.R. (Vol. IV), pp. 544–45.
[5] Ibid. (Vol. IV), p. 543.

"Roosevelt realized in 1941 the strategic importance of India (because of her geographical position) being a base of operations in the war. Mr Berle, the [U.S.] Assistant Secretary of State, pointed out in a memorandum that on every consideration of principle and policy India's wholehearted support for the war effort was essential; her vast manpower and material resources and the wholesome repercussions of her achievement of freedom on the countries of the Middle East suggested immediate steps being taken by the British Government to give India a sense of partnership with the other units of the Commonwealth. But Mr Cordell Hull, the [U.S.] Secretary of State, failed to get a positive response to the suggestions from Lord Halifax, the British Ambassador in Washington. Gandhiji's pacifist attitude and Hindu-Muslim tensions were cited as formidable difficulties.

"Mr Winant, the American Ambassador in London, was, however, in complete agreement with Mr Berle. 'A friendly India,' he told the President, 'could be a valuable ally in the war' and restrain Japan from participation on the Nazi side. The promise of Dominion Status to India 'to be implemented within a stated period following the cessation of hostilities,' Mr Winant thought, would be acceptable to a number of members of the British Cabinet, though not to Mr Churchill.

"By August ... [1941] the further deterioration in the war situation seemed to the President a valid reason for a fresh approach in regard to India."[1]

While Nehru was still confined in jail, the Viceroy finally expanded the Executive Council, creating a special War Advisory Council. L. S. Amery, British Secretary of State for India, attempted to reassure India concerning the ultimate attainment of self-government, as well as full and equal partnership in the British Commonwealth. He maintained, however, that communal rivalry was the major block to India's achieving freedom.]

8 | Tagore and Gandhi—Letter from Jail— Release from Prison

Evolution of Attitude toward Tagore (up to time of Tagore's Death, August 7, 1941), and to Gandhi

[This reminiscence is included at this point, even though written later, due to the fact that Tagore died in August, 1941, while Nehru was in Dehra Dun Jail.]

[1] I.N. (Feb. 22, 1963), p. 8. (From article *Roosevelt and India*, by B. Shiva Rao.)

I . . . find it rather difficult to write about persons who, in their greatness and magnificence, have over-shadowed my life as indeed they over-shadowed the life of the nation. Such were Gandhi and Tagore. With Gandhi it was not only his greatness but also his intimacy that comes in my way; with Rabindranath Tagore my physical contacts were limited and cannot be considered to have been very intimate. And yet, the same reluctance seizes me and perhaps a sense of humility, even though I do not normally suffer from this feeling.

Who am I to write about or pass judgement on a person who was so deep in his humanity and so many-sided in his greatness? Many eminent persons have [already written of Tagore]. Can I write anything that might be considered significant and that might add to our understanding of [him]?

Gandhi came on the public scene in India like a thunderbolt shaking us all, and like a flash of lightning which illumined our minds and warmed our hearts; Tagore's influence was not so sudden or so earth-shaking for Indian humanity. And yet, like the coming of the dawn in the mountains, it crept on us and permeated us. I belong to a generation which grew up under his influence. Perhaps we did not fully realize it at the time because of the powerful impact of Gandhi's thunderbolt. I speak more for the non-Bengali-speaking people in India, and more especially students and the younger intellectuals who did not have the advantage of reading Tagore in the original Bengali. In Bengal his influence was no doubt deeper and more pervasive because his songs reached the masses of the people.

I have always been fascinated by these two towering personalities, Gandhi and Tagore, both by their contrasts and what they had in common. Externally and in the course of their lives, there was a great deal of difference, and yet both were close to each other and had the greatest affection and admiration for one another. Both were rebels in their own way and fearless in denouncing what they considered evil. Both were attached to truth as they saw it, to the dynamic character of the living truth, and it is this that gave them their enormous strength. Both, fully conscious of the modern world and reacting to it in somewhat different ways, were heirs to the spiritual tradition of India. And thus both of them gave a spiritual basis to our demand for freedom. They laid stress on the life of the spirit and believed in the religion of Man. Both, in varying degrees, were against the bondage of tradition and denounced superstition and ritual, even though they attached the greatest importance to our inheritance from the past and sought to build upon it in the present. Tagore referred to "the unfortunate people who have lost the harvest of their past, who have lost the present age ", and spoke about them as one of the " disinherited peoples of the world ". Gandhi, laying stress on India's past treasures of the mind and spirit, told us not to close our doors and windows to the winds that blew in from the four quarters of the world; but he warned us not to be uprooted or blown away by these winds.

And yet how different the two were! Tagore was the poet and the singer; Gandhi was the man of action, the true revolutionary, single-minded in his aim and going as the arrow from the bow. To Tagore poetry and music were the essence of life which gave it rhythm, and his philosophy was one of living in harmony with nature. Gandhi did not talk or perhaps read much of poetry or art, and yet his life . . . was a poem in action, and he wanted to put himself in harmony not only with nature, but with the lowest in nature. And so Gandhi crept into the hearts of those who were disinherited and whose life was one long tale of unhappiness.

I remember my first visit to Santiniketan [the educational institution founded by Tagore]. I think it was in 1921, when I went there with Gandhi. Greatly attracted as I was to Tagore, I still felt a little irritated that he should criticize some of the aspects of the new movement that Gandhi had started. It seemed to me then that Gandhi having thrown the challenge to British Imperialism, it was every Indian's duty to join the army of liberation. Basically, I still think so in the context of things as they were in that year 1921. But the more I have read what Tagore wrote then, the more I have appreciated it and felt in tune with it. . . .

In later years, my attraction to Tagore grew. I felt a great deal of kinship with his thought and with his general outlook on life. I visited him at Santiniketan on several occasions, during the intervals of my life outside prison. I sent my daughter, Indira, to Santiniketan hoping that she would imbibe something of the atmosphere of the place and, more particularly, profit by the presence of and contact with Gurudev.

I remember particularly when he sent for me in the late thirties and expressed his great concern at the political trends, more especially in Bengal. That was probably my last visit to him, as soon after I was imprisoned again. It was in the Dehra Dun Jail that the news of Tagore's death came to me. In the solitude of prison life, I felt particularly desolate at the passing away of a man who had come to mean so much to me as to vast numbers of others. From an intellectual appreciation of his ideas and his outlook on life, an emotional bond had grown up between us.

It was war time when Rabindranath died, the Second World War was in full swing. Just before he died his last great essay came out—" Crisis in Civilization "—in which he laid bare the agony of his heart and we saw how

deeply wounded he had been by the course of events and by the treatment
accorded to India. . . .

For all his Indianness [Tagore] was essentially a person of international
mould and thinking. Nationalism is sometimes apt to become a narrowing
creed. Tagore helped, to some extent, to break these barriers and yet he
believed firmly in a people growing from their own soil and according to
their own genius. He drew inspiration from outside sources. He loved the
English language and took the trouble to learn German so that he could
read Goethe and other great German writers in the original. But he was
irritated when our young men, fresh from their visits and studies abroad,
spoke of Indian culture. In an article on education, in which he criticized
the educational methods then prevailing in India, he wrote: "I have heard
the West repeatedly ask, 'Where is the voice of India?' But when the
inquirers from the West come to India and listen at her door, they simply
hear a feeble echo of their own Western voice and it sounds like a parody!
I too have noticed that modern Indians fresh from their study of Max
Müller have always sounded like European brass bands, irrespective of
whether they are bragging about their own ancient civilization or condemning and repudiating the West."

For his aim in education, as for much else, he went back to the *Upanishads*. He suggested a motto for our Indian educational institutions: "He
who sees all things in his own self and his own self in all things, he does
not remain unrevealed."

He gave to all traditional ideas a new meaning and a new interpretation:
"How to be free from arrogant nationalism is today the chief lesson to be
learnt. Tomorrow's history will begin with a chapter on internationalism,
and we shall be unfit for tomorrow if we retain any manners, customs, or
habits of thought that are contrary to universalism. There is, I know,
such a thing as national pride, but I earnestly wish that it never makes me
forget that the best efforts of our Indian sages were directed to the abolition of disunity . . . 'He who has realised the unity of man by identifying
himself with the universe is free from ignorance and sorrow.'"

Both Tagore and Gandhi were against the earlier politics in India of
praying and petitioning: "I try to make my countrymen see that man does
not have to beg for his rights, he must create them for himself. Man lives
by his inner nature and there he is his own master. To depend on gains
from outside is to hurt one's true self. The denial of our political rights was
indeed less grievous than the shameful burden of our prayers and petitions.

"I underlined the fact that we must win over our country, not from
some foreigner, but from our own inertia, our indifference.

"At this dawn of the world's awakening, if our own national endeavour holds no intimations of a universal message, the poverty of our spirit will be laid piteously bare."

[Tagore] wanted our students to learn foreign languages, but he was deeply convinced that education must be given in the mother tongue. "For the proper irrigation of learning, a foreign language cannot be the right medium." Music and art were to him essential ingredients of education and indeed of life.

During my last visit to him I requested him to compose a National Anthem for the new India. He partly agreed. At that time I did not have "Jana-Gana-Mana", our present National Anthem, in mind. He died soon after. It was a great happiness to me when some years later after the coming of Independence, we adopted "Jana-Gana-Mana" as our National Anthem. I have a feeling of satisfaction that I was partly responsible for this choice, not only because it is a great national song, but also because it is a constant reminder to all our people of Rabindranath Tagore.

He was in line with the *rishis*, the great sages of India, drawing from the wisdom of the ancient past and giving it a practical garb and a meaning in the present. Thus he gave India's own message in a new language in keeping with the *Yugadharma*, the spirit of the times.

This great and highly sensitive man was not only a poet of India, but also a poet of humanity and of freedom everywhere, and his message is for all of us. More particularly that message is for his own people. Even as he tried to create an atmosphere in his school at Santiniketan, so he tried to produce that atmosphere in the whole of India. I earnestly trust that that living message will always be with us, guiding us in our life and our endeavours.[1]

Letter from District Jail, Dehra Dun, to Krishna Hutheesing— October 28, 1941

My mind is quite clear about relative values in life and what my own duties and obligations are. But if the mind is not clear then difficulties arise and endless and inconclusive argument. Going to jail is a trivial matter in the world today which is being shaken to its foundations. As a mere routine it has no doubt some value and I think does one good. But that

[1] R.T.C., pp. xiii–xvi.

value is not very great unless there is an inner urge to do it. If an inner urge is present [then] little else matters, for that represents something vital. . . .

The large and joint families of the past no doubt served a useful purpose and fitted in with the social structure we had evolved through long ages. But that structure is cracking up now and it cannot survive in its old form. It is pulled in two different directions at the same time—the individual asserting his right to his own way of living, and the larger social group, the community or nation, demanding a unified pattern and equal opportunities for all. Between these two pulls, the middle pull of the joint family becomes less and less; it comes in the way of the individual life as well as the larger natural life. It does not fit in with the thought and elemental forces that move the world today. So it must fade away, as it is indeed doing. But we are such a huge country, and with such deep roots in the past, that major changes take time. Yet in these days time itself moves quickly.

I do believe that the family as a unit is important, especially the smaller family, and fulfils a psychological need. It will survive. But the economic bonds that tie up large numbers of persons in a joint family tend to become real bonds, helping the individual often but also suppressing him and preventing growth. Where a common outlook on life is lacking they become a nuisance to all concerned and a constant source of irritation. There is a feeling . . . that the burden falls on some and not on others, that some are not pulling their weight, that some sow while others reap, and so on. One cannot argue against this for it all depends on our sense of values. Is money-making our test or some other also?

Then again consider even money-making today. Only a fool or an infinitely wise man will dare to prophesy for the future in a changing world. But even a man of average intellect can say that everything is going to change during the next few years all over the world, including India. It is indeed changing before our eyes, and it is quite likely that the millionaire may become a thing of the past. The whole conception of money may change and all our friends who are piling up gold or silver, or mostly paper in the form of securities or currency notes, may suddenly find the bottom knocked out of their treasure chest, and the chest empty. . . .

In time of storms and stress the only capital that counts is intelligence, individual capacity to face a crisis calmly and to overcome it. The Bank of France and the French millionaires did not save France—indeed they helped in her downfall—and now they have to part with their millions also. If we in India as individuals and as a nation have the necessary intelligence, moral fibre and staying power, it will go well with us; otherwise not.

Do not forget that India and China, in spite of their present difficulties, have shown tremendous staying power for ages past. They have done so, I believe, because of their sense of moral values.

I have written quite an essay and I could write on almost indefinitely. But I must have pity on you and desist. The point is that a time comes in the life of every individual when there should be some certitude of his way of life—objectives etc. He may change repeatedly with changing circumstances even afterwards but all the essential adaptations and the background remains much the same, or it changes subtly producing more certainty. Without this there is continuous shifting and consequent distress of mind.

I do not know what life holds for me but I am not afraid of it and I do not think anything is likely to happen to India or the wide world which will bowl me over. At least so I think in my conceit. I am slowly developing a measure of serenity, of poise, of strength, of purpose which is impersonal. It does not matter if I die, as die I must sometime or other. Millions are dying daily in war or otherwise. The smaller and more personal problems gradually lessen their hold on me and I feel more detached. I want to be unburdened, if not entangled personally. I do not know that I shall succeed, or indeed that I want to do so. For I am attached enough to life and its diversity and richness. I am perfectly willing to face it as pleasantly as I can and to take such joy from it as is possible, subject to my own mental limitations. But I want to be equally willing and prepared for the full stop when that comes.

Meanwhile there is much to do and I want to do it with every ounce of energy. And if, as at present, I cannot indulge in activity I prepare myself for it, physically and mentally and store up energy.[1]

Release from Prison, 1941

[On December 3, 1941, the Government of India issued a communiqué expressing confidence that all responsible opinion in India would support the war effort until victory was secured; that those civil disobedience prisoners—approximately six or seven thousand in number—whose offenses had been formal or symbolic in character[2] could be set free, including Nehru. Temporarily, at least, it was believed that the military danger had somewhat abated.

[1] N.L.H.S., pp. 81–84.
[2] Based on H.I.N.C. (Vol. II), p. 285.

Just after Nehru's release from jail, the military situation altered to a considerable degree. On December 7, Japan made a surprise attack on Pearl Harbor, immediately declaring war on the U.S. and Britain. The following day the U.S. and Britain each made a counter-declaration of war against Japan. On December 11, Germany and Italy declared war on the U.S.

After Pearl Harbor, the war spread disastrously in the Pacific arena, endangering not only Burma, but eventually penetrating even into India.]

9 | Statements after Release from Prison, 1941

[Virtually the same problems remained to be resolved after Nehru was liberated from jail on December 4, 1941 as had existed when he was imprisoned. (There is a tale, perhaps apocryphal, yet nevertheless apposite and poignant, to the effect that, upon being released from prison after a long confinement for speeches he had made, Nehru went directly to a large meeting, stood up and stated quite unaffectedly, "As I was saying. . . ."[1])

After leaving jail at the end of 1941, Nehru came increasingly to the forefront on the Indian political scene. Especially after Pearl Harbor he found himself in marked disagreement with Gandhi on the issue of non-violence against aggression. "There is no doubt", stated Nehru, "that the progressive forces of the world are aligned with the group represented by the United States, Britain, Russia and China."[2] By the beginning of 1942, he declared: "When we face the enemy, as in the case of Assam, which may be bombed, it would be preposterous indeed to advise the people to offer passive resistance against the war."[3]]

[Statement—Lucknow, December 4, 1941.] To all my comrades, to Congressmen, to the people, my greetings. It is good to meet old friends [once more] . . . face to face, to feel the warmth of the welcoming

---

[1] When I asked Nehru about the above story's validity, he simply smiled ambiguously. (D.N.)

[2] T.F., p. viii.

[3] Ibid.

smile and embrace and grip, to see the wide fields and crowded streets and the ever changing panorama of humanity. But it is not good to go in and out of prison at the bidding of alien authority. It is not good to come out of the narrow confines of jail into a larger prison that is India to-day. The time will come surely when we break through and demolish all the prison walls that encompass our bodies and minds, and function as a free nation. But the time is not yet and we may not forget this or rejoice at a trivial change which has no meaning.

In this world of infinite suffering where violence and hatred and the spirit of destruction seem to [be] supreme there is no rest or avoidance of travail. In India, where foreign and authoritarian rule oppresses and strangles us, there is no peace for us and the call for action in the interests of a free India and a free world comes insistently to our ears. The call of India is there for those who wish to hear. The call of suffering humanity becomes more agonising from day to day. So there is no rest for us but to carry the burden of the day and hold fast to our anchor. We have watched from afar the heroic courage and infinite sacrifice of other people struggling for freedom, especially of the people of China, and the people of Soviet Russia pouring their heart's blood and destroying their own mighty achievements, so that freedom may live. Our conditions are different, our ways of struggle are not the same. Yet there is the same call for sacrifice and discipline and iron determination.

The call of India continues to resound in our ears and tingle the blood in our veins. So let us go forward then along the path of our choice and take all trials and tribulations with serenity and confidence and with smiling countenance.[1]

[The Agony of the World—Lucknow, December 8, 1941.] I should like India to use her strength and resources in favour of possible good changes. In the grouping of powers struggling for the mastery of the world, [there seem to be dreams of world domination on the part of Governments on both sides]. Undoubtedly this is so on the part of Hitler. It is not proclaimed as such on the [part of other Governments].

I have no doubt that any attempt at world domination by any group of powers will be harmful and must be resisted. Still I think that in the grouping that exists, there is also no doubt that progressive forces of the world are aligned with the group represented by Russia, China, America and Britain. In addition to these progressive forces, this group has

[1] B.A.I., pp. 196–97. [The date of the above speech is taken from H.I.N.C. (Vol. II), p. 287.]

[included] strongly entrenched reactionary forces as evidenced by the treatment accorded to India. This treatment inevitably governs our own policy. Yet at the same time we must sympathise and wish well the group which contains these progressive forces. . . .

Every sensitive person must feel to [a] greater or lesser degree the agony of the world to-day. No individual or nation can or should think in terms of narrow self-interest in the face of this great catastrophe. We have to take the wider outlook ultimately even in terms of self-interest for there can be no doubt that national self-determination is dead and the future is hardly [going] to consist of a large number of separate national entities. Whatever attitude we . . . take up in India, we must keep these wider aspects in view. . . .

In regard to India, we have among us many differences of opinion, some of which are vital. Yet I think that so far as Indians are concerned, to whatever group they might belong, one thing should be [of common interest: India's freedom]. It should be possible for all of us to [agree upon this] common [goal] for the present [and] to co-operate. . . . Working together in spite of our differences will help in resolving [them]. . . . We are up against very big [forces]. . . . None of us can forget this without becoming petty. . . . We have seen how some countries in Asia have, in the course of this war, lost their independence. We must, therefore, take [a broad] view . . . working together for the independence of India within the framework of . . . larger world freedom.

Mahatmaji's leadership has been brilliant. He has stood firm as a rock on certain fundamental principles and not allowed himself to be diverted by various smaller happenings. It is very easy for me or anyone else to criticise certain minor developments with which we may not wholly agree but looking at the scene as a whole, I think that Gandhiji's leadership has not only been right and sound but brilliant.

In regard to non-violence, I have been unable in the past to accept all the implications of the doctrine so far as their [practical] application is concerned. But I had held [this to be] an ideal worth striving for, with all our might, and even this world war has demonstrated the utter folly of continued application of violence to . . . settlement [of] any problem. In fact, violence to-day can be used by only three or four big powers; the others [can only be] hangers-on. . . .

I am convinced that the only way out for the world is complete disarmament or else more or less complete destruction. I can conceive, however, of general disarmament being accompanied by [an] international Air Force [to] be used for police purposes. But it is essential that this should not be under the control of a few Great Powers, who can thus impose their will upon the others. National freedom for each nation is essential before any such step can be taken. . . .

The Congress position was fully stated in the declaration of September . . . 1939, and subsequently added to by A.I.C.C. resolutions. It remains [the same until] modified. Its application must necessarily depend on many factors. For instance, if it were made clear by the British Government that they accept [our] position completely, [this] would be a major international event, changing the whole character of the world. Inevitably the many drawbacks and obstacles [preventing us from] giving support to the Allied cause would then be removed. How India would give practical effect to its undoubted moral support to that cause would then be a matter [to which we could give our full attention, but as] representatives of the Indian people. . . .

I have never been able to understand the significance of Indianisation in anything, whether it is the Government or the army. One does not talk of the Anglicisation of the British army or the British Government. One talks about the nationalisation of the country's Government or army. One talks of power being transferred. The question therefore is not one of Indianisation but of transfer of power and authority controlling that power. If the Executive Council of the Viceroy [consists] of Indians of his choice, under the present circumstances, [what is decided by his Council can] make no difference to the seat of power. But if [there were a Council set up by] an independent responsible Government, [the power of the Viceroy would fade away]. . . .

It is very difficult to weigh moral issues. The fundamental [value of] the satyagraha movement during the past twenty-two years has been [to strengthen] the Indian people. I think it has succeeded in ample measure, not only in so far as Congressmen are concerned but even those who may not be in the Congress. In a sense India has gained tremendously by it. Further it has put forward before the world a method of peaceful struggle, which, though it may fall into error owing to human frailty . . . undoubtedly [represents] a great evolution in the world of thought and action.

In the present instance I feel that the satyagraha movement has enabled us to maintain the self-respect and dignity of India, to prevent the demoralisation which a passive submission to a foreign authority brings . . . and to impress the world not only with [the] Indian demand for freedom but also with the value of [a] peaceful technique of struggle while inhuman war goes on in a great part of the world.[1]

[1] Ibid., pp. 204–07.

3 + N. II

[On the fast changing world—December 14, 1941.] After thirteen months spent in isolation I have now been trying to regain my contact with people and ... adjust myself to the activities of the fast changing world. ... A momentous session of the Working Committee will be held. ... Whatever steps we take should be concerted, firm and in keeping with the dignity of our [nationalist movement]. ... The questions before us are very clear—India's freedom and our attitude towards this war. The problem of India's freedom is not a national but a world problem. We cannot say that it concerns Hindus, Muslims, or any other narrow group or body. The world is [so] much linked together [it] makes the problem of the freedom of four hundred million Indians a world problem. If we go down, the world goes down. Similarly with China. India and China together mean half the world and our freedom is of a piece with the entire picture of the world war and world [peace].[1]

[On Indian independence—December 15, 1941.] In relation to the question of India's independence it is impossible for me to think of dominion status even with a time limit. What we contemplate is complete independence. Those who talk of dominion status, however high placed and sincere, are doing a disservice to the country. We are not an offshoot of Britain and England is not our mother country. Nor are we to accept the position of [being the] cultural offspring of Britain ... [of having] to wait to come of age and ... be given responsibility and powers gradually. We have a cultural heritage and history of our own.

Besides in a fast-changing world ... a time limit has no meaning. What we want is independence. That means severance of connections with Britain. Of course, that does not mean a position of isolation for us. What it does mean is that we should form part of the new [world] order [according to] our own light. On this question of independence of India, there can be no compromise either with [the] British Government or any group in India.[2]

[India can only be a rebel—Bombay, December 17, 1941.] For the past few months that I have been in jail, I have been watching the British Government's policy and the activities of their officials in India and my conviction has been confirmed a thousand-fold that in these circumstances India can only be a rebel against the British Government which has had the insolence and audacity to speak so often through their officials in

[1] Ibid., p. 199.
[2] B.I.S.J.N. (Vol. I), p. 197.

patronising terms about moral, political and spiritual values, when they themselves have demonstrated to the world that they possess none of these. . . .

During the last few days that I have been out of jail . . . I have dealt with the general question of . . . our policy. Recently the question of violence and non-violence has cropped up. . . . This is a [subject] which has been frequently discussed in India for years past and everyone knows Mahatma Gandhi's views on it as well as [the] general reaction of the Congress. . . . No doubt [Mahatmaji] personally goes further [than Congress] but as [its] leader . . . he [has] accepted [its view] and adapted himself to it. For my part I accept it completely. I would like to say that during the past year of war and world-wide disaster I have been drawn even nearer to the ideal of political non-violence and disarmament. I cannot say that this can be applied *in toto* regardless of circumstances, for as the A.I.C.C. has said, internal factors and internal conditions will have to be considered. But I do think that we should try our utmost [to go] in that direction. . . .

When people talk about any kind of co-operation between India and Britain, they seem to forget . . . that the bitterness of the people to-day is greater than ever against . . . British policy in India. Anyone who takes the trouble to find out what the people's feeling is, has only to speak to the man in the street from Peshawar to Cape Comorin.

During my past twenty-five years of political experience I have never known feeling so strained and bitter. No politician, whatever his views might be, can ignore this background. . . . It is absurd for anyone to imagine that we can [at present] co-operate with [the British]. It is true, [however, that in view of] the international situation, all manner of considerations arise which induce us to give our sympathy to the . . . powers fighting against the Axis. . . .

Some people and some organisations talk about what might happen after the war is over or a year or two later. I am totally unable to understand this attitude. I am only concerned with to-day and here and now. It will not be Mr. Amery or the British Government who will shape things in the future but the vast elemental forces that are already rising in the world. . . . Only by [following] an entirely different policy based on the ending of [her] empire and imperialist policy can [Britain] win the mass sympathy of the [Indian] people.[1]

[1] Ibid., pp. 202–04.

PART SEVEN

1942

We do not want to be slaves of Japan or Germany. We would fight against any nation that wishes to enslave us.

The German and Japanese radio announce daily that they are fighting to liberate nations and desire also to give independence to India. I do not believe this. We should never be misled by such announcements. We are ready to defend our own country. . . .

The influence of Congress is growing. India will achieve "swaraj" and establish relations with other nations, in addition to England.[1]

*

" 'If you come to my place,' said an Indian university professor [to Nehru] . . . 'I can arrange for you to meet a few groups of keen students trying to think.'

"Nehru paced the corridor in which they stood.

"'Ah, yes,' he said, stopping suddenly before the professor and grasping his arm. 'But what about the groups inside me?' "[2]

*

We can make no complaint that life has treated us harshly, for ours has been a willing choice, and perhaps life has not been so bad to us after all. For only those can sense life who stand often on the verge of it, only those whose lives are not governed by the fear of death. In spite of the mistakes we have made, we have saved ourselves from triviality and an inner shame and cowardice. That, for our individual selves has been some achievement.[3]

[1] Based on B.A.I., p. 229.
[2] Quoted in M.J.N., p. 43.
[3] C.D.N., pp. 57–58.

I | Military Situation and Developments in East—International and Domestic Issues

Military Situation and Developments in the East

[On January 16, 1942, the All-India Congress Committee repeated its offer of conditional cooperation in the war effort. As in the past, there were divergent views within the Committee about the manner in which co-operation might take place. Although Nehru and Gandhi continued to disagree about the course of action to be taken, there was to be no real break between them. It was, in fact, precisely while the two men seemed most at odds that the Mahatma was again moved to designate Nehru as his successor. In so doing he declared: "It will require much more than differences of opinion to estrange us. We have had differences from the moment we became co-workers, and yet I have said for some years and say now that . . . Jawaharlal will be my successor. He says he does not understand my language, and that he speaks a language foreign to me. This may or may not be true. But language is no bar to a union of hearts. And I know this, that when I am gone he will speak my language." [1]

Matters became so desperate after the Japanese entry into Rangoon in March that Churchill, fearing that India might be threatened by a potentially disastrous military defeat, finally found it necessary to make certain concessions. (The military situation, combined with the prodding of the Chiang Kai-sheks and President Roosevelt, led to the sending of Sir Stafford Cripps to India with fresh proposals that might, it was hoped, prove more acceptable than had previous British plans with respect to India's future status.)

In 1942 a British declaration stated that it was recognized that British policy toward India had developed independently of the war, and that, strictly speaking, British Government statements regarding the future of India had little to do with the latter's own war and peace aims. It was nevertheless admitted that the very fact that treatment of a "dependent" people was receiving so much attention in Britain's discussions of war and peace aims justifiably could be considered in relationship to the immediate military need to enlist the full support of the Indian people in the war effort.

[1] Quoted in M.B., p. 275.

The British further described the evolution of their policy toward India, and the stalemate that had been reached as a result of the war situation: "India is approaching self-government as the result of a series of statutes and revisions extending over a quarter of a century. During World War I, India was associated with the self-governing Dominions in the Imperial War Conference and it became an original member of the League of Nations. In 1920, the Government of India Act granted a degree of self-government but less than had been hoped for by Indian nationalist leaders. In 1921, fiscal autonomy was granted. In 1929, Dominion status was designated as the goal of India's development. In 1935, a more advanced Government of India Act was passed providing for a federal union of British India and the Indian States. The part of this Act referring to provincial governments went into effect in 1937, and most subjects formerly reserved to the Governor were put in the hands of Indian ministers. In the central government certain powers were still reserved to the Viceroy and Governor-General and his appointed Council of seven members, three of whom were Indians. The outbreak of World War II caused postponement of the negotiations to bring the Government of India Act into full effect."[1]

As a result of a series of spectacular Japanese victories in Hong Kong, the Philippines, Malaya, Burma and elsewhere, the Allied military situation in the East continued steadily to deteriorate.

Beginning early in 1942, the Japanese entered Singapore, which swiftly surrendered. In the Burma campaign, the British withdrew from Rangoon. Batavia, capital of the Dutch East Indies, fell to the Japanese, who also occupied Rangoon. Dutch, British and American troops in Java surrendered unconditionally immediately thereafter. By April the Bataan peninsula (Philippine Islands) fell to the Japanese, as did Mandalay in May (the invaders having reached northern Burma).]

International and Domestic Issues

[No sympathy with Hitler—Bombay, January 3, 1942.] We have no sympathy with Hitler. We are under no delusion that he will give us our freedom. We know that our freedom cannot be a gift, either from Britain or from Hitler. Thanks to Britain we may not be able to oppose the aggressor by force of arms but we will never submit either to the rule of Hitler or Japan. It is therefore futile to hold out . . . threats to us. It is equally futile to suggest that because of [possible hazards] we must [cling to] our slavery.[2]

[1] W.P.A.U.N., pp. 278–79.
[2] B.I.S.J.N. (Vol. I), pp. 207–08.

[The pace of events—Bombay, January 5, 1942.] In India and else-where the pace of events during the past two years has made a tremendous difference to the people's minds, and none of us, even if we so willed, can ignore this solid background of reality. We are not functioning like the legendary ascetics but ... trying to come to grips with the reality of to-day and the coming reality of to-morrow. It is the British Government which lives in the yesterdays that are no more. Not only [with respect to India but] to everything else, they stick [in] the old ruts, and the world advances and changes, leaving them behind. Just as war to-day requires novel and aggressive tactics in order to be effective, even more so do other major problems of to-day and the picture of the peace that we hanker after require novel and aggressive methods and [a] capacity to take risks. It is not enough to be on the defensive, to seek to maintain the old and the out-of-date, for that is already doomed. To stick to it is to catch the infection of decay.... As far as I can see a country cannot go ahead in the way [it] desires, so long as that country is bound hand and foot by an authoritarian Government.[1]

[Political situation in India—February, 1942.] Fourteen months have elapsed since the Working Committee held their last meeting and during this period the world has fallen ever deeper into the abyss of war and rushed headlong towards self-destruction. The members of the Committee have met again on their release from prison and given earnest thought to all the national and international developments during this fateful period of human history. The burden of guiding the Congress and the nation at this critical stage when old problems assume a new significance and war approaches the frontiers of India bringing new problems in its train, is a heavy one which the Committee can only shoulder worthily with the full co-operation of the people of India. The Committee have endeavoured to keep in view the principles and objectives for which the Congress has stood during these past many years and considered them in the larger context of world conditions and world freedom. The Committee are convinced that full freedom for the people of India is essential even, and more especially, in the present state of world turmoil, not only for India's sake but for the sake of the world. The Committee also hold that real peace and freedom can only be established and endure on the basis of world co-operation between free nations. ...

British policy [has been] one of deliberate insult to Indian nationalism,

[1] Ibid., pp. 208–09.

3*

of a perpetuation of unrestrained authoritarianism, and the encouragement of disruptive and reactionary elements. Not only has every offer
made by the Congress for an honourable compromise been rejected, but
public opinion voiced by organisations regarded as moderate has also
been flouted.

The Congress was, therefore, compelled, in order to defend the
honour and the elementary rights of the Indian people and the integrity
of the nationalist movement, to request Gandhiji to guide the Congress
in the action that should be taken. Mahatma Gandhi, desirous of avoiding
embarrassment to his opponent as far as possible, especially during the
perils and dangers of war, limited the satyagraha movement which he
started to selected individuals who conformed to certain tests he had
laid down. That satyagraha has now proceeded for over fourteen months
and about twenty-five thousand Congressmen have suffered imprisonment, while many thousands of others who offered satyagraha in the
Frontier Province and elsewhere were not arrested. The Committee desire
to express their respectful appreciation of Gandhiji's leadership and of
the response of the nation to it, and are of [the] opinion that this has
strengthened the people.

Throughout this period the attitude of the British Government has
been hostile to Indian freedom and it has functioned in India as a completely authoritarian government, insulting the deeply cherished convictions and feelings of the people. Neither the professions of freedom
and democracy, nor the perils and catastrophes that have come in the
wake of war, have affected this attitude and policy, and such changes as
have taken place have been for the worse.

The recent release of a number of political prisoners has no significance
or importance, and the circumstances attending it, and official pronouncements made, make it clear that it is not connected with any change of
policy. Large numbers of detenus, who are kept in prison, under the
Defence of India Act without trial, and whose only offence seems to be
that they are ardent patriots impatient of foreign rule and determined to
achieve the independence of the country, still remain in prison. Recent
arrests of prominent persons and their treatment in prison also indicate
that the old policy is being pursued as before.

While there has been no change in Britain's policy towards India, the
Working Committee must nevertheless take into full consideration the
new world situation that has arisen by the development of the war into a
world conflict and its approach to India. The sympathies of the Congress
must inevitably lie with the peoples who are the subject of aggression

from any quarter and who are fighting for their freedom. But only a free and independent India can be in a position to undertake the defence of the country on a national basis and be of help in the furtherance of the large causes that are emerging from the storm of war. The whole background in India is one of hostility and of distrust of the British Government and not even the most far-reaching promise can alter this background, nor can a subject India offer voluntary or willing help to an arrogant imperialism which is indistinguishable from fascist authoritarianism.[1]

	Visit to India of Madame and General
2	Chiang Kai-shek—U.S. and Chinese
	Efforts in Behalf of Indian Freedom

Visit to India of Madame and General Chiang Kai-shek

[In the midst of the war (and of Congress upheavals), Madame and General Chiang-Kai-shek, whom Nehru had met during his 1939 trip to China, paid a visit to India in February, 1942. The Generalissimo pleaded fervently that "real political power" be promptly transferred to the Indian people so that they might more willingly participate in the war against the Axis powers. Since the Chiang-Kai-sheks were pleading for India's freedom, and since Indian nationalists were not in control of arrangements for welcoming distinguished visitors, Nehru deeply regretted the inability of Congress adequately to pay its respects to the Generalissimo and his wife.]

[On the occasion of the visit of the Chiang-Kai-sheks—New Delhi, February 11, 1942.] I only feel one thing, that we are not in a position to accord a reception such as we would wish to, as we are not free. . . .

India will not accept any other rule, Japanese or German, but only the rule of the masses of India. . . .

On the arrival of [the] Generalissimo in Delhi, I found a whisper that we [the Congress were] going to change our policy, but this is not a fact. Our decisions are made after mature thought: we never decide anything

[1] C.B. (Feb., 1942), pp. 17 ff. (From Ms. copy.)

in a hurry. Responsible bodies can never decide anything in a hurry. . . .
The world is passing through an ocean of revolution and nobody knows
what is going to happen. . . . Nobody [knows] if the coming changes [will]
be for [the] good or [not] . . . It [is] certain [we must] never shirk [our]
responsibility. . . . We [cannot] afford to forget our discipline and run
away when . . . trouble comes.[1]

[Let us be brave—Calcutta, February 21, 1942.] Let us be brave, take
courage from the example of [our] Chinese brothers and sisters and face any
oppressor, any aggressor; face any person who dares to think in terms of
oppressing and dictating to India.

Let us preserve our unity, forget our petty differences, work under
the programme that has been put forward by the Congress, build it up,
and see that its structure is kept intact.

I have come this time to Calcutta on a very special mission as you
know, because Generalissimo Chiang-Kai-shek and Madame Chiang
happened to come to Calcutta. I wanted very much to be of such service
to them as I could be while they were on . . . Indian soil. It was a sorrow
to me, and I have no doubt to you, that their visit to India to which we
have looked forward so much and which has been a great honour to us,
should have taken place in such circumstances, and that many of you
have been unable to see them, even from a distance.

We should like to honour them and through them China, which they
have led so magnificently. We have failed to honour them in public and
in many other ways. Nevertheless, it has been a great honour to India,
and it has been, I think, something that will affect, if I may say so, the
history of India and China. It has really been a historic visit, historic in
the sense that it will mark a new epoch in the relations of India and China.
For my part, for long years I have dreamt that India and China should
hold together in [the] present and . . . future, and I went to Chungking
with [that] hope in mind; and when I got there I found that the leaders of
China were anxious themselves to develop . . . relations between India
and China. I rejoiced and . . . was happy because I saw the future, in
which India and China would go hand in hand. I am quite definite that
there could be no peace or solution of . . . world problems unless the problem of India and China were solved because primarily India and China are
huge parts of the earth's surface and they comprise nearly half the total
population of the world. There can be no solution of the world's problems
—economic or political—unless India's and China's problems are solved.

[1] B.A.I., p. 213.

[Marshal Chiang] is a remarkable man and has proved himself a very great leader and captain in war. He is . . . one of the very few names that . . . stand out very prominently in the world today. Far greater [than] as a captain in war, he has proved himself . . . a leader of men. Today if you go to China you will find no group or individual who will not agree [on] one thing, that is, that Marshal Chiang-Kai-shek, is not only a very great leader but the only leader China could have. . . .

This great consort of the Marshal [Madame Chiang] has not only been his partner in life's journey, but [has] been a fellow warrior with him, who has donned armour to stand side by side with him in China's battle for freedom. She has become the symbol of China's invincibility [in] her magnificent spirit of resistance. It [was] an honour to India to have them here in [this] city. Those who [were] fortunate [enough] to meet them [will] not forget them and their cause. I feel convinced in my heart that we shall stand shoulder to shoulder and shall render whatever help we can to each other in the furtherance of that cause. . . .

What is happening in the world today? Proud empires are falling before our eyes, huge structures of Governments are collapsing. No one knows what will happen in the course of [the] next six months. No one knows when this war will end. No part of the world can escape the war. The question is: how to face it? We cannot face it by cursing this man or that.

Long before this war started, the National Congress . . . declared its policy in regard to Fascism and aggression. Do you think we are likely to change our opinion because Germany and Japan are the foes of Britain? We have always said that we would neither have British imperialism nor any other type of imperialism, Fascism or Nazism. Do not fall into that terrible error, that in order to get rid of one we should ask the aid of the other. Therein lies danger, and if any one of us thinks like that then he is a coward and a slave. Why should we think in terms of some outsider ruling India? We must measure all . . . dangers and take a vow not to bow before them.[1]

U.S. and Chinese Efforts in Behalf of Indian Freedom

[During February, 1942, John G. Winant, American Ambassador to Britain, urged President Roosevelt to use his personal influence with

[1] Ibid., pp. 215–16.

Churchill in behalf of Indian freedom, in spite of Roosevelt's "earlier hesitation to intervene in what 'in a strict sense [was] not our business'. From China, General Chiang Kai-shek sent a similar message to Mr Roosevelt but in much stronger terms. The Indian situation, both military and political, struck him as 'shocking'. 'It would be too late,' warned Chiang Kai-shek, 'if the British waited for Japanese planes to bomb India or [until] after the entry of the Japanese army into the country. On the other hand, if the political situation in India were changed for the better, it might prevent the enemy from having any ambitions to enter India.'

"The Senate Foreign Relations Committee in Washington took an equally firm stand: 'We should demand that India be given a status of autonomy. The only way to get the people of India to fight is to get them to fight for India. Gandhi's leadership in India becomes part of America's military equipment.' From London, Mr Averell Harriman, after a talk with Mr Churchill, informed [Roosevelt] that discussions were going on about a declaration of Dominion Status for India, with the right to secession to be exercised at her will. The British Prime Minister was personally full of misgivings about India 'being thrown into chaos on the eve of [the Japanese] invasion'. Madame Chiang Kai-shek did not think Dominion Status would satisfy India. . . .

"This was the genesis of the Cripps Mission in April 1942. Mr Roosevelt, in a long dispatch to Mr Churchill, suggested a constitutional convention being summoned in India broadly on the lines of the convention which framed the American Constitution." [1]

Roosevelt went even further, suggesting in a cable to Churchill on March 11, 1942 "that the communal difficulty" in India "was exaggerated. All that was needed, in his opinion", he stated bluntly, "was that a temporary government should be set up in India, headed by a small representative group covering different castes, occupations, religions, and geographies, which would be recognised as a temporary Dominion Government". [2] Less than a week later he warned of the possibility that Calcutta might be bombed by the Japanese.

Roosevelt's prodding, as well as the weakness of Allied resistance in Burma, caused in large part by support given to the Japanese by dissatisfied Burmese, doubtless strengthened pressure on Britain for a fresh initiative in relationship to India. On March 11, Churchill announced in the House of Commons that the War Cabinet had agreed concerning present and future action in India, and that Sir Stafford Cripps would go to India to present the Cabinet's proposals. [3]

Nehru received the following letter written by Madame Chiang Kai-shek, March 13, 1942: "The Generalissimo and I . . . feel that we owe it to our Indian friends to speak the truth as we see it, although as we were

[1] I.N. (Feb. 22, 1963), p. 8.
[2] M.G.L.I., p. 413.
[3] D.A.F.R. (Vol. IV), p. 545.

guests of the British government, politeness constrains us from openly criticising the assertion that real power cannot be given to India because of the lack of unity among her people etc. I saw in the papers today that the London *Chronicle* made quite a case of this, and was I furious. . . .

"The Generalissimo has been telegraphing Roosevelt on Indian conditions. Our latest news from him is this: Roosevelt wired that at the Peace Conference the representative from India should be chosen by *Congress*, and represent real national India. . . . . He thinks that a solution of the Indian problem might be found in dividing India into two, namely Moslem and Hindu. Both the Generalissimo and I wired to my brother T. V. [Soong] that the second premise is entirely wrong, and should not be considered for one single second. India is as indivisible as China. The fact that there are religious differences amongst her people does not mean that politically they cannot agree if given the opportunity to settle their diversity of views uninterfered with and unabetted by a third party.

"The Generalissimo is calling me to stop . . . as a message [has come] from Roosevelt".[1]]

	The Cripps Mission—Congress Resolution Concerning Mission—
3	Breakdown of Mission—Roosevelt's Efforts to Avert Breakdown— Further Statements

The Cripps Mission

[Sir Stafford Cripps arrived in New Delhi during the last week of March, bringing with him a British draft declaration, generally referred to as the Cripps Offer of 1942. The Offer stated:

"His Majesty's Government, having considered the anxieties expressed in [England] and in India as to the fulfilment of the promises made in regard to the future of India, have decided to lay down in precise and clear terms the steps which they propose shall be taken for the earliest possible realization of self-government in India. The object is the creation of a new Indian Union which shall constitute a Dominion, associated with the United Kingdom and the other Dominions by a

¹ B.O.L., pp. 476–78.

common allegiance to the Crown, but equal to them in every respect, in no way subordinate in any aspect of its domestic or external affairs.

"His Majesty's Government therefore make the following declaration:

(a) Immediately upon the cessation of hostilities, steps shall be taken to set up in India, in the manner described hereafter, an elected body charged with the task of framing a new Constitution for India.

(b) Provision shall be made, as set out below, for the participation of the Indian States in the constitution-making body.

(c) His Majesty's Government undertake to accept and implement forthwith the Constitution so framed subject only to:

(I) the right of any Province of British India that is not prepared to accept the new Constitution to retain its present constitutional position, provision being made for its subsequent accession if it so decides.

With such nonacceding Provinces, should they so desire, His Majesty's Government will be prepared to agree upon a new Constitution, giving them the same full status as Indian Union, and arrived at by a procedure analogous to that here laid down.

(II) the signing of a Treaty which shall be negotiated between His Majesty's Government and the constitution-making body. This Treaty will cover all necessary matters arising out of the complete transfer of responsibility from British to Indian hands; it will make provision, in accordance with the undertakings given by His Majesty's Government, for the protection of racial and religious minorities; but will not impose any restriction on the power of the Indian Union to decide in the future its relationship to the other Member States of the British Commonwealth.

Whether or not an Indian State elects to adhere to the Constitution, it will be necessary to negotiate a revision of its Treaty arrangements, so far as this may be required in the new situation.

(d) The constitution-making body shall be composed as follows, unless the leaders of Indian opinion in the principal communities agree upon some other form before the end of hostilities:

Immediately upon the result being known of the provincial elections which will be necessary at the end of hostilities, the entire membership of the Lower Houses of the Provincial Legislatures shall, as a single electoral college, proceed to the election of the constitution-making body by the system of proportional representation. This new body shall be in number about one-tenth of the number of the electoral college.

Indian States shall be invited to appoint representatives in the same proportion to their total population as in the case of the representatives of British India as a whole, and with the same powers as the British Indian members.

(e) During the critical period which now faces India and until the new Constitution can be framed, His Majesty's Government must inevitably bear the responsibility for and retain control and direction of the defense of India as part of their world war effort, but the task of organizing to the full the military, moral, and material resources of India must be the responsibility of the Government of India with the co-operation of the peoples of India. His Majesty's Government desire and invite the immediate and effective participation of the leaders of the principal sections of the Indian people in the counsels of their country, of the Commonwealth, and of the United Nations. Thus they will be enabled to give their active and constructive help in the discharge of a task which is vital and essential for the future freedom of India."[1]

Like the Congress, which had little enthusiasm for the Cripps proposals, the Muslim League termed the interim arrangements vague, refusing to express a final opinion about them until the entire plan might be further clarified.

Other Indian parties and groups were similarly dissatisfied. The Hindu Mahasabha feared the Cripps offer would lead to partition, the Sikhs that a Muslim majority in the Punjab would opt out of the Indian Union, the Untouchables that they would be at the mercy of caste-conscious Hindus.

Many Congress leaders found the Cripps offer unacceptable. Nehru felt quite depressed by it, although, initially, he attempted to work out a compromise in connection with it. He finally came to the conclusion, however, that while in India Cripps shifted his ground—allegedly watering his new offer down to the August 1940 proposal—at which point a settlement seemed impossible of attainment.

Both the Congress and the Muslim League finally were to reject the Cripps Offer but for "almost diametrically opposed reasons. The Working Committee balked at 'the uncertain future' surrounding the commitment to self-determination, the 'novel principle of non-accession for a province', which encouraged separation, and 'the introduction of non-representative elements', namely the Princes, in the Constituent Assembly. The short-run proposals were also criticized because no real change was contemplated. . . . Nehru . . . was especially troubled by the apparent acceptance of the [Muslim] League demand for Pakistan and the danger of widespread fragmentation of the sub-continent."[2]

Congress felt uneasy about "the powers to be entrusted to the contemplated provisional national government for the interim period. . . . [It] insisted upon a cabinet government, with the Viceroy voluntarily undertaking not to exercise his veto powers, and it wanted an Indian minister [to have] an effective share in . . . defense. It recognized fully the desirability of leaving the military operations in charge of the British Commander-in-Chief, but felt that without [the other changes it sought] it could not rouse [fervor for the war effort] among the masses. . . . [It felt that the reforms desired by] Congress would have served as a symbol of change from domination to cooperation."[3]

The Muslim League also found the Cripps Offer unacceptable, even while expressing "gratification that the possibility of Pakistan [was] recognized by implication".[4]

[1] T.A.Y. (XII–XIII), pp. 329–30.
[2] Based on M.B., p. 278.
[3] F.E.S. (Mar. 22, 1943), p. 57.
[4] D.A.F.R. (Vol. IV), p. 555.

The British Government proposal to arrange for representation of the Government of India in the War Cabinet and the Pacific War Council in London by no means impressed Indian public opinion.[1]

Even when two Indian leaders ultimately were appointed to the British War Cabinet, and an Indian representative was later placed on the Pacific Council (on July 2, 1942), this gesture had equally little meaning for those it was designed to satisfy. Whereas the Viceroy's Council was finally enlarged from twelve to fifteen members—eleven Indians and four Europeans—again, such concessions had no significance whatsoever for Congress leaders who yearned instead for complete independence. Equally unpalatable was the fact that the Cripps proposals had "to be accepted or rejected as a whole", and that an Indian Constituent Assembly was to be set up only after the war, whereas no constitutional changes could be affected during its duration.[2]

In view of the virtual certainty that Congress would refuse to accept the Cripps proposals, Sir Stafford wrote the following plea to Nehru while in Delhi, in April, 1942: "Let me make a final appeal to you, upon whom rests the great burden of decision—a decision so far-reaching in its bearing upon the future relations of our two peoples that its magnitude is indeed portentous.

"We can and must carry our people through to friendship and co-operation—I in my sphere, you in yours.

"The chance which now offers cannot recur. Other ways may come if this fails but never so good a chance to cement the friendship of our people.

"Leadership—the sort of leadership you have—can alone accomplish the result. It is the moment for the supreme courage of a great leader to face all the risks and difficulties—and I know they are there—to drive through to the desired end.

"I know your qualities, and your capacity and I beg you to make use of them now."[3]]

Resolution of Congress Working Committee, Released April 11, 1942, in Conjunction with Cripps Mission

[Of the following Resolution, H. N. Brailsford has written: "Gandhi may have been present [when it was written], but the draft reads like Nehru's work."[4]]

"The Working Committee have given their full and earnest consideration to the proposals made by the British War Cabinet in regard to

[1] Ibid., p. 545.
[2] Based on I.W.N., p. 24.
[3] B.O.L., p. 478.
[4] B.S.I., p. 75.

India and the elucidation thereof by Sir Stafford Cripps. These proposals, which have been made at the very last hour because of the compulsion of events, have to be considered not only in relation to India's demand for independence, but more specially in the present grave war crisis, with a view to meeting effectively the perils and dangers that confront India and envelop the world.

"The Congress has repeatedly stated, ever since the commencement of the War in September 1939, that the people of India would line themselves with the progressive forces of the world and assume full responsibility to face the new problems and shoulder the new burdens that had arisen, and it asked for the necessary conditions to enable them to do so to be created. An essential condition was the freedom of India, for only the realisation of present freedom could light the flame which would illumine millions of hearts and move them to action. At the last meeting of the All India Congress Committee after the commencement of the War in the Pacific, it was stated that: 'Only a free and independent India can be in a position to undertake the defence of the country on a national basis and be of help in the furtherance of the larger causes that are emerging from the storm of war.'

"The British War Cabinet's new proposals relate principally to the future upon the cessation of hostilities. The Committee, while recognising that self-determination for the people of India is accepted in principle in that uncertain future, regret that this is fettered and circumscribed and certain provisions have been introduced which gravely imperil the development of a free and united nation and the establishment of a democratic State. Even the constitution-making body is so constituted that the people's right to self-determination is vitiated by the introduction of non-representative elements. The people of India have as a whole clearly demanded full independence and the Congress has repeatedly declared that no other status except that of independence for the whole of India could be agreed to or could meet the essential requirements of the present situation. The Committee recognise that future independence may be implicit in the proposals but the accompanying provisions and restrictions are such that real freedom may well become an illusion. The complete ignoring of the ninety millions of the people of the Indian States and their treatment as commodities at the disposal of their rulers is a negation of both democracy and self-determination. While the representation of an Indian State in the constitution-making body is fixed on a population basis, the people of the State have no voice in choosing those representatives, nor are they to be consulted at any stage, while decisions vitally affecting them are being taken. Such States may in many ways become barriers to the growth of Indian freedom, enclaves where foreign authority still prevails and where the possibility of maintaining foreign armed forces has been stated to be a likely contingency, and a perpetual menace to the freedom of the people of the States as well as of the rest of India.

"The acceptance beforehand of the novel principle of non-accession for a province is also a severe blow to the conception of Indian unity and an apple of discord likely to generate growing trouble in the provinces, and which may well lead to further difficulties in the way of the Indian States merging themselves in the Indian Union. The Congress has been wedded to Indian freedom and unity and any break in that unity, especially in the modern world when people's minds inevitably think in terms of ever larger federations, would be injurious to all concerned and exceedingly painful to contemplate. Nevertheless the Committee cannot think in terms of compelling the people in any territorial unit to remain in an Indian Union against their declared and established will. While recognising this principle, the Committee feel that every effort should be made to create conditions which would help the different units in developing a common and co-operative national life. The acceptance of the principle inevitably involves that no changes should be made which result in fresh problems being created and compulsion being exercised on other substantial groups within that area. Each territorial unit should have the fullest possible autonomy within the Union, consistently with a strong national state. The proposal now made on the part of the British War Cabinet encourages and will lead to attempts at separation at the very inception of a union and thus create friction just when the utmost co-operation and goodwill are most needed. This proposal has been presumably made to meet a communal demand, but it will have other consequences also and lead politically reactionary and obscurantist groups among different communities to create trouble and divert public attention from the vital issues before the country.

"Any proposal concerning the future of India must demand attention and scrutiny, but in today's grave crisis, it is the present that counts, and even proposals for the future are important in so far as they affect the present. The Committee have necessarily attached the greatest importance to this aspect of the question, and on this ultimately depends what advice they should give to those who look to them for guidance. For this present the British War Cabinet's proposals are vague and altogether incomplete, and it would appear that no vital changes in the present structure are contemplated. It has been made clear that the Defence of India will in any event remain under British control. At any time defence is a vital subject; during wartime it is all important and covers almost every sphere of life and administration. To take away defence from the sphere of responsibility at this stage is to reduce that responsibility to a farce and a nullity, and to make it perfectly clear that India is not going to be free in any way and her Government is not going to function as a free and independent government during the pendency of the War. The Committee would repeat that an essential and fundamental prerequisite for the assumption of responsibility by the Indian people in the present is their realisation as a fact that they are free and are in charge of maintaining and defending their freedom. What is most wanted is the enthusiastic response of the people which cannot be evoked without the fullest trust in them and the devolution of responsibility on them in the matter of defence. It is only thus that even at this grave eleventh hour it may be possible to galvanise the people of India to rise to the height of the occasion. It is manifest that the present Government of India, as well as its provincial agencies, are lacking in competence, and are incapable of shouldering the burden of India's defence. It is only the people of India, through their popular representatives, who may shoulder this burden worthily. But that can only be done by present freedom, and full responsibility being cast upon them.

"The Committee, therefore, are unable to accept the proposals put forward on behalf of the British War Cabinet." [1]

Breakdown of Mission

[After the Congress Working Committee and the Muslim League had rejected the British proposals, Sir Stafford informed the press on April 11 "that the British Government's offer to India had been withdrawn, as the replies received had resulted in his regretfully advising the Government 'that there is not such measure of acceptance of their proposals as to justify their making a declaration in the form of the draft'".[2]

Nehru's reference in the following passage to being currently willing to organize guerilla warfare against Japan is a further indication of his two-fold manner of assessing methods of action to be utilized in relation to internal and external events.

As for Congress' position, it did not concurrently "ask for 'some complete and fundamental constitutional change', as Cripps later argued, but merely a political change involving the transfer of real and sufficient power in order to enable the national government to mobilize the country for [the war effort]".[3]]

[At press conference, New Delhi—after breakdown of Cripps negotiations—April 12, 1942.] Our extreme desire in India was not to break [off] the [Cripps Mission] negotiations but to come to a settlement which would be honourable. . . .

Before the last interview with Sir Stafford . . . there was a seventy-five per cent chance of settlement. Sir Stafford had talked about a National Government. He had said that the Viceroy would act like a constitutional monarch. His language had led us to conclude that the new government would function as a cabinet and that the Viceroy would not intervene. Later Sir Stafford Cripps retreated from this position.

In our last interview with Sir Stafford we were astonished to find that the premises of our discussions were wrong. I do not want to be unjust

[1] I.W.F., pp. 72–74.
[2] D.A.F.R. (Vol. IV), p. 545.
[3] F.E.S. (Mar. 22, 1943), p. 59.

to Sir Stafford, but on the night of April 10th he shot off the mark completely. What he said was a repetition of the farrago of nonsense that Mr. Amery, Secretary of State for India, has been uttering all these years. What Sir Stafford Cripps was giving us was practically the August [1940] offer with minor changes. Sir Stafford felt hurt when we told him this. He said to me, "Do you think I would be such a fool as to come out here with a mere repetition of Mr. Amery's August offer?" It was difficult for me courteously to give a direct answer to that. A rose may smell as sweet by any other name, but not the Viceroy's Council.

For an eminent lawyer and constitutionalist like Sir Stafford to use such terms as "tyrannical majority" (as Cripps did when speaking of the sort of cabinet Congress would form if their proposals were accepted by the British Government) is extraordinary and fantastic nonsense. That is all I can say.

However we cannot afford to be bitter because bitterness clouds the mind and affects judgment during a great crisis.

To-day India is the crux of the war for us. The other really important theatre of war is the Soviet Union.

Much will depend on the Russo-German war in the next three months. A great deal in India will also depend upon what happens between Germany and the Soviet Union because India is going to be the crux of the war during those three months.

I cannot tolerate the idea that I should sit idle, or that people should sit idle in their houses, while the battle for India is being fought out between foreign armies and the Japanese are invading the country.

We are not going to surrender to the Japanese invader just as we have not given in to the British during the last twenty-two years. I want to fight this idea that we must remain passive, that we cannot do anything against the Japanese. I do feel definitely that it would be a tragedy for the world if Germany and Japan won this war and dominated the world. I do not want this to happen. I would have liked to play my part in this world drama more effectively. That is why I went to the limit to come to terms with the British government.

India will make a difference both to the length and intensity of the war.

Every country in the world realises this, except of course, the big people in New Delhi and Whitehall—they are slow in understanding and comprehension—that is why India hears frantic radio appeals from Germany and Japan.

We were prepared to put aside our objections to the future and consider the present situation; the British government could have said "We will make India independent." Sir Stafford contended "We cannot change the constitution of India in law during the war".

We suggested that it was quite possible for Parliament to pass half a dozen clauses of a bill declaring the independence of India, leaving our differences to be settled later. If such an enactment was made it would change the whole picture. Sir Stafford, however, did not agree to this proposal.

We did not press this. We did not make this a fundamental point.

For the first time in twenty-two years I swallowed many a bitter pill when I said I was prepared somehow or other to reach agreement. I did want to throw all my sympathy and energy into the organisation of events in India. In my conception of the defence of India I wanted a hundred million Indians in the army. It was not a conception of just an army functioning but of every man and woman doing something—making it a people's war—and carrying on defence even where trained armies failed. The popular conception of resistance is no surrender at any cost. That is the conception China has given us, the conception seen in Russia, and that is the conception we want in India.

We wanted to give a national tinge to the Indian army. We wanted to raise a citizens' army. We cannot fight a war in the present lackadaisical manner. Under a national government there would be no place for slackers either Indian or English. It would not be an evening dress affair; it is not tea-parties, balls and dances that will win the war. . . .

It does not matter how hard a few brass hats work. If to-day a national government of India were to say "we are going to arm the Indian people. We may not have the best modern army, aeroplanes and tanks; but we are going to arm them with such guns as we can make"; think how the world situation would change; think what reaction it would have on Germany and Japan, and also on the allied countries.

We want production to go full speed ahead. We want people to stay at their jobs and not run away from them. We cannot participate in Britain's war effort because our problem is to organize our own war effort on our own basis of a free and independent India. I hope that the All-India Congress Committee will consider this matter and tell us what to do about it.

The fundamental factor is not what Britain does for us or what we do for them. The fundamental factor is India's peril and what we are going to do about it. Therefore in spite of all that has happened we are not going to embarrass the British war effort or the effort of our American friends who may come here.

If I were the National Government I would burn or destroy everything that helped the enemy, but I am terribly afraid that a British government will follow the scorched earth policy in a manner which will harm the Japanese less and the Indians more. [I suggest] that there should be a scheme for compensation for war damage in India, and that the government should give a guarantee that they [will] help in re-building destroyed buildings and factories. . . .

At no stage [is] it suggested that the Commander-in-Chief [General Wavell] should be deprived of his normal powers. We [have] to take a realistic view of the situation. But Sir Stafford Cripps' attitude on Defence [is] rigid. . . . He sent us a list of [suggestions on] Defence subjects which was not to our liking. [The] list was comic. It made the position of [the] Indian Defence Minister ridiculous [according to Sir Stafford's formula] in the eyes of the public.

It [is] not clear whether a National Government would have been permitted to organize [a citizens' army]. . . . What we were ultimately told was that the matter would lie within the discretion of the Commander-in-Chief, and that he would not come in the way [of our actions] —that in certain circumstances a Commander-in-Chief might agree [with us]. If he did not, we had the option to resign! We felt that that was not the way to bring about a settlement. Our approach was one of lighting a spark in hundreds of millions of minds in India. The only thing that troubled us all the time was: can we make . . . India hum as an organised unit of resistance, and make the people feel that this [is] their war?

For Sir Stafford Cripps to say that we are bargaining and using the language of the market place, or of a pettifogging lawyer, shows that he considers the whole question, like most British statesmen, from the standpoint which in this wide world is peculiar only to England—the singularly complacent attitude that they alone are right and that all those who are against them are not only wrong but damnably wrong.

Congress is the only party in India that could deliver the goods.

The fundamental factor to-day in India . . . is the distrust or dislike of the people for the British government. It is not a pro-Japanese, it is an anti-British, sentiment. That may occasionally lead individuals to an expression of a pro-Japanese view. This is short-sighted. This is a slave sentiment. It distresses me that any Indian should talk of the Japanese liberating India. Japan comes here either for imperialist reasons, or to fight Britain—not to liberate India.

I am not going to give in to Britain if she wants to exploit or rule India.

Much less do I want the Indian people to give in or be passive towards the Japanese. I want us to resist them to the uttermost.

Our policy [concerning] the Japanese invasion is that we are out to embarrass [Japan] to the utmost.

There is a difference in our approach to the kind of resistance we offer to the old invader and the new. We submit to neither, but there is a difference because there is a difference between the old invasion and the new. The British invasion is a played-out affair, the new invasion may not prove to be such. . . .

The best thing [the United Nations] can do is to acknowledge India as an independent nation. I welcome the friendship of any nation or nations . . . prepared to recognise India as an independent nation. I am quite convinced that America would like a real, popular war effort in India. . . .

Only the State can defend the country. We cannot now raise a citizen army; nevertheless, since this crisis came we have started an intensified programme of self-sufficiency and self-protection in rural and urban areas in respect of food and clothing if and when transport fails. Naturally [the] units [that have been established] could not resist an invading army, [but] they form the background of any resistance . . . the State or we might organise. It may be that we should have to take up guerrilla warfare.[1]

[In connection with the issues at stake, Azad has noted: " . . . I particularly asked Gandhi [during the period of the Cripps' negotiations] about the application of non-violence under the present circumstances. I am happy to say that this aspect of the problem is quite clear in his mind. As a man of action he cannot ignore the conditions prevailing around him. He told me that his personal views about non-violence need not be re-enunciated and his position remained unchanged, but at the same time he knew that it was not the position of the Congress, nor of other parties, nor of the majority of Indian people [who] consider defence to be armed defence only. Therefore, if a free National Government was established in India with an understanding to defend her against the invader it was obvious that it could be only an armed defence, not a non-violent one."

Gandhi further told his colleagues at the time of the Cripps Mission: "Non-violence with me is a creed. . . . But it is never as a creed that I placed it before India. . . . I placed it before the Congress as a political method. . . . As a political method it can always be changed, modified, altered, or even given up in preference to another. . . . If you can get

[1] Based on I.W.N., pp. 9–14.

what you want you will strike the bargain, and you may be sure that I will not shed a single tear."[1]

After Congress had rejected Britain's offer, Cripps telegraphed to London from India, "'I have tonight received long letter from Congress President stating that Congress is unable to accept proposals. . . . There is clearly no hope of agreement and I shall start home on Sunday.'

"Later the same day, Sir Stafford sent a further telegram to the [British] Prime Minister: 'My own view is that despite failure the atmosphere has improved quite definitely. Nehru has come out in a fine statement for total war against the Japanese. Jinnah has pledged me unwavering support of the Moslems. . . . We are not depressed, though sad at the result. Now we must get on with the job of defending India.'"[2]

Of President Roosevelt's Efforts to Avert Breakdown of Cripps Mission

["President Roosevelt's personal envoy in New Delhi, Colonel Louis Johnson, in a last-minute effort to avert a breakdown of the Cripps Mission, begged the President to intercede with Mr Churchill; otherwise, he warned him, it was 'doomed to failure', adding that Sir Stafford agreed with this view. But Colonel Johnson's . . . intervention was creating complications in London. Mr Harry Hopkins cabled to the President that 'Cripps very naturally is using Johnson who, in turn, uses your name very freely. I have told the Prime Minister and Eden that Johnson is not acting as a mediator on your behalf, but whatever he is doing he is doing at the specific request of Cripps.'

"After the final breakdown, Johnson informed Washington that he was convinced, 'London wanted a refusal (by the Congress). . . . Nehru has been magnificent in his co-operation with me. The President would like him, and on most things they would agree.' In the same message, he observed, 'Cripps, through no fault of his own, has failed.'

"Colonel Johnson sought to soften the disastrous results of the failure of the Cripps Mission by persuading Mr Nehru to write to the President."[3]]

[Letter to Franklin D. Roosevelt—New Delhi, April 12, 1942.] I am venturing to write to you as I know that you are deeply interested in the Indian situation today and its reactions on the war. The failure of Sir Stafford Cripps' mission to bring about a settlement between the British Government and the Indian people must have distressed you, as it has

[1] Quoted in F.E.S. (Mar. 22, 1943), p. 59.
[2] As quoted in B.J., p. 139.
[3] I.N. (Feb. 22, 1963), p. 8.

distressed us. As you know we have struggled for long years for the independence of India, but the peril of today made us desire above everything else that an opportunity should be given to us to organise a real national and popular resistance to the aggressor and invader. We were convinced that the right way to do this would have been to give freedom and independence to our people and ask them to defend it. That would have lighted a spark in millions of hearts, which would have developed into a blazing fire of resistance which no aggressor could have faced successfully.

If that was not to be as we wished it and considered necessary for the purposes of the war, the least that we considered essential was the formation of a truly national government today with power and responsibility to organise resistance on a popular basis. Unfortunately even that was not considered feasible or desirable by the British Government. I do not wish to trouble you with the details of what took place during the negotiations that have unfortunately failed for the present. You have no doubt been kept informed about them by your representatives here. I only wish to say how anxious and eager we were, and still are, to do our utmost for the defence of India and to associate ourselves with the larger causes of freedom and democracy. To us it is a tragedy that we cannot do so in the way and in the measure we would like to. We would have liked to stake everything [on] the defence of our country, to fight with all the strength and vitality that we possess, to count no cost and no sacrifice as too great for repelling the invader and securing freedom and independence for our country.

Our present resources may be limited, for the industrialisation of our country has been hindered by the policy pursued in the past by the British Government in India. We are a disarmed people. But our war potential is very great, our man power vast and our great spaces, as in China, would have helped us. Our production can be speeded up greatly with the cooperation of capital and labour. But all this war potential can only be utilised fully when the government of the country is intimately associated with and representative of the people. A government divorced from the people cannot get a popular response which is so essential; much less can a foreign government, which is inevitably disliked and distrusted, do so.

Danger and peril envelop us and the immediate future is darkened by the shadows of possible invasion and the horrors that would follow, as they have followed Japanese aggression in China. The failure of Sir Stafford Cripps' mission has added to the difficulties of the situation and reacted unfavourably on our people. But whatever the difficulties we shall face them with all our courage and will to resist. Though the way of our choice may be closed to us, and we are unable to associate ourselves with the activities of the British authorities in India, still we shall do our utmost not to sumbit to Japanese or any other aggression and invasion. We, who have struggled for so long for freedom and against an old aggression, would prefer to perish rather than submit to a new invader.

Our sympathies, as we have so often declared, are with the forces fighting against fascism and for democracy and freedom. With freedom in our own country, those sympathies could have been translated into dynamic action.

To your great country, of which you are the honoured head, we send [greetings] and good wishes for success. . . . To you, Mr. President, on whom so many all over the world look for leadership in the cause of freedom, we would add our assurances of our high regard and esteem.[1]

["Somewhat later, Colonel Johnson told President [Roosevelt]: 'Nehru's hands would be immensely strengthened if Britain, China and the United States could issue a joint statement on Pacific war aims, specifically including freedom and self-determination for India and a resolution to defend India at all costs.'"[2]]

Further Statements

[From text of cable dispatched from New Delhi, April 13, 1942, delivered in London, April 23, 1942.] The decisions of the Indian National Congress on the proposals brought to India by Sir Stafford Cripps are contained in its long resolution and the letters of the Congress President to Sir Stafford. In the resolution passed on April 2nd, we expressed our disagreement with the British proposal offering India Dominion Status in the future and reasserted our claim for independence. We also condemned the provision in the proposals for the possible division of India, while accepting the principle of non-compulsion of territorial areas against their declared will, but subject to certain conditions.

We strongly condemned the provisions in the British proposals that the rulers of the Indian States [the princes] should nominate the representatives of the States to the Constituent Assembly, thus ignoring the rights of the entire population of the States. These rulers, while they

[1] B.O.L., pp. 479–80.
I.N. (Feb. 22, 1963), p. 8.

would influence the making of the constitution [through their nominees in the constitution-making body would], however, have the option of remaining outside the proposed Indian Union. The whole conception on which these proposals are based would lead to the break up of India, with British armed forces guarding the Princes' States and British power interfering with the freedom of the new Indian Union and encouraging disruptive tendencies.

The proposals relating to the present are vague with such reservations in regard to defence as [to] make any transfer of power illusory and prevent the development of defence on a mass basis, which is now essential.

Congress, however, emphasised that in view of the national crisis, it was prepared to set aside all proposals for the future provided that a responsible national government, in control of defence, were formed now, leaving the control of the armed forces with the Commander-in-Chief.

Sir Stafford made it clear in the early stages that he envisaged a National Cabinet with the Viceroy as a constitutional head, like the King in the United Kingdom, subject only to the reservation of defence.

Discussion therefore centred round defence. Sir Stafford suggested the division of functions between the popular Defence Minister and the War Minister, which latter position would be filled by the Commander-in-Chief. The functions proposed for the Defence Minister proved trivial and unacceptable to Congress. Further formulae for defence were discussed.

Ultimately Sir Stafford stated that no substantial change was possible.

He also stated that there was no possibility of forming a national cabinet with joint responsibility, nor could assurance be given about the Viceroy's use of his powers of intervention or veto. This, he said, was entirely a matter for the Viceroy's discretion, and might be discussed with the Viceroy later [on.] *The Viceroy would also function as Prime Minister*.

Thus no major change was contemplated, but only the addition of popular representatives to the Viceroy's Executive Council. Not only would the legal position stand unaltered, but no assurances were forthcoming even about conventions. Thus we were faced practically with the repetition of the offer of August 8th, 1940, with the addition of certain minor variations.

This presents an entirely different picture from that which Cripps originally suggested. It would be impossible to call this a national government or to evoke enthusiasm for it from the people.

At no stage during the talks did any communal or minority difficulty occur, as Congress is claiming power and responsibility for the National Government as a whole and the question of the formation of the Government was deferred.

To our surprise, Sir Stafford's last letter stated that there was no possibility of a national cabinet with joint responsibility as this meant the rule of a tyrannical majority. This plea at the last stage, after the breakdown of the talks, without previous discussion in relation to this issue, is most unfair and unjustified. The objection is not applicable to a cabinet and in any case the occasion for it did not arise then.

Since that time Cripps has been emphasising the communal issue in the old Amery manner and has been endeavouring to divert attention from the real issues. He is also stressing constitutional issues which had not been discussed. His whole approach has been wrong and vitiated by the communal outlook.

Congress went to the uttermost limit during the negotiations by giving up their most precious objectives. The crux of the matter was the organisation of national defence on a popular mass basis, but this is possible only under a free national government.

Bitterness is increasing here and, in future, it will be impossible to accept anything short of complete national freedom.

The United Nations should acknowledge the independence of India.

Meanwhile we are urging the people to oppose the aggressor and on no account to submit to the invader. But individual resistance is of little avail.[1]

[From press conference—Calcutta, April 25, 1942.] We are going to make no approach to the British Government and we shall face our problems and perils with such wisdom and endurance as we may have.

We shall prefer to perish rather than submit to an arrogant imperialism or a new invader. If ... Cripps thinks that the position of India has improved by his visit, he is grievously mistaken. The gulf is greater to-day than ever before. It is true that events are compelling us to think of what we shall do to meet them, but whatever we may do we will have nothing to do with the question of co-operating with the British efforts in India. Indeed to talk of co-operation is in itself a misnomer. What is meant is subservice. We can only co-operate as free men and a free National Government with those who [are acknowledged] as such.

Sir Stafford has said, we shirk responsibility. That is a curious charge when the responsibility we sought was denied to us. Certainly we are not

[1] C.M., pp. 2–4.

excited [by] the heavy responsibility of running canteens and stationery shops, etc., which we are told we could have [under] the defence minister.... Sir Stafford has made it even more clear than before that there is no common ground between the British Government and the Congress. It surprises me that the British Government should still talk in its old pre-war patronising language and . . . pose [before others as favouring] a kind of arbitration in India. They do not appreciate that the world has changed and that India and the world will change still further without awaiting the approval and consent of the British War Cabinet. As the position of the British Government is being made clear, it is right that the position of the Congress should also be clearly understood.[1]

[From letter to Evelyn Wood—June 5, 1942.] Cripps surprised me greatly. I have liked Cripps as a man. . . . But on this occasion I was surprised at his woodenness and insensitiveness, in spite of his public smiles. He was all the time the formal representative of the War Cabinet, in fact he was the War Cabinet speaking to us with a take it or leave it attitude. Always he seemed to impress on us that he knew the Indian problem in and out and he had found the only solution for it. Anyone who did not agree with it was, to say the least of it, utterly misguided. Indeed, I made it perfectly plain to him that there were limits beyond which I could not carry the Congress and there were limits beyond which the Congress could not carry the people. But he thought that all this was totally beside the point.[2]

[In considering the Cripps proposals, it may be helpful to observe that, according to the census of 1941, the entire population of India, including the Indian States, was approximately three hundred and ninety million. This total included two hundred and twenty-five million Hindus; ninety-two million Muslims; six million Indian Christians; five and a half million Sikhs.
According to the same census, the population of Bengal was sixty million, of whom thirty-three million were Muslims. The population of the Punjab was twenty-eight million, sixteen million being Muslim.
In 1942, Hindu-Muslim coalition governments existed in Bengal, the Punjab and the Province of Sind. They were reported to be functioning successfully and in amity.
In view of the great emphasis the British placed on communal friction, as a reason for not adhering to Congress' aspirations, it is of interest to

---

[1] B.A.I., p. 221.
[2] Quoted in M.B., p. 281.

note that, by his own admission, Cripps did not discuss the Hindu-
Muslim problem with Indian leaders during his entire visit to India
in 1942.[1]]

4 | Post-Cripps Mission Period—Congress Resolution on Possible Invasion of India— India's Day of Reckoning—Other Statements of the Period—Press Interview, July

Post-Cripps Mission Period

[The period following the Cripps Mission was again a troubled one for
Nehru. His basic dilemmas of the war period became even further
accentuated. Despite his symphty for the Allies, he could not rid himself
of a deep distrust of Britain, vis-à-vis India. The thought continued to
haunt him that if England could make her generous offer of union with
France, why should she not adopt an equally enlightened attitude toward
India?

Yet, even despite the failure of the 1942 Cabinet Mission, after Cripps
had left India, Nehru stated, with characteristic generosity, that although
he had no desire "to embarrass the British war effort . . . the problem
for us is how to organize our own."[2] He continued to favor guerilla
warfare against the Japanese during this period.]

From All-India Congress Committee Resolution on Possible Invasion—April, 1942

"In case an invasion takes place, it must be resisted. Such resistance can
only take the form of non-violent non-cooperation, as the British Government has prevented the organization of national defence by the people in
any other way. . . . We may not bend the knee to the aggressor nor obey

[1] Quoted in T.A.Y. (X–XI), p. 53.
[2] Quoted in M.B., p. 283.

any of his orders. We may not look to him for favours nor fall to his bribes. . . . We will refuse to give . . . up [homes and property] even if we have to die in the effort".[1]

India's Day of Reckoning

[The] vital problems that confront India . . . are no longer our concern only; they are of world concern, affecting the entire international situation today. More so will they affect the shaping of future events. Whether we consider them from the point of view of the terrible world conflict that is going on, or in terms of the political, economic, and commercial consequences of this war, the future of 400 million human beings is of essential importance. These millions are no longer passive agents of others, submitting with resignation to the decrees of fate. They are active, dynamic, and hungering to shoulder the burden of their own destiny and to shape it according to their own wishes.

The Indian struggle for freedom and democracy has evoked a generous response from many an American, but the crisis that faces us all is too urgent for us merely to trade in sympathy or feel benevolent toward each other. We have to consider our major problems objectively and almost impersonally and endeavor to solve them, or else these problems will certainly overwhelm us, as indeed they threaten to do. That has been the lesson of history, and we forget it at our peril. It is therefore not merely from a humanitarian point of view, though humanitarianism itself is good, but rather in the objective spirit of science that we should approach our problems.

The next hundred years, it has been said, are going to be the century of America. America is undoubtedly going to play a very important role in the years and generations to come. It is young and vital and full of the spirit of growth. The small and stuffy countries of Europe, with their eternal conflicts and wars, can no longer control the world. Europe has a fine record of achievement of which it may well be proud. That achievement will endure and possibly find greater scope for development when its accompaniment of domination over others is ended.

If the next century is going to be the century of America, it is also going to be the century of Asia, a rejuvenated Asia deriving strength from its ancient cultures and yet vital with the youthful spirit of modern

[1] Ibid., p. 284.

4+N. II

science. Most of us are too apt to think of Asia as backward and decadent because for nearly two hundred years it has been dominated by Europe and has suffered all the ills, material and spiritual, which subjection inevitably brings in its train. We forget the long past of Asia when politically, economically, and culturally it played a dominant role. In this long perspective the past two hundred years are just a brief period that is ending, and Asia will surely emerge with new strength and vitality as it has done so often in the past. One of the amazing phenomena of history is the way India and China have repeatedly revived after periods of decay, and how both of them have preserved the continuity of their cultural traditions through thousands of years. They have obviously had tremendous reserves of strength to draw upon. India was old when the civilization of Greece flowered so brilliantly. Between the two there was intimate contact and much in common, and India is said to have influenced Greece far more than Greece did India. That Grecian civilization, for all its brilliance, passed away soon, leaving a great heritage, but India carried on and her culture flowered again and again. India, like China, had more staying power.

Asia is no suppliant for the favors of others, but claims perfect equality in everything and is confident of holding her own in the modern world in comradeship with others. The recent visit of Generalissimo Chiang Kai-shek and Madame Chiang to India was not only of historic significance but has given us a glimpse of the future when India and China will cooperate for their own and the world's good. The Generalissimo pointed out a remarkable fact: that India and China, with a common land frontier of 3,000 kilometers, had lived at peace with each other for a thousand years, neither country playing the role of aggressor, but both having intimate cultural and commercial contacts throughout these ages. That in itself shows the peaceful character of these two great civilizations.

Keeping this background in mind, it will be evident how unreal and fantastic is the conception of India as a kind of colonial appendage or offshoot of Britain, growing slowly to nationhood and freedom as the British dominions have done. India is a mother country, which has influenced in the past vast sections of the human race in Asia. She still retains that storehouse of cultural vitality that has given her strength in the past, and at the same time has the natural resources, the scientific, technical, industrial, and financial capacity to make her a great nation in the modern sense of the word. But she cannot grow because of the shackles that tie her down, nor can she play her part, as she should, in the war crisis today. That part can be a great one not only because of the manpower at India's disposal but because, given a chance, she can rapidly become a great industrial nation.

The world war is obviously part of a great revolution taking place throughout the world. To consider it in only military terms is to miss the real significance of what is happening. Causes lie deep, and it would be foolish to imagine that all our present troubles are due to the vanity and insatiable ambition of certain individuals or peoples. Those individuals or peoples represent evil tendencies. But they also represent the urge for change from an order that has lost stability and equilibrium and that is heartily disliked by vast numbers of people. Part of the aggressors' strength is certainly due to their challenge to this old system. To oppose these inevitable changes and seek to perpetuate the old, or even to be passive about them, is to surrender on a revolutionary plane to the aggressor countries. Intelligent people know these aggressors are out to impose tyranny far worse than any that has existed, and therefore they should be opposed. To submit to them is to invite degradation of the worst type, a spiritual collapse far worse than even military defeat. We see what has happened in Vichy France. We know what has taken place in Central Europe and in Northern China. And yet [the] fear of a possible worse fate is not enough, and certainly it does not affect the masses of population who are thoroughly dissatisfied with their present lot. They want some positive deliverance to shake them out of their passivity, some cause that immediately affects them to fight for. A proud people do not accept present degradation and misery for fear that something worse may take its place.

Thus the urgent need is to give a moral and revolutionary lead to the world, to convince it that the old order has gone and a new one really based on freedom and democracy has taken its place. No promises for the future are good enough, no half measures will help; it is the present that counts; for it is in the present that the war is going to be lost or won, and it is out of the present that the future will take shape. President Roosevelt has spoken eloquently about this future and about the four freedoms, and his words have found an echo in millions of hearts. But the words are vague and do not satisfy, and no action follows those words. The Atlantic Charter is again a pious and nebulous expression of hope, which stimulates nobody, and even this, Mr. Churchill tells us, does not apply to India.

If this urgent necessity for giving a moral and revolutionary lead were recognized and acted upon, then the aggressor nations would be forced to drop the cloak that hides many of their evil designs, and new forces of vast dimensions would rise up to check them. Even the peoples of Europe now under Nazi domination would be affected. But the greatest effect would be produced in Asia and Africa. And that may well be the turning point of the war. Only freedom and the conviction that they are fighting for their own freedom can make people fight as the Chinese and Russians have fought.

We have the long and painful heritage of European domination in Asia. Britain may believe or proclaim that she has done good to India and other Asiatic countries, but the Indians and other Asiatics think otherwise, and it is after all what we believe that matters now. It is a terribly difficult business to wipe out this past of bitterness and conflict, yet it can be done if there is a complete break from it, and the present is made entirely different. Only thus can those psychological conditions be produced that lead to cooperation in a common endeavor and release mass effort.

It was in this hope that the National Congress issued a long statement in September, 1939, defining its policy in regard to the European war and inviting the British Government to declare its war aims in regard to imperialism and democracy and, in particular, to state how these were to be given effect in the present. For many years past the Congress had condemned Fascist and Nazi doctrines and the aggressions of the Japanese, Italian, and German governments. It condemned them afresh and offered its cooperation in the struggle for freedom and democracy.

That offer was made two and a half years ago and it has been repeated in various forms subsequently. It was rejected—and rejected in a way that angered India. The British Government has made it clear beyond a doubt that it clings to the past; and present and future, in so far as Britain can help it, will resemble that past. It is not worth while to dwell on the tragic history of these two and a half years that have added to our problems and the complexity of the situation. Events have followed each other in furious succession all over the world and, in recent months, parts of the British Empire have passed out of England's control. And yet, in spite of all this, the old outlook and methods continue and England's statesmen talk the patronizing language of the nineteenth century to us. We are intensely interested in the defense of India from external aggression but the only way we could do anything effective about it is through mass enthusiasm and mass effort under popular control.

We cannot develop our heavy industries, even though wartime requirements shout out for such development, because British interests disapprove and fear that Indian industry might compete with them after the war. For years past Indian industrialists have tried to develop an automobile industry, airplane manufacture, and shipbuilding—the very industries most required in wartime. The way these have been successfully obstructed is an astonishing story. I have been particularly interested in industrial problems in my capacity as Chairman of the National Planning Committee. This committee gathered around it some of the ablest talent in India—industrial, financial, technical, economic, scientific—and tackled the whole complex and vast problem of planned and scientific development and coordination of industry, agriculture, and social services. The labors of this committee and its numerous subcommittees would have been particularly valuable in wartime. Not only was this not taken advantage of but its work was hindered and obstructed by the government.

Two and a half years ago we had hoped to be able to play an effective role in the world drama. Our sympathies were all on one side; our interests coincided with these. Our principal problem is after all not the Hindu-Moslem problem, but the planned growth of industry, greater production, juster distribution, higher standards, and thus gradual elimination of the appalling poverty that crushes our people. It was possible to deal with this as part of the war effort and coordinate the two, thus making India far stronger, both materially and psychologically, to resist aggression. But it could only have been done with the driving power that freedom gives. It is not very helpful to think of these wasted years, now that immediate peril confronts us and we have not time, as we had then, to prepare for it. We may have to meet this peril differently now, for in no event do we propose to submit to aggression.

It is said that any transfer of power during wartime involves risks. So it does. To abstain from action or change probably involves far greater risks. The aggressor nations have repeatedly shown that they have the courage to gamble with fate, and the gamble has often come off. We must take risks. One thing is certain—that the present state of affairs in India is deplorable. It lacks not only popular support but also efficiency. The people who control affairs in India from Whitehall or Delhi are incapable even of understanding what is happening, much less of dealing with it.

We are told that the independence of Syria is recognized, that Korea is going to be a free country. But India, the classic land of modern imperialist control, must continue under British tutelage. Meanwhile daily broadcasts from Tokyo, Bangkok, Rome, and Berlin in Hindustani announce that the Axis countries want India to be independent. Intelligent people know how false this is and are not taken in. But many who listen to this contrast it with what the British Government says and does in India. We have seen the effect of this propaganda in Malaya and Burma. India is far more advanced politically and can therefore resist it more successfully. She is especially attracted to China and has admired the magnificent resistance of the Russian people. She feels friendly toward the democratic ideals of America. But with all that she feels helpless and frustrated and bitter against those who have put her in her present position.

Some of the problems are of our own making, some of British creation. But whoever may be responsible for them, we have to solve them. One of these problems, so often talked about, is the Hindu-Moslem problem. It is often forgotten that Moslems, like Hindus, also demand independence for India. Some of them (but only some) talk in terms of a separate state in the Northwest of India. They have never defined what they mean and few people take their demand seriously, especially in these days when small states have ceased to count and must inevitably be parts of a larger federation. The Hindu-Moslem problem will be solved in terms of federation, but it will be solved only when British interference with our affairs ceases. So long as there is a third party to intervene and encourage intransigent elements of either group, there will be no solution. A free India will face the problem in an entirely different setting and will, I have no doubt, solve it.

What do we want? A free, democratic, federal India, willing to be associated with other countries in larger federations. In particular, India would like to have close contacts with China and Soviet Russia, both her neighbors, and America. Every conceivable protection, guarantee, and help should be given our minority groups and those that are culturally or economically backward.

What should be done now? It is not an easy question, for what may be possible today becomes difficult tomorrow. What we might have done two years ago we have no time to do now. But this war is not going to end soon, and what happens in India is bound to make a great difference. The grand strategy of war requires an understanding of the urges that move people to action and sacrifice for a cause. It requires sacrifice not only of lives of brave men but of racial prejudices, of inherited conceptions of political or economic domination and exploitation of others, of vested interests of small groups that hinder the growth and development of others. It requires conception and translation into action, in so far as possible, of the new order based on the political and economic freedom of all countries, of world cooperation of free peoples, of revolutionary leadership along these lines, and of capacity to dare and face risks. What vested interests are we going to protect for years to come when the interests of humanity itself are at stake today? Where are the vested interests of Hong Kong and Singapore?

It is essential that whatever is to be done is done now. For it is the present that counts. What will happen after the war nobody knows, and to postpone anything till then is to admit bankruptcy and invite disaster.

I would suggest that the leaders of America and Britain declare: First, that every country is entitled to full freedom and to shape its own destiny, subject only to certain international requirements and their adjustment by international cooperation. Second, that this applies fully to countries at present within the British Empire, and that India's independence is recognized as well as her right to frame her own constitution through an assembly of her elected representatives, who will also consider her future relations with Britain and other countries. Third, that all races and peoples must be treated as equal and allowed equal opportunities of growth and development. Individuals and races may and do differ, and some are culturally or intellectually more mature than others. But the door of advancement must be open to all; indeed those that are immature should receive every help and encouragement. Nothing has alienated people more from the Nazis than their racial theories and the brutal application of these theories. But a similar doctrine and its application are in constant evidence in subject countries.

Such a declaration clearly means the ending of imperialism everywhere with all its dominating position and special privileges. That will be a greater blow to Nazism and Fascism than any military triumph, for Nazism and Fascism are an intensification of the principle of imperialism. The issue of freedom will then be clean and clear before the world, and no subterfuge or equivocation will be possible.

But the declaration, however good, is not enough, for no one believes in promises or is prepared to wait for the hereafter. Its translation into present and immediate practice will be the acid test. A full change-over may not be immediately possible, yet much can be done now. In India a change-over can take place without delay and without any complicated legal enactments. The British Parliament may pass laws in regard to it or it may not. We are not particularly interested, as we want to make our own laws in the future. A provisional national government could be formed and all real power transferred to it. This may be done even within the present structure, but it must be clearly understood that this structure will then be an unimportant covering for something that is entirely different. This national government will not be responsible to the British Government or the Viceroy but to the people, though of course it will seek to cooperate with the British Government and its agents. When opportunity offers in the future, further changes may take place through a constituent assembly. Meanwhile it may be possible to widen the basis of the present central assembly and make it a representative assembly to which the provisional national government will be responsible.

If this is done in the central government, it would not be at all difficult to make popular governments function in the provinces where no special changes are necessary and the apparatus for them exists already.

All this is possible without upsetting too suddenly the outer framework. But it involves a tremendous and vital change, and that is just what is needed from the point of view of striking popular imagination and gaining popular support. Only a real change-over and realization that the old system is dead past revival, that freedom has come, will galvanize the people into action. That freedom will come at a moment of dire peril and it will be terribly difficult for any one to shoulder this tremendous responsibility. But whatever the dangers, they have to be faced and responsibility has to be shouldered.

The changes suggested would give India the status of an independent nation, but a peaceful change-over presumes mutual arrangements being made between representatives of India and Great Britain for governing their future relations. I do not think that the conception of wholly sovereign independent nations is compatible with world peace or progress. But we do not want international cooperation to be just a variation of the imperial theme with some dominant nations controlling international and national policies. The old idea of dominion status is unlikely to remain anywhere and it is peculiarly inapplicable to India. But India will welcome association with Britain and other countries, on an equal basis, as soon as all taint of imperialism is removed.

In immediate practice, after the independence of India is recognized, many old contacts will continue. The administrative machinery will largely remain, apart from individual cases, but it will be subject to such changes as will make it fit in with new conditions. The Indian Army must necessarily become a national army and cease to be looked upon as a mercenary army. Any future British military establishment would depend on many present and changing factors, chiefly the development of the war. It cannot continue as an alien army of occupation, as it has done in the past, but as an allied army its position would be different.

It is clear that if the changes suggested were made, India would line

up completely with the countries fighting aggression. It is difficult, however, to prophesy what steps would be most effective at this particular
juncture. If the military defense of India, now being carried on beyond
her frontiers, proves ineffective, a new and difficult military situation
arises that may require other measures. Mr Gandhi, in common with
others, has declared that we must resist aggression and not submit to any
invader; but his methods of resistance, as is well known, are different.
These peaceful methods seem odd in this world of brutal warfare. Yet,
in certain circumstances, they may be the only alternative left us. The
main thing is that we must not submit to aggression.

One thing is certain: whatever the outcome of this war, India is going
to resist every attempt at domination, and a peace that has not solved the
problem of India will not be of long purchase. Primarily this is Britain's
responsibility, but its consequences are worldwide and affect this war.
No country can therefore ignore India's present and her future, least of
all America, on whom rests the vast burden of responsibility and toward
whom so many millions look for right leadership at this crisis in world
history.[1]

Other Statements of the Period

[A warning to the British—Jhansi, May 29, 1942.] I wish to warn the
[British] Government that if it pursues its repressive policy . . . we will
resist. . . .

We are placed in a dilemma. If we oppose the Government and carry the
fight against it, we will invite Japan [into] our country. The Government
does not want our real co-operation on honourable terms. It is following
[the] same old methods. In this difficult situation, the Congress has tried
to guide the people, and [the] latest resolution of the All-India Congress
Committee urged . . . us to become . . . self-sufficient. . . . Some people
ridicule the idea of opposing Japan by non-violence and non-co-operation
but they do not realise that the Congress has not advised the armed
forces to adopt this weapon. It is intended for the civil population only.[2]

[On June 20, 1942, Gandhi wrote to Chiang Kai-shek stating that, if
India were given independence, he stood for resistance against Japan.

As quoted from statement by C. R. Rajagopalachari: "If Nehru were

[1] F. (Apr. 1942), pp. 67B, C, D; 187–89.
[2] B.A.I., p. 225.

4*

the leader of an Indian National Government, then Gandhi's pacificism would make no trouble and Nehru would fight this war against the Axis. Nehru was anti-Fascist when some members of the present British Government were fawning on Hitler and on Mussolini and appeasing the Japanese. You don't have to worry about Nehru or . . . a great many other Indian leaders who want to fight this war if the British would let them".[1]]

[India must be independent—variations on a theme. From letter to Lampton Berry (addressed to Office of Personal Representative of President of United States in New Delhi), June 23, 1942.] I can quite understand that some of Mr Gandhi's recent statements have been mis-understood in the United States. Perhaps his later statements have helped to clear up this misunderstanding. One thing is certain: Mr Gandhi wants to do everything in his power to prevent a Japanese invasion and occupation of India. He wants to rouse up the people of the country to resist and not to submit. He has been oppressed by the fact that British policy in India is producing just the opposite results and antagonising the people so much that they are developing a mood which prefers any change, however bad, to the existing state of affairs. This is a dangerous and harmful tendency which he wishes to combat.

After Malaya and Burma there is a widespread belief in India that so far as the British Government in India is concerned there is no serious intention or capacity to resist Japanese invasion, especially in Bengal. Confidential circulars issued by the authorities in Bengal to their officers dealt fully with the methods of evacuation and how superior officers should get away leaving their subordinates in charge. These subordinates were actually told to carry on their normal work under the orders of the enemy, as this was apparently in accordance with international law. Such instructions do not encourage resistance. They are essentially defeatist. The way the Madras Government behaved about two months ago was also extraordinary. At the rumour of a possible invasion (which turned out later to be untrue) they fled.

Even if the intention is to offer determined resistance at a later stage, the mere fact that Bengal has fallen will have far-reaching repercussions all over India. It is quite likely that in many rural areas, far from any troop concentrations, civil administration may gradually fade away. This again will inevitably affect the military situation and weaken it.

How far American planes and other kinds of help have altered the situation I do not know. But essentially the situation cannot be very

[1] Quoted in T.A.Y. (X–XI), p. 58.

different from what it was two months ago. No Indian can view this prospect with equanimity. It means Japanese occupation of important parts of the country and a growing chaos in many other parts. And yet we feel that this can be checked. In a purely military sense we cannot do much in the near future and operations must depend on the Allied forces in India. But the acknowledgement of Indian independence and the establishment of a National Government here will electrify the atmosphere and make all the difference in the world. Even if unfortunately the Japanese occupy certain parts of the country, the rest [of India will not] crack up but [will carry] on aggressively as [does] China. A spirit of passive resignation [can give place] to active opposition and resistance.

Indian independence therefore becomes of paramount importance today for purposes of Indian defence, in cooperation with the Allied forces, as well as for helping China. It is only in this context of today's problem that it has to be considered.

For those of us who have to shoulder a measure of responsibility, it is not enough to function as individuals, although that has also to be done. We must get others to act and generally to influence public opinion in the right direction. I have been endeavouring to do this. On no account do I want India to be submissive to any aggression. I want active and continuous resistance to it. But if that is to be at all effective, then the British Government in India must give place to a free national government. This will not interfere with the military dispositions or arrangements for defence.[1]

[To British and American press correspondents—July 8, 1942.] The Congress position is very much changed since . . . Cripps departed.

The Congress is not prepared to accept what it was willing [to accept] then. The rank and file felt great relief when negotiations failed. I would have [obtained] passive approval of the Congress [for] the settlement with Cripps, but now it is not possible . . . to secure [such] approval. . . .

Things are shaping [themselves] in such a manner that the people are becoming more passive and suddenly submissive. My fear is that if things are allowed to take [the present] course [the people] will [become] prepared to submit to the Japanese. . . .

It is obvious that any step we take against the British Government may be full of perils, but on the other hand not taking any step is still more perilous. We have [to] choose the lesser evil. It has become highly important to raise the spirit of resistance . . . to . . . the Japanese. By

[1] B.O.L., pp. 492–93.

passively submitting to things in India today that spirit of resistance is actually [being] crushed. The problem before the Congress is ... to increase the people's spirit of resistance in such a way ... as to avoid creating a situation which might temporarily help Japan or any invader. This may be possible for the time [being] because the step we propose to take might involve non-submission to British authority, creating further complications. But in whatever we do, our desire and intentions are clear, that we do not wish to injure the cause of China or the defence of India.[1]

[Further attempt to gain India's freedom—Delhi, July 19, 1942.] To create a resolution against the slavery of our country is our profession, and it should be the duty of everyone to raise his voice against slavery. The Congress [has been true to] its own principle [in reacting to] the background of this war and therefore we raised our voice when Japan invaded China and Italy conquered Abyssinia. . . . We condemned these [acts] and other [similar ones carried out by] Hitler and Mussolini. The Working Committee has clearly explained that they do not want to make Japan stronger by starting [a] civil disobedience movement. It is our duty now not to sit silent, but [to] fight for the freedom of India.[2]

["Can Indians Get Together?" Reprinted from *New York Times*, July 19, 1942.] Can the Indians get together! Yes, certainly, if impediments in their way created by foreign authority are removed, if they can face their problems without external interference. Every problem finally will be solved either by peaceful means or by conflict, though this may give rise to new problems. Independent India will solve her problems or cease to be. The past history of India shows us how she has successfully tackled her problems and out of every conflict of opposing forces has produced a new synthesis. Synthesis is a dominant trait of India's civilization and history.

Except for China, there is no great country in the world which has shown such powerful unity throughout the ages as India. That unity took political shape only rarely as it could not be stabilized until relatively recent developments in transport and communications made this easy. If these developments had not taken place it is possible that the United States of America might not have been a single nation.

Britain's rule over India led to political unity and also was a means to bring the industrial revolution to India. Development of that revolution

[1] B.A.I., pp. 230–31.
[2] Ibid., p. 232.

was, however, hindered by the British, who encouraged feudal elements and prevented industrial growth. The continuing process of synthesis also was stopped by this rule and disruptive forces were encouraged.

For the first time in India's history, here was the rule of a foreign people who had their political, financial, industrial and cultural roots elsewhere and who could only remain as foreigners exploiting the country for their own advantage. There could be no synthesis with them, and perpetual conflict was inevitable. Yet out of this very conflict rose the powerful All-India Nationalist movement, which became and is the symbol of political unity.

Independence, democracy and unity were the pillars of this movement. In accordance with old Indian traditions, toleration, fullest protection and autonomy were promised to all minorities, subject only to the essential unity of the country and to the democratic basis of its constitution. Independence meant severance from the British Empire, but in the New World it was realized that isolated national existence was not possible or desirable. So India was prepared to join any international federation on an equal basis. But that could come only after recognition of her independence and through her free will. There could be no compulsion. In particular, India wanted to associate herself closely with China.

There is now a demand on the part of some Moslems, represented by the Moslem League, for partition of India, and it must be remembered that this demand is a very recent one, [only a few] years old. It must also be remembered that there is a large section of Moslems in India who oppose it. Few people take it seriously, as it has no political or economic background. Americans who fought the Civil War to keep their Union together can appreciate how a proposal to divide the country is resented by vast numbers of the Indian people.

Thirty years ago the British Government introduced the principle of separate religious electorates in India, a fatal thing which has come in the way of development of political parties. Now they have tried to introduce the idea of partitioning India, not only into two but possibly many separate parts. This was one of the reasons which led to bitter resentment of the Cripps proposals. The All-India Congress could not agree to this, yet it went far and said if any territorial unit clearly declared its desire to break away, the Congress could not think in terms of compelling it to stay in the Union.

So far as minorities are concerned, it is accepted and common ground that they should be given fullest constitutional protection, religious, cultural, linguistic and every other way. Backward minorities or classes should in addition be given special educational and other privileges to bring them rapidly to the general level.

The real problem so often referred to is that of the Moslems. They are hardly a minority, as they number about 90,000,000, and it is difficult to see how even a majority can oppress them. As it happens, they are largely concentrated in particular provinces. It is proposed to give full provincial autonomy to every province, reserving only certain All-India subjects for the central government, and this will give every opportunity for self-development in each cultural area. Indeed, there may even be smaller autonomous cultural areas within the province.

It is possible to devise many ways to give satisfaction to every conceivable minority claim. The Congress has said this must be done by agreement, not by a majority vote. If agreement is not possible on any point, then impartial arbitration should be accepted. Finally, if any territorial unit insists on breaking away after the experience of working in the union, there is going to be no compulsion to force it to stay, provided such severance is geographically possible.

It must be remembered that the problem of Indian minorities is entirely different from nationalities with entirely different racial, cultural . . . linguistic backgrounds. This is not so in India where, except for a small handful of persons, there is no difference between Hindus and Moslems in race, culture or language. The vast majority of Moslems belong to the same stock as the Hindus and were converted to Islam. . . .

Can . . . Indians get together? I have no doubt that they can and they will. Even today there is an amazing unity of outlook among them and whatever their internal differences might be they stand for independence. The real obstacle in the way of real unity and progress is foreign domination. From every point of view it has become an urgent and immediate necessity that Britain should relinquish her hold in India and recognize Indian independence. There is no other way and it is certain, whether Britain likes it or not, that India must be given complete independence.

The approach of war to India has made this an even more vital question. Independent India would treat America and Britain as allies in a common enterprise to release her vast energy and resources against every aggressor who invaded her territory. But Indians can no longer function as slaves and underlings in their own country or outside or tolerate being treated as chattels by dominant foreign authority. Submission to this is for them the worst kind of spiritual degradation.

The East will put up with it no longer. Asia will come back to her own through whatever travail and suffering fate may have in store for her.

China has poured out her heart's blood in defense of her freedom. India would do likewise if the opportunity came to her to fight for her freedom. She seeks no dominion over others, but she will put up with no dominion over herself. Only independence will release her from long bondage and allow her to play her part fittingly in the terrible drama of the world today.[1]

[In conjunction with Nehru's observation in the above article that few took seriously the demand on the part of some Muslims for partition of India, he was convinced at the time that only Jinnah, and an upper-class stratum of Muslims, who possessed large agricultural holdings—and feared social reforms—favored Partition; that the reasons for their doing so were economic, not religious; that the Muslim masses had far more to gain as a result of remaining part of a united, democratic-socialist, secular nation, than a truncated, separatist Pakistan.]

From Press Interview—Allahabad, July 31, 1942

[Nehru declared, in response to a suggestion that India's problems might be solved by a further Round Table Conference, that, unless the country's desire for independence was clearly recognized, any attempt by Britain to call such a conference would be unacceptable to Congress. The holding of such a conference, in accordance with any previously utilized formula, he asserted, necessarily must end in failure. It could but serve as a trap: "The whole conception of having to sit at the feet of power is repugnant to us."

Queried about whether American and Chinese intervention in India against the Axis Powers would be acceptable in the present situation, Nehru stated that it would, but only if India were independent and able to act as an equal ally.

Asked what value he attached to the declared dissatisfaction of the Muslim League, the Hindu Mahasabha and the depressed classes, with the present stand of Congress, Nehru replied that it would be arrogance on his part to say that he attached no value to it but, on the other hand, he did not attach over-much importance to it. He said that there could be no disagreement on the fundamental issue of a desire for India's immediate independence. With respect to a Provisional National Government, it could be of a composite nature, representing all of the major parties, including the Congress and Muslim League. There was no room, he maintained, for negotiation on the question of Indian independence, even though details were always negotiable between the parties and groups concerned.

Nehru was further questioned concerning how he would react to Subhas Bose's leading an Indian "contingent of liberation" against India.

[1] C.I.G.T., pp. 3–7. © 1942 by the New York Times Company. Reprinted by permission.

Since Bose's sympathies continued to be with Japan, on the theory that a Japanese victory would lead to the defeat of the British Empire, Nehru replied that he would oppose Bose, and fight him, because Bose would be operating under Japanese auspices and control, and more for the advantage of Japan than of India. Nehru asserted, further, that Bose was quite wrong in thinking that he could achieve the freedom of India with the help of the Japanese.[1]]

5 | India and China

["India Can Learn from China." From *Asia and The Americas*, January, 1943—written shortly before August, 1942.] In the late summer of 1938 when the fate of Czechoslovakia hung in the balance, I met at the house of an English friend in London some people who had recently come from China. They were both Chinese and English, and they told us of the early beginnings of a village cooperative movement to produce goods which China lacked so much and to prevent an influx of Japanese commodities. It was a brave idea, but it was still in its infancy and one could hardly imagine then that it would grow and grow till it made a vital difference to events in China.

Later when I was back in India, small pamphlets and folders came to me from time to time from Hong Kong and Chungking telling me of the rapid growth of the Chinese Industrial Cooperatives. My interest in them grew, not only because of China, but because of our own village industry movement in India. When I went to China in August, 1939, I was eager to find out more about the C.I.C. and to visit, if possible, some of their centers. Some more information I gathered in Chungking, but my visit was suddenly cut short by the war in Europe and I hurried home.

Pamphlets and sometimes articles, chiefly in American magazines, gave further information and as I read these my excitement grew. I referred to "Indusco" in my speeches and in articles in the newspapers, and many letters came to me asking for further details. I suggested that some of our village industry experts should go to China to study the

[1] Based on B.A.I., pp. 233, 248.

Chinese cooperatives on the spot, and some C.I.C. experts should be invited to pay a visit to India. But war developments brought new complications in India and all our attention was diverted to these. I went to prison. . . .

It is obvious that there is a particular demand for information about the Chinese Cooperatives in India, for in many ways we have to face the same problems as in China. One of the problems that India has thought of for many years has been the relation of big industry with village industries. Is there an inherent conflict between them, and must one of them survive at the expense of the other? Is there no way of coordinating the two? The experience of China is of inestimable value to us, and I am sure we can learn much from it.

I have long held that the industrialization of India is essential in order to increase rapidly our production and our national wealth and thus to raise our standards of living. I do not think that we can solve our poverty problem without industrialization and the growth of big industry. I do not think that any nonindustrialized country can be economically independent.

And yet I have worked for the spread and growth of village industries, not merely as a matter of political discipline but because I believed in them. Many of my friends have not appreciated this dual urge of mine, and have charged me with a lack of faith in this or that, and with attempting to reconcile the irreconcilable. They have not convinced me, and I still hold that in India we must push both big industry and village industries and coordinate the two. I recognize that this cannot be easily done under the present capitalist system. Change that system then. Indeed it is bound to go under the stress of this war and its after-effects, and give place to a planned economy.

Gandhiji has, I think, done a great service to India by his emphasis on village industry. Before he did this, we were all, or nearly all, thinking in a lop-sided way and ignoring not only the human aspect of the question but the peculiar conditions prevailing in India. India, like China, has enormous man power, vast unemployment and underemployment. It is no good comparing it with the tight little countries of Europe which gradually became industrialized with small and growing populations. Any scheme which involves the wastage of our labor power or which throws people out of employment is bad. From the purely economic point of view, even apart from the human aspect, it may be more profitable to use more labor power and less specialized machinery. It is better to find employment for large numbers of people at a low income level than to keep most of them unemployed. It is possible also that the total wealth produced by a large number of cottage industries might be greater than that of some factories producing the same kind of goods.

The objective aimed at should be maximum production, equitable distribution and no unemployment. With India's vast population this cannot be achieved by having big industry only, or cottage industry only. The former will certainly result in much greater production of some commodities, but the unemployment problem will remain more or less as it is, and it will be difficult to have equitable distribution. It is also likely that our total production will be far below our potential because of the wastage of labor power. With cottage industries only, there will be more equitable distribution but the total production will remain at a low level and hence standards will not rise. In the present state of India, of course, even widespread cottage industry can raise standards considerably above the existing level. Nevertheless they will remain low. There are other factors also which make it almost impossible for any country to depend entirely on cottage industry. No modern nation can exist without certain essential articles which can be produced only by big industry. Not to produce these is to rely on imports from abroad and thus to be subservient to the economy of foreign countries. It means economic bondage and probably also political subjection.

Therefore it seems essential to have both big industries and cottage industries in India and to plan them in such a way as to avoid conflict. Big industry must be encouraged and developed as rapidly as possible, but the type of industry thus encouraged should be chosen with care. It should be heavy and basic industry, which is the foundation of a nation's economic strength and on which other industries can gradually be built up. The development of electric power is the prerequisite for industrial growth. Machine-making, shipbuilding, chemicals, locomotives, automobiles and the like should follow. All these, and others like them, are wealth-producing industries and work-producing industries which do not create unemployment elsewhere. Lighter industries should not be encouraged to begin with, partly because the capital at our disposal is limited and required for heavy industry, partly because they are likely to come into conflict with cottage industries and thus create unemployment.

Unfortunately industrial growth in this country has been confined to the lighter industries. The few attempts that our industrialists made to develop heavy industry were effectively scotched by the British Government. British industrialists, thinking of the brave new world to come, were more anxious to preserve their economic stranglehold in postwar India than to help win the war by allowing basic industries to develop there.

This ordered development of industry in India and coordination between large-scale, medium and cottage industries, can only be achieved by national planning. There can be no effective planning without political and economic freedom. Nor can there be any planning without a great deal of state control. The basic industries and public utilities and transport services should in any event be owned or fully controlled by the state. The measure of control over other industries might be less. But it it desirable that any big industry which might come into conflict with a cottage industry encouraged by the state, should be fully controlled by the state.

The use of electric power has made an enormous difference to industry, and it is now possible to decentralize even big industries. This works greatly in favor of small and cottage industries.

All these considerations apply to normal times. War conditions have, however, enormously enhanced the value of small and cottage industries, and it is here especially that the example of China is of great importance to us. It seems to be ideally suited to war conditions and for resistance to an invader. What has amazed me is the extraordinary production ratio of these industrial cooperatives. The monthly production value is stated to be two times greater than capital investment. This may be due to war factors; nevertheless it is astounding.

The democratic basis of these cooperatives and their development on this basis in this warring world are full of interest and significance. On this basis political democracy may survive; it is doubtful if it can do so on any other basis.

Neither India nor China is now going to have a normal capitalist industrial development. Yet go ahead industrially we must, or we perish. We shall have to find our own way, to seek our own equilibrium. Possibly the future will lead us and others to a cooperative commonwealth. Possibly the whole world, if it is to rise above its present brutal level of periodic wars, will have to organize itself in some such way.[1]

[From letter to a young Chinese journalist—Bombay, August 8, 1942.] To the Chinese people I repeat that we shall keep faith with them whatever happens. We shall do so not only because China's freedom is very precious to us but also because with it is intertwined the freedom of India. With China unfree our own freedom will be endangered and worth little purchase. Whatever we do now, constrained by circumstances, is aimed at the achievement of India's independence so that we

[1] I.C.L.C. (Jan., 1943), pp. 25-26.

may fight with all our strength and will against the aggressor in India and China. Free India can do so effectively, not so subject India with all her great strength chained up. So in this time of danger and peril we renew our faith in China. We believe that this great war is a mighty revolution which will only succeed on the basis of freedom for all peoples. Without Indian freedom now, it will fail of its purpose and lead us all into blind and dangerous alleys. This is the reason why India's freedom becomes an urgent and immediate necessity and cannot be postponed to the hereafter. The very peril that surrounds us calls for it.

To the people of China and their great leaders, Generalissimo and Madame Chiang Kai-shek, I send greeting and pay homage to the heroism which has shone like a bright star during these past five years of war and infinite suffering.[1]

[On June 26, 1942—before the Congress Working Committee made its July Demand, and subsequently passed the August Quit India Resolution—(see following Section) Madame Chiang Kai-shek wrote a further note to Nehru: "You and India have been constantly in my thoughts. . . . The Generalissimo . . . telegraphed to Washington, urging that America and China should take concerted action. The Generalissimo . . . wants me to impress upon you that nothing whatever should be done until the result of his negotiations with Washington is definitely known. That is to say, to start any movement at all now, whether by Gandhi or Congress, would be most inadvisable until definite word is received from the Generalissimo.

"This he cannot send at the present moment, but as soon as he gets any definite information he will let you know. Once started, a movement cannot be stopped without most disastrous consequences. The Generalissimo is doing his utmost on India's behalf. Telegrams are shuttling to and fro, from China and Washington and vice versa, and we may be able to take advantage of Mr Churchill's presence in Washington.

"In the meantime, rest assured that both the Generalissimo and myself have a most sincere desire to do all we can for India and that if a successful outcome be possible no lack of effort on our part will delay it. . . .

"P.S. I know how hard you must have worked on Gandhiji to make him commit himself to the extent he has written, for if you remember, when we saw him in Calcutta, his whole attitude towards possible Japanese invasion was that of non-violence and non-cooperation. And now for him to say that he approves of India resisting Japan is indeed a great step forward." [2]]

[1] Printed in Life Magazine (Mar. 1, 1943), p. 30. (This letter was written just before
   Nehru was imprisoned for the ninth time, on August 9, 1942.)
[2] B.O.L., p. 495.

6 | Quit India Movement, Summer, 1942—
Comments on Quit India Resolution—
Ninth Prison Sentence—Consequences of
Movement and Jailing of Congress
Leaders—British Statements—
Further U.S. Interest in Indian
Independence—*The Discovery of India*—
Afterthoughts on August, 1942 Struggle—
Jinnah and the Muslim League—India's
Communists—Letters from Jail

Quit India Movement, Summer, 1942

[During the summer of 1942, the Congress Working Committee passed one of the most crucial resolutions in its history, demanding immediate cessation of British rule. The resolution, promptly labelled "Quit India", was inspired by Gandhi, who so admired a phrase Nehru utilized in conjunction with it—to the effect that what was envisioned was evidently a "non-violent revolution"—that he began to use the latter term himself. Gandhi's ardent hope that the British Government would pay serious attention to the wishes of Congress, and would agree to accept India as a "free and independent partner" in the Allied struggle against Axis aggression, was rapidly to vanish, however.

With respect to the term "Quit India", Pyarelal has noted that it was an apocryphal and much misunderstood phrase fathered upon Gandhi; that it was, in fact, coined by an American Press correspondent in the course of an interview with Gandhi, which "caught on", the actual expression used by the Mahatma originally having been "orderly British withdrawal".

According to Pyarelal, "The 'Quit India' demand was explained by Gandhiji in the course of a talk with Horace Alexander, a Quaker friend of Gandhiji, as follows: 'My firm opinion is that the British should leave India now in an orderly manner and not run the risk that they did in Singapore, Malaya, and Burma. That act would mean courage of a high

order, confession of human limitation, and right doing by India. It was
a disorderly withdrawal from there. For they left Burma and Malaya
neither to God nor to anarchy, but to the Japanese. Here I say, "Don't
repeat that story here. Don't leave India to Japan, but leave India to
Indians in an orderly manner"'.''[1]]

[Congress Working Committee Resolution on the National Demand—
July, 1942.]

"Events happening from day to day, and the experience that the people
of India are passing through, confirm the opinion of Congressmen that
British rule in India must end immediately, not merely because foreign
domination, even at its best, is an evil in itself and a continuing injury
to the subject people, but because India in bondage can play no effective
part in defending herself and in affecting the fortunes of the war that is
desolating humanity. The freedom of India is thus necessary not only in
the interest of India but also for the safety of the world and for the
ending of nazism, fascism, militarism and other forms of imperialism,
and the aggression of one nation over another.

"Ever since the outbreak of the world war, the Congress has studiedly
pursued a policy of non-embarrassment. Even at the risk of making its
satyagraha ineffective, it deliberately gave it a symbolic character, in the
hope that this policy of non-embarrassment, carried to its logical extreme,
would be duly appreciated, and that real power would be transferred
to popular representatives, so as to enable the nation to make its fullest
contribution towards the realisation of human freedom throughout the
world, which is in danger of being crushed. It has also hoped that negatively nothing would be done which was calculated to tighten Britain's
stranglehold on India.

"These hopes have, however, been dashed to pieces. The abortive
Cripps proposals showed in the clearest possible manner that there was
no change in the British Government's attitude towards India and that
the British hold on India was in no way to be relaxed. In the negotiations
with Sir Stafford Cripps, Congress representatives tried their utmost to
achieve a minimum, consistent with the national demand, but to no
avail. This frustration has resulted in a rapid and wide-spread increase
of ill-will against Britain and a growing satisfaction at the success of
Japanese arms. The Working Committee view this development with
grave apprehension as this, unless checked, will inevitably lead to a
passive acceptance of aggression. The Committee hold that all aggression
must be resisted, for any submission to it must mean the degradation of
the Indian people and the continuation of their subjection. The Congress
is anxious to avoid the experience of Malaya, Singapore and Burma and
desires to build up resistance to any aggression on or invasion of India
by the Japanese or any foreign Power.

"The Congress would change the present ill-will against Britain into
goodwill and make India a willing partner in a joint enterprise of

[1] M.L.P. (Vol. I), p. 707.

securing freedom of the nations and peoples of the world and in the trials and tribulations which accompany it. This is only possible if India feels the glow of freedom.

"The Congress representatives have tried their utmost to bring about a solution of the communal tangle. But this has been made impossible by the presence of [a] foreign power whose long record has been to pursue relentlessly the policy of divide and rule. Only after the ending of foreign domination and intervention, can the present unreality give place to reality, and the people of India, belonging to all groups and parties, face India's problems and solve them on a mutually agreed basis. The present political parties, formed chiefly with a view to attract the attention of and influence the British Power, will then probably cease to function. For the first time in India's history, realisation will come home that princes, jagirdars, zamindars and propertied and monied classes, derive their wealth and property from the workers in the fields and factories and elsewhere, to whom essentially power and authority must belong. On the withdrawal of British rule in India, responsible men and women of the country will come together to form a Provincial Government, representative of all important sections of the people of India which will later evolve a scheme whereby a Constituent Assembly can be convened in order to prepare a constitution for the Government of India acceptable to all sections of the people. Representatives of free India and representatives of Great Britain will confer together for the adjustment of future relations and co-operation of the two countries as allies in the common task of meeting aggression. It is the earnest desire of the Congress to enable India to resist aggression effectively with the people's united will and strength behind it.

"In making the proposal for the withdrawal of British rule from India, the Congress has no desire whatsoever to embarrass Great Britain or the Allied Powers in their prosecution of the war, or in any way to encourage aggression on India or increased pressure on China by the Japanese or any other Power associated with the Axis group. Nor does the Congress intend to jeopardise the defensive capacity of the Allied Powers. The Congress is therefore agreeable to the stationing of the armed forces of the Allies in India, should they so desire, in order to ward off and resist Japanese or other aggression, and to protect and help China.

"The proposal of withdrawal of the British Power from India was never intended to mean the physical withdrawal of all Britishers from India, and certainly not of those who would make India their home and live there as citizens and as equals with the others. If such withdrawal take place with goodwill, it would result in establishing a stable Provisional Government in India and co-operation between this Government and the United Nations in resisting aggression and helping China.

"The Congress realises that there may be risks involved in such a course. Such risks, however, have to be faced by any country in order to achieve freedom and, more especially at the present critical juncture, in order to save the country and the larger cause of freedom the world over from far greater risks and perils.

"While, therefore, the Congress is impatient to achieve the national purpose, it wishes to take no hasty step and would like to avoid, in so far as is possible, any course of action that might embarrass the United Nations. The Congress would plead with the British Power to accept the very reasonable and just proposal herein made, not only in the interest of India but also that of Britain and of the cause of freedom to which the United Nations proclaim their adherence.

"Should, however, this appeal fail, the Congress cannot view without the gravest apprehension the continuation of the present state of affairs, involving a progressive deterioration in the situation and weakening of India's will and power to resist aggression. The Congress will then be reluctantly compelled to utilise all the non-violent strength it might have gathered since 1920, when it adopted non-violence as part of its policy for the vindication of political rights and liberty. Such a widespread struggle would inevitably be under the leadership of Gandhiji. As the issues raised are of the most vital and far-reaching importance to the people of India as well as to the peoples of the United Nations, the Working Committee refer them to the All India Congress Committee for final decision. For this purpose the A.I.C.C. will meet . . . on August 7, 1942."[1]

[Quit India Resolution—August 7, 1942.]
"The All India Congress Committee has given the most careful consideration to the reference made to it by the Working Committee in their resolution dated July 14, 1942, and to subsequent events, including the development of the war situation, the utterances of responsible spokesmen of the British Government, and the comments and criticisms made in India and abroad. The Committee approves of and endorses that resolution and is of [the] opinion that [subsequent events] have given it further justification, and have made it clear that the immediate ending of British rule in India is an urgent necessity both for the sake of India and for the success of the cause of the United Nations. The continuation of that rule is degrading and enfeebling India and making her progressively less capable of defending herself and of contributing to the cause of world freedom.

"The Committee has viewed with dismay the deterioration of the situation on the Russian and Chinese fronts and conveys to the Russian and Chinese peoples its high appreciation of their heroism in defence of their freedom. This increasing peril makes it incumbent on all those who strive for freedom and who sympathise with the victims of aggression to examine the foundations of the policy so far pursued by the Allied Nations, which have led to repeated and disastrous failure. It is not by adhering to such aims and policies and methods that failure is inherent in them. These policies have been based not on freedom so much as on the domination of subject and colonial countries, and the continuation of the imperialist tradition and method. The possession of empire, instead

[1] C.B. (Nov. 1, 1945). (From Ms. copy.)

of adding to the strength of the ruling Power, has become a burden and a curse. India, the classic land of modern imperialism, has become the crux of the question, for by the freedom of India will Britain and the United Nations be judged, and the peoples of Asia and Africa be filled with hope and enthusiasm. The ending of British rule in this country is thus a vital and immediate issue on which depend the future of the war and the success of freedom and democracy. A free India will assure this success by throwing all her great resources in the struggle for freedom and against the aggression of nazism, fascism and imperialism. This will not only affect materially the fortunes of the war, but will bring all subject and oppressed humanity on the side of the United Nations, and give these Nations, whose ally India would be, the moral and spiritual leadership of the world. India in bondage will continue to be the symbol of British imperialism and the taint of that imperialism will affect the fortunes of all the United Nations.

"The peril of today, therefore, necessitates the independence of India and the ending of British domination. No future promises or guarantees can affect the present situation or meet that peril. They cannot produce the needed psychological effect on the mind of the masses. Only the glow of freedom now can release that energy and enthusiasm of millions of people which will immediately transform the nature of the war.

"The A.I.C.C. therefore repeats with all emphasis the demand for the withdrawal of the British Power from India. On the declaration of India's independence, a Provisional Government will be formed and Free India will become an ally of the United Nations, sharing with them in the trials and tribulations of the joint enterprise of the struggle for freedom. The Provisional Government can only be formed by the co-operation of the principal parties and groups in the country. It will thus be a composite government, representative of all important sections of the people of India. Its primary functions must be to defend India and resist aggression with all the armed as well as the non-violent forces at its command, together with its Allied powers, to promote the well-being and progress of the workers in the fields and factories and elsewhere to whom essentially all power and authority must belong. The Provisional Government will evolve a scheme for a Constituent Assembly which will prepare a constitution for the Government of India acceptable to all sections of the people. This constitution, according to the Congress view, should be a federal one, with the largest measure of autonomy for the federating units, and with the residuary powers vesting in these units. The future relations between India and the Allied Nations will be adjusted by representatives of all these free countries conferring together for their mutual advantage and for their co-operation in the common task of resisting aggression. Freedom will enable India to resist aggression effectively with the people's united will and strength behind it.

"The freedom of India must be the symbol of and prelude to the freedom of all other Asiatic nations under foreign domination. Burma, Malaya, Indo-China, the Dutch Indies, Iran and Iraq must also attain their complete freedom. It must be clearly understood that such of these countries as are under Japanese control now must not subsequently be placed under the rule or control of any other colonial Power.

"While the A.I.C.C. must primarily be concerned with the independence and defence of India in this hour of danger, the Committee is of [the] opinion that the future peace, security and ordered progress of the world demands a World Federation of free nations, and on no other basis can the problem of the modern world be solved. Such a World Federation would ensure the freedom of its constituent nations, the [protection] of national minorities, [and] the advancement of all backward areas and peoples. The establishment of such a World Federation [would make] disarmament practicable in all countries, [and thus] national armies, navies and air forces would no longer be necessary. A World Federal Defence Force would keep the world peace and prevent aggression.

"An independent India would gladly join such a World Federation and co-operate on an equal basis with other nations in the solution of international problems.

"Such a Federation should be open to all nations who agree with its fundamental principles. In view of the war, however, the Federation must inevitably, to begin with, be confined to the United Nations. Such a step taken now will have a most powerful effect on the war, on the peoples of the Axis countries and on the peace to come.

"The Committee regretfully realises, however, that despite the tragic and overwhelming lessons of the war and the perils that overhang the world, the Governments of few countries are yet prepared to take this inevitable step towards World Federation. The reactions of the British Government and the misguided criticisms of the foreign press also make it clear that even the obvious demand for India's independence is resisted, though this has been made essentially to meet the present peril and to enable India to defend herself and help China and Russia in their hour of need. The Committee is anxious not to embarrass in any way the defence of China or Russia, whose freedom is precious and must be preserved, or to jeopardise the defensive capacity of the United Nations. But the peril grows both to India and these nations, and inaction and submission to a foreign administration at this stage is not only degrading India and reducing her capacity to defend herself and resist aggression, but is no answer to that growing peril and is no service to the peoples of the United Nations. The earnest appeal of the Working Committee to Great Britain and the United Nations had so far met with no response and the criticisms made in many foreign quarters have shown an ignorance of India's and the world's need, and sometimes even hostility to India's freedom, which is significant of a mentality of domination and racial superiority which cannot be tolerated by a proud people conscious of their strength and of the justice of their cause.

"The A.I.C.C. would yet again, at this last moment, in the interest of world freedom, renew this appeal to Britain and the United Nations. But the Committee feels that it is no longer justified in holding the nation back from endeavouring to assert its will against an imperialist and authoritarian government which dominates over it and prevents it from functioning in its own interest and in the interest of humanity. The Committee resolves, therefore, to sanction for the vindication of India's inalienable right to freedom and independence, the starting of a mass struggle on non-violent lines on the widest possible scale, so that the country might utilise all the non-violent strength it has gathered during the last twenty-two years of peaceful struggle. Such a struggle must inevitably be under the leadership of Gandhiji and the Committee requests him to take the lead and guide the nation in the steps to be taken.

"The Committee appeals to the people of India to face the dangers and hardships that will fall to their lot with courage and endurance, and to hold together under the leadership of Gandhiji, and carry out his instructions as disciplined soldiers of India's freedom. They must remember that non-violence is the basis of this movement. A time may come when it may not be possible to issue instructions or for instructions to reach our people, and when no Congress Committee can function. When this happens, every man and woman who is participating in this movement must function for himself or herself within the four corners of the general instructions issued. Every Indian who desires freedom and strives for it must be his own guide urging him on along the hard road where there is no resting place and which leads ultimately to the independence and deliverance of India.

"Lastly, whilst the A.I.C.C. has stated its own view of the future government under free India, the A.I.C.C. wishes to make it quite clear to all concerned that by embarking on [a] mass struggle it has no intention of gaining power for the Congress. The power, when it comes, will belong to the whole people of India." [1]

[Nehru moved the Quit India Resolution when the All-India Congress Committee met in August, 1942. Although the Committee approved the proposed measure, Nehru had little enthusiasm for it. He by no means favored the technique Gandhi believed would make the resolution effective. He nevertheless loyally assured Congress members that the "Quit India" concept stemmed not from narrow nationalism, but rather from an international attitude.]

Comments on Quit India Resolution

[From Nehru's All-India Congress Committee speeches—August 7-8, 1942.] We are accused by some newspapers that we are blackmailing. It is a curious charge for a people to make who themselves had for generations carried on a struggle for freedom. If by demanding freedom we are called

[1] Ibid.

blackmailers then surely our understanding of the English language has been wrong. Whatever may happen in Whitehall it is not going to stop us from working for Independence. We live for it and will die for it. I do not want to say anything at the present moment which might add to the feeling of bitterness that exists everywhere. I know that this war—and this is one of the worst effects of the war—has produced great emotional reactions in people's minds which make it very difficult for people to think straight and not to think in terms of violent hatred.

Nobody in Whitehall can think straight, I suppose. There is falsity everywhere. You listen to the radios, London, Berlin or to Tokyo. One does not know which is the truth. I am prepared to make many allowances for the emotional background in England and in America. I do not really mind if people get angry. But I am sorry for the people in England and in America who have a perverted way of looking at the Indian question. They are so wrong that they [will] land themselves in difficulty. After all, think just what would be the course of history, particularly that of Britain, if she had done the right thing by India in the last two years. If Britain had done rightly, the entire history of the war would have been different. England has stuck to her Imperialism and Empire. The fact is patent to me that the British Government and for certain the Government of India think the Indian National Congress to be Enemy Number One. If the Government of India is going to treat the people of India like this, then we know how to treat them. We have seen in the last few months an unparalleled example of [the] inefficiency and incompetency of this Government. The system is a rotten one. I do not want to associate myself with the creaking, shaking machinery that the Government of India is. As for the so-called National War Front there is neither the nation nor the war nor any front in it.[1]

[August 8, 1942.] This resolution is not a threat. It is an invitation. It is an explanation. It is an offer of co-operation. It is all that. But still, behind it, there is a clear indication that certain consequences will follow if certain events do not happen. It is an offer of co-operation of a free India. On any other terms there will be no co-operation. On any other terms, our resolution promises only conflict and struggle. . . .

Let there be no mistake about it. We are on the verge of a precipice and we are in dead earnest. . . . [The Quit India Resolution when passed, will not only represent the decision of the A.I.C.C., it will represent the voice of the whole of India. I would even go a step further and say that

[1] A.I.C.C. Report (Aug. 7, 1942), p. 239.

it represents the voice of the entire oppressed humanity of the world.] If Britain had accepted this resolution and acted according to its demands, it would have seen a vast change not only in India but all over the world. The whole nature of the war would have been changed. A real revolutionary background would have been given to it. . . . The essential thing about this war [is] that it [is] something infinitely more than a mere war. It [is] a world-war . . . but greater than that; it [is] a prelude to and a precursor of a vast revolution that [is] enveloping the whole world. The war might end now or it might be carried on for some time more, but no peace [can] be established, no equilibrium attained until this revolution [runs] its appointed course. It is a great misfortune . . . that the leaders in the West [have] not realized, or if they [have] realized [it, have] not acted as if they had realized the revolutionary significance of the war. They [are] still carrying on this war on the old lines and [think] that they [can] win it only by building more ships and more aeroplanes. Probably, in their position, [I] would have done the same thing. They [are] not thinking in terms of a vast surge of the elemental emotions of humanity. Until they [do] that, they [can] never attain success, but [will] only go from failure to failure. [I hope] that they [will] learn the lesson. [I can] only hope that they [will] not learn it too late. . . . Mr Churchill and other Britishers [have] not got over thinking in terms of the Anglo-Saxon race . . . [I recall] a recent speech of Mr Churchill [in which] he visualized the day when the Anglo-Saxon would march through the world in dignity and majesty. . . . [I must remind the British and Americans that there are other races in the world beside the Anglo-Saxon race, and its sense of racial superiority can no longer be tolerated.] . . . The Allied cause [is] only negatively right, in the sense that Germany and Japan [are] worse. But Indian freedom would change the whole nature of the war and make it right positively. . . . [I regret] that people in England, America and elsewhere [are] looking at every question from the narrow soldier's point of view. But it [does] not matter to them how other people [view] the Indian question. . . . [I make] an earnest appeal to all people in India that they should not forget their high aims and objectives . . . they [are] fighting not only in the interests of India but in the interests of all countries of the world including China and Russia. [I am] a Nationalist, and [am] proud to be a Nationalist . . . but [the Indian people] should not settle down to narrow nationalism. . . . They must always remember [to] . . . develop [the] right internationalism. . . . [We] are going to face great difficulties in the days ahead. All [I can] say to those Englishmen and Americans who [consider] that the Congress [is] not right [is] for the

Indian people to decide for themselves. They know what it [is] to be under subjection. . . . After all, it [is] the Indians who [will] have to undergo enormous sufferings and privations if there [is] a Japanese invasion of India.[1]

[The Communal Issue.] We have entered the fire and we have now to come out of it successfully or be consumed by it. . . . How many attempts have we not made, and how often have we not been frustrated in our attempts? We are prepared to pay any price for unity except the price of Independence. How many obstructions have not been placed in our path which have had no relation to the real issue?

I can talk and negotiate with anybody who recognises democratic freedom for India, but I cannot negotiate with anyone who refuses to recognise the fundamental issue, the freedom of India. I was told during the Cripps negotiations that a certain leader insisted on behalf of Muslims that the Viceroy's power of veto should not be removed or in any way qualified. If any section [wanted] . . . the British Viceroy [to] exercise his veto-power against the decision of his Indian Cabinet, it [meant] clearly that [the] section [was] against the freedom of India. I do not want to injure any one's feeling especially at a time when we are about to launch a great struggle for freedom. I tried, for one whole year, to find out what the [Muslim] League wanted, and I was unable to understand what they [did] want.

I have not been able to find . . . a parallel to such a situation in the history of the world. I have not come . . . across such a situation [anywhere else], except in the land of Hitler. The Sudeten crisis bears similarity to the situation here. For purposes of negotiation, we are not even allowed to select our own representatives. We are told that we cannot send Muslims to represent the Congress. This is an insult to our great organisation and to our revered President [Maulana Azad]. . . . We were prepared to stake everything consistent with our dignity and self-respect towards finding a satisfactory settlement. Whenever we knocked we found the doors were bolted, and we knocked ourselves against a wall. Are we beggars to be treated like this? Are we going to be so dishonourable as to sacrifice our mansion of Indian freedom which we want to build? Are we going to be kicked about by men who have made no sacrifice for the freedom of India and who can never think in terms of freedom at all?

Our conscience is clear. We have [done] everything that is humanly

[1] Ibid., pp. 252–53.

possible [to arrive] at a settlement. The Muslim masses are not reactionary. We have made strenuous and sincere attempts to resolve the
issue, and all our attempts have either been sabotaged or frustrated.[1]

Ninth Prison Sentence

[On August 9, 1942, as a reaction to the Quit India Resolution, the
British arrested various Congress leaders responsible for it; among them
Gandhi, Nehru and Maulana Azad.

Nehru was taken to Ahmadnagar Fort, where he was imprisoned for
his ninth and longest jail sentence. Although Congress leaders gradually
were dispersed from prison after March 28, 1945, beginning on that date
Nehru was sent to various other jails in the United Provinces. He was not
finally released until June 15, 1945.

In a letter sent to the Viceroy on August 14, 1942, Gandhi described
Nehru's dilemma during the period preceding the Quit India Resolution.
Fearing the impending ruin of China and Russia, wrote Gandhi, "Nehru
'tried to forget his old quarrel with imperialism. . . . I have argued with
him for days together. He fought against my position with a passion
which I have no words to describe. But the logic of facts overwhelmed
him. He yielded when he saw clearly that without the freedom of India
that of the other two was in great jeopardy. Surely you are wrong in
having imprisoned such a powerful friend and ally.'"[2]]

Consequences of Movement and Jailing of Congress Leaders

[Because the most important leaders in Congress were the instigators of
the Quit India Movement, and were imprisoned for over three years
during World War II, there was little, if any, hope that they might
encourage the Indian masses to become involved in the war effort. In
view of the strained military situation in the East, this was a development
troubling both to the British and the United States. Another disturbing
factor at the time—to Nehru, as to the Allies—was the continuing pro-
Japanese, even pro-German, activity of the militant Indian leader,
Subhas Chandra Bose.

In the period during which Nehru and other Congress members were
confined in jail, the British neither withdrew the Cripps offer, nor would
they agree to release Congress leaders who had favored the Quit India
Resolution, short of their altering their position in regard to the latter
statement.]

[1] Ibid. (Aug. 8, 1942), pp. 253–54.
[2] M.B., p. 286.

British Statements

[To the astonishment of Congress leaders and the Indian people at large, Winston Churchill stated in London on November 10, 1942: "We have not entered this war for profit or expansion but only for honor and to do our duty in defending the right.

"Let me, however, make this clear, in case there should be any mistake about it in any quarter: we mean to hold our own. I have not become the King's First Minister in order to preside over the liquidation of the British Empire. For that task, if ever it were prescribed, some one else would have to be found, and under a democracy I suppose the nation would have to be consulted." [1]

As late as May 6, 1944—the very day on which Gandhi was set free from the Aga Khan's Palace, in which he had been imprisoned since August, 1942—the British Ambassador to the United States, Lord Halifax, declared in Washington that "The Atlantic Charter contained nothing that had not been British policy for half a century!" He added, "Simple self-determination would not work in the case of Palestine and India because of the existence of religious and racial problems." [2]]

Further U.S. Interest in Indian Independence

[On August 1, 1942, a week before the adoption of the Quit India Resolution, President Roosevelt had written to Gandhi to assure him that the "U.S.A. was 'constantly striving for and supporting policies of fair dealing and fair play'. The war, which was 'a result of Axis dreams of a world conquest', could be won 'only through a supreme effort by those who believed in freedom'. The letter concluded: 'I shall hope that our common interest in democracy and righteousness will enable your countrymen and mine to make common cause against a common enemy.'" [3]

Because of Cordell Hull's understanding of India's sincere desire for freedom, and the war-time exigencies involved, toward the end of 1942 —when William Phillips was in New Delhi as President Roosevelt's special envoy—Hull made renewed efforts to have British negotiations with India resumed. (A note from Hull to Phillips indicated that President Roosevelt "'and I and the entire Government earnestly favor freedom for all dependent peoples at the earliest date practicable'. India was mentioned as 'receiving the President's constant attention.'" [4])

[1] W.P.A.U.N., p. 264.
[2] M.L.P. (Vol. I), p. 19.
[3] I.N. (Feb. 22, 1963), p. 8.
[4] Ibid., p. 8.

On December 8, 1942, Lord Linlithgow's term of office as Indian Viceroy was extended to October, 1943.]

"The Discovery of India"

[Nehru wrote his important volume, *The Discovery of India*, in Ahmadnagar Fort Prison, during five months—April to September, 1944. He dedicated the book (published in March, 1946), to his "colleagues and co-prisoners in the Ahmadnagar Fort prison camp from August 9, 1942 to March 28, 1945".[1]]

Afterthoughts on August, 1942 Struggle

[With regard to the August, 1942 struggle—fourteen years later.] I don't think that the action we took in 1942 could have been avoided or ought to have been avoided. It might have been in slightly different terms; that is a different matter. Circumstances drove us into a particular direction. If we had been passive then, I think we would have lost all our strength.[2]

Jinnah and Mounting Power of Muslim League

[With so many of its guiding spirits in prison, Congress activities were vastly curtailed from August, 1942 until virtually the end of World War II. Jinnah's influence, on the other hand—he was not involved in the Quit India Movement—grew appreciably during the same period. Thus it is often claimed that the Quit India Movement ultimately helped to increase the power of the Muslim League, and to strengthen the forces in favor of Partition.

Nehru has suggested that the League's growth also was due to two other essential factors: "The encouragement given to it by the British Government . . . and a vague mass following on . . . religious ground[s]."[3]]

[Further analysis of Jinnah and the Muslim League—from letter to Syed Mahmud, Allahabad, February 2, 1942.] Essentially, I think, the attitude of Jinnah and the Muslim League is governed by the desire to prevent radical changes or the democratisation of India *not* because of a

---

[1] D.I., Dedication.
[2] Quoted M.B., p. 294.
[3] Quoted in ibid., p. 294.

5+N. II

Hindu majority but because the radical elements will put an end to semi-feudal privileges, etc. You hint at this in your letter. The whole conception of the Constituent Assembly is to bring out mass elements and urges which will not view the communal problem or other problems from the middle class point of view which has landed us [in] this impasse. Personally I see no solution of the problem, however hard we may try, so long as the third party (the British) is not eliminated. We shall inevitably come near a solution when we are forced to agree by circumstances, the alternative being conflict on a big scale. That can only happen when it is clear that neither party can seek the help of the British or any other alien authority.

The correct course for both Congress and the Muslim League (as well as others) would have been to agree to one thing only, retaining, if necessary, all their other differences, including if you like Pakistan. That one thing is to join forces against all alien authority and intervention. Once this alien authority is excluded we fall back upon ourselves and either agree or fight. In all likelihood we then agree for the prospect of a real struggle will not be a pleasant one for anybody.

Jinnah puts the cart before the horse. He says no political progress till his conditions are accepted. Under present circumstances that means a veto to progress. The right course would be to say: I stick to Pakistan and everything else that goes with it and I shall never be satisfied with less, but I am perfectly willing to join hands with others to push out the alien authority. After that I shall fight for my rights if necessary. It is clear that he wants present conditions to continue and his position thus becomes indefensible.

Fortunately the world is changing and our hardest problems are in a sense solving themselves through the clash of events. While the cultural approach is right and desirable, it takes time and events today rush past us and bring big changes in their train. I think we shall see these changes before very long.[1]

India's Communists

[Like Muslim League leaders, India's Communists, who made common cause with the British in the war effort, also were out of jail in the early forties. Although the Communists' first loyalty was to Soviet Russia, rather than to England, this fact failed visibly to disturb the British in

[1] B.O.L., pp. 473–74.

view of the help they received from the Indian Communists in prose-
cuting the war, and the failure of the latter group to agitate for independence. Hence both the Communists and the Muslim League—being in
the good graces of England—gained power in India during the war,
precisely while Congress leaders were in prison, and were most severely
opposed by the British.]

Letters from Jail to Krishna Hutheesing

I. [October 26, 1942.] Nothing is so bad as to remain for ever in the ruts
of life and that is especially so in these days of storm and change all over
the world. There is so much sorrow and frustration everywhere that we
cannot really understand it emotionally unless in a sense we become
part of it. So out of sorrow itself comes a new understanding and a new
strength.[1]

II. [November 10, 1942.] Time creeps on inexorably, as it does regardless
of our wishes and desires, and we adapt ourselves, as best we may, to its
blind cause. We have adapted ourselves to it here and the days go by
without incident. Petty happenings disturb us sometimes or some piece
of news agitates the mind. But, on the whole, there is a certain calm on
the surface of the waters of the mind. Wavelets pass over time. Underneath there is more often a turmoil, a thinking furiously of the witches'
cauldron that is the world today, and our attempt to pierce this veil of
the future. In prison, the present almost ceases to be, for active sensations
and emotions in regard to it are usually absent. Only the past and the
future count, and some lose themselves in the past and some face the
trackless future. To some extent all indulge in retrospection of the past
for that appears to be the only thing that can be visualized without much
difficulty, and anyway it is easier to allow the mind to wander rather
aimlessly in known grooves. For my part I am almost always more concerned with the future. It is a far more exciting quest and the unknown
has a fatal fascination. Also it satisfies one's conceit to imagine that one
might be able to mould this as it emerges from the slime and mud of the
present, as a potter with his clay. An empty conceit probably, but
nevertheless good for the soul.[2]

III. [December 10, 1942.] Abnormal happenings are apt to upset the
nerves of all of us and for a moment we lose the proper perspective on life.

[1] N.L.H.S., p. 93.
[2] Ibid., pp. 94-95.

We have had and are having an abundance of abnormality everywhere and it is not surprising that this affects each one of us in various ways. Yet we cannot afford to have our eyes bloodshot even though that might be the temporary condition of other people's eyes. We must look straight and act straight and if we do so, our nerves behave themselves. I think, on the whole, I succeed in this endeavour. You need not worry about my not being settled down here. I can easily adapt myself to new surroundings and I have done so here and lead an ordered life keeping my mind and body as fit as possible. The body reacts on the mind so much and vice versa of course, and I try to keep some kind of an equilibrium between them. Being active by nature, I seek some kind of activity of the body where my mind has of necessity to lie fallow. Hence my enthusiasm for gardening, especially the physical aspects of it. Latterly, since it has been a little colder I take a sun bath in the early morning before the sun gets too hot. That gives me a feeling of health and vitality. And I read of course. . . . We get some newspapers and so, to that extent, can keep in touch with the news. Newspapers in prison give a curiously distant view of the world. There is something unreal about it, something impersonal, though not always so.[1]

[1] Ibid., pp. 98–99.

PART EIGHT

1943–1945

Our main stake in world affairs is peace, to see that there is racial equality and that people who are still subjugated should be free. For the rest we do not desire to interfere in world affairs and we do not desire that other people should interfere in our affairs. If, however, there is interference, whether military, political, or economic, we shall resist it.[1]

*

We in India do not have to go abroad in search of the Past and the Distant. We have them here in abundance. If we go to foreign countries it is in search of the Present. That search is necessary, for isolation from it means backwardness and decay. . . . Old barriers are breaking down; life becomes more international. We have to play our part in this coming internationalism. . . . But a real internationalism is not something in the air without roots or anchorage. It has to grow out of national cultures, can only flourish today on a basis of freedom and equality and true internationalism.[2]

[1] I.A., p. 242.
[2] D.I., p. 578.

I | The War, 1943—Phillips–Roosevelt Efforts in Behalf of Indian Freedom— Famine

The War, 1943

[Although the Allied military position had improved by the end of 1942, the danger that the Japanese might invade India remained imminent.

On September 21, 1942, Russian forces repulsed the Germans at the gates of Stalingrad. On November 4, 1942, the British offensive under General Montgomery proved successful against the Axis in Egypt. (During the same week the U.S. armed forces landed in North Africa. They were supported by the British Navy and Air Force. In November, also, the "Free French" under Charles de Gaulle refused to accept arrangements to establish a Vichy régime in Africa. The Japanese abandoned the Guadalcanal area on February 9, 1943. Roosevelt conferred with Churchill and other military leaders at Casablanca on January 14. Roosevelt and Churchill met in Washington on May 11; in Quebec on August 17. Stalin announced the termination of the Comintern (Communist International) on May 21. Mussolini resigned, July 25. On September 8, Italy unconditionally surrendered to the Allies. Two days later the Germans shelled and seized Rome. Italy declared war on Germany, October 13, 1943. Toward the end of November, 1943, Roosevelt, Churchill and Chiang Kai-shek participated in the Cairo Conference. On December 4, Roosevelt, Churchill and Stalin met at Teheran.

Although India suffered from inflation and other dislocations as a result of the war, there were certain countervailing forces. Her raw materials and industrial products were more widely saleable. New factories and industries were founded, old ones expanded. The country was transformed from a debtor to a creditor nation. Yet neither such developments, nor the enlargement of the Indian armed forces, brought comfort to Congress leaders confined in jail, who envisioned, and were preoccupied by, distinctly other goals.

In spite of occasional overtures by the British Government, it was clear that India was not to win her independence during the war period.]

Phillips–Roosevelt Efforts in Behalf of Indian Freedom

[In February, 1943, while Gandhi was imprisoned in the Aga Khan's Palace, he undertook a three-week protest-fast against Britain's repressive actions with regard to the Indian independence movement. At the time of the fast, William Phillips, President Roosevelt's Special Envoy in New Delhi, was authorized by Washington to express to the Viceroy, Lord Linlithgow, the President's profound concern about the possibility that Gandhi might die, and the potential consequences of so tragic an event.

From letter to Roosevelt written by Phillips on May 14, 1943 after his four-month mission to India: "Assuming that India is known to be an important base for our future operations against Burma and Japan, it would seem to be of highest importance that we should have around us a sympathetic India rather than an indifferent and possibly a hostile India. It would appear that we will have the prime responsibility in the conduct of the war against Japan. There is no evidence that the British intend to do more than give token assistance. If that is so, then the conditions surrounding our base in India become of vital importance.

"At present, the Indian people are at war only in a legal sense, as for various reasons the British Government declared India in the conflict without the formality of consulting Indian leaders or even the Indian Legislature. Indians feel they have no voice in the Government and therefore no responsibility in the conduct of the war. They feel that they have nothing to fight for, as they are convinced that the professed war aims of the United Nations do not apply to them.

"The British Prime Minister, in fact, has stated that the provisions of the Atlantic Charter are not applicable to India, and it is not unnatural therefore that Indian leaders are beginning to wonder whether the Charter is only for the benefit of white races. The present Indian army is purely mercenary and only that part of it which is drawn from the martial races has been tried in actual warfare and these martial soldiers represent only 33 per cent of the army.

"General Stilwell has expressed his concern over the situation and in particular in regard to the poor morale of the Indian officers.

"The attitude of the general public toward the war is even worse. Lassitude and indifference and bitterness have increased as a result of the famine conditions, the growing high cost of living and continued political deadlock.

"While India is broken politically into various parties and groups, all have one object in common—eventual freedom and independence from British domination.

"There would seem to be only one remedy to this highly unsatisfactory situation in which we are unfortunately but nevertheless seriously involved, and that is to change the attitude of the people of India toward the war, make them feel that we want them to assume responsibilities to the United Nations and are prepared to give them facilities for doing so and that the voice of India will play an important part in the reconstruction of the world. The present political conditions do not permit of any improvement in this respect.

"Even though the British should fail again, it is high time that they should make an effort to improve conditions and re-establish confidence among the Indian people that their future independence is to be granted. Words are of no avail. They only aggravate the present situation.

"It is time for the British to act. This they can do by a solemn declaration from the king emperor that India will achieve her independence at a specific date after the war and as a guarantee of good faith in this respect a provisional representative coalition government will be re-established at the center and limited powers transferred to it.

"I feel strongly, Mr President, that in view of our military position in India, we should have a voice in these matters. It is not right for the British to say this is none of your business when we alone presumably will have the major part to play in the struggle with Japan.

"If we do nothing and merely accept the British point of view that conditions in India are none of our business, then we must be prepared for various serious consequences in the internal situation in India which may develop as a result of the despair and misery and anti-white sentiments of hundreds of millions of subject people.

"The peoples of Asia—and I am supported in the opinion by other diplomatic and military observers—cynically regard this war as one between fascist and imperialist powers.

"A generous British gesture to India would change this undesirable political atmosphere. India itself might then be expected more positively to support our war effort against Japan. China, which regards the Anglo-American bloc with misgivings and mistrust, might then be assured that we are in truth fighting for a better world.

"And the colonial people conquered by the Japanese might hopefully feel that they have something better to look forward to than simply a return to their old masters.

"Such a gesture, Mr President, will produce not only a tremendous psychological stimulus to flagging morale through Asia and facilitate our military operations in that theatre, but it will also be proof positive to all peoples—our own and the British included—that this is not a war of power politics, but a war for all we say it is."[1]

The British Information Service denied Ambassador Phillips' statement. Yet when President Roosevelt suggested to Mr Phillips that he have a talk with Mr Churchill, who was then on a visit to Washington, and Phillips did so, he reported that a "stormy session" followed. According to Phillips: "Churchill was annoyed, and annoyed with me; that was clear. He got up and walked rapidly back and forth. . . . It was hopeless to argue." Despite these difficulties, "The President did not abandon hope. He suggested to Mr Churchill that Mr Eden might be sent to India 'to explore the situation [by talking] . . . to leaders of all parties and groups, Gandhi included,' and report his findings to Mr Churchill. If the suggestion proved acceptable, Mr Phillips could return to India and assist Mr Eden. It was not Mr Eden who came out to India, but Lord Wavell, as Lord Linlithgow's successor."[2]

[1] N.Y.T. (Sept. 3, 1944), p. 17.
[2] I.N. (Feb. 22, 1963), p. 8.

5*

It is noteworthy that Ambassador Phillips' ideas in 1943 about what Britain should do in relation to India were virtually identical with the dominant Congress position.]

Famine

[In 1943 India suffered a tragic famine—most disastrously so in Bengal. It is claimed that approximately three million Indians were permitted to starve to death. Congress leaders accused the British Government in India of taking no effective action whatsoever with regard to averting or dealing with the famine.]

[Three years after the 1943 Bengal famine, June 26, 1946.] What would have happened if some settlement had been arrived at at the time of the Cripps Offer [of 1942] . . . is difficult to say definitely. . . . But I think it is pretty clear that any such settlement would have led not only to a greater sensitiveness to the various problems affecting the people, especially the food problem, but also to a greater efficiency and co-ordination in dealing with them.

What the Bengal famine has shown is a complete collapse of both the Central and Provincial Governments as well as the executive services in regard to the food situation. As the official report has shown this was completely ignored for a long time and then wrong directions were issued, and then the directions were changed repeatedly and complete confusion prevailed.

It is quite inconceivable that any other [arrangements] of Government could have failed quite so miserably as the Government arrangements did in 1943. Apart from the failure of Governmental apparatus, certain psychological reactions leading to a moral decay and disruption of official apparatus have been very evident.

No big problem can ultimately be solved without full co-operation between the people and the Government of [a] country. Instead of . . . co-operation there was hostility and conflict. Obviously, if a National Government had been formed in 1942 there would have been a great deal of co-operation with the people. . . . I am quite convinced that the Bengal famine [could then either have] been avoided or at any rate very greatly minimised.[1]

Famine came [to India in 1943], ghastly, staggering, horrible beyond words. In Malabar, in Bijapur, in Orissa, and above all in the rich and

[1] B.A.I., pp. 351-52.

fertile province of Bengal, men and women and little children died in their thousands daily for lack of food. They dropped down dead before the palaces of Calcutta, their corpses lay in the mud huts of Bengal's innumerable villages and covered the roads and fields in its rural areas. Men were dying all over the world and killing each other in battle; usually a quick death, often a brave death, death for a cause, death with a purpose, death which seemed in this mad world of ours an inexorable logic of events, a sudden end to the life we could not mold or control. Death was common enough everywhere.

But here death had no purpose, no logic, no necessity; it was the result of man's incompetence and callousness, man-made, a slow creeping thing of horror with nothing to redeem it, life merging and fading into death, with death looking out of the shrunken eyes and withered frame while life still lingered for a while. And so it was not considered right or proper to mention it; it was not good form to talk or write of unsavory topics. To do so was to "dramatize" an unfortunate situation. False reports were issued by those in authority in India and in England. But corpses cannot easily be overlooked; they come in the way.

While the fires of hell were consuming the people of Bengal and elsewhere, we were first told by High Authority that owing to wartime prosperity the peasantry in many parts of India had too much to eat. Then it was said that the fault lay with provincial autonomy, and the British government in India or the India Office in London, sticklers for constitutional propriety, could not interfere with provincial affairs. That constitution was suspended, violated, ignored or changed daily by hundreds of decrees and ordinances issued by the Viceroy under his sole and unlimited authority. That constitution meant ultimately the unchecked authoritarian rule of a single individual who was responsible to no one in India, and who had greater power than any dictator anywhere in the world. That constitution was worked by the permanent services, chiefly the Indian Civil Service and the police, who were mainly responsible to the Governor, who was the agent of the Viceroy, and who could well ignore the ministers when such existed. The ministers, good or bad, lived on sufferance and dared not disobey the orders from above or even interfere with the discretion of the services supposed to be subordinate to them.

Something was done at last. Some relief was given. But a million had died, or two millions, or three; no one knows how many starved to death or died of disease during those months of horror. No one knows of the many more millions of emaciated boys and girls and little children who just escaped death then, but are stunted and broken in body and spirit.

And still the fear of widespread famine and disease hovers over the land. President Roosevelt's Four Freedoms. The Freedom from Want. Yet rich England and richer America paid little heed to the hunger of the body that was killing millions in India, as they had paid little heed to the fiery thirst of the spirit that is consuming the people of India. Money was not needed, it was said, and ships to carry food were scarce owing to wartime requirements. But in spite of governmental obstruction and desire to minimize the overwhelming tragedy of Bengal, sensitive and warmhearted men and women in England and America and elsewhere came to our help. Above all, the governments of China and Eire, poor in their own resources, full of their own difficulties, yet having had bitter experience themselves of famine and misery, and sensing what ailed the body and spirit of India, gave generous help. India has a long memory, but whatever else she remembers or forgets, she will not forget these gracious and friendly acts.

In Asia and Europe and Africa, and over the vast stretches of the Pacific and Atlantic and Indian Oceans, war has raged in all its dreadful aspects. Nearly seven years of war in China, over four and a half years of war in Europe and Africa, and two years and four months of world war. War against fascism and nazism and attempts to gain world domination.[1]

2 | Reveries in Jail

[During his long and lonely imprisonment in the early forties, Nehru remained deeply concerned by the massive problems confronting India. He wrote prolifically, planning for the future; attempting to clarify his position on any number of international, as well as domestic, issues. He concentrated to a great degree, as he has noted, on "discovering India", both its unity and diversity. Simultaneously, he contemplated the irony involved in the Allied fight against the Axis in the name of democracy, in view of India's own prolonged subjugation. He continued to dream of a liberated, secular, democratic-socialist, developed India; to dread the possibility that it might be partitioned along religious lines, despite becoming independent.]

[1] D.I., pp. 4-6.

[Written in Ahmadnagar Fort, 1944.] It is a curious turn of fate's wheel that I and people like me should spend our days in prison while war against fascism and nazism is raging, and many of those who used to bow to Hitler and Mussolini and approve of Japanese aggression in China should hold aloft the banner of freedom and democracy and antifascism.

In India the change is equally remarkable. There are those here as elsewhere, "governmentarians", who hover round the skirts of Government and echo the views which they think will be approved by those whose favor they continually seek. There was a time, not so long ago, when they praised Hitler and Mussolini and held them up as models and when they cursed the Soviet Union with bell, book, and candle. Not so now, for the weather has changed. They are high government and state officials, and loudly they proclaim their antifascism and antinazism and even talk of democracy, though with bated breath, as something desirable but distant. I often wonder what they would have done if events had taken a different turn. And yet there is little reason for conjecture, for they would welcome with garlands and addresses of welcome whoever happened to wield authority.

For long years before the war my mind was full of the war that was coming. I thought of it, spoke of it and wrote about it and prepared myself mentally for it. I wanted India to take an eager and active part in the mighty conflict, for I felt that high principles would be at stake and out of this conflict would come great and revolutionary changes in India and the world. At that time I did not envisage an immediate threat to India, [or] any probability of actual invasion. Yet I wanted India to take her full share. But I was convinced that only as a free country and an equal could she function. . . .

That was the attitude of the National Congress, the one great organization in India which consistently for all these years had been antifascist and antinazi, as it had been anti-imperialist. It had stood for republican Spain, for Czechoslovakia, and throughout for China.

And now for nearly two years the Congress has been declared illegal, outlawed and prevented from functioning in any way. The Congress is in prison. Its elected members of the provincial parliaments, its speakers of these parliaments, its ex-ministers, its mayors and presidents of municipal corporations, are in prison.

Meanwhile the war goes on for democracy and the Atlantic Charter and the Four Freedoms.[1]

---

[1] D.I., pp. 7–8.

[On Racialism and Imperialism.] Since Hitler emerged from obscurity and became the *Führer* of Germany, we have heard a gread deal about racialism and the nazi theory of the *Herrenvolk*. That doctrine has been condemned and is today condemned by the leaders of the United Nations. Biologists tell us that racialism is a myth and there is no such thing as a master race. But we in India have known racialism in all its forms ever since the commencement of British rule. The whole ideology of this rule was that of the *Herrenvolk* and the Master Race, and the structure of government was based upon it; indeed the idea of a master race is inherent in imperialism. There was no subterfuge about it; it was proclaimed in unambiguous language by those in authority. More powerful than words was the practice that accompanied them, and generation after generation and year after year India as a nation and Indians as individuals were subjected to insult, humiliation, and contemptuous treatment. The English were an Imperial Race, we were told, with the God-given right to govern us and keep us in subjection; if we protested we were reminded of the "tiger qualities of an imperial race". As an Indian, I am ashamed to write all this, for the memory of it hurts, and what hurts still more is the fact that we submitted for so long to this degradation. I would have preferred any kind of resistance to this, whatever the consequences, rather than that our people should endure this treatment. And yet it is better that both Indians and Englishmen should know it, for that is the psychological background of England's connection with India, and psychology counts and racial memories are long.[1]

[Letter from jail to Krishna Hutheesing—May 14, 1943.] It is astonishing how people constitute themselves the judges of other people's private lives and activities, without even troubling to understand those other people.

Each one, I suppose, develops some kind of a philosophy of life, and if he does not do so even in his later years, he is very superficial and his opinions are of little value. They are not opinions really but reactions, emotional and sentimental, to events and personalities. That approach is seldom a helpful one. Yet inevitably all of us are governed by it to some extent. I have tried hard to grow out of it, and to develop some poise and equilibrium which is not easily upset by life's vagaries. It is difficult for me to say how far I have succeeded.

I am an aggressive kind of person, trying often enough to force my will on others—both on the group and the individual. Nevertheless I am

[1] Ibid., p. 327.

growing more and more doubtful about the desirability of my, or anyone else, interfering with the private life and growth of individuals, except for the gravest reasons. In the mass, I suppose, I shall continue to interfere for I want to change many things utterly. But I do not want to come in the way of a young growing thing and thus possibly create all manner of frustrations and complexes. . . . Remember that we are surrounded by overwhelming problems from which none of us can run away. The small things do not matter, this way or that. It is the big things that count and that will make the final difference. Life is difficult enough and it grows in complexity. There is a shabbiness and shallowness about it which hurts continually, if we have the misfortune to be sensitive and to have any ideals. Yet we must face it, understand it and accept it, while at the same time we have to struggle against its evil and crudity. We are all the prisoners of the myths of the past and the emotions of the present with just a little elbow room perhaps. Yet that little might make a difference. So we hope and act and with that hope we face an unknown future.[1]

3	Industrialization in India—Religion, Philosophy and Science—"The Discovery of India"—Letters from Jail

Industrialization in India

The Congress has . . . always been in favor of the industrialization of India, and at the same time has emphasized the development of cottage industries and worked for this. Is there a conflict between these two approaches? Possibly there is a difference in emphasis, a realization of certain human and economic factors which were overlooked previously in India. Indian industrialists and the politicians who supported them thought too much in terms of the nineteenth-century development of capitalist industry in Europe and ignored many of the evil consequences that were obvious in the twentieth century. In India, because normal

[1] N.L.H.S., pp. 120–22.

progress had been arrested for a hundred years, those consequences were likely to be more far-reaching. The kind of medium-scale industries that were being started in India, under the prevailing economic system, resulted not in absorbing labor but in creating more unemployment. While capital accumulated at one end, poverty and unemployment increased at the other. Under a different system and with a stress on big-scale industries absorbing labor, and with planned development, this might well have been avoided.

This fact of increasing mass poverty influenced Gandhi powerfully. It is true, I think, that there is a fundamental difference between his outlook on life generally and what might be called the modern outlook. He is not enamored of ever-increasing standards of living and the growth of luxury at the cost of spiritual and moral values. He does not favor the soft life; for him the straight way is the hard way, and the love of luxury leads to crookedness and loss of virtue. Above all he is shocked at the vast gulf that stretches between the rich and the poor, in their ways of living and their opportunities of growth. For his own personal and psychological satisfaction, he crossed that gulf and went over to the side of the poor, adopting, with only such improvements as the poor themselves could afford, their ways of living, their dress or lack of dress. This vast difference between the few rich and the poverty-stricken masses seemed to him to be due to two principal causes: foreign rule and the exploitation that accompanied it, and the capitalist industrial civilization of the West as embodied in the big machine. He reacted against both. He looked back with yearning to the days of the old autonomous and more-or-less self-contained village community where there had been an automatic balance between production, distribution, and consumption; where political or economic power was spread out and not concentrated as it is today; where a kind of simple democracy prevailed; where the gulf between the rich and the poor was not so marked; where the evils of great cities were absent and people lived in contact with the life-giving soil and breathed the pure air of the open spaces.

There was all this basic difference in outlook as to the meaning of life itself between him and many others, and this difference colored his language as well as his activities. His language, vivid and powerful as it often was, drew its inspiration from the religious and moral teachings of the ages, principally of India but also of other countries. Moral values must prevail; the ends can never justify unworthy means, or else the individual and the race perish.

And yet he was no dreamer living in some fantasy of his own creation, cut off from life and its problems. He came from Gujrat, the home of hardheaded businessmen, and he had an unrivaled knowledge of the Indian villages and the conditions of life that prevailed there. It was out of that personal experience that he evolved his program of the spinning wheel and village industry. If immediate relief was to be given to the vast numbers of the unemployed and partially employed, if the rot that was spreading throughout India and paralyzing the masses was to be stopped, if the villagers' standards were to be raised, however little, *en masse*, if they were to be taught self-reliance instead of waiting helplessly like derelicts for relief from others, if all this was to be done without much capital, then there seemed no other way. Apart from the evils inherent in foreign rule and exploitation, and the lack of freedom to initiate and carry through big schemes of reform, the problem of India was one of scarcity of capital and abundance of labor—how to utilize that wasted labor, that manpower that was producing nothing. Foolish comparisons are made between manpower and machine power; of course a big machine can do the work of a thousand or ten thousand persons. But if those ten thousand sit idly by or starve, the introduction of that machine is not a social gain, except in long perspective which envisages a change in social conditions. When the big machine is not there at all, then no question of comparison arises; it is a net gain both from the individual and the national point of view to utilize manpower for production. There is no necessary conflict between this and the introduction of machinery on the largest scale, provided that machinery is used primarily for absorbing labor and not for creating fresh unemployment.

Comparisons between India and the small, highly industrialized countries of the West, or big countries with relatively sparse populations, like the U.S.S.R. or the U.S.A., are misleading. In western Europe the process of industrialization has proceeded for a hundred years and gradually the population has adjusted itself to it; the population has grown rapidly, then stabilized itself, and is now declining. In the U.S.A. and the U.S.S.R. there are vast tracts with a small, though growing, population. A tractor is an absolute necessity there to exploit the land for agriculture. It is not so obvious that a tractor is equally necessary in the densely populated Gangetic valley, so long as vast numbers depend on the land alone for sustenance. Other problems arise, as they have arisen even in America. Agriculture has been carried on for thousands of years in India, and the soil has been exploited to the utmost. Would the deep churning up of the soil by tractors lead to impoverishment of this soil as well as to soil erosion? When railways were built in India and high embankments put up for the purpose, no thought was given to the natural drainage of the country. These embankments interfered with this drainage system, and as a result we have had repeated and ever-increasing floods, soil erosion, and malaria has spread.

I am all for tractors and big machinery and I am convinced that the rapid industrialization of India is essential to relieve the pressure on land, to combat poverty and raise standards of living, for defense, and a variety of other purposes. But I am equally convinced that the most careful planning and adjustment are necessary if we are to reap the full benefit of industrialization and avoid many of its dangers.[1]

Gandhiji's attitude to the use of machinery seemed to undergo a gradual change. "What I object to," he said, "is the craze for machinery, not machinery as such. . . . If we could have electricity in every village home, I shall not mind villagers plying their implements and tools with electricity." The big machine seemed to him to lead inevitably, at least in the circumstances of today, to the concentration of power and riches: "I consider it a sin and injustice to use machinery for the purpose of concentration of power and riches in the hands of the few. Today the machine is used in this way." He even came to accept the necessity of many kinds of heavy industries and large-scale key industries and public utilities, provided they were state-owned and did not interfere with some kinds of cottage industries which he considered essential. Referring to his own proposals, he said: "The whole of [our] program will be a structure on sand if it is not built on the solid foundation of economic equality."

Thus even the enthusiastic advocates for cottage and small-scale industries recognize that big-scale industry is, to a certain extent, necessary and inevitable; only they would like to limit it as far as possible. Superficially, then, the question becomes one of emphasis and adjustment of the two forms of production and economy. It can hardly be challenged that, in the context of the modern world, no country can be politically and economically independent, even within the framework of international interdependence, unless it is highly industrialized and has developed its power resources to the utmost. Nor can it achieve or maintain high standards of living and liquidate poverty without the aid of modern technology in almost every sphere of life. An industrially backward country will continually upset the world equilibrium and encourage the aggressive tendencies of more developed countries. Even if it retains its political independence, this will be nominal only and economic control will tend

[1] D.I., pp. 409-11.

to pass to others. This control will inevitably upset its own small-scale economy which it has sought to preserve in pursuit of its own view of life. Thus an attempt to build up a country's economy largely on the basis of cottage and small-scale industries is doomed to failure. It will not solve the basic problems of the country or maintain freedom, nor will it fit in with the world framework, except as a colonial appendage.

Is it possible to have two entirely different kinds of economy in a country—one based on the big machine and industrialization, and the other mainly on cottage industries? This is hardly conceivable, for one must overcome the other, and there can be little doubt that the big machine will triumph unless it is forcibly prevented from doing so. Thus it is not a mere question of adjustment of the two forms of production and economy. One must be dominating and paramount, with the other complementary to it, fitting in where it can. The economy based on the latest technical achievements of the day must necessarily be the dominating one. If technology demands the big machine, as it does today in a large measure, then the big machine with all its implications and consequences must be accepted. Where it is possible, in terms of that technology, to decentralize production, this would be desirable. But in any event, the latest technique has to be followed, and to adhere to outworn and out-of-date methods of production, except as a temporary and stop-gap measure, is to arrest growth and development. . . .

The real question is not one of quantitative adjustment and balancing of various incongruous elements and methods of production, but a qualitative changeover to something different and new, from which various social consequences flow. The economic and political aspects of this qualitative change are important, but equally important are the social and psychological aspects. In India especially, where we have been wedded far too long to past forms and modes of thought and action, new experiences, new processes, leading to new ideas and new horizons, are necessary. Thus we will change the static character of our living and make it dynamic and vital, and our minds will become active and adventurous. New situations lead to new experiences, as the mind is compelled to deal with them and adapt itself to a changing environment.

It is well recognized now that a child's education should be intimately associated with some craft or manual activity. The mind is stimulated thereby, and there is a co-ordination between the activities of the mind and the hands. So also the mind of a growing boy or girl is stimulated by the machine. It grows under the machine's impact (under proper conditions, of course, and not as an exploited and unhappy worker in a factory) and opens out new horizons. Simple scientific experiments, peeps into the microscope, and an explanation of the ordinary phenomena of nature bring excitement in their train, an understanding of some of life's processes and a desire to experiment and find out instead of relying on set phrases and old formulae. Self-confidence and the co-operative spirit grow, and frustration, arising out of the miasma of the past, lessens. A civilization based on ever-changing and advancing mechanical techniques leads to this. Such a civilization is a marked change, a jump almost, from the older type, and is intimately connected with modern industrialization. Inevitably it gives rise to new problems and difficulties, but it also shows the way to overcome them.

I have a partiality for the literary aspects of education and I admire the classics. But I am quite sure that some elementary scientific training in physics and chemistry and especially biology, as also in the applications of science, is essential for all boys and girls. Only thus can they understand and fit into the modern world and develop, to some extent at least, the scientific temper. There is something very wonderful about the high achievements of science and modern technology (which no doubt will be bettered in the near future), in the superb ingenuity of scientific instruments, in the amazingly delicate and yet powerful machines, in all that has flowed from the adventurous inquiries of science and its applications, in the glimpses into the fascinating workshop and processes of nature, in the fine sweep of science, through its myriad workers, in the realms of thought and practice, and above all in the fact that all this has come out of the mind of man. . . .

The three fundamental requirements of India, if she is to develop industrially and otherwise, are: a heavy engineering and machine-making industry, scientific research institutes, and electric power. These must be the foundations of all planning, and the National Planning Committee laid the greatest emphasis on them. We lacked all three, and bottlenecks in industrial expansion were always occurring. A forward policy could have rapidly removed these bottlenecks, but the government's policy was the reverse of forward and was obviously one of preventing the development of heavy industry in India. Even when World War II started, the necessary machinery was not allowed to be imported; later shipping difficulties were pleaded. There was neither lack of capital nor skilled personnel in India, only machinery was lacking, and industrialists were clamoring for it. If opportunities had been given for the importation of machinery, not only would the economic position of India have been infinitely better, but the whole aspect of the war in the Far Eastern theaters might have changed. Many of the essential articles which had to be brought over, usually by air and at great cost and under considerable difficulties, could have been manufactured in India. India would really have become an arsenal for China and the East, and her industrial progress might have matched that of Canada or Australia. But imperative as the needs of the war situation were, the future needs of British industry were always kept in view, and it was considered undesirable to develop any industries in India which might compete with British industries in the postwar years. This was no secret policy; public expression was given to it in British journals, and there were continuous reference to it and protests against it in India.[1]

Religion, Philosophy and Science

India must break with much of her past and not allow it to dominate the present. Our lives are encumbered with the dead wood of this past; all that is dead and has served its purpose has to go. But that does not mean a break with, or a forgetting of, the vital and life-giving in that past. We can never forget the ideals that have moved our race, the dreams of the Indian people through the ages, the wisdom of the ancients, the buoyant energy and love of life and nature of our forefathers, their spirit of curiosity and mental adventure, the daring of their thought, their splendid achievements in literature, art, and culture, their love of truth and beauty and freedom, the basic values that they set up, their understanding of life's mysterious ways, their toleration of other ways than theirs, their capacity to absorb other peoples and their cultural accomplishments, synthesize them and develop a varied and mixed culture; nor can we forget the myriad experiences which have built up our ancient race and lie embedded in our subconscious minds. We will never forget them or cease to take pride in that noble heritage of ours. If India forgets them, she will no longer remain India and much that has made her our joy and pride will cease to be.

It is not this that we have to break with, but all the dust and dirt of ages that have covered her up and hidden her inner beauty and significance, the excrescences and abortions that have twisted and petrified her spirit, set it in rigid frames, and stunted her growth. We have to cut away these excrescences and remember afresh the core of that ancient wisdom and adapt it to our present circumstances. We have to get out of traditional

[1] Ibid., pp. 413-16.

ways of thought and living which, for all the good they may have done in a past age, and there was much good in them, have ceased to have significance today. We have to make our own all the achievements of the human race and join up with others in the exciting adventure of Man, more exciting today perhaps than in earlier ages, realizing that this has ceased to be governed by national boundaries or old divisions and is common to the race of man everywhere. We have to revive the passion for truth and beauty and freedom which gives meaning to life, and develop afresh that dynamic outlook and spirit of adventure which distinguished those of our race who, in ages past, built our house on these strong and enduring foundations. Old as we are, with memories stretching back to the early dawns of human history and endeavor, we have to grow young again, in tune with our present time, with the irrepressible spirit and joy of youth in the present and its faith in the future.

Truth as ultimate reality, if such there is, must be eternal, imperishable, unchanging. But that infinite, eternal, and unchanging truth cannot be apprehended in its fullness by the finite mind of man which can only grasp, at most, some small aspect of it limited by time and space, and by the state of development of that mind and the prevailing ideology of the period. As the mind develops and enlarges its scope, as ideologies change and new symbols are used to express that truth, new aspects of it come to light, though the core of it may yet be the same. And so, truth has ever to be sought and renewed, reshaped and developed, so that, as understood by man, it may keep in line with the growth of his thought and the development of human life. Only then does it become a living truth for humanity, supplying the essential need for which it craves, and offering guidance in the present and for the future.

But if some one aspect of the truth has been petrified by dogma in a past age, it ceases to grow and develop and adapt itself to the changing needs of humanity; other aspects of it remain hidden, and it fails to answer the urgent questions of a succeeding age. It is no longer dynamic but static, no longer a life-giving impulse but dead thought and ceremonial and a hindrance to the growth of the mind and of humanity. Indeed, it is probably not even understood to the extent it was understood in that past age when it grew up and was clothed in the language and symbols of that age. For its context is different in a later age, the mental climate has changed, new social habits and customs have grown up, and it is often difficult to understand the sense, much less the spirit, of that ancient writing. Moreover, as Aurobindo Ghose has pointed out, every truth, however true in itself, yet, taken apart from others which at once

limit and complete it, becomes a snare to bind the intellect and a misleading dogma; for in reality each is one thread of a complex weft, and no
thread must be taken apart from the weft.

Religions have helped greatly in the development of humanity. They
have laid down values and standards and have pointed out principles for
the guidance of human life. But with all the good they have done, they
have also tried to imprison truth in set forms and dogmas, and encouraged
ceremonials and practices which soon lose all their original meaning and
become mere routine. While impressing upon man the awe and mystery
of the unknown that surrounds him on all sides, they have discouraged
him from trying to understand not only the unknown but what might
come in the way of social effort. Instead of encouraging curiosity and
thought, they have preached a philosophy of submission to nature, to the
established church, to the prevailing social order, and to everything that is.
The belief in a supernatural agency which ordains everything has led to a
certain irresponsibility on the social plane, and emotion and sentimentality
have taken the place of reasoned thought and inquiry. Religion, though it
has undoubtedly brought comfort to innumerable human beings and
stabilized society by its values, has checked the tendency to change and
progress inherent in human society.

Philosophy has avoided many of these pitfalls and encouraged thought
and inquiry. But it has usually lived in its ivory tower cut off from life and
its day-to-day problems, concentrating on ultimate purposes and failing
to link them with the life of man. Logic and reason were its guides, and
they took it far in many directions, but that logic was too much the product of the mind and unconcerned with fact.

Science ignored the ultimate purposes and looked at fact alone. It
made the world jump forward with a leap, built up a glittering civilization,
opened up innumerable avenues for the growth of knowledge, and added
to the power of man to such an extent that for the first time it was possible
to conceive that man could triumph over and shape his physical environment. Man became almost a geological force, changing the face of the
planet earth chemically, physically, and in many other ways. Yet when
this sorry scheme of things entirely seemed to be in his grasp, to mold it
nearer to the heart's desire, there was some essential lack and some vital
element was missing. There was no knowledge of ultimate purposes and
not even an understanding of the immediate purpose, for science had told
us nothing about any purpose in life. Nor did man, so powerful in his
control of nature, have the power to control himself, and the monster he
had created ran amuck. Perhaps new developments in biology, psychology,

and similar sciences, and the interpretation of biology and physics, may help man to understand and control himself more than he has done in the past. Or, before any such advances influence human life sufficiently, man may destroy the civilization he has built and have to start anew.

There is no visible limit to the advance of science, if it is given the chance to advance. Yet it may be that the scientific method of observation is not always applicable to all the varieties of human experience and cannot cross the uncharted ocean that surrounds us. With the help of philosophy it may go a little further and venture even on these high seas. And when both science and philosophy fail us, we shall have to rely on such other powers of apprehension as we may possess. For there appears to be a definite stopping place beyond which reason, as the mind is at present constituted, cannot go. "*La dernière démarche de la raison*," says Pascal, "*c'est de connaître qu'il y a une infinité de choses qui la surpassent. Elle est bien faible si elle ne va jusque-là.*"

Realizing these limitations of reason and scientific method, we have still to hold on to them with all our strength, for without that firm basis and background we can have no grip on any kind of truth or reality. It is better to understand a part of truth, and apply it to our lives, than to understand nothing at all and flounder helplessly in a vain attempt to pierce the mystery of existence. The applications of science are inevitable and unavoidable for all countries and peoples today. But something more than its application is necessary. It is the scientific approach, the adventurous and yet critical temper of science, the search for truth and new knowledge, the refusal to accept anything without testing and trial, the capacity to change previous conclusions in the face of new evidence, the reliance on observed fact and not on preconceived theory, the hard discipline of the mind—all this is necessary, not merely for the application of science but for life itself and the solution of its many problems. Too many scientists today who swear by science forget all about it outside their particular spheres. The scientific approach and temper are, or should be, a way of life, a process of thinking, a method of acting and associating with our fellow men. That is a large order, and undoubtedly very few of us, if any at all, can function in this way with even partial success. But this criticism applies in equal or even greater measure to all the injunctions which philosophy and religion have laid upon us. The scientific temper points out the way along which man should travel. It is the temper of a free man. We live in a scientific age, so we are told, but there is little evidence of this temper in the people anywhere or even in their leaders.

Science deals with the domain of positive knowledge, but the temper which it should produce goes beyond that domain. The ultimate purposes of man may be said to be to gain knowledge, to realize truth, to appreciate goodness and beauty. The scientific method of objective inquiry is not applicable to all these, and much that is vital in life seems to lie beyond its scope—the sensitiveness to art and poetry, the emotion that beauty produces, the inner recognition of goodness. The botanist and zoologist may never experience the charm and beauty of nature; the sociologist may be wholly lacking in love for humanity. But even when we go to the regions beyond the reach of the scientific and visit the mountaintops where philosophy dwells and high emotions fill us, or gaze at the immensity beyond, that approach and temper are still necessary.

Very different is the method of religion. Concerned as it is principally with the regions beyond the reach of objective inquiry, it relies on emotion and intuition. And then it applies this method to everything in life, even to those things which are capable of intellectual inquiry and observation. Organized religion, allying itself to theology and often more concerned with its vested interests than with things of the spirit, encourages a temper which is the very opposite to that of science. It produces narrowness and intolerance, credulity and superstition, emotionalism and irrationalism. It tends to close and limit the mind of man, and to produce [the] temper of a dependent, unfree person.

Even if God did not exist, it would be necessary to invent him, so Voltaire said—"*si dieu n'existait pas, il faudrait l'inventer.*" Perhaps that is true, and indeed the mind of man has always been trying to fashion some such mental image or conception which grew with the mind's growth. But there is something also in the reverse proposition: even if God exists, it may be desirable not to look up to him or to rely upon him. Too much dependence on supernatural factors may lead, and has often led, to a loss of self-reliance in man and to a blunting of his capacity and creative ability. And yet some faith seems necessary in things of the spirit which are beyond the scope of our physical world, some reliance on moral, spiritual, and idealistic conceptions, or else we have no anchorage, no objectives or purpose in life. Whether we believe in God or not, it is impossible not to believe in something, whether we call it a creative life-giving force, or vital energy inherent in matter which gives it its capacity for self-movement and change and growth, or by some other name, something that is as real, though elusive, as life is real when contrasted with death. Whether we are conscious of it or not, most of us worship at the invisible altar of some unknown god and offer sacrifices to it—some ideal, personal, national, or international; some distant objective that draws us on, though reason itself may find little substance to it; some vague conception of a perfect man and a better world. Perfection may be impossible of attainment, but the demon in us, some vital force, urges us on, and we tread that path from generation to generation.

As knowledge advances, the domain of religion, in the narrow sense of the word, shrinks. The more we understand life and nature, the less we look for supernatural causes. Whatever we can understand and control ceases to be a mystery. The processes of agriculture, the food we eat, the clothes we wear, our social relations, were all at one time under the dominion of religion and its high priests. Gradually they have passed out of its control and become subjects for scientific study. Yet much of this is still powerfully affected by religious beliefs and the superstitions that accompany them. The final mysteries still remain far beyond the reach of the human mind and are likely to continue to remain so. But so many of life's mysteries are capable of and await solution, that an obsession with the final mystery seems hardly necessary or justified. Life still offers not only the loveliness of the world but also the exciting adventure of fresh and never-ceasing discoveries, of new panoramas opening out and new ways of living, adding to its fullness and ever making it richer and more complete.

It is therefore with the temper and approach of science, allied to philosophy, and with reverence for all that lies beyond, that we must face life. Thus we may develop an integral vision of life which embraces in its wide scope the past and the present, with all their heights and depths, and look with serenity toward the future. The depths are there and cannot be ignored, and always by the side of the loveliness that surrounds us is the misery of the world. Man's journey through life is an odd mixture of joy and sorrow; thus only can he learn and advance. The travail of the soul is a tragic and lonely business. External events and their consequences affect us powerfully, and yet the greatest shocks come to our minds through inner fears and conflicts. While we advance on the external plane, as we must if we are to survive, we have also to win peace with ourselves and between ourselves and our environment, a peace which brings satisfaction not only to our physical and material needs but also to those inner imaginative urges and adventurous spirit that have distinguished man ever since he started on his troubled journey in the realms of thought and action. Whether that journey has any ultimate purpose or not we do not know, but it has its compensations, and it points to many a nearer objective which appears attainable and which may again become the starting point for a fresh advance.

Science has dominated the Western world and everyone there pays tribute to it, and yet the West is still far from having developed the real temper of science. It has still to bring the spirit and the flesh into creative harmony. In India in many obvious ways we have a greater distance to travel. And yet there may be fewer major obstructions on our way, for the essential basis of Indian thought for ages past, though not its later manifestations, fits in with the scientific temper and approach, as well as with internationalism. It is based on a fearless search for truth, on the solidarity of man, even on the divinity of everything living, and on the free and co-operative development of the individual and the species, ever to greater freedom and higher stages of human growth.[1]

"The Discovery of India"

The discovery of India—what have I discovered? It was presumptuous of me to imagine that I could unveil her and find out what she is today and what she was in the long past. Today she is four hundred million separate individual men and women, each differing from the other, each living in a private universe of thought and feeling. If this is so in the present, how much more difficult is it to grasp that multitudinous past of innumerable successions of human beings. Yet something has bound them together and binds them still. India is a geographical and economic entity, a cultural unity amidst diversity, a bundle of contradictions held together by strong but invisible threads. Overwhelmed again and again, her spirit was never conquered, and today when she appears to be the plaything of a proud conqueror, she remains unsubdued and unconquered. About her there is the elusive quality of a legend of long ago; some enchantment seems to have held her mind. She is a myth and an idea, a dream and a vision, and yet very real and present and pervasive. There are terrifying glimpses of dark corridors which seem to lead back to primeval night, but also there is the fullness and warmth of the day about her. Shameful and repellent she is occasionally, perverse and obstinate, sometimes even a little hysteric, this lady with a past. But she is very lovable and none of her children can forget her wherever they go or whatever strange fate befalls them. For she is part of them in her greatness as well as her failings, and they are mirrored in those deep eyes of hers that have seen so much of life's passion and joy and folly and looked down into wisdom's well. Each one of them is drawn to her, though perhaps each has a different reason for

[1] Ibid., pp. 520–26.

that attraction or can point to no reason at all, and each sees some different aspect of her many-sided personality. From age to age she has produced great men and women, carrying on the old tradition and yet ever adapting it to changing times. Rabindranath Tagore, in line with that great succession, was full of the temper and urges of the modern age and yet was rooted in India's past, and in his own self built up a synthesis of the old and the new. "I love India," he said, "not because I cultivate the idolatry of geography, not because I have had the chance to be born in her soil, but because she has saved through tumultuous ages the living words that have issued from the illuminated consciousness of her great ones." So many will say, and yet others will explain their love for her in some different way.

The old enchantment seems to be breaking today and she is looking around and waking up to the present. But however she changes, as change she must, that old witchery will continue and hold the hearts of her people. Though her attire may change, she will continue as of old, and her store of wisdom will help her to hold on to what is true and beautiful and good in this harsh, vindictive, and grasping world.

The world of today has achieved much, but for all its declared love for humanity, it has based itself far more on hatred and violence than on the virtues that make man human. War is the negation of truth and humanity. War may be unavoidable sometimes, but its progeny are terrible to contemplate. Not mere killing, for man must die, but the deliberate and persistent propagation of hatred and falsehood, which gradually become the normal habits of the people. It is dangerous and harmful to be guided in our life's course by hatreds and aversions, for they are wasteful of energy and limit and twist the mind and prevent it from perceiving the truth. Unhappily there is hatred in India and strong aversions, for the past pursues us and the present does not differ from it. It is not easy to forget repeated affronts to the dignity of a proud race. Yet, fortunately, Indians do not nourish hatred for long; they recover easily a more benevolent mood.

India will find herself again when freedom opens out new horizons and the future will then fascinate her far more than the immediate past of frustration and humiliation. She will go forward with confidence, rooted in herself and yet eager to learn from others and co-operate with them. Today she swings between a blind adherence to her old customs and a slavish imitation of foreign ways. In neither of these can she find relief or life or growth. It is obvious that she has to come out of her shell and take full part in the life and activities of the modern age. It should be equally obvious that there can be no real cultural or spiritual growth based on imitation. Such imitation can only be confined to a small number who cut themselves off from the masses and the springs of national life. True culture derives its inspiration from every corner of the world, but it is home-grown and has to be based on the wide mass of the people. Art and literature remain lifeless if they are continually thinking of foreign models. The day of a narrow culture confined to a small fastidious group is past. We have to think in terms of the people generally and their culture must be a continuation and development of past trends, and must also represent their new urges and creative tendencies.[1]

Letters from Jail to Krishna Hutheesing (1944–1945)

I. [February 18, 1944.] If [our nationalist activity has meaning it stems from] continually challenging fate, defying it if you will, and accepting, without murmur, what it had to say in reply. The initiative was ours, not fate's, and though foreknowledge of events is not given to us, there was no lack of apprehension of results and consequences. And so, though life may have been hard and bitter occasionally, it could seldom surprise us or stun us. How far we succeeded in this attitude, it is impossible for one involved in it to judge or say. Others, and perhaps others of a different day, will be in a better position to judge. But even [to try now] has value: it gives a certain dignity and poise to life's adventure, and those deeper experiences of the spirit which pass us by in our normal routine. If we miss something that makes life full, we gain something else of perhaps greater significance in the long run, and so the balance is not tipped against us.[2]

II. [March 22, 1944.] Life is full of untoward happenings and since the world began persons with sensitive minds and those who are called philosophers have tried to understand its complex and baffling texture. Others, dissatisfied with many of its aspects, have sought to alter them. In the course of time it has changed gradually but it still fails to satisfy our minds or our impulses. Everywhere there is what is called the strength of life. In its crude aspects this is evident enough, but it is equally evident in the sphere of the mind. All action is really a challenge to life. Only

[1] Ibid., pp. 575–77.
[2] N.L.H.S., p. 145. (From Ahmadnagar Fort.)

those minds who are in the ruts and fearful of any change, refuse this challenge, and yet even they cannot escape the hard knocks of life. Possibly they get them more, or sense them more, because they fear them more and are often taken unawares. The only real conflict which is oppressive is the conflict of the mind which arises from doubt and indecision—the old question of Hamlet—to be or not to be, to do or not to do. If one decides one way or the other, it is done with whatever the consequences. The conflict is over, though other conflicts will no doubt trouble the mind. To look back continually with regret is to lose oneself in the unchangeable past and thus miss both the present and the future. And so more regrets follow and we wallow in a very ocean of regret, never catching up to the living moment. Surely that is not a satisfactory state of affairs. Often enough it is the little things of life that pursue us and trouble us far more than the big things. And yet it is the big things that count. We may be having a bad time in India, but think of the horror that has enveloped so many of our friends in Europe and China and elsewhere. For years now I have had no word, no news, from some dear friends in France. Am I to complain then, because of what happens to me?

To lose our perspective in life is to lose our bearings. To look back is necessarily to look away from the present and the future which count. We must face the ever-changing present and have the power of quick decisions. Decide this way or that after weighing the pros and cons and act up to the decision. Not to decide is to live in a fog of doubt, and misgiving. Whether it is a matter relating to the narrow sphere of the family or the larger sphere of life, one must solve and resolve our problems as they arise and go ahead, not regretting overmuch or pining for what is not, not complaining, not holding others responsible for something that might have been otherwise.

That is the only way to face life even in more or less normal times. Much more is it so during abnormal times, such as we live in.

So many things happen which are not to one's liking. We cannot allow ourselves to be swept by this or else we become straw tossed hither and thither by conflicting waves of emotion. That produces unhappiness. If we attach ourselves to any big purpose we have to attain strength and equilibrium.[1]

III. [April 11, 1944.] Most of us, I suppose, are hardly conscious of having ... a definite philosophy and would find it hard enough to

[1] Ibid., pp. 149-50.

describe it. Yet, consciously or unconsciously, we hold to a certain framework and function within it, and sometimes we rebel, but even so our little rebellion is within that general framework. Normally each individual's attitude to life is that of his social group or the more intimate circle in which he or she moves. That lays down the standard to be aimed at with minor varieties. When there is revolutionary change in the air, we are affected by it, we talk of it, and yet that talk has little reality behind it, and we find it difficult to pull ourselves out of accustomed ways of life and thought. Sometimes we are compelled to do so by circumstances and we submit, as we must, but unwillingly and rather ungraciously. We become then the slaves of circumstance rather than its masters or even its equals. To a large extent we are all such slaves of happenings which are beyond our individual control. Yet there is a difference.

Every parent wants his or her child to have all the virtues, all the good fortune. But we can seldom, if ever, have all of everything. We have to choose or to emphasize some aspects rather than others. There are what are loosely called the masculine virtues and those that are termed the feminine virtues. Both good and desirable and yet just slightly inconsistent with each other. In India, the feminine virtues seem to be more obvious today at any rate, though of course the masculine virtues are present also. Our outlook seems to favour the former.

Then again much depends on the period we are living in. In a more or less static period, certain virtues and accomplishments are more useful: in a rapidly changing period other virtues and capacities assume importance. But whatever the period, self-reliance, fitness of body and keenness of mind and a harmony between the two, and a certain basic sense of values are always desirable.[1]

IV. [August 29, 1944.] An unending panorama of human life with its sweet and bitterness, its ups and downs. One would think that with all this age-long experience and personal and racial memories, nothing very novel can be expected. The old cycle repeats itself again and again. And yet whenever a person arrives, it is something absolutely new, like others and still unique in its own way. Nature goes on repeating itself but there is no end to its infinite variety and every spring is a resurrection, every new birth a new beginning. Especially when that new birth is intimately connected with us, it becomes a revival of ourselves and our old hopes centre round it.[2]

[1] Ibid., pp. 151–52.
[2] Ibid., pp. 162–63.

V. [February 6, 1945.] I have lost touch with so many of [the people I have known in the past] . . . not only during the two and a half years of my stay in Ahmadnagar Fort but even previously. When I have met them occasionally in the past there have been two dominant and rather contradictory sensations. The older generation seemed to have remained where it was, more or less unchanged in a changing world, static and moving in the same old groove, only growing older and more wrinkled, like some old picture which is slowly fading off and developing cracks and is covered with film and dust. The growing generation [changes] rapidly in appearance, as growing children do . . . almost [unrecognizably] rather attractive, some of the girls particularly so, and apparently full of promise. Yet somehow as they grow older that promise is seldom fulfilled and they tend to become replicas of their static parents. Because of some external changes, or few new habits and ways of living, they imagine and we imagine that some inner change has also taken place. Perhaps in a very few this does take place, but they appear to be very few and soon, they settle down in the old grooves. Even those few who adopt more aggressive roles in life are different on the surface only and the depths, if there are any, are not affected. It may be that I am mistaken about the very young today for I do not know them. Even these years, and especially years full of tension, make a difference. Change there must have been and must continue. But the slowness of the process is depressing. Our middle classes, I fear, are a singularly devitalized lot as a whole, or they are too confused between the old and the new, and, being terribly cautious and afraid of taking risks, cling on to the remarks of the old.

It made me happy to read your account of the Anand Bhawan [the Nehru residence] garden. I visualized it and a picture of bright flowers and hedges and garden paths rose up before me, another prospect was pleasing—perhaps even more pleasing than if I had seen it myself. It brought to mind the continuation of life and beauty in nature in spite of the petty troubles that fill our minds temporarily.[1]

VI. [March 25, 1945.] There has been so much talk in the papers and elsewhere about our impending transfer to other jails that I have become rather fed up with it. Yet it seems that at last something of the kind is going to happen in the near future. Some of us have been formally told that we should be ready to leave within the next few days. Where we are being sent to of course remains a state secret and a deep mystery. You will know that soon enough. I do not mention any further details about the

[1] Ibid., pp. 177–78.

dates of our respective departures as the censor will not approve of it. It really does not matter, for by the time you get this letter, or very soon after, you will get to know of them.[1]

VII. [April 19, 1945.] It is just three weeks since we left Ahmednagar Fort, and spending a day in Naini Prison en route, reached here. This uprooting and transplanting business ... has naturally an unsettling effect. But we gradually settle down again and throw out fresh roots and tendrils. Now ... I ... have got used to our new routine in the new environment of a regular jail, which is somewhat different from the military barracks of Ahmednagar. We have developed the capacity to adapt ourselves and that is a useful accomplishment. ...

I see that some of you, deluded by our wishful newspapers, have been expecting our early release. Do not do so. The release will come, early or late, when the time is ripe for it. To live in expectation of it, either for those inside prison or outside, is folly. Wherever we are we have to carry on our jobs, and when any change comes we accept it and adapt ourselves to it immediately. So, as I have said, we have learnt the art of adaptation, and that is one of the secrets of life.[2]

4 | Further Course of World Events, 1944–1945: End of War in Europe—Fresh British Proposals—After Prison, 1945—Pious Platitudes

Further Course of World Events, 1944–45 : End of War in Europe

[While Congress leaders remained confined in jail, World War II relentlessly continued to take its heartbreaking toll.

[1] Ibid., pp. 179–80.
[2] Ibid., pp. 181–82. (From Izatnagar Central Prison, Bareilly.)

6+N. II

The Moscow Declaration of October 30, 1943 affirmed the determination of the U.S., the U.K., the U.S.S.R. and China to continue hostilities against the Axis powers until the latter would agree to surrender unconditionally. On March 22, 1944 the Japanese first penetrated into India, moving westward from Burma. Rome fell to the Allies on June 4. The Allied invasion of German-occupied France began on June 6. On September 5, a Finnish-Soviet armistice ended the three-year war between the two countries. The Dumbarton Oaks Conference, held in Washington, issued proposals on October 9, 1944, for the establishment of an international organization to function under the title of the United Nations. Stalin did not brand Japan an aggressor until November 6, 1944.

A number of crucially significant events occurred both in India and abroad during 1945. The text of the controversial Report of the Crimea Conference held at Yalta by Roosevelt, Churchill and Stalin was released on February 12, 1945. Two months later, on April 12, President Roosevelt died. Hitler's mountain chalet at Berchtesgaden was bombed by the British Royal Air Force on April 25.

On April 28, 1945, Mussolini was executed. Hitler was reported dead by May 1. The following day the German Army surrendered in Italy.

Since Lord Wavell, who became Viceroy of India in 1943, sensed that India would be of increasingly great strategic importance in a prolonged conflict with Japan, he decided that Indo-British relations must be improved. With so many of India's most respected leaders in jail, and a sense of frustration so prevalent throughout the country, Wavell feared that England's position might all too easily be jeopardized if the Japanese were to mount a strong offensive in the East. Because he felt this so urgently, he went to London during the spring of 1945 to ascertain whether Britain might not make some positive gesture toward India.

While Lord Wavell was in England discussing what plans might be devised to improve Anglo-Indian relations, Germany's unconditional surrender became effective on May 8–9. Simultaneously there was a cessation of military operations in Europe.

On June 5 a Four-Power Declaration signed in Berlin proclaimed the completion of Germany's defeat and assumption of supreme authority in the Reich by the U.S., the U.K., the U.S.S.R. and France.

After the European phase of the war had ended in May, 1945 (Japan did not surrender until August, 1945), Lord Wavell announced fresh British plans with regard to India on June 14, 1945.

Winston Churchill resigned during May, 1945, thereby forcing a General Election to be held in Britain for the first time in ten years. He remained in office until after the July election, at which time the Labour Party came into power. Clement Attlee, long sympathetic to the Indian Nationalist Movement, became Prime Minister.

The Charter of the newly organized United Nations was signed by approximately fifty nations in San Francisco, June 26, 1945. India was one of the original members of the U.N.

On June 30, 1945, Chinese troops invaded Indo-China. On July 4 the liberation of the Philippine Islands was announced.]

Fresh British Proposals

[From Lord Wavell's statement on June 14, 1945: In order to "enable the main communities and parties [in India] to co-operate more closely together and with the British to the benefit of the people of India as a whole ... [the British Government] would be prepared to see an important change in the composition of the Viceroy's Executive. ... It is proposed that the Executive Council should be reconstituted and that the Viceroy should in future make his selection for nomination to the Crown for appointment to his Executive from amongst leaders of Indian political life at the Centre and in the Provinces, in proportions which would give a balanced representation of the main communities, including equal proportions of Moslems and Caste Hindus.

"In order to pursue this object, the Viceroy will call into conference a number of leading Indian politicians who are the heads of the most important parties or who have had recent experience as Prime Ministers of Provinces, together with a few others of special experience and authority. The Viceroy intends to put before this conference the proposal that the Executive Council should be reconstituted as above stated and to invite from the members of the conference a list of names. Out of these he would hope to be able to choose the future members whom he would recommend for appointment by His Majesty to the Viceroy's Council, although the responsibility for the recommendations must of course continue to rest with him, and his freedom of choice therefore remains unrestricted. ...

"The members of the Executive would be Indians with the exception of the Viceroy and the Commander-in-Chief, who would retain his position as War Member. This is essential so long as the defence of India remains a British responsibility.

"Nothing contained in any of these proposals will affect the relations of the Crown with the Indian States through the Viceroy as Crown Representative."[1]

As Brecher has noted of the Wavell proposals, "By a slight change of terminology, *political parity*, which the Congress [had] never officially accepted, was transformed into *communal parity*, a tactical objective of the League, and was incorporated into [the] official statement of British policy. [The Wavell] proposals, which were 'not an attempt to obtain or impose a constitutional settlement', [were to] be discussed at a conference of representative political leaders in Simla on 25 June. To ease Congress acceptance of the invitation, all members of the Working Committee (but no other Congress prisoners) were to be released [from jail] immediately."[2] Thus Nehru finally was permitted to leave prison on June 15, 1945.

A Congress Working Committee meeting, which Nehru attended, was

---

[1] E.I.P., p. 377.
[2] M.B., p. 301.

promptly held in Bombay to consider the Wavell pronouncement before
the Simla Conference was convened.]

After Coming Out of Prison—Summer, 1945

I am told the British officials are displeased with my speeches. I cannot
help it. The fire is kindling in my heart which does not permit me to
tolerate . . . present conditions. The struggle of the last three years has
produced [an] India which can neither be suppressed nor [bent].[1]

Pious Platitudes—Summer, 1945 (just before the British General Election)

One of the fundamental problems of the day everywhere is how to co-
ordinate the two conceptions of a central socialised organisation of society
and the state with the greatest amount of individual freedom.

Both aspects are important. I have no doubt that in the modern world
the New World Order will have very large elements of Socialism as its
basis. I hope, however, that individual freedom will also be preserved in a
large measure.

Possibly, in the transition period and the upheavals that are taking
place there will be many difficulties in this co-ordination.

So far as India is concerned, I should like her to keep this in view and
to co-operate with all other nations in achieving such a world order which,
while developing international activities on an ever wider scale, would
not interfere with the individual genius and freedom of the various peoples
and countries.

[In order to preserve peace in the post-war world, there must be] the
elimination, as far as possible, of political and economic conflicts between
countries and an equitable international order to organise international
relations.

It is obviously essential that such an order be based on the national
freedom of [the] various countries involved, and that no country should
have a sense of alien domination and suppression.

It seems also necessary that some kind of International Police Force
be organised, but there is grave danger of such a Force being exploited
by the dominant Powers to their own advantage. Realities have to be

[1] B.A.I., p. 331.

faced to-day, and the reality is the outstanding position of some great Powers.

I think it would have been better, from every point of view, to give a far bigger status to the smaller powers in any international settlement. Otherwise, the small Powers, in fear and self-defence, will group themselves around each Big Power, and big and hostile blocs might face each other....

The British Labour Party does represent various progressive forces in Britain and, therefore, I wish it success in the elections. But under the present leadership that Party means just nothing to India. It surprises me how the leaders of that party make references to India which exhibit not only colossal ignorance of this country but an amazing insensitiveness to the dominant feelings of India....

[I know] that many people in Britain, both among ... intellectuals and the working classes, [have] great sympathy for Indian freedom. But it must be obvious ... that, as a whole, the British people pay no attention whatever to India, except in so far as they give expression occasionally to pious platitudes. This applies to all the major parties and certainly to their leaders.[1]

5 | The Simla Conference, June, 1945—
Statements on Other Matters, Summer,
1945

The Simla Conference, June, 1945

["The [British Government] invitation to Simla was accepted [by the Congress Working Committee]. But [a Muslim] League claim to the right to appoint all Muslim members of the Executive Council [to be set up] was emphatically rejected [by Congress] in advance.

"Twenty-one persons were invited to Simla: the eleven provincial Premiers, most of whom were appointees of the Viceroy because of the resignation of the Congress ministries in 1939; the Congress and League leaders in the Central Assembly and the Council of State; the leaders of the

[1] Ibid., pp. 352–53.

insignificant Nationalist Party and the European Group in the Assembly; one delegate each for the Untouchables and the Sikhs; and Gandhi and Jinnah, 'as the recognized leaders of the two main political parties'. Conspicuously missing was an invitation to the (Muslim) President of the Congress, Maulana Azad. Gandhi declined [to attend] on the ground that this was an official conference and he was not even a member of the Congress. However, he agreed to go to Simla as an observer, in response to the Viceroy's persistent request. He also gently reminded Wavell that Azad was the official Congress spokesman and the 'error' was duly rectified.

"Optimism prevailed at the outset of the Conference, but this rapidly gave way to frustration. Stripped of the façade of multi-party and communal representation—for it was really a contest between the Congress and the League—the fate of the 1945 Simla Conference hung on one issue. The League insisted on the right to appoint *all* Muslims to the Executive Council and the Congress refused to abdicate its status as a national organization. Conversations took place between Jinnah and Pandit Pant [a prominent Congress leader] (for the League President refused to meet the Muslim President of the Congress) but the deadlock remained. Wavell then tried to mediate. He requested both parties to submit lists of persons for the proposed Executive Council from which he would make the final selection. Jinnah sought a prior assurance that the five Muslims nominated by the League would be accepted *en bloc* (which would have eliminated the possibility of a Congress Muslim being appointed) but Wavell was non-committal. By 7 July all groups except the League had complied. For another week the Viceroy tried to win Jinnah's co-operation, but in vain. Finally, on the 14th, he terminated the Conference.

"The manner in which this was done indicates the pattern to follow in the next two years. Confronted with Jinnah's intransigence, Wavell prepared his own list for an Executive Council, including non-League Muslims. 'When I explained my solution to Mr Jinnah, he told me that it was not acceptable to the Muslim League and he was so decided that I felt it would be useless to continue the discussion. In the circumstances, I did not show my selections as a whole to Mr Jinnah and there was no object in showing them to the other leaders. The conference has therefore failed.'

"The Viceroy's explanation reveals the twin sources of collapse. Jinnah threatened to boycott the Executive Council unless his demands were met; and Wavell acquiesced. The Conference failed because Wavell allowed Jinnah to veto its decisions, a precedent that strengthened Jinnah's hand in the crucial battles to follow. The League claim to represent all Muslims at that time was dubious: of the four Muslim-majority provinces, the North-West Frontier was under Congress control, the Punjab was governed by the Unionists, and Sind was dependent on Congress support for a stable ministry."[1]

Although Nehru attended the Simla Conference, his role was a relatively minor one. Convened on June 25, the Conference terminated on July 14, 1945.]

[1] M.B., pp. 301–03.

[On the Wavell Plan—Simla, July 11, 1945.] The Congress is prepared to proceed with participation in the new "interim" Government under the terms of the Wavell Plan, to which it has already agreed, even though the Muslim League has decided against entering such a Government. But the Congress will ask that the "door be left open" to the League. . . .

Of course, this matter is not entirely in our hands because there are other parties involved, one of which is the British Government, but we hope that if the League decided not to come in that decision will be only a temporary one and they will change their minds and come in later.[1]

From Statements on Matters Other than Simla Conference— Summer, 1945

[The Indian Communists—Bombay, June 22.] Fundamentally, Communist policy is not [created] from the standpoint of the country [in which] it functions, but from the standpoint of Russian foreign policy. I have every sympathy for Russia and the great advance Russia has made but from many points of view, I do not think [another] nation's policy can be bound up by . . . Russian foreign policy. The general question [for India is] whether their policy has been injurious to the cause of India.[2]

[On Foreign Affairs—Simla, July 11—from interview with Associated Press.] Nazism and Fascism . . . are immensely dangerous to any country and to the world at large. I am as firmly opposed to them as ever before. The mere fact of Nazis, as such, having disappeared from Germany does not affect one's reactions. [Nazism] might grow again in any country other than Germany under some other name.

[In answer to question relating to Russian neutrality in war against Japan.] Fascism and Nazism have nothing to do with the war against Japan, in the technical sense of the word. Japan is a militaristic and aggressive nation. Her militarism and aggression have got to be checked. . . . It is presumptuous for me to judge Russia's or any other country's attitude. . . . In spite of every sympathy for the so-called democratic countries—that is for England and France—when the German war broke out, America did not join it because of various internal and other factors, till she was compelled to do so by the Japanese attack. . . .

There is always the danger of a new militarism growing up in the act

[1] B.A.I., p. 236.
[2] Ibid., p. 86.

of suppressing an existing militarism. . . . The only possible way of eliminating this is by the creation of an effective world organization. How far the efforts in this direction will succeed in the near future, it is difficult to say.[1]

[Further statement—Simla, July 11.] In democracy there are no heirs to political positions. . . .

In foreign relations, if we are to have any, it is very important that we establish contact with popular opinion in America and that there should be an exchange of knowledge, as to the popular will in our two countries. The same is true of Russia. The situation internationally to-day is that there are two powers which really count and [these] two are America and Russia.

Regardless of what happens in the next few weeks or months or even the next year or two, ultimately popular opinion will prevail and make the decisions and that is why it is important that we should know what the popular will is abroad.[2]

| 6 | End of World War II—Fresh Examination of "Indian Problem"—For an Undivided, Progressive India—Britain's Decision to Convene Constitution-Making Body for India, and to Create Representative Executive Council |

End of World War II

[The first atomic bomb to be utilized for war purposes was dropped by a U.S. B-29 plane on Hiroshima, Japan, August 6, 1945. On August 8 Russia declared war on Japan. The second atomic bomb was dropped on

[1] Ibid., p. 354.
[2] Ibid., p. 237.

Nagasaki, Japan, August 9. On August 14, the Japanese Government communicated its acceptance of Allied peace terms.

On August 15 Japan surrendered unconditionally. On September 12, Admiral Mountbatten, accompanied by his Commanders-in-Chief and principal staff officers in Singapore, received the total surrender of all Japanese forces—land, sea and air—in South-East Asia.

An inevitable corollary of Japan's surrender was the provocation of a major political explosion in India in the months that followed. The explosion involved "remnants of the Indian forces which, in the course of the war, had been raised and trained under Japanese supervision and control in order to take part in the campaign against the Allies in South-East Asia. These forces bore the name, 'The Indian National Army'"[1] (see Section 7).]

Fresh Examination of "Indian Problem"—Late Summer, Autumn, 1945

["On 21 August [1945] the Viceroy was summoned to London for a fresh examination of the entire 'Indian problem'. It was announced simultaneously that general elections to the central and provincial legislatures [in India], the first since 1937, would be held [during] the winter. Before another month had passed, Wavell returned to Delhi and a new policy statement appeared: provincial autonomy would be restored immediately after the elections; a constitution-making body for India would be established as soon as possible ... the Viceroy's Executive Council would be reconstituted in consultation with the principal Indian parties.

"The Congress agreed to participate in the elections, though with some misgivings: 'There is little difference between Conservative Churchill and Laborite Attlee', wrote the party's General-Secretary. 'The present elections were devised merely to gain time'. . . .

"The Congress election manifesto [pledged] equal . . . opportunities for all men and women and a 'free democratic state with fundamental rights guaranteed in the Constitution'. These combined the freedoms of the liberal West with party commitments dating from the [Congress] Karachi Resolution on Fundamental Rights in 1931: the abolition of untouchability; free and compulsory basic education; special safeguards for the Scheduled (Backward) Tribes; and neutrality in religious matters, i.e., secularism. Also deriving from the Karachi Resolution was the stress on the eradication of poverty and the raising of living standards through planning; state control or ownership of key industries; and regulation of banking and insurance. The provision about land reform attempted to satisfy both peasants and landlords; the removal of intermediaries by 'equitable compensation'; the scaling down of rural indebtedness; and encouragement to co-operative farming and cottage industries. Urban

[1] A.C.B., p. 793.
6*

labour was promised a minimum wage and the right to form unions. To allay Muslim fears about their status in a united India the Congress called for a federal constitution 'with autonomy for its constituent parts [and] a minimum list of common and essential federal subjects'. Finally, it reaffirmed the principles enunciated in the 'Quit India' Resolution.

"The Muslim League fought the elections on the issue of Hindu domination in a united India and the consequent need of a separate Muslim homeland, i.e., Pakistan."[1]

As previously suggested, while Congress leaders were in jail from 1942 to 1945, Muslim League propaganda had free reign. Although British patronage and encouragement actively helped the League to consolidate its power, the results of the 1945 Indian elections were nevertheless surprising. The League captured almost all of the Muslim seats in the Central Assembly, as well as in all of the Provincial Legislatures, with the exception of the North-West Frontier Province. In the latter province Congress captured both the majority of seats in the Assembly, and the majority of Muslim seats. It also obtained almost all of the other seats at the Centre, as well as in the Provinces, including some of the Muslim seats. It established Ministries in eight of eleven Provinces and entered into a coalition with the Unionist Party, which cut across communal alignments, in the Punjab. The League was consequently able to form Ministries only in Bengal and Sind.

"The stage was thus set for the reconstitution of the Viceroy's Executive Council with the support of the main political parties and for convening a constitution-making body, as announced by the Viceroy in September, 1945. Rightly sensing the prevailing mood in India, the British Government decided this time not to leave the work of negotiating a settlement of the Indian question in the hands of the Viceroy alone",[2] as will be described in Part Nine.

(There was "a fundamental difference" between the manner in which the Congress and League functioned "during the period 1945-1947. The League spoke with one voice and its policy was determined by Jinnah alone. The Congress spoke with three or more voices and was subject to the strains of a more heterogeneous organization. Moreover, the Congress was inclined to negotiate in public, with a variety of statements which perforce could not follow a standard line. These factors" were to strengthen "the League's bargaining power in the last stages of the constitutional battle.")[3]

For an Undivided, Progressive India

[Nehru actively participated in the 1945 campaign for the election of Congress candidates.]

[1] M.B., pp. 303-04.
[2] M.L.P. (Vol. I), p. 170.
[3] M.B., p. 331.

India . . . is a vast country, and instead of raising . . . minor issues of Pakistan, [one] should think of planning . . . [of] increasing . . . resources and . . . the removal of unemployment. . . .

The Sikhs and the Muslims [are] brave communities and they [have] nothing to fear from the Hindus. The Congress has declared that Pakistan [is] injurious both to India as a whole and to those who [demand] it. . . . However, if the [Muslims insist] on it they [will] have it . . . The Congress [has] conceded the right of self-determination to . . . Muslims but the question [is] how the [idea of] Pakistan [is] to be enforced. [It] should [be considered] with a cool head. It [is] a great complicated problem and that [is] why the Muslim League [has] not so far defined it. . . . Even if India [is] divided, the division [will] be temporary. . . .

The Congress is strongly of the opinion that India should not be divided into units. The need of the hour, both for economic and defensive reasons, [is] that India should remain a united country. Small states in the world of tomorrow have no future. . . . The tendency of Big Powers is to form [into a] federation or confederation. India will be finished if it is divided. I stand for a South Asia Federation of India, Iraq, Iran, Afghanistan and Burma. . . .

In this age of [the] Atomic Bomb and [a] rapidly changing world, problems like that of Pakistan have no bearing and use. The real problem for various countries is not that of separation but of confederation and unification, to save themselves from destruction.[1]

Separate electorates must go. All the present communal troubles in India are due to separate electorates. . . .

Theoretically [communal settlement is] not essential. The removal of untouchability, and settlement between Hindus and Muslims would obviously make India's freedom battle easier, but it might happen that before these things are totally achieved India [will attain] freedom. The foundation of [a] progressive and stable society . . . [is] harmony, unity and social equality. Unless they [are] achieved there [will] be a constant obstruction to the running of government. If communal unity is achieved beforehand, nothing like that [will happen]. . . .

The Congress [has] its political programme—to fight for complete Independence of all irrespective of caste and creed. Its door [is] open to all communities who [believe] in its politics. This [makes] it a political body. On the other hand, the Muslim League's door [is] not open to all, but to Muslims alone. This [makes] it a religious group, attempting to function as a political group, which [gives] it [a] medieval character. . . .

[1] B.A.I., pp. 80–82.

The League can demand separation only of those areas where the Muslims are in an overwhelming majority. It must be remembered that this means division of the Punjab and Bengal. You cannot ask people of [the]areas of Bengal and the Punjab where non-Muslims are in [a] majority to go with Pakistan. Will the Punjabis or Bengalis, whether Muslims or Hindus, like their provinces, which are homogeneous linguistic units, to be divided? These are the problems to be faced. If the Muslims want separation, no power can stop them, but I myself shall try my best to convince all that separation is not in the interest of anyone, certainly not of the Muslims.[1]

In the free India to come there [will] be no Hindu raj as [the] Hindu Mahasabha [has] dreamed, nor a Muslim raj, nor a Sikh raj. It will be a people's raj—a raj of all, Hindus, Muslims, Sikhs, Christians and others—with power resting in the hands of the people as a whole. It [will] not be the raj of [a] handful . . . for this would make no more difference than would . . . replacement of a few white officials by Indians. [We shall have a raj representing the] combined rule of all the elements that make India. . . .

The Congress thinks in terms of India minus the British Government. . . . The communal bodies can hardly imagine India minus the British Government and they go to the British Government to press their separate claims.[2]

Britain's Decision to Convene Constitution-Making Body for India, and to Create Representative Executive Council

[The Viceroy, in a broadcast of September 19, 1945, authorized by the British Government, stated: "'It is the intention of His Majesty's Government to convene as soon as possible a constitution-making body, and as a preliminary step they have authorised me to undertake, immediately after the elections, discussions with representatives of the Legislative Assemblies in the Provinces to ascertain whether the proposals contained in the 1942 declaration are acceptable or whether some alternative or modified scheme is preferable.'

"His Excellency said that discussions should also be undertaken with representatives of the Indian States with a view to ascertaining in what [way] they could best take their part in the constitution-making body.

"The Viceroy added: 'His Majesty's Government have further authorised me, as soon as the results of the provincial elections are published,

[1] Ibid., pp. 78–80.
[2] B.L.J.N., pp. 176–77.

to take steps to bring into being an Executive Council which will have the support of the main Indian parties.'"[1]

7 | The Indian National Army and Military Disaffection

[The origins of the Indian National Army (I.N.A.), about which organization Nehru hesitated to speak until after the war (as indicated in his post-war remarks that follow), lay with the sixty thousand Indians who were taken prisoners in Malaya during World War II. Since Japanese soldiers had been "instructed to be lenient to the Indian community in Malaya and Singapore . . . prisoners were given inducements to transfer their allegiance. Almost immediately after the conquest of the peninsula in February 1942 the Japanese [had] created Indian Independence Leagues with prominent Indian residents as figureheads. Those prisoners who were prepared to take an oath to Japan were released and given special amenities. The movement was clearly Japanese-sponsored.

"It was not until the arrival [in Malaya] of Subhas Bose [whose allegiances have been described in previous Sections] in the summer of 1943 that the Independence Leagues acquired mass popularity. Under his fiery leadership about twenty thousand prisoners joined the newly-formed Indian National Army, many lured by the prospects of power and prestige in the 'Free India' that Bose promised his followers. On 21 October 1943 he proclaimed the Provisional Government of Free India with himself as Head of State, Commander-in-Chief of the I.N.A., War Minister and Foreign Minister. Three days later he declared war on the U.S. and Britain.

"The I.N.A.'s performance on the battlefield sowed the seeds of its rapid disintegration. The Japanese held it in reserve until the threat to their own armies became acute. In April 1944 it was thrown into the battle of Imphal and suffered a savage defeat from which it never recovered. Bose reverted to propaganda war, but enthusiasm faded rapidly. Only the inspiring leadership of the *Netaji*—the Leader—as Bose was called by his followers, kept the movement alive. With his death in an aeroplane accident in August 1945 the I.N.A. collapsed. . . .

"The I.N.A. was the most attractive deviation from the principles of non-violence which guided Indian nationalism during its Gandhian era, from 1920 to 1947. Thus, when the Government of India made known

[1] H.I.N.C. (Vol. II), p. 790.

its intention of punishing some I.N.A. officers, nationalists rallied to their defence. Nehru was no exception. 'Whatever their failing and mistakes . . . [he said] they are a fine body of young men . . . and their dominating motive was love for India's freedom.'" Pleading for generous treatment for the officers, Nehru "claimed that they 'functioned as a regular, organized, disciplined and uniformed combatant force' and were therefore entitled to treatment as prisoners-of-war. They only allied themselves with Japan to facilitate Indian freedom. He rejected the charge that Bose was a war criminal . . . and stated that he never doubted Bose's passion for Indian freedom. He welcomed the trial of alleged war criminals. . . .

"Nehru's attitude to the I.N.A. expressed the Congress mood just after V-J Day. Nor was his support confined to words. The Congress set up an I.N.A. Defence Committee consisting of some of the ablest lawyers in the country. . . [among them] Nehru. For the first time in almost thirty years he donned his legal robes and attended court. It was only a symbolic act, but thousands were roused by the sight of Nehru [and his colleagues] approaching the Red Fort where the trials were held. The Congress also appointed an I.N.A. Relief and Inquiry Committee of twelve members, including Nehru.

"By the time the trials began in November 1945 all eyes were on the I.N.A. The drama . . . was intensified by the inter-communal character of the first and most important trial. . . . A Muslim . . . a Sikh, and . . . a Hindu, were put on trial . . . for rebellion, [and for an] additional charge of abetment to murder. . . . All were convicted, but under pressure from Nehru, Gandhi and others the sentences were suspended. The I.N.A. officers were lionized throughout the country, to the horror of British (and some Indian) officers."

As for "Nehru's motives in defending the I.N.A. . . . political necessity may have been one. National pride was certainly involved. . . . Yet he was not uncritically devoted to the I.N.A. When a Muslim member of the Central Assembly urged the release of all I.N.A. personnel convicted of specific crimes, Nehru objected forcefully, saying that it consisted of morally good, bad and indifferent men."[1]

Among the attractions the I.N.A. had for many Indians was, quite naturally, its independence of, and opposition to the British. It was well trained and free of communalism. In view of its power to spread disaffection in the "regular" army in India, there were inevitably those who hoped that it—rather than the Allies—would succeed in "liberating" India, in spite of Bose's pro-Japanese, pro-Axis leanings.]

[Of the Indian National Army—after end of World War II.] There is one matter which has been paining and troubling me for sometime, but to which I have made no reference so far, because any mention of it might have been misunderstood. But now that the war has ended, there is no such reason for remaining silent. . . . This concerns the twenty thousand

[1] M.B., pp. 305-08.

or more prisoners of the so-called Indian National Army, which had been formed in Malaya and Burma. I was of the opinion three years ago, and am still of the opinion, that the leaders and others of this army had been misguided in many ways, and had failed to appreciate the larger consequences of their unfortunate association with the Japanese.

Three years ago I was asked in Calcutta what I would do if Subhas Bose led an army into India on the plea of liberating India. I replied then that I would not hesitate to resist this invasion even though I did not doubt that Subhas Bose and his Indian colleagues and followers were motivated by the desire to free India, and were in no way mere tools of the Japanese. Nevertheless, they had put themselves on the wrong side, and were functioning under . . . Japanese auspices. No person could come to India in this way or under such foreign auspices. Therefore, whatever the motive behind [such] people, they had to be resisted in India or outside.

But the situation has completely changed with the end of war. And a very large number of officers and soldiers of this Indian National Army, as it is called, are prisoners, and some of them, at least, have been executed.

Though proper information is lacking, it is reliably stated that very bad treatment is being given to them in prisons and forts, where they are kept, and many of them live in the shadow of death. I do not wish to complain to the British for the strict military rule. They could plead justification for treating with rebels in any way they like. But as an Indian, and as one representing, in this respect, the views of almost all Indians of whatever party or group, I would say that it would be [a] supreme tragedy if these officers and men are liquidated by way of punishment.

Whatever their feeling and mistakes may have been in the past, and these were serious, there can be no doubt that they are a fine body of young men taken as a whole—fine officers and fine rank and file—and that their dominating motive was love for India's freedom. At any time it would have been wrong to treat them too harshly, but at this time, when it is said that big changes are impending in India, it would be a very grave mistake, leading to far-reaching consequences, if they were treated just as ordinary rebels. The punishment given to them would, in effect, be a punishment for all India and all Indians, and a deep wound would be created in millions of hearts. In this matter, fortunately, there is no communal question, for these officers and men are Hindus, Muslims and Sikhs.

From such accounts as have come to me, it appears probable that this Indian National Army first took shape when Singapore was almost surrounded by the Japanese and most of the British army left by boats. The

Indian Army in Malaya was, therefore, left stranded by the fortunes of war, and was completely at the mercy of the Japanese.[1]

[From later letter to Sardar Baldev Singh (prominent Sikh leader)—December 25, 1946.] I am writing to you especially about the I.N.A. men still in prison. I know that the Commander-in-Chief feels rather strongly about this matter, but I should like you and him to consider the broader aspects of this question. Indeed, I should have liked to discuss this with him and, perhaps, we might be able to fix up a meeting some time later for this purpose.

Quite apart from the merits of each individual involved, and I understand there are only a very few persons in prison now, we have to consider the consequences of either keeping them in prison or of discharging them. You will remember that the matter came up [in] a resolution before the Central Legislative Assembly. Both the Congress members and the Muslim League members, as well as others would, normally speaking, have unanimously passed the resolution asking for their release. It was only because of the Commander-in-Chief's wishes in the matter that we got the resolution postponed. Naturally, in any such matter we have to give full weight to what the Commander-in-Chief feels and we do not want to go against any decision of his. He represents the Army and army discipline has to be maintained. On the other hand, it is exceedingly difficult for us to ignore a very widespread public sentiment. The result of ignoring it is bound to lead to public agitation and possibly some trouble.

The adjourned resolution will come up right at the beginning of the next Central Assembly session and our policy in regard to it should be clearly defined beforehand. You must have seen reports of a growing agitation in the Punjab among I.N.A. men demanding the release of the persons in jail. I have tried my utmost to prevent any such agitation developing, but I do not know if I shall succeed. Once any such thing happens, public attention will be drawn to it all over the country and it will be quite impossible for the Central Assembly to ignore this. The consequences will be bad both for the Army and the public.

I would earnestly request you, therefore, to place these considerations before the Commander-in-Chief. The I.N.A. people in prison have been there now for over a year and from any point of view there would be nothing abnormal about their discharge. I understand that some kind of review takes place of these cases periodically, and that January is the time

[1] B.A.I., pp. 159–60.

fixed for such a review. If, as a result of this review, the Commander-in-Chief himself decides to release them, this would be in the fitness of things and would be greatly appreciated by all concerned. It is far better that the initiative for this came from the Commander-in-Chief and that we are not hustled by public agitation in the matter.

We have so many big problems to face that our natural desire is not to allow relatively minor matters to come in our way and produce new conflicts in the public mind. If we delay a decision in the early stages, the issue will force itself upon us somewhat later. We shall not be able to ignore it, or to postpone it then. Therefore, it is highly desirable that some clear decision should be arrived at in the course of the next two or, at most, three weeks.

As I have suggested above, I shall gladly meet the Commander-in-Chief to discuss this matter.[1]

8 | Dialogue with Gandhi—Message to Youth of Ceylon—Anti-National Policy of Communist Party of India—End of 1945

[Growing evidence of concern about the freedom of other colonial peoples, and of making common cause with them, is clearly evidenced in the passages that follow.]

Continuation of Dialogue With Gandhi

[From Gandhi letter to Nehru—October 5, 1945: "The first thing I want to write about is the difference of outlook between us. If the difference is fundamental then I feel the public should also be made aware of it. It would be detrimental to our work for Swaraj to keep them in the dark. I have said that I still stand by the system of Government envisaged in *Hind Swaraj*. These are not mere words. All the experience gained by me since 1908 when I wrote the booklet has confirmed the truth of my belief. Therefore if I am left alone in it I shall not mind, for I can only bear witness to the truth as I see it. I have not *Hind Swaraj* before me as I write.

[1] A.C.B., pp. 855-56.

It is really better for me to draw the picture anew in my own words. And whether it is the same as I drew in *Hind Swaraj* or not is immaterial for both you and me. It is not necessary to prove the rightness of what I said then. It is essential only to know what I feel today. I am convinced that if India is to attain true freedom and through India the world also, then sooner or later the fact must be recognised that people will have to live in villages, not in towns, in huts, not in palaces. Crowds of people will never be able to live at peace with each other in towns and palaces. They will then have no recourse but to resort to both violence and untruth. I hold that without truth and non-violence there can be nothing but destruction for humanity. We can realise truth and non-violence only in the simplicity of village life and this simplicity can best be found in the Charkha and all that the Charkha connotes. I must not fear if the world today is going the wrong way. It may be that India too will go that way and like the proverbial moth burn itself eventually in the flame round which it dances more and more furiously. But it is my bounden duty up to my last breath to try to protect India and through India the entire world from such a doom. The essence of what I have said is that man should rest content with what are his real needs and become self-sufficient. If he does not have this control he cannot save himself. After all the world is made up of individuals just as it is [of] drops that constitute the ocean. I have said nothing new. This is a well known truth.

"But I do not think I have stated this in *Hind Swaraj*. While I admire modern science, I find that it is the old looked at in the true light of modern science which should be reclothed and refashioned aright. You must not imagine that I am envisaging our village life as it is today. The village of my dreams is still in my mind. After all every man lives in the world of his dreams. My ideal village will contain intelligent human beings. They will not live in dirt and darkness as animals. Men and women will be free and able to hold their own against any one in the world. There will be neither plague, nor cholera nor small pox; no one will be idle, no one will wallow in luxury. Everyone will have to contribute his quota of manual labour. I do not want to draw a large scale picture in detail. It is possible to envisage railways, post and telegraph offices, etc. For me it is material to obtain the real article and the rest will fit into the picture afterwards. If I let go the real thing, all else goes.

"On the last day of the Working Committee it was decided that this matter should be fully discussed and the position clarified after a two or three days session. I should like this. But whether the Working Committee sits or not I want our position *vis-à-vis* each other to be clearly understood by us for two reasons. Firstly, the bond that unites us is not only political work. It is immeasurably deeper and quite unbreakable. Therefore it i that I earnestly desire that in the political field also we should understan each other clearly. Secondly neither of us thinks himself useless. We bot live for the cause of India's freedom and we would both gladly die for i We are not in need of the world's praise. Whether we get praise or blam is immaterial to us. There is no room for praise in service. I want to liv to one hundred and twenty-five for the service of India but I must adm that I am now an old man. You are much younger in comparison and I have therefore named you as my heir. I must, however, understand my heir and my heir should understand me. Then alone shall I be content."[1]]

[Letter to Gandhi—Allahabad, October 9, 1945.] Briefly put, my view is that the question before us is not one of truth versus untruth or non-violence versus violence. One assumes as one must that true cooperation and peaceful methods must be aimed at and a society which encourages these must be our objective. The whole question is how to achieve this society and what its content should be. I do not understand why a village should necessarily embody truth and non-violence. A village, normally speaking, is backward intellectually and culturally and no progress can be made from a backward environment. Narrow-minded people are much more likely to be untruthful and violent.

Then again we have to put down certain objectives like a sufficiency of food, clothing, housing, education, sanitation, etc. which should be the minimum requirements for the country and for everyone. It is with these objectives in view that we must find out specifically how to attain them speedily. Again it seems to me inevitable that modern means of transport as well as many other modern developments must continue and be developed. There is no way out of it except to have them. If that is so inevitably a measure of heavy industry exists. How far [will that] fit in with a purely village society? Personally I hope that heavy or light industries should all be decentralised as far as possible and this is feasible now because of the development of electric power. If two types of economy exist in the country there should be either conflict between the two or one will overwhelm the other.

The question of independence and protection from foreign aggression, both political and economic, has also to be considered in this context. I do not think it is possible for India to be really independent unless she is a technically advanced country. I am not thinking for the moment in terms of just armies but rather of scientific growth. In the present context of the world we cannot even advance culturally without a strong background of scientific research in every department. There is today in the world a tremendous acquisitive tendency both in individuals and groups and nations, which leads to conflicts and wars. Our entire society is based on this more or less. That basis must go and be transformed into one of cooperation, not of isolation which is impossible. If this is admitted and is found feasible then attempts should be made to realise it not in terms of

B.O.L., p. 507.

an economy which is cut off from the rest of the world, but rather one which cooperates. From the economic or political point of view an isolated India may well be a kind of vacuum which increases the acquisitive tendencies of others and thus creates conflicts.

There is no question of palaces for millions of people. But there seems to be no reason why millions should not have comfortable up-to-date homes where they can lead a cultured existence. Many of the present overgrown cities have developed evils which are deplorable. Probably we have to discourage this overgrowth and at the same time encourage the village to approximate more to the culture of the town.

It is many years ago since I read *Hind Swaraj* and I have only a vague picture in my mind. But even when I read it twenty or more years ago it seemed to me completely unreal. In your writings and speeches since then I have found much that seemed to me an advance on that old position and an appreciation of modern trends. I was therefore surprised when you told us that the old picture still remains intact in your mind. As you know, the Congress has never considered that picture, much less adopted it. You yourself have never asked it to adopt it except for certain relatively minor aspects of it. How far it is desirable for the Congress to consider these fundamental questions, involving varying philosophies of life, it is for you to judge. I should imagine that a body like the Congress should not lose itself in arguments over such matters which can only produce great confusion in people's minds resulting in inability to act in the present. This may also result in creating barriers between the Congress and others in the country. Ultimately of course this and other questions will have to be decided by representatives of free India. I have a feeling that most of these questions are thought of and discussed in terms of long ago, ignoring the vast changes that have taken place all over the world during the last generation or more. It is thirty-eight years since *Hind Swaraj* was written. The world has completely changed since then, possibly in a wrong direction. In any event any consideration of these questions must keep present facts, forces and the human material we have today in view, otherwise it will be divorced from reality. You are right in saying that the world, or a large part of it, appears to be bent on committing suicide. That may be an inevitable development of an evil seed in civilisation that has grown. I think it is so. How to get rid of this evil, and yet how to keep the good in the present as in the past is our problem. Obviously there is good too in the present.

These are some random thoughts hurriedly written down and I fear they do injustice to the grave import of the questions raised. You will forgive me, I hope, for this jumbled presentation. Later I shall try to write more clearly on the subject. . . .

You may have seen in the papers an invitation by the President of the newly formed Indonesian Republic to me and some others to visit Java. In view of the special circumstances of the case I decided immediately to accept this invitation subject of course to my getting the necessary facilities for going there. It is extremely doubtful if I shall get the facilities, and so probably I shall not go. Java is just two days by air from India, or even one day from Calcutta. The Vice-President of this Indonesian Republic, Mohammad Hatta, is a very old friend of mine. I suppose you know that the Javanese population is almost entirely Muslim.[1]

[From Gandhi letter to Nehru—Poona, November 13, 1945: "Our talk of [yesterday] made me glad. I am sorry it could not be longer. I feel it cannot be finished in a single sitting, but will necessitate frequent meetings between us. I am so constituted that, if only I were physically fit to run about, I would myself overtake you, wherever you might be, and return after a couple of days' heart-to-heart talk with you. I have done so before. It is necessary that we understand each other well and that others also should clearly understand where we stand. It would not matter if ultimately we might have to agree to differ so long as we remained one at heart as we are today. The impression that I have gathered from our yesterday's talk is that there is not much difference in our outlook. To test this I put down below the gist of what I have understood. Please correct me if there is any discrepancy.

"(1) The real question, according to you, is how to bring about man's highest intellectual, economic, political and moral development. I agree entirely.

"(2) In this there should be an equal right and opportunity for all.

"(3) In other words, there should be equality between the town-dwellers and the villagers in the standard of food and drink, clothing and other living conditions. In order to achieve this equality today people should be able to produce for themselves the necessaries of life i.e. clothing, foodstuffs, dwellings and lighting and water.

"(4) Man is not born to live in isolation but is essentially a social animal independent and interdependent. No one can or should ride on another's back. If we try to work out the necessary conditions for such a life, we are forced to the conclusion that the unit of society should be a village, or call it a small and manageable group of people who would, in the ideal, be self-sufficient (in the matter of their vital requirements) as a unit and bound together in bonds of mutual cooperation and inter-dependence."[2]]

[1] Ibid., pp. 508–10.
[2] Ibid., pp. 511–12.

From Message to Youth of Ceylon—October 9, 1945

The great men who have come have always been rebels against the existing order. Two thousand and five hundred years ago the great Buddha proclaimed his gospel of social equality and fought against all privileges, priestly and otherwise. He was a champion of the people against all who sought to exploit them. Then came another great rebel, Christ, and then the Prophet of Arabia, who did not hesitate to break and change almost everything he found. They were realists who saw that the world had outgrown its ancient practices and customs and sought to bring it back to reality. Even so we have out-grown the creeds and rituals of yesterday and as realists we must not hesitate to discard them wherever they clash with reality. The avatars of to-day are great ideas which come to reform the world. And the idea of the day is social equality. Let us listen to it and become its instruments to transform the world and make it a better place to live in.

I may be a weak instrument capable of doing little by myself in spite of my ardent desire to do much. And you individually may be able to do little. But you and I together can do much. . . . Let our elders seek security and stability. Our quest must be adventure, but adventure in a noble enterprise which promises to bring peace to a distracted world and security and stability to the millions who have it not.

It is not those who are continually seeking security and have made a god of discretion who reform the world. It is not the sleek and shiny people having more than their share of this world's goods who are the apostles of change. The world changes and progresses because of those who are disaffected and dissatisfied and who are not prepared to tolerate the evils and injustice of things as they are. . . .

So long, therefore, as the world is not perfect, a healthy society must have the seeds of revolt in it. It must alternate between revolution and consolidation. It is the function of youth to supply this dynamic element in society; to be the standard-bearers of revolt against all that is evil and to prevent older people from suppressing all social progress and movement by the mere weight of their inertia.

Religion has in the past often been used as an opiate to dull men's desire for freedom. Kings and Emperors have exploited it for their own benefit and led people to believe in their divine right to rule. Priests and other privileged classes have claimed a divine sanction for their privileges. And with the aid of religion the masses have been told that their miseries are due to kismat or the sins of a former age.

The freedom of India is dear to all of us here. But there may be many ... who have the ordinary conveniences of life and are not hard put to it to find their daily bread. Our desire for freedom is a thing more of the mind than of the body, although even our bodies often suffer for the lack of freedom. But to the vast masses of our fellow countrymen present conditions spell hunger and deepest poverty, an empty stomach and a bare back. For them freedom is a vital bodily necessity, and it is primarily to give them food and clothing and the ordinary amenities of life that we should strive for freedom. The most amazing and terrible thing about India is her poverty. It is not a dispensation from Providence or an inevitable condition of society. India has enough or can have enough for all her children if an alien Government and some of her own sons did not corner the good things and so deprive the masses of their due.

"Poverty," said Ruskin, "is not due to natural inferiority of the poor or the inscrutable laws of God, or drink, but because others have picked their pockets."

Have great ideals before you and do not lower them by ignoble compromise. Look deep down to where the millions toil in field and factory and look across the frontiers of India to where others like you are facing problems similar to yours. Be national, the sons and daughters of your ancient motherland working for her liberation; and be international, members of the Republic of Youth, which knows no boundaries or frontiers or nationalities and works for the liberation of the world from all thraldom and injustice.

"To do great things," said a Frenchman many years ago, "a man must live as if he had never to die."

None of us can evade death, but youth, at least, does not think of it. Old men work for the span of years that still remain for them; the young work for eternity.[1]

On Anti-National Policy of Communist Party of India— October 23, 1945

The cause of Communism and the name of Russia have suffered most at the hands of the Communist Party of India. . . .

When the second great war started, the Congress agreed to join hands with the anti-Fascist forces, provided the national freedom of the country was assured. This demand was not a bargain, because as the situation

[1] B.L.J.N., pp. 186–88.

stood, neither the Congress nor its biggest leaders could have organised the national forces against Fascism without the assurance of National Independence. The Communist Party was the one party that tried to do what the Congress could not do, namely, organize the national forces without the assurance of Independence, and it failed.

The role of the Communist Party of India . . . has made all Nationalist India its . . . [opponent]. Opposition to the Indian Communists [is] not merely political. The whole nation [is] angry with them. When lakhs of [Indians] staked their all for the country's cause . . . the Communists were in the opposite camp, which cannot be forgotten. The common man associates the Communist Party with Russia and Communism. But the actions of the Communist Party of India have prejudiced both Russia and Communism. We don't want to spoil relations with Russia, with whom we are looking forward [to] closer relations when India becomes free. . . .

From the inception of the [Communist] Party till 1935, it had been doing propaganda against the Congress from underground. In 1936 the Party changed its policy to one of [a] joint front with the Congress. It worked within the Congress for three years. When the Congress offered individual civil disobedience, the Communists criticised [it] for not taking a stronger course of action against . . . British power. But when Russia joined the war against Germany, the Imperialist War became an object of attack. The Congress Organisation began to be disturbed from within. The Communists played against the Congress policy. But the Congress [is] even now following the least offensive policy towards the Communists. . . .

No other political organisation would deal so leniently with its opponents. . . . For the Congress, National Independence [is] the prime objective, while the Communists [give] primary importance to other issues. The last three years have been a clear indicator as to where a particular person or organisation [stands] in relation to the struggle for National Independence. It is no use fighting a battle of words when the issues have been clearly decided in action. The Communist Party itself has brought on . . . its present position. No one should be misguided by the blooming name of Russia and Communism uttered by the Communist Party.[1]

End of 1945

[Bombay, November 12, 1945.] It is the duty of every Indian who is a slave to revolt and carry on the revolt till he is a free man. Every country

[1] E.I.P., pp. 367–68.

which is dominated by another nation must revolt against that authority. I am using the world "revolt" after great consideration and thought. The question of when and how a subject country should revolt should be carefully considered. A nation, which has not sufficient strength to rise against an alien authority, is a dead nation. It is our duty first and foremost to rebel against that foreign authority which rules over us.

We have been following the path of revolution during the last twenty-five years openly. Before that period we had talks about revolt, but all the talks were conducted under cover. The first revolt against the British authority in India was in 1857 and thereafter there were small and sporadic fights.

When we recall these incidents in the history of our national struggle for freedom, it becomes increasingly clear that India is not a dead nation. During the last twenty-five years we have seen various phases in the struggle for freedom. These included [the] Satyagraha, civil disobedience and Khilafat movements. [Which does not mean, therefore,] that we should bow our heads to our enemy even while we follow the lead given by our great leader Mahatma Gandhi. The issue of freedom assumes greater importance day after day. After all, the strength of this great country of four hundred millions is not negligible. It is not an easy task to lead the millions of our countrymen on the path of revolution. . . .

It is useless to say that we have not committed mistakes during the last twenty-five years since we raised the banner of revolt. But it is true that we have never allowed the flag to be dishonoured or lowered. It is, therefore, proper that we are proud of it. To err is human and in every country there are weak-hearted people. But the real issue is to judge how far we have contributed to the real strength of the nation.

We have kept the flag of revolution in our hands firmly during the last twenty-five years and it will remain high till our country attains her independence.[1]

[The dropping of the atomic bomb on Japan in August, 1945, had aroused widespread distress throughout the Pacific area. In India, with its respect for Gandhian non-violence, there was special concern about the dangers of atomic warfare.]

[From Press Conference—November 13, 1945: In answer to question about the menace of the atom bomb.] [The bomb] cannot be checked effectively unless the fundamental causes which create friction and war

[1] B.A.I., pp. 246–47.

are removed. So long as these causes exist, there will be war. So long as
[there are] wars ... they will use the atom bomb, or something worse
than that. ... [The] revolution [caused by discoveries having to do with
atomic energy] can either destroy human civilisation, or take it up to
unheard-of-levels.

[In answer to question about nationalization of industries.] There is
always a great difficulty in answering [such a] question, because [the]
answer ... depends [upon] who owns the state.[1]

[In December, 1945 the Attlee Government announced that a parliamentary delegation was to depart from London to make a fresh investigation
of the Indian political situation.]

9 | On Development of Indian Literature
as a Uniting Force: Address at P.E.N.
Symposium, 1945

You have done me the honour of making me a Vice-President of the
Indian Centre of the P.E.N., and I deem it a privilege. But you know very
well that my work has been in another direction, and that other activities
have absorbed my attention far too much. I am not untouched by "the
spiritual paralysis of politics" [as it has been phrased]. And yet I have
sometimes strayed into other fields by accident. ... By accident I became a
writer, and so found my way into the P.E.N. ...

The subject [to be discussed] is: "The Development of ... Indian
Literatures as a Uniting Force." It is a fascinating subject, and I wish I
knew more about it except that there is so much to know if one really is to
deal with it in any proper style, which is truly beyond me.

The questions that strike me in this connection are these:—Are
Indian literatures a uniting force or not? Do we take it for granted that
they are a uniting force or that they are going to be a uniting force? A
superficial survey would, I am afraid, tend to show that they create or
might create greater provincialism and erect new barriers to unity. As you

[1] Ibid., pp. 245, 246.

know, one of the questions to which frequent reference is made nowadays is the so-called "language question" of India. When we talk about the "language question," we do not refer to the dozen or so languages—the principal languages—of India, but rather to Hindi and Urdu, which are one language with different literary forms drawing inspiration from the same fountain-head. That is the language question! There is hardly any cause, so far as I know, for any conflict between the different languages in their different spheres; but conflict appears sometimes with regard to Hindi or Urdu. . . .

However, it is interesting to trace the development of Indian languages. For long years, long centuries, they formed a happy joint family, very much dependent on their parent language, Sanskrit,—so dependent, indeed, that they did not grow at all. Later, Persian came into the field, superficially on the top. Persian also affected our languages, but it was a restraining force which would not allow them to grow, since learned people then thought it beneath their dignity to write or speak at select assemblies like this in any language but Sanskrit or Persian. If anything worth while was to be written, surely it must be written in Sanskrit, not in Hindi or Bengali or some other dialect; and to some extent that happened later with regard to Persian. People talked or wrote in Sanskrit or Persian. Of course, only a very small circle could talk those languages, and that is why, I suppose, this divorce between that small circle at the top talking or writing in Sanskrit or Persian and the vast numbers talking in other languages, more living languages, prevented the growth of these latter, and the growth also of our modern literatures.

Now when I say that Sanskrit and Persian were a restraining influence, please do not imagine that I am condemning Sanskrit or Persian at all. Sanskrit is of course something of which every Indian is infinitely and rightly proud. Sanskrit really has performed a great unifying task throughout the ages, and as a unifying force it has obviously been the greatest instrument of the continuity of our culture for thousands of years. There is therefore no question whatever of my condemning Sanskrit.

Persian came late in the field of development of the Indian languages, and yet it played a fairly important part in later centuries, affecting almost all our provincial languages considerably—and thus Persian too became a part of our national heritage. In this way Persian also became a unifying force, at any rate for the upper classes, though not so much for the masses.

Sanskrit, then, pre-eminently, and Persian to some extent, have played a great part in Indian literary life. . . .

However that may be, the fact we should remember is that our provincial languages were controlled by these two aristocratic languages, by Sanskrit especially; and it took a tremendous lot of time for the provincial languages to grow. Gradually, by force of circumstances, out of the hundreds of original dialects, Hindi developed, Bengali developed, Marathi and Gujarati and other languages developed. In the South, of course, there was a different family of languages, which, though different, became through Sanskrit intimately associated with the other languages of India,—and so we have now about a dozen principal languages of India.

One of the remarkable instances of the development of languages in India is provided by Urdu, which grew up and exhibited the interplay of . . . various forces that flowed in India during the last two hundred years, and became essentially an Indian language, with probably 80% of words that are common to it and Hindi, but of course with a number of Persian words as well. The main difference between Hindi and Urdu is not so much in the vocabulary but in their respective literary forms. The Hindi literary form has been, I suppose, derived directly from Sanskrit— I speak with diffidence in this matter—and all the metaphors and similes and ways of thought and expression have been likewise derived from Sanskrit, and also from the common background of life in India. Thus the literary and other forms of Hindi are Indian no doubt, for no outside influence has permeated them, but they are very old, and long after they have ceased to have any meaning, some of them are still being used.

Urdu, the same language as Hindi with almost the same vocabulary, with a few words thrown in from outside, developed as an entirely different literary form. Its ways of expression were not derived from Indian life as a rule; its similes and metaphors were derived from Central Asia, or the Caucasus or Iran, and today in our colloquial Hindustani or Hindi so many of these expressions, similes and metaphors, which are not really Indian in origin, have become very common.

As I have said already, the language question mainly deals with Hindi and Urdu. Why there should be so much argument and so much heat and passion, I do not know. But, of course, it is hardly a question of language. It has become a question of selection of a common language for India, and that is why, perhaps, there is so much heat and passion. It has become a political question in a way, or rather, in a way politics affects the question very much.

The result is obvious. In Hindi and Urdu we have formed certain literary devices, or have certain sophisticated patterns, which attract those who are orthodox. But these devices and patterns have lost their vitality or popular appeal, and must progressively grow more and more stale in spite of a certain beauty in them, because those forms are wholly unconnected with the life of the common people. They remain the same, oblivious to the changing environment. That, of course, applies not only to Hindi and Urdu but to so many aspects of our life. We are sticking to ancient forms so much in our social life, sometimes without any perceptible sense in those forms, that some of our activities are a puzzle even to people just outside our province in our own country. And language, after all, is something which reflects the life of the people. If the life of the people is confined to a narrow circle of old-fashioned forms, then inevitably their language also is bound to be like that. And it is no use blaming the standard of this or that language, if that language became isolated from the life of the people. I refer only to the literary language, because [our] popular languages ... [have] revealed their vitality in popular songs and the rest. Though these popular songs were quite vital in their own way, they had no chance of gaining importance in the centres of learned people for, say, a hundred years. In our popular languages we find folk songs, ballads, poems, etc., while ... prose works [have been] limited to Sanskrit or Persian. Every serious work was, in fact, written in Sanskrit or Persian. But the popular languages flourished among the common people and in the households. So this divorce between the language of the common people and the language of the learned persons has had, I suppose, a very harmful effect on the growth of our languages. That divorce, in a sense, has had its harmful effect, not only on [our] languages, but on life itself. Many of our ills in India, I think, are probably the result of that. Well, anyhow these popular languages grew, in spite of all the obstructions and the various influences restricting their growth, because life has to grow. But they grew so slowly, and in fact much of their growth has taken place in poetry, in which some of our languages are very rich. Almost all the growth of ... our Indian languages has taken place during the last two hundred years or less—here, again, I am subject to correction. . . .

Now the growth of these provincial languages has not, so far as I know, tended at all towards disunity. To some extent, no doubt, it may have accentuated a certain provincialism, or given a little push to provincial culture. A Bengali is very rightly proud of his Bengali language, Gujaratis of their Gujarati, Maharashtrians of Marathi, and so on. They have their legitimate prides, but I do not think that there is any conflict between this feeling and the larger feeling of national identity, because the whole basis of India's thought, as I know it, has been never a mere regimentation of people's ideas, but of unity plus diversity, plus variety. Therefore the two do not conflict, because each province, each linguistic area, taking pride in its own past cultural achievements, realizes that it is but part of a larger whole. In the past, the cultural unit of India was maintained, not only by one language, Sanskrit, but also by a special philosophy which was common to the whole of India. The old philosophical outlook was later on superseded to some extent at least, and therefore I feel that it is not now strong enough to be a unifying force to the extent, to the degree it was in the past. Other things have happened. Possibly, the unifying force today would be not so much national but something more international, something which is common to all nations, —which, again, would not mean the submergence of the national identity in its entirety, but rather the two existing together.

I do not personally see any need to answer the questions which I put at the beginning. I do not see anything tending towards disunity or towards ... essential separatism in the growth of provincial languages in India. There is also another factor to consider. In fact, if I may quote the instance of Rabindranath Tagore, it is extraordinary how a man like Tagore who wrote in the Bengali language influenced every other language in India, Hindi certainly, and also the other languages. It shows how ... cultural giants grow across provincial barriers. If one language grows, it surely helps others to grow. It does not hinder the others. It does not come into conflict with them. That is my chief grievance with those people who fight and argue about Hindi and Urdu. I have no doubt in my mind that if Hindi grows rich it will help Urdu, and if Urdu grows rich it will help Hindi.

I am quite sure at the same time that Hindi and Urdu are bound to grow nearer to each other, not because you and I may like it or not like it, but because circumstances are forcing us to develop them as a common language. It seems to me a sheer waste of energy that [the] champions of Urdu should so strongly object to Hindi influence, and *vice versa.*

Therefore, I do feel that [the] renaissance of our provincial languages that has taken place is a thing which helps towards unification, and can never be a destructive factor in India. But apart from the language question, it depends again on the background of politics as they develop in India, because languages will be affected by them. For example, there is the Pakistan controversy. Suppose, for a moment, that Urdu becomes the official language in Pakistan and Hindi in the rest of India. If that leads to the destruction of Indian unity, it is not the fault of the languages but of certain arguments on the political front that are taking place in India. Languages by themselves, I am convinced, are not a destructive factor, not at all a factor leading to disunity, partly because the languages are akin to each other and the growth of one helps to build up the others, and anyhow they are not going to hinder each other's growth.

Apart from this question of politics behind them, ultimately it all depends mainly on whether we have some kind of a common philosophy, common ethical standards, common artistic standards. If they differ greatly, then those divergences may show themselves in our languages and may lead to unfortunate consequences. If there are vital differences or fundamental differences in our philosophy of life, then the barriers between nations will remain high. If we have certain standards of conduct in common, we can get along amicably, even if we may differ physically, spiritually and artistically. If not, I can only guess what the future is going to be. I am not ... competent to know for certain which will triumph, the good in life or the evil in life.

One thing more ...: in literature everything depends on how much freedom there is to function. Freedom of thought, freedom of expression, freedom of occupation, and freedom generally to function as we believe, are all essential for the growth of literature. The slowness in the development of many of our languages is largely due to the absence of political freedom. Lack of political freedom comes in the way of all progress. But even in a politically free India, if there is no freedom of speech and expression, [this] can only be an obstruction in the way of the growth of our languages and it may even lead to unhealthy and disuniting forces growing up. Restrictions on freedom of speech and expression will prevent the language from affecting the mind of the people at large. That means that you are creating barriers to ... self-expression, that you are separating some people at the top from the vast masses at the bottom and thereby creating a select coterie which functions in an artificial atmosphere. There is nothing more dangerous than this idea of authority. Personally, I rebel against that idea in all its phases. In this connection, I was surprised at the whole body of the P.E.N. standing up when a princely message was read this morning, even though it may be in accordance with the traditions of the State.

So it seems to me that the very essence of our growth is this essential freedom, political freedom, because ... other types of freedom depend on this. [In addition to which] the words that we use, the language that we use, should keep in touch with changing conditions. We are a conservative people and we still stick to false values. This sticking to outmoded values obstructs the growth of one's culture. It has already done us immense harm. Sanskrit lost its popularity because it did not keep in touch with the life of the people. One reason why provincial languages and literatures are more vital today than they were before is because they went back to the life of the people and drew inspiration from it. That, again, is another reason why they should develop as a uniting force, because the life of the people in India, taken as a whole, does not differ greatly. The difference—such as it is—is at the top. If you once go down to the large masses, you come to something that is common,—whether you express it in this language or in that language does not matter.

Well, now I leave it to more learned persons to continue this discussion.[1]

[1] I.W.C., pp. 34-42.

PART NINE
1946 : Year of Decision

[To Lord Pethick-Lawrence, British Secretary of State for India and Member of 1946 British Cabinet Mission.] Do not forget that if you and I come to an agreement, you are laying down a burden and I am picking it up.[1]

*

At no stage during the years in which the Congress has fought His Majesty's Government has Congress preached hatred against the British people. Even now we can go about quite freely because our struggle has not been against individuals, but against British rule.[2]

*

[At the height of Congress dispute with Muslim League, 1946.] Mr Jinnah complains that I am out to create new situations. I *am* out to create new situations.[3]

*

Sardar Patel: "There is only one genuinely nationalist Muslim in India—Jawaharlal."[4]

*

All of us, to whatever religion we may belong, are equally children of India, with equal rights, privileges and obligations.[5]

[1] Quoted in S.N., p. 111.
[2] Based on V.I. (Jan. 1947), inside cover.
[3] Quoted in M.J.N., p. 490.
[4] Quoted in M.B., p. 315.
[5] Based on B.L.J.N., p. 188.

I | Developments, Early 1946: Cross-Section of Statements

[1946 was to be a year of fateful decisions. During the period immediately following the war it became overwhelmingly evident that the power of the British Empire was rapidly waning. In India, as in other areas of South and South-East Asia, it was equally clear that the desire for independence had been growing at such an accelerated rate that freedom from foreign rule would have to be granted without further delay; that the principles enunciated in the Atlantic Charter must be as fully applicable to the awakening East as to the West.

With respect to India, in particular, Britain was finding it difficult to maintain her dominant position, if for no other reason than a financial one.

Nehru's words of the period, while echoing his dreams of earlier years, adumbrated also the manner in which he was subsequently to work more directly with leaders of other nations in the Middle East, South and South-East Asia, as well as Africa; how, in turn, the subjected peoples of those areas were more and more openly to make common cause with India. (It should be recalled further that, in 1946, United Nations membership was predominately European and American. Asians and Africans, whose countries were still in search of independence, were virtually without a voice in the council of nations. The latter groups were increasingly drawn together both in order to be heard, and in the hope of jointly improving their lot.)

Nehru's dicta of 1946 continued to reflect his prodigious impatience with imperialism, militarism, dictatorship, aggression; with the world-wide failure to eliminate racial prejudice, economic inequities, international tensions. He was no more in favor of efforts to maintain the *tatus quo* in reactionary fashion outside of India, than within its confines. Freedom and world-order remained twin and paramount goals.

In February, 1946—as will be further elaborated—Britain began to ake certain important steps that, at long last, were to pave the way for ndian independence.

In Congress' first Presidential election since 1940, Nehru was elected 'resident for the fourth time, on May 9, 1946. On July 6, Gandhi tated: "I told Jawaharlal that he must wear the crown of thorns for he sake of the nation and he has agreed."[1]

M.B., p. 314.

In 1946, famine again hovered over India.

In the sections that follow, more detailed documentation than has hitherto been provided is included, in part because Nehru wrote less himself at this time than in previous periods; in part because of the complexity of the events described, and their crucial relationship to the evolution of a finally independent, although divided India.]

[Message to Japan—January, 1946.] I am asked by the Japanese news-papers to give . . . plain advice to Japan, especially [to say how] I think Japan [can] gain [the] respect and confidence of [other] nations. That is not easy [to do], for it is always difficult and often presumptuous to advise . . . other nations and peoples, and it becomes still more difficult to advise those . . . [who have been] stricken down by defeat and misfortune. Also I cannot speak for the United Nations as a whole, or for the Four Big Powers who dominate the councils of [those] nations. Perhaps I can have some insight into the mind of India, and to a lesser extent into the mind of Asia, and so I shall say a few words as an Indian.

There was a time when Indians looked up to the Japanese and admired their great achievements. Then there came a time when the Japanese began [to] resemble too closely . . . the aggressive imperialist powers of the West, and instead of being the champions of Asiatic freedom, their lust for domination and imperialist expansion led them to the conquest of Asiatic countries. Korea was deprived of her freedom, and China, in the birth-pangs of new freedom, was continually harassed and threatened and later attacked. All this changed India's attitude to Japan, and the old admiration gave place to resentment. Our sympathies flowed to China and other countries attacked by Japan.

Now Japan has met with disaster in her imperialistic adventure—[a] fate which will befall every nation to-day which aims at world domination Both world considerations and narrow national interests must induce Japan to give up her old dreams of conquest and expansion. Nor should she think in terms of revenge, for there is no end to the cycle of hatred and revenge. The Japanese have shown extraordinary qualities which were turned in a wrong direction. They must now use them to build anew on sounder foundations; they must reject militarism and imperialism and make of Japan a country of free democratic institutions, which threatens none, and is feared by none. They must build their economic order on the basis of equality and equal opportunities for all their people and not aim at economic domination of any other country. Thus will they create afresh [a] prosperous and progressive Japan on friendly terms with her neighbour members of the Asiatic family, as well as the world brotherhood of nations. Japan has caused deep injury to China both materially and spiritually and, therefore, Japan's special task must be to gain [the] goodwill of the Chinese people. Ultimately the peace of the Far East depends on co-operation of the Chinese and . . . Japanese, and such co-operation can only be based on freedom. If this policy is followed by Japan, she will not only gradually heal the deep scars of war, but will also cure deeper spiritual injuries caused to herself and to others, and bridge the gulf which now separates her from other nations. India and other countries of Asia will outlive yesterday's anger and resentment, and join hands with Japan in the furtherance of Asiatic freedom and co-operation, within the larger framework of world peace.[1]

[Message to United Nations—New Delhi, January 21, 1946.] If the Axis Powers had won the war, their victory would have been disastrous for freedom and democracy throughout the world. . . . However . . . the present victory of the United Nations has thus far been a victory in war only, and not in peace. It remains to be seen what . . . [it] makes of peace. While there are some elements of hope, there are obvious reasons for grave misgivings. What is happening, not only in [the] higher councils of the Big Powers, but also in Indonesia and Indo-China [is not conducive to] peace and freedom.

The people [who have waged] and ultimately won [the] war thought too little of the real aims and objects which they loudly proclaimed. Many of them wanted the "status quo" to continue. But that, of course, never happens, and so we have a conflict [that still goes on]. . . . Big problems await solution, and real peace is as far away as ever. . . .

I believe that if the leaders of the United Nations had pursued a different course, the duration of the last war would have been lessened considerably, and the consequences to-day would have been infinitely better for the whole world. That chance was lost at a cost of millions of lives and infinite suffering. Other chances are [appearing] now, and the big question is whether they will be seized or not, and whether they will be considered with vision and judgment, or in [the] discredited [terms] of power politics.

The age of atomic energy is upon us, and there is no escape from [the] alternatives—a solution of . . . world problems based on freedom everywhere and a world order, or world conflict and destruction on a colossal scale. To put it in another way, there will be either a free association of

B.A.I., pp. 383-84.

nations in the world, or the domination by one power of a shattered world. . . .

I am convinced that co-ordination of various countries in the Middle East, India and South-East Asia is not only possible, but exceedingly likely in the future. The question of an Asiatic Federation is perhaps premature, but some kind of closer association between these countries is necessary, both for defence and trade purposes. In Egypt in the West, and Indonesia in the East, there is to-day a common feeling which is bringing them nearer to each other. For the moment [the feeling has to do] chiefly with the attainment of freedom, but other questions are looming up in the present-day context of [the] world, which affect [both nations] intimately; to some extent jointly. . . .

[The] closer union of a number of Asian countries will be in no way anti-European or anti-anything else.

European aggression, as such, is fast fading out. All of us stand for an international order, and, if proper international order is established, [involving] free nations, there will be no need for any smaller federations. [Until such a time arrives, the] long-oppressed nations of Asia will inevitably seek to protect themselves by holding together as far as possible, and presenting a joint front in the councils of the world. . . . [Even now Asia] is rather ignored in the United Nations . . . although it is apparent that [it] is going to play a big part in [the] future. . . .

I have suggested that a conference be held by various Asian countries, as well as Egypt, to consider common problems. The best place for this conference will be India, which is centrally situated, and which in future is bound to play an important role. . . .

The problems before the countries of Asia [are] more or less similar— defence, getting rid of feudal structures, and establishment of democratic institutions; development of industry and agriculture, and rapid raising of the standard of living of the masses. In the solution of these problems we should gladly co-operate with the rest of the world, and take [its] help, but that help cannot be accepted if there is any element of domination [in] it.[1]

[Political friendship—February 10, 1946.] Of course I expect a peaceful and friendly settlement with Britain. If such a settlement is reached, India's relations with Great Britain will naturally be closer, as there are

[1] B.I.S.J.N. (Vol. I), pp. 384–85.

so many ties already developed between our two peoples, some good, many bad....

But ... such friendly relations can only grow between independent countries which can co-operate with each other. Otherwise the past will pursue us and poison our relations....

From no point of view can India fit into [a current] Dominion Status pattern....

Days of national isolation have gone forever. It is clear from the point of view of defence, and [the] future progress [of] industry, trade and communications, that the mutual good relations of the countries of [the] Middle East, as well as of South East Asia, will largely depend on India. In this I include Australia and New Zealand.

I firmly believe that China will ... in the near future, [be] a strong, powerful State, closely associated with India, and playing an important [role] in the Pacific region....

Russia being a neighbour, we shall presumably have closer contact [with her]. The United States can play a great part in India's industrial development.[1]

[February 10, 1946.] A clear declaration of the recognition of India's independence is vital for any constitutional solution of Indian problems. Transfer [of power] should be made to Indian representatives, or the constitution-making body [that] will come into existence.... The constitution which this body will frame must be accepted as final.

For the interim period, while the [Indian] Constitution is being [created] ... [I envisage] a [Central Government], as responsible as possible, to carry on the administration, with the help of ... democratic conventions, and without [a] Viceroy's veto....

Pakistan cannot be discussed in the present atmosphere. Mr. Jinnah's demand [for Partition] is completely impossible.... The Muslims, [however], and other minorities [have] been offered [all kinds of safeguards by the Congress—] cultural, [legal] and others.[2]

[February 15, 1946.] There [is] no intermediate way between Swaraj and foreign domination: either [the] alien Government [of Britain] should quit India, or we [shall] perish....

India is on the threshold of tremendous changes. She is restless and fully prepared to wrest power from unwilling hands....

[1] B.I.S.J.N. (Vol. I), p. 356.
[2] Based on ibid., pp. 356–57.

On the one hand, India is gaining in strength and, on the other, Britain is growing weaker. When Britain is confronted with her own difficult problems, how can she be expected to solve the mighty problems facing the people of our country—the problems of hunger and unemployment.

The British administration to-day ... is unfit even to maintain its police raj, [which] knows one duty, that is, of firing on people in India. The tehsildars, the deputy collectors, patwaris and all the relics of the vanishing order cannot be expected to solve problems of poverty and unemployment, and the dozens of other problems, without the active co-operation of the teeming millions of our country.

The truth of the matter is that the British Government, as it is to-day, is utterly unfit to rule India, and there can be no peace in our country unless we achieve freedom.

In the context of the problems of hunger, want, and sickness, [where] does the communal problem fit in?

When we are [involved] with the work of rebuilding our devastated country, shall we sit down to consider what [should] be the proportion of Hindu and Muslim engineers, or should we entrust the work to those who will work with efficiency, be they Muslims, Hindus or Christians, or any other community of India? We have to look at [our] Indian problems from this angle.

To-day [our major problems have to do with] achieving independence, and ... building the country anew. Can the Muslim League or the [Hindu] Mahasabha tackle these problems? I stagger to think that these problems do not even figure in their programme: they have not given any serious consideration to them. I ask what they have done during the last thirty years towards solving these problems, except [to raise] a hue and cry.

It is easy for the Muslim League and the Mahasabha to sow seeds of discord, but I warn them that the results [will] be disastrous for the whole of India. Can Hindus or Muslims rule the country on communal lines? ...

The country can no longer tolerate the present state of affairs.[1]

[1] Ibid., pp. 334–36.

Mounting Tensions: Naval Mutiny—
Acts of Violence in Bombay and Related
2 Problems—Announcement of Cabinet
Mission

Mounting Tensions : Naval Mutiny

[During the winter months of 1945–46, tensions in India had been steadily increasing. By 1946 there was a mounting wave of student demonstrations, strikes and violence. The position of Congress leaders was becoming more overtly intransigent. Not only had Indian National Army (I.N.A.) activities caused manifold difficulties for the British, but so also had growing disaffection in the armed forces.

Early in 1946, the Royal Air Force (R.A.F.) mutinied in Calcutta, as well as elsewhere in India and the Middle East. Such disruptive actions "were followed by hunger strikes in the R.I.A.F. (Royal Indian Air Force) and minor cases of indiscipline in the R.I.N. (Royal Indian Navy)". On February 18, 1946 an explosive incident occurred that was to have far-reaching consequences: a naval mutiny in Bombay. During the ensuing five days, both the leading base of the R.I.N., and Bombay itself "presented the appearance of a minor battlefield, though there was little bloodshed.

"There were strong political overtones to the mutiny. Congress and Muslim League flags were flown from ... 'captured' ships and shore establishments. Left-wing parties called for a 'union of Hindus and Muslims at the barricades'. Communist influence was evident in the Sailors' Central Strike Committee. Congress leaders sympathized with the sailors' grievances but opposed their reliance on the Communists and the talk of violence. ... The mutiny spread to other naval bases. ...

"Genuine grievances were at the root of the mutinies, along with the restlessness common to all servicemen at the end of a war. However, there can be little doubt that the loss of 'face' by the Government of India as a result of the I.N.A. affair contributed to the belief in the armed forces generally that mutiny was not a serious offence."[1]

The British Government already had intimated in December, 1945 (see Part Eight) that more decisive steps must be taken to review the Indian political situation. But, as Brecher points out, it seems more than a mere coincidence that one day after the outbreak of the mutiny—on February 19, 1946—it was announced that a fresh British Cabinet Mission would be sent to India.]

[1] M.B., p. 308.

7*

On Acts of Violence in Bombay and Related Problems

What has happened [in Bombay] ... clearly demonstrates how anti-social elements in a vast city like Bombay exploit a situation. In every free country there is this problem, but in our country [it] is complicated by our fight for freedom. The time has come when we should direct our energies along the channel of constructive work. What happened in Bombay shows that the constructive tendency is lacking. . . .

For the past twenty-five years the people of India have made tremendous sacrifices in the cause of winning our national independence. Our freedom is near at hand today. We have all the virtues for winning our freedom, but I confess that we lack the discipline which is essential for a free country.[1]

[From Press Conference—as reported March 1, 1946. Nehru commented upon "naval ratings"—one of the "overt" causes of the February demonstrations in Bombay, generally referred to as a "mutiny".]

I understand in official army and any other parlance there is no such thing as a strike. Everything is a mutiny. If two persons sign a letter together, it is a mutiny. A letter of protest or any kind of joint letter, I believe, officially ... is considered a mutiny. [It] is a matter for people who know the English language to determine what is the right word. I do not see why we should worry ourselves as to what a particular word means or does not mean. But it is obvious that where rules are so rigid that even a simple joint protest, however respectfully worded ... might be ... considered a [mutiny], it becomes impossible for any kind of constitutional or semi-constitutional or any other action to be indulged in which ... is not a [mutiny]. Either one does nothing at all or one, in official language, mutinies.

I understand ... that ... instructions have been issued, which can only be interpreted to mean that there is going to be a great deal of victimisation ... and not only victimisation but a measure of terrorisation. That is, ratings ... in the navy are being ... picked out for some kind of action against them. Secondly, where there is not even evidence for that, it is suggested something should still be done so as to have an opportunity of punishing people against whom there is [no] evidence, with the object, of course, of frightening and terrorising others. Now that kind of course of action obviously is in direct conflict both in spirit and letter with the assurances given in the Assembly. . . .

[1] M.J.N., p. 314.

Such a course of action is bound to have repercussions not only [on] public opinion but on the armed forces in the country. It shows ... quite an extraordinary lack of foresight from even the narrowest point of view.

As to what the Congress [proposes] to do in case of such victimisation ... we ask for a public trial. Where there is ... to be a trial, it should be public. Secondly the Congress proposes to organise [the] defence of those who are being tried.

That [is] as far as [I can] ... see for the moment in regard to these matters. ...

[I do] ... not quite know how things [will] shape themselves and what the Defence Consultative Committee should do. But ... this question like any other question [can] not be [simply] isolated from both the larger question of the army and its grievances and the still larger question of the political future of India.

Most of our difficulties ... arise from the fact that we are in a period of intense transition. It is absurd for high army authorities to continue to think in terms of some years back—[in] pre-war terms—when the army was isolated from the people and was a relatively small force—a small professional force. They will have to revise their outlook completely and realise that the present army, navy and air force are of a different calibre, and further that the Indian public is greatly interested in them. ...

Obviously there was tremendous sympathy in the city of Bombay for ... naval ratings. ... A great deal of excitement has been caused by gunfire which was more or less harmless ... but ... which made people think that a pitched battle was being fought in the Bombay harbour, which it was not. When there is excitement, it is very easy to put a spark to [it]. There are all manner of groups in the city, who immediately rush in to exploit such a situation, to the advantage of their own respective groups [which] call themselves revolutionary [but which] cannot function normally in ... public, because their revolution is of the eighteenth century variety.

The Communists ... consider themselves ... very revolutionary ... but I consider them counter-revolutionary. ... Far from being revolutionary [they] are actually conservative.

["Should not the city of Bombay observe a hartal in response to the Royal Indian Naval ratings appeal?"] The R.I.N. Central Strike Committee had no business to issue such an appeal. ... Fifteen men, however much I [may] like them, knowing nothing about the situation in Bombay, in India or the world; [having gone] over the heads of everyone in Bombay [—and all recognised political parties—have issued] ... an appeal that there should be a hartal. The obvious course open to the Strike Committee was not to issue such an appeal to the three million citizens of Bombay over the heads of everyone in Bombay, but to meet the recognized leaders, and put before them their case and ask whether a hartal was feasible. ... [It] was for the political leaders—be they Congress or ... League—to decide, after taking various factors into consideration.

["Was it not necessary to adopt a 'revolutionary programme of significance'?"] A revolutionary programme of significance does not mean the breaking of heads ... [the] destruction of property. My conception of a revolutionary programme of significance is one aimed at increasing the standard of living of the people of India, within a space of five or ten years. If a programme toward this end is drawn up, and practical methods [are] suggested to implement it, I could call it a "revolutionary programme of significance". But if some people think that a "revolutionary programme of significance" means merely the breaking of heads, I would emphatically say that the breaking of heads does not necessarily mean that a new social or economic order will follow.

[On underground activity.] During the last two or three years when effective functioning was difficult, one can understand other kinds of functioning. ... But when there are numerous avenues of functioning in the open, it is absurd to function in secret or otherwise, because it really means you are not functioning in secret from ... Governmental authority. You are functioning in secret from your people and no mass movements are built up by underground methods. ...

Generally speaking ... I do not approve of underground movements at all, except when [they offer] the only way of action. Underground movements strike at the root of mass action. ...

[Referring to the underground movement in the West.] The background of the whole of the European revolutionary movement [is] one of underground activity. But in India conditions [are] different, chiefly because our whole method of action is different. [The] method of action [involved here] may be good or bad. But it does permit of [an] activity of a type ... not ... tolerated in Europe by ... governmental authorities. On the whole, underground activity in Europe has not achieved any remarkable success. In the case of Russia it is completely different. Very extraordinary circumstances preceded the Russian revolution. But we cannot duplicate [such circumstances] anywhere else. ...

The best way of combating communalism [is] by placing greater stress on economic issues.

[On non-violence.] There [is] considerable confusion in the country about violence and non-violence. . . . I can only express my opinion for the moment, but it may represent many other people's opinion also. . . . I think . . . in our fight for freedom today as yesterday, non-violence, the general non-violent technique . . . is the only desirable technique, both in regard to internal conditions in India and in regard to world conditions. It seems to me obvious that if one thinks in terms of violence, one must think in terms of superior violence. It is folly to put up inferior violence to oppose superior violence. . . .

Of course, in moments of crisis, people act as they might feel at the moment. When you are considering these problems you think, not in terms of a particular crisis, but in terms of a general policy. I have not a shadow of doubt that the right policy is the non-violent policy for us in India today.[1]

Announcement of Cabinet Mission, February 19

["On [the] 19th February 1946 it was announced in both Houses of Parliament that 'in view of the paramount importance not only to India and to the British Commonwealth but to the peace of the world of a successful outcome of the discussions with the leaders of Indian opinion', the Government had decided to send out to India a special Mission of Cabinet Ministers 'to seek in association with the Viceroy an agreement with these leaders on the principles and procedure relating to the constitutional issue'. The members of the Mission were to be Lord Pethick-Lawrence, the Secretary of State for India, Sir Stafford Cripps, the President of the Board of Trade, and Mr. A. V. Alexander, the First Lord of the Admiralty."

Further statements by the British threw additional light upon the nature of the Mission's task, which "was essentially to help the Viceroy . . . give effect to the programme outlined in his statement of September 19th [1945], that is to say, the bringing into being of, first, a constitution-making body and, secondly, an interim Executive Council supported by the main Indian parties. There was no intention that the Mission should take part in framing a constitution for India; that was the responsibility of Indians themselves. Nor would they, like Sir Stafford Cripps in 1942, take with them definite proposals on which to base their negotiations.

"There was, however, one point in the [previous] Cripps Offer which was now reaffirmed even more unambiguously," namely "that India

[1] A.B.P. (Mar. 1, 1946), last page.

would be at liberty to choose her own future position in the world, whether inside or outside the Commonwealth." [1]

In spite of the announcement of the new British Cabinet Mission, anti-British demonstrations continued to occur in India throughout the remainder of February.

"On February 23, Patel's persuasions, to which were added those of Nehru and Jinnah, had their effect, and the mutineers surrendered. There were minor simultaneous outbreaks in Calcutta and Madras, and on February 21-22 a more serious one in Karachi, which was summarily suppressed by the military commander on the spot, with considerable loss of life and casualties among the mutineers." [2]]

[Further deprecation of recent acts of hooliganism—March 9, 1946.] Setting buildings afire is to ruin ... national property. The buildings will certainly belong to the people ultimately. I am fully cognizant of the great forces [at work, that have given rise to rebellious acts] of which the recent uprisings gave only a hint. These forces will have to be directed and organized through the proper channels. They should not be allowed to be dissipated in thoughtless actions. [3]

3 | Reactions to Cabinet Mission Proposals—Colonialism Must Go— India and the Future

Reactions to 1946 Cabinet Mission Proposals—from Press Conference February 27, 1946

[Nehru stated that Congress would enter into talks with members of the British Cabinet Mission, in the hope and belief that a satisfactory solution of the Indian problem would be evolved.]

[1] L.T.P.I., pp. 71-72.
[2] A.C.B., p. 829.
[3] Based on S.A.B.P. (Mar. 10, 1946), unnumbered page.

[Concerning prospects of the success of the proposed Cabinet Mission.] We are apt to consider [such a question] too much in the personal context. I am so often asked what is so and so like and what is your reaction to such and such a person. As a matter of fact while [the] personal equation counts and does make a difference, in larger problems, one has to consider other impersonal questions. . . . Therefore in considering this question of India and England, we should consider it in the context of the world to-day.

We must realise that each country in the final analysis works for its own interests. [On] the international plane, it only works for what might be considered international interests when they are in harmony with its own interests. So you can take it that the British Delegation will work for the interests of Britain and the Indians who meet them will work for the interests of India. But that is only part of the question. . . . What do British interests . . . require today? And what do Indian interests from our point of view require?

In the final analysis Britain has to choose between two possible developments. It is inevitable that in the course of the next few years India will be independent, even if Britain opposes [her]. If India gains her independence in spite of Britain, India for a long time is likely to be a country hostile to Britain, ranged in a camp hostile to Britain in the world context. On the other hand, if India attains independence more or less immediately by cooperating with the British, it might be possible for Britain to salvage some goodwill, as well as other things in India. Therefore from the British point of view, it may well be to their interest, even in the near future, and much more so in the distant future, to recognise Indian independence now, [rather] than to be forced to recognise it some years later after having lost everything.

Similarly India naturally would prefer a peaceful solution to [one that would] . . . entail [a] great deal of loss and suffering, which might delay India's progress later . . . in the economic field. The costs of conflict are always great and the heaviest of these costs is the trail of hatred and bitterness that follows. We should like to avoid all this and therefore we should like to do our utmost to have a peaceful solution of India's problem. But it is dead clear that . . . settlement can only be [reached] on the basis of Indian independence and on no other. There is a desire and [a] strong urge on both sides to come to a peaceful settlement, and it may well be that success [will] come . . . to us. On the other hand there are powerful factors working in a contrary direction. The most powerful factor working in a contrary direction is the one hundred and fifty year old tradition in British minds which has putrefied British thinking in regard to India. Britishers even to-day and even including the Cabinet Ministers and the Prime Minister of England cannot get rid of their tradition which has eaten into their minds and they still talk of India often enough in a language [reminiscent] of a generation or two ago. They forget that they are addressing a sensitive, proud and virile people who will not put up with any patronage or anything smacking of superiority.

It is obvious that India today is a volcano of four hundred million human beings. There are fair chances of some agreement based on independence emerging out of the talks that are to come, and even if the chances were less, it is the right policy for us to work for such an agreement to the utmost, provided always that we stick to our anchor. It is neither good policy nor statesmanship to enter into any talks with a foreign power or authority after deciding or declaring that the talks are likely to be fruitless.[1]

Colonialism Must Go—March 3, 1946

The future of the colonies? The obvious answer is that there is no future for them as colonies, that the whole system known as colonialism has to go. It has to go for a variety of reasons. It is evident that the dependent peoples of the colonial empires are in [a] rebellious mood and cannot be suppressed for long, and every attempt to suppress them is a drain on the ruling country, which weakens it.

It is even more evident that the old-style empires are decadent as empires and show signs of cracking up. In some instances, indeed, they have cracked up and the attempts that are being made to pin together the broken pieces show a lack of wisdom and statesmanship which is amazing. One decadent empire tries to help another still more ramshackle empire and in this process speeds up the process of its own dissolution.

All these are signs of an inevitable change and transition from an era of colonialism to another era which has yet to be given a shape, a form and a name. The fundamental fact behind all this is that colonialism is obsolete in the modern world and does not fit in with the political and economic structure that is gradually evolving.

The problem of the colonies and dependent countries thus is a vital part of the world problem, and an attempt to isolate it results in other problems becoming far more difficult of solution. Behind that problem

[1] A.B.P. (Mar. 1, 1946), last page.

today lie the passion and hunger for freedom, equality and better living conditions which consume hundreds of millions of people in Asia and Africa. That passion cannot be ignored, for anything that drives vast numbers of human beings is a powerful factor in the dynamics of today.

But essentially it is not the sentimental appeal to freedom that is so important as the lack of food, clothing, housing and of the barest necessities of life which lies behind that urge. This lack can no longer be made good even in part by continuation of colonial administration in any form.

The problem should therefore be considered apart from sentiment in the wider context of world problems, political and economic, because the peace and well-being of the world depend to a large extent on its solution. Colonies and dependencies have been fruitful sources of conflict in the past between acquisitive powers and expanding economies. They lead to an accentuation of power politics. If internal conditions in different countries are in a state of continuous tension and conflict they spread their contagions outside and affect world peace.

It may be difficult to do away with power politics entirely, for they represent to some extent the reality of today trying to find a new equilibrium. But it is certainly possible to lessen their importance and to reduce the area of potential conflict. The elimination of colonialism and imperialism would certainly have this effect and thus help in solving the other major problems of the age. Any variation of the old theme of a covering up of old processes under new names would have the reverse effect and add to the bitterness and conflict.

Effective war today means total war, drawing upon the entire resources of the nation. Effective peace and solution of national and international problems demand also a comprehensive and cooperative effort not only on the part of Governments but also on the part of the people. Any lack of cooperation between the Government and the people leads to failure. There can obviously be no cooperation between an alien and authoritarian Government and the people, and hence no proper solution of any problem.

This has been evident in India for a long time past and problems have accumulated till they seem to be almost insoluble. The war accentuated this progress and the Bengal famine [of 1943, described in Part Eight] was a terribly tragic reminder of the chaos and incompetence that is called government in India today. We are now facing another crisis on an even bigger scale and the shadow of wide-spread famine darkens the land.

No alien Government can deal with this situation satisfactorily, nor can it have the cooperation of the people which is so essential both from the psychological and practical points of view. This is not the game of politics, but something that deeply moves masses of our people. We have seen this Government going from disaster to disaster and making a mess of everything.

It is not an easy matter to refashion the destiny of hundreds of millions of people. The uprooting of the British Empire, as of other empires, which is happening before our eyes, is bound to lead to numerous upsets and it may take some time to establish a new equilibrium on a surer foundation. The problem of the future of colonies and dependencies is no doubt difficult, as is every major problem today. And yet it is essentially simple, or rather the first big step is simple enough. That step is a clear renunciation of colonialism and imperialism and recognition of the national independence of the dependent countries within the larger framework of the world order that is slowly evolving. It is only after that unequivocal declaration has been made and immediate steps taken to implement it that other questions can be discussed as between equals.

It is only then that the foundation can be laid for friendly and cooperative relations between the opponents of yesterday. Everyone realizes that independence today cannot and must not mean isolation or an absolute independence. Everyone knows, or should know, that the only hope for the world lies in cooperation and interdependence and the building up of a world order of free nations. It is in this context that the independence of the nations that are dependent today is sought.

It is also realized that there should be no monopolies in materials or markets or in the natural resources of the world. These should be shared equitably for the advantage of all. But it must be remembered that the peoples of Asia and Africa have been exploited and deprived of their natural riches and resources for many generations, and others have profited enormously by these one-sided transactions. It has to be remembered that this [has] resulted in terrible poverty and backward conditions. The balance has to be righted.

The break-up of the old empires based on colonial economy may lead to harder conditions of life and to somewhat lower standards in the countries which have so far been dominant and have drawn upon the resources of their dependencies. In the long run this should not be so as new techniques are adding tremendously to the wealth of the world. But in the near future some falling back seems probable.

We do not want any lowering of standards anywhere, even where they are higher than ours: we want to raise our own standards to the highest level. But it is obvious that high standards elsewhere based on an economy which results in low standards in Asian and African countries cannot be allowed. If the people of any country can maintain high standards by their own productive efforts they are welcome to do so, but such standards must not be at the expense of starvation and misery elsewhere.

Indeed low standards and the brood of poverty will tend to pull down standards in other places and will also disturb the economy and peace of the world. We have to aim at the raising of the level of the common man everywhere and for that purpose we have to pay especial attention to Asia and Africa which have suffered most in the past. The world has to pull together or not at all.

India is inevitably the crux of the colonial problem by virtue of her size and population, her millennia of cultured life, her contributions to civilization, her capacity and vast resources, her potential power and her strategic position. Historically she has been during the one hundred and fifty years the classic land of colonial imperialism.

Because of her dependence other countries, notably those of the Middle East, have suffered subjection so that the routes to India might be protected and insured for imperialist purposes. The freedom of many other countries thus depends largely on the freedom of India. With India free the old imperialism ends and world politics refashion themselves in new, stabler and more peaceful contest. But it must be remembered that there are no halfway houses to freedom or independence and any attempt to limit freedom will result in conflict.

India has her internal problems largely owing to the arrested growth of a hundred years and more. They are difficult problems, essentially economic problems, and they are insistent and urgent. They cannot be dealt with by the British or any other authority at the top cut off from the people. Nor can they be made excuses for the postponement of independence, for freedom is the prerequisite for their solution. Delay will lead to conflict and disaster and an intensification of those very problems and will affect the political and economic structure of the world.

In Indonesia we have been witnessing a clear case of a shattered imperialism trying to hold on with the help of another imperialist power. Here is a country well capable of looking after itself, with a functioning Government which has obviously the support of the mass of the people, where there would certainly be peace and security if outsiders did not intervene.

The story of Indonesia during the past few months has been fantastic and significant in the extreme and the part the British have played there has injured them more than they perhaps realize. The independence of Indonesia has to be accepted and the Government recognized.

So also in Indo-China. This principle has to be applied to all Asian countries under subjection as well as to Egypt, which should be freed from external control.

The only limiting conditions should be those which apply to world peace and economy, for no country can be allowed to be a law unto itself so as to endanger world peace or to monopolize what is meant for the world. There would be little difficulty in discussing these conditions on the basis of national freedom and independence. But the discussion has to take place in a world context and in [a] world forum and not for the private advantage of this or that nation.

In certain parts of Africa it may perhaps not be immediately possible to establish independent states of the kind mentioned above. Even so, independence in the near future should be aimed at and [a] large measure of it granted immediately, with suitable provision for rapid advance in education, economic and allied fields.

A free India will link together the Middle East with China. India is so situated as to form the center of a group of Asian nations for defense as well as trade and commerce. Her cultural contacts with all these countries date back thousands of years. Already there is considerable talk about a closer union between the countries in the Indian Ocean region, which would include Australia and New Zealand. It has been proposed that a conference of representatives of Asian countries should be held in India.

This is not immediately feasible owing to governmental travel restrictions, but it is likely to be held as soon as conditions permit. There has already been favorable response to the proposal.

The freedom of colonial and dependent countries will raise many new problems, internal to them as well as external. But there can be no doubt that this would be a powerful stabilizing factor in the world and would tend to reduce the conflicts inherent in power politics by removing some of the major causes. These countries, with their newly achieved freedom, will be intent on their progress for they will have to make up for lost time. Their weight will always be thrown on the side of world peace, for any war would be disastrous to them. India in particular is wedded to peace and her powerful influence will make a difference.

If, however, freedom is delayed or circumscribed, and colonies and dependencies are used as pawns in the game of the power politics of a few great powers, then these dependent or semi-dependent countries will also play their part in power politics to the extent they can, and side with this or that power as suits their convenience and advantage. They will add to the confusion and chaos of a distracted world and be victims, together with others, of the inevitable disaster.

The end of colonialism and imperialism will not mean the splitting up of the world into a host of additional national states intent on their isolated independence. It will lead to [a] new grouping together of all nations, a new outlook, to cooperation gradually replacing competition and conflict, to the utilization of the wonders of modern technique and the vast sources of energy at the disposal of man for the advancement of the human race as a whole. It will lead to that One World of which wise statesmen have dreamed and which seems to be the inevitable and only outcome of our present troubles, if we survive disaster.[1]

India and the Future

I. [Speech—Calcutta University, March 9, 1946.] Immediately India moves out of the orbit of subjection it jumps into a new orbit, not only [with respect to] independence, but also the elder-sisterly relationship with all countries round about it. . . .

The centre of world events [is] now shifting from Europe to Asia and . . . India . . . [will] have to play a big part in world affairs. . . .

All over the world—in Asia, in India—[we are] facing [an] extraordinary crisis in human affairs. We read about critical situations arising in political, economic and other domains. We read about wars and disasters, and also the possibility of coming wars. Nevertheless . . . it seems to me that there has been hardly any time in the course of history when humanity has faced such an enormous possibility of changes and conditions as we face today. Possibly the whole structure of human life will be changed, maybe also the structure of [the] human mind to some extent. . . . If one thing is certain, it is . . . that the political and economic structure of the world which has led to so many disasters during the last quarter of a century has failed. If it does not change completely it will fail again and again. There must be a refashioning of the whole structure if we are to prevent war and have peace. But if that refashioning is still based on the old structure—political or economic—inevitably it is bound to fail.

[1] N.Y.T.M. (Mar. 3, 1946), pp. 9, 53–54. © 1946 by the New York Times Company. Reprinted by permission.

The history of the period between the two big wars is a record of [such] failure. True, people tried and tried honestly and earnestly to solve the problems of the age, but always on the basis of the political and economic structure which had continued and which they wished to continue. The strange thing is that in spite of this tremendous disaster there is not sufficient realisation of the fact that [it is] . . . due to a political and economic structure which has failed.

While I speak to you about political and economic matters I do feel that the crisis of today is something deeper than that—call it psychological, call it spiritual if you like . . . something in the spirit of man himself. It seems to me that the world is going through a deep spiritual crisis, not in the narrow religious meaning of the word—I am not a man of religion . . . but in a larger sense. All of us, whether as individuals or as groups or as nations—or taking humanity as a whole—have to face [this] crisis. What the outcome . . . will be I do not know. Out of this crisis is coming that great transformation of the human race which seems to me to be overdue. That is a big question about which I have little competence to speak. . . . It is . . . especially [for] the young [to realize] . . . that we stand on the verge of great happenings which may lead either to disaster or to a new and brighter phase of human existence.

If we look back to our history we find that some hundreds of years ago a change [took place]. . . . Europe . . . began to play an increasing role in [Asian] affairs. . . . Then it began to play an aggressive part in the history of Asia. The scene of world events shifted to Europe during the last two hundred years or so. In the last two hundred years Europe played a prominent part in world history not merely by force of arms but by virtue of its thought, its science and many other factors. Undoubtedly Asia went down or ceased to play any effective part in . . . world history because of the lack of those qualities in Asia. Asia became utterly static, unmoving, unchanging or at any rate ceased thinking in terms of changes.

What do we find happening to-day? The centre of world events is now shifting from Europe to other parts of the world, to America certainly, and partly to Asia, though the process in this respect is slower. In future both the seats of trouble as well as progress are going to be more and more in Asia. Europe to-day is a shattered continent with many valiant peoples in it. Most of the countries in Europe from the point of view of fall in birth rate alone are likely to be hardly aggressive in [the] future. On the other hand Asia is gradually and fairly rapidly coming back to what it was some hundreds of years ago. Exactly what shape it will take

I do not know. I am not thinking in terms of military power, because we have arrived at a stage when if countries continue to think in terms of military power they are likely to destroy themselves completely. Some solution other than that of military might has got to be found. So I am thinking in terms of vital energy that takes possession of people and pushes them on and then the people begin to develop in all the various departments of life and human activities. I feel in India and in a large part of Asia we lost that vitality which we possessed long ago in an abundant measure.

I believe we are regaining that vitality. Asia is going to play a big part in the future of world affairs and I believe certainly India will play a very big part. . . .

India, fortunately for the world, is a country which has stood more than most other countries for peace. Therefore, when we think [of peace] it is not with a view to having [an] alliance with this group or that country as opposed to any [other] group or country, because every intelligent person realises that if there is going to be any real progress and peace in the world, it must be on the basis, not of [a] military alliance of big groups or races facing each other, but of some kind of . . . world commonwealth growing up, of which all . . . countries will be free members. So, [it is necessary] to think in terms of . . . renascent Asia and a new India playing a very important role, inevitably situated [as they are], so as to form a connecting link between the various parts of Asia, [the] Middle East, [and the] South East. That does not mean we shall not be bound to other countries, because India is bound to stand for peace. . . . It is obvious that the period of history that we have gone through during the last [one hundred and fifty years of] British rule is coming to an end. It is obvious that the British Empire in India is fading away, more or less has faded away. India will have to function according to its own ability and strength. . . .

My vision of a free India [involves] something bigger, more magnificent than just political freedom. It is a freedom in which four hundred million people can live the life which man should live . . . in which every individual . . . [shall] have the door of opportunity open to him; in which every person [will be provided with the necessities] of life, and those who have leisure can explore the . . . regions of science and the mind and start again on [the] great field of adventure . . . which [was embarked upon] in this country so many thousand years ago.

We will leave behind the past, and with hope, march [again] in that adventure . . . which has no end. The process of travel will give us the satisfaction that we have functioned in our brief life as we should function.[1]

II. [Interview with Associated Press—Bombay, March 15, 1946.]

[In response to question about what position independent India might take in the event that the Russian military were to move southward in Iran, and Russian demands on Turkey were to be pressed.] Indian opinion, as a whole, will strongly resent any aggression [against] Iran or Turkey by any power. . . . News from the Middle East and from Turkey has been confusing. . . . There is a general impression in India that we have been getting one side of the news.

It appears that in Iran there is a continuation of the old contest for possession of oil by rival powers. Iran has become the plaything of these rival powers and there is much concern in India about Iran's fate. . . .

The Big Powers are continuing the old imperialist game, which already has led to two world wars. They have not learned anything from the tragic history of the past and, if they do not learn soon . . . they will plunge again into disaster. . . .

On the one hand, there appears to be Russian aggression; on the other, the desire of Britain not only to hold on to oil, but also to preserve the so-called life-lines of the Empire. Rival Iranian groups are exploited by either party. . . .

There are many seeds of conflict, but certainly one of the principal ones is subjection of one country by another. If one great power [subjects another, the other] follows [suit] immediately, for fear that the former may gain an advantage, and so the mad race goes on.

The real solution of this problem must be preceded by a complete renunciation of imperialism, and the domination of one country by another. Foreign armies should be withdrawn [from subject countries]. Then the United Nations Organization could consider how the world's resources could be utilized in an equitable manner for all countries concerned, for there should be no monopoly on something the world needs.

Every country, in the final analysis, puts its own interests first in considering an international situation. . . .

Obviously India will be attracted more to those countries which favour her own independence and progress. Her general policy is sure to be one of promoting world peace, preventing aggression anywhere, and helping, in so far as possible, in the attainment of freedom by the subject countries of Asia and Africa. She will try to maintain friendly relations with all

[1] S.A.B.P. (Mar. 10, 1946), first and last pages.

countries and help in the evolution of a world order. More particularly, she will inevitably have closer contacts with her neighbour countries. The Indian Ocean region depends for its defence greatly on India, which is strategically situated in the centre. Thus both South-East Asia and the Middle East defence arrangements will partly depend on India.

It is difficult to say what the international [situation] may be in the future, but the above considerations will generally govern Indian policy.

[In answer to question about whether an independent India would seek a military alliance with Britain or other countries.] We want to be friendly with the three principal powers—America, Russia and England—but this can only be [accomplished] on the basis of complete freedom.

We shall choose our own friends and cannot accept any imposition.

It is impossible for me to say what military or other alliances a free India may . . . [approve]. . . . Generally speaking, she would not like to entangle herself with other people's feuds and imperialist rivalries.

[In answer to a question about the future of India's armed forces and their possible size.] Presumably India will maintain defence forces and, obviously, she will try to keep them as efficient as possible. The whole question of defence in future warfare is so much in a fluid state, owing to scientific developments . . . it is difficult to prophesy about the future.[1]

4 | Publication of *The Discovery of India*—Trip to South-East Asia—First Meeting with Lord and Lady Mountbatten—Statements on Return to India, April

Publication of "The Discovery of India"

[In March, 1946, Nehru's *The Discovery of India*, written while in jail, was published. On March 17, just before the British Cabinet Mission was to arrive in India, he left for a tour of South-East Asia, where he witnessed a political awakening somewhat comparable to that being experienced by

[1] B.A.I., pp. 358–60.

his own people. While traveling, Nehru discussed issues involved in India's battle for independence, as well as a variety of other subjects.]

Trip to South-East Asia

[Singapore—March 18, 1946.] There are strong forces at work to-day which are forcing England to recognize the freedom of India. Most intelligent people realise that freedom cannot be held back. The possession of India is gradually ceasing to be of profit in any way. . . . It is becoming a burden. . . . There are several factors in favour of something satisfactory emerging from the forthcoming [Cabinet Mission] talks.

There are two extraordinary problems—the conception of the British people that they possess India as though it were a landlord's estate and the economic inertia of the British administration in India. . . .

It is a different matter, however, to say that we will not come to an agreement about certain matters which affect British interests. . . .

The independence India wants is not for herself. You cannot have the world half free and half slave. If India aspires for freedom, it is in a free world, and when India is free, every ounce of her energy shall be used for the freedom of all subject nations. This is true of Indonesia, Malaya or any other country in the world.[1]

[March 21, 1946.] Mr Jinnah has never been a revolutionary nor has he anything out of which he can summon a revolt. The Congress [stands] for a sane self-determination for which Mr Jinnah is supposed to be fighting. The Congress is prepared to agree to the greatest amount of autonomy [for] the federating units, reserving the minimum essential powers for the Centre, and further it does not want to compel any unit to stay inside the Federation if by a free definite vote any unit decides to break away. But at the same time no well-defined area of a unit can be compelled to join the seceding unit against the desires of the people living in that area.[2]

[Statement during Malayan Tour—from Kuala Lumpur, March 24, 1946.] In [the] renaissance and resurgence of Asia obviously India is going to play a big part, as obviously as China is going to do so. . . . India is so situated that even apart from . . . historical tradition, geography . . .

[1] B.I.S.J.N. (Vol. II), p. 480.
[2] A.B.P. (Mar. 23, 1946).

compels us to play a big part. India happens to be [a] pivot. If you think of [the] Middle East you must think of what is happening in India. If you think of South-East Asia you must [consider] what is happening in India.

India must be closely associated with China, otherwise unfortunate consequences might be the outcome. Fortunately there is no fear of that because one very enlightening fact of history is that during . . . thousands of years there has been an intimate contact and intercourse between India and China. They have had a common culture, and during these thousands of years there has been no cause [for] conflict between China and India. You will find it very difficult to see such [a] parallel in the history of any continent. But the co-operation between India and China is not going to be an aggressive co-operation against anybody else. it will be a co-operation for peace in Asia and all over the world.[1]

First Meeting with Lord and Lady Mountbatten

[An incident of far-reaching consequences occurred during Nehru's 1946 visit to Malaya and Singapore. While there, he met Lord and Lady Mountbatten for the first time under rather extraordinary circumstances, during a period when none of them possibly could have known that Mountbatten was to become India's last Viceroy.

As Rear Admiral, Mountbatten easily might have been embarrassed by Nehru's plan, while in Malaya, to unveil a memorial to the Indian National Army, whose activities already have been described.

In February, 1946, according to Ray Murphy, when Mountbatten had been in New Delhi visiting Lord Wavell, then Viceroy of India, the latter had told him that Nehru, President of Congress at the time, "proposed to visit the large Indian community in Malaya, and suggested that it would be a good thing if he were invited to do so. Another reason the Viceroy might have given was that Nehru was scheduled to become the first Prime Minister of India and . . . it might be wise to be as agreeable to him as possible, an attitude which had not characterized official British behaviour towards him hitherto. As it would have been diplomatically difficult for Wavell to entertain [Nehru] in New Delhi, it was thought best that Mountbatten should do so in Malaya. . . .

"Mountbatten had been away on tour of his theatre while arrangements for [Nehru's] visit were being made. The British military authorities were displeased and did not propose even to put a car at Nehru's disposal to facilitate his getting round to see his fellow Indians. Possibly

[1] Ibid. (Mar. 28, 1946), p. 5.

this attitude on their part had been caused to some extent by the trouble they had had with the Indian National Army [which Nehru was planning to honor and] which had been formed by the Japanese out of the Indian contingents that had surrendered after the fall of Malaya to fight against the British. . . . It was well understood . . . that the British administration at Singapore intended to ignore [Nehru's] visit except by posting armed M.P.s all over the city in case there should be rioting by the Indians or demonstrations in favour of the Indian National Army. The city was alive with rumours of what might happen. . . .

"Two days before Nehru was to arrive Mountbatten returned to Singapore. He took a very firm line with the military authorities about Nehru's coming reception. If the military authorities thought Nehru ought not to come, because his coming might lead to difficulties with the Indian population and the Indian troops, they should have made that quite clear before he was invited; but a guest visiting Malaya was entitled to the ordinary courtesies, and, in the case of a man of Nehru's standing, to much more than those. The military authorities arranged to place a car at Nehru's disposal only after Mountbatten had told them he would let Nehru have his own car if they did not produce one.

"After Mountbatten's return the official attitude changed overnight. Two hundred passes were issued to leading members of the Indian community to the airport at Kalang so they could suitably welcome the Pandit, and British trucks were put at the disposal of Indians in outlying districts to bring them into Singapore to greet the Pandit on his arrival. . . .

"The order to line the streets with M.P.s was countermanded, presumably because Mountbatten feared there might be a repetition of an incident which had taken place a month before, when young and somewhat panicky British military police had fired into an unarmed mob of Chinese. . . .

"Driving through the streets of Singapore on the morning scheduled for Nehru's arrival was a startling experience, for thousands of Indians, most of whom had served in the Indian National Army, lined the streets waiting patiently in orderly ranks for the Pandit.

"As it turned out he was several hours late, for his 'plane had had 'engine trouble' over Rangoon and had made a forced landing in a field near that city. It was considered by some to be a significant coincidence that the leaders of the Indian community in Rangoon should have happened to be waiting on the field when the Pandit made his 'forced landing'. It was also thought worth noting that the pilot of Nehru's 'plane, who was an ardent supporter of the Indian Congress, had been forced down near Rangoon, for the British had short-sightedly refused Nehru permission to stop there on his way to Singapore.

"When Nehru finally arrived he was received by prominent local Indians and then went direct to Government House, where Mountbatten had invited high-ranking Service and civilian authorities to meet him at a quick and informal lunch. Next on the programme for Nehru was a drive through the streets, where the Indian community was waiting to catch a glimpse of him. . . . Mountbatten waved Nehru into [a] large open car . . . [whereupon they] drove side by side through the cheering crowds. . . .

"When it had become known to high-ranking officers on Mountbatten's staff that he proposed to drive through the streets with Nehru, he had been bombarded with advice to do nothing so unwise, if not actually dangerous. If he were so fortunate as to escape assassination, he would at least be guilty of enhancing Nehru's prestige by lending him his own. Mountbatten, as always, listened to [his officers'] arguments carefully, but decided that he was right. . . .

"Never have I seen or heard anything quite so extraordinary as the welcome accorded Nehru and Mountbatten on that drive. The streets, packed with Indians, seemed to shake with the cries of enthusiasm which greeted them."[1]

To everyone's surprise, Lord Mountbatten declared that he would escort Nehru to the memorial meeting for the I.N.A.

Nehru has added still further details: "When I reached the airport at Singapore, several hours late, as something happened at Penang I think, to delay me, I found a crowd of people waiting for me and an A.D.C. of Lord Mountbatten with a message suggesting that I might go straight to Government House to see him. I agreed to do so and went and had tea with him. . . . Mountbatten told me that he had directed two of the Indian officers to be with me during my tour of Malaya and to help me in every way. . . . After discussing my programme in Singapore and Malaya, Mountbatten suggested that we might go together to the Indian soldiers' canteen where his wife would be waiting for us. I went with him in an open carriage through crowded streets. Mountbatten told me that he had asked the police to keep away from the streets which had been left to Indian volunteers. These volunteers kept perfect order. We arrived at the canteen and I met Lady Mountbatten there. We then moved in from the porch or portico to a room inside. Just then there was a wild rush of Indian soldiers, presumably wanting to see me. When we reached the room inside, Edwina Mountbatten was nowhere to be seen. I think I got up on a chair to have a look around. Soon Lady Mountbatten crawled out of the milling crowd. She had evidently been knocked down by the soldiers rushing in. That was an unusual introduction for us."[2] (It has been stated by Murphy that Mountbatten and Nehru rescued Lady Mountbatten.) Lord and Lady Mountbatten and Nehru later dined together. The long conversation that they had that evening well may have established the basis for a future friendship of extraordinary importance. Lord and Lady Mountbatten at once developed a most cordial rapport with Nehru, who did not meet them again until their arrival in India in March, 1947, when Mountbatten was to serve as Viceroy.]

[1] R.M.L.V., pp. 232–34.
[2] From letter to D.N., Oct. 12, 1963.

Statements on Return to India, April

[On South Africa—Delhi, April 5, 1946.] What the future is going to be in South Africa I cannot say, but I can say with the utmost conviction that we are not going to tolerate [the policy being carried out there], and we are going to face all the consequences of opposing [that] policy, not only in South Africa, but in Asia as a whole, and in the world, because it raises a fundamental racial issue which applies to all Asians and Africans, and the so-called coloured races. . . . [As] long as this issue is not solved satisfactorily, it is going to be a menace to the peace of the world. . . .

To me, the [United Nations Organization] will be an absurdity if it tolerates racialism of this type. I do not expect [it] to go along with South Africa on this issue, but I do expect [it] and the rest of the British Empire—if they are in earnest—to dissociate themselves from South Africa, and cut her away from the family of nations, if she follows this Nazi doctrine. If the U.N.O., Europe, or America do not do that, the time will soon come when all [of] Asia may do [it], and so might Africa—where South Africa is situated.[1]

[Nehru's preoccupation with the fate of other Asian countries had been steadily increasing. Interference with the birth of the free Republic of Indonesia accelerated his decision to call a Conference of Asian Nations in New Delhi.]

[On Conference of Asian Nations—Delhi, April 5, 1946.] [I disapprove] of Great Britain's foreign policy, particularly in relation to Indonesia . . . [which] leads me to India's relations with her neighbour countries of Asia. Whatever our relations may be with other countries in the world, and I hope they will all be friendly, it is inevitable that we will draw closer to Asian countries, East of India, South-East, and West. Indeed, you can say they are joined together already. All over Asia there is not merely a revival of old memories and historical traditions, although that is important, but much more important is the compulsion of geography and of developing events.

I have suggested and some others have done likewise that we should have a conference of representatives from Asiatic countries meet . . . here in India to consider common problems. This suggestion has met with approval, to my knowledge, in many countries, but at present there are so many difficulties in the way that it is not easy to organise such a conference. But it will be possible to do so before very long.[2]

[1] Based on B.A.I., p. 259.
[2] Ibid., pp. 258–59.

5 | Clarification of Purpose of Cabinet Mission—Arrival of Mission in India

Clarification of Purpose of Cabinet Mission

[On March 15, the 1946, the British Prime Minister further clarified the February 19 announcement of the forthcoming Cabinet Mission. "I hope", Attlee declared, "that the Indian people may elect to remain within the British Commonwealth. I am certain that [India] will find great advantages in doing so. . . . But if she does so elect, it must be by her own free will. The British Commonwealth and Empire is not bound together by chains of external compulsion. It is a free association of free peoples. If, on the other hand, [India] elects for independence, in our view she has a right to do so. It will be for us to help to make the transition as smooth and easy as possible.[1] India herself must choose what will be her future constitution."[2]

As for the Muslim League's goal of Pakistan, Attlee proclaimed—also on March 15, 1946: "I am well aware, when I speak of India, that I speak of a country containing a congeries of races, religions and languages. . . . We are very mindful of the rights of minorities [who] should be able to live free from fear. On the other hand, we cannot allow a minority to place a veto on the advance of the majority. . . . There is the problem of the Indian States. . . . I do not believe for a moment that the Indian Princes would desire to be a bar to the forward march of India. But, as in the case of any other problems, this is a matter that Indians will settle themselves."[3]]

Arrival of Cabinet Mission in India

[When the 1946 Cabinet Mission arrived in India during the last week of March, it set out to reconstitute the Viceroy's Executive Council as a coalition Interim Government, and to secure agreement on the setting up of a constitution-making body.

On March 25, Lord Pethick-Lawrence stated: "While the Congress are representative of larger numbers . . . [than the Muslim League] it would not be right to regard the . . . League as merely a minority political

[1] L.T.P.I., p. 72.
[2] M.B., p. 309.
[3] M.L.P. (Vol. I), p. 171.

party—they are in fact majority representatives of the great Muslim community." Sir Stafford Cripps stated at a later Press Conference: "As in everything else, the importance of minorities, their position and their influence may well have changed in the last five or six years, and that may change the application of any ... statement ... made in the past. We really want to start ... on a fresh basis. If we [go] back to interpret everything that has been said from Queen Victoria down to today I think we will get into an awful muddle. The best way of approach is: We want to give independence to India as quickly and smoothly as we can."[1]

The Cabinet Mission's talks with Congress and Muslim League representatives continued throughout the spring of 1946. Both Indian parties agreed to confer on "fundamental principles" with British Ministers at Simla, concerning acceptable methods of terminating British rule in India. When the Simla talks took place in May, it became eminently clear, however, that Congress and Muslim League leaders were in basic disagreement on virtually all important issues.[2] Whereas, among other measures, Congress leaders favored prompt withdrawal of the British, and continued to oppose partition, the League was not at all interested in various "iron-clad guarantees" that were of vast moment to Congress. They pressed instead—hard and consistently—for a separate Pakistan.

(As defined by a Muslim writer, Choudhury Rahmat Ali, the name of the proposed new nation was said to have most complex connotations: "Pakistan", wrote Ali, "is both a Persian and Urdu word. It is composed of letters taken from the names of all our homelands—'Indian' and 'Asian'. That is, Punjab, Afghania (North West Frontier Province), Kashmir, Iran, Sindh (including Kutch and Kathiawar), Tukharistan, Afghanistan and Balochistan. It means the land of the Paks—the spiritually pure and clean. It symbolizes the religious beliefs and ethnical stocks of our people; and it stands for all the territorial constituents of our original Fatherland.")[3]]

[From Singapore—March 21, 1946.] The fundamental factor for success [in] the coming [Cabinet Mission] negotiations ... is a clear recognition of Indian independence, after which, as between equals, with certain common interests, the representatives of India and Britain [can] proceed to negotiate terms. The imperial mind, however consciously desirous [it] may be to throw off the thoughts of imperialism, still tends to proceed on the assumption that it can concede only ... Dominion Status with a right later for the Dominion to break away.[4]

[1] L.T.P.I., pp. 73–74.
[2] M.B., p. 310.
[3] Quoted in B.J., p. 125.
[4] Based on A.B.P. (Mar. 23, 1946).

[Variations on a theme: differences between the Congress and Muslim League—spring, 1946.]

April 3: The Constitution-making body . . . should have final authority, but any [area] not willing to join should not be compelled [to do so].

April 5: Congress is not going to agree to the Muslim League's demand for Pakistan under any circumstances whatsoever, even if the British Government agrees to it. Nothing on earth, not even [the United Nations Organization], is going to bring about the Pakistan which Jinnah wants.

April 13: [I am] prepared to view with respect a demand for Pakistan if it is made after the freedom of the country has been achieved.

[On April 27th a letter from Lord Pethick-Lawrence told the Presidents of the two Parties—Congress and the Muslim League—that the Cabinet Mission had decided to make one further attempt "to obtain agreement between them. It would be useless, however, to ask them to meet unless there could be placed before them a basis of negotiation which might lead to agreement."[1]]

6 | Simla Conference Proposals—Mission's Further Offer, and Failure of Conference— The Princes: General Congress-League Controversies

Simla Conference Proposals

["The [Simla] Conference [of 1946] opened on May 5th. Not since the first Simla Conference nearly a year before had Congress and League leaders met round the same table; and a further sign of an improved atmosphere appeared when Nehru and Jinnah met twice outside the Conference for private talks, mainly concerned with an abortive proposal for the appointment of an Umpire to settle matters of difference between the two parties."

The Conference sent both parties a document containing suggested points for agreement, which elaborated the idea already put forward that there should be a constitutional structure in three tiers, consisting of a Union, Groups and Provinces.

"The Union would consist of a Government and a Legislature, each containing an equal number of representatives of the Hindu-majority and Muslim-majority Provinces, together with representatives of the States. It would deal not only with Foreign Affairs, Defence, and Communications but also with fundamental rights, and would have the power to obtain the finance required for all these subjects. All the remaining powers would vest in the Provinces, but an intermediate tier might be formed by Provinces joining themselves into Groups, which might set up their own Executives and Legislatures. It would be for the Groups to decide which of the Provincial subjects they would take in common. The Union and Group constitutions would provide that any Province might by a majority vote of its Legislative Assembly call for a reconsideration of the terms of the constitution at the end of ten years. The document also made suggestions for the composition and procedure of the Constituent Assembly.

"The essence of the compromise was the option to form Groups. The Mission hoped to be able to persuade the League that if the Muslim-majority Provinces were able to group themselves into organisations which could regulate in common such matters as religion, culture, education, trade and industry, they need have no fear of the extinction of their own way of life under the pressure of the Hindu majority; so that they would be willing to co-operate in an All-India Union with minimum powers, in which they would have equal representation with the Hindu-majority Provinces. The scheme was in fact designed to give them the advantages of Pakistan without the disadvantages inherent in the division of India. Equally the Mission hoped that Congress would recognise that the formation of Groups and a weak Union were lesser evils than the 'vivisection' of the country." [1]]

Mission's Further Offer, and Failure of Conference

[After the Cabinet Mission had met from May 5 to 12, it suggested further points for possible agreement; that, "as a concession to the Congress viewpoint the original list of the Union subjects, viz., Foreign Affairs, Defence and Communications [could be] enlarged by the addition of 'Fundamental Rights' and . . . that the Union Government should have the necessary powers to obtain for itself the finances it required for those subjects. To make the Union acceptable to the League it was suggested that the Constituent Assembly should divide up into three sections, one representing the Hindu-majority Provinces, the second representing the Muslim-majority Provinces and the third representing the States. The first two sections would then meet separately and decide Provincial constitutions for their groups and, if they wished, group constitutions. To counter-balance the Congress objection to the compulsory grouping of

[1] L.T.P.I., pp. 80–81.

Provinces in [a] Section, the Cabinet Mission proposed that a Province should have the freedom to opt out of the original group and go to another group or remain out of any group by a majority of the votes of its representatives, if the Provincial or group constitution was not acceptable to it. The three sections would then meet together to frame the Union constitution.

"Under the Union constitution, there would thus be three sub-federations: one of the Muslim-majority Provinces, another of the Hindu-majority Provinces and the third of the States. The Muslim-majority Provinces would have a parity of representation in the Union Legislature as well as in the Union Government with the Hindu-majority Provinces irrespective of whether the Provinces in question formed themselves into groups or not. Further, to compensate the League for the possible loss, through opting out of the N.-W. F. P. [North-West Frontier Province] from the Muslim-majority group and for the exclusion of Assam from the same, which the League demanded for the Muslim-majority group, it was proposed that there should be the additional safeguard that no measure affecting a communal issue in the Union constitution would be passed unless the majority of both the major communities voted in its favour.

"The Congress was prepared to accept the formation of groups provided it was entirely optional. It, however, held that this would be for the representatives of the Provinces to decide *after* the Constituent Assembly had framed the constitution for the all-India Federal Union. The Muslim League, on the other hand, demanded that there should be a separate constitution-making body for the six "Muslim Provinces", namely, the Punjab, the N.-W. F. P., Baluchistan, Sind, Bengal and Assam (although Assam was a Hindu-majority Province) from the very beginning. After the constitutions of the Pakistan Federal Government and the Provinces were framed the constitution-making bodies of the two groups—[the] Pakistan group and the Hindustan group—sitting together would deal with the three subjects, namely, Foreign Affairs, Defence and 'Communications necessary for Defence'.

"There were other points of difference. The Congress wanted the Union Government to have the power to raise the finances required for the discharge of its functions by taxation. The Muslim League insisted that the Federal Union should in no event have the power to raise revenues in its own right but only by contribution. The League further wished] that no decision—legislative, executive or administrative—should be taken by the Union in regard to any matter of a controversial nature except by a majority of three-fourths."

Whereas Congress agreed to optional grouping of Provinces and a Muslim veto on communal issues "in order to allay the anxiety of the Muslims so that Hindus and Muslims might be able to live together as one nation in their common motherland, the Muslim League regarded" the proposals that had been made "as a strategic gain in its battle for Pakistan."

Congress, on the other hand, was of the opinion that it was not up to the Simla Conference to arrange for division of India.

"As had been feared from the very beginning, the difficulty about parity in regard to the executive or the legislature as between seven Hindu-majority Provinces, comprising a population of nineteen crores and the five Muslim-majority Provinces with a population of little over nine crores, proved insurmountable. 'This is worse than Pakistan,' wrote Gandhiji to Sir Stafford Cripps on the 8th May. As a way out he suggested that an 'impartial non-British tribunal should [make an] award on this [issue] as on any other matters of difference otherwise incapable of adjustment' between the League and the Congress. . . .

"The Congress was prepared to do anything within the bounds of reason to remove fear and suspicion from the mind of any Province or community, but it felt itself unable to endorse" any suggestions that "went against the 'basic method of democracy' on which [it] hoped to build up [a] constitution.

"Failure of the conference . . . seemed inevitable. The Congress, thereupon, suggested that an umpire should be appointed by the Congress and the Muslim League to settle matters of difference between [them]. The suggestion was turned down by the League.

"On the 12th May, it was announced that the conference had failed to bring the Congress and the League to an agreement. The members of the Cabinet Mission thereupon returned to Delhi."[1]]

The Princes: General Congress-League Controversies—Delhi, April 5, 1946

[I am] glad that some of [the Indian Princes have] taken up more or less an attitude [that] might be summed up as "Let there be independence immediately, including withdrawal of the British army, and we shall solve our problems among ourselves." That is a dignified attitude for any Indian, whatever his party views may be, and that is the only real attitude, because ultimately there can be no doubt that problems will be solved by the Indian people themselves and by no outside authority.

Redistribution of provincial boundaries is essential and inevitable . . . because we [want] provinces which are autonomous units, culturally and linguistically, as far as possible. [We want] such cultural and linguistic units to grow . . . with a sense of freedom, and without a sense of compulsion. . . .

An Indian State joining the federation [we envisage] . . . will be an equal unit [within] the federation, having the same responsibilities, privileges and obligations as any other unit. Every State would . . . have to

[1] M.L.P. (Vol. I), pp. 205–08.

[maintain the same] level of administration and democratic liberty [as] the rest of India. It might be that the exact form [would] vary slightly, but it [is] impossible to conceive of varying levels of feudalism and democracy in different States forming part of the federation.

Difficult problems in India ... [are] not so much those about which people talk and [become] heated, such as Pakistan, although [such problems exist], but the primary problem [for] India is the economic problem: [to solve] as far as we can the problem of poverty and [raise] the standard of living.

I say the economic problem is the essential problem. That does not mean it is the first problem, because the economic problem cannot be tackled before the political problem is solved. ...

I should like every person and every political party to put forward its views and demands in relation to [the] ... economic problem of India, because if [they are] not so related, then [what is demanded must be] unreal and superficial. I should like to consider the problem of Pakistan from the point of view of [the] economic problem: from the point of view of defence and of international affairs.

I am quite convinced that [once] independence [is] recognised and [brought into being] and the solution of all problems [is] definitely [placed] in the hands of Indians, whatever the consequences, we shall solve the problems that face us such as Pakistan, or the Indian States.

Inevitably, we have a large number of matters to consider [in conjunction with our relations with Britain], and they should be considered by ... representatives of the Constituent Assembly and those of the British Government [eventually] in [the] context of independence.

It will be [possible for] us to have close and friendly relations, economic and [otherwise], with Britain. [Such relations] will depend on the national interests of the parties concerned.[1]

[1] Based on B.A.I., pp. 257-58.

7 | Cabinet Mission's Own Plan, May 16—
Formation of Interim Government

Cabinet Mission's Own Plan

[After the failure of the Simla Conference, the Cabinet Mission set forth its own long-range plan on May 16, with respect to a possible constitutional settlement. Attlee announced the Mission's opposition to Jinnah's claims regarding partition. The Viceroy also favored a united India. Thus there was no official British approval whatever, at the time, of the League's demand "that the Moslem majority provinces should have full autonomy". There was, in fact, British resistance to what Maulana Azad termed Muslim League leaders' loose talk "of the partition of [India] and the establishment of an independent state for the Moslem majority areas".

The British Cabinet Mission Plan of May 16, 1946 clearly stated: "A separate sovereign State of Pakistan on the lines claimed by the Moslem League would not solve the communal minority problem. . . . We are therefore unable to advise the British government that the power which at present resides in British hands should be handed over to two entirely separate sovereign states."[1]

The May 16 Cabinet Mission Plan further "provided that only three subjects would belong compulsorily to the Central Government. These were defence, foreign affairs and communications. . . . It divided the country into three zones, A, B and C, as the members of the Mission felt that this would give a greater sense of assurance to the minorities. Section B would include the Punjab, Sind, the N.W.F.P. and British Baluchistan. This would constitute a Moslem majority area. In Section C, which included Bengal and Assam, the Moslems would have a small majority over the rest. The Cabinet Mission thought that this arrangement would give complete assurance to the Moslem minority, and satisfy all legitimate fears of the League. . . . (Section A would include all the predominantly Hindu territory between Section B in western India and Section C in eastern India.) . . .

"Moslems in the majority provinces would . . . exercise almost complete autonomy. Only certain agreed subjects would be dealt with at the sectional level. Here also the Moslems were assured of a majority in Sections B and C and would be able to satisfy all their legitimate hopes. So far as the Centre was concerned, there were only three subjects [as above] which from the nature of the case could not be provincially administered. . . .

[1] I.W.F., pp. 170, 171 footnote.

"At first Mr Jinnah was completely opposed to the scheme. The Moslem League had gone so far in its demand for a separate independent state that it was difficult for it to retrace its steps. The Mission had stated in clear and unambiguous terms that they could never recommend the partition of the country and the formation of an independent state. Lord Pethick-Lawrence and Sir Stafford Cripps said repeatedly that they could not see how a state like the Pakistan envisaged by the Moslem League could be viable and stable. . . .

"Lord Pethick-Lawrence said more than once . . . that in the beginning the Moslem majority provinces would delegate to the Central Government only three subjects and thus ensure complete autonomy for themselves. The Hindu majority provinces would on the other hand voluntarily agree to transfer to the Central Government several more subjects. The Cabinet Mission thought there was nothing wrong in this. In a true federation, the federating units must have the freedom to decide on the number and nature of the subjects to be transferred to the central government.

"The Moslem League Council met for three days before it could come to a decision. On the final day, Mr Jinnah had to admit that there could be no fairer solution of the minority problem than that presented in the Cabinet Mission Plan. In any case he could not get better terms. He told the Council that the scheme presented by the Cabinet Mission was the maximum that he could secure. As such, he advised the Moslem League to accept the scheme and the Council voted unanimously in its favor." [1]

Formation of Interim Government

[On June 3, Lord Wavell offered the League and Congress "equal representation" in the proposed Interim Government, adding two other members, one representing the Sikhs, the other the Untouchables. Although at first Jinnah agreed to this plan, a few days later the Viceroy decided to add Parsee and Anglo-Indian representatives. On June 16, after conferring with the Cabinet Mission, the Viceroy stated that he hoped "all parties, especially the two major" ones, would "co-operate for the successful carrying on of an Interim Government". He proclaimed further that, in the event of the two major parties—or either of them—proving unwilling to join, he would himself "proceed with the formation of an Interim Government", which would be "as representative as possible" of those who accepted the Cabinet Mission plan.

[1] Ibid., pp. 175–76. (The full text of the Cabinet Mission's and Viceroy's Statement of May 16, 1946, is to be found in Appendix IV, T.P.I., pp. 466–75. T.P.I. also contains a detailed account of events that occurred during 1946, preceding the final transfer of power from Britain to an independent India. 1946 negotiations also are described in H.I.N.C.)

"The Muslims read into this an assurance that, if the members of Congress were 'unwilling' to co-operate, the Viceroy would still form his government without them." [1]

The Cabinet Mission, the Muslim League and Congress continued to be at odds over the interpretation of various words utilized in Britain's series of proposals. In considering adjacent passages, it should be borne in mind that what the British termed their "long-range plan" for India was their proposal for a constitutional settlement, offered on May 16. (In the following section, Britain's "short-range plan" for formation of an Interim Government for India is presented in the Statement of June 16.)

Not only did the Muslim League and Congress continually fail to reach agreement with one another, they almost never agreed with Britain's proposals either. Even the proposals, themselves, seemed seldom to be fully clarified.]

8	Cabinet Mission's and Viceroy's June 16 Statement—Journey to Kashmir— Congress and Muslim League Reactions to Britain's Proposals—Speech to Congress, July 7

Statement by Cabinet Delegation and the Viceroy—16th June, 1946

["1. His Excellency the Viceroy, in consultation with the members of the Cabinet Mission, has for some time been exploring the possibilities of forming a coalition Government drawn from the two major parties and certain of the minorities. The discussions have revealed the difficulties which exist for the two major parties in arriving at any agreed basis for the formation of such a Government.

"2. The Viceroy and the Cabinet Mission appreciate these difficulties and the efforts which the two parties have made to meet them. They consider, however, that no useful purpose can be served by further prolonging these discussions. It is indeed urgently necessary that a strong

[1] B.J., p. 162.

and representative Interim Government should be set up to conduct the very heavy and important business that has to be carried through." (The third section of the Statement listed those invited to serve as members of the Interim Government, including Nehru.)

"4. The Viceroy will arrange the distribution of portfolios in consultation with the leaders of the two major parties.

"5. The above composition of the Interim Government is in no way to be taken as a precedent for the solution of any other communal question. It is an expedient put forward to solve the present difficulty only, and to obtain the best available coalition Government.

"6. The Viceroy and the Cabinet Mission believe that Indians of all communities desire to arrive at a speedy settlement of this matter so that the process of constitution-making can go forward and that the Government of India may be carried on as efficiently as possible in the meantime.

"7. They therefore hope that all parties especially the two major parties will accept this proposal so as to overcome the present obstacles, and will co-operate for the successful carrying on of the Interim Government. Should this proposal be accepted, the Viceroy will aim at inaugurating the new Government about the 26th June.

"8. In the event of the two major parties or either of them proving unwilling to join the setting up of a coalition Government on the above lines, it is the intention of the Viceroy to proceed with the formation of an Interim Government which will be as representative as possible of those willing to accept the Statement of May 16th.

"9. The Viceroy is also directing the Governors of the Provinces to summon the Provincial Legislative Assemblies forthwith to proceed with the elections necessary for the setting up of the constitution-making machinery as put forward in the Statement of May 16th." [1]]

Journey to Kashmir

[Just after the June 16 Cabinet Mission's announcement, Nehru hurriedly went to Kashmir to aid Sheikh Saheb Abdullah, leader of the Kashmir Freedom Movement, who was on trial for treason. Whereas Jinnah won certain concessions from the Viceroy while Nehru was away, Nehru was arrested for ignoring the Maharajah of Kashmir's prohibition to enter the State. (Nehru's statement at the time of his Kashmir arrest is included in a later Section.)]

Congress Reactions to Cabinet Mission's Statements

[The Congress Working Committee subsequently considered the Cabinet Mission's Statements of May 16 and June 16. After reviewing both sets of proposals, the Committee rejected the Mission's plan for an Interim Government at the Centre, while agreeing to the long-term plan, but with

[1] H.I.N.C. (Vol. II), pp. ccxiii–iv.

8*

its own interpretation of disputed clauses. Essentially, Congress continued to desire creation of a free, united, democratic Indian Federation, with a central authority. Such a Federation would lead "to the rapid advance of the masses, economically and socially, so that their material standards [might] be raised and poverty, malnutrition, famine and the lack of the necessaries of life [might] be ended." The Congress Working Committee hoped that "all the people of the country [might] have the freedom and opportunity to grow and develop according to their genius." The Mission's proposals fell short of these objectives. Yet the Committee wished earnestly "to find some way for the peaceful settlement of India's problem and the ending of . . . conflict between India and England."

The Working Committee recommended that a meeting of the A.I.C.C. be held on July 6 and 7, 1946, in order to consider and ratify its June decisions.[1]

Meanwhile, the Cabinet Mission, "instead of recognizing the harsh reality of continued deadlock," interpreted the Congress Resolution as "acceptance" of its constitutional proposals, thereupon shelving its recommendations for an Interim Government. It consequently left for England at the end of June.[2]]

From Jinnah's Statement on Proposed Interim Government— New Delhi, June 28, 1946

["I would like to emphasize that if any attempt is made to whittle down in any way the assurances given the Moslem League or to change or modify the basis of the statement of June 16 which has been accepted by the Moslem League, it will be regarded by Moslem India as going back on the part of the Cabinet Delegation and Viceroy on their pledged word in writing and as a breach of faith. The British Government will in that case forfeit the confidence of Moslem India and those with whom they expect to work on their part according to their pledged word."[3]]

From Speech at All-India Congress Committee Meeting— July 7, 1946

[When the All-India Congress Committee met at the beginning of July Nehru presided over it as President for the fourth time.]

The Congress idea of independence is certainly different from what the Moslem League or the Viceroy thinks. Our idea of independence is tha there must be absolutely no foreign domination in India and that Indi; may even break her connections with the British. We want to establis]

[1] Ibid., pp. ccxxiii–iv.
[2] M.B., p. 313.
[3] V.I. (Sept., 1946), p. 333.

the republic of India. Arguments have been advanced [that there could now exist] a very satisfactory Constituent Assembly—something we have been asking for and now have got. On the other hand it has been stated that [such a] Constituent Assembly is futile and is being imposed on us, to which we should not attach much importance. If I am asked to give my own view I would say that it is not, obviously, something which we have desired and worked for. There are many difficulties and snags and the scales are weighed against us. On the other hand, it is obvious . . . that it is not so bad. I do think that [at] some time or other in the future we may have to summon our own proper revolutionary Constituent Assembly. That does not mean we should not take advantage of [the present offer] and [use] it for our own advantage. If we do not succeed in the Constituent Assembly we can change our tactics [in any manner we desire]. There is a good deal of talk of the Cabinet Mission's long-term plan and short-term plan. So far as I can see, it is not a question of our accepting any plan—long or short. It is only a question of our agreeing to go into the Constituent Assembly. . . . We will remain in that Assembly so long as we think it is good [for] India and we will come out when we think it is injuring our cause and then offer battle. We are not bound by a single thing except that we have decided for the moment to go to the Constituent Assembly, not certainly to deliver fine speeches but to build something to overcome some of our problems.[1]

9 | Muslim League Reactions to Cabinet Mission Plans and Congress Position— July 10 Press Conference—Criticism of Statements at Conference—Speech of July 22

Muslim League Reactions

In order to comprehend the repercussions of Nehru's July 10 Press Conference in Bombay—the text of which follows—it is necessary to assess it in relationship to the position of the Muslim League during the preceding period.

Ibid., p. 336.

Nehru's July 10 Conference has, at times, been regarded as both "explosive" and "history changing." Yet even before July 10, Nehru had explained his reservations about the Cabinet Mission's Plans (see his July 7 speech above) and the Muslim League itself had expressed reservations about the Mission's Statement of June 16 concerning negotiations for an Interim Government. The League also harbored objections, at the time, both to the Mission's long-range and short-range plans, as well as to Congress reactions to the Mission's proposals.

Although the League originally had stated that it accepted the Mission's May 16th Statement—as clarified by that of May 25th—the Indian Annual Register of July 10, 1946, clearly states that, by that date, the League already had announced its displeasure at "the breaking of solemn pledges" by both the Cabinet Mission and the Viceroy, in conjunction with the Interim Government plan. The fact that the League also expressed dismay that Congress was willing to accept the Mission's long-range plan only "conditionally," seems essentially to make the criticisms of Nehru's July 10 remarks that follow lose their *raison-d'être*.

The Indian Annual Register of July 10, 1946, called attention to the grave possibility that the League might not participate in the forth-coming Constituent Assembly, for lack of assurance that the fundamental principles of the Cabinet Mission's scheme would be adhered to. In addition to which, the League believed that Congress had merely agreed to enter the Constituent Assembly in order to frame a constitution according to its own wishes, irrespective of Cabinet Mission recommendations. Could this, inquired the League, be termed Congress acceptance of the Mission's long-range plan?

In other words, while pointing to the need for a fresh statement of Britain's intentions—before July 10—the League simultaneously blamed Congress for what was occurring. It further protested that, short of the British making a fresh statement of their intentions, it would be worse than useless to go into the proposed Constituent Assembly. The League had similar doubts about the advisability of entering into any fresh nego-tiations the Viceroy might initiate for formation of an Interim Govern-ment, after elections to a Constituent Assembly. (At the same time, the League curiously insisted that a decision on such matters rested "with the Council of the Muslim League" itself.) Moreover, political circles in New Delhi were anticipating difficulties even before Nehru's July 10 Conference, following the Muslim League announcement on July 9 that its Council was to be convened in Bombay on July 28 and 29.[1]]

From Press Conference, Bombay, July 10

[In reply to a request for amplification of the statement made in the All-India Congress Committee to the effect that Congress had made n

[1] I.A.R. (Vol. II), July 10, 1946, p. 145.

commitment with regard to either the long-term or the short-term plan of the Cabinet Mission—except to enter the Constituent Assembly.] If you read the correspondence that has passed between the Congress President and the Cabinet Mission and the Viceroy you will see [under] what conditions and circumstances we agreed to go into this Constituent Assembly. The first thing is we have agreed to go into [it] and we have agreed to nothing else. It is true that in going [into] the Constituent Assembly, inevitably, we have agreed to a certain process of going into it, that is, election of the candidates to the Constituent Assembly. What we do there, we are entirely and absolutely free to determine. We have committed ourselves [on] no single matter to anybody. Naturally even though one might not agree to commit oneself, there is a certain compulsion of facts which makes one accept this thing or that thing. I do not know what that might be in a particular context. But the nature of compulsion of facts would be not of the British Government's desires or intents but how to make the Assembly a success and how to avoid its breaking up. That will be certainly a very important consideration. But the British Government does not appear there at all.

[With respect to the Congress Statement that the Constituent Assembly was a sovereign body.] The Cabinet Mission's reply was . . . more or less "yes", subject to two considerations: [First], proper arrangement for minorities and [second], a treaty between India and England. I wish the Cabinet Mission had stated that both these matters are not controversial. It is obvious the minorities question has to be settled satisfactorily. It is also obvious that if there is any kind of peaceful change-over in India, it is bound to result in some kind of treaty with Britain.

What exactly that treaty will be I can not say. But if the British Government presumes to tell us that they are going to hold anything in India . . . because they do not agree either in regard to . . . minorities, or . . . to [a] treaty, we shall not accept that position. It will become a *casus belli*. We shall have no treaty if they seek to impose anything upon us, and we shall tear up any treaty they try to impose. If they treat us as equals and come to terms there will be a treaty. But if there is the slightest attempt at imposition, we shall have no treaty.

In regard to . . . minorities, it is our problem and we shall, no doubt, succeed in solving it. We [shall] accept no outside interference— . . . certainly not the British Government's interference— . . . and therefore, these two limiting factors to the sovereignty of the Constituent Assembly are not accepted by us.

How to make the job in the Constituent Assembly a success or not is the only limiting factor. It does not make the slightest difference what the Cabinet Mission thinks or does in the matter.

[Asked when the Provisional National Government would be formed at the Centre.] I cannot just peep into the future and tell what is going to happen. For the moment we are somewhat engaged in the Constituent Assembly elections. But remember . . . that the Constituent Assembly is not going to put up easily for long with the kind of Caretaker Government that exists today. There is bound to be conflict. . . . In fact, the Caretaker Government has no stability; nor is there any possibility of its long continuance. . . . How and when and what shape the new Government will take I cannot say. . . .

[Of the forthcoming All-India Muslim League Council meeting at Bombay.] Whatever the Congress does is always intended to create new situations. We do not follow other people's situations. I am glad that the Muslim League has realized that we have created a new situation. We propose to create many further new situations. What we shall do if the League decides to do this or that we will see what the conditions then are and decide accordingly. . . .

[Of the powers of the proposed Union Centre.] According to the Cabinet Mission's proposals there were three or four basic subjects in it, i.e., Defence, Foreign Affairs, Communications and the power to raise finances for these. Obviously, Defence and Communications have a large number of industries behind them. So these industries inevitably come under the Union Government and they are likely to grow. Defence is such a wide subject that it tends to expand its scope and activities more and more. All that comes under the Union Government.

Similarly, External Affairs inevitably include foreign trade policy. You cannot have foreign policy if you divorce foreign trade from it. [External Affairs] include all manner of things. . . .

[Referring to the question of raising finances for the Union.] No Central Government carries on on doles. . . . Inevitably . . . any Central Government must raise its finances by taxation. I cannot make a list now, but obviously Customs, including tariffs, is bound to be one [tax]. In fact, tariff is connected with foreign trade policy. It may be [that] income-tax will be another. I do not know what else. . . .

Suppose there is trouble between the Provinces or States, or an economic break-down due to famine conditions. . . . The Centre comes in again, inevitably. However limited the Centre might be you cannot help [its] having wide powers, because the past few years have shown that if there were no central authority, . . . conditions would have been far worse in India. However, the fact that there has been a central authority has not done much good to the country, because it has been incompetent. It is obvious that without [a] central authority you cannot deal with the problems mentioned above. There must be some over-all power to intervene in grave [crises], breakdown of the administration or economic breakdown or famine. The scope of the Centre, even though limited, inevitably grows, because it cannot exist otherwise.[1]

Criticism of Statements at Conference

[Maulana Azad, one of the most distinguished Muslim leaders in Congress, later described his amazement at what Nehru had said at his July 10, 1946 Press Conference. According to Azad, in his book *India Wins Freedom*, the Press Conference was "one of those unfortunate events which changed the course of history".[2] In his introduction to the same volume, Louis Fischer recounts that, after the above conference question and answer period, he, himself, had addressed Nehru: "You have changed the entire basis of the agreement with England." To which, according to Fischer, Nehru smilingly replied: "I am fully aware of that." Fischer refers to the fact that, in view of what had appeared to be an affirmative vote of the All-India Congress Committee with regard to the Mission plan, what Nehru said "changed" everything. It should be noted, in this connection, that although Fischer, as well as Azad, was perturbed by Nehru's remarks of July 10, Azad, himself, stated on the same date—as also recorded in the Indian Annual Register: "If unfortunately, any insuperable difficulties crop up in direct conflict with our fundamental principles, we shall not hesitate to kill the Constituent Assembly".[3]]

[From statement at later Press Conference, in reply to question about Azad's criticism of July 10, 1946 Press Conference.] I am sorry to confess that I have no very clear ideas of the day to day occurrences in those days; it was a great burden on all of us—a burden of decision, a burden of occurrences, events, happenings, all over, and the tremendous strain under which we were functioning in that Interim Government as it was called, inside the Government, I mean, apart from occurrences outside, because the Moslem League Party were out, as they openly said, to prevent

---

[1] I.A.R. (Vol. II), July 10, 1946, pp. 145–47.

[2] I.W.F., p. 181. [When shown I.W.F. in manuscript before its publication, although Nehru was given the opportunity to object to any passages, he insisted that, whether or not the book criticized him, it should be printed as Azad wrote it. He corrected only minor factual errors having nothing to do with criticism of himself.]

[3] I.A.R. (Vol. II), July 10, 1946, p. 144.

us from functioning satisfactorily. During the period of the Interim Government, I think in the first few weeks, I was constantly going to Lord Wavell and telling him that I had had enough of it. I must have done so—I do not know—four or five times in the course of the next two or three months, that is, verbally resigning, not actually writing, but saying that I wanted to get out. He said, "Wait and see" or something like that. So that it is a little difficult to rely on one's memory of a thing that happened twelve years ago when one was under great strain, in difficulty—not I alone, but all of us. And it is quite conceivable for people to have different recollections as to who influenced whom or what. The real fact is, I think, that personal influences count. How am I to say how I was influenced? I cannot judge. But I think the real facts were, the situation itself and the bitterness and conflicts that were growing in the communal field and the feeling that even if some arrangement could be arrived at to prevent partition, those conflicts and inner disruptions would continue, and might come in the way of any marked progress of the economy of the country later. Because we were anxious naturally to make good, after Independence, in the political and the economic spheres and others—planning and all that—and we felt that if there was some kind of a compulsory union carried on, it would prevent—all our energies would be spent in these inner tugs of war. Whether that was a right analysis or a wrong analysis, I cannot say. I am only saying that it had a powerful effect [on] our thinking. And, even in the course of the Interim Government, we had proposed the appointment of a Planning Commission. It had been opposed by the Moslem League representatives. So that, in every such matter where economic considerations and planning came in, we were likely to come up against inner pulls in different directions. That was, I think—this overwhelming sensation that any kind of a union, if it came about, would first of all not put an end to these inner pulls, secondly, it would leave the Federal Government so weak—with the transfer of power to its various constituent units—the Central Federation would be so weak, that it would not be able to act properly or adopt any effective economic measures. These were the real reasons which ultimately induced us to agree [to partition]. It was a very, very difficult choice—you can well imagine—and it is frightfully difficult to say now what one could do if one had the same choice. It is very difficult to say; it is very difficult because of what happened subsequently— the terrible things that happened—because when we decided on partition, I do not think any of us ever thought that there would be this terror of mutual killing after the partition. It was in a sense to avoid that, that we decided on partition. So we paid a double price for it, first, you might say, politically, ideologically, second, the actual thing happened that we tried to avoid.

So, how can I judge how far I am responsible? Mine was certainly part of the responsibility, and Maulana Sahib may be completely right in thinking that I acted wrongly. Only I would say this, that Maulana Sahib thinks too much in individual terms, sometimes, not in terms of historic forces at work. Individuals make a difference and have made a difference but sometimes individuals are only symbols of forces at work.[1]

Continued Suspicion of Britain's Bona Fides—Extracts from Speech—Delhi, July 22, 1946

The Constituent Assembly can be a useless thing, as well as . . . a powerful instrument for achieving freedom. Its greatest merit [is] that although it will be brought into existence by the British Government, they will have nothing to do with it after it has been set up into motion. . . . Nobody can interfere in its work. Foreign rulers may be angry with the manner wherein the Constituent Assembly conducts its business, but they cannot dissolve it. Of course it can commit suicide, but nobody else can kill it. . . . It is a fallacy to think that a constitution drawn by the Constituent Assembly will be sent to London for ratification so that the British Government may put its seal on it. . . . We shall start on the basis that the constitution drawn by us has become effective. New elections will be held under the new constitution. We may have a provisional, temporary government during [a] transition period between the drawing [up] of [a] constitution and bringing it into operation. We may [win] our freedom through peaceful methods or after a conflict with the British Government. . . . As regards the question of safeguarding the rights of minorities, we all recognize its importance. No constitution can work unless the minorities are satisfied. We shall not however brook any interference on the part of the ruling power on [that] score, if they arrogate to themselves the functions of an arbitrator. . . . I want to make it clear that we shall not accept any dictation. The treaty between the two countries must be on the basis of absolute equality.[2]

[1] I.W.F., as quoted in introduction by Louis Fischer, "Giants and Men"; pp. xxii–xxiv.
[2] V.I. (Sept., 1946), p. 334.

10 | Summer, 1946

[There were moments during the summer of 1946 when it appeared that an Interim Government might finally come into existence. Nehru, who was again Congress President at the time, continued to argue in favor of an independent Constituent Assembly, against communal hatred, for protection of minorities and a united, democratic India.

Jinnah, the Viceroy (Lord Wavell), and Nehru had constant difficulties with one another. Distrust existed on all sides. Not only Nehru, but Jinnah, himself, made numerous conditions in conjunction with proposals put forward by Britain. The manner in which an Interim Government might be set up had to be revised again and again. At times the very possibility of its existence seemed threatened.

Just a week before the Muslim League passed its July 29 Resolution calling for "Direct Action"—namely violence against non-Muslims—the Viceroy resumed his efforts to convince both Nehru and Jinnah that a coalition Interim Government at the Center should be formed, giving assurances that Britain would enter into the same close consultation with the new Interim Government and give it the same consideration as a Dominion Government; that it would give the Indian Government the greatest possible freedom in the exercise of day-to-day administration of the country. He pointed out, however, that it would not be possible for either Congress or the Muslim League to object to names submitted for the Government by the other party, provided that the names were accepted by the Viceroy. Thus Congress was now free to nominate one or more nationalist Muslims to the Interim Government, a point on which negotiations had broken down in June. In all other respects the Viceroy's offer remained unchanged.

Nevertheless Nehru informed the Viceroy that his proposal in the form in which it was offered was not acceptable to Congress, that previous talks had shown how little hope there was in following the old lines of approach.

Congress attached great importance to what it termed "independence in action" on the part of a Provisional Government. It was on the basis of such "independence" only, according to Nehru, that a satisfactory approach could be made. Since the nature of the status and power of a Provisional Interim Government must, in Nehru's view, be decided in unambiguous language, he concluded that he was wholly unable to cooperate in the formation of a Government on the terms suggested by the Viceroy.[1]

In its July 29 call for "Direct Action" to attain Pakistan, the League set up a Council of Action to remind Muslims that "it was in the month of

[1] Based on M.L.P. (Vol. I), p. 264.

Ramzan that the 'first open conflict between Islam and Heathenism' was fought and won by three hundred and thirteen Muslims in Arabia. A leaflet containing a special prayer for the crusade announced that ten crores of Indian Muslims 'who through bad luck had become slaves of Hindus and the British' would be starting 'a Jehad [holy war] in this very month of Ramzan'". A leaflet bearing a picture of Jinnah with sword in hand, stated: "We Muslims have had the Crown and have ruled. Be ready and take your swords. . . . O Kafer! . . . your doom is not far and the general massacre will come!"[1]

The League call to take up the sword proved catastrophic. Communal tensions reached a new height, resulting in what came, ominously, to be known as the Great Calcutta Killing. (August 16, 1946, was the Muslim League's Direct Action day.) In conjunction with Muslim League plans for August 16, Jinnah announced: "'Today we bid good-by to constitutional methods'. And again: 'We have . . . forged a pistol and are in a position to use it.'"[2]

Although, according to some historians, neither Congress nor the League had ever truly accepted the Cabinet Mission's long-range plan—despite having at one time or another formally approved it—the British Labor Government, and the Cabinet Mission members whom it had sent to India, were in truth "sincere in wanting to transfer power." It was simply that no one had as yet found an acceptable method of doing so.[3]

Since no further plans were currently advanced by the Viceroy, the "Direct Action" resolution passed by the Muslim League, and "withdrawal of its acceptance of the Cabinet Mission plan accomplished what Congress had failed so far to do. The reaction of the British Cabinet was reported to Gandhi . . . by a friend from London, in a letter in the first week of August: 'After Jinnah's threat (of Direct Action), the British Cabinet asked the Viceroy to send for Jinnah and tell [him] that if he was not prepared to play the game the British Cabinet had decided to hand over responsibility to the Congress and such other people as were prepared to work with them and to go ahead without Jinnah. The Viceroy pleaded that calling Jinnah immediately after the threat would give the impression that the British were frightened by [it] and suggested not seeing Jinnah. The Cabinet agreed.

"'Jinnah's outburst [gave] . . . the Ministers as well as the administration [in Britain] and in India the good shaking that they badly needed.'"

On August 6, 1946 the Viceroy, acting under instructions from London, invited Nehru to submit proposals for formation of an Interim Government.

From the Viceroy's note to Nehru: "I have decided with the concurrence of His Majesty's Government to invite you as President of the Congress to submit to me proposals for the formation of an Interim Government. . . . It will be for you to consider whether you should first

[1] Ibid., pp. 251–53.
[2] Ibid., p. 251.
[3] Based on M.B., p. 317.

discuss them with Mr Jinnah; if you were able to reach an agreement with him, I should naturally be delighted." Thus the way was "cleared ... for the Congress to accept the [Viceroy's] invitation".[1]

Nehru wrote to the Viceroy on August 10, 1946: "We would have welcomed the formation of a Coalition Government with the Muslim League." In view of the resolution adopted by, and the statements recently made on behalf of the Muslim League on July 29, it was not possible to expect that its leaders would agree to cooperate, however. "Any premature attempt to induce them to do so", stated Nehru, "might produce a contrary result. Such an attempt will inevitably become public and result in communal controversy and further delay which you rightly deprecate."

Nehru suggested that the best course—as recorded by Pyarelal— "would, therefore, be for the Viceroy to make a public announcement to the effect that he had invited the President of ... Congress to form [a] Provisional Government and that the latter had accepted his invitation." "It will then be possible", noted Nehru, "for us to approach the Muslim League and invite its cooperation. We shall welcome that cooperation, but if this is denied us, we shall be prepared to go ahead without it."

"The Viceroy accepted ... Nehru's suggestion and, on the 12th August, put out the necessary announcement. After the announcement ... Nehru made another attempt to woo Jinnah. The reception he got from him was chilling. . . .

"Hardly had the letter of invitation to ... Nehru [mentioned above] left the Viceroy's desk, than it seems, he regretted his action. He even tried to recall his letter but was informed that it was too late. Thereafter, his own effort was concentrated on counteracting it by bringing the League into the Interim Government at any cost. . . .

Even before "Nehru could submit his list of names for the Government," [the Viceroy] "wanted to send for Jinnah ... to persuade him to come into the Government."[2]

The following correspondence indicates the protracted nature of the differences that continued to exist among the various parties concerned with a potential transfer of power.]

[From letter to Wavell—August 19, 1946.] When you wrote to me that you had decided, with the concurrence of the British Government, to invite me, as President of the Congress, to make proposals for the formation of an Interim Government, we accepted this invitation on the understanding that the responsibility would be ours. . . . I approached ... Jinnah and sought the cooperation of the Muslim League. Mr Jinnah was not willing to cooperate with us. . . . We had then to proceed without him and the League. . . .

[1] M.L.P. (Vol. I), pp. 264–65.
[2] Ibid., pp. 265–66.

Your new proposal would change the whole approach to the problem
and put an end to the responsibility which, at your suggestion, we had
undertaken. We are now asked to revert to the previous stage which, we
had thought, had finally ended after months of fruitless effort.

[When Jinnah made a statement on August 18 that especially upset Lord
Wavell, the latter finally lost patience, noting: "I have read the statement by Mr Jinnah in today's paper and in the present circumstances I
agree that there would be no use in my sending for him."
    "In submitting his proposals for the formation of the Interim Govern-
ment, ... Nehru ... pressed for the number of members in the new
Cabinet to be raised to fifteen for efficient discharge of functions, as also
to enable a representative of the Anglo-Indian community to be included.
But the Viceroy ... while he saw the 'advantage of having an Anglo-
Indian representative in the Executive Council', objected to it on the
ground that it would make the League's joining the Government more
difficult, and 'the matter of paramount importance ... (was) to leave no
stone unturned to get the Muslim League to join the Executive Council.'
... Nehru took strong exception to this as also to the Interim Government being referred to as the Executive Council. The new Government,
though formed within the terms of the existing law, it was well recognised,
was in nature and formation different from its predecessors; and in the
invitation sent to the Congress and in the official announcement made in
that behalf, it had been referred to as the 'Interim Government'. Why
this reversion to the old designation? Was it again to please Jinnah?"]

[From letter to Wavell—August 22, 1946.] I do not know what your conception is of the proposed Provisional Government. Is it going to be just
another caretaker Government waiting and hoping for the Muslim League
to walk in when it feels inclined to do so? That would simply mean an
ineffective, unstable Government ... which exists more or less on sufferance ... That might well lead to a worsening of the situation and possibly
even to a repetition of the horrors of Calcutta. It is not for this that we
would care to join the Provisional Government.

[From letter to Wavell—August 28, 1946.] In your broadcast on August
24th you refer to the Constituent Assembly and the question of grouping
as follows: "I can assure the Muslim League that the procedure laid down
in the statement of May 16th regarding the framing of Provincial and
Group constitutions will be faithfully adhered to ... and that the Congress
are ready to agree that any dispute of interpretation may be referred to
the Federal Court. ..." [1]

[1] Ibid., p. 267–68.

What you said in your broadcast in this respect [about the Federal Court deciding questions of interpretation was] in conformity with what we have ourselves said. What you now suggest . . . means that there should be no reference to the Federal Court of this particular matter, and that we should accept the interpretation put upon it by the Cabinet Mission and you, as distinguished from the legal interpretation which may be put upon it by the Federal Court. You stressed this and the need for communal harmony presumably because of what has happened in Calcutta. This approach is new. The Calcutta occurrences had taken place before your broadcast in which you have referred to the Federal Court deciding questions of interpretation.

All of us are extremely anxious to do everything in our power to promote communal harmony, but the way you suggest seems to us to lead to a contrary result. To change our declared policy, which is generally acknowledged to be fair, because of intimidation is surely not the way to peace. . . .

Your reference to the non-summoning of the Constituent Assembly, unless the course suggested by you was adopted by us, seemed to us extraordinary. . . . It is both a legal and moral obligation now to go on with the Constituent Assembly. . . . It cannot be held up because some people do not choose to join it and disturbances take place in the country. . . . If they refuse to join . . . the Constituent Assembly must proceed without them. . . .[1]

[From letter to Wavell—August 29, 1946.] I agree with you that the problem is not merely a legal . . . but a practical one. . . . We have considered it in all its practical aspects. . . . If the Congress acted [upon] your present suggestion, many minorities would feel that we were ready to betray them and their interests because of pressure from some source. . . . If any change has to be made it should be through a recognised process, such as the one referred to by us, and not casually and over the the heads of many people concerned. As regards the Constituent Assembly . . . an indefinite postponement of it would not only be wrong in principle but would have harmful practical results even from the point of view of our gaining cooperation of the Muslim League which we desire.[2]

[1] Ibid., pp. 268-69.
[2] Ibid., p. 270.

11 | The Interim Government— Reactions to Communal Riots, August

The Interim Government

[After prolonged controversy, Congress decided to withdraw its final objections to entering an Interim Government. It thus became possible to form a new Government on September 2, 1946, with Nehru as Vice-President of the Viceroy's Executive Council—*de facto* Prime Minister— and Member for External Affairs and Commonwealth Relations. Despite this momentous occurrence, on the same day the Private Secretary to the Viceroy issued a directive "that Members of the Government who might be visiting an Indian State were expected to give previous information of their visit to the Political Department. Also, that Members should avoid making speeches of a 'political nature' in the Indian States."[1]]

[From letter to Wavell, of the same date, concerning the above directive— September 4, 1946.] This appears to be an old convention. . . . I do not quite understand why we should function in a State under the tutelage of the Political Department. . . . It [would] be more fitting if the Political Department brought itself in line with the present Government.[2]

[From letter to Wavell in conjunction with absence of various members from meetings of Interim Government.] I do not quite understand a portfolio remaining vacant or reverting to the Governor-General because a Member happens to be absent for a while. . . . The whole Cabinet is jointly responsible for major decisions. . . . If a Member is absent for a while, does this portfolio suddenly revert to the Governor-General and the sense of common responsibility in regard to it cease ? . . . In such cases the obvious course appears to be that the portfolio should either be handled by some other member or by me as Vice-President. . . .

As you have yourself indicated, the present Council is different in nature and content from previous ones, there is a popular basis for it, and because of this you decided that secretaries of departments should not approach you directly but only through [a] Member. . . . Your alternative to this would be that a popular Government suddenly ceases to function

[1] M.LP (Vol. I), p. 273.
[2] Ibid., pp. 273-74

in regard to some portfolios because one or more of the Members are absent for a while. . . . I do feel that the approach to this problem should be in line with the conception of a growth of popular Government under responsible Ministers.[1]

[Despite such altercations, the Interim Government finally did come into being. In his initial broadcast to the nation in his new role, Nehru gave voice to his vision of the future, of his hopes and dreams—many of which were soon to be shattered by forces beyond his control. Yet the very uttering of his beliefs gave direction and a sense of purpose not only to India, but to other nations also aspiring toward freedom, nationhood, and a peaceful world order.]

[Inaugural broadcast as *de facto* Prime Minister—New Delhi, September 7, 1946.] Six days ago my colleagues and I sat on the chairs of high office in the Government of India. A new Government came into being in this ancient land, the Interim or Provisional Government we called it, the stepping stone to the full independence of India. Many thousands of messages of greeting and good wishes came to us from all parts of the world and from every nook and corner of India. And yet we asked for no celebration of this historic event and even restrained our people's enthusiasm. For we wanted them to realize that we were yet on the march and the goal had still to be reached. There were many difficulties and obstacles on the way and our journey's end might not be so near as people thought. Any weakness now, any complacency would be fatal to our cause.

Our hearts were heavy also with the terrible tragedy of Calcutta and because of the insensate strife of brother against brother. The freedom we had envisaged and for which we had laboured, through generations of trial and suffering, was for all the people of India, and not for one group or class or the followers of one religion. We aimed at a co-operative commonwealth in which all would be equal sharers in opportunity and in all things that give meaning and value to life. Why then this strife, this fear and suspicion of each other?

I speak to you today not much of high policy or our programme for the future—that will have to wait a while—but to thank you for the love and affection which you have sent us in such abundant measure. That affection and spirit of co-operation are always welcome, but they will be needed more than ever in the difficult days ahead of us. A friend sent me the following message: "May you weather every storm, first pilot of the ship

[1] Ibid., p. 273.

of State, *bon voyage!*" A cheering message, but there are many storms ahead and our ship of State is old and battered and slow-moving and unsuited to this age of swift change. It will have to be scrapped and give place to another. But however old the ship and however feeble the pilot, when there are so many millions of willing hearts and hands to help, we can brave the high seas and face the future with confidence.

That future is already taking shape and India, this old and dear land of ours, is finding herself again through travail and suffering. She is youthful again with the bright eyes of adventure, and with faith in herself and her mission. For long years she had been narrowly confined and had lost herself in brooding. But now she looks out on the wide world and holds out her hands in friendship to the other peoples of the world, even though that world may still be full of conflict and thoughts of war.

The Interim National Government is part of a larger scheme which includes the Constituent Assembly which will meet soon to give shape to the Constitution of free and independent India. It is because of this expectation of an early realization of full independence that we have entered this Government, and we propose to function so as progressively to achieve that independence in action both in our domestic affairs and our foreign relations. We shall take full part in international conferences as a free nation with our own policy and not merely as a satellite of another nation. We hope to develop close and direct contacts with other nations and to co-operate with them in the furtherance of world peace and freedom.

We propose, as far as possible, to keep away from the power politics of groups, aligned against one another, which have led in the past to world wars and which may again lead to disasters on an even vaster scale. We believe that peace and freedom are indivisible and the denial of freedom anywhere must endanger freedom elsewhere and lead to conflict and war. We are particularly interested in the emancipation of colonial and dependent countries and peoples, and in the recognition in theory and practice of equal opportunities for all races. We repudiate utterly the Nazi doctrine of racialism, wheresoever and in whatever form it may be practised. We seek no dominion over others and we claim no privileged position over other peoples. But we do claim equal and honourable treatment for our people wherever they may go, and we cannot accept any discrimination against them.

The world, in spite of its rivalries and hatreds and inner conflicts, moves inevitably towards closer co-operation and the building up of a world commonwealth. It is for this One World that free India will work, a world in which there is the free co-operation of free peoples, and no class or group exploits another.

In spite of our past history of conflict, we hope that an independent India will have friendly and co-operative relations with England and the countries of the British Commonwealth. But it is well to remember what is happening in one part of the Commonwealth today. In South Africa racialism is the State doctrine and our people are putting up a heroic struggle against the tyranny of a racial minority. If this racial doctrine is going to be tolerated it must inevitably lead to vast conflicts and world disaster.

We send our greetings to the people of the United States of America to whom destiny has given a major role in international affairs. We trust that this tremendous responsibility will be utilized for the furtherance of peace and human freedom everywhere.

To that other great nation of the modern world, the Soviet Union, which also carries a vast responsibility for shaping world events, we send greeting. They are our neighbours in Asia and inevitably we shall have to undertake many common tasks and have much to do with each other.

We are of Asia and the peoples of Asia are nearer and closer to us than others. India is so situated that she is the pivot of Western, Southern and South-East Asia. In the past her culture flowed to all these countries and they came to her in many ways. Those contacts are being renewed and the future is bound to see a closer union between India and South-East Asia on the one side, and Afghanistan, Iran, and the Arab world on the other. To the furtherance of that close association of free countries we must devote ourselves. India has followed with anxious interest the struggle of the Indonesians for freedom and to them we send our good wishes.

China, that mighty country with a mighty past, our neighbour, has been our friend through the ages and that friendship will endure and grow. We earnestly hope that her present troubles will end soon and a united and democratic China will emerge, playing a great part in the furtherance of world peace and progress.

I have not said anything about our domestic policy, nor at this stage do I wish to do so. But that policy will inevitably have to be governed by the principles by which we have stood all these years. We shall look to the common and forgotten man in India and seek to bring him relief and raise his standard of living. We shall continue our fight against the curse of untouchability and other forms of enforced inequality, and shall especially try to help those who are economically or otherwise backward. Today millions lack food and clothing and houses, and many are on the verge of starvation. To meet this immediate need is an urgent and difficult task and we hope other countries will help us by sending foodgrains.

An equally urgent and vital task for us is to conquer the spirit of discord that is abroad in India. Out of mutual conflict we shall never build the House of India's freedom of which we have dreamt so long. All of us in this land have to live and work together, whatever political developments might take place. Hatred and violence will not alter this basic fact, nor will they stop the changes that are taking place in India.

There has been much heated argument about sections and groupings in the Constituent Assembly. We are perfectly prepared to, and have accepted, the position of sitting in sections, which will consider the question of formation of groups. I should like to make it clear, on behalf of my colleagues and myself, that we do not look upon the Constituent Assembly as an arena for conflict or for the forcible imposition of one viewpoint over another. That would not be the way to build up a contented and united India. We seek agreed and integrated solutions with the largest measure of goodwill behind them. We shall go to the Constituent Assembly with the fixed determination of finding a common basis for agreement on all controversial issues. And so, in spite of all that has happened and the hard words that have been said, we have kept the path of co-operation open and we invite even those who differ from us to enter the Constituent Assembly as equals and partners with us with no binding commitments. It may well be that when we meet and face common tasks, our present difficulties will fade away.

India is on the move and the old order passes. Too long have we been passive spectators of events, the playthings of others. The initiative comes to our people now and we shall make the history of our choice. Let us all join in this mighty task and make India, the pride of our heart, great among nations, foremost in the arts of peace and progress. The door is open and destiny beckons to all. There is no question of who wins and who loses, for we have to go forward and together as comrades and either all of us win or we all go down together. But there is going to be no failure. We go forward to success, to independence and to the freedom and well-being of the four hundred millions of India.[1]

Reactions to Communal Riots, August

[While continuing with his efforts to have the Muslim League join the Interim Government, Nehru simultaneously refused to permit either the

[1] I.A., pp. 339–43.

manner in which the new Government was to operate, or the Government itself, to be vitiated. He pressed for prompt creation of a Constituent Assembly with actual, rather than merely theoretical power. He stead-fastly argued against communalism and separatism. After the monstrous communal riots that occurred in Calcutta during August—in the wake of the Muslim League July 29 Call to Direct Action—he made various public statements in the hope of averting further violence.

"Nehru's reaction to the riots was typical of the man: deep sympathy for the victims of both communities; stern rebukes to the perpetrators of the ghastly crimes, regardless of the source; courageous tours of the worst affected areas disregarding his personal safety; appeals for communal peace supplemented by threats of military retaliation. Nehru was appalled by the crazed resort to mass murder among normally placid peasants. With the long-sought prize of independence so near, the riots struck him as a dastardly blow to his hopes for a free India. 'There appears to be a competition in murder and brutality,' he said in the course of a moving report on the riots to the Central Assembly. The shock waves were to recur time and time again, leaving indelible marks on Nehru's outlook for the future."[1]

[How to fight gangsters—August 26, 1946.] Calcutta has been a terrible lesson, and the horror and fearful tragedy of the killing and inhuman atrocities there have shaken up all of us.

The new development of violence, involving stabbing, arson and looting, chiefly in cities, obviously cannot be tolerated or else all organised life would become impossible. It has become a challenge to every decent instinct of humanity and it should be treated as such. What has led up to this, the incitements to violence, the direct invitations to the shedding of blood, is worthy of inquiry so that effective action may be taken. For the present, we are concerned with the immediate steps to be taken. It is well to remember, however, that during the past twenty-six years of repeated conflict on an intensive and mass scale between the nationalist movement and the British power in India, nothing of this kind has happened. A very few regrettable incidents have occurred, but in spite of high passion and deep feeling, our movement has been carried on at a high level of peaceful and decent behaviour, even towards our opponents. It is well to compare this with recent events.

In the present then, what are we to do? The responsibility for maintain-ing peace and order must necessarily fall on the Government and its police forces. But every citizen has also a certain responsibility and in a crisis like this it is an obligation for every citizen to discharge this respon-sibility. For the conflict is between ordinary decency and bestial behaviour.

[1] M.B., p. 321.

When such conflicts occur, there is always danger of even decent persons being swept away by passions and sinking to low levels. We cannot permit this, or else there would be no hope for India. Inevitably, when one is attacked, there has to be self-defence and organised defence by the police as well as by the people. Anti-social and gangster elements can never be allowed to dominate a situation. This requires co-operation between the people and the police and a spirit of accommodation between them so that such anti-social elements might be isolated and dealt with adequately.

It has been the usual practice, when a communal riot occurs, [to form] a peace committee ... consisting ... of some of the very elements that have caused trouble. Such peace committees may be useful but their utility is not enhanced by the presence of these elements. Troublemakers do not easily transform themselves into messengers of peace and goodwill. It is more necessary for ... average citizens to organise themselves so as to prevent trouble, or nip it in the bud as soon as it begins.[1]

[Broadcast on violence in the Punjab—Delhi, September 9, 1946.] During the last few weeks I have wandered about West Punjab and East Punjab and my mind is full [of] the horror of the things that I saw and that I heard. During these last few days in the Punjab and in Delhi, I have supped my fill of horror. That, indeed, is the only feast that we can have now....

This morning our leader, our master, Mahatma Gandhi, came to Delhi, and I went to see him and I sat by his side, for a while, and wondered how low we had fallen from the great ideals that he had placed before us.

I go to the country-side, and people with spikes and all sorts of destructive weapons, when they see me, shout "Mahatma Gandhi ki jai! Jawaharlal ki jai!" I feel ashamed to hear these cries from these people, who might have committed murder, loot and arson, in the name of Mahatma Gandhi. It is not by shouting slogans that they will wash off the evils deeds that they have done. And even we will not get over these evil deeds by just honouring the Mahatma in name, and not following what he [has] told us all these long years.

What is happening now is something directly inimical, and so directly opposed to these ideals. The very thought of it shames me, and makes me sometimes doubt if all the good work that we have done in these many years is not going to bear fruit at all. And yet that doubt cannot remain for long. For I do believe that good work must bear good results just as I do

[1] B.I.S.J.N. (Vol. I), p. 390.

believe that evil must bear evil consequences. There has been enough of
evil work in this country. Let us put an end to it, and start good work, and
try to follow the great lessons that the Mahatma has taught us.[1]

12	**Congress-League Controversy, October— Letters to Jinnah—Correspondence with Wavell**

Congress-League Controversy, October

[On October 4, 1946, a list of demands was made by Jinnah "as the basis
of the League's joining the Interim Government."[2] Meanwhile, Nehru
continued tirelessly to argue in favor of a rational method of establishing
a properly representative, secular, united, independent and democratic
Government for India. (Because of space limitations it is not possible to
include the entire Nehru-Wavell-Jinnah correspondence.[3]) Nehru's
letters that follow, reflect something of the agonizing conflicts to be
resolved.]

[From letter to Wavell: reactions to Viceroy's response to Jinnah's
October 4 demand.] (1) Mr Jinnah mentions that the six nominees of the
Congress will include one Scheduled Caste representative. And yet he
says further on that "it must not be taken that the Muslim League has
agreed to, or approves of, the selection of the Scheduled Caste representative." I do not see how the question of agreement or approval by the
Muslim League arises in regard to the nominees of the Congress. . . . It is
true that legally and constitutionally speaking the ultimate responsibility
for the appointment of Members rests with the Governor-General. But
it was understood that the legal responsibility should be exercised on the
advice of the person charged with forming the Government. . . .

(2) I am personally agreeable . . . to a Muslim League Member being

[1] M.J.N., p. 343.
[2] M.L.P. (Vol. I), p. 277.
[3] For a fuller record of negotiations of the period, see M.L.P., S.D.I.C. and H.I.N.C.

chosen as Vice-Chairman of the Co-ordination Committee of the Cabinet. . . . I feel, however, that your answer to this question introduces a new element which creates a difficulty. You say that you will arrange to nominate a Muslim League Member to preside over the Cabinet in the event of the Governor-General and the Vice-President being absent. I think that any such nomination by you would neither be constitutional nor otherwise desirable. This, however, can be done by agreement between us. . . .

(3) If we function as a Cabinet, as we must, the whole Cabinet should be consulted before any decision is arrived at. Naturally, the major parties would confer together. . . . It would seriously interfere with the Cabinet system, and the growth of the convention that Cabinet advice should be accepted, if the Governor-General consulted each group or individual Members separately and then came to his own decision in the matter.

(4) What I have stated above flows from the acceptance of the principle of Cabinet responsibility and the Governor-General's acceptance of Cabinet recommendations. . . . Our whole objective must necessarily be for the Cabinet to function together and not to be treated as consisting of separate groups which can be consulted separately as groups, thus putting an end to the cohesion and sense of joint responsibility in the Cabinet. Naturally, as you have pointed out . . . a Coalition Government either works by a process of mutual adjustments or does not work at all. . . . We have adopted the practice of meeting daily in informal Cabinet meetings to consider not only the formal Cabinet agendas but also all important matters relating to any Department. Thus, any important decision, to whatever Department it might relate, is considered by us jointly and actually becomes a joint decision as well as a joint responsibility. This avoids grouping within the Cabinet and at the same time helps in evolving an integrated solution or decision. If any procedure is adopted which encourages group functioning within the Cabinet and encourages separate groups to function separately, this would seriously militate against the whole conception of Cabinet Government which we are seeking to evolve and which we have already succeeded in evolving in a large measure during the past month.[1]

["On the 5th October . . . Nehru had a very full and, as he fancied, friendly talk with Jinnah. . . . But on the 7th October, he was surprised to receive a letter from Jinnah, which was . . . at variance with the spirit and drift of their whole talk."[2]]

[1] Ibid., pp. 278–79.
[2] Ibid., p. 282.

From Letters to Jinnah

I. [October 6, 1946.] I have consulted some of my colleagues about . . . the possibility of a rapprochement between the Muslim League and the Congress. We are all agreed that nothing could be happier and better for the country than that these two organisations should meet again as before as friends, having no mental reservations and bent on resolving all their differences by mutual consultation and never desiring or allowing the intervention of the British Government through the Viceroy or others or of any other foreign Power. We would, therefore, welcome the decision of the League to join the Interim Government [and] for it to work as a united team on behalf of India as a whole.

The points put forward by you in our conversation yesterday were:

(1) the formula suggested to you by Gandhiji [see analysis below];

(2) the League not being responsible for the members at present representing the Scheduled Castes and the Minorities;

(3) what should be done in case any vacancy should arise among the members representing the Minorities other than the Scheduled Castes;

(4) the procedure to be adopted over what may be called major communal issues; and

(5) alternating Vice-Presidentship.

Regarding No. 1, we feel that the formula is not happily worded. We do not question the purpose underlying it. We are willing, as a result of the elections, to accept the Muslim League as the authoritative representative organisation of an overwhelming majority of the Muslims of India and that as such and in accordance with democratic principles they have today the unquestionable right to represent the Muslims of India, provided that for identical reasons the League recognises the Congress as the authoritative organisation representing all non-Muslims and such Muslims as have thrown in their lot with the Congress. The Congress cannot agree to any restriction or limitations to be put upon it in choosing such representatives as they think proper from amongst the members of the Congress. We would suggest, therefore, that no formula is necessary and each organisation may stand on its merits.

Regarding No. 2, I am to say that the question of the League being responsible does not arise and, as you do not raise any objections to the present constitution of the Government in this respect, there is no question to be solved.

Regarding No. 3, I am to say that if any such vacancy arises, the whole

Cabinet will consider what should be done to replace the vacancy and advise the Viceroy accordingly. There can be no question of right in the matter of consultation with the League in regard to the representation of these minorities.

Regarding No. 4, your suggestion about the Federal Court is not feasible. Matters coming before the Cabinet cannot be made [the] subject-matter of references to a Court. We should thrash out all such matters amongst ourselves and bring up agreed proposals before the Cabinet. In the event of failure to reach an agreed decision, we should seek the method of arbitration of our own choice. We hope, however, that we will act with such mutual trust, forbearance and friendliness that there will be no occasion to go to such arbitration.

Regarding No. 5, it is out of the question to have any rotation in the vice-presidentship. We have no objection if you desire to have [an] additional Vice-Chairman for the Co-ordination Committee of the Cabinet, who can also preside at such committee meetings from time to time.

I am hoping that if your committee finally decide upon the League joining the National Cabinet, they will also decide simultaneously to join the Constituent Assembly or [make a recommendation] to your Council to this effect.

I need hardly mention that when an agreement has been reached by us, it can only be carried [out] by mutual agreement and not otherwise.[1]

II. [October 8, 1946.] I received your letter of October 7 as I was going to . . . meet you . . . last evening. I hurriedly glanced through it and was perturbed by it as it seemed to me to be at variance with the spirit of our talk the previous day. Subsequently we discussed various points and unfortunately could not convince each other.

On my return I read through your letter more carefully and consulted my colleagues. They were also disturbed not only by the letter but also by the list of points attached to it. This list had not been seen or considered by us previously. It had little relevance after our talk.

We have again given earnest consideration to the whole matter and we feel that we cannot state our position more clearly than I did in my letter to you of October 6, except for some variations which I shall indicate below. I shall, therefore, refer . . . you to that letter of mine which represents our general and specific viewpoints.

[1] H.I.N.C. (Vol. II), pp. ccliv–cclv.

9+N. II

As I have told you, my colleagues and I did not accept the formula agreed to by Gandhiji and you. The meeting between you and me was not arranged, so far as I was aware, on the agreed basis of that formula. We knew of it and were prepared to agree to the substance of that formula as stated to you in my letter of October 6. That formula contained a further paragraph which you have not quoted in your letter: "It is understood that all the ministers of the Interim Government will work as a team for the good of the whole of India and will never invoke the intervention of the Governor-General in any case."

While we still think that the formula is not happily worded, we are prepared, for the sake of the settlement we so earnestly desire, to accept the whole of it, including the paragraph left out in your letter.

In that case you will agree, I hope, that we should make our further position quite clear. It is clearly understood, of course, that the Congress has the right to appoint a Muslim out of its quota. Further, as I have stated in my previous letter, the Congress position in regard to the Nationalist Muslims and the small minorities should not be challenged by you.

In regard to points numbered two, three and four in my letter of October 6, I have stated our position and have nothing further to add. We have gone as far as we could to meet you and we are unable to go further. I trust that you will appreciate the position.

Regarding No. 5 (the question of the Vice-President) you made a suggestion yesterday that the Vice-President and the Leader of the House (the Central Assembly) should not be the same person. In the present circumstances this means that the Leader of the House should be a Muslim League member of the Cabinet. We shall agree to this.

I am writing this letter to you after full and careful consideration of all the issues involved and after consulting such of my colleagues as are here. It is in no spirit of carrying on an argument that I have written but rather to indicate to you our earnest desire to come to an agreement. We have discussed these matters sufficiently and the time has come for us to decide finally.[1]

III. [October 13, 1946.] I thank you for your letter of October 12. In this letter there are a number of mis-statements. What you have said does not fit in with my recollection of our conversations or what has taken place during the past few days. I need not, however, go into this matter now

[1] Ibid., pp. cclvi–cclvii.

as I have been informed by the Viceroy that the Muslim League have
agreed to nominate five persons on their behalf as members of the
Interim Government.[1]

From Correspondence with Wavell

[From letter to Wavell—October 14, 1946—on being informed of the
Muslim League's decision to come into the Interim Government.] It is
important for us to understand exactly how [Jinnah] proposes to join. . . .
The offer you made . . . was that five places . . . could be taken by the
Muslim League (and) . . . you made it clear that a Coalition Government
must necessarily work as a team and not as a joining together of rival
groups which did not cooperate for a common purpose (and) . . . the basis
for participation in the Cabinet must . . . be presumed to be the acceptance of the Cabinet Mission's statement of 16th May.[2]

["Jinnah's letter . . . accepting the Viceroy's offer of five seats in the
Interim Government was couched in terms of a general disapproval of the
'basis and scheme of setting up the Interim Government' and repudiation
of 'the decision already made'."[3]
  "Within ten days of taking office Nehru addressed to [General]
Auchinleck a memorandum on the problems of India's defence, 'more
especially', as he put it in his accompanying letter, 'in relation to foreign
policy'. The memorandum . . . revealed . . . a suspicion that the Army
was not yet fully a 'national' army and 'in accord with public sentiment'.
The [Prime] Minister was also anxious that Indian troops should be
withdrawn from Indonesia and Iraq, and British troops from India.
  "Since Auchinleck had spent the past twelve months and more trying
to forestall criticisms of this character and had anticipated, with a high
degree of sympathetic intuition, most of the demands which Nehru and
his colleagues would make when they were in power, it was not difficult
for him to answer the memorandum satisfactorily. . . . He had some experience [at the time] of politicians' interest in matters of defence."
  At the beginning of October, the Viceroy decided to have "further
talks with Jinnah, as a result of which Jinnah declared that he had received
better satisfaction. On October 15 the Interim Government was reconstituted; five Muslim League nominees joined it, under the leadership of
Liaquat Ali Khan. But co-operation between the two main wings was

[1] Ibid., p. cclviii. (Jinnah's letters of October, 1946, to Nehru are to be found in
H.I.N.C. (Vol. II).)
[2] M.L.P. (Vol. I), pp. 282–83.
[3] Ibid., p. 283.

beyond achieving," despite Liaquat's claim that "'We have come into the Government with the intention of working in harmony with our other colleagues—but you cannot clap with one hand'. . . . On the day he and his friends joined the Government, Nehru told the Viceroy that he deeply regretted the choice of candidates, which indicated a desire for conflict rather than co-operation.

"When Wavell urged that one of the three senior portfolios—External Affairs, Defence or Home Affairs—be transferred to one of the Muslim League members Nehru refused [claiming] . . . 'that this would have an unsettling effect all over the country'. When Wavell persisted, Nehru threatened to resign."[1]

When the Muslim League finally consented to enter a somewhat reconstituted Interim Government at the Viceroy's invitation on October 15, five Muslim League nominees were included in the new Government, "among them an Untouchable. . . . That the League had no intention of working in co-operation with the Congress became crystal clear. . . ." It stated firmly: "'We are going into the Interim Government to get a foothold to fight for our cherished goal of Pakistan. . . . The Interim Government is one of the fronts of the Direct Action Campaign.' Jinnah's motives for joining the Government, even though few of his demands had been met, appear to have been twofold. From the negative standpoint, continued League boycott would perpetuate the Congress monopoly of power at the Centre and would jeopardize the goal of Pakistan. Added to this was a desire to demonstrate that the two communities could not function in harmony and that Pakistan was the only way out of the impasse.

"Nehru was aware of the danger in such a coalition but he was powerless to alter the course of events."[2]]

[From letter to Wavell—October 15, 1946.] We have not raised any objection to the names proposed on behalf of the Muslim League. . . . But I think I owe it to you to tell you privately and personally that I regret deeply the choice [of candidates] which the . . . League has made. That choice itself indicates a desire to have conflict rather than to work in cooperation. . . .[3] Our past experience does not encourage us to rely on vague and ambiguous phrases. . . . It is desirable . . . to be precise . . . and to know exactly where we stand.[4]

[1] A.C.B., pp. 849–50.
[2] M.B., p. 323.
[3] M.L.P. (Vol. I), p. 283.
[4] Quoted in M.B., p. 323.

[On October 23, 1946, Lord Wavell wrote to Nehru: "I have made it clear to Mr Jinnah . . . that the Muslim League's entry into the Interim Government is conditional on the acceptance of the scheme of . . . May 16th . . . and that he must call his Council at an early date to agree to this.

"As I have told you, Mr Jinnah has assured me that the Muslim League will come into the Interim Government and the Constituent Assembly with the intention of cooperating. . . .

"I consider that the Muslim League are entitled to one out of the three following portfolios: External Affairs, Home and Defence. I would be grateful if you would let me know which of these portfolios you advise should be given to the . . . League." (This insistence, notes Pyarelal, in spite of Nehru's feeling that it would be improper to change the three portfolios, was more than the latter could accept.)[1]]

[From letter to Wavell—October 23, 1946.] We feel . . . that it would be an entirely wrong step, leading to most unfortunate consequences, if any change was made in the portfolios of Defence and Home. . . .

In regard to the portfolio of External Affairs, some similar considerations arise. . . . It seems to us essential that even before the question of portfolios is considered, other matters should be cleared up.

[Nehru already had told the Viceroy that Patel would rather resign than continue in the Cabinet if his portfolio was tampered with.] Whatever might have been done at the time of the formation of the Government if the Muslim League had then come in, at the present moment to ask . . . Patel to leave his portfolio would be an act of extreme discourtesy to him. He had been made a special target of attack by the official organ of the Muslim League and it becomes, therefore, still more unbecoming for us to ask him to leave this portfolio. Indeed, I do not think he will care to remain in the Government if he is asked to do so.[2]

[From further communications to the Viceroy, October 23, 1946.]

I am glad that Mr Jinnah has assured you that the . . . League is coming into the Interim Government and Constituent Assembly with the intention of cooperating . . . (and) that . . . [its] entry into the Interim Government is conditional on . . . acceptance of . . . the Cabinet Delegation [scheme] of May 16th. While you have made this clear to Mr Jinnah, it is not equally clear what the . . . League's view is on this subject.[3]

[1] M.L.P. (Vol. I), pp. 285–86.
[2] Ibid., p. 286. (October 15, 1946.) Sardar Patel was to become Home, and Information and Broadcasting Minister.
[3] Ibid., p. 285.

You know how arguments and difficulties have arisen in the past over any matter left vague. It would be exceedingly unfortunate if we did not clarify the position completely before starting this new experiment. . . .[1]

In my correspondence with you and in your letter addressed to me as well as to Mr Jinnah it was made clear that the . . . League's joining the Interim Government meant inevitably their acceptance of the long-term scheme of the Cabinet Delegation contained in the statement of May 16. I need not trouble you with reference to this in various letters. It was pointed out then that a formal decision of the . . . League to this effect would have to be taken by the Council of the League, as they had originally passed the resolution of non-acceptance. Nevertheless, it was made clear that the Working Committee of the League would itself recommend the acceptance of this scheme and the formality could follow soon after. It was on this basis that we proceeded. We suggest, therefore, that these two points should be cleared up.[2]

Now it is by no means clear what the position of the . . . League is in regard to the long-term arrangement. . . . So far as we know, the Council of the . . . League (has not) been convened. . . . I was told (by the Viceroy during the talk on the previous day) that Mr Jinnah . . . and his Working Committee have not agreed to accept the statement of May 16th unless something further happens.[3]

The . . . League's acceptance of the long-term scheme as embodied in the statement of May 16, [is] subject only to a formal ratification by the Council of the League at an early date, which should be fixed. The approach of the League to the Interim Government . . . [must be clarified]. . . .

If this clarification is satisfactory, the next step to be taken is the allotment of portfolios. The second step cannot precede the first, for it is dependent upon it and governed by it.

From past experience, you will appreciate how this clarification and precision are necessary in order to avoid future trouble. This is all the more necessary because the . . . League are not joining the Interim Government after an agreement with the Congress. Even as it is, we welcome their coming in, but that coming in would have little value and in fact might even be harmful to all concerned if it was really a prelude to inner as well as to outer conflicts.[4]

[1] Ibid., p. 284
[2] S.D.I.C. (Vol. II), pp. 653-54.
[3] M.L.P. (Vol. I), p. 284.
[4] S.D.I.C. (Vol. II), p. 654.

[From letter to Wavell, October 24, 1946.] I have consulted my colleagues.
. . . We cannot continue in the Government if a decision is imposed upon
us against our will. . . . We would not have attached importance to the
allocation of portfolios but for the implications and circumstances which
I have already mentioned and which compel us to do so.

Two months ago I was asked to form the Interim Government and I
undertook the responsibility. This was done as a result of all the talks and
negotiations which preceded it with the concurrence of H.M.G. [His
Majesty's Government]. Now that a crisis has arisen which is leading to
our resignation and termination of this Government, I think H.M.G.
should be informed of all the developments.

["Lord Wavell was not prepared for this. His only desire was to bring . . .
the League [into the Government]. So he capitulated on the question of
portfolios and the Congress continued in office."[1]]

13 | Of Subjects other than the Impending Independence of India: Statements at Time of Arrest in Kashmir, on Atomic Bomb, Racial Issues, Foreign Policy, Food Situation, African Aspirations, Communalism (Summer–Autumn, 1946)

[Nehru made numerous pronouncements on subjects other than the Cabinet Mission proposals, League-Congress tensions, the Interim Government and the Constituent Assembly, during the summer and autumn of
1946. As previously noted, he was arrested at the time of his trip to
Kashmir, in June, 1946, when he rushed there to defend his colleague,
Sheikh Saheb Abdullah, a popular Kashmiri leader on trial for treason for
his pro-Independence activities. The District Magistrate in Kashmir
served an externment order against Nehru which demanded that he leave
the territory and not return without written permission, since his presence

[1] M.L.P. (Vol. I), p. 286.

might cause a breach of the public peace. Nehru defied the order, refusing to leave the State territory, despite the fact that the Magistrate reminded him that he was defying valid orders of a legally constituted authority.]

[Interchange with District Magistrate—Kashmir, June, 1946.]
[Nehru.] "During the past twenty-five years I have never obeyed a single order of the British Government in India or any Maharajah which came in my way. . . . When once a course of action is taken [I] never [go] back, [but] forward; if you think otherwise, then you don't know [me]. No power on earth can prevent me from going anywhere in India unless I am arrested or forcibly removed." [The District Magistrate.] "The Military and the police are here and untoward incidents are likely to happen. . . ." [Nehru.] "I am going to be callous about it; it does not matter if a few people die in a movement, one day we will all have to die, and it is immaterial if some die now for a cause." [The District Magistrate.] "When you get into Government do you expect your orders to be carried out?" [Nehru.] "That Government will be a popular Government with the people's backing and not a corrupt Government like that of Kashmir; the orders of the popular Government will be carried out and if necessary enforced."[1]

[From speech—Bombay, June 26, 1946.] It [is] a very grave responsibility for any country [to use] atom bombs. A very great responsibility rests with the United States. It justified the use of [the] atomic bomb on the ground that it stopped [the] war, but by unleashing such a weapon it [has] created a dangerous situation. The atomic bomb brought a measure of hope also. Faced with such a destructive weapon, people might wake up. . . .
   [As] long as the world [is] constituted as it [is], every country [will] have to devise and use the latest scientific devices for its protection. [I have] no doubt India [will] develop her scientific researches and [I hope] Indian scientists [will] use the atomic force for constructive purposes. But if India [is] threatened, she [will] inevitably try to defend herself by all means at her disposal. [I hope] India, in common with other countries, [will] prevent the use of atomic bombs[2]

[From speech—July, 1946.] It is not my habit to raise racial issues. Indeed I have always laid stress on the fact that our quarrel was and is

[1] V.I. (Sept., 1946), p. 332.
[2] B.A.I., pp. 353-54.

with [a] system of government and not with any particular race or nationality. . . . If that system of government continues even after the withdrawal of British dominance, that would give little freedom or relief to India. . . .

I realise that every government considers it its first duty to maintain itself and to resist and suppress any attack upon it. Of that I [make] no complaint. But there are certain limits of decency and humanity which no government or its officers are supposed to transgress. All these limits were passed in these past years in India and numerous cases of almost inhumane and atrocious behaviour have come to light. A government which values its fair name should investigate all such charges and punish those who are found guilty. But our present Government is afraid of nothing more than of such an investigation and tries to prevent it.

For my part what has happened in India, and whatever may happen, will not induce me to introduce racial issues in the argument. I came to the conclusion long ago that no race or people can be condemned wholesale, and I know too many decent and honourable Englishmen to cast the blame on them as a race or nationality. But that has nothing to do with my judgment on what happened in India [from the time of the "Quit India" Movement of 1942, throughout the remainder of the war period]. None of us who experienced these years, or have knowledge of the facts, can ever forget what happened then.[1]

[On India's Foreign Policy—Press Conference—September 27, 1946. From a cross-section of subjects touched upon.]

So far [as] her near neighbours are concerned India will watch with close interest the development of events in Palestine, Iran, Indonesia, China, Siam and Indo-China, as well as in the foreign possessions in India itself, with every sympathy [for] the aspiration of the peoples of these lands for the attainment of internal peace, freedom (where they lack it) and of their due place in the comity of nations.

With the U.S.A. and China, India already has a form of diplomatic contact. The relations thus already existing will, it is hoped, shortly be strengthened by the exchange of [representatives] on an independent diplomatic footing.

The first step necessary for India's separate representation abroad is the creation of an Indian Foreign Service to man diplomatic, Consular

[1] Ibid., pp. 357–58.

9*

and commercial posts in foreign countries as well as countries in the British Empire. . . .

The period of India's separate representation abroad must begin with the best material available, and care will be taken to ensure that persons in all walks of life who possess the requisite qualifications are able to offer themselves for selection. The training of . . . older recruits will necessarily be brief, [since] they will be required to take up appointments as soon as possible; but it is intended that new recruits should receive instruction in such subjects as economics, world history, international affairs and foreign languages, and . . . spend a part of their training period at a foreign university. Other matters of detail, such as salaries and allowances, the syllabus of the entrance examination, are still under consideration.

At present there are Indian diplomatic officials in the U.S.A. and China, and High Commissioners in Australia and South Africa. . . .

[We now also have] representatives in Burma, Ceylon and Malaya and Trade Commissioners in several countries. With the creation of the new service the existing posts will be strengthened and new ones opened. It will be necessary to work out a system of priorities, but obviously first consideration must be given to countries with which we already have contacts and to our neighbours in the East as well as in the West.

[The] Government propose as soon as practicable to examine, in consultation with all the interests concerned, the problem of the tribal areas of the North-West Frontier. The question is one of All-India importance, for the tribes are the guardians of the northern doorway to India and the security and well-being of these areas is, therefore, a definite factor in the defence of this country.

I should like to make it quite clear that in reviewing the problem there is no intention whatever of depriving the tribes of their existing freedom which they have defended so jealously and valiantly for many years, still less to impose any scheme on them against their will. It follows that Government's approach to the problem will be essentially a friendly one seeking co-operation and consultation with the tribes' ways and means of solving their economic difficulties, promoting their welfare generally and bringing them into a happy and mutually beneficial association with their neighbours in the settled districts.

I have said that the question is one of All-India importance. So it is, but there is a wider aspect to it than this. The tribal areas of the North-West Frontier lie along an international frontier—the frontier which divides India from its friendly neighbour, Afghanistan. From this situation arises an international obligation, for our friends, the Afghans, look to us to preserve peace and order in the tribal areas in the [interest] of the tranquillity of their own country. They may rest assured that in seeking a new approach to the problem the fullest regard will be paid to our obligations.

It will fall to the Constituent Assembly in consultation with the interests concerned, to decide in what way Baluchistan will enter the new Indian body politic and how the Baluchistan of the future will be administered. But in view of the comparative backwardness of political development in Baluchistan, Government are already considering the question of forming as soon as practicable an Advisory Council drawn from representative institutions and organisations in Baluchistan to assist the Agent to the Governor-General. This would be a preliminary to the introduction of a fuller democratic system of administration.

It is the intention of Government to consult at every stage the wishes of the inhabitants of Baluchistan and not to ignore such indigenous institutions as the tribal jirgas. . . .

Towards the United Nations Organization India's attitude is that of whole-hearted co-operation and unreserved adherence, in both spirit and letter, to the charter governing it. To that end, India will participate fully in its various activities and endeavour to play that role in its councils to which her geographical position, population and contribution towards peaceful progress entitle her. In particular, the Indian Delegation will make it clear that India stands for the independence of all colonial and dependent peoples and their full right to self-determination. . . .

The most important item on the agenda from India's point of view is the case against South Africa. It is understood that South Africa will contend that the matter is not within the jurisdiction of the General Assembly as it is essentially one of domestic jurisdiction. With this contention the Government of India do not agree. In their view the treatment of Indians in South Africa is fundamentally a moral and human issue which, in view of the "purposes" and "principles" so clearly stated in the Charter of the United Nations, the General Assembly cannot disregard.

A further important matter will be that of the new International Trusteeship system. The Indian Delegation will stress the point that sovereignty everywhere vests in the people of a country. If for any reason immediate independence is not feasible, then India would not object to the territory being placed under United Nations trusteeship for a limited period. The attitude of the delegation will be that all Asians and the people of dependent countries stand together for freedom and for emancipation from foreign control, as this is the only way to bring about world peace and progress.

Another item of importance concerns the Union of South Africa's wish to absorb the Mandated Territory of South-West Africa. This proposition India's delegation will oppose on a point of principle; the Government of India consider that Annexation of a Mandated Territory would be fundamentally opposed to the conception of mandates and trusteeship and that sovereignty resides ultimately in the people of a territory, whose wishes and interests are paramount. The correct course, in their view, would be for S.-W. Africa to be placed first under trusteeship of the Trusteeship Council and General Assembly of the United Nations and then to consider its future.

Two items on the agenda have to do with the privilege of veto enjoyed by the Five Great Powers in the Security Council—or as those countries prefer to term it, the "rule of great power unanimity." The attitude of the delegation towards this controversial issue will be that, although on principle India cannot like such an essentially undemocratic provision in the Charter, she attaches the greatest importance to the continuance of great power unanimity and co-operation within the framework of the United Nations and would do nothing to prejudice that position.

Progress in the conference now in session in Paris to decide terms of peace with Italy, Rumania, Bulgaria, Hungary and Finland has been regrettably, but perhaps understandably slow. India's delegation has wherever possible followed an independent line of fair compromise, and has supported those proposals which seemed to offer the solution most generally equitable. The delegation has throughout borne clearly in mind the humanitarian aspect of each problem confronting the conference.

For two reasons India has refrained from presenting a formal claim for reparations from Italy: first, because she has no wish to reduce the amount of reparations available for distribution to countries whose claims may be entitled to priority of consideration, and second, because she preferred not to add to that heavy burden which Italy must carry up the steep hill towards economic recovery. The delegation has, however, reserved the right to utilize Italian assets in India towards liquidating Indian nationals' claim to compensation for damage arising out of the war, and for meeting in part certain other claims.

India's concern in the future of the ex-Italian Colonies in Africa has been made fully apparent. . . .

[Of Ceylon.] Unfortunately, there has been, for some time past, a kind of impasse with regard to our relations with Ceylon. . . .

But we have tried our utmost, and we propose to continue trying, to approach the people of Ceylon and the Ceylon Government in a friendly manner, because it is inevitable that Ceylon and India must pull together in future and we do not want a trace of bad blood between us.

[Of Burma.] We welcome [formation of a new Government] from many points of view, first of all, in the hope that this will lead rapidly to the freedom and independence of Burma. And, secondly, we do not only hope but expect that the relations between our Government and the new Burmese Government will be friendly and cordial. . . .

It [is] a very well known fact that Indians [are] a hundred per cent in sympathy with the Indonesian Republic. . . . We want them to win through and establish their freedom . . . and we should like to help and support them in every way in their task. We have not recognised the Indonesian Republic in the formal sense that nations recognise other nations, but in practice we recognise it. . . .

We are entirely opposed to policing other countries, and more especially opposed to the use of any Indian resources, men or money, in opposition to the national movement in any other country. We should like to have all our Indian troops back in India, wherever they may be. We have been assured that this process is going on. It seems to us that it has taken longer than it need have done, but the principle is admitted that they must come back. For instance, from Indonesia many have come back. A fair number still remain there, but we are told that all of them will be back by the end of November. Apart from the question of shipping whenever the question of troops comes in, one has to deal with complicated and rather static organisms like War Offices. . . .

Nepal is an independent country so far as we are concerned. If, in future, Nepal chooses to have some kind of closer union with India, we shall welcome it.[1]

[Appeal to permit foodstuffs to sail: (from personal message to Will Clayton, Acting Secretary of State, United States of America—September 20, 1946).] In view of the very serious food situation in India, which is being aggravated by the delay in the arrival of promised allotments due to shipping strikes in America, we . . . earnestly request you, and through [your] labor leaders, to permit and arrange for the earliest despatch of food ships to India. We would be very grateful to you and the labor leaders concerned if they will make a special exception in favor of sending foodgrains abroad which will bring urgently needed relief to millions of people.[2]

[1] H.I.N.C. (Vol. II), Appendix, pp. ccxlv–ccli.
[2] V.I. (Oct., 1946), p. 340.

[Always sympathetic to African aspirations for greater political autonomy and economic well-being, Nehru remained consistently opposed to the inhuman forms of South African racial discrimination. During the forties he had become increasingly aware that Asia and Africa must make common cause in their battle for freedom and equality; for respect for the integrity of the individual, without regard to race, creed, color or previous servitude.]

[From letter to African Leaders—New Delhi, September 27, 1946.] We have long struggled for the freedom and independence of India, but always we have thought of this freedom as a common heritage for all, and more especially for those who have been deprived of it.

India, I hope, will always stand and work for this wider freedom. We are particularly interested in the people of Africa, who have suffered so much [in] the past and who are suffering still from exploitation by foreign elements.

You can rest assured that the voice of India will always be raised in the cause of African freedom. . . .

I like the idea that African students should come to the Universities and technical institutes of India and we shall try to encourage this in so far as we can.

You have referred to the Inter-Asian Relations Conference which we propose to hold in March next in New Delhi. As its name implies, this Conference is more or less limited to Asia, but I am sure that friendly observers from Africa will be welcome at this Conference and we can then confer together as to what we should do for developing closer relations between Asia and Africa.[1]

[On widespread communal riots—Central Assembly, New Delhi—November 14, 1946.] To give an account of the communal trouble in the country is to deal with a chain of events going back to the past. One evil action leads to another which again becomes the ostensible cause of further evil. The preaching and practice of hatred and violence inevitably sow seeds which yield bitter fruit. If we sow the wind we have to reap the whirlwind.

Ever since the Interim Government took charge of affairs they have been intensely occupied with these communal troubles. The House will remember that this Government took office very soon after what is called the great Calcutta killing which began on the 16th August. All our work was shadowed by these events and we tried our utmost to deal with this

[1] I.I. (Oct. 15, 1946), p. 218.

situation. The House knows that the Government of India may not interfere, under the existing constitution, with . . . Provincial autonomy. In so far as any one can interfere under the constitution, it is the Governor-General. . . . Nevertheless, as Indians in responsible positions to whom the country looked for guidance, we tried our utmost to help. Throughout this unhappy period, whether it was in Calcutta or elsewhere in India . . . the Government were acutely conscious of their responsibilities and keenly desirous of combating the peril that had encompassed the country. There has been much public criticism of our seeming inaction because necessarily we could not function in public in regard to these matters. If [the] facts were known, I do not think that this criticism would be considered to be justified.

A succession of events, which are known to this House, led to the great Calcutta killing. That was followed by [further] great tragedy . . . and that again led to the terrible happenings in Bihar. And now Bihar is leading to other outbursts of brutality and violence. There appears to be a competition in murder and brutality, and unless we put a stop to this, the immediate future of our country is dark. That it can be put a stop to, I have little doubt. Not by a reliance on mere armed force, though that may be necessary occasionally, but by the efforts of all those who influence public opinion, can we put an end to this horror, which comes in the way of all political and social progress, and indeed which is already making life a burden for many of us. It must be clearly accepted that we cannot settle any problem by the methods of hatred and violence.

Recently I have come into intimate contact with masses of people in Bihar and I saw horrors that a simple and likeable peasantry can perpetrate when it loses all balance and sanity. I found that during the Calcutta killing a large number of Biharis had lost their lives. Their relatives had returned to Bihar, together with many other refugees, and had spread out all over the rural areas carrying stories of what had happened in Calcutta. The people of Bihar were stirred profoundly. Then came news of Noakhali and East Bengal. These stories, and more especially the accounts of abduction and rape of women and forcible conversion of large numbers of people, infuriated the populace. For some time they looked to the Central Government and hoped that this would give them relief and afford protection. When they did not see any such help or protection forthcoming, they grew bitter, [criticizing] strongly the Interim Government for its apparent inactivity.

Various incidents occurred in Bihar which added to the general excitement. Towards the end of October there was trouble . . . [that] was soon suppressed. Then came . . . [what] was in essence a mass uprising, large numbers of peasants burning and killing mercilessly. As always happens on such occasions, criminal and anti-social elements took part and even took the lead in certain areas. One of the difficulties of the situation was that the areas [in question] could not be easily reached because of lack of communications and flooded conditions.

This mass uprising lasted almost exactly one week. Just as it started suddenly, it ended almost equally suddenly. This rapid ending of a wide-spread movement, which was on the verge of spreading to other districts, was remarkable. The military, of course, came in at a somewhat later stage and helped in restoring order. But a much more powerful factor in this restoration of order was the effort of a large number of people, chiefly Biharis, who spread out all over the villages and came face to face with the peasant masses. The news of Mahatma Gandhi's proposed fast also had a powerful effect.

Grossly exaggerated accounts have appeared of the number of casualties during these troubles caused both by infuriated mobs and by military firing. It is difficult to give at present even approximately accurate figures of casualties. But it can be said with certainty that some of the figures appearing in newspapers are completely wrong. They are usually based on accounts of panic-stricken refugees who [have] lost all balance or judgment.

The Bihar situation was brought completely under control after a week and is quiet now. Evidence of a return to normality is the desire of people to return to their villages. The great problem . . . now is how to rehabilitate these people. The Bihar Government have undertaken responsibility to lodge, feed and provide other necessaries including medical relief to the evacuees. I understand that they also propose to give financial assistance to the sufferers in order to help rehabilitation.

As I have stated, the news [of casualties] created a very profound feeling in Bihar and the rest of India. . . . Recent reports from reliable witnesses have drawn particular attention to the vital problem of restoring women [in East Bengal] who were abducted and forcibly converted. This problem is not only important in itself but also because of its All-India repercussions. It is, therefore, urgently necessary that every possible step should be taken with all possible speed to restore [the women] to their people. Only then can beginnings . . . of rehabilitation [be made] in East Bengal.

It is clearly the duty of the State to give every possible assistance to the sufferers from these disturbances. I hope that Provincial Governments will undertake this duty in adequate measure. This will help also in producing a feeling of security among the people and a psychological atmosphere for a return to normality. . . .

It is time that we put an end to all this sorry business all over India, and I trust that every sensitive Indian, whatever his political views might be, will co-operate with others in this vital and urgent task.[1]

| 14 | Congress-Muslim League Tensions, November |

["If there was any doubt about . . . the League's motives in joining the Government, Jinnah set these at rest in mid-November: 'We shall resist anything that militates against the Pakistan demand', he said. League ministers were instructed to oppose any Government action of substance which prejudiced this goal. Then, as if to taunt the Congress, he denied the existence of a species called Indian; four thousand years of history evaporated in a sentence. He pressed for an indefinite postponement of the Constituent Assembly."[2] On November 21, Jinnah went still further, issuing a directive that no representative of the Muslim League would participate in the Constituent Assembly, and that the Muslim League Council resolution of 29th July, withdrawing its acceptance of the Cabinet Mission Plan, still stood.[3]

Having stated that the atmosphere in the Interim Government, after the League's entry, had become so strained that Congress members had twice threatened to resign, Nehru declared: "Our patience is fast reaching the limit. . . . If . . . things continue [on the same basis] a struggle on a large scale is inevitable." He further charged Lord Wavell with failure to carry on the Interim Government in the spirit in which he had started it: "[Wavell] is gradually removing the wheels of the car and this is leading to a critical situation."

According to Nehru, ever since the Muslim League had entered the Interim Government, it had pursued its aim to enlist British support. He had written to Jinnah that differences between the Congress and League in the Interim Government should be settled by themselves, without the

[1] E.I.P., pp. 387–89.
[2] M.B., p. 324.
[3] Based on M.L.P. (Vol. I), p. 288.

Viceroy's intervention. But, noted Nehru, "There is a mental alliance between the League and senior British officials".[1]]

[As reported in the Indian Annual Register on November 21, 1946—in conjunction with Congress' decision to enter the Constituent Assembly— Nehru stated that if the League failed to accept the Cabinet Mission's proposals of May 16—as Jinnah had intimated—there was no room for League representatives in the Interim Government.] While [the League is] welcome to join the Constituent Assembly, let me make it clear that, whether [it comes in, or keeps] out, we will go on. I am not enamoured of this Constituent Assembly. But we have accepted it and we shall . . . get the fullest advantage out of it. I do not regard it as by any means the last Constituent Assembly. It may be that, after India achieves ample freedom, another Constituent Assembly will be called.

The only good thing about this Constituent Assembly is that . . . British power will not be directly represented in it, though we may not be able to check its indirect representation by the back door.

[Nehru reiterated his determination that the Congress go into the Constituent Assembly in full strength and fully organised.] We will enter it, not in order to quarrel over petty things but to establish the Indian Republic.[2]

[In answer to the League replies to Nehru's charges.] Whatever might be the League's intention, its policy of stressing the legal position and preventing the Government from functioning as a Cabinet must inevitably make it into a kind of King's Party and increase the power and influence of the Viceroy.[3]

[On November 25, 1946 Jinnah said of Nehru's insistence that the Viceroy's Executive Council be termed a Cabinet: "Little things please little minds and you cannot turn a donkey into an elephant by calling it an elephant." This verbal fencing revealed the crux of the disagreement between the two men. Congress and the League read different meanings into the same words. The Viceroy, unfortunately, failed sufficiently to clarify matters.[4]]

[1] Based on I.A.R. (Vol. II), Nov. 21, 1946, p. 279.
[2] Based on ibid.
[3] L.T.P.I., pp. 123–24.
[4] Based on M.B., p. 325.

15 | London Conference, December—
     | Creation of Constituent Assembly

London Conference, December

[At the point at which there seemed to be no way out of the current impasse, Attlee issued an invitation by way of the Viceroy to "two representatives of the Congress, two from the League, and one Sikh, to confer in London in an effort to reconcile the warring parties." Nehru and the Congress Working Committee, sensing a trap, were initially wary of accepting the invitation to attend the London Conference.[1] Attlee assured Nehru, however, that there was no intention of abandoning either the Constituent Assembly's decision to meet, or the plan advanced by the Cabinet Delegation; that it was his Government's desire to implement the plan in full. Attlee simultaneously assured Jinnah that there was nothing in the plan to "prejudice full consideration of all points of view."[2]]

[From letter to Wavell—November 26, 1946.] With reference to our conversation today, in the course of which you conveyed His Majesty's Government's invitation to some of us to visit London this week, I have consulted my colleagues and we have given careful thought to the proposal. I need hardly say that we are grateful to His Majesty's Government for their invitation, but we feel we cannot, at this stage, go to London. We would be agreeable to consultations with the representatives of the British Government in India.

It would appear that the proposal involves a reopening and a reconsideration of the various decisions arrived at since the visit of the British Cabinet Delegation to India. The Muslim League accepted places in the Government on the very clear understanding that they also accepted the long-term proposals contained in the Cabinet Mission's statement of May 16. Indeed they could not join the Government otherwise. But now, the League have announced very definitely that they will not participate in the Constituent Assembly. We attach, as you are aware, great importance to the holding of the meeting of the Constituent Assembly on the date fixed, namely, December 9. The invitation to us to go to London

[1] Based on M.B., p. 325.
[2] M.L.P. (Vol. I), p. 475.

appears to us to reopen the whole problem which was settled to a large extent by the Cabinet Mission's statement and the formation of the Interim Government. Any impression in the public mind that these decisions are reopened would, in our opinion, be fatal.

It was because we felt that it was necessary in the public interest to emphasize that problems have been finally settled that we insisted on the holding of the Constituent Assembly on the date fixed for it. Even this date, it must be remembered, was given months after the election of the members. Any further postponement in the present context would, in all probability, result in the abandonment of the plan and create a feeling of uncertainty all round which is not only undesirable but actually, at the present juncture, would encourage various forms of violent propaganda.

It is difficult enough at this stage for us to leave the country even for a short while. We have also to prepare for the Constituent Assembly meeting which will take place in less than two weeks. If any useful purpose would have been served by our going out now, we should have done so in spite of these difficulties. We are convinced, however, that our leaving India now would mean that at the instance of the League the Cabinet Mission's plan is going to be abandoned or substantially varied and that we are parties to it. It would mean giving in to the League's intransigence and incitement to violence and this would have disastrous consequences. The first thing to be certain about is that plans agreed to will be implemented and that there will be a continuity about policy. There has been suspicion enough. Any addition to it will wreck the whole scheme and make it difficult to replace it by another. We feel, therefore, that we cannot, at this stage, proceed to London, but we would welcome, whenever necessary, consultations with the representatives of the British Government in India. A brief visit now on our part to England cannot bear fruit. It is likely to have a contrary result. We, therefore, regret we are unable to accept His Majesty's Government's invitation conveyed to us through you. I trust you will convey the contents of this letter to His Majesty's Government.[1]

[From cable to Attlee, November 28, 1946.] I am grateful to you for your message and appreciate your desire to ensure a successful meeting of the Constituent Assembly on December 9 and onwards. We are all anxious that the Constituent Assembly should meet on the date fixed and should proceed harmoniously to fulfil its task and we shall do our utmost to this end and in co-operation with others.

[1] S.D.I.C. (Vol. II), pp. 657–58.

As we have repeatedly stated, we accept the Cabinet Delegation's plan in its entirety. In regard to certain interpretations we made our position perfectly clear to the Delegation and we have proceeded accordingly since then. We have further stated that in the event of different interpretations the matter should be referred to the Federal Court and we shall abide by the Court's decision.

It appears from the statements made on behalf of the British Government in Parliament yesterday that the only point to be considered is this interpretation. In regard to this, our position is quite clear and we are completely committed to it. We are unable to change it and have no authority to do so. Hence our visiting London for this purpose is not necessary.

The first session of the Constituent Assembly will deal with matters of procedure and appointment of committees. The question of interpretation as regards subsequent activities will not arise at this stage. It is, therefore, easily possible for all to co-operate in this session and, if necessity arises, to refer any matter over which agreement has not been reached to the Federal Court.

It would be more suitable and convenient for us to visit London, if necessary, after the first brief session of the Constituent Assembly. This would allow more time for consultations.

In view of these considerations and also because of the great difficulty in leaving India at present we feel that our visit to London now would serve no useful purpose; but if in spite of this or because you wish to consider other matters you desire us to come, we shall endeavour to do so. But we shall have to return by December 9 in time for the Constituent Assembly.[1]

[Attlee announced that Lord Wavell, Nehru, Jinnah, Liaquat Ali Khan and Sardar Baldev Singh (the latter representing the Sikhs) were to arrive in London to confer, "in an effort to save the Cabinet Mission plan".[2]

After having raised numerous objections to going to London, Nehru finally agreed to attend the London Conference during December, 1946. Once there, however, he was greatly perturbed by what he felt to be the continued ambivalence of the British. He claimed that "obstructions were placed in our way, new limitations were mentioned, . . . no imagination" was shown "in the understanding of the Indian problem".

Attlee's invitation to the Conference had been accepted, Nehru maintained, in order to leave the door open for the League to enter the

Constituent Assembly. Rejection of the London invitation might have given an opportunity to the British to change or withdraw the May 16th Cabinet Mission plan, whereupon the Constituent Assembly might have been radically changed.

Again, according to Nehru, Congress decided to participate in the London Conference in order not to "add to our enemies", or be accused in any way of rejecting the British plan to transfer power.[1]]

Creation of Constituent Assembly

[Three days after the London Conference convened, the Constituent Assembly was formally established. Although the Muslim League was absent, the Sikhs, initially opposed to attending, had been persuaded by Nehru and Patel to do so. Congress had an overwhelming majority—two hundred and five of the two hundred and ninety-six seats allotted to British India. The Princes had not yet joined the proceedings. Gandhi remained in Bengal, trying to heal the wounds caused by communal riots.

"Since the late 'twenties Nehru had been the principal advocate of a Constituent Assembly to express the national will. With the passage of time the Assembly had become an article of faith, a symbol of independence. The dream had now come to pass. It was a moment of personal and national pride."[2]]

16 | After Return from London: Resolution Concerning Independent Sovereign Republic

An Independent Sovereign Republic—Speech Moving Objectives Resolution, Constituent Assembly—New Delhi, December 13, 1946

I beg to move that:

(1) This Constituent Assembly declares its firm and solemn resolve to proclaim India as an Independent Sovereign Republic and to draw up for her future governance a Constitution;

[1] Based on M.B., pp. 327–28.
[2] Based on ibid., p. 328.

(2) Wherein the territories that now comprise British India, the territories that now form the Indian States, and such other parts of India as are outside British India and the States as well as such other territories as are willing to be constituted into the Independent Sovereign India, shall be a Union of them all; and

(3) Wherein the said territories, whether with their present boundaries or with such others as may be determined by the Constituent Assembly and thereafter according to the Law of the Constitution, shall possess and retain the status of autonomous Units, together with residuary powers, and exercise all powers and functions of government and administration, save and except such powers and functions as are vested in or assigned to the Union, or as are inherent or implied in the Union or resulting therefrom; and

(4) Wherein all power and authority of the Sovereign Independent India, its constituent parts and organs of government, are derived from the people; and

(5) Wherein shall be guaranteed and secured to all the people of India justice, social, economic and political: equality of status, of opportunity, and before the law; freedom of thought, expression, belief, faith, worship, vocation, association and action, subject to law and public morality; and

(6) Wherein adequate safeguards shall be provided for minorities, backward and tribal areas, and depressed and other backward classes; and

(7) Whereby shall be maintained the integrity of the territory of the Republic and its sovereign rights on land, sea and air according to justice and the law of civilized nations; and

(8) This ancient land attain its rightful and honoured place in the world and make its full and willing contribution to the promotion of world peace and the welfare of mankind. . . .

We have still much to do . . . before we can proceed to the real step, to the real work of this Constituent Assembly, that is, the high adventure of giving shape, in the printed and written word, to a nation's dream and aspiration. But even now, at this stage, it is surely desirable that we should give some indication to ourselves, to those who look to this Assembly, to those millions in this country who are looking up to us and to the world at large, as to what we may do, what we seek to achieve, whither we are going. It is with this purpose that I have placed this Resolution before this House. It is a Resolution and yet it is something much more than a resolution. It is a Declaration. It is a firm resolve. It is a pledge and an undertaking and it is for all of us, I hope, a dedication. And I wish that this

House, if I may say so respectfully, should consider this Resolution not in a spirit of narrow legal wording, but rather look at the spirit behind the Resolution. Words are magic things often enough, but even the magic of words sometimes cannot convey the magic of the human spirit and of a nation's passion. And so, I cannot say that this Resolution at all conveys the passion that lies in the hearts and the minds of the Indian people today. It seeks very feebly to tell the world what we have thought or dreamt of so long, and what we now hope to achieve in the near future. It is in that spirit that I venture to place this Resolution before the House and it is in that spirit that I trust the House will receive it and ultimately pass it. And may I, Sir, also, with all respect, suggest to you and to the House that, when the time comes for the passing of this Resolution, let it not be done in the formal way by the raising of hands, but much more solemnly, by all of us standing up and thus taking this pledge anew. . . .

We have undertaken a tremendous task and we seek the co-operation of all people in that task; because the future of India that we have envisaged is not confined to any group or section or province, but it comprises all the four hundred million people of India, and it is with deep regret that we find some benches empty and some colleagues, who might have been here, absent. I do feel that they ought to come, I do hope that they will come and that this House, in its future stages, will have the benefit of the co-operation of all. Meanwhile, there is a duty cast upon us and that is to bear the absentees in mind, to remember always that we are here not to act for one party or one group, but always to think of India as a whole and always to think of the welfare of the four hundred millions that comprise India. We are all now, in our respective spheres, party men, belonging to this or that group and presumably we shall continue to act in our respective parties. Nevertheless, a time comes when we have to rise above party and think of the nation, think sometimes even of the world at large of which our nation is a great part. And when I think of the work of this Constituent Assembly, it seems to me the time has come when we should, so far as we are capable of it, rise above our ordinary selves and party disputes and think of the great problem before us in the widest and most tolerant and most effective manner so that whatever we may produce will be worthy of India as a whole and will be such that the world will recognize that we have functioned, as we should have functioned, in this high adventure. . . .

As I stand here, Sir, I feel the weight of all manner of things crowding upon me. We are at the end of an era and possibly very soon we shall embark upon a new age; and my mind goes back to the great past of

India, to the five thousand years of India's history, from the very dawn of that history which might be considered almost the dawn of human history, till today. All that past crowds upon me and exhilarates me and, at the same time, somewhat oppresses me. Am I worthy of that past? When I think also of the future, the greater future I hope, standing on this sword's edge of the present between the mighty past and the mightier future, I tremble a little and feel overwhelmed by this mighty task. We have come here at a strange moment in India's history. I do not know, but I do feel that there is some magic in this moment of transition from the old to the new, something of that magic which one sees when the night turns into day and even though the day may be a cloudy one, it is day after all, for when the clouds move away, we can see the sun again. Because of all this I find a little difficulty in addressing this House and putting all my ideas before it and I feel also that in this long succession of thousands of years, I see the mighty figures that have come and gone and I see also the long succession of our comrades who have laboured for the freedom of India. And now we stand on the verge of this passing age, trying, labouring, to usher in the new. I am sure the House will feel the solemnity of this moment and will endeavour to treat this Resolution which it is my proud privilege to place before it in a correspondingly solemn manner. I believe there are a large number of amendments coming before the House. I have not seen most of them. It is open to the House, to any member of this House, to move any amendment and it is for the House to accept it or reject it, but I would, with all respect, suggest that this is not the moment for us to be technical and legal about small matters when we have big things to face, big things to say and big things to do, and, therefore, I hope that the House will consider this Resolution in a broad-minded manner and not lose itself in wordy quarrels and squabbles.

I think also of the various Constituent Assemblies that have gone before and of what took place at the making of the great American nation when the fathers of that nation met and fashioned a Constitution which has stood the test of so many years, more than a century and a half, and of the great nation which has resulted, which has been built up on the basis of that Constitution. My mind goes back to that mighty revolution which took place also over one hundred and fifty years ago and the Constituent Assembly that met in that gracious and lovely city of Paris which has fought so many battles for freedom. My mind goes back to the difficulties that that Constituent Assembly had to face from the King and other authorities, and still it continued. The House will remember that when these difficulties came and even the room for a meeting was denied to that

Constituent Assembly, they betook themselves to an open tennis court and met there and took the oath, which is called the Oath of the Tennis Court. They continued meeting in spite of Kings, in spite of the others, and did not disperse till they had finished the task they had undertaken. Well, I trust that it is in that solemn spirit that we too are meeting here and that we too, whether we meet in this chamber or in other chambers, or in the fields or in the market place, will go on meeting and continue our work till we have finished it.

Then my mind goes back to a more recent revolution which gave rise to a new type of State, the revolution that took place in Russia and out of which has arisen the Union of the Soviet Socialist Republics, another mighty country which is playing a tremendous part in the world, not only a mighty country, but for us in India, a neighbouring country.

So our mind goes back to these great examples and we seek to learn from their success and to avoid their failures. Perhaps we may not be able to avoid failures, because some measure of failure is inherent in human effort. Nevertheless, we shall advance, I am certain, in spite of obstructions and difficulties, and achieve and realize the dream that we have dreamt so long. In this Resolution which the House knows has been drafted with exceeding care we have tried to avoid saying too much or too little. It is difficult to frame a resolution of this kind. If you say too little, it becomes just a pious resolution and nothing more. If you say too much, it encroaches on the functions of those who are going to draw up a Constitution, that is, on the functions of this House. This Resolution is not a part of the Constitution we are going to draw up, and it must not be looked upon as such. This House has perfect freedom to draw up that Constitution and when others come into this House, they will have perfect freedom too to fashion that Constitution. This Resolution, therefore, steers between these two extremes and lays down only certain fundamentals which, I do believe, no group or party and hardly any individual in India can dispute. We say that it is our firm and solemn resolve to have an Independent Sovereign Republic. India is bound to be sovereign, it is bound to be independent and it is bound to be a Republic. I will not go into the arguments about monarchy and the rest but obviously we cannot produce monarchy in India out of nothing. It is not there. If it is to be an independent and sovereign State, we are not going to have an external monarchy and we cannot begin a search for a legal heir from among local monarchies. It must inevitably be a Republic. Now, some friends have raised the question: "Why have you not put in the word 'democratic' here?" Well, I told them that it is conceivable, of course, that a Republic may not be democratic, but the whole of our past is witness to the fact that we stand for democratic institutions. Obviously, we are aiming at democracy and nothing less than a democracy. What form of democracy, what shape it may take is another matter. The democracies of the present day, many of them in Europe and some elsewhere, have played a great part in the world's progress. Yet it may be doubtful if those democracies may not have to change their shape somewhat before long if they [are] to remain completely democratic. We are not going just to copy, I hope, a certain democratic procedure or an institution of a so-called democratic country. We may improve upon it. In any event, whatever system of government we may establish here must fit in with the temper of our people and be acceptable to them. We stand for democracy. It will be for this House to determine what shape to give to that democracy, the fullest democracy, I hope. The House will notice that in this Resolution, although we have not used the word "democratic", because we thought it obvious that the word "republic" contains the meaning of that word and we did not want to use unnecessary words and redundant words, ... we have done something much more than using the word. We have given the content of democracy in this Resolution and not only the content of democracy but the content, if I may say so, of economic democracy in this Resolution. Others might take objection to this Resolution on the ground that we have not said that it should be a Socialist State. Well, I stand for socialism and, I hope, India will stand for socialism and that India will go towards the constitution of a Socialist State and I do believe that the whole world will have to go that way. What form of socialism again is another matter for your consideration. But the main thing is that in such a Resolution, if, in accordance with my own desire, I had put in that we wanted a Socialist State, we would have put in something which might be agreeable to many and might not be agreeable to some and we wanted this Resolution not to be controversial in regard to such matters. Therefore, we have laid down, not theoretical words and formulas, but rather the content of the thing we desire. This is important and I take it there can be no dispute about it. Some people have pointed out to me that our mentioning a Republic may somewhat displease the rulers of Indian States. It is possible that this may displease them. But I want to make it clear personally, and the House knows, that I do not believe in the monarchical system anywhere, and that in the world today monarchy is a fast disappearing institution. Nevertheless, it is not a question of my personal belief in this matter. Our view in regard to the Indian States has been, for many years, first of all that the people of those States must share completely in the freedom to come. It is quite inconceivable to me that there should be different standards and degrees of freedom as between the people of the States and the people outside the States. In what manner the States will be parts of that Union is a matter for this House to consider with the representatives of the States. And I hope that, in all matters relating to the States, this House will deal with the real representatives of the States. We are perfectly willing, I take it, to deal in such matters as appertain to them, with the rulers or their representatives also, but finally when we make a Constitution for India, it must be through the representatives of the people of the States as with the rest of India, who are present here. In any event, we may lay down or agree that the measure of freedom must be the same in the States as elsewhere. It is a possibility and personally I should like a measure of uniformity too in regard to the apparatus and machinery of Government. Nevertheless, this is a point to be considered in co-operation and in consultation with the States. I do not wish, and I imagine this Constituent Assembly will not like, to impose anything on the States against their will. If the people of a particular State desire to have a certain form of administration, even though it might be monarchical, it is open to them to have it. The House will remember that even in the British Commonwealth of Nations today, Eire is a Republic and yet in many ways it is a member of the British Commonwealth. So it is a conceivable thing. What will happen, I do not know, because that is partly for this House and partly for others to decide. There is no incongruity or impossibility about a certain definite form of administration in the States, provided there is complete freedom and responsible government there and the people really are in charge. If monarchical figure-heads are approved of by the people of the State, of a particular State, whether I like it or not, I certainly would not interfere. So I wish to make it clear that so far as this Resolution or Declaration is concerned, it does not interfere in any way with any future work that this Constituent Assembly may do, with any future negotiations that it may undertake. Only in one sense, if you like, it limits our work, if you call that a limitation, i.e., we adhere to certain fundamental propositions which are laid down in this Declaration. These fundamental propositions, I submit, are not controversial in any real sense of the word. Nobody challenges them in India and nobody ought to challenge them, but if anybody should challenge them, well, we shall accept that challenge and hold our position.

Well, Sir, we are going to make a Constitution for India and it is obvious that what we are going to do in India is going to have a powerful effect on the rest of the world, not only because a new free independent nation comes out into the arena of the world, but because of the very fact that India is such a country that by virtue, not only of her large size and population, but of her enormous resources and her ability to exploit those resources, she can immediately play an important and a vital part in world affairs. Even today, on the verge of freedom as we are today, India has begun to play an important part in world affairs. Therefore, it is right that the framers of our Constitution should always bear this larger international aspect in mind.

We approach the world in a friendly way. We want to make friends with all countries. We want to make friends, in spite of the long history of conflict in the past, with England also. The House knows that recently I paid a visit to England. I was reluctant to go for reasons which the House knows well. But I went because of a personal request from the Prime Minister of Great Britain. I went and I met with courtesy everywhere. And yet at this psychological moment in India's history when we wanted, when we hungered for messages of cheer, friendship and co-operation from all over the world, and more especially from England, because of the past contact and conflict between us, unfortunately, I came back without any message of cheer, but with a large measure of disappointment. I hope that the new difficulties that have arisen, as every one knows, because of the recent statements made by the British Cabinet and by others in authority there, will not come in our way and that we shall succeed yet in going ahead with the co-operation of all of us here and those who have not come. It has been a blow to me, and it has hurt me that just at the moment when we were going to stride ahead, obstructions were placed in our way, new limitations were mentioned which had not been mentioned previously and new methods of procedure were suggested. I do not wish to challenge the *bona fides* of any person, but I wish to say that whatever the legal aspect of the thing might be, there are moments when law is a very feeble reed to rely upon, when we have to deal with a nation which is full of the passion for freedom. Most of us here during many years past, for a generation or more, have often taken part in the struggle for India's freedom. We have gone through the valley of the shadow. We are used to it, and if necessity arises, we shall go through it again. Nevertheless, through all this long period, we have thought of the time when we should have an opportunity, not merely to struggle, not merely to destroy, but to construct and create. And now, when it appeared that the time had come for constructive effort in a free

India to which we looked forward with joy, fresh difficulties were placed in our way at such a moment. It shows that, whatever force might be behind all this, people who are able and clever and very intelligent somehow lack the imaginative daring which should accompany great offices. For, if you have to deal with any people, you have to understand them imaginatively; you should understand them emotionally; and, of course, you have also to understand them intellectually. One of the unfortunate legacies of the past has been that there has been no imagination in the understanding of the Indian problem. People have often indulged in, or have presumed to give us advice, not realizing that India, as she is constituted today, wants no one's advice and no one's imposition upon her. The only way to influence India is through friendship and co-operation and goodwill. Any attempt at imposition, the slightest trace of patronage, is resented and will be resented. We have tried, I think honestly, in the last few months, in spite of the difficulties that have faced us, to create an atmosphere of co-operation. We shall continue that endeavour. But I do very much fear that that atmosphere will be impaired if there is not sufficient and adequate response from others. Nevertheless, because we are bent on great tasks, I hope and trust that we shall continue that endeavour and I do hope that, if we continue, we shall succeed. Where we have to deal with our own countrymen, we must continue that endeavour even though in our opinion some of our countrymen take a wrong path. For, after all, we have to work together in this country and we have inevitably to co-operate, if not today, tomorrow or the day after. Therefore, we have to avoid in the present anything which might introduce a new difficulty in the creation of that future which we are working for. Therefore, as far as our own countrymen are concerned, we must try our utmost to gain their co-operation in the largest measure. But co-operation cannot mean the giving up of the fundamental ideals on which we have stood and on which we should stand. It is not co-operation to surrender everything that has given meaning to our lives. Apart from that, as I said, we seek the co-operation of England even at this stage, even when we are full of suspicion of each other. We feel that if that co-operation is denied, it will be injurious to India, certainly to some extent, probably more so to England, and, to some extent, to the world at large. We have just come out of a world war and people talk vaguely and rather wildly of new wars to come. At such a moment is this New India taking birth—renascent, vital, fearless. Perhaps it is a suitable moment for this new birth to take place out of this turmoil in the world. But we have to be clear-eyed at this moment,—we, who have the heavy task of constitution-building. We have to think of this tremendous prospect of the present and the greater prospect of the future and not get lost in seeking small gains for this group or that. In this Constituent Assembly we are functioning on a world stage and the eyes of the world are upon us and the eyes of our entire past are upon us. Our past is witness to what we are doing here and though the future is still unborn, the future too somehow looks at us, I think, and so I would beg of this House to consider this Resolution in the mighty perspective of our past, of the turmoil of the present and of the great and unborn future that is going to take place soon.[1]

[In reply to Churchill's statement that London would not be bound by the decisions of the Constituent Assembly, Nehru stated: "Whatever form of Constitution we may decide [upon] in the Constituent Assembly will become the Constitution of free India—whether Britain accepts it or not. . . . We have now altogether stopped looking towards London. . . . We cannot and will not tolerate any outside interference."[2]]

17 | Appointment of Lord Mountbatten as Viceroy

[The British Government, according to Prime Minister Attlee, was most disturbed by the political tension existing between the Congress and Muslim League. In the hope of improving the situation the principal members of the Cabinet concluded "that a new personal approach was perhaps the only hope", and that "the need for closer personal contacts with" Indian leaders was paramount.

Thus, in mid-December, Attlee invited Lord Mountbatten to succeed Lord Wavell as Viceroy of India.

Mountbatten had various reservations concerning acceptance of Attlee's invitation. He maintained that the earliest possible time-limit should be set for the final transfer of power to India. By December 20, 1946 he decided that, "while appreciating the honour" paid to him, he begged to be excused from becoming the Viceroy unless he could go to India at the express invitation of her own leaders.

[1] I.A., pp. 344–53.
[2] M.B., p. 330.

Finally, after being assured that the transfer of power from Britain to India was definitely to be accomplished within a certain time-limit, Mountbatten accepted Attlee's invitation. As for the British reaction to Mountbatten's decision, he felt that "there would be considerable public sympathy for him in taking on the job at all, and popular support would probably back him up in whatever measures he saw fit to take." [1] (His appointment was made public only in February, 1947. Accompanied by Lady Mountbatten, he arrived in India in March, 1947, to take up his duties as the last Viceroy of India.)]

[1] M.M., pp. 18–19.

PART TEN
Year of Independence : 1947

[To an English friend before independence.] I have had to put up with a great deal which might have embittered me and filled me with hate . . . and yet I have survived. I feel pretty lonely often enough, but not bitter against anybody. Why . . . succumb to . . . bitterness and hate?[1]

*

[To an American journalist.] I have learned that a Prime Minister cannot afford to be sensitive.[2]

*

[It does not] matter what kind of a signboard is put up outside the India Office. The real thing is that the whole conception lying behind the India Office should go.[3]

[1] Quoted in M.J.N., p. 400.
[2] Ibid., p. 441.
[3] B.I.S.J.N. (Vol. I), p. 352.

I | Upheaval and Transition—Of Gandhi and Difficulties within Congress

Upheaval and Transition

[Early 1947 was a period of upheaval and transition in India. Liberation from foreign rule seemed more nearly attainable than ever before, yet innumerable crucial questions remained unanswered. Among them: how to make Congress more effective, so that it might help transform the lives of India's downtrodden millions in at least somewhat satisfying fashion? How to avoid both communal violence and partition? How to build a modern, united, democratic-socialist, secular state?

In March, 1947, Lord Mountbatten became the last Viceroy of India. He was to play a most sympathetic and effective role during the period of the final transfer of power.

August 15, 1947 marked the momentous birth of independent India. Freedom gave rise to an enormous release of energy, a cultural renaissance, an improvement in the standard of living of the Indian masses. Nevertheless the problems to be solved at times seemed to loom quite as large as the gains achieved.

Once partition became what seemed to be an irreversible reality, it served to intensify rather than lessen communal tensions. Incidents of violence, involving Muslims, Hindus and Sikhs, increased in harrowing fashion. Whereas Muslim League leaders were exultant at the creation of Pakistan, in the eyes of Congress leaders bi-furcation of the Indian sub-continent remained a major disaster, even after being regretfully accepted.

Gandhi's consistent choice of Jawaharlal as leader, first of Congress, then of free India, inevitably helped to make Nehru one of the country's foremost political figures. Gandhi long had contended that Jawaharlal would be by far the most idealistic, progressive champion of the well-being of the people. Yet, had the nation's youth, as well as the most politically aware sections of the populace as a whole, not agreed with the Mahatma's judgment, even his advocacy of Nehru could not possibly have had the impact that it did. Thus with the approach of independence Jawaharlal quite naturally was named India's first Prime Minister.

Sardar Patel, whose role in Congress had long been highly significant, became first Home Minister of India and Deputy Prime-Minister.

Patel was not only an outstanding administrator and organizer, but his success in achieving the peaceful integration of India's nearly six hundred princely States—with the Princes' own acquiescence—well may be considered one of the most remarkable occurrences in modern Indian history.

Although Patel was far more conservative than Nehru, the two men complemented one another—in spite of their periodic divergences of opinion.

During 1947 Nehru began to assume an increasingly important role, not only on the Indian scene, but on that of Asia in general.

Despite the many disagreements even his closest colleagues had had with Gandhi over the years, the Mahatma had set so high a standard, and was so effective and natural a leader, that he remained the symbolical focus of the Indian independence movement, even while refusing to hold any official position.

It long since had become a habit for Congress's most powerful members to ask Gandhi for advice and, by and large, to take it. It was difficult, therefore, to forego the privilege of continuing to do so. By 1946, however, the Mahatma had removed himself from the Center in an attempt—through his exemplary way of life and his calming influence—to quell the seemingly never-ending surge of communal atrocities that occurred. He continued to remain away from New Delhi in order to continue with his demanding task.

Nehru's early 1947 letters to, and writings about Gandhi—as well as his other statements of the period—reveal his continuing attachment to the Mahatma, in contrast to his growing misgivings about Congress. The pressure of work increased in conjunction with the potential transfer of power. It became more and more difficult to concentrate upon problems confined to the Congress Organisation. There were manifold other causes for the deep anguish suffered at the time, even though independence was about to be attained.

During 1947 not only partition and the intensified two-way flow of refugees, but the tragedy of Kashmir and other related problems served to counterbalance the tremendous joy experienced at the gaining of freedom.]

Of Gandhi and Difficulties within Congress

This little man has been and is a colossus before whom others, big in their own way and in their own space and time, are small of stature. In this world of hatred and uttermost violence and the atom bomb, this man of peace and good will stands out, a contrast and a challenge. In an acquisitive society madly searching for new gadgets and new luxuries, he takes to his loincloth and his mud hut. In man's race for wealth and authority and power, he seems to be a nonstarter, looking the other way and yet that authority looks out of his gentle but hard eyes, that power seems to fill his slight and emaciated frame, and flows out to others. Wherein does his strength lie, wherein this power and authority? . . .

Often we do not understand him; we argue with him and get angry sometimes. But the anger passes leaving us rather ashamed of our lack of balance and restraint. Only that pervasive influence remains and he seems to become the vehicle and embodiment of some greater force of which even he is perhaps only dimly conscious. Is that the spirit of India, the accumulated experience of the millennia that lie behind our race, the memory of a thousand tortured lives? [1]

[To Gandhi—January 30, 1947.] Conditions all over India to some extent are very unsatisfactory. There is a certain disruptive tendency at work which affects our work in every direction. The whole Congress organisation is suffering from it and we, who are in the Government, have no time at all to give to any work except the immediate problems which confront us. . . . I want you to realize that there is in some ways a progressive deterioration in the situation and I feel very unhappy about it. . . .

When our own approach is not quite clear and there are different view-points and pulls, then it becomes even more difficult to deal with the problem.[2]

I know that we must learn to rely upon ourselves and not run to you for help on every occasion. But we have got into this bad habit and we do often feel that if you had been easier of access our difficulties would have been less.[3]

[1] N.O.G., pp. ix–x.
[2] M.L.P. (Vol. II), pp. 30–31.
[3] Ibid. (Vol. I), p. 568.

	Congress Resolution—Mountbatten
2	Accepts Invitation to Become Viceroy— Constituent Assembly Acceptance of Objectives Resolution

Congress Resolution

[At meeting of All-India Congress Committee, Delhi: From Resolution moved by Nehru—January 5, 1947.]

"The All-India Congress Committee is firmly of the opinion that the constitution for a free and independent India should be framed by the people of India on the basis of as wide an agreement as possible. There must be no interference whatsoever by any external authority and no compulsion of any province or part of a province by another province. The All-India Congress Committee realises and appreciates the difficulties placed in the way of some provinces. . . . The Congress cannot be a party to any . . . compulsion or imposition against the will of the people concerned, a principle which the British Government have themselves recognised.

"The A.I.C.C. is anxious that the Constituent Assembly should proceed with the work of framing a constitution for free India with the goodwill of all the parties concerned and with a view to removing the difficulties that have arisen owing to varying interpretations. . . .

"It must be clearly understood, however, that this must not involve any compulsion of a province. . . . In the event of any attempt at such compulsion, a province or part of a province has the right to take such action as may be deemed necessary in order to give effect to the wishes of the people concerned.

"The future course of action will depend upon the developments that take place and the All-India Congress Committee therefore directs the Working Committee to advise upon it, whenever circumstances so require, keeping in view the basic principle of provincial autonomy." [1]

Mountbatten Accepts Invitation to Become Viceroy

[On January 15, 1947, Lord Mountbatten's acceptance of the Viceroyalty was finally firm, the British Government accepting the principle

[1] T.P.I., pp. 332–33.

of a time-limit with respect to the transfer of power without, however, setting an exact date for it. The second half of 1948 was suggested as a deadline, even though Mountbatten became increasingly convinced that Britain should leave India in June, 1948, rather than in December. He warned his Government against the danger of giving the impression that he had been appointed to perpetuate the Viceregal system, or to impose British arbitration. Fortunately Attlee accepted the principle of terminating British rule by a specific date earlier than the appointed time-limit, provided that the various Indian factions could "agree on a constitution and form a Government".[1] Meanwhile, to Nehru's despair, communal tensions and violence persisted.]

Constituent Assembly Acceptance of Objectives Resolution

[In his January 22, 1947 speech to the Constituent Assembly, Nehru expressed disappointment at the delay in passing his "Objectives" Resolution (see Part Nine) and urged the Assembly to adopt it. He regretted also the absence of certain opposition forces and Princes, whose failure to be present served to postpone what Nehru sought so passionately to accomplish, by way of the Constituent Assembly.]

It was my proud privilege . . . six weeks ago, to move [the Objectives] Resolution before this Honourable House. . . . The Resolution represented the agony and hopes of the nation coming at last to fruition.

As I stood here on that occasion I felt the past crowding round me, and I felt also the future taking shape. We stand on the razor's edge of the present, and as I was addressing not only this Honourable House but the millions of India who were vastly interested in our work and because I felt that we were coming to the end of an age, I had a sense of our forebears watching this undertaking of ours and possibly blessing it, if we moved aright, and the future of which we became trustees, almost . . . [taking on] a living shape and moving before our eyes. It was a great responsibility to be trustees of the future, and it was some responsibility also to be inheritors of our great past. And between the great past and the great future which we envisage, we stood on the edge of the present and the weight of that occasion, I have no doubt, impressed itself upon this Honourable House.

So I placed this Resolution before the House, and I had hoped that it could be passed in a day or two and we could start our other work immediately. But after a long debate this House decided to postpone

[1] M.M., p. 19.

further consideration of this Resolution. May I confess that I was a little disappointed, because I was impatient that we should go forward? I felt that, by lingering on the road we were not true to the pledges that we had taken. It was a bad beginning that we should postpone such an important Resolution about objectives. Would that imply that our future work would go along slowly and be postponed from time to time? Nevertheless, I have no doubt that the decision this House took in its wisdom in postponing this Resolution was a right decision, because we have always balanced two factors, one, the urgent necessity of reaching our goal, and the other, that we should reach it in proper time and with as great a unanimity as possible. It was right, therefore, if I may say with all respect, that this House decided to adjourn consideration of this motion and thus has not only demonstrated before the world our earnest desire to have all those people here who have not so far come, but also to assure the country and everyone else how anxious we were to have the co-operation of all. Since then six weeks have passed, and during these weeks there has been plenty of opportunity for those who wanted to come. Unfortunately, they have not yet decided to come and they still hover in a state of indecision. I regret that, and all I can say is this, that we shall welcome them at any future time when they may wish to come. But it should be made clear without any possibility of misunderstanding that no work will be held up in future, whether any one comes or not. There has been waiting enough. Not only . . . six weeks' waiting but many in this country have waited for years and years, and the country has waited for some generations now. How long are we to wait? And if we, some of us, who are more prosperous can afford to wait, what about the waiting of the hungry and the starving? This Resolution will not feed the hungry or the starving, but it brings a promise of many things—it brings the promise of freedom, it brings the promise of food and opportunity for all. Therefore, the sooner we set about our task the better. We waited for six weeks, and during these six weeks the country thought about it, pondered over it, and other countries also and other people who are interested have thought about it. Now, we have come back here to take up the further consideration of this Resolution. We have had a long debate and we stand on the verge of passing it. . . . [It also] appears now that there is no one in this House who does not fully accept this Resolution as it is. It may be that some would like it to be slightly differently worded or the emphasis placed more on this part or on that part. But taking it as a whole, it is a Resolution which has already received the full assent of this House, and there is little doubt that it has received the full assent of the country.

There have been some criticisms of it, notably from some of the Princes. Their first criticism was that such a Resolution should not be passed in the absence of the representatives of the States. In part I agree with that criticism, that is to say, I should have liked all the States to be properly represented here, the whole of India, every part of India to be properly represented here when we pass this Resolution. But if they are not here it is not our fault. It is largely the fault of the scheme under which we are working, and we have this choice before us: are we to postpone our work, because some people cannot be here? That would be a dreadful thing if we stopped not only this Resolution, but possibly so much else, because representatives of the States are not here. As far as we are concerned, they can come in at the earliest possible moment; we shall welcome them if they send proper representatives of the States. As far as we are concerned, even during the last six weeks or a month we have made some effort to get into touch with the Committee representing the States rulers to find a way for their proper representation here. It is not our fault that there has been delay. We are anxious to get every one in, whether it is the representatives of the Muslim League or the States or anyone else. We shall continue to persevere in this endeavour so that this House may be as fully representative of the country as it is possible to be. So we cannot postpone this Resolution or anything else, because some people are not here.

Another point has been raised: the idea of the sovereignty of the people which is enshrined in this Resolution does not commend itself to certain rulers of the Indian States. This is a surprising objection and, if I may say so, if that objection is raised in all seriousness by anybody, be he a ruler or a minister, it is enough to condemn the Indian States system that exists in India. It is a scandalous thing for any man to say, however highly placed he may be, that he is here by special divine dispensation to rule over human beings today. That is a thing which is an intolerable presumption on any man's part, and it is a thing which this House will never allow and will repudiate if it is put before it. We have heard a lot about this Divine Right of Kings; we have read a lot about it in past histories and we thought that we had heard the last of it and that it had been put an end to and buried deep down in the earth long ages ago. If any individual in India or elsewhere claims it today, he will be doing so without any relation to the present in India. So I would suggest to such persons in all seriousness that, if they want to be respected or considered with any measure of friendliness, no such idea should even be hinted at, much less said. On this there is going to be no compromise.

10*

But, as I made plain on the previous occasion when I spoke, this Resolution makes it clear that we are not interfering in the internal affairs of the States. I even said that we are not interfering with the system of monarchy in the States, if the people of the States want it. I gave the example of the Irish Republic in the British Commonwealth and it is conceivable to me that, within the Indian Republic, there might be monarchies if the people so desire. That is entirely for them to determine. This Resolution, and presumably, the Constitution that we make, will not interfere with that matter. Inevitably, it will be necessary to bring about uniformity in the freedom of the various parts of India, because it is inconceivable to me that certain parts of India should have democratic freedom and certain others should be denied it. That cannot be. That will give rise to trouble, just as in the wide world today there is trouble, because some countries are free and some are not. There will be much more trouble if there is freedom in parts of India and lack of freedom in other parts.

But we are not laying down in this Resolution any strict system in regard to the governance of the Indian States. All that we say is this: that they, or such of them as are big enough to form unions or group themselves into small unions, will be autonomous units with a very large measure of freedom to do as they choose, subject no doubt to certain central functions in which they will co-operate with the Centre, in which they will be represented at the Centre and in which the Centre will have control. So that, in a sense, this Resolution does not interfere with the inner working of those Units. They will be autonomous and, as I have said, if those Units choose to have some kind of constitutional monarchy at their head, they will be welcome to do so. For my part, I am for a Republic in India as anywhere else. But, whatever my views may be on that subject, it is not my desire to impose my will on others; whatever the views of this House may be on this subject, I imagine that it is not the desire of this House to impose its will in these matters.

So the objection of the ruler of an Indian State to this Resolution becomes an objection in theory to the theoretical implications and the practical implications of the doctrine of the sovereignty of the people. To nothing else does any one object. That is an objection which cannot stand for an instant. We claim in this Resolution the right to frame a Constitution for a Sovereign Independent Indian Republic—necessarily [a] Republic. What else can we have in India? Whatever [a] State may have or may not have, it is impossible and inconceivable and undesirable to think in any terms but those of a Republic in India.

Now, what relation will that Republic bear to the other countries of the world, to England and to the British Commonwealth and the rest? For a long time past we have taken a pledge on Independence Day that India must sever her connection with Great Britain, because that connection had become an emblem of British domination. At no time have we ever thought in terms of isolating ourselves in this part of the world from other countries or of being hostile to countries which have dominated over us. On the eve of this great occasion, when we stand on the threshold of freedom, we do not wish to carry a trail of hostility with us against any other country. We want to be friendly to all. We want to be friendly with the British people and the British Commonwealth of Nations.

But what I would like this House to consider is this: [since] these words and these labels are fast changing their meaning—and in the world today there is no isolation—you cannot live apart from the others. You must co-operate or you must fight. There is no middle way. We wish for peace. We do not want to fight any nation if we can help it. The only possible real objective that we, in common with other nations, can have is the objective of co-operating in building up some kind of world structure, call it One World, call it what you like. The beginnings of this world structure have been laid in the United Nations Organization. It is still feeble; it has many defects; nevertheless, it is the beginning of [a] world structure. And India has pledged herself to co-operate in its work.

Now, if we think of that structure and our co-operation with other countries in achieving it, where does the question come [in] of our being tied up with this group of nations or that group? Indeed, the more groups and blocs are formed, the weaker will that great structure become.

Therefore, in order to strengthen this big structure, it is desirable for all countries not to insist, not to lay stress on separate groups and separate blocs. I know that there are such separate groups and blocs today, and because they exist today, there is hostility between them, and there is even talk of war among them. I do not know what the future will bring us, whether peace or war. We stand on the edge of a precipice and there are various forces which pull us on one side in favour of co-operation and peace, and on the other, push us towards the precipice of war and disintegration. I am not enough of a prophet to know what will happen, but I do know that those who desire peace must deprecate separate blocs which necessarily become hostile to other blocs. Therefore, India, in so far as it has a foreign policy, has declared that it wants to remain independent and free of all these blocs and that it wants to co-operate on equal terms with all countries. It is a difficult position, because, when people are full of fear of one another, any person who tries to be neutral is suspected of sympathy with the other party. We can see that in India and we can see that in the wider sphere of world politics. Recently an American statesman criticized India in words which show how lacking in knowledge and understanding even the statesmen of America are. Because we follow our own policy, this group of nations thinks that we are siding with the other and that group of nations thinks that we are siding with this. That is bound to happen. If we seek to be a free, independent, democratic Republic, it is not to dissociate ourselves from other countries, but rather as a free nation to co-operate in the fullest measure with other countries for peace and freedom, to co-operate with Britain, with the British Commonwealth of Nations, with the United States of America, with the Soviet Union, and with all other countries, big and small. But real co-operation would only come between us and these other nations when we know that we are free to co-operate and are not imposed upon and forced to co-operate. As long as there is the slightest trace of compulsion, there can be no co-operation.

Therefore, I commend this Resolution to the House and I commend this Resolution, if I may say so, not only to this House but to the world at large so that it can be perfectly clear that it is a gesture of friendship to all and that behind it there lies no hostility. We have suffered enough in the past. We have struggled sufficiently, we may have to struggle again, but under the leadership of a very great personality we have sought always to think in terms of friendship and goodwill towards others, even those who opposed us. How far we have succeeded, we do not know, because we are weak human beings. Nevertheless, the impress of that message has found a place in the hearts of millions of people of this country, and even when we err and go astray, we cannot forget it. Some of us may be little men, some may be big, but whether we are small men or big, for the moment we represent a great cause and therefore something of the shadow of greatness falls upon us. Today in this Assembly we represent a mighty cause and this Resolution that I have placed before you gives some semblance of that cause. We shall pass this Resolution, and I hope that this Resolution will lead us to a Constitution on the lines suggested by this Resolution. I trust that the Constitution itself will lead us to the real freedom that we have clamoured for and that real freedom in turn will bring food to our starving people, clothing for them, housing for them and all manner of opportunities for progress; that it will lead also to the freedom of the other countries of Asia, because in a sense, however unworthy we may be, we have become—let us recognize it—the leader of the freedom movement of Asia, and whatever we do, we should think of ourselves in these larger terms. When some petty matter divides us and we have difficulties and conflicts amongst ourselves over these small matters, let us remember not only this Resolution, but this great responsibility that we shoulder, the responsibility of the freedom of four hundred million people of India, the responsibility of the leadership of a large part of Asia, the responsibility of being some kind of guide to vast numbers of people all over the world. It is a tremendous responsibility. If we remember it, perhaps we may not bicker so much over this seat or that post, over some small gain for this group or that. The one thing that should be obvious to all of us is this, that there is no group in India, no party, no religious community, which can prosper if India does not prosper. If India goes down, we go down, all of us, whether we have a few seats more or less, whether we get a slight advantage or we do not. But if it is well with India, if India lives as a vital, free country then it is well with all of us to whatever community or religion we may belong.

We shall frame the Constitution, and I hope it will be a good Constitution, but does anyone in this House imagine that, when a free India emerges, it will be bound down by anything that even this House might lay down for it? A free India will see the bursting forth of the energy of a mighty nation. What it will do and what it will not, I do not know, but I do know that it will not consent to be bound down by anything. Some people imagine that what we do now may not be touched for ten years or twenty years; if we do not do it today, we shall not be able to do it later. That seems to me a complete misapprehension. I am not placing before the House what I want done and what I do not want done, but I should like the House to consider that we are on the eve of revolutionary changes, revolutionary in every sense of the word, because when the spirit of a nation breaks its bonds, it functions in peculiar ways and it should function in strange ways. It may be that the Constitution this House frames may not satisfy an India that is free. This House cannot bind down the next generation or the people who will duly succeed us in this task. Therefore, let us not trouble ourselves too much about the petty details of what we do; these details will not survive for long, if they are achieved in conflict. What we achieve in unanimity, what we achieve by co-operation is likely to survive. What we gain here and there by conflict and by overbearing manners and by threats will not survive long. It will only leave a trail of bad blood. And so now I commend this Resolution to the House and may I read the last paragraph of this Resolution? But, one word more, Sir, before I read it.

India is a great country, great in her resources, great in manpower, great in her potential, in every way. I have little doubt that a free India on every plane will play a big part on the world stage, even on the narrowest plane of material power, and I should like India to play that great part on that plane. Nevertheless, today there is a conflict in the world between forces in different planes. We hear a lot about the atom bomb and the various kinds of energy that it represents and in essence today there is a conflict in the world between two things, the atom bomb and what it represents and the spirit of humanity. I hope that while India will no doubt play a great part in all the material spheres, she will always lay stress on the spirit of humanity and I have no doubt in my mind that ultimately in this conflict that is confronting the world the human spirit will prevail over the atom bomb. May this Resolution bear fruit and the time may come when in the words of this Resolution, this ancient land will attain its rightful and honoured place in the world and make its full and willing contribution to the promotion of world peace and the welfare of mankind.[1]

[In spite of the Muslim League's previous disapproval of the course of events in India, when the Constituent Assembly reconvened towards the end of January and Nehru spoke in behalf of his Objectives Resolution, the measure was unanimously approved. The League persisted, however, in criticizing both the Assembly and the Objectives Resolution, defiantly calling upon Britain to proclaim its own recent Cabinet Mission plan a failure, and to dissolve the Assembly. While the League continued to concentrate its attention upon obtaining a separate Pakistan, Congress requested removal of League Ministers from the Interim Government in February, short of League participation in the Assembly. At just this point Britain made its momentous declaration about the final transfer of power. The year of decision regarding achievement of Indian independence was about to begin, even though internal dissensions had by no means come to an end. (Despite Nehru's ardent opposition to the Axis Powers during the thirties, his increasing adherence to non-alignment became evident in the late forties. This development is to be understood within the context of India's geographical situation, the fact that the new division of Power Blocs appeared to have taken on fresh connotations, and it seemed imperative to utilize all possible domestic resources to alleviate the poverty of India's millions. Above all, the existence of the atomic bomb made the very contemplation of war impossible).]

[1] I.A., pp. 354–61.

3 | Attlee's February 20 Statement—From Letters to Gandhi—Jinnah's Decision to Cooperate with Congress: Proposal to Divide the Punjab—On the Punjab

Attlee's February 20 Statement

[On February 20 Attlee made a statement in Parliament announcing His Majesty's Government's definite intention to take the necessary steps peacefully to transfer power into responsible Indian hands by a date not later than June 1948. It wished to hand over its responsibility to authorities established by a constitution approved by all parties in India in accordance with the Cabinet Mission Plan, but unfortunately there was no clear prospect that such a constitution and such authorities would emerge. "If then, it should appear that an agreed constitution would not have been worked out [by a fully representative Constituent Assembly] by June 1948, it would have to consider to whom [the] transfer [of] the powers of the central Government [should be made] 'whether as a whole to some form of central Government for British India, or in some areas to the existing provincial Governments, or in such other way as may seem most reasonable and in the best interests of the Indian people.'"[1]

The fact that a definite date was set for the final transfer of power seemed so extraordinary that it was initially difficult for the majority of Congress leaders, including Nehru, to believe in it as a reality.

At the time of Attlee's February statement, it was publicly announced that Lord Wavell—whose appointment it was explained, had been "a wartime one"—was to be succeeded as Viceroy in March by Admiral the Viscount Mountbatten. Mountbatten was to transfer "to Indian hands responsibility for the government of British India" in a manner that would best insure the future happiness and prosperity of the country.[2] Paramountcy in conjunction with the princely states also was to terminate with the transfer of power.]

[Reaction to Attlee's Statement of February 20, 1947.] The statement made by Prime Minister Attlee in the House of Commons on February

---

[1] T.P.I., p. 338. (The full text of Attlee's February 20, 1947 statement is to be found in T.P.I., Appendix IX.)

[2] Ibid., p. 338.

20 in regard to [Indian] policy has received and is receiving the earnest attention of all those who are vitally interested in bringing the present transition period to a satisfactory conclusion.

The statement is obscure in some places and requires careful consideration. The outstanding feature of it, however, is the decision of the British Government to transfer power to Indian hands not later than June, 1948.

It has further been stated that preparatory measures must be put in hand in advance. This is important, [as] only thus can we secure a rapid and effective transference of power within this period. My colleagues and I are giving the fullest thought to this statement, and early next month the Congress Working Committee will meet and give its considered views on the new situation that has arisen.

I should like to say, however, even at this stage, that the decision of the British Government is a wise and courageous one. The clear and definite declaration that the final transference of power will take place by a date not later than June, 1948, not only removes all misconception and suspicion, but also brings reality and a certain dynamic quality to the present situation in India.

That decision will undoubtedly have far-reaching consequences and puts a burden and responsibility on all concerned. It is a challenge to all of us and we shall try to meet it bravely in the spirit of that challenge. I trust that we shall all endeavour to get out of the rut and end the internal conflicts that have frustrated our efforts and delayed our advance, and accept this burden and responsibility, keeping only the independence and advancement of India in view.

The work of the Constituent Assembly must now be carried on with greater speed so that the new and independent India may take shape and be clothed with a constitution worthy of her and bringing relief and opportunity to all her children. In this great work we invite afresh all those who have kept aloof, and we ask all to be partners in this joint and historic understanding, casting aside fear and suspicion, which ill become a great people on the eve of freedom.

The Constituent Assembly, however constituted, can only proceed with its work on a voluntary basis. There can be no compulsion, except the compulsion of events, which none can ignore.

The moment British rule goes the responsibility for the governance of India must inevitably rest on her people and their representatives alone. They will have to shoulder that responsibility. Why then should we not accept this responsibility now and work together to find integrated solutions of our problems? No external authority is going to help or hinder us in future.

The British Government on behalf of their people have expressed their goodwill and good wishes to the people of India. We have had a long past of conflict and ill-will. But we earnestly hope that this past is over. We look forward to a peaceful and co-operative transition and to the establishment of close and friendly relations with the British people for the mutual advantage of both countries and for the advancement of the cause of peace and freedom all over the world.[1]

From Letters to Gandhi

I. [February 24, 1947.] You must have seen my statement on the new declaration made by the British Government. The statement was considered carefully by all our colleagues in the Interim Government minus, of course, the Muslim Leaguers. . . . Mr Attlee's statement contains much that is indefinite and likely to give trouble. But I am convinced that it is in the final analysis a brave and definite statement. It meets our oft-repeated demand for quitting India. . . . Matters will move swiftly now or at any rate after Mountbatten comes. . . . The Working Committee is meeting on the 5th March. . . . Your advice at this critical moment would help us greatly. But you are too far away for consultation and you refuse to move out of East Bengal [where there had been rioting]. Still if you could convey to us your ideas on the subject, we would be very grateful.

II. [February 28, 1947.] The Working Committee is meeting here soon and all of us were anxious to have you here on the occasion. We considered the question of sending you a joint telegram appealing to you to come. But we decided ultimately not to send it. We felt sure that you would not come at this stage and our telegram would only be an embarrassment.

But though we are not sending the telegram we feel very strongly that your advice during the coming weeks is most necessary. It is possible of course for one or two of us to visit you but that is not a satisfactory way of doing things. It is a full discussion among all of us that we would have liked to have. At present it is exceedingly difficult for any of us to leave Delhi even for two or three days. For several to go together would upset work completely. There is the budget in the Assembly, the Committees of the Constituent Assembly, the negotiations with the Princes,

[1] T.L. (Feb. 24, 1947).

the change in Viceroys and so many other things that demand constant attention. So we cannot go away and if you will not come how are we to meet?[1]

[Gandhi refused to go to New Delhi, stating that he would be useless there, unless he could accomplish something to bring about communal peace right where he was—in the Indian countryside.[2]]

Jinnah's Decision to Cooperate with Congress: Proposal to Divide the Punjab

[In early March, even before Mountbatten's arrival in India, and in spite of Muslim League activities during January, Jinnah suddenly agreed to co-operate with Congress. Why this should have occurred after Attlee's February statement—a declaration that had, as is generally agreed, helped greatly to assure partition—can be explained, perhaps, primarily by the fact that Jinnah hoped thereby to improve his bargaining position. (The Muslim League was in control of only two of the six provinces claimed for Pakistan at the time, namely Bengal and Sind. The League could expect support, in addition, only from the rather weak Baluchistan —a Chief Commissioner's Province. Congress, on the other hand, was in power in Assam and the North-West Frontier Province, a Unionist Congress-Sikh coalition also holding office in the Punjab.)

That Attlee's February statement was widely looked upon as "a Pakistan Award" is further indicated by the fact that the Hindus and Sikhs in eastern Punjab, as well as the Hindus of western Bengal, interpreted it as such. In consequence of which these groups, fearing that they might be "swallowed in a Muslim state", urged Congress leaders to seek partition of their two provinces, in order to protect minority groups.

There was a growing feeling even among Congress leaders "that the alternative to partition was chaos." Thus, on March 8, the Working Committee finally acknowledged the essence of the British Government's policy declaration: "It has been made clear that the constitution framed by the Constituent Assembly will apply only to those areas which accept it." In an effort to salvage the non-Muslim majority areas of the Punjab and Bengal, Congress claimed that "any Province or part of a Province which accepts the constitution and desires to join the Union cannot be prevented from doing so", simultaneously proposing partition of the Punjab into two provinces and inviting "the League to a joint conference for [that] purpose", in an effort to help reduce communal friction.[3]

[1] M.L.P. (Vol. I), pp. 566–67.
[2] Based on ibid., pp. 567–68.
[3] M.B., pp. 336–40.

The question inevitably arises: Could Congress totally have avoided either communal violence or partition? Since, according to Gandhi, it was felt that to combat violence with violence was to employ a wrong means—no matter how desirable the end—no violent method of accomplishing either objective could have been employed by Congress under his aegis. Conversely, the argument that failure to take drastic measures against violence, as well as other divisive tendencies, was, in effect, to condone them, raises as many questions as it seems to answer. In any event, because communal atrocities tended steadily to increase rather than the reverse, and Congress leaders were unable to stem this unfortunate trend, the philosophy that they had adopted was bound to come under fire.

Acceptance of partition doubtless may be construed as the necessity to face a reality in the final instance, since the causes of what was occurring were not sufficiently comprehended and dealt with in the beginning. It is possible, however—whatever the failures involved—that if no attempt whatever had been made to meet violence with non-violence, the spiritual values symbolized by Gandhi's approach would not have been given an opportunity to be tested directly within India itself. It is equally tenable to assert that there is no single answer to the highly complex problems involved.

With respect to Nehru, his commitment to a modern, secular, democratic, peacefully united nation remained unshaken. His position was so unassailable that he found it virtually incomprehensible that anyone could be impressed by the to him essentially destructive, negative, and retrogressive vision of Jinnah. Insight into his manner of functioning in this connection well may help to make other events, often initially equally difficult to understand, more readily comprehensible.

Nehru's ultimate concurrence in the decision to divide the Punjab has, at times, been interpreted as opening the door to partition of the entire sub-continent. This is obviously a superficial view, when one considers the many previous actions and events that have been similarly interpreted. Nevertheless, since Nehru had so consistently—and for so long—opposed dividing India in any manner whatever, his final agreement to partitioning of the Punjab inevitably must seem at least somewhat surprising. In this connection, his statement of March 25, 1947 that follows, may be of special interest.

During the period of Nehru's tour of the Punjab in March, 1947—at which time he spoke out fearlessly against the monstrous communal violence being committed—constitutional government in the province was virtually at a standstill. As a result of mounting communal tensions, the most distressing factor involved was formation of private armies— the Muslim Guard, the R.S.S.S. (a right-wing Hindu organization), and the army of the Sikhs. (Congress had no army.)

At the beginning of March, 1947, after the Premier of the Punjab had resigned, and the Sikhs—like the Muslim League—had called for "action", the British took over administration of the province. Serious rioting occurred both in various cities and throughout the countryside.]

On the Punjab

[Of repeated atrocities—Lahore Press Conference, March 17, 1947.]
There is never need for panic whatever happens, much less today when
the situation is more or less under control. The man who is panicky is a
useless citizen and a danger to others.

I propose to say little about my Punjab visit this time. I have seen
ghastly sights and I have heard of behaviour by human beings which
would degrade a brute. The first thing to be done is to put an end to every
kind of disorderly action. The second thing is to protect and rescue
people who may be threatened or are in danger, more especially must
women, who have been abducted or removed by force, be brought back
to their homes. Then other problems like the care of refugees and rehabilitation have to be [faced].

I think that the present disturbances will be completely ended within
a very few days. So far as I have been able to see the military are acting
efficiently and with rapidity.

Obviously all that has happened is intimately connected with political
affairs. I propose to say nothing about that aspect except this: if politics
are to be conducted in this way then they cease to be politics and become
some kind of jungle warfare which reduces human habitation to the state
of a desert. If there is any grace of intelligence in a person, he must
realize that whatever political objective he may aim at, this is not the way
to attain it. Any such attempt must bring, as it has in a measure brought,
risks in its train.

Let people struggle for their political aim if they want to. But let them
do so as human beings with a measure of human dignity. I am not enamoured of slogans anywhere. . . . There may be times when slogans are
useful and good, but when we are up against these hard facts which we
face to-day, they cease to have any meaning. . . . Slogans accusing and
denouncing others are particularly unbecoming and objectionable. . . .

India will go . . . along her destined path to her destined end of Independence and nothing that has happened is going to stop her. So, I am
sure, will the Punjab as a part of India, in spite of everything that has
happened and that is likely to happen. Mighty historic forces are at work
driving us all in that direction in spite of our own follies. It is up to us,
however, to march ahead with dignity, and with head erect, or crawl like
animals in the field.

The Punjab has had a hard lesson. Let it learn from it and not lose itself in a sea of hatred and reprisal, which can only lead to mutual destruction and infamy. Let us all build together and prepare ourselves for the great things to come.

A relief fund has been started and an appeal has been issued on its behalf. I hope that this fund will be liberally subscribed to, and that it will be employed to give help to the large number of sufferers from . . . disturbances, regardless of creed or any other distinction.[1]

[Nehru spoke of the proposal to divide the Punjab on March 25. Although, in his speeches, Nehru publicly belittled the brutalities being committed in the Punjab in order to calm the populace, it nevertheless was necessary to face what was occurring as stark reality. The spirit of non-violence was by no means abroad in the land.]

About our proposal to divide [the] Punjab, this flows naturally from our previous decisions. These were negative previously, but now a time for decision has come and merely passing of resolutions giving expression to our views means little. I feel convinced and so did most of the members of the [Congress] Working Committee that we must press for this immediate division so that reality might be brought into the picture. Indeed this is the only answer to partition as demanded by Jinnah. I found people in the Punjab agreeable to this proposal—except Muslims as a rule. For the present it means an administrative decision without any change in law.[2]

4 | Inter-Asian Relations Conference

[An Inter-Asian Relations Conference—convened in New Delhi during March, 1947 at Nehru's request—happened quite accidentally to coincide with Lord Mountbatten's scheduled arrival in India as Viceroy.

As Pyarelal has recorded, the Delhi Conference of 1947 "brought together nearly two hundred and fifty delegates from twenty-two countries, representing more than half the population of the world. The Conference symbolised the development of a definite 'Asia sentiment', and the keen desire of the people of Asia to take their due share in the affairs of the

[1] B.A.I., pp. 422–23.
[2] M.L.P. (Vol. II), p. 35.

world", a wish that had been developing in accelerated manner since the war.

Nehru, with his "one world" outlook, had set his heart upon holding the Delhi meeting, as previously noted. His profound concern that colonial peoples seeking freedom should make common cause dated back to the 1920s. "We are having a very distinguished and representative gathering . . . from all the countries of Asia", he wrote to Gandhi at the time of the 1947 Conference.[1]

The 1947 Inter-Asian Relations Conference in Delhi was called to review the position of Asia in the post-war world, to exchange ideas about problems common to all Asian countries and to study ways and means of promoting closer contacts, as well as to serve as a sounding board for Asians, many of whom were conferring with one another for the first time.

"Almost all countries of Asia from the west, the east and the south, including the Arab countries, Tibet and Mongolia, and the countries of South-East Asia as well as the Asian Republics of the Soviet Union were represented. . . . Various European and American Governments took great interest and sent their observers to attend the Conference. . . . Japan was not represented as, under the occupation, the Japanese were not allowed to leave their country for such purposes. Conspicuous by its absence was also the Muslim League. . . . It could not help betraying the green eye even in a matter of all-Asia concern. One would have thought that this at least would be regarded as common ground by all groups and sections. But, instead, it dubbed the Conference as a 'thinly disguised attempt on the part of the Hindu Congress to boost itself politically as the prospective leader of the Asian people' and regretted that 'a number of organisations in Muslim countries should have been beguiled . . . to participate in this Conference!' And this in spite of the fact that the Conference was held not at the invitation of the Congress, nor even under the official auspices of the Governments of any of the countries concerned, but on a wholly unofficial basis. Its sole object was to bring together the leading men and women from various Asian countries on a common platform to foster mutual contacts and focus attention on their social, economic and cultural problems. The Indian Council of World Affairs, under whose auspices the Conference was held, was a non-political organisation. Political problems, particularly of a controversial nature . . . relating to the internal affairs of any country, were deliberately excluded from the agenda of the Conference. At the very outset it was made clear that the Conference would adopt no formal resolution or address any recommendations to anybody, lest it should jeopardise the status of the Council of World Affairs as a nonpartisan body. . . .

"Before dispersing, the Conference resolved to form an Asian Relations Organisation. . . . Nehru was unanimously elected President of its Provisional General Council."[2]]

[1] M.L.P. (Vol. II), p. 89.
[2] Ibid. (Vol. II), pp. 89–90.

["Asia Finds Herself Again"—from speech inaugurating Asian Conference, New Delhi, March 23, 1947.] Friends and fellow Asians, what has brought you here, men and women of Asia? Why have you come from the various countries of this mother continent of ours and gathered together in the ancient city of Delhi? Some of us, greatly daring, sent you invitations for this Conference and you gave a warm welcome to that invitation. And yet it was not merely the call from us, but some deeper urge that brought you here.

We stand at the end of an era and on the threshold of a new period of history. Standing on this watershed which divides two epochs of human history and endeavour, we can look back on our long past and look forward to the future that is taking shape before our eyes. Asia, after a long period of quiescence, has suddenly become important again in world affairs. If we view the millennia of history, this continent of Asia, with which Egypt has been so intimately connected in cultural fellowship, has played a mighty role in the evolution of humanity. It was here that civilization began and man started on his unending adventure of life. Here the mind of man searched unceasingly for truth and the spirit of man shone out like a beacon which lighted up the whole world.

This dynamic Asia from which great streams of culture flowed in all directions gradually became static and unchanging. Other peoples and other continents came to the fore and with their new dynamism spread out and took possession of great parts of the world. This mighty continent became just a field for the rival imperialisms of Europe, and Europe became the centre of history and progress in human affairs.

A change is coming over the scene now and Asia is again finding herself. We live in a tremendous age of transition and already the next stage takes shape when Asia takes her rightful place with the other continents.

It is at this great moment that we meet here and it is the pride and privilege of the people of India to welcome their fellow Asians from other countries, to confer with them about the present and the future, and lay the foundation of our mutual progress, wellbeing and friendship.

The idea of having an Asian Conference is not new and many have thought of it. It is indeed surprising that it should not have been held many years earlier, yet perhaps the time was not ripe for it and any attempt to do so would have been superficial and not in tune with world events. It so happened that we in India convened this Conference, but the idea of such a conference arose simultaneously in many minds and in many countries of Asia. There was a widespread urge and an awareness that the time had come for us, peoples of Asia, to meet together, to hold together and to advance together. It was not only a vague desire, but the compulsion of events that forced all of us to think along these lines. Because of this, the invitation we in India sent out brought an answering echo and a magnificent response from every country of Asia.

We welcome you, delegates and representatives from China, that great country to which Asia owes so much and from which so much is expected; from Egypt and the Arab countries of Western Asia, inheritors of a proud culture which spread far and wide and influenced India greatly; from Iran whose contacts with India go back to the dawn of history; from Indonesia and Indo-China whose history is intertwined with India's culture, and where recently the battle of freedom has continued, a reminder to us that freedom must be won and cannot come as a gift; from Turkey that has been rejuvenated by the genius of a great leader; from Korea and Mongolia, Siam, Malaya and the Philippines; from the Soviet Republics of Asia which have advanced so rapidly in our generation and which have so many lessons to teach us; and from our neighbours Afghanistan, Tibet, Nepal, Bhutan, Burma and Ceylon to whom we look especially for co-operation and close and friendly intercourse. Asia is very well represented at this conference, and if one or two countries have been unable to send representatives, this was due to no lack of desire on their part or ours, but circumstances beyond our control came in the way. We welcome also observers from Australia and New Zealand, because we have many problems in common, especially in the Pacific and in the South-East region of Asia, and we have to co-operate together to find solutions.

As we meet here today, the long past of Asia rises up before us, the troubles of recent years fade away, and a thousand memories revive. But I shall not speak to you of these past ages with their glories and triumphs and failures, nor of more recent times which have oppressed us so much and which still pursue us in some measure. During the past two hundred years we have seen the growth of Western imperialisms and of the reduction of large parts of Asia to colonial or semi-colonial status. Much has happened during these years, but perhaps one of the notable consequences of the European domination of Asia has been the isolation of the countries of Asia from one another. India always had contacts and intercourse with her neighbour countries in the North-West, the North-East, the East and the South-East. With the coming of British rule in India these contacts were broken off and India was almost completely isolated from the rest of Asia. The old land routes almost ceased to function and our chief window to the outer world looked out on the sea route which led to England. A similar process affected other countries of Asia also. Their economy was bound up with some European imperialism or other; even culturally they looked towards Europe and not to their own friends and neighbours from whom they had derived so much in the past.

Today this isolation is breaking down because of many reasons, political and other. The old imperialisms are fading away. The land routes have revived and air travel suddenly brings us very near to one another. This Conference itself is significant as an expression of that deeper urge of the mind and spirit of Asia which has persisted in spite of the isolationism which grew up during the years of European domination. As that domination goes, the walls that surrounded us fall down and we look at one another again and meet as old friends long parted.

In this Conference and in this work there are no leaders and no followers. All countries of Asia have to meet together on an equal basis in a common task and endeavour. It is fitting that India should play her part in this new phase of Asian development. Apart from the fact that India herself is emerging into freedom and independence, she is the natural centre and focal point of the many forces at work in Asia. Geography is a compelling factor, and geographically she is so situated as to be the meeting point of Western and Northern and Eastern and South-East Asia. Because of this, the history of India is a long history of her relations with the other countries of Asia. Streams of culture have come to India from the west and the east and been absorbed in India, producing the rich and variegated culture which is India today. At the same time, streams of culture have flowed from India to distant parts of Asia. If you would know India you have to go to Afghanistan and Western Asia, to Central Asia, to China and Japan and to the countries of South-East Asia. There you will find magnificent evidence of the vitality of India's culture which spread out and influenced vast numbers of people.

There came the great cultural stream from Iran to India in remote antiquity. And then that constant intercourse between India and the Far East, notably China. In later years South-East Asia witnessed an amazing efflorescence of Indian art and culture. The mighty stream which started from Arabia and developed as a mixed Irano-Arabic culture poured into India. All these came to us and influenced us, and yet so great was the powerful impress of India's own mind and culture that it could accept them without being itself swept away or overwhelmed. Nevertheless, we all changed in the process and in India today all of us are mixed products of these various influences. An Indian, wherever he may go in Asia, feels a sense of kinship with the land he visits and the people he meets.

I do not wish to speak to you of the past, but rather of the present. We meet here not to discuss our past history and contacts, but to forge links for the future. And may I say here that this Conference, and the idea underlying it, is in no way aggressive or against any other continent or country? Ever since news of this Conference went abroad some people in Europe and America have viewed it with doubt imagining that this was some kind of a Pan-Asian movement directed against Europe or America. We have no designs against anybody; ours is the great design of promoting peace and progress all over the world. Far too long have we of Asia been petitioners in western courts and chancellories. That story must now belong to the past. We propose to stand on our own feet and to co-operate with all others who are prepared to co-operate with us. We do not intend to be the playthings of others.

In this crisis in world history Asia will necessarily play a vital role. The countries of Asia can no longer be used as pawns by others; they are bound to have their own policies in world affairs. Europe and America have contributed very greatly to human progress and for that we must yield them praise and honour, and learn from them the many lessons they have to teach. But the West has also driven us into wars and conflicts without number and even now, the day after a terrible war, there is talk of further wars in the atomic age that is upon us. In this atomic age Asia will have to function effectively in the maintenance of peace. Indeed, there can be no peace unless Asia plays her part. There is today conflict in many countries, and all of us in Asia are full of our own troubles. Nevertheless, the whole spirit and outlook of Asia are peaceful, and the emergence of Asia in world affairs will be a powerful influence for world peace.

Peace can only come when nations are free and also when human beings everywhere have freedom and security and opportunity. Peace and freedom, therefore, have to be considered both in their political and economic aspects. The countries of Asia, we must remember, are very backward and the standards of life are appallingly low. These economic problems demand urgent solution or else crisis and disaster may overwhelm us. We have, therefore, to think in terms of the common man and fashion our political, social and economic structure so that the burdens that have crushed him may be removed, and he may have full opportunity for growth.

We have arrived at a stage in human affairs when the ideal of One World and some kind of a World Federation seem to be essential, though there are many dangers and obstacles in the way. We should work for that ideal and not for any grouping which comes in the way of this larger world group. We, therefore, support the United Nations structure which is painfully emerging from its infancy. But in order to have One World, we must also, in Asia, think of the countries of Asia co-operating together for that larger ideal. . . .

We seek no narrow nationalism. Nationalism has a place in each country and should be fostered, but it must not be allowed to become aggressive and come in the way of international development. Asia stretches her hand out in friendship to Europe and America as well as to our suffering brethren in Africa. We of Asia have a special responsibility to the people of Africa. We must help them to their rightful place in the human family. The freedom that we envisage is not to be confined to this nation or that or to a particular people, but must spread out over the whole human race. That universal human freedom also cannot be based on the supremacy of any particular class. It must be the freedom of the common man everywhere and full opportunities for him to develop.

We think today of the great architects of Asian freedom . . . whose labours have borne fruit. We think also of that great figure whose labours and whose inspiration have brought India to the threshold of her independence—Mahatma Gandhi. We miss him . . . [but he] is engrossed in the service of the common man in India, and even this Conference could not drag him away from it.

All over Asia we are passing through trials and tribulations. In India also you will see conflict and trouble. Let us not be disheartened by this; this is inevitable in an age of mighty transition. There are a new vitality and powerful creative impulses in all the peoples of Asia. The masses are awake and they demand their heritage. Strong winds are blowing all over Asia. Let us not be afraid of them, but rather welcome them for only with their help can we build the new Asia of our dreams. Let us have faith in these great new forces and the dream which is taking shape. Let us, above all, have faith in the human spirit which Asia has symbolized for those long ages past.[1]

[1] I.A., pp. 295-301.

5 | Mountbatten's Arrival in India and Subsequent Developments, March–April

[The variety of problems confronting Lord Mountbatten on his arrival in India on March 22 was overwhelming. Communal violence had reached new heights in the Punjab, as had League agitation in the North-West Frontier Province and Assam. The Interim Government was plagued by tensions, the Congress by conflicts between industrialists and socialists. The country's administration was functioning against vast odds. Congress and the Sikhs continued to hope for maintenance of a united India, the Muslim League for creation of a divided sub-continent. Paramountcy was to return to the Indian Princes, but no machinery had been set up either for direct negotiation to provide a new relationship with the successors of British India or with anyone else. Thus there was danger that the existence of virtually six hundred separate princely States might serve to Balkanize the country. The Punjab, composed of Hindus, Muslims, and Sikhs, continued to be governed by emergency decree. Britain's Viceregal plan provided only for "a phased military evacuation".[1]

India continued to be confronted by a series of bewildering, and seemingly irreconcilable British proposals: The Cabinet Mission Statement of May 16, 1946, with its provisions for a united India; the London Declaration of December, 1946, which had so disturbed Nehru, and which had "opened a wedge for Pakistan;" Attlee's Statement of February 20, 1947, "which added more confusion by its vagueness".[2]

Immediately after his arrival, Mountbatten had "interviews with . . . Gandhi, Jinnah, Nehru, Liaquat Ali Khan and Patel. From the outset he was drawn to Nehru whom he had met in Malaya a year before. . . .

"For Gandhi [Mountbatten] had much respect but their outlooks were fundamentally different and the Mahatma remained on the periphery during the last stage of . . . negotiations [for the transfer of power].

"The most striking feature of Mountbatten's diplomacy was the rapidity with which he arrived at decisions. A series of interviews with Jinnah and Nehru persuaded him that the League leader would persevere to the end, that the Congress leaders were more amenable to compromise, that the Indian situation was rapidly deteriorating into chaos, and that the Cabinet Mission plan for a united India would have to be scrapped in favour of partition."[3]

[1] Based on M.M., p. 40.
[2] M.B., p. 343.
[3] Ibid., pp. 343–44.

During his first interview with Mountbatten on March 25, 1947, Nehru reviewed the major developments that had occurred since the arrival of the Cabinet Mission of 1946. Mountbatten considered Nehru's account substantially accurate, that it "tallied with information he had gathered in London. In Nehru's view, Wavell had made one serious blunder in inviting the Moslem League to come into the Interim Government, instead of waiting a little longer for them to ask to be brought in. He spoke of a private Moslem League meeting at which Jinnah had in fact already capitulated on this issue."

When Mountbatten asked Nehru his estimate of Jinnah, Nehru replied that the essential thing to realise was that Jinnah was a man to whom success had come very late in life, at over sixty. Before that, said Nehru, Jinnah "had not been a major figure in Indian politics. He was a successful lawyer, but not an especially good one . . . Nehru stressed the necessity of making this particular distinction in Jinnah's case. The secret of his success—and it had been tremendous, if only for its emotional intensity—was in his capacity to take up a permanently negative attitude. This he had done with complete singleness of purpose" since 1935, even while realizing that Pakistan could never stand up to constructive criticism, to which he had made certain it would "never be subjected".

When Mountbatten inquired what he considered the biggest single problem facing India, Nehru "replied at once, the economic one. Thereupon Mountbatten asked him whether he was satisfied with the way the Interim Government was tackling it. Nehru said he was not, but the position was made impossible by the League, who were determined to sabotage any economic planning from the centre. Such planning, if it succeeded, would *ipso facto* undermine the case for Pakistan with regard to the Punjab. Nehru put forward a proposal he [had] made before of a tripartite administration of the Province divided . . . on communal lines, with a central authority to deal with certain major non-communal subjects. He was convinced this was the only way to break the intolerable deadlock . . . which Wavell had had to impose. . . .

"In Mountbatten's view, Nehru was extremely frank and fair, and astounded him by actually suggesting at one point an Anglo-Indian union involving nothing less than common citizenship—in effect, a far closer bond than Commonwealth status, which Nehru felt was psychologically and emotionally unacceptable.

"At the end of the interview, as Nehru was about to take his leave, Mountbatten said to him, 'Mr Nehru, I want you to regard me not as the last Viceroy winding up the British Raj, but as the first to lead the way to the new India.' Nehru turned, looked intensely moved, smiled and then said, 'Now I know what they mean when they speak of your charm being so dangerous.'" [1]

Mountbatten was at once convinced that the need for a political solution in India was far more pressing than had been apparent in London, and that the earliest possible time-limit was of paramount importance. Otherwise,

[1] M.M., pp. 44–45.

he feared political collapse, and that the Congress, League and Sikhs would be unable to achieve a viable solution.[1]

By mid-April Mountbatten had begun to evolve a Plan that he hoped would resolve existing difficulties in India, having swiftly recognized that a united India could be maintained only as a result of a bitter and costly civil war.

A Simla Conference was planned for early May. Just before it was convened, the essential principles of the draft Mountbatten Plan, about to be presented for consideration, had been formulated. Responsibility for Pakistan—if it materialized—was to rest upon the Indians themselves. The Provinces in general were to possess the right to determine their own future. Bengal and the Punjab would be partitioned for purposes of voting. The predominately Muslim Sylhet district in Assam, contiguous to Bengal, would be given the option of joining the Muslim Province created by a partitioned Bengal. A general election was to be held in the North-West Frontier Province.[2]

By April 18, Congress had conditionally accepted the idea of partition, although the precise form it might take was still to be decided upon.]

[From speech to All-India States People's Conference—April 18, 1947.] The Congress . . . [has] recently on practical considerations passed a resolution accepting the division of the country.[3]

[End of April, 1947.] The Muslim League can have Pakistan if they want it . . . but on the condition that they do not take away other parts of India which do not wish to join Pakistan.[4]

[On May 10 Mountbatten gave Nehru his draft plan to read, as revised and approved by London. Nehru, having read it, vehemently turned it down, being convinced that it involved a major departure in principle from the original draft prepared by Mountbatten and his staff, that had been taken back to London at the beginning of the month.

Nehru believed that both in the Cabinet Mission Plan, which he was at pains to stress was still not dead, and in the original Mountbatten draft, his concept of India as a continuing unity had been preserved. The London draft, however, struck him as amounting to little less than connivance at Balkanization. He wanted it to be fully established that India and the Constituent Assembly were the successors to, and Pakistan and the Muslim League the seceders from, British India. The changes he felt had been made aroused in Nehru his old suspicions of London as the

[1] Based on ibid., p. 55.
[2] Based on ibid., p. 62. (For further details of the final Mountbatten Plan of June 3, 1947, see following pages.)
[3] M.B., p. 345.
[4] L.T.P.I., p. 155.

home of an alien Civil Service whose hearts were hard, and whose understanding was strictly limited when it came to handling present-day India.

"The one immediate result of his attitude [was] to make it necessary for Mountbatten and his staff . . . to push ahead at once with a second revised draft at the highest speed." [1]

Because of the need to redraft the plan, the Simla meeting planned for May 17 was changed to June 2.

A "compromise [Plan]" was finally hammered out at Simla . . . where, for a while, the issue hung on the thread of trust. . . .

"The bone of contention [remained] not the principle of partition, which Nehru had already accepted, but a number of technicalities relating to the transfer of power. The most important was the issue of constitutional continuity." Nehru's claim that the Union of India was the rightful successor to the British Raj, whereas Pakistan amounted merely to the secession of a few provinces from British India "proved to be of some importance for the subsequent international status of the Indian Union: the U.N. recognized this claim." The way out of the dilemma that was posed proved finally to be a Dominion Status formula[2] finally acceptable to a free India.

When V. P. Menon first discussed Mountbatten's Plan concerning how best finally to transfer power with Nehru, he met a blank wall. It was only at Simla that Menon finally succeeded in winning Nehru's approval of remaining in the Commonwealth. (Nehru was unaware at the time that Patel already had expressed similar agreement.)

Once India's powerful "duumvirate" had jointly approved Dominion Status—but with the terms "King Emperor", "Empire", and any allegiance to the crown strictly eliminated from the formula to be adopted —Congress concurrence was bound to follow. After Patel and Nehru had accepted the concept of Dominion Status—albeit reluctantly, despite the fact that India would be independent—even Gandhi's opposition could have been of no avail.]

[1] Based on M.M., p. 89.
[2] M.B., pp. 345–46.

6 | Developments, May 18–June 2— The Mountbatten Plan

Developments, May 18–June 2

[Lord Mountbatten left for London on May 18, 1947 to report to the British Government. He returned to India at the end of the month. While he was away Jinnah made a demand for an eight-hundred-mile corridor that would link an East and a West Pakistan.]

[From Interview—May 24, 1947.] Mr Jinnah's recent statement [about a corridor] is completely unrealistic and indicates that he desires no settlement of any kind. The demand for a corridor is fantastic and absurd. We stand for a union of India with the right to particular areas to opt out. . . . We envisage no compulsion. If there is no proper settlement on this basis without further claims being advanced, then we shall proceed with making and implementing the constitution for the union of India.[1]

[June 2, 1947: "Having made his last formal attempt to resuscitate the [1946] Cabinet Mission Plan, and Jinnah having for the last time formally rejected it, Mountbatten [again] turned to the dilemma presented by Partition." At this point, "Congress, he said, did not agree to the principle of the partition of India, but, if this were unavoidable, insisted on the partition of Provinces to avoid the coercion of Moslem or Hindu majority areas, while on the other hand Jinnah resisted the partition of Provinces but demanded the division of India."

Mountbatten then introduced a new paragraph in his Plan, about to be formally presented the following day, under the heading of "Immediate Transfer of Power." The paragraph defended the idea of "Dominion Status not from the imputation of Britain's desire to retain a foothold beyond her time but from the possible charge of quitting on her obligations. Therefore", Mountbatten stated, "it was abundantly clear that British assistance should not be withdrawn prematurely if it was still required".[2]]

[1] M.M., p. 96.
[2] Ibid., pp. 99–100.

From The Mountbatten Plan, Presented June 3

["1. On February 20th, 1947, His Majesty's Government announced their intention of transferring power in British India to Indian hands by June 1948. His Majesty's Government had hoped that it would be possible for the major parties to co-operate in the working out of the Cabinet Mission's Plan of May 16th, 1946, and evolve for India a Constitution acceptable to all concerned. This hope has not been fulfilled.

"2. The majority of the representatives of the Provinces of Madras, Bombay, the United Provinces, Bihar, Central Provinces and Berar, Assam, Orissa and the North-West Frontier Provinces, and the representatives of Delhi, Ajmer-Merwara and Coorg have already made progress in the task of evolving a new Constitution. On the other hand, the Muslim League Party, including in it a majority of the representatives of Bengal, the Punjab and Sind as also the representative of British Baluchistan, has decided not to participate in the Constituent Assembly.

"3. It has always been the desire of His Majesty's Government that power should be transferred in accordance with the wishes of the Indian people themselves. This task would have been greatly facilitated if there had been agreement among the Indian political parties. In the absence of such agreement, the task of devising a method by which the wishes of the Indian people can be ascertained has devolved upon His Majesty's Government. After full consultation with. political leaders in India, His Majesty's Government have decided to adopt for this purpose the plan set out below. His Majesty's Government wish to make it clear that they have no intention of attempting to frame any ultimate Constitution for India; this is a matter for the Indians themselves nor is there anything in this plan to preclude negotiations between communities for a united India.

"4. It is not the intention of His Majesty's Government to interrupt the work of the existing Constituent Assembly. Now that provision is made for certain provinces specified below, His Majesty's Government trust that, as a consequence of this announcement, the Muslim League representatives of those provinces, a majority of whose representatives are already participating in it, will now take their due share in its labour. At the same time it is clear that any constitution framed by this Assembly cannot apply to those parts of the country which are unwilling to accept it. His Majesty's Government are satisfied that the procedure outlined below embodies the best method of ascertaining the wishes of the people of such areas on the issue whether their Constitution is to be framed:
(a) in the existing Constituent Assembly; or
(b) in a new and separate Constituent Assembly consisting of the representatives of those areas which decide not to participate in the existing Constituent Assembly.

"When this has been done, it will be possible to determine the authority or authorities to whom power should be transferred.

"5. The Provincial Legislative Assemblies of Bengal and the Punjab (excluding the European members) will, therefore, each be asked to meet in two parts, one representing the Muslim majority districts and the other the rest of the province. For the purpose of determining the population of districts the 1941 census figures will be taken as authoritative. The Muslim majority districts in these two provinces are set out in the Appendix to this announcement.[1]

"6. The members of the two parts of each Legislative Assembly sitting separately will be empowered to vote whether or not the province should be partitioned. If a simple majority of either part decides in favour of partition, division will take place and arrangement will be made accordingly.

"7. Before the question as to partition is decided, it is desirable that the representative of each part should know in advance which Constituent Assembly the province as a whole would join in the event of the two parts subsequently deciding to remain united. Therefore, if any member of either Legislative Assembly so demands, there shall be held a meeting of all members of the Legislative Assembly (other than Europeans) at which a decision will be taken on the issue as to which Constituent Assembly the province as a whole would join if it were decided by the two parts to remain united.

"8. In the event of partition being decided upon, each part of the Legislative Assembly will, on behalf of the areas they represent, decide which of the alternatives in paragraph 4 above to adopt.

"9. For the immediate purpose of deciding on the issue of partition, the members, of the legislative assemblies of Bengal and the Punjab will sit in two parts according to Muslim majority districts (as laid down in the Appendix) and non-Muslim majority districts. This is only a preliminary step of a purely temporary nature as it is evident that for the purposes of final partition of these provinces a detailed investigation of boundary questions will be needed; and as soon as a decision involving partition has been taken for either province a boundary commission will be set up by the Governor-General, the membership and terms of reference of which will be settled in consultation with those concerned. It will be instructed to demarcate the boundaries of the two parts of the Punjab on the basis of ascertaining the contiguous majority areas of Muslims and non-Muslims. It will also be instructed to take into account other factors. Similar instructions will be given to the Bengal Boundary Commission. Until the report of a boundary commission has been put into effect, the provisional boundaries indicated in the Appendix will be used.

"10. The Legislative Assembly of Sind (excluding the European members) will at a special meeting also take its own decision on the alternatives in paragraph 4 above.

"11. The position of the North-West Frontier Province is exceptional. Two of the three representatives of this province are already participating

---

[1] A listing of the Muslim majority districts of the Punjab and Bengal, according to the 1941 census, is to be found in I.W.F., p. 286. It comprises the Appendix to the Mountbatten Plan of June 3, 1947.

in the existing Constituent Assembly. But it is clear, in view of its geographical situation and other considerations, that if the whole or any part of the Punjab decided not to join the existing Constituent Assembly, it will be necessary to give the North-West Frontier Province an opportunity to reconsider its position. Accordingly, in such an event a referendum will be made to the electors of the present Legislative Assembly in the North-West Frontier Province to choose which of the alternatives mentioned in paragraph 4 above they wish to adopt. The referendum will be held under the aegis of the Governor-General and in consultation with the provincial Government.

"12. British Baluchistan has elected a member, but he has not taken his seat in the existing Constituent Assembly. In view of its geographical situation, this province will also be given an opportunity to reconsider its position and to choose which of the alternatives in paragraph 4 above to adopt. His Excellency the Governor-General is examining how this can most appropriately be done.

"13. Though Assam is predominantly a non-Muslim province, the district of Sylhet which is contiguous to Bengal is predominantly Muslim. There has been a demand that, in the event of the partition of Bengal, Sylhet should be amalgamated with the Muslim part of Bengal. Accordingly if it is decided that Bengal should be partitioned, a referendum will be held in Sylhet District under the aegis of the Governor-General and in consultation with the Assam Provincial Government to decide whether the district of Sylhet should continue to form part of Assam Province or should be amalgamated with the new province of Eastern Bengal. [A] boundary commission with terms of reference similar to those for the Punjab and Bengal will be set up to demarcate the Muslim majority areas of Sylhet District and contiguous Muslim majority areas of adjoining districts, which will then be transferred to East Bengal. The rest of Assam Province will in any case continue to participate in the proceedings of the existing Constituent Assembly.

"14. If it is decided that Bengal and the Punjab should be partitioned, it will be necessary to hold fresh elections to choose their representatives on the scale of one for every million of population according to the principle contained in the Cabinet Mission's Plan of May 16, 1946. Similar election will also have to be held for Sylhet in the event of it being decided that this district should form part of East Bengal. . . .

"15. In accordance with the mandates given to them, the representatives of the various areas will either join the existing Constituent Assembly or form the new Constituent Assembly.

"16. Negotiations will have to be initiated as soon as possible on the administrative consequences of any partition that may have been decided upon:—

(a) Between the representatives and the respective successor authorities about all subjects now dealt with by the Central Government including defence, finance, and communications.

(b) Between different successor authorities and His Majesty's Government for treaties in regard to matters arising out of the transfer of power.

(c) In the case of provinces that may be partitioned, as to the administration of all provincial subjects, such as the division of assets and liabilities, the police and other services, the high courts, provincial institutions etc.

"17. Agreements with tribes of the North-West Frontier of India will have to be negotiated by the appropriate successor authority.

"18. His Majesty's Government wish to make it clear that the decisions announced above relate only to British India and that their policy towards Indian States contained in the Cabinet Mission's memorandum of 12th May, 1946 remains unchanged.

"19. In order that the successor authorities may have time to prepare themselves to take over power, it is important that all the above processes should be completed as quickly as possible. To avoid delay, the different provinces or parts of provinces will proceed independently as far as practicable within the conditions of this plan. The existing Constituent Assembly and the new Constituent Assembly (if formed) will proceed to frame constitutions for their respective territories; they will, of course, be free to frame their own rules.

"20. The major political parties have repeatedly emphasized their desire that there should be the earliest possible transfer of power in India. With this desire His Majesty's Government are in full sympathy and they are willing to anticipate the date of June 1948, for the handing over of power by the setting up of an Independent Indian Government or Governments at an even earlier date. Accordingly, as the most expeditious, and indeed the only practicable way of meeting this desire, His Majesty's Government propose to introduce legislation during the current session for the transfer of power this year on a Dominion Status basis to one or two successor authorities according to the decisions taken as a result of this announcement. This will be without prejudice to the right of the Indian Constituent Assemblies to decide in due course whether or not the part of India in respect of which they have authority will remain within the British Commonwealth.

"His Excellency the Governor-General will from time to time make such further announcements as may be necessary in regard to procedure or any other matters for carrying out the above arrangements." 1]

1 I.W.F., pp. 282–86.

	Acceptance of Mountbatten Plan—
7	Commonwealth Relations and
	Dominion Status

Acceptance of Mountbatten Plan

[The Mountbatten Plan was officially announced on June 3, after all the parties concerned had approved it.

After objections had been voiced, and suspicions made obvious for one reason or another, Mountbatten attempted to explain that "the creation of two new States [India and Pakistan] would inevitably mean two strong central governments which could not afford to delegate their powers, instead of one weak one for the whole sub-continent which could. On the other hand, he felt that the acceptance of Dominion Status . . . both offered a measure of protection as well as compensation to those Princes who had stood so loyally by their alliances and friendship with Britain. Whatever decisions they reached, he advised them to cast their minds forward ten years and to consider what the situation in India and the world was likely to be by then."[1]

News of India's Partition, and the potential agreement of various Indian leaders to the proposed bi-furcation of the sub-continent of India, was immediately "flashed across the world."[2] Once the Mountbatten Plan was released, Nehru made the statement about it that follows, after explaining that, whereas the Plan never could meet with Congress' complete approval, on balance it was being accepted.

"I doubt," Alan Campbell-Johnson has noted, "whether any draft agreement was thrashed out with such exhaustive line by line . . . paragraph by paragraph discussion at such a high political level as the June 3rd Plan. It was the reverse of an award. . . ."[3] (Even Mountbatten "did not conceal his preference for a unitary solution" with regard to the final transfer of power, however, "in his broadcast of the 3rd June".[4])]

[Broadcast Message—New Delhi, June 3, 1947.] Nearly nine months ago, soon after my assumption of office,[5] I spoke . . . from this place. I told you then that we were on the march and the goal had still to be

[1] M.M., p. 105.
[2] Ibid., p. 107.
[3] T.A.R. (July, 1952), p. 164.
[4] Ibid., p. 169.
[5] As *de facto* Prime Minister of the Interim Government.

reached. There were many difficulties and obstacles on the way and our journey's end might not be near, for that end was not the assumption of office in the Government of India but the achievement of the full independence of India and the establishment of a co-operative commonwealth in which all will be equal sharers in opportunity and in all things that give meaning and value to life.

Nine months have passed, months of sore trial and difficulty, of anxiety and sometimes even of heartbreak. Yet looking back at this period with its suffering and sorrow for our people there is much on the credit side also, for India has advanced nationally and internationally, and is respected today in the councils of the world.

In the domestic sphere something substantial has been achieved though the burden on the common man still continues to be terribly heavy and millions lack food and cloth and other necessaries of life. Many vast schemes of development are nearly ready and yet it is true that most of our dreams about the brave things we are going to accomplish have still to be realized.

You know well the difficulties which the country had to face, economic, political and communal. These months have been full of tragedy for millions and the burden on those who have the governance of the country in their hands has been great indeed. My mind is heavy with the thought of the sufferings of our people in the areas of disturbance—the thousands who are dead and those, especially our womenfolk, who have suffered agony worse than death. To their families and to the innumerable people who have been uprooted from their homes and rendered destitute I offer my deepest sympathy and assurance that we shall do all in our power to bring relief. We must see to it that such tragedies do not happen again.

At no time have we lost faith in the great destiny of India which takes shape, even though with travail and suffering. . . .

Today I am speaking to you on another historic occasion when a vital change affecting the future of India is proposed. You have just heard an announcement on behalf of the British Government. This announcement lays down a procedure for self-determination in certain areas of India. It envisages on the one hand the possibility of these areas seceding from India; on the other, it promises a big advance towards complete independence. Such a big change must have the full concurrence of the people before effect can be given to it, for it must always be remembered that the future of India can only be decided by the people of India, and not by any outside authority, however friendly.

These proposals will be placed soon before the representative assemblies of the people for consideration. But meanwhile, the sands of time run out and decisions cannot await the normal course of events. So while we must necessarily abide by what the people finally decide we had to come to certain decisions ourselves and to recommend them to the people for acceptance. We have, therefore, decided to accept these proposals and to recommend to our larger committees that they do likewise. It is with no joy in my heart that I commend these proposals to you, though I have no doubt in my mind that this is the right course. For generations we have dreamt and struggled for a free, independent and united India. The proposal to allow certain parts to secede if they so will is painful for any of us to contemplate. Nevertheless, I am convinced that our present decision is the right one even from the larger viewpoint. The united India that we have laboured for was not one of compulsion and coercion but a free and willing association of a free people. It may be that in this way we shall reach that united India sooner than otherwise and then she will have a stronger and more secure foundation.

We are little men serving a great cause, but because the cause is great something of that greatness falls upon us also. Mighty forces are at work in the world today and in India, and I have no doubt that we are ushering in a period of greatness for India. The India of geography, of history and tradition, the India of our minds and hearts, cannot change.

On this historic occasion each one of us must pray that he might be guided aright in the service of the motherland and humanity at large. We stand on a watershed dividing the past from the future. Let us bury that past in so far as it is bad and forget all bitterness and recriminations; let there be moderation in speech and in writing; let there be strength and perseverance in adhering to the cause and the ideals we have at heart. Let us face the future not with easy optimism or any complacency or weakness but with confidence and firm faith in India.

There has been violence, shameful, degrading and revolting violence, in various parts of the country. This must end. We are determined to end it. We must make it clear that political ends are not to be achieved by methods of violence, now or in the future.

On this eve of great changes in India we have to make a fresh start with clear vision and firm mind, with steadfastness and tolerance and with a stout heart. We should not wish ill to anyone but think always of every Indian as our brother and comrade. The good of the four hundred millions of Indians must be our supreme objective. We shall seek to build anew our relations with England on a friendly and co-operative basis forgetting the past which has lain so heavily on us.

I should like to express on this occasion my deep appreciation of the labours of the Viceroy, Lord Mountbatten, since his arrival here at a critical juncture in our history.

Inevitably, on every occasion of crises and difficulties we think of our great leader Mahatma Gandhi who has led us unfalteringly for over a generation through darkness and sorrow to the threshold of our freedom. To him we once again pay our homage. His blessings and wise counsel will happily be with us in the momentous years to come as always.

With a firm faith in our future I appeal to you to co-operate in the great task ahead and to march together to the haven of freedom for all in India.[1]

[From speech to All-India Congress Committee, June 15, 1947, at time of Congress' formal approval of Mountbatten Plan.] There is a certain inherent paramountcy in the Government of India which cannot lapse . . . which must remain because of the very reasons of Geography, History, Defence, etc. . . . The States cannot remain in a void . . . if they do not join the Union, there must be a suzerain relationship . . . the Congress would not permit any act jeopardizing Indian security. . . .

[A warning to Foreign States, i.e., Pakistan and the United Kingdom.] The recognition of any princely State as independent will be considered an unfriendly act.[2]

Commonwealth Relations and Dominion Status

[Nehru's stand on what India's ultimate relationship with Britain should be had gone through various phases over the years. Yet had he, and others of like mind, not insisted upon complete freedom for India throughout the nationalist struggle, it is doubtful whether the measure of independence finally achieved within the Commonwealth would have been as great as it was.

Even as late as 1936, for example, Nehru had proclaimed, as on many other occasions, that the very idea of becoming a dominion seemed "fantastic . . . the whole conception of Dominion Status seems to me to be an acceptance of the basic fabric of British imperialism". Complete independence, on the other hand, had signified for him the total "separation of India from England at the time" even though this approach

[1] S.D.I.C. (Vol. II), pp. 681–83.
[2] Quoted in M.B., p. 354.

occasionally was tempered by such an observation as: "Personally I can conceive and welcome the idea of a close association between India and England on terms other than those of Imperialism"—i.e., once India would be liberated from British rule.[1] Finally, in January 1947, Nehru was further to declare: "At no time have we ever thought in terms of isolating ourselves in this part of the world from other countries or of being hostile to countries which have dominated over us ... we want to be friendly with the British people and the British Commonwealth of Nations."[2]]

[On accepting Dominion Status.] I wanted the world to see that India did not lack faith in herself ... and that [she] was prepared to cooperate even with those whom she had been fighting in the past, provided the basis of cooperation today was honorable, that it was a free basis ... which would lead to the good not only of ourselves but of the world also. .... We have to wash out the past with all its evil.[3]

8 | Indian Independence Act— Problem of Princely States and Patel's Role in Integrating Them

Indian Independence Act

[The Indian Independence Act of July 4 provided for the setting up of two new independent dominions—India and Pakistan—after August 15, 1947. The new Act substituted certain new provisions for previous ones contained in the Government of India Act of 1935.[4] Powers hitherto exercised by the British Parliament, and the Government in British India, would be transferred to the two new dominions, also on August 15.

[1] Ibid., pp. 413–14.
[2] I.A., p. 358.
[3] V.S.N., pp. 142–43. © Copyright 1960 by Vincent Sheehan.
[4] The entire text of the Indian Independence Act of 1947 is to be found in T.P.I., pp. 516ff.

11*

In the 1947 Independence Act "the territories of the Dominions were defined, with appropriate qualifications for the areas about to determine their choice by referendum or by vote of their legislature. Each Dominion was to be headed by a Governor-General, but it was expressly stipulated that one person might serve in a dual capacity, in the hope that Mountbatten would be acceptable to both. The absence of a legally constituted Parliament in either of the proposed Dominions was overcome by giving both Constituent Assemblies the dual status and function of legislature and constitution-making body. The 1935 Government of India Act and its accompanying Orders-in-Council would remain in force (pending alteration or the drafting of new constitutions by the successor authorities), subject to the removal of the reserved and special powers vested in the Governor-General and the provincial Governors. All laws in force in British India on 15 August 1947 would remain in force until amended by the new Dominion legislatures. There was also a provision for continuity in the terms of employment of members of the Services. . . .

"Two provisions of the Act gave rise to vigorous controversy, even before the formal transfer of power: the Governor-Generalship and the constitutional future of the princely States. The Congress proposed Mountbatten as Governor-General of the Dominion of India, undoubtedly on the assumption that the League would do likewise. To the consternation of many, Jinnah decided to occupy that post in Pakistan. In reality it made little difference to the power pyramid in Pakistan during the first year, for Jinnah remained the dominant personality until his death in September 1948. . . .

"The Muslim League accepted the implied doctrine of freedom of action for the Princes, probably because the few States on the Pakistani side of the border would have no real choice. Moreover, the exercise of such freedom by some of the large princely States in India, notably Hyderabad, would imperil the territorial integrity and stability of Pakistan's more powerful neighbour. For precisely opposite reasons the Congress rejected the British Government's interpretation of Paramountcy and declared that it would resist territorial fragmentation."

The A.I.C.C. approved Nehru's strong line by "stating that it could not 'admit the right of any State in India to declare its independence and to live in isolation from the rest of India'.

"The Viceroy, too, was acutely conscious of the constitutional vacuum created by the Indian Independence Act and the danger of Balkanization. He readily agreed to the establishment of a Ministry of States early in July. On 25 July he addressed the Princes in an effort to persuade them to accede to one or the other Dominion, depending upon their geographical position and the communal composition of their population. His speech was a resounding success. By the time power was formally transferred all but three princely States had signified their intention of doing so. Yet the three holding out—Kashmir, Hyderabad and Junagadh —were to cause bitterness and dislocation of such a magnitude that the achievement was overlooked.

"Within the Interim Government tension continued. The Congress members insisted on the necessity of maintaining the normal administrative functions of a central government; the League members blocked every decision of substance. Early in July Nehru was on the verge of resignation over this issue. As soon as the Independence Act received royal assent, on 18 July, Mountbatten solved the problem by splitting the Interim Government into two provisional administrations for the successor states. In the Punjab communal conflict increased as the day of Partition approached. . . . Friction was further intensified by uncertainty over the boundaries." [1]

By default the Indian Independence Act seemed to give the Princes freedom to accede to India or to Pakistan, or to become independent. The vagueness involved with respect to this problem presented difficulties that might well have led to instability and fragmentation. This threat was especially grave for India because all but a dozen of the over five hundred princely States were contiguous to Indian territory. Thus any uncertainty was bound to contribute to the dangerous tension between the two Dominions from the very day of their formation. In particular it was partly responsible for the tragic conflict over Kashmir which was to succeed in poisoning Indo-Pakistani relations after partition. [2]

The Indian Independence Bill was introduced in the British House of Commons on July 4. It was promptly approved by both Houses of Parliament.]

The Problem of the Princely States and Sardar Patel's Role in Integrating Them : Hyderabad, Kashmir, Junagadh

[It was contemplated by Mr Attlee that, during the period before the final transfer of power, the relations of the Crown with individual States might be adjusted by agreement, Mountbatten having been given a very wide mandate concerning what he might do in connection with this matter. [3]

Concerning the problem of the Indian States, and Mountbatten's advice to the Princes, Alan Campbell-Johnson has noted: "To have given no advice at all would merely have intensified the Princes' . . . uncertainties and opened up endless opportunities for intrigue. To have advised the Princes to stand out would . . . in the context of [a] declared intention to transfer power to British India have been a wrecking act. . . . To transfer power to two sovereign states covering two-thirds of the sub-continent and to leave a power vacuum in the remaining third would . . . have been

[1] M.B., pp. 351-55.
[2] Ibid., p. 353.
[3] Based on M.M., p. 22.

morally far more questionable and politically more explosive than to pursue the course in fact adopted." (The essence of the treaties of paramountcy that existed between the Princely States and Britain involved the establishment of a relationship with the paramount power which provided for the Indian Princes a status less than that of either independence or full national sovereignty. The purpose of these treaties was presumably to stabilize the power of the Raj within the limits of its resources.) [1]

During his own seven days' negotiations with the Princes in February, 1947, Nehru already had stressed no fewer than five times both "the voluntary nature of any agreement" to be made with Congress, and Congress "refusal to coerce any unwilling partner". Yet the decision facing the Princes—in view of the approach of independence—was inevitably "to join or perish". [2]

As head of the Ministry of States, from the time of its creation in July, 1947, Sardar Patel was to perform superbly as directing genius of the difficult, yet nevertheless peacefully achieved integration of over five hundred Princely States into the new union of India. Lord Mountbatten and V.P. Menon also played a highly significant part in bringing about their successful integration—as did Nehru in helping to frame policy—in consequence of which India was saved from the tragedy of Balkanization.

It was intended that the "integration" of the States was to involve both the question of accession and democratization. As already indicated, all of the Princely States except Junagadh, Hyderabad and Kashmir decided to accede to India or Pakistan by the time power finally was transferred in August, 1947. (Bloodshed occurred only in conjunction with the accession of the latter two states, as will be described in succeeding pages.) Junagadh, predominantly Hindu, non-contiguous to Pakistan, and under a Muslim ruler, at first acceded to Pakistan. When India opposed this act, sending in its Army to hold a plebiscite in order to ascertain the wishes of the populace, it was found, according to Indian sources, that ninety per cent favored accession to India, which was thereupon carried out.

To the surprise of most Indians, as well as the world at large, the majority of India's Princes finally were deprived of their special privileges with their own acquiescence.]

[1] Based on T.A.R., p. 169.
[2] Based on M.M., p. 48.

9 | On the Eve of Freedom—
Independence: Creation of Pakistan

On the Eve of Freedom

[From cable, New Delhi, published August 4, 1947.] Owing to the secession of some parts of India the immediate problem is to finalize the partition and settle down to work in the new conditions. The food situation is very serious. This has been worsened by the Dutch action in Indonesia in seizing rice stacks meant for India. We have to take urgent steps to obtain foodstuffs from abroad and to add to our domestic production. Lack of foreign exchange comes in the way both in importing food and in buying capital equipment from abroad. Hence the release of sterling balances is of vital importance to us.

We have already a dozen big projects in hand for damming rivers, developing power resources, irrigation, etc. Some of these are as big in area as the T.V.A. We shall push these on as rapidly as possible. We propose to appoint a planning commission to develop industry, agriculture and social services in an organized and planned manner. Scientific research will have first priority.

Our provincial governments are already committed to far-reaching land reforms to result in the abolition of the landlord system and also to the development of popular education. These will be fully supported by the central government.

A great majority of British civil servants will be leaving India by August 15. Probably very few British civil servants or military officers will be left in India after March, 1948. Only a few who might be required by us for special purposes will be invited to remain. It is our definite policy completely to Indianize the civil and defense services by next April.

We propose to have a relatively small but highly efficient army, a growing air force and, to begin with, a small navy. Training schools for these are being enlarged or being established.

Foreign capital will be welcome in India for our schemes of development on profitable terms, but the control of Indian industry must remain in Indian hands. Some of our basic industries and public utilities are likely to be controlled by the state.

It is difficult to prophesy about the future, but it seems inevitable that India and Pakistan must have much in common and will have to cooperate in many fields. This cooperation should lead to closer relations and possibly to some kind of union. That can only come with mutual good will and the force of circumstances.

In our foreign relations we have emphasized our desire not to be entangled in power politics and rival blocs but to try to be friendly with all nations. We are anxious to develop our own resources and raise our standards of living, and we shall do our utmost to preserve peace. . . .

Today, on the eve of independence, India's mood is strange and perplexed. There is a feeling of quiet confidence and triumph at her achievement and, at the same time, deep sorrow for all that has happened during the past year and the secession of part of the country. We realize fully that we have to face a multitude of very difficult problems both nationally and internationally. This is a sobering thought and yet the ultimate feeling is one of confidence in ourselves and in our future.[1]

[Toward the end of July, 1947, after a protracted struggle between the Indonesian Republic and the Netherlands, the Dutch began to wage a military attack against Indonesia, labelled police action to prevent international interference.]

[On Indonesia—August 4, 1947.] We have been greatly disturbed by the recent happenings in Indonesia. Military aggressive action on a big scale involving organized destruction by bombing of the nerve centers of the country is a negation of the United Nations Charter. If there is any dispute between nations it must be referred to arbitration or to the U.N. For any power to refuse arbitration and to take unilateral action is to strike a grievous blow at the United Nations.

The League of Nations failed because the individual powers ignored it and went ahead with their own expansionist schemes. The U.N. will suffer a like fate if it remains passive when warlike operations are started without any reference to it. This is a matter which affects Asia intimately but it affects the whole world, for in it lie the seeds of war and of destruction of world cooperation for the maintenance of peace. Indonesia has become a symbol and a test for all the powers and more especially for the United Nations.[2]

[The question of the Indian National Army (I.N.A.), discussed in earlier sections, continued to have a certain importance in India, that

[1] T.N.R. (Aug. 4, 1947), p. 9.
[2] Ibid., p. 9.

could not be ignored on the eve of independence. Nehru's meeting with Lord Mountbatten in Malaya in 1946, and Mountbatten's imaginative behaviour at that time (also previously described), doubtless made the following letter readily comprehensible to the Viceroy.]

[To Admiral Mountbatten—July 19, 1947.] You will remember that the case of the I.N.A. prisoners was considered at length some time ago and ultimately it was decided to refer it to the judges of the Federal Court. I made a statement to this effect in the Legislative Assembly. I do not know how far this consideration by the Federal Court judges has proceeded and when we are likely to have their recommendations.

As you will no doubt appreciate, an entirely new situation arises, because of the political changes that have taken place. Normally speaking it would be entirely inappropriate for any political prisoners, or those who are considered as political prisoners to be kept [on] in prison after the declaration of Indian independence. There would be a widespread feeling among the people that this independence was not real and was only a façade if such prisoners continued to be detained. It seems to me essential therefore that on or before August 15 I.N.A. prisoners should be released. I am quite certain that if this release does not take place, the matter will be raised in the Constituent Assembly which will be functioning then as a sovereign Legislative Assembly.

There is another aspect of this case. It is possible that the Pakistan Government may take some action in this matter and release the prisoners in their charge. If this happens, as it very probably will, then the retention in prisons at the instance of the India Government would be very difficult if not impossible, and would give rise to tremendous public opinion.

In view of this situation I wish to suggest to you that very early steps should be taken to release these prisoners. This can be done quite appropriately and without any reference to the past in view of the new political status of India. If this is not done soon, a new public demand will arise and then we shall have to do it in response to that demand. It is thus far better to keep the initiative with ourselves than to be compelled by circumstances to take action.[1]

Independence : Creation of Pakistan

[At midnight, August 14, 1947, India attained her freedom, to the accompaniment of tumultuous demonstrations. Simultaneously the new state of Pakistan was created.

[1] A.C.B., p. 895.

In New Delhi, Nehru addressed the Constituent Assembly. The follow-ing day Lord Mountbatten became Governor-General of India. He swore in the new Cabinet, with Nehru as Prime Minister. Jinnah (who died on September 11, 1948) became Governor-General of Pakistan, Liaquat Ali Khan its first Prime Minister.]

["A Tryst With Destiny"—Constituent Assembly, New Delhi, August 14, 1947.] Long years ago we made a tryst with destiny, and now the time comes when we shall redeem our pledge, not wholly or in full measure, but very substantially. At the stroke of the midnight hour, when the world sleeps, India will awake to life and freedom. A moment comes, which comes but rarely in history, when we step out from the old to the new, when an age ends, and when the soul of a nation, long suppressed, finds utterance. It is fitting that at this solemn moment we take the pledge of dedication to the service of India and her people and to the still larger cause of humanity.

At the dawn of history India started on her unending quest, and track-less centuries are filled with her striving and the grandeur of her success and her failures. Through good and ill fortune alike she has never lost sight of that quest or forgotten the ideals which gave her strength. We end today a period of ill fortune and India discovers herself again. The achievement we celebrate today is but a step, an opening of opportunity, to the greater triumphs and achievements that await us. Are we brave enough and wise enough to grasp this opportunity and accept the chal-lenge of the future?

Freedom and power bring responsibility. That responsibility rests upon this Assembly, a sovereign body representing the sovereign people of India. Before the birth of freedom we have endured all the pains of labour and our hearts are heavy with the memory of this sorrow. Some of those pains continue even now. Nevertheless, the past is over and it is the future that beckons to us now.

That future is not one of ease or resting but of incessant striving so that we may fulfil the pledges we have so often taken and the one we shall take today. The service of India means the service of the millions who suffer. It means the ending of poverty and ignorance and disease and inequality of opportunity. The ambition of the greatest man of our generation has been to wipe every tear from every eye. That may be beyond us, but as long as there are tears and suffering, so long our work will not be over.

And so we have to labour and to work, and work hard, to give reality to our dreams. Those dreams are for India, but they are also for the world, for all the nations and peoples are too closely knit together today for any one of them to imagine that it can live apart. Peace has been said to be indivisible; so is freedom, so is prosperity now, and so also is disaster in this One World that can no longer be split into isolated fragments.

To the people of India, whose representatives we are, we make an appeal to join us with faith and confidence in this great adventure. This is no time for petty and destructive criticism, no time for ill-will or blaming others. We have to build the noble mansion of free India where all her children may dwell.

I beg to move, Sir,

"That it be resolved that:

(1) After the last stroke of midnight, all members of the Constituent Assembly present on this occasion, do take the following pledge: 'At this solemn moment when the people of India through suffering and sacrifice, have secured freedom, I,............, a member of the Constituent Assembly of India, do dedicate myself in all humility to the service of India and her people to the end that this ancient land attain her rightful place in the world and make her full and willing contribution to the promotion of world peace and the welfare of mankind;'

(2) Members who are not present on this occasion do take the pledge (with such verbal changes as the President may prescribe) at the time they next attend a session of the Assembly."[1]

["First Servant of the Indian People"—Indian Independence Day Broadcast, New Delhi, August 15, 1947.] Fellow countrymen, it has been my privilege to serve India and the cause of India's freedom for many years. Today I address you for the first time officially as the First Servant of the Indian people, pledged to their service and their betterment. I am here because you willed it so and I remain here so long as you choose to honour me with your confidence.

We are a free and sovereign people today and we have rid ourselves of the burden of the past. We look at the world with clear and friendly eyes and at the future with faith and confidence.

The burden of foreign domination is done away with, but freedom brings its own responsibilities and burdens, and they can only be shouldered in the spirit of a free people, self-disciplined, and determined to preserve and enlarge that freedom.

We have achieved much; we have to achieve much more. Let us then

[1] I.A., pp. 3-4.

address ourselves to our new tasks with the determination and adherence to high principles which our great leader has taught us. Gandhiji is fortunately with us to guide and inspire and ever to point out to us the path of high endeavour. He taught us long ago that ideals and objectives can never be divorced from the methods adopted to realize them; that worthy ends can only be achieved through worthy means. If we aim at the big things of life, if we dream of India as a great nation giving her age-old message of peace and freedom to others, then we have to be big ourselves and worthy children of Mother India. The eyes of the world are upon us watching this birth of freedom in the East and wondering what it means.

Our first and immediate objective must be to put an end to all internal strife and violence, which disfigure and degrade us and injure the cause of freedom. They come in the way of consideration of the great economic problems of the masses of the people which so urgently demand attention.

Our long subjection and the World War and its aftermath have made us inherit an accumulation of vital problems, and today our people lack food and clothing and other necessaries, and we are caught in a spiral of inflation and rising prices. We cannot solve these problems suddenly, but we cannot also delay their solution. So we must plan wisely so that the burdens on the masses may grow less and their standards of living go up. We wish ill to none, but it must be clearly understood that the interests of our long-suffering masses must come first and every entrenched interest that comes in their way must yield to them. We have to change rapidly our antiquated land tenure system, and we have also to promote industrialization on a large and balanced scale, so as to add to the wealth of the country, and thus to the national dividend which can be equitably distributed.

Production today is the first priority, and every attempt to hamper or lessen production is injuring the nation, and more especially harmful to our labouring masses. But production by itself is not enough, for this may lead to an even greater concentration of wealth in a few hands, which comes in the way of progress and which, in the context of today, produces instability and conflict. Therefore, fair and equitable distribution is essential for any solution of the problem.

The Government of India have in hand at present several vast schemes for developing river valleys by controlling the flow of rivers, building dams and reservoirs and irrigation works and developing hydro-electric power. These will lead to greater food production and to the growth of industry and to all-round development. These schemes are thus basic to all planning and we intend to complete them as rapidly as possible so that the masses may profit.

All this requires peaceful conditions and the co-operation of all concerned, and hard and continuous work. Let us then address ourselves to these great and worthy tasks and forget our mutual wrangling and conflicts. There is a time for quarrelling and there is a time for co-operative endeavour. There is a time for work and there is a time for play. Today, there is no time for quarrelling or overmuch play, unless we prove false to our country and our people. Today, we must co-operate with one another and work together, and work with right goodwill.

I should like to address a few words to our Services, civil and military. The old distinctions and differences are gone and today we are all free sons and daughters of India, proud of our country's freedom and joining together in our service of her. Our common allegiance is to India. In the difficult days ahead our Services and our experts have a vital role to play and we invite them to do so as comrades in the service of India. Jai Hind.[1]

["The Appointed Day"—message to the Press, New Delhi—August 15, 1947.] The Appointed Day has come—the day appointed by destiny, and India stands forth again after long slumber and struggle, awake, vital, free and independent. The past clings on to us still in some measure and we have to do much before we redeem the pledges we have so often taken. Yet the turning point is past, history begins anew for us, the history which we shall live and act and others will write about.

It is a fateful moment for us in India, for all Asia and for the world. A new star rises, the star of freedom in the East, a new hope comes into being, a vision long cherished materializes. May the star never set and that hope never be betrayed!

We rejoice in that freedom, even though clouds surround us, and many of our people are sorrow-stricken and difficult problems encompass us. But freedom brings responsibilities and burdens and we have to face them in the spirit of a free and disciplined people.

On this day our first thoughts go to the architect of this freedom, the Father of our Nation, who, embodying the old spirit of India, held aloft the torch of freedom and lighted up the darkness that surrounded us. We have often been unworthy followers of his and have strayed from his message, but not only we but succeeding generations will remember this message and bear the imprint in their hearts of this great son of India, magnificent in his faith and strength and courage and humility. We shall

[1] Ibid., pp. 7-9.

never allow that torch of freedom to be blown out, however high the wind or stormy the tempest.

Our next thoughts must be of the unknown volunteers and soldiers of freedom who, without praise or reward, have served India even unto death.

We think also of our brothers and sisters who have been cut off from us by political boundaries and who unhappily cannot share at present in the freedom that has come. They are of us and will remain of us whatever may happen, and we shall be sharers in their good and ill fortune alike.

The future beckons to us. Whither do we go and what shall be our endeavour? To bring freedom and opportunity to the common man, to the peasants and workers of India; to fight and end poverty and ignorance and disease; to build up a prosperous, democratic and progressive nation, and to create social, economic and political institutions which will ensure justice and fullness of life to every man and woman.

We have hard work ahead. There is no resting for any one of us till we redeem our pledge in full, till we make all the people of India what destiny intended them to be. We are citizens of a great country, on the verge of bold advance, and we have to live up to that high standard. All of us, to whatever religion we may belong, are equally the children of India with equal rights, privileges and obligations. We cannot encourage communalism or narrow-mindedness, for no nation can be great whose people are narrow in thought or in action.

To the nations and peoples of the world we send greetings and pledge ourselves to co-operate with them in furthering peace, freedom and democracy.

And to India, our much-loved motherland, the ancient, the eternal and the ever-new, we pay our reverent homage and we bind ourselves afresh to her service.[1]

[1] Ibid., pp. 5–6.

IO | In the Wake of Independence

[In the wake of independence, renewed communal rioting in the Punjab involved manifold and horrifying atrocities—violence, arson, looting, rape, carnage—followed by uprooting and all manner of other agonies to defy the imagination.

Nehru continued courageously and consistently to oppose communalism in all forms; to play an important role—second only to that of Gandhi —in helping to stem the overwhelming tide of hatred and terrorism that seemed both never-ending and inhuman beyond belief.]

["This Unhappy Land of the Five Rivers"—Broadcast, New Delhi, August 19, 1947.] On the 15th and 16th August, India celebrated the coming of independence; not only India but Indians wherever they happened to be in this wide world. I have received thousands of messages of greetings from abroad. They have come from representatives of great nations, from famous men and from Indians from every remote corner of the world. While I have been deeply moved by these messages from the leaders of other countries welcoming India into the fellowship of free nations, nothing has affected me more than the very touching messages from our countrymen overseas. Cut away from their Motherland they have hungered for India's freedom even more perhaps than we have, and the coming of this freedom has been a tremendous event in their lives. May the New India always remember her children abroad who look to her with such pride and affection and give them all the succour she can.

Nearly the whole of India celebrated the coming of independence, but not so the unhappy land of the five rivers. In the Punjab, both in the east and the west, there was disaster and sorrow. There was murder and arson and looting in many places and streams of refugees poured out from one place to another.

One of the first tasks of our Government was to think of the Punjab and so I hurried thither on the morning of the 17th, accompanied by [one of my Indian colleagues and by] Mr Liaquat Ali Khan, the Prime Minister of Pakistan, and some of his colleagues. I want to tell you what we found there and what we did there. There have been wild rumours enough and people's minds all over India are naturally agitated because whatever happens, the people of the Punjab, whether they live to the east or to the west, are our own kith and kin and anything that affects them affects us.

You must remember that till the 15th August there was a different regime in the [entire province of the] Punjab. . . . The change over took place on the 15th and the new Provincial Governments thus are only four days old. So also are the new Central Governments. These Governments, Central or Provincial, are directly responsible only since the 15th August. The Provincial Governments of East and West Punjab had to face a terrible crisis in the very hour of their birth, even before they had settled down to work or had proper offices functioning.

The story of disastrous happenings in the Punjab takes us back many months to March of this year. One disaster has followed another, each producing its reaction elsewhere. . . .

In both Amritsar and Lahore we heard a ghastly tale and we saw thousands of refugees, Hindu, Muslim and Sikh. There were some fires still burning in the city and reports of recent outrages reached us. We were . . . unanimously of [the] opinion that we must deal firmly with the situation as we found it and not enter into acrimonious debate about the past, and that the situation demanded that crime must be put an end to immediately at whatever cost.

The alternative was complete chaos and ruin for the land and for every community. Anti-social elements were abroad, defying all authority and destroying the very structure of society. Unless these elements were suppressed, to whatever community they belonged, there was no freedom or even security for any person; and so, all of us who were present, whether we belonged to the two Central or the two Provincial Governments, or whether we were leading members of the various communities, pledged ourselves to do our utmost to put an end to this orgy of murder and arson.

We have taken effective steps to this end, effective not only from the administrative and military point of view, but, what is even more important, from the point of view of a popular approach to all our people. We have established high level committees of the two Provincial Governments of the Punjab and liaison officers between the civil and the military authorities, so that there should be the fullest amount of co-operation between the two Provincial Governments and the military forces. We have pledged the Central Governments to help in this task. Popular leaders have assured us of their fullest co-operation.

I am convinced that we shall deal with this situation effectively and that fairly soon security will return to the Punjab, but that requires the utmost effort and constant vigilance from all concerned, whether they are Government officers or others. Each one of us who cares for his country must help in this business of restoring peace and security.

In the past we have unfortunately had communal troubles on a large scale. They are not going to be tolerated in the future. So far as the Government of India are concerned, they will deal with any communal outbreak with the greatest firmness. They will treat every Indian on an equal basis and try to secure for him all the rights which he shares with others.

Our State is not a communal state, but a democratic state in which every citizen has equal rights. The Government is determined to protect these rights.

I have been assured by Mr Liaquat Ali Khan that this is also the policy of the Pakistan Government.

We have made arrangements for the transport of refugees from Lahore [now in Pakistan] to Amritsar [India] or Amritsar to Lahore. They will be carried by railway trains and motor lorries and we hope that very soon most of those who so want will be carried to their destinations. We are further making arrangements for their proper accommodation and food. . . .

We are appointing a Deputy High Commissioner in Lahore to look after our interests there, and, more especially, to look after the refugees who wish to come to East Punjab. We hope to provide a number of tents to the East Punjab Government for accommodating the refugees. In every way that is possible to us we shall help the unfortunate sufferers in the Punjab. So far as Eastern Punjab is concerned, it is our direct responsibility and we shall act accordingly.

While we shall give every help to those who wish to come to East Punjab, we would not like to encourage mass migration of peoples across the new borders, for this will involve tremendous misery for all concerned. We hope that very soon peace and order will be established and people will have security to carry on their avocations.

[No matter what we have done], ultimately the future depends on the co-operation we receive from the people. It is with confident expectation of this co-operation that we are proceeding and declaring with conviction that we shall settle this Punjab problem soon. We can make no progress there or elsewhere in India if these horrible disturbances continue. I appeal, therefore, to all people concerned to face this task with firmness and courage and thus to demonstrate how free India can handle a difficult situation.

The Punjab problem is one of first priority with us and I propose to go there again soon, or whenever needed. Because we seek the co-operation of the people, we must also take them into our confidence. I have, therefore, spoken to you today and I propose to do so again whenever necessity arises. Meanwhile, I hope that people will not give credence to wild rumours which spread so easily and influence people's opinions. The reality has been bad enough, but rumour makes it worse.

To those who have suffered during these dark days in the Punjab, our deepest sympathy goes out. Many have lost their lives, many others have lost everything else that they possessed. We cannot restore the dead, but those who are alive must certainly receive aid from the State now, which should later rehabilitate them.[1]

[To Diplomatic Corps in Government House—September 12, 1947.] The history of India has been one of assimilation and synthesis of the various elements that have come in. . . . It is perhaps because we tried to go against the trend of the country's history that we are faced with [the tragedy of communal rioting]. . . . It is for our common good that the situation must be controlled as soon as possible. Otherwise tremendous injury will be done to both Dominions. . . . Of course it is easier to come to conclusions at the conference table than to put them into effect.[2]

[On Muslim League Methods—New Delhi, October 3, 1947.] India has been able to maintain her culture and civilisation through thousands of years mainly because it has always been a composite state. That way, let it be clearly understood, lies the hope of life in the future also. . . .

India had for thirty years been drilled into non-violence by Mahatma Gandhi. Why, then, suddenly did violence break out in the country ?. . . . The rise of racism in Europe led to the acceptance of the doctrine of brutality as an article of faith for certain nations. In India fascism won its earnest votary in the Muslim League. The League was a moribund, upper class organisation for whom the ideas of Hitler [have] had special appeal. Hitler taught the earlier leaders of the League the way to stem the tide of democracy which Congress had unleashed in the country. . . .

When I returned to India from Europe in 1938 . . . I observed how the League was trying to follow the example of the Fascists, and how some

[1] I.A., pp. 43–46.
[2] M.M., p. 187.

of its responsible leaders had begun to echo fascist tirades against democracy as a form of government. . . .

Nazis were wedded to a negative policy. So also was the League. The League was anti-Hindu, anti-Congress and anti-national. What it was positively, nobody [can] say. The negative policy of the Nazis was, also . . . the League [policy]. The Nazis raised a cry of hatred against the Jews: the League [has] raised [its] cry against the Hindus.

Pakistan [is] the logical outcome of these developments. . . . There could be nothing more negative or destructive than the division of the country into two. But political developments made the establishment of Pakistan almost inevitable.

The League's success in attaining Pakistan led some people to believe its methods had to be adopted if India were to become strong and powerful. But these people forgot that Congress could never be a party to the tactics of the League, because the fundamental conception behind the Congress movement [has been] democratic.[1]

[Although totally reliable figures with respect to what occurred during the tragic mass migrations stemming from communal violence caused by fear of partition are not available with respect to all matters, it has been reliably estimated that "while Muslims lost the most lives, Hindus and Sikhs lost the most property. As regards the number of persons compelled to migrate," according to Penderel Moon, "reasonably accurate figures are available. Between August 1947 and March 1948 about four and a half million Hindus and Sikhs migrated from West Pakistan to India and about six [seven million according to Pakistan authorities] million Muslims moved in the reverse direction. A great part of this huge migration took place within the short space of three months."[2] In addition to the many and varying casualties that occurred, it is generally agreed that no fewer than two hundred thousand lost their lives. It is often asserted that, in fact, millions were killed, and that there was a two-way mass migration of over twelve million persons.]

I I | The Tragedy of Kashmir

[Until August 15, 1947 Jammu and Kashmir comprised an autonomous State in treaty relations with and subject to the Paramountcy of the

[1] G.I.S.S. (Oct. 8, 1947).
[2] D.Q ., p. 268.

Crown of England. When, on the above date, the Indian Independence Act came into force, the Indian States were free to decide whether they would accede to one or the other of the two new Dominions, India or Pakistan. Since the State of Jammu and Kashmir delayed its decision about accession, it sought temporarily to enter into a Standstill Agreement with each of the Dominions.[1]

Whereas Pakistan agreed to have a Standstill Agreement with Kashmir regarding communications, supplies, postal and telegraphic arrangements, India requested that a representative be sent to negotiate and settle the terms of a similar agreement, while expressing the desire that "existing agreements and administrative arrangements" be maintained.[2]

The objective of the Kashmir Standstill Agreement with Pakistan was to provide for the continuance of economic and administrative relations between the State and Pakistan, on the same basis that had existed before creation of the new Dominions.[3]

According to the Indian Government, invasion of Kashmir in October, 1947, prevented the carrying out of further negotiations, even though existing agreements and administrative arrangements still prevailed.[4]

The situation was especially difficult in Kashmir because of the communal disturbances that occurred in the two Punjabs after the announcement of partition. According to India, reports were made throughout September concerning infiltration into Kashmir from the border districts of Pakistan. Claims were made that when representations were presented to the authorities of those districts, denials resulted, but no action was taken.[5]

India accused Pakistan of violating agreements reached between the two governments as early as October 12, 1947, claiming that, as a result of such violations, the already great "misery and suffering involved in the readjustment of Indian populations" was intensified[6].

When the Indian Government first called attention to incursions into Kashmir, it asserted that the majority of the invaders came from the North-West Frontier Province, and that they entered the State by the thousands on October 22, 1947. India further claimed that by October 24 such numerous raids and disturbances had occurred that it received the first request from Kashmir for military aid at that time.[7]

Since, when Kashmir made its initial request to India for aid, the two Governments had no agreement, either military or political, and no plans for sending troops had, up to that time, been considered by the Indian Army, it was decided that none should be sent. As Lord Mountbatten argued, "the essential prerequisite" to sending troops "was accession,

[1] Based on W.P.J.K., p. 2.
[2] K.U.N., p. 2.
[3] Based on W.P.J.K., p. 2.
[4] Based on K.U.N., p. 2.
[5] Based on W.P.J.K., p. 2.
[6] G.I.I.S. (Oct. 22, 1947).
[7] Based on K.F.S., pp. 5-6.

and unless it was made clear that this accession was not just an act of acquisition, this in itself might touch off a war." Even when the Maharajah of Kashmir finally did decide to accede to India, Mountbatten, in the reply he was requested to dispatch to Kashmir in behalf of India accepting accession, suggested that it be "conditional on the will of the people being ascertained as soon as law and order" were restored. "This principle was at once freely accepted and unilaterally proposed by Nehru".[1] (Subsequent U.N. Resolutions, to be found in the Appendix, explain the basis on which a plebiscite might be held.)

The Maharajah of Kashmir decided to accede to India on October 26, whereupon Indian troops were sent to the State by air on October 27, following the signing of the Instrument of Accession the previous night.

When the Maharajah acceded, this act was not only legal, but it also was carried out on the advice of Sheikh Abdullah, leader of the All-Jammu and Kashmir National Conference, the political party commanding the widest popular support in the State.[2] Sheikh Saheb, who had been imprisoned by the Maharajah, had been released to become head of a Provisional Kashmir Administration.

After the Maharajah had executed the Instrument of Accession with India, a few hundred Indian troops were flown into Kashmir to support the "resistance offered by the people. These troops arrived just in time to stem the tide of invasion which had almost reached the capital."[3]

Gandhi supported Nehru wholeheartedly on the dispatch of troops to the Vale of Kashmir on the grounds that India had a moral obligation to come to the aid of victims of aggression.[4]

As described in Government of India documents, the invaders of Kashmir "indulged in indiscriminate plunder, arson and rape" committing "savage atrocities against men, women and children and [reducing] to scorched earth the towns and villages through which they passed".[5] Had they not committed such deeds, it was claimed that they might have reached the capital, Srinagar, and been victorious. India further claimed that the invaders possessed bases, sources of supply and reinforcements in Pakistan.]

["Kashmir Has Gone Through Fire"—Statement before Constituent Assembly (Legislative), New Delhi, November 25, 1947.] I am glad to have this opportunity of explaining to the House the course of events that have led to our intervention in Kashmir with the aid of armed forces, and the attitude of the Government of India to the grave problems that have arisen in that State.

[1] M.M., p. 225.
[2] Based on W.P.J.K., p. 3.
[3] K.F.S., p. 6.
[4] M.B., p. 382.
[5] K.F.S., p. 6.

The House is aware that on the lapse of Crown Paramountcy on the 15th August, this year, Kashmir did not accede to either Dominion. We were of course vitally interested in the decision that the State would take. Kashmir, because of her geographical position with her frontiers with three countries, namely, the Soviet Union, China and Afghanistan, is intimately connected with the security and international contacts of India. Economically also Kashmir is intimately related to India. The caravan trade routes from Central Asia to India pass through the Kashmir State.

Nevertheless, we did not put the slightest pressure on the State to accede to the Indian Dominion, because we realized that Kashmir was in a very difficult position. We did not want a mere accession from the top but an association in accordance with the will of her people. Indeed, we did not encourage any rapid decision. Even in regard to a standstill agreement, no speedy steps were taken by us, although Kashmir had entered into a standstill agreement with Pakistan soon after the 15th August.

We learnt later that serious external pressure was being applied on Kashmir by the Pakistan authorities refusing to send to Kashmir supplies vital to the needs of the people, such as food-grains, salt, sugar and petrol. Thus an attempt was being made to strangle Kashmir economically and force her to accede to Pakistan. This pressure was serious, because it was not easy for Kashmir to obtain these essential supplies from India on account of the difficulty of communications.

In September, news reached us that tribesmen of the North-West Frontier Province were being collected and sent to the Kashmir border. In the beginning of October events took a grave turn. Armed bands moved into the Jammu province from the neighbouring districts of West Punjab, committed serious acts of depredation on the local inhabitants, burnt villages and towns and put a large number of people to death. Refugees from these areas poured into Jammu.

On the Jammu side of the border the local inhabitants, who are chiefly Hindu and Rajput, took retaliatory measures and drove out the Muslims living in those border villages. In these border conflicts a very large number of villages were destroyed or burnt by both parties, on either side of the frontier.

The raiders from West Punjab into the Jammu province increased in number and spread out over that province. The Kashmir State Army which had to meet these raids at numerous points soon found itself broken into small fragments and gradually ceased to be a fighting force.

The raiders were highly organized, had competent officers and modern arms. They succeeded in occupying a considerable part of the Jammu province. . . .

About this time the State authorities asked us to supply them with arms and ammunition. We agreed to do so in the normal course. But in fact no supply was made till events took a more serious turn. Even at this stage no mention was made of accession to India.

The leader of the popular organization in Kashmir, Sheikh Mohammed Abdullah, President of the Kashmir National Conference, was released from prison during this period and we discussed the situation in Kashmir with him as well as with the representatives of the Maharaja of Kashmir. We made it clear to both of them that while we would welcome the accession of Kashmir we did not want any hurried or forced accession and we would rather wait for the people to decide. Sheikh Abdullah was himself of this opinion.

On the 24th October we heard that large armed bands consisting both of tribesmen from the Frontier and ex-servicemen had broken through Muzzafarabad and were marching to Srinagar. These raiders had crossed Pakistan territory and they were equipped with Bren guns, machine guns, mortars and flame-throwers and had at their disposal a large number of transport vehicles. They moved rapidly down the valley, sacking and burning and looting all along the way. We gave earnest consideration to this situation in our Defence Committee on the 25th and 26th October. The position on the morning of the 26th was that the raiders were marching towards Srinagar and there was no military detachment capable of stopping them. They had been stopped for two days near Uri by the State forces under a gallant commander who resisted this advance to the point of death. These two days thus gained were very valuable.

We were asked at this stage both on behalf of the Maharaja and Sheikh Abdullah to accept the accession of the State to the Indian Union and to intervene with the armed forces of the Union. An immediate decision was necessary, and in fact it is now clear that if we had delayed the decision even by 24 hours, Srinagar would have fallen. . . . It was clear to us that we could not possibly accept under any circumstances the ruin of Kashmir by brutal and irresponsible raiders. This would have been a surrender to frightfulness and fanaticism of the worst type and it would have had the most serious consequences all over India. To intervene at this stage was no easy matter and was full of risks and danger. Yet we decided to face this risk and intervene because any other course would have meant ruin to Kashmir and greater danger to India.

In accepting the accession, however, we made it perfectly clear to the Maharaja that his Government must be carried on in future according to the popular will and that Sheikh Abdullah should be charged with the formation of an interim government on the new model adopted in Mysore. Sheikh Abdullah, in our opinion, had undoubtedly the support of the large majority of the people of Kashmir, Muslims, Hindus and Sikhs. Further, we made it clear that as soon as law and order had been restored in Kashmir and her soil cleared of the invaders, the question of the State's accession should be settled by reference to the people.

I shall not detain the House by dealing with the course of the military campaign that followed. The facts are well known and redound to the credit of our military organization, our troops and our airmen. It must be remembered also that our operations have been very largely based on air transport in difficult circumstances. Our civil airlines and their air-crews functioned with remarkable success.

One fact, however, which contributed to our success, at least as much as the military operations, was the maintenance, under the leadership of Sheikh Abdullah, of the civil administration and the morale of the civilian population. The civilian population, completely unarmed, with the enemy within a few miles of the city, behaved in a manner which showed extraordinary courage and coolness. They did so, because they had a great leader and because Hindus, Muslims and Sikhs all joined together under him to throw back the enemy and to save Kashmir, their common heritage. This fact is one of the most remarkable events of recent times in India and one from which the rest of the country may well take a profitable lesson. It was certainly a factor of the most vital importance in the saving of Srinagar.

The present position is that [the terrain in which] our troops . . . are fighting is difficult and mountainous and the roads and approaches have been destroyed by the raiders. Progress is [thus] slow. In the Poonch area occupied by the raiders several massacres of the non-Muslim inhabitants have taken place involving large numbers of persons.

I should like to say here that certain events happened near Jammu early in November which I regret very deeply. The Muslim convoys of evacuees were being taken away from Jammu when they were attacked by non-Muslim refugees and others and a large number of casualties were inflicted. The troops escorting them did not play a creditable role. I might add that none of our troops were present or had anything to do with this. We have issued the most stringent orders to our troops to protect the people, to act with impartiality and indeed to make friends with the loca population. I am glad to say that they have carried out these instructions.

The House is aware that the Pakistan Government have protested emphatically against our action in Kashmir. In doing so they have used language which is not becoming in any government and have alleged fraud and conspiracy on our part. I need only say that I am completely convinced that every action that the Government of India have taken in regard to Kashmir has been straight and above board and I can defend it at any time before the world. We have indeed been over-scrupulous in this matter so that nothing may be done in the passion of the moment which might be wrong. The behaviour of our army has all along been good and worthy of our traditions.

I cannot say this of the Pakistan Government. Their case is that the genesis of the trouble was the extensive killing of Muslims in Eastern Punjab and Kashmir and that the raid on Kashmir was a spontaneous reaction to this on the part of the tribesmen. I think this is completely untrue. I regret deeply that in parts of the Jammu province Muslims were killed and driven out. This of course has had nothing to do with our Government or our forces. But this mutual killing has been a very tragic feature during these past months in the Punjab, and Jammu was powerfully affected by this. We have sufficient evidence in our possession to demonstrate that the whole business of the Kashmir raids both in the Jammu province and in Kashmir proper was deliberately organized by high officials of the Pakistan Government. They helped the tribesmen and ex-servicemen to collect, they supplied them with the implements of war, with lorries, with petrol and with officers. They are continuing to do so. Indeed, their high officials openly declare so. It is obvious that no large body of men could cross Pakistan territory in armed groups without the goodwill, connivance and active help of the authorities there. It is impossible to escape the conclusion that the raids on Kashmir were carefully planned and well organized by the Pakistan authorities with the deliberate object of seizing the State by force and then declaring accession to Pakistan. This was an act of hostility not only to Kashmir but to the Indian Union. It is only necessary to see the semi-official organs of the Muslim League and the Pakistan Government to find out the attitude of that Government. If we had allowed this scheme to succeed, we would have been guilty of the betrayal of the people of Kashmir and of a grave dereliction of duty to India. The results of these on the communal and political situation all over India would have been disastrous.

The Pakistan Government have proposed a simultaneous withdrawal of our forces and the raiders from Kashmir. This was a strange proposal and could only mean that the raiders were there at the instance of the Pakistan Government. We cannot treat with freebooters who have murdered large numbers of people and tried to ruin Kashmir. They are not a State, although a State may be behind them. We have gone to Kashmir to protect the people and as soon as this duty is discharged our forces need not remain there and we shall withdraw our forces. We cannot desert the people of Kashmir till the danger is passed. If the Pakistan Government are sincere, they can stop the entry of these raiders and thus accelerate the return of peace and order. After that let the people of Kashmir decide and we shall accept their decision. But if this armed conflict continues, no opportunity is given to the people to decide by peaceful means, and the decision gradually takes shape through the sacrifice and power of the people in this conflict.

In order to establish our *bona fides*, we have suggested that when the people are given the chance to decide their future, this should be done under the supervision of an impartial tribunal such as the United Nations Organization.

The issue in Kashmir is whether violence and naked force should decide the future or the will of the people. The raiders encouraged by Pakistan have sought to enforce by the sword accession to Pakistan against the obvious wishes of large numbers of the people in Kashmir. We cannot permit the success of this method to achieve political ends. It is a tragedy that Pakistan should ally itself to such methods instead of devoting itself to the urgent tasks of economic and social reconstruction.

Kashmir has gone through fire and I am sure that the House would like me to communicate their sympathy to the people of Kashmir for the tribulations they have been going through in recent weeks. This fair land, which Nature has made so lovely, has been desecrated by people who have indulged in murder, arson, loot and foul attacks on women and children. The people have suffered greatly from shortage of the most vital necessities of life and yet, under the inspiring lead of Sheikh Abdullah, they have stood together in the hour of calamity and showed to the rest of India an example of what communal unity can achieve. Whatever the future may hold, this chapter in the history of Kashmir will be worth reading and we shall never regret that in their hour of distress we have been able to be of assistance to this gallant people. Kashmir and India have been bound together in many ways from ages past. These last few weeks have forged a new link which no one can sunder.[1]

[1] I.A., pp. 60–65.

12	Hyderabad—India's Foreign Policy— "The Universities Have Much to Teach"

Hyderabad—October, 1947

[For over two months after Independence Day, the Nizam of the Princely State of Hyderabad—a non-Congress Muslim area, and allegedly in close contact with Pakistan leaders—failed to accede either to India or Pakistan. Neither had the Nizam signed a Standstill Agreement with India, of whose territory the State of Hyderabad was an integral part. By October, 1947, although a Draft Standstill Agreement with India was prepared, and was signed by the Nizam, by the end of the month his true intentions remained undisclosed. Hence a final document did not as yet exist. Further developments in conjunction with the Hyderabad issue will be found in Part Eleven.]

India's Foreign Policy—Constituent Assembly (Legislative)—New Delhi, December 4, 1947

The main subject in foreign policy today is vaguely talked of in terms of "Do you belong to this group or that group?" That is an utter simplification of issues. . . .

We have proclaimed during this past year that we will not attach ourselves to any particular group. That has nothing to do with neutrality or passivity or anything else. If there is a big war, there is no particular reason why we should jump into it. Nevertheless, it is a little difficult nowadays in world wars to be neutral. Any person with any knowledge of international affairs knows that. . . .

We are not going to join a war if we can help it: and we are going to join the side which is to our interest when the time comes to make the choice. There the matter ends.

But talking about foreign policies, the House must remember that these are not just empty struggles on a chess board. Behind them lie all manner of things. Ultimately, foreign policy is the outcome of economic policy, and until India has properly evolved her economic policy, her foreign policy will be rather vague, rather inchoate, and will be groping. It is well for us to say that we stand for peace and freedom and yet that does not convey much to anybody, except a pious hope. We do stand for peace and freedom. . . . When we say that we stand for . . . freedom of Asian countries and . . . the elimination of imperialistic control over them. There is some meaning in that.

Undoubtedly it has some substance, but a vague statement that we stand for peace and freedom by itself has no particular meaning, because every country is prepared to say the same thing, whether it means it or not. What then do we stand for? Well, you have to develop this argument in the economic field. As it happens today, in spite of the fact that we have been for some time in authority as a Government, I regret that we have not produced any constructive economic scheme or economic policy so far. Again my excuse is that we have been going through such amazing times which have taken up all our energy and attention that it was difficult to do so. Nevertheless, we shall have to do so and when we do so, that will govern our foreign policy, more than all the speeches in this House.

We have sought to avoid foreign entanglements by not joining one bloc or the other. The natural result has been that neither of these big blocs looks on us with favour. They think that we are undependable, because we cannot be made to vote this way or that way.

Last year when our delegation went to the United Nations, it was the first time that a more or less independent delegation went from India. It was looked at a little askance. They did not know what it was going to do. When they found that we acted according to our own will, they did not like it. We were unpopular last year at the United Nations. I do not mean individually, but in regard to our policy. They could not quite make out what we were or what we were aiming at. There was a suspicion in the minds of the first group that we were really allied to the other group in secret, though we were trying to hide the fact, and the other group thought that we were allied to the first group in secret though we were trying to hide the fact.

This year there was a slight change in this attitude. We did many things which both the groups disliked, but the comprehension came to them that we were not really allied to either group, that we were trying to act according to our own lights and according to the merits of the dispute as they seemed to us. They did not like that, of course, because the position today is that there is so much passion and so much fear and suspicion of each other between these great rival Powers and groups that anybody who is not with them is considered against them. So they did not like what we did in many instances: nevertheless, they respected us much more, because they realized that we had an independent policy, that we were not going to be dragooned this way or that, that we might make a mistake just like anyone else, nevertheless, we were going to stick to our own policy and programme, so that while possibly we irritated some of our friends even a little more than last year, we got on much better with everybody, because they understood that we did stand for something. . . .

In the key places of the world the ideal Ambassador must be some kind of a superman. It is so difficult now not only to understand the intricacies,—that is not difficult,—but to remain friends with everybody and yet to advance your cause. After all we have in the past discussed foreign affairs from the outside, in other assemblies, or here perhaps, rather in an academic way, rather as in a college debating society. That is, we talked of high policies, but we did not come to grips with them when we had to say "yes" or "no" to a question and face the consequences. . . .

Foreign affairs are utterly realistic today. A false step, a false phrase, makes all the difference. The first thing that an Ambassador of ours has to learn is to shut his mouth and give up public or even private speaking. It is not a habit which we have developed in our past careers—that of being completely silent. Yet this habit has to be developed, and in private one has to be silent lest what one says injures the cause of the nation, creates international ill-will.

It is in this background that I should like the House to consider international affairs—this realistic background, this notion that it is not merely some naughty men playing about and quarrelling with one another, some statesmen in America and the U.S.S.R. or British imperialism lurking behind the curtain in the distance. We have talked so much about British imperialism that we cannot get rid of the habit.

To come to grips with the subject, in its economic, political and various other aspects, to try to understand it, is what ultimately matters. Whatever policy you may lay down, the art of conducting the foreign affairs of a country lies in finding out what is most advantageous to the country. We may talk about international goodwill and mean what we say. We may talk about peace and freedom and earnestly mean what we say. But in the ultimate analysis, a government functions for the good of the country it governs and no government dare do anything which in the short or long run is manifestly to the disadvantage of that country.

Therefore, whether a country is imperialistic or socialist or communist, its Foreign Minister thinks primarily of the interests of that country. But there is a difference, of course. Some people may think of the interests of their country regardless of other consequences, or take a short-distance view. Others may think that in the long-term policy the interest of another country is as important to them as that of their own country. The interest of peace is more important, because if war comes everyone suffers, so that in the long-distance view, self-interest may itself demand a policy of co-operation with other nations, goodwill for other nations, as indeed it does demand.

Every intelligent person can see that if you have a narrow national policy it may enthuse the multitude for the moment, just as the communal cry has done, but it is bad for the nation and it is bad internationally, because you lose sight of the ultimate good and thereby endanger your own good. Therefore, we propose to look after India's interests in the context of world co-operation and world peace, in so far as world peace can be preserved.

We propose to keep on the closest terms of friendship with other countries unless they themselves create difficulties. We shall be friends with America. We intend co-operating with the United States of America and we intend co-operating fully with the Soviet Union.[1]

"The Universities Have Much to Teach"—Allahabad University, December 13, 1947

During these past fifteen months I have lived in New Delhi, next door to Old Delhi City. What do these two cities convey to us, what pictures and thoughts do they bring to our minds? When I think of them, the long vista of India's history stretches out before me, not so much the succession of kings and emperors, but rather that of the inner life of a nation, its cultural activities in many fields, its spiritual adventures and its voyages in the realms of thought and action. The life of a nation, and more especially of a nation like India, is lived principally in the villages. Nevertheless, it is the cities that represent the highest cultural achievements of the age, as they also do sometimes the more unpleasant aspects of human life. So these cities remind me of the cultural growth of India, of that inner strength and balance which come from long ages of civilization and culture. We have been very proud of this inheritance of our in India, and rightly so. And yet, where do we stand today?...

I.A., pp. 200-05.

The universities have much to teach in the modern world and their scope of activity ever enlarges. I am myself a devotee of science and believe that the world will ultimately be saved, if it is to be saved, by the method and approach of science. But whatever path of learning we may pursue, and however profitable it might seem to us, there is a certain basis and foundation without which the house of learning is built on shifting sands. It is for a university to realize and to lay stress on this essential basis and foundation, those standards of thought and action, which make an individual and a nation. Above all this is necessary today, during this extremely rapid phase of transition, when old values have almost left us and we have adopted no new ones. Freedom came to us, our long-sought freedom, and it came with a minimum of violence. But immediately after, we had to wade through oceans of blood and tears. Worse than the blood and tears was the shame and disgrace that accompanied them. Where were our values and standards then, where was our old culture, our humanism and spirituality and all that India has stood for in the past? Suddenly darkness descended upon this land and madness seized the people. Fear and hatred blinded our minds and all the restraints which civilization imposes were swept away. Horror piled on horror and a sudden emptiness seized us at the brute savagery of human beings. The lights seemed all to go out; not all, for a few still flickered in the raging tempest. We sorrowed for the dead and the dying and for those whose suffering was greater than death. We sorrowed even more for India, our common mother, for whose freedom we had laboured these long years.

The lights seemed to go out. But one bright flame continued to burn and shed its light on the surrounding gloom. And looking at that pure flame, strength and hope returned to us and we felt that whatever momentary disaster might overwhelm our people, there was the spirit of India, strong and unsullied, rising above the turmoil of the present and not caring for the petty exigencies of the day. How many of you realize what it has meant to India to have the presence of Mahatma Gandhi during these months? We all know of his magnificent services to India and to freedom during the past half century and more. But no service could have been greater than the one he has performed during the past four months when in a dissolving world he has been like a rock of purpose and a lighthouse of truth, and his firm low voice has risen above the clamours of the multitude, pointing to the path of rightful endeavour.

And because of this bright flame we could not lose faith in India and her people. And yet the surrounding gloom was in itself a menace. Why should we relapse into this gloom when the sun of freedom had arisen? It is necessary for all of us, and more especially young men and young women in the universities, to pause and think for a while on these basic matters, for the future of India is taking shape in the present, and the future is going to be what millions of young men and women want it to be. There is today a narrowness and intolerance and insensitiveness and lack of awareness which rather frighten me. We have recently passed through a great world war. That war has not brought peace and freedom, but it should teach us many lessons. It brought the downfall of what had been called Fascism and Nazism. Both of these creeds were narrow and overbearing and based on hatred and violence. I watched their growth in their respective countries as well as elsewhere. They brought a certain prestige to their people for a while, but they also killed the spirit and destroyed all values and standards of thought and behaviour. They ended by ruining the nations they sought to exalt.

I see something very similar to that flourishing in India today. It talks in the name of nationalism, sometimes of religion and culture, and yet it is the very opposite of nationalism, of true morality and of real culture. If there was any doubt of this, the past few months have shown us the real picture. For some years we have had to contend against the policy of hatred and violence and narrow communalism on the part of a section of the community. Now, that section has succeeded in forming a State carved out of certain parts of India. Muslim communalism, which had been such a danger and obstruction to Indian freedom, now calls itself a State. It has ceased to be a living force in India proper today, because its strength is concentrated in other parts. But it has resulted in degrading other sections of the community who seek to copy it and sometimes even to improve upon it. We have now to face this reaction in India and the cry is raised for a communal State, even though the words used may be different. And not only a communal State is demanded, but in all fields of political and cultural activity the same narrowing and strangling demand is put forward.

If we look back at India's long history we find that our forefathers made wonderful progress whenever they looked out on the world with clear and fearless eyes and kept the windows of their minds open to give and to receive. And, in later periods, when they grew narrow in outlook and shrank from outside influences, India suffered a setback, politically and culturally. What a magnificent inheritance we have, though we have abused it often enough. India has been and is a vital nation, in spite of al the misery and suffering she has experienced. That vitality in the realm of constructive and creative effort spread to many parts of the Asian world and elsewhere and brought splendid conquests in its train. Those conquests were not so much of the sword, but of the mind and heart which bring healing and which endure when the men of the sword and their work are forgotten. But that very vitality, if not rightly and creatively directed, may turn inward and destroy and degrade.

Even during the brief span of our lives we have seen these two forces at play in India and the world at large—the forces of constructive and creative effort and the forces of destruction. Which will triumph in the end? And on which side do we stand? That is a vital question for each one of us and, more especially, for those from whom the leaders of the nation will be drawn, and on whom the burden of tomorrow will fall. We dare not sit on the fence and refuse to face the issue. We dare not allow our minds to be befuddled by passion and hatred when clear thought and effective action are necessary.

What kind of India are we working for, and what kind of world? Are hatred and violence and fear and communalism and narrow provincialism to mould our future? Surely not, if there has been any truth in us and in our professions. Here in this city of Allahabad, dear to me not only because of my close association with it, but also because of its part in India's history, my boyhood and youth were spent in dreaming dreams and seeing visions of India's future. Was there any real substance in those dreams or were they merely the fancies of a fevered brain? Some small part of those dreams has come true, but not in the manner I had imagined, and so much still remains. Instead of a feeling of triumph at achievement, there is an emptiness and distress at the sorrow that surrounds us, and we have to wipe the tears from a million eyes.

A university stands for humanism, for tolerance, for reason, for progress, for the adventure of ideas and for the search for truth. It stands for the onward march of the human race towards even higher objectives. If the universities discharge their duty adequately, then it is well with the nation and the people. But if the temple of learning itself becomes a home of narrow bigotry and petty objectives, how then will the nation prosper or a people grow in stature?

A vast responsibility, therefore, rests on our universities and educational institutions and those who guide their destinies. They have to keep their lights burning and must not stray from the right path even when passion convulses the multitude and blinds many amongst those whose duty it is to set an example to others. We are not going to reach our goal through crookedness or flirting with evil in the hope that it may lead to good. The right end can never be fully achieved through wrong means.

Let us be clear about our national objective. We aim at a strong free and democratic India where every citizen has an equal place and full opportunity of growth and service, where present-day inequalities in wealth and status have ceased to be, where our vital impulses are directed to creative and co-operative endeavour. In such an India communalism, separatism, isolation, untouchability, bigotry, and exploitation of man by man have no place, and while religion is free, it is not allowed to interfere with the political and economic aspects of a nation's life. If that is so, then all this business of Hindu and Muslim and Christian and Sikh must cease in so far as our political life is concerned and we must build a united but composite nation where both individual and national freedom are secure.

We have passed through grievous trials. We have survived them but at a terrible cost, and the legacy they have left in tortured minds and stunted souls will pursue us for a long time. Our trials are not over. Let us prepare ourselves for them in the spirit of free and disciplined men and women, stout of heart and purpose, who will not stray from the right path or forget our ideals and objectives. We have to start this work of healing and we have to build and create. The wounded body and spirit of India call upon all of us to dedicate ourselves to this great task. May we be worthy of the task and of India.[1]

[1] Ibid., pp. 115–19.

PART ELEVEN

1948

"One day in a Punjab village Jawaharlal was surrounded by a crowd of about a thousand villagers who greeted him with the cry *Bharat Mata ki jai!*

"'What does it all mean?' he asked them.

"They did not know.

"'Who is this *mata* you salute?' Nehru persisted.

"'It is *dharti*' (the earth), said a peasant.

"'Whose earth?' Nehru questioned. 'Your village earth? Your province? India? The world?'

"They were silent again, and then some voices suggested that Nehru himself should explain it to them.

"Nehru did. He told them that Bharat Mata was Mother India and that they were all her children, they and other Indians who resided in the north, south, east and west. When they said *jai* they were hailing the people of India, Bharat Mata's sons and daughters.

"'Who are these sons and daughters?' Nehru asked them. 'They are you, all of you, and I. So when you cry *jai*, you are shouting your own *jai* as well as the *jai* of all our brothers and sisters throughout Hindustan. Remember this. *Bharat Mata* is you, and it is your own *jai*.'"[1]

*

Jinnah, in 1948: "If I hadn't been a fanatic there would never have been Pakistan."[2]

*

[January, 1948.] The loss of Mahatma Gandhi's life would mean the loss of India's soul.[3]

[1] M.J.N., p. 262.
[2] Quoted in B.J., p. 167.
[3] T.D.G. (Vol. VIII), p. 311.

I | January, 1948

[By 1948, free India's complex problems—political, social and economic—had multiplied with formidable rapidity. On January 1, 1948, the Indian Government lodged a formal complaint concerning Kashmir against Pakistan in the Security Council of the United Nations.

Among the most distressing aftermaths of years of communal tensions —in addition to partition and the Kashmir situation—were the two-way flow of millions of refugees between Pakistan and India, and the often equally tragic plight of vast number of persons displaced within India, or otherwise adversely affected by communal violence.

On January 30, 1948 Gandhi was brutally assassinated by an extremist, right-wing Hindu, whose heartless deed is said to have resulted from fanatical outrage at the Mahatma's tolerance of Muslims.

Gandhi's death caused profound shock and a sense of unutterable loss within India. The country's grief was shared by the Mahatma's vast number of admirers elsewhere. Even those who disagreed with Gandhi in theory, scarcely could fail to recognize the extraordinary moral force of his non-violent approach to resolving conflict—whether among individuals, peoples or nations; the vast symbolical power of his courageous example of "turning the searchlight inward"; his unequalled role in gaining India's freedom. Nehru's own overwhelming sorrow upon hearing the news of Gandhi's death is echoed in his eloquent broadcast, included in the following pages.]

2 | Assassination of Gandhi

To Nehru from Gandhi—January 18, 1948, preceded by Nehru note:
[*Below is an English translation of a letter which Gandhiji sent me. The original is in Hindi. It was written on the day he broke his fast which had*

*already lasted a number of days and which was undertaken to indicate his
unhappiness at the communal tension in Delhi.*

*I was rather upset at events in Delhi as well as Gandhiji's fast and for a
day or two I did not take any food. This was not a regular fast but rather a
personal reaction to events which hardly anyone knew. Somehow, Gandhiji
got to know of it and hence his advice to me to put an end to it.*

The reference to a "jewel of India" is a pun on my name JAWAHAR *which
means jewel.*

*This was the last letter [Gandhiji] wrote to me. Twelve days later, on
January 30th 1948, he died at the hands of an assassin.]*

"My dear Jawaharlal,
   Give up your fast. . . . May you live long and continue to be the jewel
of India."[1]

Gandhi's tragic assassination occurred in the garden of Birla House,
New Delhi, during one of the Mahatma's daily prayer meetings.]

["The Light Has Gone Out"—Broadcast, New Delhi, January 30.] Friends
and comrades, the light has gone out of our lives and there is darkness
everywhere. I do not know what to tell you and how to say it. Our beloved
leader, Bapu as we called him, the Father of the Nation, is no more. Perhaps I am wrong to say that. Nevertheless, we will not see him again as we
have seen him for these many years. We will not run to him for advice
and seek solace from him, and that is a terrible blow, not to me only, but
to millions and millions in this country. And it is a little difficult to soften
the blow by any other advice that I or anyone else can give you.

The light has gone out, I said, and yet I was wrong. For the light that
shone in this country was no ordinary light. The light that has illumined
this country for these many many years will illumine this country for
many more years, and a thousand years later, that light will still be seen
in this country and the world will see it and it will give solace to innumerable hearts. For that light represented something more than the immediate
present, it represented the living, the eternal truths, reminding us of the
right path, drawing us from error, taking this ancient country to freedom.

All this has happened when there was so much more for him to do. We
could never think that he was unnecessary or that he had done his task.
But now, particularly, when we are faced with so many difficulties, his not
being with us is a blow most terrible to bear.

A madman has put an end to his life, for I can only call him mad who
did it, and yet there has been enough of poison spread in this country

[1] B.O.L., pp. 513-15.

during the past years and months, and this poison has had an effect on people's minds. We must face this poison, we must root out this poison, and we must face all the perils that encompass us, and face them not madly or badly, but rather in the way that our beloved teacher taught us to face them.

The first thing to remember now is that none of us dare misbehave because he is angry. We have to behave like strong and determined people, determined to face all the perils that surround us, determined to carry out the mandate that our great teacher and out great leader has given us, remembering always that if, as I believe, his spirit looks upon us and sees us, nothing would displease his soul so much as to see that we have indulged in any small behaviour or any violence.

So we must not do that. But that does not mean that we should be weak, but rather that we should, in strength and in unity, face all the troubles that are in front of us. We must hold together and all our petty troubles and difficulties and conflicts must be ended in the face of this great disaster. A great disaster is a symbol to us to remember all the big things of life and forget the small things of which we have thought too much. In his death he has reminded us of the big things of life, that living truth, and if we remember that, then it will be well with India. . . .

It was proposed by some friends that Mahatmaji's body should be embalmed for a few days to enable millions of people to pay their last homage to him. But it was his wish, repeatedly expressed, that no such thing should happen, that this should not be done, that he was entirely opposed to any embalming of his body, and we so decided that we must follow his wishes in this matter, however much others might have wished otherwise.

And so the cremation will take place on Saturday in Delhi city by the side of the Jumna river. . . . I trust that [there will be] silence [and no] demonstrations. That is the best way and the most fitting way to pay homage to this great soul. Also, Saturday should be a day of fasting and prayer for all of us.

Those who live elsewhere out of Delhi and in other parts of India will no doubt also take such part as they can in this last homage. For them also, let this be a day of fasting and prayer. And at the appointed time for cremation, that is 4 P.M. on Saturday afternoon, people should go to the river or to the sea and offer prayers there. And while we pray, the greatest prayer that we can offer is to take a pledge to dedicate ourselves to the truth, and to the cause for which this great countryman of ours lived and for which he has died. That is the best prayer that we can offer him and his memory. That is the best prayer that we can offer to India and ourselves.[1]

[The following is a translation of a speech in Hindustani delivered on February 12, 1948, to a crowd of over a million people assembled to watch the immersion of Gandhi's ashes in the holy waters of the Ganges, at the confluence of the sacred rivers, the Ganges and the Jumna, at Allahabad.]

The last journey has ended. The final pilgrimage has been made. For over fifty years Mahatma Gandhi wandered all over our great country, from the Himalayas and the North Western Frontier and the Brahmaputra in the North East to Kanya Kumari (Cape Comorin) in the far South. He visited every part and corner of this country, not as a mere tourist or visitor for the sake of amusement, but in order to understand and serve the Indian people. Perhaps no other Indian in history has travelled so much in India or got to know the common people so well and served them so abundantly. And now his journey in this world is over, though we have still to continue for a while. Many people are moved to grief, and this is proper and natural. But why should we grieve? Do we grieve for him or for something else? In his life as in his death there has been a radiance which will illumine our country for ages to come. Why then should we grieve for him? Let us grieve rather for ourselves, for our own weaknesses, for the ill-will in our hearts, for our dissensions and for our conflicts. Remember that it was to remove all these that Mahatmaji gave his life. Remember that during the past few months it was on this that he concentrated his vast energy and service. If we honour him, do we honour his name only or do we honour what he stood for, his advice and teachings, and more especially what he died for?

Let us, standing here on the banks of the Ganga, search our own hearts and ask ourselves the question: how far have we followed the path shown to us by Gandhiji and how far have we tried to live in peace and cooperation with others? If even now we follow the right path, it will be well with us and well with our country.

Our country gave birth to a mighty soul and he shone like a beacon not only for India but for the whole world. And yet he was done to death by one of our own brothers and compatriots. How did this happen? You might think that it was an act of madness, but that does not explain this tragedy. It could only occur because the seed for it was sown in the poison-

[1] I.A., pp. 17-19.

of hatred and enmity that spread throughout the country and affected so many of our people. Out of that seed grew this poisonous plant. It is the duty of all of us to fight this poison of hatred and ill-will. If we have learnt anything from Gandhiji, we must bear no ill-will or enmity towards any person. The individual is not our enemy. It is the poison within him that we fight and which we must put an end to. We are weak and feeble, but Gandhiji's strength passed to us also to some extent. In his reflected glory we also gained in stature. The splendour and the strength were his and the path he showed was also his. We stumbled often enough and fell down in our attempts to follow that path and serve our people as he wanted us to serve them.

Our pillar of strength is no more. But why do we say that? His image is enshrined in the hearts of the million men and women who are present here today, and hundreds of millions of our countrymen, who are not present here, will also never forget him. Future generations of our people, who have not seen him or heard him, will also have that image in their hearts because that image is now a part of India's inheritance and history. Thirty or forty years ago began in India what is called the Gandhi Age. It has come to an end today. And yet I am wrong, for it has not ended. Perhaps it has really begun now, although somewhat differently. Thus far we have been leaning on him for advice and support, from now onwards we have to stand on our own feet and to rely on ourselves. May his memory inspire us and his teachings light our path. Remember his ever recurring message: "Root out fear from your hearts, and malice, put an end to violence and internecine conflict, keep your country free."

He brought us to freedom and the world marvelled at the way he did it. But at the very moment of gaining our freedom we forgot the lesson of the Master. A wave of frenzy and fanaticism overtook our people and we disgraced the fair name of India. Many of our youth were misled and took to wrong paths. Are we to drive them away and crush them? They are our own people and we have to win them over and mould them and train them to right thought and action.

The communal poison, which has brought disaster upon us, will put an end to our freedom also if we are not vigilant and if we do not take action in time. It was to awaken us to this impending danger that Gandhiji undertook his last fast two or three weeks ago. His self-crucifixion roused the nation's conscience and we pledged before him to behave better. It was only then that he broke his fast.

Gandhiji used to observe silence for one day in every week. Now that voice is silenced for ever and there is unending silence. And yet that voice resounds in our ears and in our hearts, and it will resound in the minds and hearts of our people and even beyond the borders of India, in the long ages to come. For that voice is the voice of truth, and though truth may occasionally be suppressed it can never be put down. Violence for him was the opposite of truth and therefore he preached to us against violence not only of the hand but of the mind and heart. If we do not give up this internecine violence and have the utmost forbearance and friendliness for others, we are doomed as a nation. The path of violence is perilous and freedom seldom exists for long where there is violence. Our talk of Swarajya and the people's freedom is meaningless, if we have internal violence and conflict.

I see a large number of soldiers of the Indian Army in this audience. It is their proud privilege and duty to defend the integrity and honour of this country of ours. They can only do so if they stand together and function together. If they were to fall out amongst themselves, what would their strength be worth and how could they then serve their country?

Democracy demands discipline, tolerance and mutual regard. Freedom demands respect for the freedom of others. In a democracy changes are made by mutual discussion and persuasion and not by violent means. If a government has no popular support, another government which commands that popular support takes its place. It is only small groups who know that they cannot get sufficient popular support that resort to methods of violence, imagining in their folly that they can gain their ends in this way. This is not only utterly wrong but it is also utterly foolish. For the reaction to the violence of the minority, which seeks to coerce the majority, is to provoke the majority into violence against them.

This great tragedy has happened because many persons, including some in high places, have poisoned the atmosphere of this country of ours. It is the duty of the Government as well as the people to root out this poison. We have had our lesson at a terrible cost. Is there anyone amongst us now who will not pledge himself after Gandhiji's death to fulfil his mission—a mission for which the greatest man of our country, the greatest man in the world, has laid down his life?

You and I and all of us will go back from these sands of our noble river, the Ganga. We shall feel sad and lonely. We shall never see Gandhiji again. We used to run to him for advice and guidance whenever we were confronted with any great problem or when we felt ill at ease or in doubt. There is none to advise us now or to share our burdens. It is not I alone or a few of us who looked up to him for help. Thousands and hundreds of thousands of our countrymen considered him their intimate friend and counsellor. All of us felt that we were his children. Rightly he was called the Father of our Nation and in millions of homes today there is mourning as on the passing away of a beloved father.

We shall go away from this river bank sad and lonely. But we shall also think with pride of the high and unique privilege that has been ours to have had for our chief and leader and friend this mighty person, who carried us to great heights on the way to freedom and truth. And the way of struggle that he taught us was also the way of truth. Remember also that the path he showed us was one of fighting for the good and against evil and not the way of sitting quietly on the peaks of the Himalayas. And so we have to fight on and not seek escape or rest. We have to do our duty and fufil the pledges we have given him. Let us tread the path of truth and Dharma. Let us make India a great country in which goodwill and harmony prevail and every man and woman, irrespective of faith and belief, can live in dignity and freedom.

How often we have shouted, "Mahatma Gandhi ki Jai". By shouting this slogan we thought we had done our duty. Gandhiji always felt pained to hear this shouting, for he knew what little it meant and how often it just took the place of action or even of thought. "Mahatma Gandhi ki Jai"— "Victory to Mahatma Gandhi", what victory could we wish him or give him? He was the Victorious One in life and in death. It is you and I and this unfortunate country who have to struggle for victory.

Throughout his life he thought of India in terms of the poor and the oppressed and the downtrodden. To raise them and free them was the mission of his life. He adopted their ways of life and dress so that no one in the country might feel lowly. Victory to him was the growth of freedom of these people.

What kind of triumph did Gandhiji wish for us? Not the triumph for which most people and countries strive through violence, fraud, treachery and evil means. That kind of victory is not stable. For the foundations of a lasting victory can only be laid on the rock of truth. Gandhiji gave us a new method of struggle and political warfare and a new kind of diplomacy. He demonstrated the efficacy of truth and goodwill and non-violence in politics. He taught us to respect and co-operate with every Indian as a man and as a fellow-citizen, irrespective of his political belief or religious creed. We all belong to Mother India and have to live and die here. We are all equal partners in the freedom that we have won. Every one of our three or four hundred million people must have an equal right to the opportunities and blessings that free India has to offer. It was not a few privileged persons that Gandhiji strove and died for. We have to strive for the same ideal and in the same way. Then only shall we be worthy to say, "Mahatma Gandhi ki Jai".[1]

["A Glory Has Departed"—February 2, 1948.] I have a sense of utter shame both as an individual and as the head of the Government of India that we should have failed to protect the greatest treasure that we possessed. It is our failure, as it has been our failure in the many months past, to give protection to many an innocent man, woman and child; it may be that the burden and the task was too great for us or for any government. Nevertheless, it is a failure. And today the fact that this mighty person whom we honoured and loved beyond measure has gone because we could not give him adequate protection is a shame for all of us. It is a shame to me as an Indian that an Indian should have raised his hand against him, it is a shame to me as a Hindu that a Hindu should have done this deed and done it to the greatest Indian of the day and the greatest Hindu of the age.

We praise people in well-chosen words and we have some kind of a measure for greatness. How shall we praise him and how shall we measure him, because he was not of the common clay that all of us are made of? He came, lived a fairly long span of life and has passed away. No words of praise of ours in this House[2] are needed, for he has had greater praise in his life than any living man in history. And during these two or three days since his death he has had the homage of the world; what can we add to that? How can we praise him ... we who have been children of his, and perhaps more intimately his children than the children of his body, for we have all been in some greater or smaller measure the children of his spirit, unworthy as we were?

A glory has departed and the sun that warmed and brightened our lives has set and we shiver in the cold and dark. Yet, he would not have us feel this way. After all, that glory that we saw for all these years, that man with the divine fire, changed us also—and such as we are, we have been moulded by him during these years; and out of that divine fire many of us also took a small spark which strengthened and made us work to some extent on the lines that he fashioned. And so if we praise him, our words seem rather small and if we praise him, to some extent we also praise ourselves. Great men and eminent men have monuments in bronze and marble set up for them, but this man of divine fire managed in his lifetime to became enshrined in millions and millions of hearts so that all of us became somewhat of the stuff that he was made of, though to an in-

[1] Ibid., pp. 24-28.
[2] Constituent Assembly (Legislature), New Delhi.

finitely lesser degree. He spread out in this way all over India not in palaces only, or in select places or in assemblies but in every hamlet and hut of the lowly and those who suffer. He lives in the hearts of millions and he will live for immemorial ages.

What then can we say about him except to feel humble on this occasion? To praise him we are not worthy—to praise him whom we could not follow adequately and sufficiently. It is almost doing him an injustice just to pass him by with words when he demanded work and labour and sacrifice from us; in a large measure he made this country, during the last thirty years or more, attain to heights of sacrifice which in that particular domain have never been equalled elsewhere. He succeeded in that. Yet ultimately things happened which no doubt made him suffer tremendously though his tender face never lost its smile and he never spoke a harsh word to anyone. Yet, he must have suffered—suffered for the failing of this generation whom he had trained, suffered because we went away from the path that he had shown us. And ultimately the hand of a child of his—for he after all is as much a child of his as any other Indian—a hand of that child of his struck him down.

Long ages afterwards history will judge of this period that we have passed through. It will judge of the successes and the failures—we are too near it to be proper judges and to understand what has happened and what has not happened. All we know is that there was a glory and that it is no more; all we know is that for the moment there is darkness, not so dark certainly because when we look into our hearts we still find the living flame which he lighted there. And if those living flames exist, there will not be darkness in this land and we shall be able, with our effort, remembering him and following his path, to illumine this land again, small as we are, still with the fire that he instilled into us.

He was perhaps the greatest symbol of the India of the past, and may I say, of the India of the future, that we could have had. We stand on this perilous edge of the present between that past and the future to be and we face all manner of perils and the greatest peril is sometimes the lack of faith which comes to us, the sense of frustration that comes to us, the sinking of the heart and of the spirit that comes to us when we see ideals go overboard, when we see the great things that we talked about somehow pass into empty words and life taking a different course. Yet, I do believe that perhaps this period will pass soon enough.

Great as this man of God was in his life, he has been great in his death and I have not the shadow of a doubt that by his death he has served the great cause as he served it throughout his life. We mourn him; we shall always mourn him, because we are human and cannot forget our beloved Master. But I know that he would not like us to mourn him. No tears came to his eyes when his dearest and closest passed away—only a firm resolve to persevere, to serve the great cause that he had chosen. So he would chide us if we merely mourn. That is a poor way of doing homage to him. The only way is to express our determination, to pledge ourselves anew, to conduct ourselves in a befitting manner and to dedicate ourselves to the great task which he undertook and which he accomplished to such a large extent. So we have to work, we have to labour, we have to sacrifice and thus prove, to some extent at least, worthy followers of his.

It is clear, [as has been said], that this happening, this tragedy, is not merely the isolated act of a madman. This comes out of a certain atmosphere of violence and hatred that has prevailed in this country for many months and years and more especially in the past few months. That atmosphere envelops us and surrounds us and if we are to serve the cause he put before us we have to face this atmosphere, to combat it, to struggle against it and root out the evil of hatred and violence.

So far as this Government is concerned, I trust they will spare no means, spare no effort to tackle it, because if we do not do that, if we, in our weakness or for any other reason that we may consider adequate, do not take effective means to stop this violence, to stop this spreading of hatred by word of mouth or writing or act, then indeed we are not worthy of being in this Government; we are certainly not worthy of being his followers and we are not worthy of even saying words of praise for this great soul who has departed. So on this occasion or any other when we think of this great Master who has gone, let us always think of him in terms of work and labour and sacrifice, in terms of fighting evil wherever we see it, in terms of holding to the truth as he put it before us, and if we do so, however unworthy we may be, we shall at least have done our duty and paid proper homage to his spirit.

He has gone, and all over India there is a feeling of having been left desolate and forlorn. All of us sense that feeling, and I do not know when we shall be able to get rid of it, and yet together with that feeling there is also a feeling of proud thankfulness that it has been given to us of this generation to be associated with this mighty person. In ages to come, centuries and maybe millennia after us, people will think of this generation when this man of God trod on earth and will think of us who, however small, could also follow his path and tread the holy ground where his feet had been. Let us be worthy of him.[1]

[1] Ibid., pp. 20–23.

["The Greatest Indian"—New Delhi, February 14, 1948.] Two weeks have passed since India and the world learnt of that tragedy which will shame India for ages to come. Two weeks of sorrow and searching of heart, and strong and dormant emotions rising in a flood, and of tears from millions of eyes. Would that those tears had washed away our weakness and littleness and made us a little worthy of the Master for whom we sorrowed! Two weeks of homage and tribute from every corner of the globe, from kings and potentates and those in high authority to the common man everywhere who instictively looked to him as a friend, a comrade and a champion.

The flood of emotion will tone down gradually as all such emotions do, though none of us can ever be the same as we were before. . . .

[Though Gandhiji] was intensely religious and came to be called the Father of the Nation which he had liberated, yet no narrow religious or national bonds confined his spirit. And so he became the great internationalist, believing in the essential unity of man, the underlying unity of all religions, and the needs of humanity, and more specially devoting himself to the service of the poor, the distressed and the oppressed millions everywhere.

His death brought more tributes than [have] been paid at the passing of any other human being in history. Perhaps what would have pleased him best [were] the spontaneous tributes that came from the people of Pakistan. On the morrow of the tragedy, all of us forgot for a while the bitterness that had crept in, the estrangement and conflict of these past months, and Gandhiji stood out as the beloved champion and leader of the people of India, of India as it was before partition cut up this living nation.

What was his great power over the mind and heart of man due to? Ages to come will judge and we are too near him to assess the many facets of his extraordinarily rich personality. But even we realize that his dominating passion was truth. That truth led him to proclaim without ceasing that good ends can never be attained by evil methods, that the end itself is distorted if the method pursued is bad. That truth led him to confess publicly whenever he thought he had made a mistake—Himalayan errors he called some of his own mistakes. That truth led him to fight evil and untruth wherever he found them regardless of the consequences. That truth made the service of the poor and the dispossessed the passion of his life, for where there is inequality and discrimination and suppression, there is injustice and evil and untruth. And thus he became the beloved of all those who have suffered from social and political evils, and the great representative of humanity as it should be. Because of that truth in him, wherever he sat became a temple and where he trod was hallowed ground. . . .

He was the great unifier in India, who taught us not only a bare tolerance of others but of a willing acceptance of them as our friends and comrades in common undertakings. He taught us to rise above our little selves and prejudices and see the good in others. His last few months and his very death symbolize to us this message of large-hearted tolerance and unity. A little before he died we pledged ourselves to this before him. We must keep that pledge and remember that India is a common home to all those who live here, to whatever religion they may belong. They are equal sharers in our great inheritance and they have equal rights and obligations. Ours is a composite nation, as all great nations must necessarily be. Any narrowness in outlook, any attempt to confine the bounds of this great nation, will be a betrayal of his final lesson to us and will surely lead to disaster and to the loss of that freedom for which he laboured and which he gained for us in large measure.

Equally important is the service of the common man in India who has suffered so much in the past. His claims must be paramount and everything that comes in the way of his betterment must have second place. Not merely from moral and humanitarian grounds but also from the point of view of political commonsense, has it become essential to raise the standard of the common man and to give him full opportunity of progress. A social structure which denies him this opportunity stands self-condemned and must be changed.

Gandhiji has gone though his flaming spirit envelops us. The burden is upon us now and the immediate need is that we should endeavour to the utmost of our ability to discharge that burden. We have to hold together and fight the terrible poison of communalism that has killed the greatest man of our age. We must root this out not in any spirit of ill-will to misguided individuals but in militant opposition to the evil itself wherever it may be. That evil has not ended by the killing of Gandhiji. It was an even more shameful thing for some people to celebrate this killing in various ways. Those who did so or feel that way have forfeited their rights to be called Indians.

I have said that we must all hold together in this hour of crisis for our nation and must avoid public controversy as far as possible and lay stress on the points of agreement on essential matters. I would make a special appeal to the Press to help in this urgent task and to avoid personal or other criticisms which encourage fissiparous tendencies in the country. I would appeal more especially to the millions of my colleagues and comrades in the Congress who have followed, often haltingly enough, the leadership of Mahatma Gandhi.

It has distressed me beyond measure to read in newspapers and otherwise learn of whisperings about vital differences between Sardar Patel and myself. Of course, there have been for many years past differences between us, temperamental and other, in regard to many problems. But India at least should know that these differences have been overshadowed by fundamental agreements about the most important aspects of our public life and that we have co-operated together for a quarter of a century or more in great undertakings. We have been sharers in joy and sorrow alike. Is it likely that at this crisis in our national destiny either of us should be petty-minded and think of anything but the national good? May I pay my tribute of respect and admiration to Sardar Patel not only for his life-long service to the nation but also for the great work he has done since he and I have served together in the Government of India? He has been a brave captain of our people in war and peace, stout-hearted when others might have wavered, and a great organizer. It has been my privilege to have been associated with him for these many years and my affection for him and appreciation of his great qualities have grown with the passing of time. . . .

I plead therefore for tolerance and co-operation in our public life and a joining together of all the forces which want to make India a great and progressive nation. I plead for an all-out effort against the poison of communalism and narrow provincialism. I plead for a cessation of industrial conflict and a joint endeavour of all concerned to build up India. In these great tasks I pledge myself and I earnestly trust that it may be given to us of this generation to realize somewhat the dreams that Gandhiji had. Thus will we honour his memory and erect a worthy memorial for him.[1]

3 | Kashmir Developments: January

[Facts relating to Kashmir—Press Conference, New Delhi, January 2, 1948.] As is well known now, the Government of India has made a

[1] Ibid., pp. 29-32.

reference to the Security Council of the UNO in regard to the invasion of Kashmir by persons coming from or through Pakistan.

The Government desires to take the Press and the public into full confidence in so far as it can, having regard to diplomatic decorum and propriety. It has waited thus far because it would have been proper for the Security Council to consider the matter first before any publicity was given to it, but, in view of references being made to this subject by the Foreign Minister of Pakistan and by others, it is desirable to state the facts briefly.

I have previously, on several occasions, placed before the country the facts relating to Kashmir ever since we sent our troops there on October 27, 1947. Our troops succeeded in saving the valley of Kashmir and the city of Srinagar and drove back the enemy to Uri along the Jhelum Valley road.

Since then, fighting has taken place on a large front along almost the entire border of the Kashmir State and Pakistan. Very large numbers of armed men, in battle formation and fully equipped with modern arms, have entered Kashmir State territory at many places, and still larger concentrations of these men have been made along the border on the Pakistan side.

These border areas of Pakistan have become the base of operations for these invaders and, from the security of these bases, large numbers come across and raid, burn and loot on Kashmir State territory which is Indian Dominion territory.

The Government of India would have been justified, in self-defence, to strike at these bases, and thus put an end to the sources of supply of these invaders. It has, however, scrupulously avoided doing so, so as to limit the field of operations and in the hope that the Pakistan Government will cease aiding and abetting these invaders.

During the last two months, repeated requests have been made to the Pakistan Government to prevent the use of its territory for aggression on India. It has not only not done so, but it is an established fact that these invaders, among whom are a large number of Pakistan nationals, have been helped in every way by the Pakistan Government.

They are allowed transit through Pakistan territory by motor transport and railway trains, supplied petrol, food and accommodation; and the arms they possess are manifestly the arms of the Pakistan Army. Pakistan Army personnel have also been captured by our troops in the operations in Kashmir.

Not only has the Pakistan Government not taken effective steps to prevent this invasion, but it has refused even to call upon the invaders to desist from their active aggression.

The Government of India cannot tolerate the use of a friendly and neighbouring country as a base for the invasion of Indian territory but, in its desire to avoid any action, unless it is compelled by circumstances to take it, it has decided to refer this matter to the Security Council of the UNO.

On December 22, 1947, a formal request was made in writing to the Prime Minister of Pakistan. In this letter, the acts of aggression of Pakistan and the forms of aid given by Pakistan to the invaders were briefly stated and the Government of Pakistan was asked to call upon Pakistan nationals to cease participating in the attack on the Jammu and Kashmir State and to deny to the invaders: (1) all access to and use of Pakistan territory for operations against the Kashmir State; (2) all military and other supplies; (3) all other kinds of aid that might tend to prolong the present struggle.

The Government of India expressed its earnest desire again to live on terms of friendship with Pakistan and hoped that its request would be acceded to promptly and without reserve. It pointed out, however, that, failing such response, it would be compelled to take such action, with due regard to its rights and obligations as a member of the UNO, as it might consider necessary to protect its own interests and those of the Government and people of Jammu and Kashmir State.

As no reply was received to this formal request, two reminders were sent. Ultimately, on December 30, a formal reference was made to the Security Council of the UNO through the representative of the Government of India with UNO. On December 31, a copy of this reference was sent by telegram to the Pakistan Government.

This reference stated the facts of the case and pointed out that they indisputably pointed to the following conclusions:

(a) that the invaders are allowed transit across Pakistan territory;
(b) that they are allowed to use Pakistan territory as a base of operations;
(c) that they include Pakistan nationals;
(d) that they draw much of their military equipment, transport and supplies (including petrol) from Pakistan; and
(e) that Pakistan officers are training, guiding and otherwise helping them.

There was no source other than Pakistan from which such quantities of modern military equipment, training and guidance could have been obtained. The Government of India requested the Security Council, therefore to ask the Government of Pakistan:

(1) to prevent Pakistan Government personnel, military and civil, participating in or assisting the invasion of the Jammu and Kashmir State;

(2) to call upon other Pakistan nationals to desist from taking any part in the fighting in the Jammu and Kashmir State;

(3) to deny to the invaders: (a) access to and use of its territory for operations against Kashmir; (b) military and other supplies; (c) all other kinds of aid that might tend to prolong the present struggle.

The reference to the Security Council is thus limited to the matters mentioned above. There is an urgency about these matters, for the first step that must be taken is to put a stop to the fighting and this can only be done if the invaders withdraw. It must be remembered that all the fighting has taken place on Indian Union territory and it is the inherent right of the Government of India to drive back any invaders on its territory. Till the Kashmir State is free of the invaders, no other matter can be considered.

The Government of India deeply regrets that this serious crisis has arisen. It is not of its seeking, and it has been thrust upon it by invading armies from outside who have committed acts of barbarism against the inhabitants of the Kashmir State and destroyed and burnt a large number of villages and some towns. No Government can tolerate such an invasion.

In its desire, however, to avoid any act which might lead to further complications, it has shown the greatest forbearance and made repeated appeals to the Pakistan Government. Those appeals have been in vain, and hence it decided to refer this particular question to the Security Council. It has naturally reserved to itself freedom to take such action in self-defence as the situation may require. . . .

The Kashmir issue stands by itself. If the methods of invasion of friendly territory by a barbarous foe are encouraged and submitted to, there is no future either for India or for Pakistan and therefore this has to be and will be resisted by us to the utmost, and the Kashmir State will have to be freed completely. Even from the narrowest viewpoint of self-interest, the Government of Pakistan should realize that the encouragement of such an invasion is perilous to its own future, because, once the forces of unbridled violence are let loose, they endanger the whole security of any State.

It must be remembered that in Kashmir there is no communal issue as such. Large numbers of Kashmiris, Muslims, Hindus and Sikhs are fighting the invaders. It is a national issue for them to preserve their freedom, and we have gone there to support them. We have pledged our honour to them and we shall stand by our pledge.[1]

[On January 17, 1948 the Security Council of the United Nations called upon Pakistan and India: "(1) to take immediately all measures within their power (including public appeals to their people) calculated to improve the situation [regarding Kashmir] and to refrain from making any statements and from doing or causing to be done or permitting any acts which might aggravate the situation; (ii) to inform the Security Council immediately of any material change in the situation which occurs or appears to either of them to be about to occur while the matter is under consideration by the Council, and consult with the Council thereon."[2]

On January 20, 1948, a resolution was adopted by the majority of the members of the Security Council, appointing "a Commission to investigate the facts [in Kashmir] and to exercise mediatory influence."[3]]

4 | Economic Policy—Foreign Policy

India's Economic Policy—February 17, 1948

We have to go ahead step by step so as not to break up something we have got without replacing it immediately with something better.... We cannot over-look the other factors ... but production comes first and I am prepared to say that everything that we do should be judged from the point of view of production. If nationalisation adds to production we shall have to nationalise at every step. If it does not, let us see how to bring it about in order not to impede production....

As far as Congress is concerned it accepted the principle of nationalisation of defence and key industries about seventeen years ago, and I believe such industries had to be nationalised at some time or other. But when you come down to giving effect to this, we have to think as to [what] to choose first, and how to do it without upsetting the present structure

[1] I.A., pp. 66–70.
[2] K.U.N., p. 5.
[3] K.F.S., p. 41.

and without actually interfering with production. It is far better for the state to concentrate on certain specific vital new industries, rather than go about nationalising the many old ones, though in the case of some specific vital industries of national importance that might be done. If we squander our resources in merely acquiring for the state the existing industries for the moment, we may have no other resources left, and we [might have] stopped the field for private enterprise too. Therefore, we should conserve our resources and start new industries. . . . As a result of the progress being made in technology and science new sources of power will [evolve] which could upset all the methods of production that exist today. It is, therefore, most important [that] . . . new and novel sources of production should always remain in the hands of the state, and that we should not allow these methods to go into private hands and thus become private monopolies.[1]

Foreign Policy

[In the field of foreign policy, new and complex problems continued to arise during 1948. In spite of all pressures to the contrary, Nehru remained consistently opposed to India's becoming aligned with, or part of, either of the two great power blocs, preferring to judge each international issue separately, as it might arise, on its own merits. This was due, in part, to a reaction shared by many Indians as a result of having been deprived for so long—while subjected to foreign rule—of the freedom to make up their own minds; in part, to a sincere hope of lessening world tensions; in part, to the dire necessity of expending every possible ounce of energy upon building a new nation, whose resources were pitifully underdeveloped.]

["India Keeps Out of Power Blocs"—Speech, Constituent Assembly, New Delhi, March 8, 1948.] In criticizing the foreign policy of the Government of India during the last year, I should like this House for an instant to turn its mind to any country today and think of its foreign policy —whether it is the U.S.A., the United Kingdom, the U.S.S.R., China or France. These are supposed to be the great Powers. Just think of their foreign policy and tell me if you would say that the foreign policy of any one of those countries has succeeded from any point of view, from the point of view of moving towards world peace or preventing world war, succeeded even from the mere opportunist and individual point of view of that country.

[1] Based on G.I.I.S. (Feb. 20, 1948), pp. 1–2.

I think if you will look at this question from this point of view, you will find that there has been a miserable failure in the foreign policy of every great Power and country. It is in that context that we shall have to view these matters. It is not really the failure of the foreign policy of any particular Power, though perhaps two or three major Powers do influence foreign policy greatly.

Now, surely the responsibility for the deterioration of the international situation might lie with some Powers. In India, our responsibility is very little. We may have acted well or badly on the international stage, but we are not, frankly speaking, influential enough to affect international events very much. Therefore, if a great deterioration has taken place in the international sphere it is not due to our policy. We suffer from it just as every other nation suffers from it and I think it is this vague feeling that we have suffered that induces the members of the House to search for reasons why we have suffered.

I think that is a very right approach, because we must find the reasons for our having erred, how we might have bettered our lot and so on and so forth. Nevertheless, I think the real reason is that the causes lie entirely outside any policy that we have pursued. There are bigger and deeper causes affecting the world and we, like the strongest of nations, are pulled hither and thither by these forces. That is one fact that I should like the House to bear in mind.

Another factor—and that is more applicable to us—is that owing to the unfortunate events that have happened in India since the 15th August, 1947, anything we did in the world outside suddenly lost weight or lost weight for a time. We counted for something, not very greatly, of course, more potentially than in actuality, indeed, potentially we counted for a great deal, though actually we need not have counted for much. But the events that occurred after 15th August in India and Pakistan,—Pakistan I might say naturally did not count for much because it had no background; it was a newcomer; it was we who counted—those events suddenly brought down our credit in the international domain tremendously.

It affected the United Nations when they met last October to consider the South Africa issue. Undoubtedly the events in India affected the decision of the United Nations General Assembly in regard to the South Africa issue; so also in regard to other matters. All these facts have nothing to do with foreign policy.

The point I wish to make before the House is this, that it may be desirable for us to adopt this or that foreign policy one of which is called a policy of neutrality or, [as it also has been called], a more positive one.

But all this has no relationship, it has nothing to do, with what has happened. Other factors govern it. If you like, it was a fault, but we have been rather passive about [certain matters, the very ones about which some of our] Honourable Members desire us to be more active. We are asked to collect the smaller nations of the world around us. . . . [which activity is called] idealistic; I do not think it is purely idealistic; I think it is, if you like, opportunist in the long run—this policy that we have so far pursued before we became a Government, and to some extent after we became a Government. That is, [we have stood] up, in so far as we could, for the weak and the oppressed in various continents. [This] is not a policy which is to the liking of the great Powers who directly or indirectly share in their exploitation. It is this that puts us in the wrong with them.

There has been a lot said about other matters. Here is Indonesia. It is a clear issue before this House. We have done precious little in the way of actual active help; we are not in a position to do so. But we have sympathy for the Indonesians and we have expressed it as publicly as possible. Because we give our sympathy and some degree of help to Indonesia and because this offends and irritates some of the major Powers of the world, are we to withdraw that help? Are we to submit tamely and say, "No, this might irritate this Power or that", because it does irritate this or that Power and there is no doubt about it?

Naturally, we cannot as a Government go as far as we might have [gone] as a non-official organization in which we [could] express our opinions as frankly and . . . aggressively as possible. Speaking as a Government we have to moderate our language. We have sometimes to stop doing things which we might otherwise do. Nevertheless, the fundamental thing is, do we sympathize and openly sympathize with a country like Indonesia in her struggle for freedom, or do we not? That applies not to Indonesia only, but to several other countries. In each case, we have to face the passive hostility of various interests, not only the direct interests involved, but also the indirect interests involved, because the direct and the indirect interests hang together in such matters.

It has been an astonishing thing to see how for many months, the Good Offices Committee functioned in Indonesia—all good people—and as it happens the Secretary of the Committee was an Indian. The way it has functioned and the results it has produced are not at all satisfactory. If this House is dissatisfied with what the Security Council has done this year or considered in regard to Kashmir, they would be still more dissatisfied, I think, if they considered the Indonesian Good Offices Committee's work. Unfortunately, their approach to such problems is an approach with which this House cannot agree, on account of our past traditions, on account of our ideals.

Now, I am not talking in terms of this bloc or that bloc; I am talking independently of the blocs as they have appeared on the world stage. We have either to pursue our policy generally within limitations—because we cannot pursue it wholeheartedly, nevertheless openly—or give it up. I do not think that anything could be more injurious to us from any point of view—certainly from an idealistic and high moral point of view, but equally so from the point of view of opportunism and national interest in the narrowest sense of the word—than for us to give up the policies that we have pursued, namely, those of standing up for certain ideals in regard to ... oppressed nations, [instead of aligning] ourselves with this great Power or that and becoming its camp follower in the hope that some crumbs might fall from [the] table.

I think that would undoubtedly be, even from the narrowest point of view of national interest, a bad and harmful policy.

I can understand some of the smaller countries of Europe or some of the smaller countries of Asia being forced by circumstances to bow down before some of the greater Powers and becoming practically satellites of those Powers, because they cannot help it. The power opposed to them is so great and they have nowhere to turn. But I do not think that consideration applies to India.

We are not citizens of a weak or mean country and I think it is foolish for us to get frightened, even from a military point of view, of the greatest of the Powers today. Not that I delude myself about what can happen to us if a great Power in a military sense goes against us; I have no doubt it can injure us. But after all in the past, as a national movement, we opposed one of the greatest of World Powers. We opposed it in a particular way and in a large measure succeeded in that way, and I have no doubt that if the worst comes to the worst—and in a military sense we cannot meet these great Powers—it is far better for us to fight in our own way than submit to them and lose all the ideals we have.

Therefore, let us not be frightened too much of the military might of this or that group. I am not frightened and I want to tell the world on behalf of this country that we are not frightened of the military might of this Power or that. Our policy is not a passive policy or a negative policy. . . .

Now, we agree . . . that the United Nations, in spite of its failings and weaknesses, is . . . good. It should be encouraged and supported in every way, and should be allowed to develop into some kind of world government or world order. ... It is an odd contrast today that while in the official councils of the United Nations we may not perhaps pull the weight we ought to, nevertheless, in the unofficial councils outside, our weight has considerably increased. Why is this so? Because progressively, people see that within the United Nations things are done far from idealistically or morally, or in terms of the underdog, the smaller nations, or the Asian nations, and so more and more of these people try to find someone else and in their search for someone else who might perhaps give a lead in these matters, almost automatically their eyes turn towards India.

Now, I do not wish to enter into any comparisons with other countries, and certainly we have done nothing in India to merit leadership of anybody. It is for us to lead ourselves, then only can we lead others properly and I do not wish to place the case of India at any higher level. We have to look after ourselves.

That is why I am, if I may say so, in spite of being Minister in charge of External Affairs, not interested in external affairs so much as internal affairs at the present moment. External affairs will follow internal affairs. Indeed, there is no basis for external affairs if internal affairs go wrong. Therefore, I am not anxious to widen the scope of our representation all over the world. It is fairly wide already. That too we have been almost compelled by circumstances to do, because as an independent nation we simply cannot do without that representation, but I am not anxious to extend it any further unless some very special reason arises.

That being so, the fact remains that we stand for certain things. Now, when we come into contact with the external world, do we stand for them or do we not? We have to choose. I have no doubt at all, as I said right at the beginning of my remarks, that in the long run, it is to the great advantage of India to try to attract to itself the sympathy and the hope of millions of people in the world without offending others. It is not our purpose to offend others or to come into conflict with others. The world, however, is in a pretty bad way and it is easy enough for people to tell me, "Oh, you talk idealistically, you should be practical."

May I remind the House that we have seen, these many years, the results of persons and things being very practical? I have had about enough of this practicalness, which leads to incessant conflict and which leads to all the misery and suffering that we have seen. If that is the meaning of being practical, the sooner we are not practical, the better.

But that is not being practical. That is being grossly impractical. To march without looking to the left or to the right, each group just contracting into an ever smaller circle, full of danger for the other group, trying to win over other small or big nations by offering some immediate advantage. I do not say that this is good enough for this country and we really are not even compelled by circumstances to submit to it. We might have been compelled by circumstances, but we are not compelled by circumstances to give up . . . our independence in order to gain the goodwill of this country or that country.

I think that not only in the long run, but also in the short run, independence of opinion and independence of action will count. This again does not mean that we should not associate closely with particular countries in certain activities. [Someone has] referred to the necessity for our developing economically, militarily and otherwise. Surely this House realizes that nothing is more important in the opinion of this Government than to make India economically strong and militarily—not strong in the Big Power sense, because that is beyond our capacity,—but as strong as we can to defend ourselves if anybody attacks us.

We want to do that. We want the help of other countries; we are going to have it and we are going to get it too in a large measure—I am not aware of this having been denied to us to any large extent. Even in accepting economic help, or in getting political help, it is not a wise policy to put all your eggs in one basket. Nor should one get help at the cost of one's self-respect. Then you are not respected by any party; you may get some petty benefits, but ultimately even these may be denied you.

Therefore, purely from the point of view of opportunism, if you like, a straightforward honest policy, an independent policy is the best. What that policy should be at a particular moment, it is very difficult for me or for this House to say, because things change rapidly from day to day. It may be that we have to choose what might be a lesser evil in certain circumstances—we must always choose the lesser evil.

We stand in this country for democracy, we stand for an independent Sovereign India. Now obviously, anything that is opposed to the democratic concept—the real, essentially democratic concept, which includes not only political but economic democracy—we ought to oppose. We will resist the imposition of any other concept here or any other practice. . . .

[On the one hand, certain Members] talk about our standing up for the weak and the oppressed against imperialism, and on the other hand, they ask us more or less to side with a Power here or there which may stand for imperialism. . . . I can quite conceive of . . . siding even with an imperialist Power—I do not mind saying that; in a certain set of circumstances that may be the lesser of the two evils. Nevertheless, as a general policy it is not worthy policy or a worthwhile policy. May I state another fundamental difficulty before us? Because of our past record in India, that is the anti-imperialist record, we have not been *persona grata* with many groups and peoples outside. We have not yet overcome their antipathy. With the best will in the world, those people do not like us. Those people govern opinion elsewhere, they govern the Press. . . .

What does joining a bloc mean? After all it can only mean one thing: give up your view about a particular question, adopt the other party's view on that question in order to please it and gain its favour. It means that— it means nothing else as far as I can see, because if our view is the view of that party, then there is no giving up and we do go with that bloc or country. The question only arises when we are opposed to it on that point; therefore we give up our view-point and adopt the other one in order to gain a favour.

Now, I am prepared to agree that on many occasions, not only in international conferences, but in this House, one gives up one's point to gain a compromise, and I am not prepared to rule out the possibility of our subordinating our viewpoint in international conferences in order to gain something worthwhile. That is perfectly legitimate, and it is often done. But this general approach is the worst possible approach to get anything from another country. I should like this House to realize that even if we wanted to adopt that policy, this approach is the worst approach to get a thing done.

The fact of the matter is that in spite of our weakness in a military sense—because obviously we are not a great military Power, we are not an industrially advanced Power—India even today counts in world affairs, and the trouble that you see in the United Nations or the Security Council is because she does count, not because she does not count. That is a fact you should remember. If we had been some odd little nation somewhere in Asia or Europe, it would not have mattered much. But because we count, and because we are going to count more and more in the future, every thing we do becomes a matter for comment, and many people do not like our counting so much. It is not a question of our viewpoint or of attaching ourselves to this or that bloc; it is merely the fact that we are potentially a great nation and a big Power, and possibly it is not liked by some people that anything should happen to strengthen us.[1]

[1] I.A., pp. 210-19.

5 Launching of S.S. *Jala-Usha* (first ocean-going steamer made in India): March 14

India is an old country and I have always thought of [her] as the off-spring of mountains and seas, the Himalayas and the Indian Ocean embracing her on two sides. So I have always thought of India not as a country isolated from the rest of the world, but a country eminently suited for the closest and widest intercourse with the other countries of the world. Unfortunately, in recent years—two hundred years, more especially during the last one hundred and fifty years—it has become isolated both by mountain and by sea. All our contacts with the western countries of the world, chiefly England, have been only by sea. But other contacts were ended and cut off. We lost touch with the highland of Central Asia and eastern and western Asia. Indian history tells us of greater enterprises across the seas and across mountains and we were not an isolated people in those days. We looked forward as we ventured across the seas and took our metal and culture to far off countries. . . .

Narrow-mindedness was unheard of in those days. But with the passage of time we have developed narrow-mindedness in the name of religion. What kind of religion is it that prevents man from meeting man? In the name of religion, it has been called a sin to undertake a sea voyage. What kind of religion is it that prevents a man from going to his mother and trusting his mother? If one is not to trust his mother, father, and brother how can one live and progress? We have had enough of this religion and narrow-mindedness in outlook. We grow afraid of the sea, our mother. If we grow afraid of our mother and distrust her, where can we rest and take shelter in times of danger? Now, we must go back to the sea, our mother, and send our ships fearlessly. Let that sea be a symbol for us in the future. Let us send the ship of State, that is India, into the sea with a stout heart and in this way not only develop India, but enhance her stature and co-operate with other nations and venture with a stout heart more and more in future.

Isolation means, in future, death and ruin of the country. To every great country, however big, isolation means standing apart from the world. It means falling behind in the progress of the world. We are not looking forward to interfering with the lives of other countries. We seek no

dominion over others. We seek the friendship of all and co-operation
with all. At the same time we brook no interference from outside. . . .

[In a speech just made] a strange and rather astounding phrase [was]
used; that is about harmonious relations between the Government and
industry. Is industry a rival of our Government? The Government
will help industry in every way. If industry does not function efficiently,
the Government interferes and takes it over. The Government is going to
encourage industry. Industry will become one hundred per cent Government if it does not function efficiently. . . . Whatever happens, take it
from me, the technical personnel and managerial personnel who contribute
to the making of magnificent things will not undergo any change. They
remain the same. It is only that somewhere at the top certain changes
affecting policy and profits will come about. . . . I think one of the most
important things for us to realize today is that industrial warfare injures
and weakens the nation at any time, of course, but more especially today,
when we have just launched our ship of State. If the crew of the ship starts
non-co-operation how will the ship start its voyage? . . .

We are a democratic country . . . We want to give the largest measure
of freedom of opinion . . . action and . . . expression to each group, even
though we may differ from it. Freedom, however, does not mean violence
or instigation to violence. If there is [such] instigation . . . it [must] be
dealt with seriously. We are living in critical times, not only in [India]
but in the world. None knows what the morrow will bring. At times swift
action, wherever necessary, will have to be taken to keep the ship of State
moving even though the waters may be stormy. All the world over, things
are becoming rougher and rougher. Therefore, we must not entangle
ourselves with the world's difficulties and problems. Yet we cannot escape
them either. We have to look at things in their proper perspective. We
have to keep an effective eye on the maintenance of peace in the country.
If we lead a disciplined life and solve our own problems, industrial and
other, I hope industry will prosper. Industry will have above all to seek
and solve its own problems, certainly with the help of the Government.
I hope the workers, too, will realize [that there are] . . . many perils and
dangers ahead.[1]

[1] I.A., pp. 364-67.

6 | Kashmir Developments—March, April

[By March, 1948, India asserted that Pakistan had sent its regular armies into Kashmir.]

Instead of discussing and deciding our references in a straightforward manner, the nations of the world sitting in [the U.N. have] got lost in power politics. . . . It is neither the realities of the situation [in Kashmir] nor the ability with which a case is put forward that [weighs] with these powers.[1]

[The Government of India, as well as Nehru, continued to make numerous detailed statements relating to Kashmir. In the following speech, Nehru places the Kashmir issue in the wider context of the "Integration of the States," in general.]

["The Sweep of History"—Statement, Constituent Assembly (Legislative), New Delhi, March 5, 1948.] Sir, I crave your leave and the indulgence of the House to make a statement on Kashmir. I would beg the House to bear with me for a while, because there is a great deal to say, however briefly I might say it,—not that I am going to make any sensational disclosures, there is nothing very secret about what I am going to say and the facts have appeared in the public Press and in other places frequently enough during the last few months. Nevertheless, it is right that I should place before the House some kind of a consecutive account of what has happened. In order to lessen my task and to help Members of the House, we have prepared a White Paper on Kashmir [that brings] matters right up-to-date. . . . It is not an absolutely complete paper . . . but, on the whole, most of the messages that passed between us and the Government of Pakistan, or connected messages have been given in this White Paper.

Now, before I speak on this particular Kashmir issue, I should like by your leave to say a few words on a wider issue of which the Kashmir issue is a part. We have been living through strenuous days; we have been passing through a period of dynamic history in India. Much has happened during the past six months, much that was good and much that was very bad. But, perhaps, when the history of India comes to be written, when much of the horror of today has been forgotten, one of the biggest things that will be mentioned will be the change that has come over India and that is coming over India in regard to the Indian States. We see something very remarkable happening. It is perhaps difficult for us who live in the middle of this change to appreciate the bigness of what has happened. But it is the upsetting in a very curious way—a peaceful way—of a structure that has endured in India for the past one hundred and thirty or one hundred and forty years, more or less ever since the beginning of the nineteenth century.

We see the sweep of history suddenly coming, the big broom of history, . . . changing this one hundred and thirty-year-old structure and putting something else in its place. We cannot definitely and absolutely say what the final and precise outcome of all this will be, though the picture is clearing up fairly rapidly. It would almost appear that there is the hand of destiny at work. What is happening is nothing that we did not expect. In fact, many of us for many years past have had certain objectives in regard to the Indian States and we have worked for them both through our political and other organizations in India, through the people of the States, through the people of the provinces and otherwise. And, on the whole, what is happening today is in line with the objectives we had laid down. So it is not surprising. Yet, may I confess to you, Sir, that even I who have been rather intimately connected with the States peoples' movement for many years, if I had been asked six months ago what the course of developments would be in the next six months since then, I would have hesitated to say that such rapid changes would take place. Many factors have gone to bring about these rapid changes. Ultimately, I suppose, they are the forces of history working,—the unleashing of all manner of forces which had been repressed for so long. For we had during these one hundred and thirty years a strange phenomenon. The British Government had constructed a State structure in the course of a quarter of a century in the early days of the nineteenth century. Whether it fitted in, in reality, with conditions then existing in India or not, it is a little difficult to say what would have happened minus the British Government. Anyhow, the dominant power of the British created this system, no doubt for their own advantage as they thought fit. That system continued, not because of any inherent strength, as is obvious today, but because of the continuance of that dominant power, of the paramount power as it was called. All manner of changes were going on in India and in the outside world and yet the Indian States structure continued. Many of us said that it was rather archaic, it was out of date, it had to change and must change and so on. But now that the protecting hand of a foreign Government has been removed, the repressions also are removed. The forces that had been kept in check suddenly began to function and we see them in action,—in rapid action. The forces are there of course; they have not been curbed by any of us, but I think in the manner of dealing with this situation,—an intricate and difficult situation—this House will agree with me that we owe a debt of gratitude to my friend and colleague, the Deputy Prime Minister.

So it is in this mighty context of a changing India in regard to the States that we have to view any particular aspect of it. We saw unfortunately six months back the partition of India, the splitting up of India, a part of India going out of India. Immediately after that process of cutting off, another process started, or rather we have . . . had these two processes [partition and integration of] India. We have seen this process of integrating India going on in regard to the States, and not only in regard to the States but, to some extent, even in regard to the provinces, but much more so in regard to the States. So these two things have gone on together—a process of cutting away and a process of integration—and in the balance it is difficult to say how far we have gained and how far we have lost. It is difficult to say also how far this process of integration will go and whither it will take us ultimately. Nevertheless, it is interesting for us living through this rather strange and dynamic period of India's history, to look at it in some perspective, not as actors in the drama but rather as historians looking back on what has happened. The historian who looks back will no doubt consider this integration of the States into India as one of the dominant phases of India's history.

Well, Sir, the process is taking various shapes. There has been an actual merger of a large number of small States with India; there has been a bringing together of a number of States into Unions of States which form units of the Union of India and a certain number of major States remain as separate entities. But what is equally important—and if I may say so, even more important—is not this integration externally but the inner integration, that is, the growth of democratic institutions and responsible government in the States, because that brings about a real integration, not at the top level of government but at the level of the people. Both these processes have gone on and both these processes, may I remind the House, are in line with the objectives for which we have laboured for many years.

Now, it is in this context of changes in the States system that I would like this House to consider the particular case of Kashmir, although it stands apart and many other factors come into play. Today in India two States stand quite apart from the rest in regard to these processes. These States are Hyderabad and Kashmir. I am not going at this moment to say anything about Hyderabad. In regard to Kashmir, it stands apart for many reasons, partly because it has got entangled in external politics, that is to say, it has got entangled in the relations between India and Pakistan and so the two essentially State issues there are somewhat submerged. It is an odd thing that it should get so entangled. That it got entangled is not odd, but the manner of its entanglement, because the Government of Pakistan have assured us time and again that they have nothing to do with the recent events in Kashmir, raids and invasions, etc.—they go on repeating that; nevertheless, they seek to profit by those events. They seek political advantages out of those events, so that while disclaiming all responsibility for what has happened they do want to share in whatever they might get out of it. Anyhow, the Kashmir problem stands apart.

But for the moment, leaving out this external implication of the Kashmir problem, if you consider it, it is essentially the same problem, that is to say, a problem of the growth of the freedom of the people and the growth also of a new integration. Now, we have been aiming, the Government of India and the States Ministry, at the growth of this inner freedom of the people of all the States. If many of the States have agreed to merge with India or come into closer contact with her, it is not because the State Ministry took a big stick and threatened them with consequences. It is because of those forces, arising from the people, and other forces, and fundamentally the sudden withdrawal of an external force which had kept the States together, or rather the States system together, the might of the British Government and the sanctions behind it. That disappearing, immediately the structure began to collapse and it is an astonishing thing— this sudden collapse of a structure which seemed so solid just a few months or a year ago—not surprising to those who knew the facts, but undoubtedly surprising to those people who take a superficial view of things. So essentially we have been aiming at the freedom of the people, knowing and realizing that ultimately it will be for the people of the States to decide what their future will be. We are not going to compel them. We do no propose to compel them, and indeed we cannot compel them in the context of the world today in any State. There are other compulsions, the compulsions of geography. That is true; one cannot ignore it. There are many other compulsions. And naturally in considering the problem, we that is, the Government of India, have always to consider the interests of India as a whole, the interests of India in regard to security, defence, etc but apart from that, we do not wish to exercise any other compulsion in the slightest, over the growth of freedom. In fact, we want to encourage it in the people of the States. We know well that if there is that growth of freedom and freedom of decision by the people of the States, then it will be a powerful factor in bringing them nearer to our people, because we hope that whatever constitution we may adopt in India, it will be based completely on the will of the people.

Now, may I say a few words before I go on to the Kashmir issue and that is this: in this matter I feel a slight difficulty, because the matter is being or going to be discussed again in the Security Council of the United Nations and I would not like to say anything which might be construed, shall I say, [as] putting difficulties in the way of coming to a settlement either in the Security Council or elsewhere. Because we earnestly desire a settlement, we earnestly desire that these great forces should be allowed to function normally and to achieve their results; any other result will be an artificial result. We cannot impose a result—certainly Pakistan cannot impose a result. Ultimately there is no doubt in my mind that in Kashmir as elsewhere, the people of Kashmir will decide finally, and all that we wish is that they should have freedom of decision without any external compulsion.

Now, there is one other factor which I should like to put before the House in regard to Kashmir. We have become too used in India, unfortunately, to thinking of every problem or many problems in terms of communalism, of Hindu versus Muslim or Hindu and Sikh versus Muslim and so on. That has been an unfortunate legacy of ours, and the extent to which it took us cannot be forgotten by us nor the tragedies that it has led to. We are trying, I hope, to get rid of the spirit of communalism, in India at least. We hope to put an end to it, not suddenly perhaps, but certainly fairly rapidly.

Now, in this context of communal conflict the case of Kashmir stands apart, because Kashmir is not a case of communal conflict; it may be a case of political conflict, if you like; it may be a case of any other conflict, but it is essentially not a case of communal conflict. Therefore, this struggle in Kashmir, although it has brought great suffering in its train to the people of Kashmir and placed a burden on the Government of India and the people of India, nevertheless it stands out as a sign of hope that there we see a certain co-operation, combination and co-ordination of certain elements, Hindu and Muslim and Sikh and others on an equal level, and for a political fight for their own freedom. I wish to stress this because it is continually being said by our opponents and critics on the other side that

13*

this is a communal affair and that we are there to support the Hindus or the Sikh minorities as against the Muslim masses of Kashmir. Nothing can be more fantastically untrue. We could not for an instant send our armies and we would not be there if we were not supported by very large sections of the population, which means the Muslims of Kashmir. We would not have gone there in spite of the invitation of the Maharajah of Kashmir, if that invitation had not been backed by the representatives of the people of Kashmir and may I say to the House that in spite of our armies having functioned with great gallantry, even our armies could not have succeeded except with the help and co-operation of the people of Kashmir. Now, we are blamed by people outside, beyond the borders of India, for going to Kashmir to support an autocratic monarch. The House will remember that one of the conditions that we made at that critical moment, when we had to decide whether to send the Indian Army or not, whether to accept accession or not, one of the conditions was that there must be a popular government there, not as a goal and an ideal, but immediately. It was an immediate thing and it was given effect to immediately in so far as it could be given effect to. So it is strange that this charge should be brought against us. Look at this charge in another context. Those people, men and women of Kashmir, who are with us and who are fighting for their freedom and liberty there, they are not new-comers in the struggle for freedom: for the greater part of a generation, they have fought for the freedom of Kashmir, in Kashmir; they have suffered for it and some of us have deemed it a privilege to be associated with them in this fight for the freedom of Kashmir against autocratic rule. These people are with us today. Who are their opponents, who are against them in Kashmir or elsewhere? What has been their record in the past ten, twenty years in regard to the freedom of Kashmir? It is an interesting speculation and an interesting inquiry, because these gentlemen who talk about the autocracy of the Ruler of Kashmir, who talk about autocracy there, what did they do during these last ten, twenty years? They never fought for the freedom of the people of Kashmir; most of them supported that autocracy; most of them opposed the freedom movement in Kashmir. Now, because of entirely different reasons, they have become the champions of the freedom of Kashmir. And what is the type of freedom they have brought into Kashmir today? The freedom so-called that they have brought into Kashmir is the licence to loot and murder and burn that lovely country and to abduct and carry away the beautiful women of the Jammu and Kashmir State; and not only carry them away, but place some of them in the open market place for sale! So let us have this background before us when we consider this Kashmir story. It is a stirring background of events and many of us have been distressed at the strangely narrow view that people in the Security Council have taken on this matter. I do not desire to enter into the details of what happened or did not happen in the Security Council, but I do feel that this background must be appreciated. It is not a Hindu-Muslim question in Kashmir; it is not a question certainly of our standing for any autocracy or anything. We have already, during the last fifteen or twenty years, shown where we stand in regard to the States people and their rules. In regard to Kashmir, more particularly, we have shown by our actions from the very first day we went there, from October last until today, and I shall have something more to say about it before I finish as to how we feel about the freedom of Kashmir. . . .

The House will remember the circumstances in which we had sent our forces to Kashmir. Kashmir State territory, that is, after accession, Indian Dominion territory, was being invaded to the accompaniment of murder, arson, loot and the abduction of women. The whole countryside was being ruined. Fresh raiders were continually coming from Pakistan territory into the Kashmir State. All the fighting was taking place in Indian Dominion territory. The invaders had their principal bases across the border in Pakistan, received supplies and reinforcements from them, and could go back there to rest and recuperate in safety. Our troops had strict orders not to enter Pakistan territory. The normal course to prevent raids on Indian territory would have been to deny the use of any bases to them in Pakistan. Since Pakistan was unwilling to co-operate with us in this manner, the alternatives left to us were to send our armed forces across Pakistan territory to deal effectively with the invaders, or to request the United Nations to ask Pakistan to do so. Any resort to the first course would have involved armed conflict with Pakistan. We were anxious to avoid this and to try every available method to find a peaceful solution. Therefore, the only course left open to us was to make a reference to the Security Council.

I shall not take up the time of the House with a detailed account of the proceedings of the Security Council; these have been fairly fully reported in the Press. I must confess that I have been surprised and distressed at the fact that the reference we made has not even been properly considered thus far and other matters have been given precedence. If the facts we stated in our reference were correct, as we claim they were, then certain consequences naturally followed from them, both in law and from the point of view of establishing peace and order.

On behalf of Pakistan, there was a repetition of the fantastic charges against India which [already] had been made. . . . Pakistan refused to act at once, to deny assistance in men and material to our enemies in Jammu and Kashmir, to prevent further incursions through Pakistan into the State, and to ask the tribesmen and Pakistanis now in the State to withdraw unless a previous agreement had been reached and announced to the effect that the Indian Armed Forces would be withdrawn completely from the Jammu and Kashmir State, and the administration of the State would be replaced by another administration. There were some other matters in dispute also but the principal ones were the two I have mentioned above.

In effect, Pakistan not only admitted that they were aiding the raiders but made it clear that they would continue to do so till certain political objectives of theirs were achieved by them. This was a proposal to which the Government of India could not agree. For such an agreement would have been a betrayal not only of the people of Kashmir to whom they had pledged their word, but also a surrender to methods of violence and aggression which would have had disastrous consequences both for India and Pakistan. It was impossible for us to withdraw our forces without grave danger to the State and without handing over the people of the State who trusted in us to an unscrupulous and cruel invader who had already brought so much misery to the State and its people. Nor could we share the responsibility of protecting the people of Kashmir with any other outside force. It was equally impossible for us to agree to the replacement of Sheikh Abdullah's administration by any other. The Government of Jammu and Kashmir is now no longer an autocratic government; it is a government representing the largest popular party in the State and is under a leader who, during these many months of unparalleled stress, has sustained the morale of his people, maintained an effective administration over the greater part of the State, and, generally, has inspired effective resistance to the brutal attempts of the invaders to overrun and destroy Kashmir. There is no alternative administration possible in Kashmir, unless that administration rested on coercion. If Sheikh Abdullah was not there by the will of the people, he could not have survived, much less could he have accomplished what he has done during these difficult months. It is for him to choose any national of Kashmir to assist him in his Government and it would be improper for us to interfere with his discretion in this matter.

I regret greatly that the representative of Pakistan before the Security Council should have made many statements and charges against India which have no foundation in fact. A great deal has happened in India and Pakistan during the last six months or more which has brought shame on all of us and I am prepared to admit at any stage and at any time the errors of our own people, for I do not think that it is good for the individual or the nation to lapse from truth. That is the lesson our Master taught us and we shall hold on to it to the best of our ability. Many horrible things have happened in India and Pakistan during these past months and while we hold strong views as to the initial responsibility for all the frightfulness that has occurred, all of us, in a greater or lesser degree, have a certain responsibility for it. But so far as the events in Kashmir are concerned, I am convinced in my mind that every action that the Government of India has taken has been straight and above board and inevitable in the circumstances. Our going there at the end of October was thrust upon us by the course of events. Not to have rushed to the rescue of the people of Kashmir, when they were in dire peril, would have been an eternal disgrace, a gross betrayal and a deep injury. We feel deeply about this matter and it is not merely a question of political advantage or disadvantage. It has been and is a moral issue with us, apart from other aspects of the case, and because of this, at every stage and at every step, I consulted Mahatma Gandhi and had his approval. In the confusion of a welter of charges and exaggerated statements, the basic facts are apt to be forgotten. I should like to know from anyone who studies our record in Kashmir since that fateful day when the raiders swooped down at Muzzafarabad and started their career of rapine and arson, I should like to know what major step we took that was morally or otherwise wrong.

The role of the Indian Army in this conflict, which I repeat was not [of] our own seeking, has been conspicuous for ... discipline, impartiality, endurance and gallantry. They have extended their protection to every section of the people of the State. To suggest that they should be withdrawn before complete order is restored is to suggest something which is neither practicable nor reasonable and which is further a reflection on the exemplary record of our forces in Kashmir. We are in Kashmir and our forces are there because, legally, we are on unassailable ground. . . .

We have only two objectives in the Jammu and Kashmir State; to ensure the freedom and the progress of the people there, and to prevent anything happening that might endanger the security of India. We have nothing else to gain from Kashmir, though Kashmir may profit much by our assistance. If those two objectives are assured to us, we are content.

Our making a reference on this issue to the Security Council of the United Nations was an act of faith, because we believe in the progressive realization of world order and a world government. In spite of many shocks, we have adhered to the ideals represented by the United Nations and its Charter. But those very ideals teach us also certain duties and responsibilities to our own people and to those who put their trust in us. To betray these people would be to betray the basic ideals for which the United Nations stand or should stand.[1]

[On April 21, 1948, the United Nations Security Council adopted a further resolution on Kashmir, calling upon Pakistan "'to use its best endeavour' to secure the withdrawal of tribesmen and Pakistan nationals, to prevent any 'further intrusion' into the State, and to refrain from aiding 'those fighting in the State'. India was permitted 'a minimum force to aid the Government of Kashmir in the maintenance of law and order'". In accordance with India's understanding, withdrawal of her forces was, however, not to begin until after the Commission (and not Pakistan) was satisfied that "'the tribesmen [were] withdrawing and that arrangements for the cessation of fighting [had] become effective'".[2]]

7 | Current Dilemmas

["An Age of Crises"—Broadcast to U.S.A.—Delhi, April 3, 1948.] We live in an age of crises. One crisis follows another, and even when there is peace, it is a troubled peace with fear of war and preparation for war. Tortured humanity hungers for real peace, but some evil fate pursues it and pushes it further and further away from what it desires most. It seems almost that some terrible destiny drives humanity to ever-recurring disaster. We are all entangled in the mesh of past history and cannot escape the consequences of past evil.

In the multitude of crises, political and economic, that face us, perhaps the greatest crisis of all is that of the human spirit. Till this crisis of the spirit is resolved it will be difficult to find a solution for the other crises that afflict us.

[1] I.A., pp. 73–84.
[2] K.F.S., p. 42.

We talk of World Government and One World and millions yearn for it. Earnest efforts continue to be made to realize this ideal of the human race, which has become so imperative today. And yet those efforts have thus proved ineffective, even though it becomes ever clearer that if there is to be no world order then there might be no order at all left in the world. Wars are fought and won or lost, and the victors suffer almost as much as the vanquished. Surely, there must be something wrong about our approach to this vital problem of the age, something essential lacking.

In India during the last quarter of a century and more, Mahatma Gandhi made an outstanding contribution not only to the freedom of India but to that of world peace. He taught us the doctrine of non-violence, not as a passive submission to evil, but as an active and positive instrument for the peaceful solution of international differences. He showed us that the human spirit is more powerful than the mightiest of armaments. He applied moral values to political action and pointed out that ends and means can never be separated, for the means ultimately govern the end. If the means are evil, then the end itself becomes distorted and at least partially evil. Any society based on injustice must necessarily have the seeds of conflict and decay within it so long as it does not get rid of that evil.

All this may seem fantastic and impractical in the modern world, used as it is to thinking in set grooves. And yet we have seen repeatedly the failure of other methods and nothing can be less practical than to pursue a method that has failed again and again. We may not perhaps ignore the present limitations of human nature or the immediate perils which face the statesmen. We may not, in the world as it is constituted today, even rule out war absolutely. But I have become more and more convinced that so long as we do not recognize the supremacy of the moral law in our national and international relations, we shall have no enduring peace. So long as we do not adhere to right means, the end will not be right and fresh evil will flow from it. That was the essence of Gandhiji's message and mankind will have to appreciate it in order to see and act clearly. When eyes are bloodshot vision is limited.

I have no doubt in my mind that World Government must and will come, for there is no other remedy for the world's sickness. The machinery for it is not difficult to devise. It can be an extension of the federal principle, a growth of the idea underlying the United Nations, giving each national unit freedom to fashion its destiny according to its genius, but subject always to the basic covenant of the World Government.

We talk of the rights of individuals and nations, but it must be remembered that every right carries an obligation with it. There has been far too much emphasis on rights and far too little on obligations; if obligations were undertaken, rights would naturally flow from them. This means an approach to life different from the competitive and acquisitive approach of today.

Today fear consumes us all—fear of the future, fear of war, fear of the people of the nations we dislike and who dislike us. That fear may be justified to some extent. But fear is an ignoble emotion and leads to blind strife. Let us try to get rid of this fear and base our thoughts and actions on what is essentially right and moral, and then gradually the crisis of the spirit will be resolved, the dark clouds that surround us may lift and the way to the evolution of world order based on freedom will be clear.[1]

["Democracy and Unity"—Speech, Constituent Assembly (Legislative), New Delhi, April 3, 1948.] We talk about democracy and unity and all that and I hope we shall rapidly have more and more democracy and more and more unity in this country. A democracy is not purely a political affair. The nineteenth century conception of democracy . . . [of] each person having a vote, was a good enough conception in those days, but it was incomplete and people think in terms of a larger and deeper democracy today. After all there is no equality between the pauper who has a vote and the millionaire who has a vote. There are a hundred ways of exercising influence for the millionaire which the pauper has not got. After all there is no equality between the person who has tremendous educational advantages and the person who has had none. So educationally, economically and otherwise, people differ greatly. People will, I suppose, differ to some extent. All human beings are not equal in the sense of ability or capacity. But the whole point is that people should have equality of opportunity and that they should be able to go as far as they can go.

Now it is patent in India today that there are huge differences between certain groups, classes and individuals. There is a big hiatus between those at the top and those at the bottom. If we are to have democracy it becomes necessary and essential for us not merely to bridge [the] gap but to lessen it . . . to bring [people] closer together as far as [their] opportunities are concerned, as far ultimately as general living conditions are concerned and in so far as the necessities of life are concerned, leaving out for the moment luxuries and the rest, though ultimately there seems to me to be no particular reason why any particular group or class should be favoured even in regard to the luxuries of life. But that is perhaps a rather distant picture. Now, because there are such great differences in India, it becomes

[1] I.A., pp. 302–03.

incumbent upon us, not only for humanitarian reasons but from the standpoint of the fulfilment of democracy to raise up those people who are low
down in the social and economic scale and to bring to them every possible
opportunity of growth and progress. That has been the generally accepted
policy of this country and it is the accepted policy of this Government. Now
in pursuance of that policy, a certain reservation of seats was granted, for
instance, to the scheduled castes, and various scholarships and educational
amenities, etc., have been granted and no doubt will be granted still more,
not only to the scheduled castes but also to other backward groups in the
country. For there are the tribal people and others who require every
help. It is no good for us to say . . . we have given a vote to [a] member of
a tribal folk and we have done our duty by him. Having for hundreds and
thousands of years not done our duty by him, [just by giving] him a vote
we consider ourselves absolved of . . . further duty. [Thus] we have to
think always in terms of raising the level of all those who have been denied
opportunities in the past. I do not personally think myself that the best
way to do that is on the political plane by the reservation of seats and the
rest. I think the best way, and the more basic and fundamental way, is to
advance them rapidly in the economic and educational spheres and then
they will stand on their own feet.

There is a great danger, whether you deal with an individual, group or
community, of giving certain props to that community which give it a
false sense of strength which does not belong to it. The props are external
to it, and when they are removed suddenly make the community weak. A
nation ultimately ought to stand on its own feet. So long as it relies on
some external prop, it is not strong. It is weak. So these external props,
as I might call them—that is, reservation of seats and the rest—may
possibly be helpful occasionally in the case of the backward groups, but
they produce a false sense of the political relation, a false sense of strength,
and ultimately, therefore, they are not so nearly as important as real educational, cultural and economic advance, which gives them inner strength
to face any difficulty or any opponent. However, I can conceive that in the
present context of affairs in regard to these unfortunate countrymen of
ours who have not had these opportunities in the past, special attempts
should be made, of course, in the educational and economic field and
even in the political field to see that they have a proper place till they find
their own legs to stand upon without any external aid.[1]

[1] Ibid., pp. 49-51.

8 | Economic Freedom for Asia

[As is clear from preceding passages, Nehru wished to help create a world in which the individual might obtain greater economic, as well as political equality and democracy. The long heritage of colonialism had made him also especially sensitive to the possibility that previously subject countries might now blindly expose themselves to a new form of outside domination. He feared that, through accepting much needed assistance for their development, from other more powerful nations— but without proper safeguards—such countries might once more be subjugated, this time primarily at the economic level.]

[Inaugural Address, Third Session, United Nations Economic Commission for Asia and the Far East—Ootacamund, Madras, June 1, 1948.] There has been talk in the past of One World in the political sense, but it is even more important to consider it in the economic sense. You are meeting here to deal with Asia and Asia's problems—problems, too, inevitably in the context of the larger world—because we cannot escape looking at almost any problem except in the global context today. Asia is big enough and the subjects you have to deal with are vast and of tremendous importance. . . .

We have to deal with human beings and the future of human beings and in this area under survey—Asia which has a population of at least a thousand million human beings. In India, including Pakistan, there are forty per cent of those thousand millions, that is four hundred millions, and we have to deal with these vast numbers—practically half the world's population—and if you look at the human aspect of it, these thousand millions with their sufferings, with their wants, with their joys and sorrows, the problem becomes something much more than a dry economic problem which you have to solve and it assumes a tremendous urgency.

Now, for many years past most of these problems have been considered in the world context and I had a feeling and I still have that feeling, that the continent of Asia is somewhat neglected, somewhat overlooked. It is not considered important enough for as much attention to be given to it as is given to certain other parts of the world. Possibly that has been so, because most of the people who were considering these problems were themselves intimately connected with other parts of the world and naturally they thought of them in the first instance. Naturally also, if I have to consider these problems, I would attach more importance to Asia, because it affects me more intimately. But that kind of reaction apart, it is quite obvious that you cannot consider the problem of Asia, or the problem of Europe, or the problem of America or the problem of Africa isolated from the problem of other countries.

It just cannot be done and if some countries which are fortunate enough today—more fortunate than others—think that they can lead their lives in isolation irrespective of what happens in the rest of the world, it is obvious that they are under a misapprehension. Today, if one part of the world goes down economically, it has a tendency to drag others with it, just as when unfortunately war breaks out other people are involved who do not want war. So it is not a question of the prosperous, merely out of the generosity of their hearts helping those that are not prosperous, though generosity is a good thing. But it is a question of enlightened self-interest, realizing that if some parts of the world do not progress, remain backward, they have an adverse effect on the whole economy of the world and they tend to drag down those parts that are at present prosperous. Therefore, it becomes inevitable to consider these problems in the global way and to pay even more attention to those parts which are relatively backward.

Now, Asia has been for generations past in a somewhat static and backward condition. But during the last few years mighty forces have been at work in Asia. These forces inevitably thought in terms of political change to begin with, because without political change it was not possible to have any far-reaching or enduring economic change. Large parts of Asia were colonial territory dominated by other countries. From that connection they have obtained some advantage sometimes. While it did undoubtedly in a sense shake up that static condition, at the same time it tended to preserve it too.

The political struggle of Asia is largely over—not entirely; there are parts of Asia still where some kind of struggle for political freedom is still going on: and it is obvious that so long as there is that type of struggle on the political plane other activities will be ignored or will be thwarted. The sooner, therefore, it is realized that politically every country in Asia should be completely free and be in a position to follow its own genius within the larger world policy that any world organization may lay down, the better it will be. If one thing is certain, it is that there will be no peace in any part of Asia if there is a tendency for another country to dominate over an Asian country by force. I regret that some such attempts continue to be made in parts of Asia. They seem to me not only undesirable in themselves, but singularly lacking in foresight, because there can be but one end to their attempts and that is the complete elimination of any kind of foreign control.

Now, generally speaking, this political aspect of the Asian struggle is drawing to its natural and inevitable culmination. But at the same time, the economic aspect continues and is bound up with all manner of economic problems affecting the world. From the Asian point of view, it has become essentially a matter of extreme urgency to deal with these problems. From the world point of view it is equally urgent really, because unless these problems are dealt with in Asia, they affect other parts of the world. I trust that you, ladies and gentlemen, who are members of this Commission, no doubt realize the importance of what I have said, and will make it clear to the United Nations that any attempt to pay inadequate attention to Asian problems is likely to defeat the end which the United Nations have in view.

In Asia, many historical forces have been at work for many years past and many things have happened which are good and many things which are not so good as always happens when impersonal historic forces are in action. They are still in action. We try to mould them a little, to divert them here and there, but essentially they will carry on till they fulfil their purpose and their historical destiny. That historical destiny can only be one complete political and economic freedom within certainly some kind of world framework. In Asia and the rest of the world, there are various systems at work, political and economic, in different countries. Obviously, it will not be possible to co-operate easily unless we proceed on the basis of not interfering with any system, political or economic, in any country, leaving it to that country to develop as it chooses within the larger sphere of world co-operation.

Now, you can look upon the problems of Asia from the long-term point of view and the short-term. The short-term problems demand immediate attention because of the urgency of solving some great difficulties. There is the aspect of food. It is an extraordinary state of affairs that in a country like India or similarly predominantly agricultural countries, we should lack food or that we should not have a sufficiency of food. There is something obviously wrong if that kind of thing happens.

I have no doubt in my mind that India can and will produce enough food for itself—not immediately, but in the course of a few years. But at the present moment, we have to face this problem. Other similar urgent problems will also come up for deliberation before you. Looking at these problems from a long-term point of view, it seems to me that various deficiencies have to be made good. We have to increase our productive capacity, agricultural and industrial. It is admitted now that industrialization should proceed in these countries of Asia. In the past, this has been rather held up by various problems and various interests.

The real limiting factor in industrialization is the lack of capital equipment. The difficulties are of getting the capital equipment and special experience from those countries which happen to possess it and who have a surplus of it. How far that can be obtained, it is for you to calculate and the producing countries to decide. If it is not obtained quickly, the process of industrialization may be somewhat delayed, but it will go on.

Now, if it is considered right in the larger interest of the world, that a country like India and other countries in the East should be industrialized, should increase, modernize agricultural production, it is in the interests of those countries that can help in this process to help the Asian countries with capital equipment and their special experience. But in doing so, it is to be borne in mind that no Asian countries will welcome any such assistance, if there are conditions attached to it which lead to any kind of economic domination. We would rather delay our development, industrial or otherwise, than submit to any kind of economic domination of any country.

That is an axiom which is accepted by everyone in India and I shall be surprised if any other country in Asia does not accept it. We want to co-operate in the fullest measure in any policy or programme laid down for the world's good, even though it might involve the surrender, in common with other countries, of any particular attribute of sovereignty, provided that it is a common surrender, all round. But a long age of foreign domination has made the countries of Asia very sensitive about anything which might lead to some visible or invisible forms of domination. Therefore, I would beg of you to remember this and to fashion your programmes and policies so as to avoid anything savouring of the economic domination of one country by another. Political domination, it is admitted, leads to economic domination, but an invisible or semi-invisible economic domination creeps in unless you are careful; if that creeps in, it will lead immediately to ill-will and not that atmosphere of co-operation which is so essential in this matter.

In a long-term view—I may speak of India—I suppose the most important thing is to develop our power resources. From that will flow the industrialization of the country, and an addition to our food production. As it is, you know that India has probably more in the shape of irrigation than any other country in the world. We hope to increase that very greatly. We have in view at least a score of various river valley schemes—some very big, some bigger than the Tennessee Valley scheme, some smaller, much smaller. We have to push the schemes through soon, constructing huge dams and reservoirs, and thereby adding to the irrigated parts of India large tracts which are not at present under cultivation.

May I say a word here about the population of India? A great deal has been said and written about our tremendous population and how it over-whelms us and how we cannot solve any problem till the Indian popula-tion is checked or decimated. Well, I have no desire for the population of India to go on increasing. I am all in favour of the population being checked, but I think there is a great misapprehension when so much stress is laid on this aspect. I entirely disagree with that. I think India is an under-populated country and I say this not because I want it to be much more populated. It is under populated, because large tracts of India are still unpopulated. It is true that if you go to the Gangetic plain it is thickly populated; parts of India are thickly populated, but many parts are not populated at all. . . .

We are over-populated, if you like, because our productive capacity is low. If we increase our production, agricultural and other, if this popula-tion is put to work for production then we are not over-populated. We have these big river valley schemes which in addition to irrigating land, preventing floods, soil erosion and malaria, will produce a very great deal of hydro-electric power and at the same time we will have industrial development. If you look at the map of India, you will see the noble range of the Himalayas from the North to the North-East. I do not think there is any part of the world similar in area which has so much concen-trated power—latent potential power, if only it can be tapped and used. Well, we intend tapping and using it. To some extent we have done it. The Himalayas are also full of a variety of mineral resources.

But my point is that not only India, but the whole of this Asian region is full of vast resources, human and material, and the question before us is how to yoke them together and produce results. It is not that we are lacking in men or material. We have both. In order to yoke them together the easiest way is to have certain assistance in capital equipment and experienced technical personnel from those countries which may have a surplus of it. From the world's point of view that will inevitably lead to the world's good. If that cannot be done, then naturally we have to act in a more limited way, but we shall have to go in that direction anyhow.

Apart from increasing production in this way—I mean new schemes and the rest—I think it is important for us to utilize our existing resources better. I do not think they are being utilized to the best advantage. We can get more out of what we have than we have been doing. That involves in India, as in the rest of Asia, many problems—the economic system, the relation of capital and labour and the satisfaction of labour. There is no doubt at all that in all or at any rate most of these Asian countries, there are long-standing social injustices; and naturally where there are these social injustices you will not get proper and satisfactory work, especially now when there is an acute sense of social wrong and social injustice.

In India I have no doubt that our production has suffered because of this acute feeling of social injustice. An individual or a community may undertake to shoulder almost any burden. We have seen during the last war how nations put up with the most enormous burdens in the shape of suffering and sacrifice; but always when there is a sense of sharing the burden inequitably, the burden being greater on some than on others, the sense of injustice becomes greater and you do not have that harmonious working and co-operation which is quite essential today, more so than in the past. Therefore, this problem has to be viewed from the human point of view, quite apart from a purely economic point of view. . . .

People vaguely talk of India's leadership in Asia. I deprecate such talk. I want [our] problems to be approached not in terms of this country or that country being the leader and pushing or pulling others, but rather in a spirit of co-operation between all the countries of Asia, big or small. . . . We should talk only in terms of co-operation between countries, whatever they may be. It is in that spirit that I should like India to approach [the problems before us, but I also] should . . . like India to play a leading part in serving the common cause, whatever the result of that may be to India.[1]

9 | Kashmir: Further Statement, Summer, 1948

'Defence of stand on U.N. Commission's power in conjunction with Kashmir—June 5, 1948.] I do not propose to enter into the merits of
[1] I.A., pp. 304–11.

Pakistan's charges against India of genocide and non-implementation of the agreements with Pakistan or against the accession of Junagadh [see earlier sections] to India. Our views have been repeatedly stated before the Security Council and also in the statements made by me and some of my colleagues. We regard the accusations of genocide and non-implementation of agreements as baseless. That we have protested against the Security Council's decision to include these charges within the scope of the functions of the Council's Commission is certainly not due, as alleged by the Prime Minister of Pakistan, to a desire to conceal anything. Because India has nothing to conceal is no reason why India should acquiesce in an investigation by an outside body in something which in our view is outside the competence of that body and which has no foundation in fact.

The Prime Minister of Pakistan has also attributed India's decision to refer the Kashmir dispute to the Security Council to a desire to gain time in which to force a military decision. The reference of India's complaint to the Security Council will show that, contrary to what [the Pakistanis have] suggested, India has all along insisted on urgency of action by the Council on her complaint against Pakistan. If such action has not been taken the fault is not India's. In referring the Kashmir dispute to the Security Council India never intended to sacrifice her freedom of military action to rid the State of Jammu and Kashmir of all invaders and to restore peace. She has both the right and the obligation to do so in respect of a State which has acceded to her. It is strange that [the Pakistanis] should complain of India's action in using her resources to achieve this legitimate and humane object.

Once more allegations have been made of atrocities by Indian troops on "defenceless old men, women and children in areas occupied by them." I most emphatically repudiate this unfounded charge. The purpose of these accusations, often repeated but without any vestige of truth, can only be to divert the attention of the world from the barbarous atrocities which the raiders, whom Pakistan has been so actively aiding and abetting, have been committing on innocent civilians, regardless of creed, sex or age, in the areas which they occupy or into which they penetrated. Such crimes against humanity can never be concealed. . . .

[The Pakistanis have] complained of Indian troops violating Pakistan's frontiers and Indian airmen bombing villages well within Pakistan's boundaries. Every complaint of violation by our troops of Pakistan's frontiers that could be investigated has been inquired into. Most of these complaints have on inquiry proved baseless. As is well known, the raiders when forced to retire from state territory often flee to Pakistan. Our troops chase them up to the frontier of the State; this is their duty as well as their right. As regards our airmen also, every complaint of Pakistan has been carefully investigated. . . . The history of two world wars shows how impossible it is to avoid damage to neutrals through *bona fide* mistakes of observation. No aggression against Pakistan [has been] intended.

[The Pakistanis have] referred to "the exemplary patience" shown by the Pakistan Government "in the face of provocations". [They have] conveniently forgotten the continuous and continuing provocation to which the Indian Government has been subjected . . . since the invasion last October by tribesmen of the Kashmir Valley, inspired by Pakistan in the shape of every kind of aid given by her to the aggressor. More recently Pakistan troops have in strength been opposing Indian troops on the Uri front. It is idle in the circumstances either to speak of the Pakistan Government's "anxiety to maintain peaceful and friendly relations with India" or to suggest that Indian action in Kashmir constitutes a "grave threat to the security of Pakistan" or a "campaign of murder and destruction" against the Moslems of Jammu and Kashmir.

Far from seeking to murder and destroy Moslems in the State, Indian forces [were] used to protect them against . . . ruthless marauders whom Pakistan let loose. An Interim Government, representative of the people, headed by a Moslem who has for years been a most outstanding leader of the popular and progressive forces in Jammu and Kashmir and composed of a majority of Moslems, has been formed in the State.

On the question of accession India has repeatedly affirmed that the freely declared will of the people of Jammu and Kashmir shall prevail. Though, short of a declaration of war, Pakistan has done everything to help the invaders of and the insurgents within the State, the Government of India have acted with unexampled restraint in the interests of peace. They still desire to live on the friendliest possible terms with the neighbour State of Pakistan.[1]

[1] G.I.I.S. (June 11, 1948), pp. 1–4. (A sequence of U.N. Resolutions on Kashmir is included in the Appendix.)

10 | Departure of Lord and Lady Mountbatten—On Partition—Socialism and Communism

Departure of Lord and Lady Mountbatten, Summer, 1948

[Lord and Lady Mountbatten were warmly regarded throughout their stay in India. When it was time for their return to Britain during the summer of 1948, Nehru's parting tribute reflected the extraordinarily high esteem in which they were held by Indians.]

[To the Mountbattens—June 20, 1948.] Your Excellencies, Your Highnesses, ladies and gentlemen—Fifteen months ago, almost to the day, some of us went to Palam airfield to welcome the new Viceroy and his wife. Some of us will go again to Palam airfield tomorrow morning to bid them goodbye. Fifteen months have passed and these fifteen months seem a long time, and yet it seems but yesterday that Lord and Lady Mountbatten and Pamela Mountbatten came here, and yet if you look again it seems that an age has gone by because of the accumulation of sensation and experience, of joy and sorrow that has come to us during these fifteen months.

I find it a little difficult to speak on this occasion, because the people about whom I am going to speak have become during this period very dear and intimate friends of ours, and it is always difficult to speak of those who are friends and who are dear to us. One may overdo it or one may, on the other hand, guard oneself unduly and underdo it. In any event, I do not know that any words of mine are needed . . . to say much about Lord and Lady Mountbatten. In the past few days, there have been numerous [events at which] they received words of praise . . . friendship and welcome, I suppose, but they did not affect me very much. They were rather formal on the whole.

I do feel that any words of mine this evening, after the demonstration in the City of Delhi three or four hours ago, will be in the nature of an anti-climax, because three or four hours ago, the City of Delhi, that is the common people of Delhi, gathered together to welcome or rather to bid goodbye . . . and that was such a wonderful demonstration of friendship and affection that any words or phrases can hardly be suited to an occasion after that event. I do not know—at the most I can only guess—how Lord and Lady Mountbatten felt on that occasion: but used as I am to these vast demonstrations here, I was much affected and I wondered how it was that an Englishman and an Englishwoman could become so popular in India during this brief period of time; and that brief period being a period certainly of achievement and success in some measure, but also a period of sorrow and disaster.

In fact, I have often wondered why the people of India put up with people like me who are connected with the governing of India after all that has happened during the last few months. I am not quite sure that if I had not been in the Government, I would put up with my Government. Quite apart from the merits or demerits, the fact is that a government should and must be responsible for everything that happens, and if everything that happens is not right, then the government ought to be held responsible. I think that is a good maxim, generally speaking. It may perhaps be possible to find sufficient excuses. So it surprised me all the more that after this period of storm and stress and difficulty, the Governor-General and his wife, who were in some sense associated with all this, should still be able to win the affection of the people to such a tremendous degree.

Obviously, this was not connected so much with what had happened, but rather with the good faith, the friendship and the love of India that these two possessed. They saw them working hard with indomitable energy, with perseverance, with optimism, which defied everything; they felt even more than they saw the friendship which they had for India and they saw that they were serving India to the best of their ability.

We have many failings and many weaknesses in India, but when we see friendship for India and service for India, our hearts go out and those who are friends of India and those who serve India are our comrades, whoever they might be or wherever they might be. And so the people of India, realizing that Lord and Lady Mountbatten undoubtedly were friendly to India and the Indian people, undoubtedly were serving them, gave you their affection and love. They could not give very much else. You may have many gifts and presents, but there is nothing more rare or precious than the love and affection of the people. You have seen yourself, Sir and Madam, how that love and affection work. If I may say so, they are the most precious of gifts. So when you have seen all this, I have little to add except to say a few words, rather personal perhaps, and also impersonal.

You have been here, in your individual capacity and in a great public capacity. We have become friends with you, many of us, and we have been thrown together at a strange moment in history, and we have been actors also in this historic scene. It is difficult for me or for anyone to judge of what we have done during the last year or so. We are too near it and too intimately connected with events. Maybe we have made many mistakes, you and we. Historians a generation or two hence will perhaps be able to judge whether we have done right and whether we have done wrong. Nevertheless, whether we did right or wrong, the test, perhaps the right test, is whether we tried to do right or did not, for if we did try to do right with all our might and main, then it does not very much matter, although it does matter in the sense that it turned out to be a wrong thing. I cannot judge our own motives, but I do believe that we did try to do right and I am convinced that you tried to do the right thing by India, and, therefore, many of our sins will be forgiven us and many of our errors also.

You came here, Sir, with a high reputation, but many a reputation has foundered in India. You lived here during a period of great difficulty and crisis, and yet your reputation has not foundered. That is a remarkable feat. Many of us who came in contact with you from day to day in these days of crisis learnt much from you, we gathered confidence when sometimes we were rather shaken, and I have no doubt that the many lessons we have learnt from you will endure and will help us in our work in the future.

To you, Madam, I should like to address myself also. The gods or some good fairy gave you beauty and high intelligence, and grace and charm and vitality, great gifts, and she who possesses them is a great lady wherever she goes. But unto those that have, even more shall be given, and they gave you something which was even rarer than those gifts, the human touch, the love of humanity, the urge to serve those who suffer and who are in distress, and this amazing mixture of qualities resulted in a radiant personality and in the healer's touch. Wherever you have gone, you have brought solace, you have brought hope and encouragement. Is it surprising, therefore, that the people of India should love you and look up to you as one of themselves and should grieve that you are going? . . . Hundreds of thousands have seen you personally in various camps and hospitals and other places, and hundreds of thousands will be sorrowful at the news that you have gone. . . .

The bonds that tie the Mountbattens to us are too strong to be broken and we hope to meet here or elsewhere from time to time, and whether we meet you or not, we shall remember you always.[1]

[1] I.A., pp. 368–71.

On Partition—July 26, 1948

We consented [to partition] because we thought that thereby we were purchasing peace and goodwill, though at a high price. . . . I do not know now, if I had the same choice, how I would decide.[1]

Socialism and Communism—Madras, July 26, 1948

I find today that people are talking in terms of socialism and more especially of communism. These are excellent gospels. I accept their fundamental principles but I do not and will not accept the manner and methods of those who call themselves communists because I find that in the name of an economic doctrine they are at present trying to coerce and commit all manner of atrocities in [our] provinces. . . . They want us in the name of civil liberty to allow them to carry on these atrocities. No Government can put up with this. If any group or people want to declare war against a state then the state is at war with them. . . .

[Nehru advised the workers not to waste their time and energy on strikes but to increase production, to enable the Government to go ahead with its development schemes, calculated to raise the economic standards of the people.] We have every sort of potential resource in India. What we lack for the present is the proper coordination of those resources with human power, in a cooperative spirit, and a spirit of discipline, so that all of us together may serve the nation and serve the people. If we do so together then very rapidly we can build up this great nation.

[Congress, according to Nehru, had always been committed, not only to a people's era, but essentially to the workers' and peasants' dominance in that era.] Our ideal is a democratic form and structure of Government, and in that structure the workers and peasants in this country will have the fullest say. . . .

The first thing before us is to get this country going, to get it properly stabilized, to increase its production and with one aim in view: that is, raising the standards of the mass of common people and making them freer and better by putting an end to poverty and unemployment. We have therefore to combat [the] anti-social forces that are at work and I call upon [the Indian people] to fight these forces.[2]

[1] Quoted in M.B., p. 374.
[2] Based on G.I.I.S. (July 30, 1948), p. 1.

| I I | Commonwealth Relations—European Trip—Last Lap of Our Journey |

Commonwealth Relations

[Toward the end of 1948, India's decision about what its relationship to the Commonwealth should be finally crystallized. Nehru's own attitude continued to be that, even while accepting Dominion Status, and a close relationship with the Commonwealth, India must be a Republic, free to make her own decisions, as well as her own associations with other nations, in accordance with her own wishes. Moreover, India must swear no allegiance to the "Crown", as did other Dominions in the Commonwealth.

"On 25 February 1948, the day before the Indian draft constitution was published . . . in an *aide-memoire* for the British Secretary of State for Commonwealth Relations, [Mountbatten] proposed certain changes in the structure of the association, 'particularly in nomenclature, to allow Asian countries to remain more easily associated with it'. Though he was unhappy with the word republic, he remarked, 'I think there can be no doubt that there is room for a Republic within the Commonwealth.'"

At the Commonwealth Prime Ministers Conference in London in October 1948—the first such Conference which Nehru attended—there was no formal discussion of the issue. Nehru and Attlee exchanged views, however, agreeing on general procedure. At this point, Nehru "'realized that membership in the Commonwealth meant independence plus, not independence minus. Having persuaded himself of its virtues, [he] had to convince his colleagues and Indian political opinion at large. Upon his return [to India] from London he noted that he had not committed India in any sense, for this was a matter to be decided by the Constituent Assembly. However, since the Congress dominated the Assembly, it became a mere formality. The issue was decided by Nehru with his Cabinet's assent.

"The Congress, complying with Nehru's wish, gave its approval . . . in December 1948. The formal arrangement was concluded at the Commonwealth Prime Ministers Conference in April, 1949 and was embodied in the Declaration of London. It was a very brief document. . . . The first [paragraph] noted the existing position, referred to the *British* Commonwealth of Nations and the common *allegiance* to the *Crown*. The second indicated that India had informed the participants of its decision to establish a sovereign independent republic, of its desire to retain full membership in the Commonwealth, and of its willingness to accept the

King as *symbol* of the free association of members and as such as *Head* of *the Commonwealth*. The participants accepted India on these terms and affirmed their status as free and equal members.

"Despite its simplicity of phrasing, the Declaration of London had many hurdles to overcome. At the Delhi end there was no real problem, for Nehru's views on foreign policy were final, and in any event Patel strongly favoured the idea. According to one prominent person who played a key role in the negotiations, the King supported the novel idea of a Republic in the Commonwealth. The Foreign Office lawyers, however, were strongly opposed. Lengthy negotiations took place, but the lawyers were adamant, saying it was impossible to devise a formula under international law which would make a Republic compatible with a Commonwealth. Initially there were about ten problems to be solved, but these were reduced to three—citizenship, reciprocity and the place of the Crown. A suggestion for Commonwealth citizenship was made. Though it was finally rejected, the substance was later incorporated into the citizenship laws of various Commonwealth countries. The core issue was the Crown. The Australians wanted the King to be designated King of the Commonwealth, but South Africa, Canada and India were opposed. There was a proposal to have the President of India formally appointed by the King, but India was opposed. Mountbatten suggested the inclusion of the Crown in the Indian flag; this, too, was rejected. Finally, [the formula was devised], 'Head of the Commonwealth'. At the last moment the Pakistanis wanted a more direct monarchical link. To break the impasse the words 'as such' were added, connecting the terms 'Head of the Commonwealth' and 'symbol of the free association of members'. . . .

"From a strictly formal point of view India took the initiative. Perhaps the most significant facet of the story was that 'absolutely no pressure was exerted by the British on [India] to remain in the Commonwealth. They wanted [India] of course, but Attlee did not lift a finger to intervene.'

"Within India the Left termed the decision relating to the Commonwealth 'the great betrayal'. Sections of the right wing Hindu Mahasabha also objected to it. The debate in the Constituent Assembly was spirited, with thirteen members voicing support of Nehru's action, six opposition. The outcome was a foregone conclusion. The main themes of the critics were that it violated previous pledges; committed India to the West; represented a loss of independence; and was immoral because of racial discrimination in South Africa. In defence of his policy Nehru declared that it did not violate previous pledges, for India's independence was unimpaired; that it was in India's self-interest, for it enabled Delhi to act more effectively in foreign affairs, even with respect to Indians in South Africa; and that it helped to promote international stability and therefore world peace.

"Various considerations influenced Nehru's decision. (In the last analysis it was his decision alone.) At the subconscious level was his affection for Britain dating from his formative years, an attachment which was deepened by his friendship with the Mountbattens. The reservoir of good-will which America possessed in India at the end of the second world war had evaporated. But by far the most important was the realization that India could not remain isolated in a world of great tension—the 'Cold War' was then a harsh reality—and that the Commonwealth link was the most advantageous. The bulk of India's trade was with the Common-wealth; its foreign exchange reserves were tied up in the Sterling Area; its armed forces depended on British-made weapons. Moreover, membership of the Commonwealth would enable India to render greater assistance to the substantial communities of Indian settlers in South Africa, Malaya, British Guiana and other parts of the Empire. Viewed in the perspective of the duumvirate, it was an act of high statesmanship, for it thwarted the danger of isolation in foreign affairs at a time of grave crisis internally and on the world scene. It marks the first real stabilizing act in India's rela-tions with the outside world.

"In the midst of his negotiations with the Commonwealth, Nehru made his formal début on the world stage as Prime Minister of India. Many people in the West knew of him as Gandhi's aide in the struggle for freedom and as an author of renown. But it was not until he addressed the U.N. General Assembly in Paris on 3 November 1948 that he" emerged as the voice of new Asia.[1]]

European Trip

[Nehru left for London during the autumn of 1948, to attend the Prime Ministers Conference.]

[To George Bernard Shaw, before leaving for London—New Delhi, September 4, 1948.] I do not quite know why I am writing to you, for we are both busy men and I have no desire to add to your work. But Devadas Gandhi [son of the Mahatma] has sent me a copy of a letter you wrote to him on the 16th July and this has produced an urge in me to write to you.

Forty years ago, when I was eighteen and an undergraduate at Cam-bridge, I heard you address a meeting there. I have not seen you again since then, nor have I ever written to you. But, like many of my generation, we have grown up in company with your writings and books. I suppose a part of myself, such as I am today, has been moulded by that reading. I do not know if that would do you any credit.

[1] Based on M.B., pp. 415–18. (Further details concerning India's Declaration in re the Commonwealth are to be found in Part Twelve, Section 2.)

Because, in a sense, you have been near to me, or rather near to my thoughts, I have often wanted to come in closer touch with you and to meet you. But opportunities have been lacking and then I felt that the best way to meeting you was to read what you had written.

Devadas apparently asked you as to what we should do with Gandhi's assassin. I suppose he will hang and certainly I shall not try to save him from the death penalty, although I have expressed myself in favour of the abolition of the death penalty in previous years. In the present case there is no alternative. But even now in a normal case, I have grown rather doubtful if it is preferable to death to keep a man in prison for fifteen or twenty years.

Life has become so cheap that it does not seem of very much consequence whether a few criminals are put to death or not. Sometimes one wonders whether a sentence to live is not the hardest punishment after all.

I must apologise to you for those of my countrymen who pester you for your views on India. Many of us have not outgrown our old habit of seeking testimonials from others. Perhaps that is due to a certain lack of faith in ourselves. Events have shaken us rather badly and the future does not appear to be as bright as we imagined it would be.

There is a chance of my going to England for two or three weeks in October next. I would love to pay you a visit, but certainly not if this means any interference with your daily routine. I would not come to trouble you with any questions. There are too many questions which fill the mind and for which there appear to be no adequate answers, or if the answers are there, somehow they cannot be implemented because of the human beings that should implement them. If I have the privilege to meet you for a while, it will be to treasure a memory which will make me a little richer than I am.[1]

[Reply from George Bernard Shaw to Nehru—London, September 18, 1948: "I was greatly gratified to learn that you were acquainted with my political writings; and I need hardly add that I should be honored by a visit from you, though I cannot pretend that it will be worth your while to spend an afternoon of your precious time making the journey to this remote village, where there is nothing left of Bernard Shaw but a doddering old skeleton who should have died years ago.

"I once spent a week in Bombay, another in Ceylon; and that is all I know at first hand about India. I was convinced that Ceylon is the cradle of the human race because everybody there looks an original. All other nations are obviously mass products.

"Though I know nothing about India except what is in the newspapers

I can consider it objectively because I am not English but Irish, and have lived through the long struggle for liberation from English rule, and the partition of the country into Eire and Northern Ireland, the Western equivalent of Hindustan and Pakistan. I am as much a foreigner in England as you were in Cambridge.

"I am wondering whether the death of Jinner [*sic*] will prevent you from coming to England. If he has no competent successor you will have to govern the whole Peninsula."[1]

Because of Nehru's crowded program in London, he could not meet Shaw, to the regret of both men.]

[From speech on India and Britain—at meeting organized by India League of London, October 12, 1948.] I should like the closest cooperation between the peoples of India and Britain. . . . Whatever has happened in India in the past many years has been essentially not a one or two or three-man show, but something bigger—something that involves the labor and sacrifice of vast numbers of human beings. One is apt to symbolize that sacrifice in individuals and it would be easy to do so in the case of men like Mahatma Gandhi, because he [was not only a symbol] but he was the man who built up [our] movement. When you think of the past years of India, certainly [you] think of the Mahatma, but think also of those vast numbers of human beings who for many years have worked on a remarkable high moral level and a high level of courage, which ultimately resulted in what [has occurred in India]. . . .

Probably when the history of this time comes to be written this change will have an important place not only because two countries and two peoples were involved, but probably because it will have even a large significance in human history. I should like to congratulate here in public the present Government of the United Kingdom and the people of Britain for the courage and vision they showed at a very critical moment in their dealings with India. I should say that that courage and vision has already—to those who can see it—yielded substantial fruits.

Remembering the past background of the generation-old struggle and bitter conflict, it is extraordinary how a sense of conflict has rapidly faded away. Not entirely perhaps, but generally speaking it has faded with remarkable rapidity. For that I think there are two causes. One certainly is the manner in which the whole struggle for freedom was conceived and carried out by Gandhiji. Undoubtedly, that is the basic fact. The othe

[1] Ibid., p. 517.

is the manner in which at the critical juncture the British Government and the British people handled the situation.

People talk of a kind of axis that might continue between England and India. They think of it in legal and other terms. I do not know at this moment exactly what shape it might take. All I can say is this: first of all I should like the closest cooperation between the people of India and the people of Britain. But whatever form it might take it is obvious that any foundation for cooperation will be a sense of comradeship, fellow-feeling and the absence of conflict between them.[1]

[Address to Special Session of United Nations General Assembly, Paris—November 3, 1948.] I am grateful for the opportunity that has been given to me to address this great Assembly. I feel a little embarrassed and a little overwhelmed by this occasion, because this Assembly represents the world community, and, whether we who are present here are big men and women or small, we represent a mighty cause and something of the greatness of that cause falls upon us too, and makes us, for the moment, greater perhaps than we are.

Therefore, in venturing to address this Assembly, I feel embarrassed. You have been dealing with intricate and difficult problems, and I do not, and I would not, venture on this occasion to say anything about those great problems that confront you. You can carry the burdens and sorrows of the world. But I have often wondered whether, in dealing with those problems, the approach that is normally made to them is the right one or not. The Charter of the United Nations, in noble language, has laid down the principles and the purposes of this great organization. I do not think it would be possible to improve upon that language.

The objectives are clear; your aim is clear; and yet, in looking at that aim, we lose ourselves often, if I may venture to say so, in smaller matters and forget the main objective that we were looking at. Sometimes it seems that the objective itself gets a little clouded and lesser objectives are before us.

I come from a country which, after a long struggle, though that struggle was a peaceful struggle, attained her freedom and her independence. In these long years of struggle we were taught by our great leader never to forget not only the objectives we had, but also the methods whereby we should achieve those objectives. Always he laid stress on this, that it was not good enough to have a good objective, that it was equally important that the means of attaining those objectives were good; means were always

G.I.I.S. (Oct. 18, 1948), pp. 2-3.

as important as ends. You will permit me to repeat that here, because I am convinced that, however good the ends, the larger ends of the United Nations, or the lesser objectives which we may from time to time have before us, either as individual nations or as groups of nations, it is important that we should remember that the best of objectives may not be reached if our eyes are bloodshot and our minds clouded with passion.

Therefore, it becomes essential for us, for a while, to think more of how we are doing things than what we are aiming at, even though we should never forget what we are aiming at. It becomes necessary for us always to remember the principles and the purposes for which this great Assembly was formed.

Now, a mere repetition of those principles and purposes would perhaps indicate to us how sometimes, with passion and prejudice, we swerve away from that path. This Assembly took shape after two mighty wars and as a consequence of those wars. What has been the lesson of those wars? Surely the lesson of those wars has been that out of hatred and violence you will not build peace. It is a contradiction in terms. The lesson of history, the long course of history, and more especially the lesson of the last two great wars which have devastated humanity, has been that out of hatred and violence only hatred and violence will come. We have got into a cycle of hatred and violence, and not the most brilliant debate will get you out of it, unless you look some other way and find some other means. It is obvious that if you continue in this cycle and have wars which this Assembly was especially meant to avoid and prevent, the result will not only be tremendous devastation all over the world, but non-achievement by any individual Power or group of its objective.

How, then are we to proceed? It may be that it is difficult to get this hatred and prejudice and fear out of our minds. Nevertheless, unless we try to proceed in this way, to cast out this fear, we shall never succeed. Of that I am quite convinced.

You meet here, representatives of all nations of the world, or nearly all Inevitably, you have behind you and before you the immediate great problems that confront more especially Europe, which has suffered so much.

May I say, as a representative from Asia, that we honour Europe for it culture and for the great advance in human civilization which it repre sents? May I say that we are equally interested in the solution of European problems; but may I also say that the world is something bigger tha Europe, and you will not solve your problems by thinking that the problem of the world are mainly European problems. There are vast tracts of th world which may not in the past, for a few generations, have taken much part in world affairs. But they are awake; their people are moving and they have no intention whatever of being ignored or of being passed by.

It is a simple fact that I think we have to remember, because unless you have the full picture of the world before you, you will not even understand the problem, and if you isolate any single problem in the world from the rest, you do not understand the problem. Today I do venture to submit that Asia counts in world affairs. Tomorrow it will count much more than today. Asia till recently was largely a prey to imperial domination and colonialism; a great part of it is free today, part of it still remains unfree; and it is an astonishing thing that any country should still venture to hold and to set forth [the] doctrine of colonialism, whether it is under direct rule or whether it is indirectly maintained in some form or other. After all that has happened, there is going to be no mere objection to that, but active objection, an active struggle against any and every form of colonialism in any part of the world. That is the first thing to remember.

We in Asia, who have ourselves suffered all these evils of colonialism and of imperial domination, have committed ourselves inevitably to the freedom of every other colonial country. There are neighbouring countries of ours in Asia with whom we are intimately allied. We look to them with sympathy; we look at their struggle with sympathy. Any Power, great or small, which in [any] way prevents the attainment of the freedom of those peoples does an ill turn to world peace.

Great countries like India who have passed out of [the] colonial stage do not conceive it possible that other countries should remain under the yoke of colonial rule.

We in Asia regard it as a vital problem, because it has been a vital problem for us, and it is a question to which I want to draw attention—that is the question of racial equality, which is something which is laid down in the provisions of the United Nations Charter. It is well to repeat that, because after all this question of racial equality has frequently been spoken about in the Assembly of the United Nations.

I do not think I need dwell on any particular aspect of [prejudice] but I would remind this Assembly of the world-wide aspects of this question. Obviously there are large regions of the world which have suffered from this question of racial inequality. We also feel that there is no part of the world where it can be tolerated in the future, except perhaps because of superior force. It is obviously sowing the seeds of conflict if racial equality is not approved. [It is] a menace to world peace and is in conflict with the principles of the United Nations Charter.

The effects of this inequality in the past have made themselves felt in Asia, Africa and other parts of the world much more than in Europe, leading towards a conflict in the future, and it is a problem which, if it is not properly understood, will not be solved.

It is a strange thing, when the world lacks so many things, food and other necessities in many parts of the world and people are dying from hunger that the attention of this Assembly of Nations is concentrated only on a number of political problems. There are economic problems also. I wonder if it would be possible for this Assembly to take a holiday for a while from some of the acute political problems which face it, and allow men's minds to settle down and look at the vital and urgent economic problems, and look at places in the world where food is lacking.

I feel that today the world is . . . tied up in fears [and] apprehensions, some of them justified no doubt. But[when]a person feels fear, bad conse- quences and evil consequences follow. Fear is not a good companion. It is surprising to see that this sense of fear is pervading great countries—fear, and grave fear of war, and fear of many things. Well, I think that it is admitted, or it will be admitted, that no aggression of any kind can be tolerated, because the very idea of aggression must upset the balance and lead to conflict. Aggression of every type must be resisted. . . . In existing circumstances it is difficult for people to say . . . they will not defend them- selves, because if there is a fear of aggression one has to defend oneself against aggression. We have to defend ourselves, but even in defending ourselves, we must not submit ourselves to this Assembly without clean hands. It is easy to condemn people. Let us not do so, for who are without blame, who cannot themselves be condemned? In a sense, all of us who are gathered here today in this continent of Europe—are there any amongst us who have not been guilty in many ways? We are all guilty men and women. While we are seeking points where error occurs, we should not forget that there is not one of us who is exempt from blame.

If we proceed to this problem, and discuss in peace the psychology of fear, if we realize the consequences of what is happening, it is possible that this atmosphere of fear may be dissipated. Why should there be this fear of war? Let us prepare ourselves against any possible aggression, let no one think that any nation, any community can misbehave. The United Nations are here to prevent any fear or hurt, but at the same time let us banish all thought of an aggressive attitude whether by word or deed. . . .

I have no doubt that this Assembly is going to solve our problems. I am not afraid of the future. I have no fear in my mind, and I have no fear,

even though India, from a military point of view, is of no great consequence. I am not afraid of the bigness of great Powers, and their armies,
their fleets and their atom bombs. That is the lesson which my Master
taught me. We stood as an unarmed people against a great country and a
powerful empire. We were supported and strengthened, because throughout all this period we decided not to submit to evil, and I think that is the
lesson which I have before me and which is before us today. I do not know
if it is possible to apply this to the problems which face the world today.
It is a terrible problem, but I think if we banish [our] fear, if we have
confidence, even though we may take risks of trust rather than risk violent
language, violent actions and in the end war, I think those risks are worth
taking.

In any event, there are risks—and great risks. If it is a question of
taking risks why take risks which inevitably lead to greater conflict? Take
the other risks, while always preparing yourself to meet any possible contingency that may arise.

It is perhaps not very proper for me to address this great Assembly in
such matters, because I have not been associated with it nor with all these
different problems in any intimate degree. However, there would have
been no point in my addressing you merely to repeat certain pious phrases.
I feel strongly about this matter, and that is why I should like to present
the views and wishes of the Indian people. And the Indian people happen
to be three hundred and thirty millions in number; it is well to remember
that. We have had a year of freedom and a year of difficulty. We have
overcome many of those difficulties and we shall overcome the others. We
propose to go ahead at a rapid pace. We propose to build and construct
and be a power for peace and for the good of the world. We propose to
meet every aggression, from whatever quarter it comes, in every possible
way open to us.

However, we do not think that the problems of the world or of India can
be solved by thinking in terms of aggression or war or violence. We are
frail mortals, and we cannot always live up to the teaching of the great
man who led our nation to freedom. But that lesson has sunk deep into
our souls and, so long as we remember it, I am sure we shall be on the
right path. And, if I may venture to suggest this to the General Assembly,
I think that if the essentials of that lesson are kept in mind, perhaps our
approach to the problems of today will be different; perhaps the conflicts
that always hang over us will appear a little less deep than they are and
actually will gradually fade away.

I should like to state to this General Assembly, on behalf of my people and my Government, that we adhere completely and absolutely to the principles and purposes of the United Nations Charter and that we shall try, to the best of our ability, to work for the realization of those principles and purposes.... No one can be optimistic enough to think that all problems will fade away simply if we feel good; that is not what I mean to say. The problems are difficult and intricate and they will take a lot of solving. But I do feel that our approach to those problems should not be the approach of anger and passion and fear. Then, perhaps, the problems will gradually appear in a different light. Perhaps, we shall understand the other side better; perhaps, the fear of one another will grow less in our minds, and then a solution may come. At any rate, even if the solution does not come, this pall of fear that surrounds us will grow less, and that in itself will be a partial solution of the world problem.[1]

The Last Lap of Our Long Journey—November 8, 1948

[Step by step, Nehru continued to help give direction to Indian policy, with respect to major and often complex issues, concerning which decisions had to be made in rapid succession. The following speech, delivered before the Constituent Assembly, relates to the Draft Constitution then under consideration.]

We are on the last lap of our long journey. Nearly two years ago . . . it was my high privilege to move a Resolution which has come to be known as the Objectives Resolution. That is rather a prosaic description of that Resolution, because it embodied something more than mere objectives, although objectives are big things in the life of a nation. It tried to embody, in so far as it is possible in cold print to embody, the spirit that lay behind the Indian people at the time. It is difficult to maintain the spirit of a nation or a people at a high level all the time and I do not know if we have succeeded in doing that. Nevertheless, I hope that it is in that spirit that we [shall] approach the framing of this Constitution and it is in that spirit that we shall consider it in detail, always using that Objectives Resolution as the yard measure with which to test every clause and phrase in this Constitution. It may be, of course, that we can improve even on that Resolution; if so, certainly we should do it, but I think that Resolution in some of its clauses laid down the fundamental and basic content of what our Constitution should be. The Constitution is after all some kind of legal body given to the ways of Governments and the life of a people. A

[1] I.A., pp. 318-24.

Constitution if it is out of touch with the people's life, aims and aspirations, becomes rather empty: if it falls behind those aims, it drags the people down. It should be something ahead to keep people's eyes and minds up to a certain high mark. I think that the Objectives Resolution did that. Inevitably since then in the course of numerous discussions, passions have been roused about what I would beg to say are relatively unimportant matters in this larger context of giving shape to a nations' aspirations and will. Not that they [are] unimportant, because each thing in a nation's life is important, but still there is a question of priority, there is a question of relative importance, there is a question ... of what comes first and what comes second. After all there may be many truths, but it is important to know what is the first truth. It is important to know what in a particular context of events is the first thing to be done, to be thought of and to be put down, and it is the test of a nation and a people to be able to distinguish between the first things and the second things. If we put the second things first, then inevitably the first and the most important things suffer a certain eclipse.

Now, I have ventured with your permission, Sir, to take part in this initial debate on this Draft Constitution, but it is not my intention to deal with any particular part of it, either in commendation of it or in criticism, because a great deal of [this nature] has already been said and will no doubt be said. But in view of that perhaps I could make some useful contribution to this debate by drawing attention to certain fundamental factors again. I had thought that I could do this even more, because in recent days and weeks, I have been beyond the shores of India, have visited foreign lands, met eminent people and statesmen of other countries and had the advantage of looking at this beloved country of ours from a distance. That is some advantage. It is true that those who look from a distance do not see many things that exist in this country. But it is equally true that those who live in this country and are surrounded all the time with our numerous difficulties and problems sometimes fail to see the picture as a whole. We have to do both; to see our problems in their intricate detail in order to understand them and also to see them in some perspective so that we may have that picture as a whole before our eyes.

Now, this is even more important during a period of swift transition such as we have gone through. We who have lived through this period of transition with all its triumphs and glories and sorrows and bitterness, we are affected by all these changes; we are changing ourselves; we do not notice ourselves changing or the country changing so much and it is quite helpful to be out of this turmoil for a while and to look at it from a

14*

distance and to look at it also to some extent with the eyes of other people. I have had that opportunity. I am glad of that opportunity, because for the moment I was rid of the tremendous burden of responsibility which all of us carry and which in a measure some of us who have to shoulder the burden of Government have to carry more. For a moment I was rid of those immediate responsibilities and with a freer mind I could [see from a] distance the rising star of India far above the horizon . . . casting its soothing light, in spite of all that has happened, over many countries of the world. [I could see those] who looked up to [us] with hope, who considered that out of this new Free India would come various forces which would help Asia . . . [and] the world somewhat to right itself, which would co-operate with other similar forces elsewhere. . . . This great continent of Asia [and] Europe and the rest of the world are in a bad way. [We] are faced with problems which might almost appear to be insurmountable. And sometimes one has the feeling that we [are] all actors in some terrible Greek tragedy which [is] moving on to its inevitable climax of disaster. Yet when I looked at this picture again from afar and from here, I had a feeling of hope and optimism not merely because of India, but because also of other things. . . . I saw that the tragedy which seemed inevitable was not necessarily inevitable, that there were many other forces at work, that there were innumerable men and women of goodwill in the world who wanted to avoid . . . disaster and tragedy, and there was certainly a possibility that they would succeed in avoiding it.

But to come back to India, we have, ever since I moved this Objectives Resolution before this House—a year and eleven months ago almost exactly—passed through strange transitions and changes. We function here far more independently than we did at that time. We function as a sovereign independent nation, but we have also gone through a great deal of sorrow and bitter grief during this period and all of us have been powerfully affected by it. The country for which we were going to frame this Constitution was partitioned and split into two. And what happened afterwards is fresh in our minds and will remain fresh with all its horrors for a very long time to come. All that has happened, and yet, in spite of all this, India has grown in strength and in freedom, and undoubtedly this growth of India, this emergence of India as a free country, is one of the significant facts of this generation, significant for us and for the vast numbers of our brothers and sisters who live in this country, significant for Asia, and significant for the world. . . . The world is beginning to realize . . . I am glad to find . . . that India's role in Asia and the world will be a beneficent [one]. Sometimes it may be with a measure of apprehension [that this is felt] because India may play some part which some people, some countries, with other interests may not particularly like. All that is happening, but the main thing is [the] great significant factor that India after being dominated for a long period has emerged as a free sovereign democratic independent country, and that is a fact which changes and is changing history. How far it will change history will depend upon us, this House in the present and other Houses like this [emerging] in the future [that] represent the organized will of the Indian people.

That is a tremendous responsibility. Freedom brings responsibility; of course, there is no such thing as freedom without responsibility. Irresponsibility itself means lack of freedom. Therefore, we have to be conscious of this tremendous burden of responsibility which freedom has brought: the discipline of freedom and the organized way of [using] freedom. But there is something even more than that. The freedom that has come to India by virtue of many things, history, tradition, resources, our geographical position, our great potential and all that, inevitably leads India to play an important part in world affairs. It is not a question of our choosing this or that; it is an inevitable consequence of what India is and what a free India must be. And because we have to play that inevitable part in world affairs, that brings another and greater responsibility. Sometimes, with all my hope and optimism and confidence in my nation, I rather quake at the great responsibilities that are being thrust upon us, and which we cannot escape. If we get tied up in . . . narrow controversies, we may forget this. Whether we forget it or not [the responsibilities are] there. If we forget [them], we fail in that measure. Therefore, I would beg of this House to consider these great responsibilities that have been thrust upon India, and because we represent India in this as in many other spheres, on us in this House.... [We must] work together in the framing of [our] Constitution, always keeping that in view. ... The eyes of the world are upon us. ... We dare not be little; if we [are] we do an ill-service to our country and to [the] hopes and aspirations of other countries that surround us. It is in this way that I would like this House to consider this Constitution: first of all to keep the Objectives Resolution before us and to see how far we are going to [live] up to it, how far we are going to build up, as we said in that Resolution: "an Independent Sovereign Republic, wherein all power and authority of the Sovereign Independent India, its constituent parts and organs of Government, are derived from the people, and wherein shall be guaranteed and secured to all of the people of India justice, social, economic and political; equality of status, of opportunity, and before the law; freedom of thought and expression, belief, faith, worship, vocation, association and action, subject to law and public morality; and this ancient land attain its rightful and honoured place in the world and make its full and willing contribution to the promotion of world peace and the welfare of mankind".

I read that last clause in particular, because that brings to our mind India's duty to the world. I should like this House when it considers the various controversies—there are bound to be controversies and there should be controversies, because we are a living and vital nation, and it is right that people should think differently—to realize that it is also right that, thinking differently when they come to decisions, they should act unitedly in furtherance of those decisions. There are various problems, some very important problems, on which there is very little controversy and we pass them—they are of the greatest importance—with a certain unanimity. There are other problems, important no doubt, possibly of a lesser importance, on which we spend a great deal of time and energy and passion also, and do not arrive at agreements in the spirit with which we should arrive at agreements. In the country today, reference has been made—I will mention one or two matters—to linguistic provinces and to the question of language in this Assembly and for the country. I do not propose to say much about these questions, except to say that it seems to me and it has long seemed to me inevitable that in India some kind of reorganization of the provinces should take place to fit in more with the cultural, geographical and economic condition of the people and with their desires. We have long been committed to this. I do not think it is good enough just to say linguistic provinces; that is a major factor to be considered, no doubt. But there are more important factors to be considered, and you have, therefore, to consider the whole picture before you proceed to break up what we have and refashion it into something new. What I would like to place before the House is that, important from the point of view of our future life and government as this question is, I would not have thought that this was a question of such primary importance that it must be settled here and now today. It is eminently a question which should be settled in an atmosphere of goodwill and calm and by scholarly discussion of the various factors of the case. I find, unfortunately, that it has raised a considerable degree of heat and passion and when heat and passion are there, the mind is clouded. Therefore, I would beg of this House to take these matters into consideration when it thinks fit, and to ... [settle them] not in a hurry when passions are roused, but at a suitable moment when the time is ripe. . . .

The same argument, if I may say so, applies to the question of language.

Now, it is an obvious thing and a vital thing that any country, much more so a free and independent country, must function in its own language. Unfortunately, the mere fact that I am speaking to this House in a foreign language and so many of our colleagues here have to address the House in a foreign language itself shows that something is lacking. It is lacking, let us recognize it; we shall get rid of that lacuna undoubtedly. But, if in trying to press for a change, an immediate change, we get wrapped up in numerous controversies and possibly even delay the whole Constitution, I submit to [you that this] is not a very wise step to take. Language is and has been a vital factor in an individual's and a nation's life and because it is vital, we have to give it every thought and consideration. Because it is vital, it is also an urgent matter; and because it is vital, it is also a matter in which urgency may ill-serve our purpose. There is a slight contradiction. Because, if we proceed in an urgent matter to impose something, maybe by a majority, on an unwilling minority in parts of the country or even in this House, we do not really succeed in what we have started to achieve. Powerful forces are at work in the country which will inevitably lead to the substitution of the English language by an Indian language or Indian languages in so far as the different parts of the country are concerned; but there will always be one all-India language. Powerful forces are also at work in the formation of that all-India language. A language ultimately grows from the people; it is seldom that it can be imposed. Any attempt to impose a particular form of language on an unwilling people has usually met with the strongest opposition and has actually resulted in something the very reverse of what the promoters thought. I would beg this House to consider the fact and to realize, if it agrees with me, that the surest way of developing a natural all-India language is not so much to pass resolutions and laws on the subject, but to work to that end in other ways. For my part I have a certain conception of what an all-India language should be. Other people's conception may not be quite the same as mine. I cannot impose my conception on this House or on the country just as any other person will not be able to impose his or her conception unless the country accepts it. I would much rather avoid trying to impose my or anyone else's conception and instead work [positively] in co-operation and amity and see how, after we have settled [major questions concerning] the Constitution . . . [and] attained an even greater measure of stability, we can take up each separate [question] and dispose of [it] in a much better atmosphere.

The House will remember that when I brought the motion of the Objectives Resolution before this House, I referred to the fact that we

were asking for or rather we were laying down that our Constitution should
be framed for an Independent Sovereign Republic. I stated at that time
and I have stated subsequently that this business of our being a Republic
is entirely a matter for us to determine, of course. It has nothing or little
to do with what relations we should have with other countries, notably
the United Kingdom or the Commonwealth that used to be called the
British Commonwealth of Nations. That [is] a question which [has] to be
determined again by this House and by no one else, independently of what
our Constitution [is] going to be. I want to inform the House that in
recent weeks when I was in the United Kingdom, whenever this subject or
any allied subject came up for private discussion—there was no public
discussion . . . [concerning what relations] we should have . . . with other
countries, inevitably the first thing I had to say . . . was that I could not
as an individual—even though I had been honoured with the high office
of Prime Ministership . . . in any sense commit . . . the Government
which I had the honour to represent. This was essentially a matter which
the Constituent Assembly of India alone could decide. That I made perfectly clear. Having made that clear, I further drew . . . attention to the
Objectives Resolution of the Constituent Assembly. I said it was, of
course, open to the Constituent Assembly to vary that Resolution as it
could vary everything else, because it was sovereign in this and other
matters. That was the direction . . . the Constituent Assembly had
given itself and . . . its Drafting Committee for [the] Constitution . . . [I
added that] as far as I knew . . . [the] Constitution would [reflect] . . .
the Objectives Resolution. Having made that clear . . . I said that it
had often been said on our behalf that we desired to be associated in
friendly relationship with other countries, with the United Kingdom and
the Commonwealth. How, in this context, it can be done, or . . . should
be done is a matter for careful consideration and ultimate decision . . . on
our part by the Constituent Assembly, on [the] part [of others] by their respective Governments or peoples. That is all I wish to say about this matter
at this stage, because in the course of this session this matter no doubt will
come up before the House in more concrete form. But in whatever form it
may come up whether now or later, the point I should like to stress is this,
that [the question] is something apart from and in a sense independent of
the Constitution that we are considering. We [can approve] the Constitution for an Independent Sovereign Democratic India, for a Republic, as we choose, and the second question is to be considered separately at
whatever time it suits this House. It does not in any sense fetter our
Constitution or limit it, because this Constitution coming from the

people of India through their representatives represents their free will with regard to the future government of India.

Now, may I beg again to repeat what I said earlier? Destiny has cast a certain role on this country. Whether anyone of us present here can be called men or women of destiny or not I do not know. That is a big word which does not apply to average human beings, but whether we are men or women of destiny or not, India is a country of destiny and so far as we represent this great country with a great destiny stretching out in front of her, we also have to act as men and women of destiny. . . .

[We can never forget] the great responsibility that freedom, that this great destiny of our country has cast upon us. [We dare not lose] ourselves in petty controversies and debates which might be useful, but which would in this context be either out of place or out of tune. Vast numbers of minds and eyes look in this direction. We have to remember them. Hundreds of millions of our own people look to us and hundreds of millions of others also look to us; and remember this that while we want [our] Constitution to be as solid and as permanent a structure as we can make it, nevertheless, there is no permanence in constitutions. There should be a certain flexibility. If you make a thing rigid and permanent, you stop a nation's growth, the growth of a living, vital, organic people. Therefore, it has to be flexible. So also, when you pass this Constitution you will, and I think it is so proposed, lay down a period of years —whatever that period may be—during which changes [in the] Constitution can easily be made without any difficulty. That is a very necessary proviso for a number of reasons. One is this: that while we, who are assembled in this House, undoubtedly represent the people of India, nevertheless, I think it can be said, and truthfully, that when a new House, by whatever name it goes, is elected in terms of [our] Constitution, and every adult in India has the right to vote—man and woman—the House that emerges . . . will certainly be fully representative of every section of the Indian people. It is right that [a] House so elected . . . should have an easy opportunity to make such changes as it wants [to make]. . . . But in any event, we should not, as some other great countries have, make a Constitution so rigid that it cannot be easily adapted to changing conditions. Today especially, when the world is in turmoil and we are passing through a very swift period of transition, what we do today may not be wholly applicable tomorrow. Therefore, while we make a Constitution which is sound and as basic as we can make it, it should also be flexible and for a period we should be in a position to change it with relative facility.

May I say one word again about certain [factions] in the country which still think in terms of separatist existence or separate privileges and the like?...[The]Objectives Resolution has set [forth]adequate safeguards to be provided for minorities, for tribal areas, depressed and other backward classes. Of course, that must be done, and it is the duty and responsibility of the majority to see that this is done and to see that they win over all minorities which may have suspicions [about] them, [or] may suffer from fear. It is right and important that we should raise the level of the backward groups in India and bring them up to the level of the rest. But it is not right that in trying to do this we create further barriers, or even keep existing barriers, because the ultimate objective is not separatism, but building up an organic nation, not necessarily a uniform nation, because we have a varied culture, and in this country, ways of living differ in various parts of the country, habits differ and cultural traditions differ. I have no grievance against that. Ultimately in the modern world there is a strong tendency for the prevailing culture to influence others. That may be a natural influence. But I think the glory of India has been the way in which it has managed to keep two things going at the same time: that is, its infinite variety and at the same time its unity in that variety. Both have to be kept, because if we have only variety, then that means separatism and going to pieces. If we seek to impose some kind of regimented unity, that makes a living organism rather lifeless. Therefore, while it is our bounden duty to do everything we can to give full opportunity to every minority or group and to raise every backward group or class, I do not think it will be ... right [for this country to do what it has done] in the past by creating barriers and by calling for protection. As a matter of fact, nothing can protect ... a minority ... less than a barrier which separates it from the majority. [Such a barrier creates] a permanently isolated group ... [preventing] it from coming closer to the other groups in the country.

I trust, Sir, that what I have ventured to submit to the House will be borne in mind when [the] various clauses [of the Constitution] are considered and that ultimately we shall pass [our] Constitution in the spirit of the solemn moment when we started this great endeavour.[1]

[1] Ibid., pp. 375–84.

12 | Hyderabad—Kashmir

Hyderabad, September, 1948

[The State of Hyderabad—like Kashmir and Junagadh—had delayed its accession after Independence. Although the Nizam of Hyderabad was a Muslim, the majority of the population was Hindu. At the time of the following speech, negotiations concerning the accession of Hyderabad had been going on for some time.]

["This Question of Hyderabad"—Statement, Constituent Assembly, New Delhi, September 7, 1948.] For over a year now, we have been making earnest attempts to come to a peaceful and satisfactory settlement with the Government of Hyderabad. In November last, our efforts led to a Standstill Agreement for a year. We hoped that this would soon be followed up by a final and satisfactory settlement. In our view, this settlement could only be based on the establishment of responsible government in the State and accession to India. That accession meant, of course, that the State would be an autonomous unit in the Indian Union enjoying the same powers and privileges as other autonomous units. What we offered Hyderabad was, in fact, an honourable partnership in the great brotherhood of the Indian Union.

Popular responsible government in Hyderabad or in any other State or province of India has long been our objective and we are glad to say that it is very near fulfilment all over India, except for the State of Hyderabad. It was inconceivable to us that, in the modern age, and in the heart of India which is pulsating with a new freedom, there should be a territory deprived of this freedom and indefinitely under autocratic rule.

As for accession, it was equally clear to us that a territory like Hyderabad, surrounded on all sides by the Indian Union and with no outlet to the rest of the world, must necessarily be part of that Indian Union. Historically and culturally, it had to be a part, but geographic and economic reasons were even more peremptory in this matter and they could not be ignored, whatever the wishes of particular individuals or groups of individuals. Any other relationship between Hyderabad and the rest of India would have involved continuing suspicion and, therefore, an ever-present fear of conflict. A State does not become independent by merely

declaring itself to be so. Independence connotes certain relationships with
independent States and recognition by them. India could never agree to
Hyderabad having independent relations with any other Power for that
would endanger her own security. Historically, Hyderabad has at no time
been independent. Practically, in the circumstances of today, it cannot be
independent.

Further, in conformity with the principles that we have repeatedly
proclaimed, we were agreeable that the future of Hyderabad should be
determined after a reference to its people, provided that such a reference
was made under free conditions. It cannot possibly be made under the
conditions of terror which prevail in Hyderabad today.

Our repeated attempts at a settlement, which came near to success on
one or two occasions, ended unfortunately in failure. The reasons for this
were obvious to us; there were sinister forces at work in the Hyderabad
State which were determined not to allow any agreement with the Indian
Union. These forces, led by completely irresponsible persons, have progressively gained in strength and now completely control the Government.
The resources of the State were and are being mobilized for war in every
way. The State army has been increased and irregular armies have been
allowed to grow up rapidly. Arms and ammunition were smuggled in from
abroad; this process, in which a number of foreign adventurers have been
taking a prominent part, is continuing. No country, situated as India is,
would have tolerated these warlike preparations by a State in its very
heart. Nevertheless, the present Government of India patiently continued
negotiations in the hope that they would lead to some settlement. The
only other step they took was to prevent, in so far as they could, the flow
of warlike material into Hyderabad.

The private armies that grew up in Hyderabad, notably the Razakars,
have become more and more aggressive and brutal within the State and
sometimes across its borders, in India. . . .

The growing terrorism and frightfulness inside . . . Hyderabad State
against all those, Muslims and non-Muslims, who are opposed to the
Razakars and their allies, both official and non-official, [have] produced
a very grave situation and . . . had . . . repercussions on the bordering areas
of the Union and in India generally. At the present moment, our immediate and most anxious preoccupation is this mounting wave of violence
and anarchy inside the Hyderabad State.

A full account of Razakar activities will take long. I shall mention only
some recent incidents and a few figures. The inhabitants of a village inside the State, which, under the spirited leadership of its headman, had

offered stout resistance to these gangsters, were, when resistance became impossible owing to the exhaustion of ammunition, put to the sword and the village itself burnt. The brave headman was decapitated and his head carried about on a pole. In another village, men, women and children were collected in one spot and shot dead by the Razakars and the Nizam's police.

A large party of villagers, fleeing in bullock carts to some haven of safety in India, was brutally attacked; the men were beaten up and the women abducted.

A train was held up, the passengers looted and a number of coaches burnt. The House is aware of the attacks on our troops seeking to enter our enclaves within Hyderabad State territory and of Razakar incursions into our own villages along the border.

According to reports received yesterday, Razakars and a unit of the regular Hyderabad army with armoured cars went into action against Indian troops on Indian territory. They were repulsed; one armoured car was destroyed and one officer and eighty-five other ranks taken prisoner. The incident further illustrates the mounting aggression against India.

Since this provocative campaign of violence started, according to information which has so far reached us, over seventy villages have been attacked inside the State, about one hundred and fifty incursions have occurred into our territory, hundreds of persons have been killed, a large number injured and many women raped or abducted, twelve trains attacked, property worth over a crore of rupees looted. Hundreds of thousands have fled from the State in order to seek refuge in the neighbouring provinces of India.

The House will agree that no civilized Government can permit such atrocities to continue to be perpetrated with impunity within the geographical heart of India; for this affects not only the security, honour, life and property of the law-abiding inhabitants of Hyderabad, but also the internal peace and order of India. We cannot have a campaign of murder, arson, rape and loot going on in Hyderabad without rousing communal passion in India and jeopardising the peace of the Dominion. Let the House consider what our predecessors in the Government of India would have done in these circumstances. For far less, they would have intervened drastically; the lapse of the Paramountcy of the British Crown cannot alter the organic inter-relation of Hyderabad and the Power whose responsibility for the security of India as a whole is, and should continue to be unquestioned, or the mutual obligations of the one to the other. We have been patient and forbearing in the hope that good sense would prevail and a peaceful solution be found. This hope has proved to be vain and not only is peace inside the State or on its borders nowhere in sight, but peace elsewhere in India is seriously threatened.

We have been criticized for having been too patient and too forbearing. That criticism may have some justification. But we have tried to act on the principle that no effort should be spared at any time to avoid conflict and to secure a settlement by peaceful methods. Except in the last resort, any other course would be a sad contradiction of the ideals and principles to which we have repeatedly pledged ourselves from the beginning to the termination of our struggle for freedom from foreign rule. But we cannot blind ourselves to cruel facts or shirk the hard responsibilities that such facts might impose. At the present moment, let me repeat the issue that compels immediate priority is that of security of life and honour in Hyderabad and the stoppage of the brutal terrorism that persists in that State. Other issues may well be taken up later, for indeed peace and order are essential for the consideration of other questions.

The Hyderabad Government have demonstrated both their unwillingness and their incapacity to put down the terrorism that has made the life of the law-abiding citizens of the State so extremely insecure that large numbers of them are fleeing to the neighbouring provinces and States. We feel that internal security in Hyderabad will not be assured at this stage unless our troops are stationed at Secunderabad as they used to be until India withdrew them early this year. In reply to a recent letter from the Nizam, His Excellency the Governor-General made this suggestion to His Exalted Highness who has replied that no such action is necessary as conditions in Hyderabad are entirely normal. This, of course, is contrary to all known facts and we have now asked the Nizam for the last time to disband the Razakars immediately and, as suggested by His Excellency the Governor-General, to facilitate the return of our troops to Secunderabad, in such strength as may be necessary to restore law and order in ... Hyderabad State. If they are so stationed, there will be a sense of security in the people and the terrorist activities of private armies will cease.

May I add a few more words? First of all, I should like to state to this House and place before this country that we have tried to look upon the question of Hyderabad as far as possible entirely [apart] from the communal point of view and I should like the country to look upon it in this non-communal way. I know, as I have just stated, that communal passions have been roused. But it should be the business of all of us, to whatever religion or community we may belong, to lift this question away from the communal plane and to consider it from other, and, I think more valid and more basic points of view.

We wish to send our troops to Secunderabad to ensure security in Hyderabad, the security of all the people there, whether they are Hindus or Muslims, or they belong to any other religion or group. If subsequently freedom comes to Hyderabad, it must come to all equally and not to a particular group. Therefore, I would like to lay stress on this and I would like those organs of public opinion which can influence the public so much at any time, and more especially during times of stress and strain, always to lay stress on this non-communal aspect. Also, whatever steps we may have to take [by way of police or any other action], our instructions are going to be definite and clear that any kind of communal trouble from any side will be most sternly dealt with.

There has been, as I mentioned to this House, a large migration from Hyderabad of terror-stricken people. I do not know how many have come out, but in the Central Provinces even now there are large camps of tens of thousands—probably several hundred thousand people may have come out in the course of the last two months. Now, if I may give advice—although the giving of this advice means the assumption of a certain responsibility —I would give this advice and take the risk that people should not migrate from Hyderabad or from any part, wherever they may be.

(An Honourable Member: And get butchered!)

Somebody said "get butchered". I can only speak in my own terms. If I were there I would not migrate, whatever happened—butchery or no butchery. I think that when we have to face a serious situation, nothing can be worse than running away from it: and especially in the present instance I see no benefit in regard to [this] matter. Because the person who runs away exposes himself to [the danger he flees] more than a person who sits or stands quietly, normally speaking. Of course I am not considering exceptional cases and some things may happen here and there. But my general point is this, that we may be on the eve of grave happenings in this country, and because of that our Government has paid the greatest and the deepest attention to these matters. We have discussed them, not only amongst ourselves, but with our advisers: we have considered various possible consequences, for every action has to be judged [in terms of its] possible consequences. . . .

We have come to certain conclusions. . . . At any time I would have advised the country to be calm and poised and I refuse to be panicky and refuse to run away from a difficult situation. At this time particularly, I do call upon everybody with all the earnestness that lies in me that we should maintain peace and calm and face any situation that may arise not only in a calm and collected and disciplined way, but also always remembering the fundamental principles and lessons that our Master placed before us.[1]

[On September 13, 1948 a Government of India police action took place in Hyderabad. By September 17 Indian military control was complete. A popularly elected government in Hyderabad came into being at the time of the 1951–52 General Elections.]

[From broadcast on Hyderabad—September 18, 1948.] We have stated clearly that the future of Hyderabad will be determined in accordance with the wishes of her people. We shall stand by that declaration. That future, I am convinced, lies in the closest association with India. Hyderabad's history, geography and cultural traditions bear witness to this fact. . . .

For the present, our military commander will be in charge of Hyderabad, for much work has to be done before normality is restored. He has been charged by us to interfere as little as possible with the normal life of the people of the State, in town and village alike, which must go on as before.

As soon as this immediate task is over, other arrangements will be made, and later we will take steps for the election of a Constituent Assembly, which will determine the constitutional structure of Hyderabad.

I would repeat that we do not consider, as we have not considered in the past, Hyderabad as something different or alien from us. Her people, whether Hindus or Moslems, are our kith and kin and sharers in the great heritage of India. . . .

I am glad His Exalted Highness the Nizam realized that he had acted wrongly and had been misled and that he wisely retraced his steps. Much misery and complication of issues might have been avoided if this right action had been taken a little earlier. . . .

It is natural that we should rejoice at this swift termination of the action we undertook after prolonged and painful thought and much deliberation. As I have repeatedly said, we are men of peace, hating war and the last thing we desire is to come into an armed conflict with anyone. Nevertheless, circumstances which you know well, compelled us to take this action in Hyderabad. Fortunately, it was brief and we return with relief to the paths of peace again.

[1] I.A., pp. 103–08.

We rejoice at the splendid way in which officers and men of our armed forces have carried out this work like true soldiers, with skill, expedition and forbearance, strictly observing all codes of honor. What has pleased me most during these past six days is the splendid response of our people, both Moslems and non-Moslems, to the call of restraint and discipline and the test of unity. It is a remarkable thing, and one which is full of good augury for the future, that not a single communal incident occurred in the whole length and breadth of this great country. I should also like to congratulate the people of Hyderabad, who during these days of trial, kept calm and helped the cause of peace. Many persons warned us of communal trouble that might besmirch our land. But our people have [proved] these prophets [false] and demonstrated that when a crisis comes they can face it with courage, dignity and calm.

Let this be an example and pledge for the future. Henceforth, let there be no talk or hint of communal antagonism. We must bury this false doctrine and the ignoble urges that have given rise to this antagonism and build firmly a United India, for which we labored for so long in the past and in which every Indian, to whatever religion he might belong, has equal rights. . . . I should like, at this moment, to appeal to the people of Pakistan, our countrymen till yesterday, and still as near to us, to cast aside their fear and suspicion and to join us in the works of peace.[1]

Kashmir—September, 1948

["The Story of Kashmir Goes On": Speech, Constituent Assembly (Legislative)—New Delhi, September 7, 1948.] In the early stages [of the Kashmir conflict] towards the end of October and in November [1947] . . . I was so exercised over Kashmir and if anything had happened or was likely to have happened to Kashmir, which, according to me, might have been disastrous for Kashmir, I would have been heart-broken. I was intensely interested, apart from the larger reasons which the Government have, for emotional and personal reasons; I do not want to hide this: I am interested in Kashmir. Nevertheless, I tried to keep down the personal and emotional aspect and consider it from the larger viewpoint of India's good and Kashmir's good. I tried to consider the question from the point of view of not straying or drifting from the high principles which we had proclaimed in the past.

[1] I.T. (Oct. 1948,) pp. 2–3.

When this question first came up, I sought guidance, as I often did in other matters, from Mahatmaji and I went to him repeatedly and put to him my difficulties. The House knows that that apostle of non-violence was not a suitable guide in military matters—and he said so—but he undoubtedly always was a guide on the moral issue. And so I put my difficulties and my Government's difficulties before him; and though it is not proper for me to drag in his name at this juncture in order to lessen my own responsibility or my Government's responsibility on this issue, which is complete, I, nevertheless, mention this matter merely to show how the moral aspect of this question has always troubled me. And more especially when I saw in India all manner of things happening, which had happened in previous months and had brought India's name into disrepute, I was greatly troubled and worried and was anxious that we should keep straight or as straight as we possibly could.

Now, this has been my attitude and on several occasions I had proclaimed it publicly. And apart from rhetoric and vague insinuations, I should like to know from anybody—friend or enemy, from that day in the last week of October, when we took the fateful decision to send our troops by air to Kashmir till today, what it is we have done in Kashmir which from any point of view and from any standard is wrong.

I want an answer to that question. Individuals may have erred here and there; but I say that the Government of India and the Indian army as a whole have done something which was inevitable, and each step that we have taken has been an inevitable step which, if we had not taken it, would have brought disgrace to us. That is how I have ventured to look at this question of Kashmir. And when I find that on the other side the whole case that has been built up on what I venture to say—using strong language—is falsehood and deceit, am I wrong? That is what I ask this House and the country and the world to consider.

Now, therefore, this is the first fact to remember; that all this case built up by Pakistan before the Security Council crumbles by [the] admission of theirs and by the proven fact that large armies of theirs are active in Kashmir, and no doubt similar armies—if you like—and others connected with them have operated in Kashmir on Indian Union territory during these ten months or so. Every subsequent proceeding should be viewed from that aspect.

Now, we come to the present, and I must add one more thing. This has been an aggression; and if it is called—as according to their own admission it must be called—an aggression, then certain consequences ought to follow. Now, my difficulty has been that in considering any question if you lose yourself in a forest of intricate detail sometimes you lose sight of the wood for the trees. There have been long discussions over the Kashmir issue and every aspect and phase and the past and present history have been considered. But what has been the major point? I repeat that ... I think the fundamental factor [has been] the aggression of Pakistan on Indian Union territory; secondly, the denial of the fact of that aggression; thirdly, the present admission of the fact. These are the governing factors of that situation. And the argument has gone on for so long, because these governing factors were slurred over and were not emphasized. We emphasized them, of course, and the problem was discussed in intricate detail.

Now, if you start from a wrong premise in an argument, obviously your whole argument goes wrong and you land yourself in difficulties. If you try to solve a problem without analyzing or stating the nature of the problem, how are you to solve it? And that has been the fundamental difficulty in this Kashmir business: the fundamental issue has been slurred over and by-passed and passed over. Therefore, we have been dealing with other matters which cannot yield a solution. Now, the basic factor is revealed by the very admission of the Pakistan Government.

Now, coming to [the] proposal of the United Nations Commission in India in regard to [a] cease-fire and truce, etc., I shall not discuss it much, because I do not wish at this moment to say anything which might embarrass that Commission. But certain papers are before you. I need hardly say that the proposal they made was not welcomed by us with joy and enthusiasm; there were many matters in it which went against the grain. But we tried to look at the matter as coolly and dispassionately as possible with a view to establishing peace in the harried State of Kashmir, to[avoid] needless suffering and shedding of blood; and we agreed to [the] cease-fire proposal after the Commission had been good enough to elucidate certain points which we had placed before them. We did not place too many points before them but only certain simple obvious points relating to the security of Kashmir. We placed these before them and they were good enough to tell us that that was their meaning. Thereupon we accepted the cease-fire proposal, accepted many things in it which we did not like, because we felt that both in the interest of peace and of international order, it was a good thing for us to go a few steps forward even though some of the steps might be unwilling ones. We did so in order to bring about ... peace and to show that we were prepared to go as far as possible to meet the wishes of an international organization like the United Nations. The original proposal of the United Nations was given to us on the 14th August. The 15th was our Independence Day. Immediately after, on the 16th, we met the members of the Commission and discussed the matter with them to find out exactly what they meant and told them exactly what we meant; and within four days, i.e. on the 20th August we sent them our reply. We did not want to delay matters as they were anxious that they should not be delayed.

The Pakistan Government had also received these proposals at the same time, on the 14th August, at 3 or 4 p.m. They also had the same amount of time. But even after the return of the Commission to Pakistan —and some members of the Commission went in between to Karachi— they were not ready with their reply. And, in fact, it was by the pressure of events or the pressure of the Commission that ultimately they gave some kind of a reply yesterday. Meanwhile, they sent long letters seeking elucidation ... [to my knowledge, thus far, rejecting the] proposals.

Now, the Commission told us that [their] proposals stood as a whole and while they were prepared to discuss any matter gladly it was difficult—in fact, it was not possible for them to accept conditional acceptances, because if we made some conditions and Pakistan naturally made other conditions, what exactly was accepted and by whom? So they said that these proposals were to be accepted as they were, and if there were conditions attached to them, it was not an acceptance but a rejection. Now, therefore, what the Pakistan Government have done is tantamount to rejection. It is for the Commission to decide and to say what they are going to do. It is not for me to advise them. So we arrive at a curious state of affairs, that the country which was the aggressor nation according to its own showing, now even rejects and refuses a proposal for a cease-fire, or puts forward conditions which are tantamount to such a refusal.

Now, certain international consequences should follow from all this. What consequences follow? In a somewhat narrow sphere, all those officers and individuals who are participating in this aggressive war against India in Kashmir territory—there are, of course, Pakistani nationals and others there too—are participating not only in an aggressive war, but in a war after the refusal of a United Nations Commission proposal for a cease-fire. Their position is worthy of consideration.

That is all that I wish to say on the Kashmir issue. Naturally the story of Kashmir goes on. It has been a saga during these ten months or so, and there has been a great deal of suffering and blood and tears involved in it. There have been high moments also. But for us in India, and for the Government of India, it has been a period of trial and difficulty from many points of view; still, at no time have we considered that we were wrong or that we had taken a step which we could not fully justify. It is in that faith that we are going to continue, and may I say that in all these consultations with the United Nations Commission and in other matters affecting Kashmir, we have kept in close touch with the Kashmir Government under Sheikh Abdullah and consulted him in all the steps that we have taken? That was natural and it is inevitable in the circumstances that we should march together in full consultation with each other. Proceeding on that basis, we shall go ahead, whether in the military sphere or in other spheres, and I am quite convinced that, if we adhere to the right course and do not stray from it, even from the opportunist point of view of some present advantage, we shall win through, and any country that bases its case on an essential falsehood cannot gain its ends.[1]

13 | Of the Father of the Nation

[Broadcast from New Delhi on the Anniversary of Mahatma Gandhi's Birthday, October 2, 1948.] Friends and comrades, what shall I say to you on this day which is specially dedicated to the memory of him who we call the Father of the Nation? I shall not speak to you today as Prime Minister of India but as Jawaharlal, a pilgrim like you in India's long journey to freedom and one whose high privilege it was to learn the service of India and of truth at the feet of the Master. Nor will I say much to you about the problems of the day, which fill our minds and demand our continuous attention. Rather I would like to speak about those basic things which Gandhiji taught us and without which life would be superficial and empty.

He taught us the love of truth and straight dealing not only in our individual lives but also in public affairs and in the intercourse of nations. He taught us the dignity of man and of man's labour. He repeated the old lesson that, out of hatred and violence, nothing but hatred and violence and destruction can result. And so he taught us the way of fearlessness, of unity, of tolerance and of peace.

How far have we lived up to this teaching? Not very far, I fear. And yet we learned much under his guidance. We achieved our country's freedom by peaceful methods. But at the very moment of deliverance we

[1] I.A., pp. 95-99.

became forgetful and strayed into evil ways, causing infinite pain to that great heart which throbbed continuously for India and for the great truths that India has embodied through ages past.

What of today? When we remember him and praise him, and sometimes childishly talk of putting up statues to him, do we give thought to the great message for which he lived and died? I fear all of us are still very far from living up to that message. But I do believe that the great forces that he set in motion are working silently but powerfully to move India in the direction of his wishes. There are other forces also, forces of disruption and untruth and violence and narrow-mindedness, which work in the opposite direction. Between the two there is unceasing conflict, as between the forces of good and evil there is conflict all over the world. If we honour the memory of Gandhiji, we must do so actively by working ceaselessly for the causes he represented.

I am proud of my country, proud of my national inheritance, proud of many things, but I speak to you not in pride but with all humility. For events have humbled me and often shamed me and the dream of India that I have had has sometimes grown dim. I have loved India and sought to serve her not because of her geographical magnitude, not even because she was great in the past, but because of my faith in her today and my belief that she will stand for truth and freedom and the higher things of life.

Do you want India to stand for these great aims and ideals which Gandhiji placed before us? If so, then you will have to think and act in accordance with them and not allow yourself to be carried away by the passion of the moment or by thoughts of petty advantage. You will have to root out every tendency that weakens the nation, whether it is communalism, separatism, religious bigotry, provincialism or class arrogance.

We have said repeatedly that we will not tolerate any communalism in this country and that we are building a free secular State, where every religion and belief has full freedom and equal honour, where every citizen has equal liberty and equal opportunity. In spite of this, some people still talk in the language of communalism and separatism. I want to tell you that I am entirely opposed to this and I expect you likewise to oppose it with all your might, if you have faith in Gandhiji's teaching.

Another evil is that of provincialism and of that we see a great deal today running riot and [a] forgetting [of] larger issues. That also has to be opposed and combated.

Some people have recently called India an aggressor nation. I can only say that they spoke in ignorance. If India took to the ways of aggression against any other nation, there would be no place left for me and for many of my colleagues in the Government of India. If we indulged in aggression, we should be false to all that we have stood for and all that Gandhiji taught us.

Our neighbour country, Pakistan, has exhibited a strange fever during the past weeks. I have been astonished to read its newspapers and the public utterances of its leaders, utterances which have no relation to fact but foster wild fears and fantasies. If the people of Pakistan have to read this literature of hatred and fear from day to day, I am not surprised that they should form a picture of India in their minds which is completely divorced from reality. I deeply regret this, for as I have said before, I cannot think of the people of Pakistan as strangers. They have been our countrymen, and neither they nor we can rid ourselves of the past or forget our close kinship, however much momentary passions may seem to divide us. I would like to utter, in all earnestness and friendship, a note of warning to those who are carrying on an unscrupulous propaganda against India in Pakistan. They are doing an ill service to their own country and to their own people.

I can assure the people of Pakistan that India has no aggressive designs against any country, least of all against Pakistan. We want Pakistan to live in peace and to progress and to have the closest ties with us. There never will be aggression from our side.

But there has been aggression of a brutal and unforgivable kind, aggression against the people of Kashmir and against the Indian Union. We met that aggression as any self-respecting country was bound to meet it. Memories are short and it is well to remember what happened a little more than eleven months ago in Kashmir. Pakistan denied its complicity and, even in the face of incontrovertible facts, continued to deny it. It built up its case in the Security Council of the United Nations on this denial and now it has had to admit that its armies are operating in Kashmir which is Indian Union territory. History offers few parallels of a case built up so greatly on a complete denial of truth. The United Nations Commission proposed a truce. We accepted it. Pakistan in its pride and arrogance rejected it.

I want to tell you as well as the people of Pakistan, and now I speak to you as the Prime Minister of India that on no account, and whatever happens, are we going to submit to this aggression. We shall fight it to the utmost, for it involves not only the freedom of Kashmir but also the honour of the Indian people and respect for the law of nations.

Many things have happened in India during the past year or more which have deeply pained me because they were evil and a falling away from the teachings of the Master. But I have no regret for what we did and are doing in Kashmir and Hyderabad. Indeed, if we had not done what we did and are doing in Kashmir and Hyderabad, there would have been infinitely greater trouble and violence and misery. I would have been ashamed of India if she had not run to the rescue of Kashmir, or gone to the aid of the people of Hyderabad who were being crushed by an unscrupulous clique.

Whatever may happen in other countries, let us remain calm and let us try to remain true to Gandhiji's teachings. If we keep faith with him, we shall keep faith with ourselves and with India, and all will be well with this country so dear to us.[1]

[1] I.A., pp. 35-38.

PART TWELVE

1949–1950
To the Founding of the Republic
of India—January 26, 1950

No person engaged in public affairs can understand
the modern world unless he understands the United
States.[1]

*

We ... support the United Nations ... which is
painfully emerging from its infancy. But in order
to have One World, we must also, in Asia, think of
the countries of Asia cooperating together for that
larger ideal.[2]

*

The world is full of strife today and disaster looms
on the horizon. In men's hearts there is hatred and
fear and suspicion which cloud their vision. Every
step, therefore, which leads to a lessening of this
tension in the world, should be a welcome step.[3]

[1] Quoted in M.J.N., p. 470.
[2] Ibid., p. 448.
[3] I.A., p. 266.

I | Eighteen Nations Conference— Emergence of India in World Affairs

[During 1949 Nehru was greatly occupied with details having to do with the founding of the Republic of India, to be formally inaugurated on January 26, 1950. While continuing to resist becoming part of either of the two great power blocs, he announced the decision to convene an Asian Conference on the Indonesian situation in New Delhi, in January, 1949. Referring to the proposed Conference, he asked for what the rival power blocs in the world stood. What, for example, was their reaction to the alleged attempt to destroy the Indonesian Republic? He confessed with sorrow that, in his view, the attitude of certain Powers had been one of tacit approval or acceptance of aggression against Indonesia.

During 1949 the refugee situation in India remained unresolved, as did Indo-Pakistan friction over Kashmir (see Appendix), and various other equally vexing issues. In October, 1949, Nehru made his initial visit to the United States of America and Canada.]

Eighteen Nations Conference on Indonesia

[The Governments of Afghanistan, Australia, Burma, Ceylon, Egypt, Ethiopia, India, Iran, the Lebanon, Pakistan, the Philippines, Saudi Arabia, Syria and Yemen were represented at the Delhi Conference on Indonesia by delegates at the ministerial level, while China, Nepal, New Zealand and Siam sent observers. The following passages are from Nehru's Presidential Address inaugurating the Conference on January 20, 1949.[1]]

I should like to express my deep gratitude to your Governments for having responded at short notice to the urgent invitation that we extended to them. That response itself is witness to the deep feelings that have been aroused all over Asia and in other parts of the world at recent happenings in Indonesia. We meet today, because the freedom of a sister country of ours has been imperilled and the dying colonialism of a past age has

[1] I.F.P., p. 407.

raised its head again and challenged all the forces that are struggling to build up a new structure of the world. That challenge has a deeper significance than might appear on the surface, for it is a challenge to a newly awakened Asia which has so long suffered under various forms of colonialism. It is also a challenge to the spirit of man and to all the progressive forces of a divided and distracted world. The United Nations—symbol of One World that has become the ideal of men of thought and goodwill— has been flouted, and its expressed will set at naught. If this challenge is not met effectively, then indeed the consequences will affect not merely Indonesia but Asia and the entire world. That would represent the triumph of the forces of destruction and disintegration and the certain sequel would be ceaseless conflict and world disorder.

Although we meet to consider a vital problem of immediate importance, my mind is filled with the historic significance of this unique gathering. Here we are, representatives of the free nations of Asia and our friends from Australia and New Zealand as well as Egypt and Ethiopia, met together for the first time to consider a matter of common concern to us. We represent, from Australia, New Zealand and the Philippines on the one side to Egypt and Ethiopia on the other, the vast area embracing half of the circumference of the globe and by far the greater part of its population. We represent the ancient civilizations of the East as well as the dynamic civilization of the West. Politically, we symbolize in particular the spirit of freedom and democracy which is so significant a feature of the new Asia. This long sweep of history passes before my eyes with all its vicissitudes for the countries of Asia, and standing on the edge of the present I look to the future that is gradually unfolding. We are the heirs of these long yesterdays of our history, but we are also the builders of the tomorrow that is shaping itself. The burden of that tomorrow has to be borne by us and we have to prove ourselves worthy of that great responsibility. If this gathering is significant today, it is still more significant in the perspective of tomorrow. Asia, too long submissive and dependent and a plaything of other countries, will no longer brook any interference with her freedom. . . .

The story of Indonesia during the last three years has been a strange and revealing one. It should be remembered that Indonesia was reconquered from the Japanese by the Allied Forces and then handed over to the Dutch. Therefore, a special responsibility attaches to the Allied Nations. Many remarkable things have happened in Indonesia during these past three years . . . [involving] broken pledges and continuous attempts to undermine and break the Republic of Indonesia.

On the 18th December of last year, the Dutch forces launched an offensive, practically without warning, against the Republic while negotiations for a peaceful settlement were still going on. Even the dulled and jaded conscience of the world reacted to this with shock and amazement. The leaders of the Republic were imprisoned and separated from one another and treated with inhumanity. The Security Council of the United Nations passed a series of resolutions asking for the release of the Republican leaders and a cessation of hostilities as an essential preliminary to the resumption of negotiations for a peaceful and honourable settlement. The directions of the Security Council have not yet been carried out and the Dutch authorities seem to be concentrating all their efforts on the formation of a so-called interim Government which they hope will be subservient to their will. Any person who is acquainted with the spirit of the Indonesian people or of Asia today, knows that this attempt to suppress Indonesian nationalism and the deep urge for freedom of the Indonesian people must fail. But if open and unabashed aggression is not checked and is condoned by other Powers, then hope will vanish and people will resort to other ways and other means even though these might involve the utmost catastrophe. One thing is certain: there can be, and will be, no surrender to aggression and no acceptance or reimposition of colonial control.

It was not without deep thought and earnest consideration that we decided to hold this Conference. Believing as we do that the United Nations must be strengthened as a symbol of the New Order, we were reluctant to take any steps which might appear to weaken its authority. But when the will of the Security Council was itself flouted, then it became clear to us that we must confer together to strengthen the United Nations and to prevent further deterioration of a dangerous situation. We meet, therefore, within the framework of the United Nations and with the noble words of the Charter before us. That Charter itself recognizes regional arrangements as a means of furthering international peace and security. Ours is, therefore, a regional conference, to which we invited both Australia and New Zealand, whose interest in the tranquillity and contentment of Indonesia is as great as that of any of us. Our primary purpose is to consider how best we can help the Security Council to bring about a rapid and peaceful solution of the Indonesian problem. We meet to supplement the efforts of the Security Council, not to supplant that body. We meet in no spirit of hostility to any nation or group of nations, but in an endeavour to promote peace through the extension of freedom. It must be realized that both freedom and peace are indivisible. I should like to make it clear that we do not wish to consider this, or any other problem, in a spirit of racialism. Racialism has been, and is even today, the policy of some other countries. We, in Asia, who have suffered so much from it are not going to encourage it, but will combat it, believing as we do that it is not only a negation of democracy, but is also the seed of conflict. Our task will be threefold:

1. To frame and submit to the Security Council proposals which would, if accepted by both parties concerned, restore peace immediately to Indonesia and promote the early realization of freedom by the Indonesian people;
2. Also to suggest to the Security Council what action it should take if either party to the dispute fails to act according to its recommendations;
3. To devise machinery and procedure by which the Governments represented here today can keep in touch with one another for purposes of mutual consultation and concerted action for the achievement of the purposes for which this Conference has met....

It seems . . . clear that our immediate objective should be to restore, as far as possible, the conditions which existed before this recent Dutch aggression, so that the Republic may be able to function freely and to negotiate as a Free Government without military or economic pressure. The next step should be to aim at the elimination of colonialism. It must be appreciated that so long as any form of colonialism exists in Asia or elsewhere, there will be conflict and a threat to peace. The situation in Indonesia is full of dangerous possibilities and requires urgent action. We have to aim, therefore, to complete our work as quickly as possible, so that the Security Council which is still considering this difficult problem should be in possession of our views within the next few days. All of us who meet here have, I believe, [a] community of outlook and our deliberations should bear fruit soon.

We are living in a revolutionary age of transition. On the one hand, we see a divided and disintegrating world, a multitude of conflicts and an ever-present fear of world war. On the other hand, we see creative and co-operative impulses seeking a new integration and a new unity. New problems arise from day to day which, in their implications, concern all of us or many of us. The Americans have already recognized a certain community of interest and have created machinery for the protection and promotion of common interests. A similar movement is in progress in Europe. Is it not natural that the free countries of Asia should begin to think of some more permanent arrangement than this Conference for effective mutual consultation and concerted effort in the pursuit of common aims—not in a spirit of selfishness or hostility to any other nation or group of nations, but in order to strengthen and bring nearer fulfilment the aims and ideals of the Charter of the United Nations? In this world of hatred, conflict and violence, let us endeavour to work jointly and in co-operation with others of goodwill to further the cause of peace and tolerance and freedom. We shall not succeed in our mission if we follow the path of violence or seek to divide the world further, but we may well make a difference to the world if we fashion ourselves in accordance with the old spirit of Asia and hold up the torch of truth and peace to a war-distracted world. May I, in all humility but also with pride, remind this Conference of the message of the Father of our Nation who led us through the long night of our subjection to the dawn of freedom? It was not through hatred or violence or intolerance of each other, he told us, that nations grow in stature or attain their freedom. It was by following his lead in some measure that we attained our independence through peaceful methods. The world has got caught in a vicious circle of fear, hatred and violence. It will never get out of that vicious circle unless it seeks other ways and practises other means. Therefore, let us adhere to the right means with the conviction that right means will inevitably lead to right ends. Thus, we shall help in the process of integration and synthesis which is so urgently needed in the world of today.[1]

Emergence of India in World Affairs: Speech, Constituent Assembly (Legislative), New Delhi, March 8, 1949

I should like to make something in the nature of a general survey not only of foreign affairs, but of India itself. . . .

The Indian Union is an . . . infant free State, a year and a half old, but remember that India is not an infant country. India is a very ancient country with millennia of history behind her—history in which she has played a vital part not only within her own vast boundaries, but in the world and in Asia in particular. India now, in this last year or more, emerges again into the main trend of human affairs. . . .

One of the major questions of the day is the readjustment of the relations between Asia and Europe. When we talk of Asia, remember that India,

[1] B.A.I., pp. 520-24.

not because of any ambition of hers, but because of the force of circumstances, because of geography, because of history and because of so many other things, inevitably has to play a very important part in Asia. And not only that; India becomes a kind of meeting ground for various trends and forces and a meeting ground between what might roughly be called the East and the West.

Look at the map. If you have to consider any question affecting the Middle East, India inevitably comes into the picture. If you have to consider any question concerning South-East Asia, you cannot do so without India. So also with the Far East. While the Middle East may not be directly connected with South-East Asia, both are connected with India. Even if you think in terms of regional organizations in Asia, you have to keep in touch with the other regions. And whatever regions you may have in mind, the importance of India cannot be ignored. . . .

In the past, especially by virtue of her economic and political domination, the West ignored Asia, or at any rate did not give her the weight that was due to her. Asia was really given a back seat and one unfortunate result of it was that even the statesmen did not recognize the changes that were taking place. There is, I believe, a considerable recognition of these changes now, but it is not enough yet. Even in the Councils of the United Nations, the problems of Asia, the outlook of Asia, the approach of Asia have failed to evoke the enthusiasm that they should. There are many ways of distinguishing between what may be called the approach of Asia and the approach of Europe. Asia today is primarily concerned with what may be called the immediate human problems. In each country of Asia—under-developed countries more or less—the main problem is the problem of food, of clothing, of education, of health. We are concerned with these problems. We are not directly concerned with problems of power politics. . . .

Europe, on the other hand, is also concerned with these problems, no doubt, in the devastated regions. Europe has a legacy of conflicts of power, and of problems which come from the possession of power. They have the fear of losing that power and the fear of some one else getting greater power and attacking one country or the other. So that the European approach is a legacy of the past conflicts of Europe.

I do not mean to say that we in Asia are in any way superior, ethically or morally, to the people of Europe. In some ways I imagine we are worse. There is, however, a legacy of conflict in Europe. In Asia, at the present moment at least, there is no such legacy. The countries of Asia may have their quarrels with their neighbours here and there, but there is no basic legacy of conflict such as the countries of Europe possess. That is a very great advantage for Asia and it would be folly in the extreme for the countries of Asia, for India to be dragged in the wake of the conflicts in Europe. We might note that the world progressively tends to become one—one in peace and it is likely to be one, in a sense of war. No man can say that any country can remain apart when there is a major conflagration. But still one can direct one's policy towards avoiding this conflict and being entangled in it.

So the point I wish the House to remember is this: first of all, the emergence of India in world affairs is something of major consequence in world history. We who happen to be in the Government of India or in this House, are men of relatively small stature. But it has been given to us to work at a time when India is growing into a great giant again. So, because of that, in spite of our own smallness, we have to work for great causes and perhaps elevate ourselves in the process.

When India became independent a year and a half ago, we chose the time, or if you like, fate and circumstance chose the time for us, which was one of exceeding difficulty. There were the damages and the consequences of the last great war. And immediately we were independent there were volcanic upheavals in India. It would have been difficult enough for us if there had been complete peace in India to face all the problems that had accumulated during the period of our arrested growth in the past, but added to that came new problems of colossal magnitude. How we faced them the House well knows, and it will be for history to record whether we failed completely or we succeeded or succeeded partially. Anyhow we survived and made good in many ways, apart from mere survival. And gradually we have overcome those problems and gradually we have made of India a single political unit.

And may I point out to this House that the political unit that is India today is, in terms of population, the largest political unit in the world? But population and numbers do not count, it is quality that counts. I would say further that from the point of view of our potential resources and our capacity to use those potential resources, we are also potentially the biggest unit in the world. I say that not in any spirit of vainglory, but let us recognize the huge trust we have in our keeping and let us then think of it in terms of the great burden and the great responsibility. . . .

We, the great majority of the members of this House and vast numbers of people in this country, have spent our lives in what might be called revolutionary activity, in conflict with authority. We are bred in the tradition of revolution and now we sit in the seat of authority and have to deal with difficult problems. That adjustment is not an easy adjustment at any time for anyone. Then again, not only were we revolutionaries and agitators and breakers up of many things, but we were bred in a high tradition under Mahatma Gandhi. . . .

And with that idealism and ethical background we now face practical problems and it becomes an exceedingly difficult thing to apply that particular doctrine to the solution of these problems. That is a conflict which individuals and groups and nations have often had to face. It came to us in very peculiar circumstances and it was intensified by those circumstances and so there has been this travail of the spirit in most of us. We have not often thought enough of Gandhiji and his great doctrine, of his great message, and while we praised it often enough, we felt: "Are we hypocrites, talking about it and being unable to live up to it? Are we deluding ourselves and the world?" Because if we are hypocrites, then surely our future is dark. We may be hypocritical about the small things of life, but it is a dangerous thing to be hypocritical about the great things of life. And it would have been the greatest tragedy if we exploited the name and prestige of our Great Leader, took shelter under it and denied in our hearts, in our activities, the message that he had brought to this country and the world. So we have had these conflicts in our minds and [they] . . . continue. . . . Perhaps there is no final solution of [them] . . . except to try continually to bridge the gulf between the idealism and the practice . . . forced upon us by circumstances. We cannot and I am quite positive that our great leader would not have had us behave as blind automatons just carrying out what he had said without reference to the changes in events. On the other hand, we have to keep in mind those very ideals to which we have pledged ourselves so often.

There is always a great difference between a prophet and a politician in their approach to a problem. We had the combination of a prophet and a great statesman; but then we are not prophets nor are we very great in our statesmanship. All we can say is that we should do our utmost to live up as far as we can to that standard, but always judging a problem by the light of our own intelligence, otherwise we will fail. There is the grave danger, on the one hand, of denying the message of the prophet, and on the other, of blindly following it and missing all its vitality. We have, therefore, to steer a middle course through these. Then a politician or a statesman, or call him what you will, has to deal not only with the truth, but with men's receptivity of that truth, because if there is not sufficient response to it from the politician's or statesman's point of view that truth is banished into the wilderness till minds are ripe for it. And certainly a statesman cannot act and much less can he act in a democratic age unless he can make people believe in that truth. So unfortunately, but inevitably, compromises have to take place from time to time. You cannot do without compromises, but a compromise is a bad compromise if it is opportunist in the sense that it is not always aiming at the truth. It may be a good compromise if it is always looking at that truth and trying to take you there. So in the past year and a half we have faced these difficult problems, and the difficulty has been obvious enough to many, but perhaps no one would have thought of this travail of the spirit under which we suffered all the time. All we can do is to pull ourselves up occasionally, look at our activities and examine them from the high standard which was laid down and try to remain as close to it as possible.

It was a curious thing that we who carried on the struggle for freedom in a non-violent and peaceful way should immediately have had to be confronted with violence of the intensest form, civil violence as well as, what may be called, military violence; that we should have had to undertake a kind of war in a part of the country. The whole thing seemed to be a complete reversal of all that we stood for; and yet circumstances were such that I am quite convinced that we had no other way and that the way we took was the right one. . . .

The broad lines of [our] policy have been laid down:

(a) that India will naturally and inevitably in the course of a few months become an Independent Republic.

(b) that in our external, internal or domestic policy, in our political policy, or in our economic policy, we do not propose to accept anything that involves in the slightest degree dependence on any other authority.

Subject to that, we are prepared to associate ourselves with other countries in a friendly way. We are associated today in the United Nations with a great number of countries in the world. Anything else that we might do will naturally have to be something that does not go against our association with the United Nations. It is only in terms of independent nations co-operating together that we can consider the problem of our association with the Commonwealth. There may be, as some people have suggested, alliances with this or that nation. Alliances usually involve military and other commitments and they are more binding. Other forms of association which do not bind in this manner, but which help in bringing together nations for the purpose of consolidation and, where

15*

necessary, of co-operation, are, therefore, far . . . preferable [to] any form of alliance which [binds]. . . .

Recently there was a conference on Indonesia held at India's instance in New Delhi and many countries from Asia attended it. . . . That conference forcibly brought several matters before the world's eye and at that conference one of the resolutions passed was that we should explore methods of closer co-operation. . . . Whatever structure of co-operation we may build up will be entirely within the scope of the Charter of the United Nations. Secondly, there will be no binding covenant in it, and this will largely be an organization for the consultation and co-operation that naturally flow from common interests.

So our policy will continue to be not only to keep aloof from power alignments, but try to make friendly co-operation possible. Fortunately we enter upon our independence as a country with no hostile background in regard to any country. We are friendly to all countries. Our hostility during the last two hundred years was mainly directed towards the dominating power here and because of India's independence that hostility has largely vanished, though it may survive in some people's minds. So we approach the whole world on a friendly basis and there is no reason why we should put ourselves at a disadvantage, if I may say so, by becoming unfriendly to any group. I think that India has a vital role to play in world affairs.

The various ideologies that confront the world today, the various *isms* which threaten conflict repeatedly may have a great deal, I think, to commend themselves, but all of them have been derived, if I may say so, from the background of Europe. Well, the background of Europe is not something apart from the background of the world and there is much in the background of Europe which is present in India or in other countries. Nevertheless, it is true that the background of Europe is not completely the background of India or the world and there is absolutely no reason why we should be asked to choose between this ideology or the other in toto.

India is a country with a tremendous vitality which it has shown through its history. It has often enough imposed its own cultural pattern on other countries not by force of arms, but by the strength of her vitality, culture and civilization. There is no reason why we should give up our way of doing things, our way of considering things, simply because of some particular ideology which emanates from Europe. I have no doubt at all that we have to learn a great deal from Europe and America and I think that we should keep our eyes and ears completely open. We should be flexible in mind and we should be receptive, but I have also no doubt at all that we should not allow ourselves, if I may use the words of Gandhiji, we must not allow any wind from anywhere to sweep us off our feet.

So we should approach these problems, whether domestic or international problems, in our own way. If by any chance we align ourselves definitely with one power group, we may perhaps from one point of view do some good, but I have not the shadow of a doubt that from a larger point of view, not only of India but of world peace, it will do harm. Because then we lose that tremendous vantage ground that we have of using such influence as we possess (and that influence is going to grow from year to year) in the cause of world peace. What are we interested in world affairs for? We seek no domination over any country. We do not wish to interfere in the affairs of any country, domestic or other. . . .

The supreme question that one has to face today in the world is, how can we avoid a world war? Some people seem to think that it is unavoidable and, therefore, they prepare for it and prepare for it not only in a military sense, but in a psychological sense and thereby actually bring the war nearer. Personally, I think that is a very wrong and a very dangerous thing. Of course, no country dare take things for granted and not prepare for possible contingencies. We in India must be prepared for all possible danger to our freedom and our existence. That is so. But to think in terms of the inevitability of world war is dangerous thinking. I should like this House and the country to appreciate what a world war means, what it is likely to mean. It just does not matter who wins in [a] world war, because it will mean such utter catastrophe that for a generation or more everything that we stand for in the way of progress and advancement of humanity will be put an end to. That is a terrible thing to contemplate and everything should be done to avoid this catastrophe.

I feel that India can play a big part, and maybe an effective part, in helping to avoid war. Therefore, it becomes all the more necessary that India should not be lined up with any group of Powers which for various reasons are full of fear of war and preparing for war. That is the main approach of our foreign policy and I am glad to say that I believe that it is more and more appreciated. . . .

I would beg the House to look upon [our policies] from the wider point of view . . . I have placed before it, that is the emergence of India and Asia in the modern trend of human affairs, the inevitability of India playing an important part by virtue of her tremendous potential, by virtue of the fact that she is the biggest political unit in terms of population today and is likely to be in terms of her resources also. She is going to play that part. . . .[1]

2 | Foreign Policy—India and the Commonwealth

Our Foreign Policy: From Speech, Indian Council of World Affairs, New Delhi, March 22, 1949

I sometimes think that it would be a good thing for the world if all the Foreign Ministers remained silent for some time. I think more trouble is being caused in foreign affairs by the speeches that the Foreign Ministers or their representatives deliver either in their own respective Assemblies or in the United Nations. They talk about open diplomacy and I suppose in theory most of us believe in it. Certainly, I have believed in it for a long time and I cannot say that I have lost that belief entirely. Open diplomacy is good enough, but when that open diplomacy takes the form of very open conflicts and accusations and strong language hurled at one another, then the effect, I suppose, is not to promote peace. It becomes a contest, an open contest in the use of violent language towards one another. Now, it is all very well to talk about foreign policy, but you will appreciate that no person charged with a country's foreign policy can say really very much about it. He can say something general about it; he can sometimes say something very specific about it when occasion arises, but there are many things connected with it which are supposed to lie in what are called top-secret files. In spite of this, they are not frightfully secret, but still they are not to be talked about in public.

Now, foreign policy in the past, I suppose, related chiefly to the relations of a country with its immediate neighbours—whether they were friendly or otherwise. . . .

Our neighbours now are all the countries of the world so that we cannot

[1] I.A., pp. 229–44.

relate our foreign policy just to a few countries around us, but have to think of practically every country in the world and take into consideration all the possible areas of conflict, trade, economic interest, etc. It has been recognized now that if there is a conflict on a big scale anywhere in the world, it is apt to spread all over the world, i.e., that war has become indivisible and, therefore, peace is indivisible. Therefore, our foreign policy cannot limit itself to the nearby countries. Nevertheless, the nearby countries always have a special interest in one another and India must, inevitably, think in terms of its relations with the countries bordering her by land and sea. What are these countries? If you start from the left, Pakistan; I would also include Afghanistan, although it does not touch India's borders; Tibet and China, Nepal, Burma, Malaya, Indonesia and Ceylon. In regard to Pakistan, the position has been a very peculiar one owing to the way Pakistan was formed and India was divided. And there have been not only all the upsets that you all know, but something much deeper, and that is, a complete emotional upset of all the people in India and Pakistan because of this. It is a very difficult thing to deal with, a psychological thing, which cannot be dealt with superficially. A year and a half or more has passed, and there is no doubt at all that our relations have improved and are improving. There is also no doubt at all in my mind that it is inevitable for India and Pakistan to have close relations— very close relations—sometime or other in the future. I cannot state when this will take place, but situated as we are, with all our past, we cannot really be just indifferent neighbours. We can either be rather hostile to each other or very friendly with each other. Ultimately, we can only be really very friendly, whatever period of hostility may intervene in between, because our interests are so closely interlinked. It is an astonishing thing— this partition that has taken place, and although we know a great deal about it, because we have lived through these troubled times, nevertheless, it is interesting to list the things that were upset by it. All our communications were upset and broken. Telegraphs, telephones, postal services, railway services and almost everything as a matter of fact was disrupted. Our Services were broken up. Our army was broken up. Our irrigation systems were broken up and so many other things happened. If we were to go on making a list of all, there would be a large number of them. But above all, what was broken up which was of the highest importance was something very vital and that was the body of India. That produced tremendous consequences . . . in the minds and souls of millions of [persons]. We saw enormous migrations as a result of them, but what was deeper than that was the hurt and injury to the soul of India. We are getting over it, as people get over almost any type of injury, and we are again developing closer relations with Pakistan. There are many problems still to be solved, and I suppose they will gradually be solved.

As far as other countries are concerned, our relations with them are quite friendly. Take for instance, Afghanistan. Our relations with Afghanistan are exceedingly friendly and our relations with Tibet, Nepal and all the neighbouring countries are also very friendly. In fact, I think I am justified in saying that there is no country in this wide world today with which our relations may be said to be inimical or hostile. Naturally we will be attracted more towards some or our trade or economic interests might link us more with some countries and less with others, but there can be no doubt about it that we are friendly with all and I think that is a good thing and some achievement.

If our neighbouring countries have in a sense first place in our minds, then the second place goes to the other countries of Asia with whom we are also fairly intimately connected. Now, India is very curiously placed in Asia and her history has been governed a great deal by the geographical factor plus other factors. Whichever problem in Asia you may take up, somehow or other India comes into the picture. Whether you think in terms of China or the Middle East or South-East Asia, India immediately comes into the picture. It is so situated that because of past history, traditions, etc., in regard to any major problem of a country or a group of countries of Asia, India has to be considered. Whether it is a problem of defence or trade or industry or economic policy, India cannot be ignored. She cannot be ignored, because, as I said, her geographical position is a compelling reason. She cannot be ignored also, because of her actual or potential power and resources. . . .

A very curious thing happened when, roughly speaking, British power came to India and British dominion was established here. This was the reason why we were cut off from our neighbouring countries of Asia. Our contacts were then with England across the seas and while we to some extent struggled against that domination and resented those contacts, nevertheless, they were there and we saw the world more and more through that window—through the British window. Very few people went to the Asian countries from India and very few came here from there. And even those few people from Asia we met, we met in Europe and not in Asia. Now in recent years that process has been reversed or is being reversed for a variety of reasons. . . .

There are many factors that join the countries of Asia together apart from geography. There is the factor that for the last one hundred and fifty to two hundred years Asia has been dominated by Europe, by certain European countries. They came here, exploited this continent, dominated it, and various consequences flowed from this. We are today rather over-whelmed with the recent history of two hundred years of European domination. But if we look at the long process of history, going back more than a few hundred years, we get a truer perspective, and in that perspec-tive, of course, whether you look at Asia, or whether you look at India, the period of foreign domination is a very limited one. And now, the foreign domination of most Asian countries has ended, and it will no doubt end soon, there is a certain process of finding oneself, which each of the Asian countries is going through in various stages of advance according to modern standards; there is this looking into oneself, finding oneself, feeling a certain assurance, self-confidence, fear also it may be in the case of some countries, because of economic and other weaknesses—but on the whole, finding oneself. This is also a certain binding factor.

Then again, the problems of Asia today are essentially problems of supplying what may be called the primary human necessities. They are not problems which may be called problems of power politics. Of course, every country to some extent has something to do with power politics in this world. But whichever countries we may take in Asia, one problem they always have, and that is the problem of preserving their freedom—the fear that somebody might take away their freedom. That problem is always there, quite apart from the fundamental problem, the problem of supplying primary necessities—food, clothing, housing, health, edu-cation and the like. These are common problems all over the world undoubtedly, but a great part of the rest of the world has advanced in its standards much further than the countries of Asia. The countries of the rest of the world have room for still further advance no doubt, and they have suffered ... tremendous losses caused by the last war.... [Since then] Europe has been tied up to a number of very grave problems and conflicts. If I may say so, the past *karma* of Europe pursues it. We cannot easily get rid of the curse of our past *karma*; it pursues our country in various ways. But there is this basic difference, I think, in the European approach to problems and the Asian approach. The whole world wants peace; I have no doubt about it. And if there are any individuals who really want war, they cannot be many, and they cannot be completely balanced in mind. But what does happen is that in the case of people wanting war, a certain obsession, a certain fear, oppresses them, and, therefore, whether they want to or not, they go towards war. This is a terrible thing, this fear complex that we see all over the world today, or nearly all over the world. Europe is full of it at the present moment. Why Europe? Other parts of the world, too. And, of course, Asia has it too, and, I suppose a good deal of it; but compared with Europe, I think, there is much less of it.

Let me put it in another way—the countries which have been the "haves" in the world are very much afraid of losing what they have, while countries not having had so much to lose are not obsessed by that fear so much. Anyhow, there are these different psychological approaches to these various problems.

Now, take the United Nations. The United Nations Organization has most of the nations of the world in it, but it is true that it is dominated more or less by certain great nations of Europe and America, with the result that the main problems discussed there are the problems of Europe and America. Naturally we are interested in those problems, because they affect us too; and if there is war, obviously we are affected. But we cannot possibly get as excited about those problems as the people of Europe and America. For instance, the problem of Indonesia is more important to us than many European problems. Geography, perhaps, is responsible if you like. Whatever the reason may be, the real reason ultimately is not merely geography, but a feeling deep down in our minds that if some kind of colonial domination continues in Indonesia, if it is permitted to continue, it will be a danger to the whole of Asia, it will be a danger to us in India as well as to other countries. Further, if it is allowed to continue there, obviously it can only continue with the passive or active acquiescence of some of the great Powers, the result being that those great powers who may acquiesce in it themselves become in the eyes of Asia partners to that guilt. This is an important point to remember, that it is not merely a political game of chess for us in India; it is, apart from the freedom of Indonesia, a most vital problem affecting the whole of Australia, Asia, and perhaps America. From this point of view, Europe and America are being tested in the eyes of Asia, just as we may be tested in the eyes of Europe and America.

I give you one instance. Now, if I may be quite frank before you, I have no doubt that the countries in Europe and America are themselves very much disturbed and distressed by what is taking place in Indonesia. They want to help Indonesia. I think they realize that Indonesian freedom is not only desirable in itself, but in the larger scheme of things which they have before them it is also desirable, and if by any chance any kind of imperialistic domination succeeds in Indonesia it will affect the larger plans they have for the future. And I realize that the Asian nations as a whole will be very much affected and our action in future may be governed by what happens in Indonesia. Therefore, I have heard that they are very anxious to solve the Indonesian problem satisfactorily and bring about freedom and independence in Indonesia. True, but then there comes the difficulty when you forget or you do not act up to certain definite principles. Any action taken in Indonesia concerns more especially the Indonesian people on the one side and the Netherlands Government on the other. Now, in an entirely different context, some of the Powers of Western Europe and America have, as you well know, arrived at a settlement in which the Netherlands Government is also included— the Atlantic Pact. They were apparently justified in looking after their interests. It is another matter, I am not discussing that. But here a conflict arises in the minds of all these countries. While, on the one hand, they wish to have Indonesian freedom, on the other, they are very anxious to have the Netherlands in their political grouping. Sometimes they do not take up the strict and direct line that they might otherwise take up, because they are pulled in other directions by these very difficulties. . . .

It [makes] a lot of difference what priorities you give to things. It makes all the difference in the world whether you give truth the first place or the second place in life and in politics. . . .

Foreign policy is normally something which develops gradually. Apart from certain theoretical propositions you may lay down, it is a thing which, if it is real, has some relation to actuality and not merely to pure theory. Therefore, you cannot precisely lay down your general outlook or general approach, but gradually it develops. We are as an independent country a fairly young country at present, although we are a very ancient country, and we have all the advantages and disadvantages of being an ancient country. Nevertheless, in the present context of foreign policy we are a young country and, therefore, our foreign policy is gradually developing and there is no particular reason why we should rush in all over the place and do something that comes in the way of this gradual development. We may and we should express our general view as to where we wish to go and how we wish to go there, but laying down our policy precisely in regard to any particular country would probably lead us into some difficulties. As I said, our general policy has been to try to cultivate friendly relations with all countries, but that is something which any one can say. It is not a very helpful thought. It is almost outside, if I may say so, of politics. It may be just a verbal statement or a moral urge. It is hardly a political urge. Nevertheless, something can be said for it even on the political plane. We cannot perhaps be friendly always with every country. The alternative is to become very friendly with some and hostile to others. That is the normal foreign policy of a country—very friendly with close relations with some, with the consequence that you are hostile to others. You may be very friendly to some countries and you cannot just be equally friendly with all countries. Naturally you are more friendly with those with whom you have closer relations, but that great friendliness, if it is active friendliness, is good; if it merely reflects hostility to some other country, then it is something different. And ultimately your hostility provokes other people's hostility and that is the way of conflict and leads to no solution. Fortunately, India has inherited no past hostility to any country. Why should we then start this train of hostility now with any country? Of course, if circumstances compel us it cannot be helped, but it is far better for us to try our utmost to keep clear of these hostile backgrounds. Naturally, again, we are likely to be more friendly to some countries than to others, because this may be to our mutual advantage. That is a different matter, but even so, our friendship with other countries should not, as far as possible, be such as brings us inevitably into conflict with some other country. Now, some people may think that this is a policy of hedging or just avoiding pitfalls, a middle-of-the-road policy. As I conceive it, it is nothing of the kind. It is not a middle-of-the-road policy. It is a positive, constructive policy deliberately aiming at something and deliberately trying to avoid hostility to other countries, to any country as far as possible.

How can we achieve this? Obviously, there are risks and dangers, and the first duty of every country is to protect itself. Protecting oneself unfortunately means relying on the armed forces and the like and so we build up, where necessity arises, our defence apparatus. We cannot take the risk of not doing so, although Mahatma Gandhi would have taken that risk no doubt and I dare not say that he would have been wrong. Indeed, if a country is strong enough to take that risk it will not only survive, but it will become a great country. But we are small folk and dare not take that risk. But in protecting oneself, we should do so in such a way as not to antagonize others and also so as not to appear to aim at the freedom of others. That is important. Also we should avoid in speech or writing anything which worsens the relationship of nations. Now, the urge to do or say things against countries, against their policies and sometimes against their statesmen is very great, because other people are very offensive at times; they are very aggressive at times. If they are aggressive we have to protect ourselves against their aggression. If there is fear of future aggression we have to protect ourselves against that. That I can understand, but there is a distinct difference between that and shouting loudly from the house tops all the time attacking this country or that— even though that country may deserve to be criticized or attacked. It does not help—this shouting business; it only makes matters worse, because this increases tremendously that fear complex to which I referred. And in the shouting that takes place on either side, logic and reason disappear, because people's passions are roused and ultimately they land themselves in war.

If war comes, it comes. It has to be faced. To some extent it has to be provided for and all the consequences of war have to be accepted with it if it comes. But surely we do not want war. As I said some time ago, I take it that the vast majority of people of this world do not want war. Then our policy should primarily aim at avoiding war or preventing war. The prevention of war may include providing for our own defence and you can understand that, but that should not include challenges, counter-challenges, mutual cursings, threats, etc. These certainly will not prevent war, but will only make it come nearer, because they frighten the other Governments and the other Governments issue similar challenges and then you are frightened and so everybody lives in an atmosphere of fear and anything may come out of such an atmosphere of fear. . . .

Can any country, can India succeed in preventing this kind of mutual recrimination? Can we succeed, as we want to, in dealing with every question on its merits? Today international questions are looked upon from the point of view of how they will affect some future conflict, with the result that you find groupings on either side forgetful of the actual merits of the case. And a country like India which talks in a different language is looked upon as a nuisance in every way; unfortunately, not only as a nuisance, but every group suspects it of joining hands with the opposite group. But now, I think, there is a certain amount of realization by other countries that we really mean what we say. . . .

May I say that I do not for an instant claim any superior vantage point for India to advise or criticize the rest of the world? I think we are merely trying not to get excited about these problems and anyhow there is no reason why we should not try. It follows, therefore, that we should not align ourselves with what are called power blocs. We can be of far more service without doing so and I think there is just a possibility—and I shall not put it higher than that—that at a moment of crisis our peaceful and friendly efforts might make a difference and avert that crisis. If so, it is well worth trying. When I say that we should not align ourselves with any power blocs, obviously it does not mean that we should not be closer in our relations with some countries than with others. That depends on entirely different factors, chiefly economic, political, agricultural and many other factors. At the present moment you will see that as a matter of fact we have far closer relations with some countries of the western world than with others. It is partly due to history and partly due to other factors, present-day factors of various kinds. These close relations will no doubt develop and we will encourage them to develop, but we do not wish to place ourselves in a position where, politically speaking, we are just lined up with a particular group or bound up to it in regard to our future foreign activities. India is too big a country herself to be bound down to any country, however big it may be. India is going to be and is bound to be a country that counts in world affairs, not I hope in the military sense, but in many other senses which are more important and effective in the end. Any attempt on our part, i.e., the Government of the day here, to go too far in one direction would create difficulties in our own country. It would be resented and we would produce conflicts in our own country which would not be helpful to us or to any other country. While remaining quite apart from power blocs, we are in a far better position to cast our weight at the right moment in favour of peace, and meanwhile our relations can become as close as possible in the economic or other domain with such countries with whom we can easily develop them. So it is not a question of our remaining isolated or cut off from the rest of the world. We do not wish to be isolated. We wish to have the closest contacts, because we do from the beginning firmly believe in the world coming closer together and ultimately realizing the ideal of what is now being called One World. . . . India, we are convinced, can help in that process far more by taking an individual stand and acting according to her own wishes whenever any crisis arises than by merging herself with others and getting tied up in hard and fast rules. . . .

But what has happened today? We find that there has developed a fatalistic tendency to think in terms of war. It is rather difficult to say anything with certainty, yet the prospect of war is so bad and the consequences of war are going to be so bad, that, regardless of the result of war, I wish every human being to try his utmost to avoid war as far as possible. We do not want war anywhere. We want at least ten or fifteen years of peace in order to be able to develop our resources. If there is war anywhere in the world, then what happens to the rest of the world? You can imagine starvation for millions following the war.

So if we strive earnestly for peace and try to take advantage of the fact that the very grave crisis of the past autumn has toned down and might tone down still further, I think we can well increase the chances of peace. As far as we are concerned, we ought to try to do that. Now, there are other conflicts—whether it is in Berlin or in other places in Europe. Apart from these, there are two other issues in the world which, unless satisfactorily solved, may well lead to conflict and a conflict on a big scale. One is the issue typified by Indonesia, that is the issue of domination of one country over another. Where there is continued domination, whether it is in Asia or Africa, there will be no peace either there or in the people's minds elsewhere. There will be a continuous conflict going on, continuous suspicion of each other and continuous suspicion of Europe in the minds of Asia and, therefore, the friendly relationship which should exist between Asia and Europe will not come about easily. It is, therefore, important that all these areas of colonial domination should be freed and they should be able to function as free countries.

The second important factor is that of racial equality. That too, in some parts of the world, you know, has come very much to the forefront. For example, take the question of Indians in South Africa. It is a matter which concerns us all. It is not merely a question of Indians or South Africans, but it is a matter of vital significance to the world, because that too symbolises something in the world. If that is to continue in the world, then there is bound to be conflict and conflict on a big scale, because it is a continuous challenge to the self-respect of a vast number of people in the world and they will not put up with it. The matter is thus before the United Nations and I hope the United Nations will help in its solution. But quite apart from the United Nations, there can be not a shadow of doubt that if such a policy is continued, it will breed conflict. And that conflict will not be confined to particular areas in South Africa or elsewhere; it will affect peoples in vast continents.

I am not touching upon the third matter, the basic matter, that is, economic policies,—it is too big a subject—except that I would like to say this in regard to it, that the only way to proceed in the world today as far as I can see is for each country to realize that it must not interfere with another country's economic policy. Ultimately the policies that deliver the goods will succeed, those that do not will not succeed. This policy of interfering aggressively with other countries' policies inevitably leads to trouble. We must realize that there are different types of economic policy in the world today, in different countries, and they are believed in by their people. Well, the only thing to do is to leave them to work out their destiny. It may be that one of them justifies this policy, another

justifies another. It may be that a third follows a middle course. Whatever
it may be, the future will show. Whatever that may be, the point is that
we must proceed on the basis of leaving every country to shift for itself
in regard to its internal affairs. Any effort to change the economic policy,
or any other internal policy, forcibly, or to bring pressure to bear upon it,
leads to counter-pressure and to continuous conflict. . . .

We are striving for One World, and what with the development of
communications and everything, we come closer to one another. We know
a great deal more about one another than we used to do. Nevertheless, I
have a feeling that our knowledge of one another is often extraordinarily
superficial, and we, living in our grooves, big or small, seem to imagine,
each country seems to imagine, that we are more or less the centre of the
world, and the rest is on the fringe, that our way of living is the right way
of living and other people's way of living is either a bad way or a mad way,
or just some kind of backward way. Now, I suppose it is a common
human failing to imagine that we are right and others are wrong. But, of
course, apart from being right or wrong, it may be, both are right, and
both are wrong; anyhow, in so far as the people's manner of living is
concerned, there may be differences, not only as between Europe,
America, Asia and Africa, but also internally in some of the continents.
Now, Europe and America, because they have been dominant countries,
with a dominant culture, have tended to think that ways of living other
than theirs are necessarily inferior. Whether they are inferior or not I do
not know. If they are inferior, probably their own people will change them.
But this method of approach of one country to another is a very limited
approach and does not indicate much wisdom, because this world is a
very varied place. Even in India, our whole culture testifies to our understanding of the variety of humanity—laying stress always on the unity,
but also on the variety, the diversity. The world is a very diverse place,
and I personally see no reason why we should regiment it along one line.
And yet there is this attitude in people's minds to some extent, to regiment
it and shape it after one particular pattern. Perhaps it may be due to the
whole philosophy of life behind us in India. Whatever we may do in our
limited outlook and failings, we have had a type of philosophy which is a
live-and-let-live philosophy of life. We have no particular desire to convert other people to any view or thought. We are prepared to talk it out
with everybody and convince him, and it is for him to accept it or not,
and we are quite happy if he goes his own way. We are not at all happy if
he interferes with our way. Other philosophies apparently are to compel
a man to think and act according to their own ways, and that leads to

conflict, apart from the fact that it is not probably, psychologically speaking, a right approach.

So if we recognize that this world is a diverse place and there are diverse ways of living and functioning and thinking in it, then let us try to get rid of the evil in the world and allow the variety of the world to continue. There are forces strong enough to unify it today, and probably it will come together, and the diversity will probably grow less. It would be unfortunate if it were to disappear one day and we were to become one regimented whole; it is a terrible thought. If it so happens, well, those who live then will face the problems of the day. Most of us will not be alive then. I suppose if we approach it in this way, there will be far greater understanding between countries. . . .

With all our failings, we are a very ancient people, and we have gone through thousands and thousands of years of human experience; we have seen much wisdom, and we have seen much folly, and we bear the traces of both that wisdom and that folly around us. We have to learn much, and we shall learn much; and perhaps we have to unlearn a great deal too. . . .

I wish all of us would give up the idea of improving others, and improve ourselves instead.[1]

India and the Commonwealth

["A Fateful and Historic Decision"—Broadcast, New Delhi, May 10, 1949, on the occasion of India's decision to continue as a member in the Commonwealth.] Three days ago I returned to Delhi after attending the meeting of the Commonwealth Prime Ministers in London. It is right that I should report to you about this meeting which resulted in a fateful and historic decision. That decision will have to be placed before the Constituent Assembly for their approval. It will also be considered by the All India Congress Committee which has been the torch-bearer of India's freedom these many years. It is for these great and representative organizations to give the final verdict on what was done by me and others in London last month.

You have already read the declaration[2] embodying the conclusions

---

[1] I.A., pp. 245–61.

[2] The Declaration *in re* the Commonwealth Decision: "The Governments of the United Kingdom, Canada, Australia, New Zealand, South Africa, India, Pakistan and Ceylon, whose countries are united as Members of the British Commonwealth of Nations and

reached by the London meeting. The impression that I have gathered since my return is that the vast majority of our people has welcomed the decision, though there are some who have criticized in strong language what I did and have even called it "a great blunder," and "an outrage on the national sentiments of the Indian people." During a fairly long career in India's service I have often been accused of errors and mistakes, but I have never yet been charged with doing anything which was against the honour and self-respect of India or her people. It is a serious matter, therefore, if even a few persons, whose opinions I value, should consider that I have committed an outrage.

I want to tell you that I have not the least doubt in my mind that I have adhered in letter and spirit to every pledge that I, in common with millions of my countrymen, have taken in regard to the independence of India during the past twenty years and more. I am convinced that far from injuring the honour or interest of India, the action I took in London has kept that honour bright and shining and enhanced her position in the world.

Though the critics are few, I would rather address myself to them than to the much larger number of my people who have already expressed their approval. I can only imagine that these critics are labouring under some misapprehension, or are under the impression that something else has been done in secret which has not seen the light of day. I wish to say that nothing has been done in secret and that no commitments of any kind limiting our sovereignty or our internal or external policy have been

---

owe a common allegiance to the Crown, which is also the symbol of their free association, have considered the impending constitutional changes in India.

"The Government of India have informed the other Governments of the Commonwealth of the intention of the Indian people that under the new constitution which is about to be adopted, India shall become a sovereign independent Republic. The Government of India have however declared and affirmed India's desire to continue her full membership of the Commonwealth of Nations and her acceptance of the King as the symbol of the free association of its independent member nations and as such as the Head of the Commonwealth.

"The Governments of the other countries of the Commonwealth, the basis of whose membership of the Commonwealth is not hereby changed, accept and recognise India's continuing membership in accordance with the terms of this Declaration.

"Accordingly the United Kingdom, Canada, Australia, New Zealand, South Africa, India, Pakistan and Ceylon hereby declare that they remain united as free and equal members of the Commonwealth of Nations, freely co-operating in the pursuit of peace, liberty and progress." (From C.A.D. Official Report, May 16, 1949, (Vol. VIII), p. 2, footnote. For Nehru's 1948 decision *in re* the Commonwealth, see Part Eleven.)

made, whether in the political or economic or military spheres. Our foreign policy has often been declared by me to be one of working for peace and friendship with all countries and of avoiding alignments with power blocs. That remains the keystone of our policy still. We stand for the freedom of suppressed nationalities and for the ending of racial discrimination. I am convinced that the Sovereign Indian Republic, freely associating herself with the other countries of the Commonwealth, will be completely free to follow this policy, perhaps in an even greater measure and with greater influence than before.

We took a pledge long ago to achieve Purna Swaraj (complete independence). We have achieved it. Does a nation lose its independence by an alliance with another country? Alliances normally mean mutual commitments. The free association of sovereign Commonwealth nations does not involve such commitments. Its very strength lies in its flexibility and its complete freedom. It is well-known that it is open to any member nation to go out of the Commonwealth if it so chooses.

It must be remembered that the Commonwealth is not a super State in any sense of the term. We have agreed to consider the King as the symbolic head of this free association. But the King has no function attached to that status in the Commonwealth. As far as the Constitution of India is concerned, the King has no place and we shall owe no allegiance to him.

I have naturally looked to the interests of India, for that is my first duty. I have always conceived that duty in terms of the larger good of the world. That is the lesson that our Master taught us and he told us also to pursue the ways of peace and of friendship with others, always maintaining the freedom and dignity of India. The world is full of strife today and disaster looms on the horizon. In men's hearts there is hatred and fear and suspicion which cloud their vision. Every step, therefore, which leads to a lessening of this tension in the world, should be a welcome step. I think it is a good augury for the future that the old conflict between India and England should be resolved in [a] friendly way which is honourable to both countries. There are too many disruptive forces in the world for us to throw our weight in in favour of further disruption and any opportunity that offers itself to heal old wounds and to further the cause of co-operation should be welcomed.

I know that much is being done in parts of the Commonwealth which is exceedingly distasteful to us and against which we have struggled in the past. That is a matter to be dealt with by us as a sovereign nation. Let us not mix things up which should be kept separate.

It has been India's privilege in the past to be a meeting place for many cultures. It may be her privilege in the present and the future to be a bridge to join warring factions and to help in maintaining that most urgent thing of today and the future—the peace of the world. It is in the belief that India could more effectively pursue this policy of encouraging peace and freedom and of lessening the bitter hatreds and tensions in the world, that I willingly agreed to the London agreement. I associated myself with the decisions taken in London at the Prime Ministers' meeting in the full belief that they were the right decisions for our country and for the world. I trust that the Indian people will also view them in that light and accept them in a manner worthy of the stature and culture of India and with full faith in our future. Let us not waste our energy at this critical moment in the world's history over empty debates, but rather let us concentrate on the urgent tasks of today, so that India may be great and strong and in a position to play a beneficent part in Asia and the world.[1]

["This New Type of Association"—Moving of Resolution for ratification of Commonwealth decision—Constituent Assembly, New Delhi, May 16, 1949.] I have the honour to move the following motion:

"Resolved that this Assembly do hereby ratify the declaration, agreed to by the Prime Minister of India, on the continued membership of India in the Commonwealth of Nations, as set out in the official statement issued at the conclusion of the Conference of the Commonwealth Prime Ministers in London on April 27, 1949."

I shall . . . point out very briefly some salient features of this declaration. It is a short and simple document in four paragraphs. The first paragraph, it will be noticed, deals with the present position in law. It refers to the British Commonwealth of Nations and to the fact that the people in this Commonwealth owe a common allegiance to the Crown. That in law is the present position.

The next paragraph of this declaration states that the Government of India have informed the Governments of the other Commonwealth countries that India is soon going to be a sovereign independent Republic further that they desire to continue her full membership of the Commonwealth of Nations, accepting the King as a symbol of the free association.

The third paragraph says that the other Commonwealth countrie accept this and the fourth paragraph ends by saying that all these coun tries remain united as free and equal members of the Commonwealth o

[1] Ibid., pp. 265-67.

Nations. You will notice that while in the first paragraph this is referred to as the British Commonwealth of Nations, in the subsequent paragraph it is referred to only as the Commonwealth of Nations. Further you will notice that while in the first paragraph there is the question of allegiance to the Crown which exists at present, later, of course, this question does not arise, because India by becoming a Republic goes outside the Crown area completely. There is a reference, in connection with the Commonwealth, to the King as the symbol of that association. Observe that the reference is to the King and not to the Crown. It is a small matter, but it has a certain significance. But the point is this that in so far as the Republic of India is concerned, her Constitution and her working are concerned, she has nothing to do with any external authority, with any king, and none of her subjects owe any allegiance to the King or any other external authority. The Republic may however agree to associate itself with certain other countries that happen to be monarchies or whatever they choose to be. This declaration, therefore, states that this new Republic of India, completely sovereign and owing no allegiance to the King, as the other Commonwealth countries do owe, will, nevertheless, be a full member of this Commonwealth and it agrees that the King will be recognized as a symbol of this free partnership or rather association.

Now, I am placing this declaration before this Honourable House for their approval. Beyond this approval, there is no question of any law being framed in accordance with it. There is no law behind the Commonwealth. It has not even the formality which normally accompanies treaties. It is an agreement by free will, to be terminated by free will. Therefore, there will be no further legislation or law if this House approves of this. In this particular declaration nothing very much is said about the position of the King, except that he will be a symbol. It has been made perfectly clear—it was made perfectly clear—that the King has no functions at all. He has a certain status. The Commonwealth itself, as such, is not a body, if I may say so; it has no organization through which to function and the King also can have no functions.

Now, some consequences flow from this. Apart from certain friendly approaches to one another, apart from a desire to co-operate, which will always be conditioned by each party deciding on the measure of co-operation and following its own policy, there is no obligation. There is hardly any obligation in the nature of commitments. But an attempt has been made to produce something which is entirely novel, and I can very well understand lawyers on the one hand feeling somewhat uncomfortable at a thing for which they can find no precedent or parallel. There may also be others who feel that behind this there may be something which they cannot quite understand, something risky, something dangerous, because the thing is so simple on the face of it. That kind of difficulty may arise in people's minds. What I have stated elsewhere I should like to repeat. There is absolutely nothing behind this except what is placed before this House.

One or two matters I might clear up which are not mentioned in this declaration. One of these, as I have said, is that the King has no functions at all. This was cleared up in the course of our proceedings; it has no doubt been recorded in the minutes of the Conference in London. Another point was that one of the objects of this kind of Commonwealth association is now to create a status which is something between being completely foreign and being of one nationality. Obviously, the Commonwealth countries belong to different nations. They are different nationalities. Normally either you have a common nationality or you are foreign. There is no intermediate stage. Up till now in this Commonwealth or the British Commonwealth of Nations, there was a binding link which was allegiance to the King. With that link, therefore, in a sense there was common nationality in a broad way. That snaps, that ends when we become a Republic, and if we should desire to give a certain preference or a certain privilege to any one of these countries, we would normally be precluded from doing so, because of what is called the "most favoured nation clause" every country would be as much foreign as any other country. Now, we want to take away that foreignness, keeping in our own hands what, if any, privileges or preferences we can give to another country. That is a matter entirely for two countries to decide by treaty or arrangement, so that we create a new state of affairs—or we try to create it—that the other countries, although in a sense foreign, are, nevertheless, not completely foreign. I do not quite know how we shall proceed to deal with this matter at a later stage. That is for the House to decide—that is to say, to take the right, only the right, to deal with Commonwealth countries, should we so choose, in regard to certain preferences or privileges. What they are to be, of course, we shall in each case be the judge ourselves. Apart from these facts, nothing has been decided in secret or otherwise which has not been put before the public.

The House will remember that there was some talk at one stage of a Commonwealth citizenship. Now, it was difficult to understand what the status of Commonwealth citizenship might be except that it meant that its members were not completely foreign to one another. That unforeignness remains, but I think it is as well that we left off talking about something vague, which could not be surely defined, but the other fact remains, as I have just stated: the fact that we should take the right to ourselves if we so chose to exercise it at any time to enter into treaties or arrangements with Commonwealth countries assuring us of certain mutual privileges and preferences.

I have briefly placed before this House this document. It is a simple document and yet the House is fully aware that it is a highly important document or rather what it contains is of great and historical significance. I went to this Conference some weeks ago as the representative of India. I had consulted my colleagues here, of course, previously, because it was a great responsibility and no man is big enough to shoulder that responsibility by himself when the future of India is at stake. For many months past we had often consulted one another, consulted great and representative organizations, consulted many members of this House. Nevertheless, when I went, I carried this great responsibility and I felt the burden of it. I had able colleagues to advise me, but I was the sole representative of India and in a sense the future of India for the moment was in my keeping. I was alone in that sense and yet not quite alone, because, as I travelled through the air and as I sat there at the Conference table, the ghosts of many yesterdays of my life surrounded me and brought up picture after picture before me, sentinels and guardians keeping watch over me, telling me perhaps not to trip and not to forget them. I remembered, as many Honourable Members might remember, that day nineteen years ago when we took a pledge . . . at the midnight hour, and I remembered the 26th January the first time and that oft-repeated pledge year after year in spite of difficulty and obstruction, and finally I remembered that day when standing at this very place, I placed a resolution before this House. That was one of the earliest resolutions placed before this Honourable House, a resolution that is known as the Objectives Resolution. Two years and five months have elapsed since that happened. In that Resolution we defined more or less the type of free Government or Republic that we were going to have. Later in another place and on a famous occasion, this subject also came up, that was at the Jaipur session of the Congress, because not only my mind, but many minds were struggling with this problem, trying to find a way out that was in keeping with the honour and dignity and independence of India, and yet also in keeping with the changing world and with the facts as they were. Something that would advance the cause of India, would help us, something that would advance the cause of peace in the world, and yet something which would be strictly and absolutely true to every single pledge that we had taken.

It was clear to me that whatever the advantages might be of any association with the Commonwealth or with any other group, no single advantage, however great, could be purchased by giving up a single iota of our pledges, because no country can make progress by playing fast and loose with the principles which it has declared. So during these months we had thought and we had discussed amongst ourselves and I carried all this advice with me. May I read to you, perhaps, just to refresh your minds, the Resolution passed at the Jaipur session of the Congress? It might be of interest to you and I would beg of you to consider the very wording of this Resolution:

"In view of the attainment of complete independence and the establishment of the Republic of India which will symbolize Independence and give to India the status among the nations of the world that is her rightful due, her present association with the United Kingdom and the Commonwealth of Nations will necessarily have to change. India, however, desires to maintain all such links with other countries as do not come in the way of her freedom of action and independence and the Congress would welcome her free association with the independent nations of the Commonwealth for their commonweal and the promotion of world peace."

You will observe that the last few lines of this Resolution are almost identical with the lines of the declaration of London.

I went there guided and controlled by all our past pledges, ultimately guided and controlled by the Resolution of this Honourable House, by the Objectives Resolution and all that had happened subsequently; also by the mandate given to me by the All India Congress Committee in that Resolution, and I stand before you to say with all humility that I have fulfilled the mandate to the letter. All of us have during these many years past been through the valley of the shadow; we have passed our lives in opposition, in struggle and sometimes in failure and sometimes success and most of us are haunted by these dreams and visions of old days and those hopes that filled us and the frustrations that often followed those hopes; yet we have seen that even from that prickly thorn of frustration and despair, we have been able to pick the rose of fulfilment.

Let us not be led away by considering the situation in terms of events which are no longer here. You will see that the Resolution of the Congress that I have read out says that because India becomes a Republic, the association of India with the Commonwealth must, of course, change. Further it says that free association may continue subject only to our complete freedom being assured. Now, that is exactly what has been tried to be done in this declaration of London. I ask you or any Honourable

Member to point out in what way the freedom, the independence of India has been limited in the slightest. I do not think it has been. In fact, the greatest stress has been laid not only on the independence of India, but on the independence of each individual nation in the Commonwealth.

I am often asked, how we can join a Commonwealth in which there is racial discrimination, in which there are other things happening to which we object. That, I think, is a fair question and it is a matter which must necessarily give us some trouble in our thinking. Nevertheless, it is a question which does not really arise. That is to say, when we have entered into an alliance with a nation or a group of nations, it does not mean that we accept their other policies; it does not mean that we commit ourselves in any way to something that they may do. In fact, this House knows that we are carrying on at the present moment a struggle, or our countrymen are carrying on a struggle in regard to racial discrimination in various parts of the world.

This House knows that in the last few years one of the major questions before the United Nations, at the instance of India, has been the position of Indians in South Africa. May I, if the House will permit me, for a moment refer to an event which took place yesterday, that is, the passing of the Resolution at the General Assembly of the United Nations, and express my appreciation and my Government's appreciation of the way our delegation has functioned in this matter and our appreciation of all those nations of the United Nations, almost all, in fact all barring South Africa, which finally supported the attitude of India? One of the pillars of our foreign policy, repeatedly stated, is to fight against racial discrimination, to fight for the freedom of suppressed nationalities. Are you compromising on that issue by remaining in the Commonwealth? We have been fighting on the South African Indian issue and on the other issues even though we have thus far been a Dominion of the Commonwealth. It was a dangerous thing for us to bring that matter within the purview of the Commonwealth. Because then the very thing to which you and I object might have taken place. That is, the Commonwealth might have been considered as some kind of a superior body which sometimes acts as a tribunal, or judges, or in a sense supervises the activities of its member nations. That certainly would have meant a diminution in our independence and sovereignty, if we had once accepted that principle. Therefore, we were not prepared and we are not prepared to treat the Commonwealth as such or even to bring disputes between member nations of the Commonwealth before the Commonwealth body. We may, of course, in a friendly way discuss the matter; that is a different matter.

We are anxious to maintain the position of our countrymen in other countries in the Commonwealth. As far as we are concerned, we could not bring their domestic policies in dispute there; nor can we say in regard to any country that we are not going to associate ourselves with that country because we disapprove of certain policies of that country.

I am afraid that if we adopted that attitude, then there would hardly be any association for us with any country, because we have disapproved of something or other that that country does. Sometimes, it so happens that the difference is so great that either you cut off relations with that country or there is a conflict. Some years ago, the United Nations General Assembly decided to recommend its member States to withdraw diplomatic representatives from Spain, because Spain was supposed to be a Fascist country. I am not going into the merits of the question. Sometimes, the question comes up in that way. The question has come up again and they have reversed that decision and left it to each member State to do as it likes. If you proceed in this way, take any great country or a small country; you do not agree with everything that the Soviet Union does; therefore, why should we have representation there or why should we have a treaty of alliance in regard to commercial or trade matters with it? You may not agree with some policies of the United States of America; therefore, you cannot have a treaty with them. That is not the way nations carry on their foreign work or any work. The first thing to realize, I think, in this world is that there are different ways of thinking, different ways of living and different approaches to life in different parts of the world. Most of our troubles arise from one country imposing its will and its way of living on other countries. It is true that no country can live in isolation, because, the world as constituted today is progressively becoming an organic whole. If one country living in isolation does something which is dangerous to the other countries, the other countries have to intervene. To give a rather obvious example, if one country allowed itself to become the breeding ground of all kinds of dangerous diseases, the world would have to come in and clear it up, because it could not afford to allow disease to spread all over the world. The only safe principle to follow is that, subject to certain limitations, each country should be allowed to live its own life in its own way.

There are at present several ideologies in the world and major conflicts flow from these ideologies. What is right or what is wrong, we can consider at a later stage, or maybe something else altogether is right. Either you want a major conflict, a great war which might result in the victory for this nation or that, or else you must allow them to live a peace in their respective territories and to carry on their way of thinking, their way of living, their structure of State, allowing the facts to prove which is right ultimately. I have no doubt at all that ultimately it will be the system that delivers the goods—the goods being the advancement and the betterment of the human race or the people of the individual countries—that will survive and no amount of theorizing and no amount of warfare can make the system that does not deliver the goods survive. I refer to this because of the argument that was raised that India could not join the Commonwealth, because it disapproved of certain policies of certain Commonwealth nations. I think we should keep these two matters completely separate.

We join the Commonwealth, obviously because we think it is beneficial to us and to certain causes in the world that we wish to advance. The other countries of the Commonwealth want us to remain, because they think it is beneficial to them. It is mutually understood that it is to the advantage of the nations in the Commonwealth and therefore they join. At the same time, it is made perfectly clear that each country is completely free to go its own way; it may be that they may go, sometimes go so far as to break away from the Commonwealth. In the world today where there are so many disruptive forces at work, where we are often on the verge of war, I think it is not a safe thing to encourage the breaking up of any association that one has. Break up the evil part of it; break up anything that may come in the way of your growth, because nobody dare agree to anything which comes in the way of a nation's growth. Otherwise, apart from breaking the evil parts of the association, it is better to keep a co-operative association going which may do good in this world rather than break it.

Now, this declaration that is placed before you is not a new move and yet it is a complete reorientation of something that has existed in an entirely different way. Suppose we had been cut off from England completely and we had then desired to join the Commonwealth of Nations, it would have been a new move. Suppose a new group of nations wanted us to join them and we joined them in this way, that would have been a new move from which various consequences would have flowed. In the present instance, what is happening is that a certain association has been in existence for a considerable time past. A very great change came in the way of that association about a year and eight or nine months ago, from August 15, 1947. Now another major change is contemplated. Gradually the conception is changing. Yet that certain link remains in a different form. Now, politically we are completely independent. Economically we

16+N. II

are as independent as independent nations can be. Nobody can be 100% independent in the sense of absolute lack of inter-dependence. Nevertheless, India has to depend on the rest of the world for her trade, for her commerce and for many supplies that she needs, today for her food unfortunately, and so many other things. We cannot be absolutely cut off from the world. Now, the House knows that inevitably during the past century and more all kinds of contacts have arisen between England and this country, many of them were bad, very bad, and we have struggled throughout our lives to put an end to them. Many of them were not so bad, many of them may be good and many of them, good or bad, irrespective of what they may be, are there. Here I am the patent example of these contacts, speaking in this Honourable House in the English language. No doubt we are going to change that language for our use, but the fact remains that I am doing so and the fact remains that most other members who will speak will also do so. The fact remains that we are functioning here under certain rules and regulations for which the model has been the British Constitution. Those laws which exist today have been largely forged by them. Gradually, the laws which are good we will keep and those that are bad we will throw away. Any marked change in this without something to follow creates a hiatus which may be harmful. Largely our educational apparatus has been influenced. Largely our military apparatus has been influenced by these considerations and we have grown up naturally as something rather like the British Army. I am placing before the House certain entirely practical considerations. If we break away completely, the result is that without making sufficient provision for carrying on in a different way, we have a period of gap. Of course, if we have to pay a price, we may choose to do so. If we do not want to pay the price, we should not pay it and face the consequences.

But in the present instance, we have to consider not only these minor gains, which I have mentioned to you, to us and to others but, if I may say so, the larger approach to world problems. I felt as I was conferring there in London with the representatives of other Governments that I had necessarily to stick completely and absolutely to the sovereignty and independence of the Indian Republic. I could not possibly compromise on the question of allegiance to any foreign authority. I also felt that in the state of the world today and in the state of India and Asia, it would be a good thing if we approached this question in a friendly spirit which would solve the problems in Asia and elsewhere. I am afraid I am a bad bargainer. I am not used to the ways of the market place. I hope I am a good fighter and I hope I am a good friend. I am not anything in between and so when you have to bargain hard for anything, do not send me. When you want to fight, I hope I shall fight and then when you are decided about a certain thing, then you must hold on to it and hold to it to the death, but about minor things I think it is far better to gain the goodwill of the other party. It is far more precious to come to a decision in friendship and goodwill than to gain a word here and there at the cost of ill will. So I approached this problem and may I say how I felt about others? I would like to pay a tribute to the Prime Minister of the United Kingdom and also to others there, because they also approached the problem in this spirit, not so much to score a debating point or to change a word here and there in this declaration. It was possible that if I had tried my hardest I might have got a word here and there changed in this declaration, but the essence could not have been changed, because there was nothing more for us to get out of that declaration. I preferred not to do so, because I preferred creating an impression and I hope the right impression that the approach of India to these and other problems of the world was not a narrow-minded approach. It was the approach based on faith and confidence in her own strength and in her own future and, therefore, it was not afraid of any country coming in the way of that faith, it was not afraid of any word or phrase in any document, but it was based essentially on this: that if you approach another country in a friendly way, with goodwill and generosity, you would be paid back in the same coin and probably the payment would be in an even larger measure. I am quite convinced that in the treatment of nations to one another, as in the case of individuals, only out of goodwill will you get goodwill and no amount of intrigues and cleverness will get you good results out of evil ways. Therefore, I thought that this was an occasion not only to impress England, but others also, in fact to some extent the world, because the matter that was being discussed at 10 Downing Street, in London, was something that drew the attention of the entire world. It drew the attention of the world, partly because India is a very important country, potentially so, and actually so too. And the world was interested to see how this very complicated and difficult problem which appeared insoluble, could be solved. It could not be solved if we had left it to eminent lawyers. Lawyers have their uses in life; but they should not be spread out everywhere. It could not have been solved by those extreme, narrow-minded nationalists who cannot see to the right or to the left, but live in a narrow sphere of their own, and, therefore, forget that the world is going ahead. It could not be solved by people who live in the past and cannot realize that the present is different from the past and that the future is going to be still more different. It could not be solved by any person who lacked faith in India and in India's destiny.

I wanted the world to see that India did not lack faith in herself, and that India was prepared to co-operate even with those with whom she had been fighting in the past; provided the basis of co-operation today was honourable, that it was a free basis, a basis which would lead to the good not only of ourselves, but of the world also. That is to say, we would not deny that co-operation, simply because in the past we had fought, and thus carry on the trail of our past *karma* along with us. We have to wash out the past with all its evil. I wanted, if I may say so in all humility, to help in letting the world look at things in a slightly different perspective, or rather try to see how vital questions could be approached and dealt with. We have seen too often in the arguments that go on in the assemblies of the world, this bitter approach, this cursing of each other, this desire, not in the least to understand the other, but deliberately to misunderstand the other, and to make clever points. Now, it may be a satisfying performance for some of us, on occasions to make clever points and be applauded by our people or by some other people. But in the state of the world today, it is a poor thing for any responsible person to do, when we live on the verge of catastrophic wars, when national passions are roused, and when even a casually spoken word might make all the difference.

Some people have thought that by our joining or continuing to remain in the Commonwealth of Nations we are drifting away from our neighbours in Asia, or that it has become more difficult for us to co-operate with other countries, great countries in the world. But I think it is easier for us to develop closer relations with other countries while we are in the Commonwealth than it might have been otherwise. This is rather a peculiar thing to say. Nevertheless, I say it, and I have given a great deal of thought to this matter. The Commonwealth does not come in the way of our co-operation and friendship with other countries. Ultimately we shall have to decide, and ultimately the decision will depend on our own strength. If we dissociate ourselves completely from the Commonwealth, then for the moment we are completely isolated. We cannot remain completely isolated, and so inevitably by stress of circumstances, we have to incline in some direction or other. But that inclination in some direction or other will necessarily be a basis of give-and-take. It may be in the nature of alliances, you give something yourself and get something in return. In other words, it may involve commitments far more than at present. There are no commitments today. In that sense, I say we are freer today to come to friendly understandings with other countries and to play the part, if you like, of a bridge for the mutual understanding of other countries. I do not wish to place this too high; nevertheless, it is no good placing it too low either. I should like you to look round the world today and look, more especially during the last two years or so, at the relative position of India and the rest of the world. I think you will find that during this period of two years or less, India has gone up in the scale of nations in its influence and in its prestige. It is a little difficult for me to tell you exactly what India has done or has not done. It would be absurd for anyone to expect that India can become the crusader for all causes in the world and bring forth results. Even in cases that have borne fruit, it is not a thing to be proclaimed from the housetops. But something which does not require any proclamation is the fact of India's prestige and influence in world affairs. Considering that she came on the scene as an independent nation only a year and a half or a little more ago, it is astonishing—the part that India has played.

One more thing I should like to say. Obviously a declaration of this type, or the Resolution that I have placed before the House is not capable of amendment. It is either accepted or rejected. I am surprised to see that some Honourable Members have sent in notice of amendments. Any treaty with any foreign power can be accepted or rejected. It is a joint declaration of eight—or is it nine countries?—and it cannot be amended in this House or in any House. It can be accepted or rejected. I would, therefore, beg of you to consider this business in all its aspects. First of all make sure that it is in conformity with our old pledges, that it does violence to none. If it is proved to me that it does violence to any pledge that we have undertaken, that it limits India's freedom in any way, then I certainly shall be no party to it. Secondly, you should see whether it does good to us and to the rest of the world. I think there can be little doubt that it does us good, that this continuing association at the present moment is beneficial for us, and it is beneficial in the larger sense, to certain world causes that we represent. And lastly, if I may put it in a negative way, not to have had this agreement would certainly have been detrimental to those world causes as well as to ourselves.

And finally, about the value I should like this House to attach to this declaration and to the whole business of those talks resulting in this declaration. It is a method, a desirable method, and a method which brings a touch of healing with it. In this world which is today sick and which has not recovered from so many wounds inflicted during the last decade or more, it is necessary that we touch upon the world problems, not with passion and prejudice and with too much repetition of what has ceased to be, but in a friendly way and with a touch of healing, and I think the chief value of this declaration and of what preceded it was that it did bring a touch of healing in our relations with certain countries.

We are in no way subordinate to them, and they are in no way subordinate to us. We shall go our way and they will go their way. But our way, unless something happens, will be a friendly way; at any rate, attempts will be made to understand one another, to be friends with one another and to co-operate with one another. And the fact that we have begun this new type of association with a touch of healing will be good for us, good for them, and I think, good for the world.[1]

[It is sometimes argued that since Commonwealth membership finally was accepted by India, after Dominion Status had for so long been rejected, earlier approval would have assured preservation of a united India, without resulting in any corresponding loss. To make such a claim is to ignore the basis on which India's freedom finally was attained, and the precise nature of the Commonwealth membership accepted. Moreover, the importance of having the freedom to make up one's own mind about an issue, after years of colonial oppression, cannot be underestimated.]

3 | Independence Day, 1949

[Delhi, August 15, 1949.] Thirty years ago there appeared on the Indian scene a mighty man of destiny who lighted our path. That light illumined our minds and hearts and large numbers of our people, forgetting their own troubles and domestic difficulties, their property and family, responded to his call. It was not for personal gain of any kind. Among these there existed a friendly competition as to who could serve the motherland better and more effectively. Our consuming obsession was the liberation of our country.

The star of a free India beckoned us forward. We dreamed of freedom from poverty and distress. We gained our political freedom at last but the other freedom still remains for us to achieve. Before we could do much to achieve it, new problems came in our way. Sixty lakhs of people

[1] I.A., pp. 268-81.

migrated to India as refugees. We faced this problem as we had faced others. I suppose we made some mistakes but no one reviewing these two years will fail to appreciate our forward march in the face of all kinds of difficulties.

Unarmed and peaceful, we faced a proud empire, not looking for aid to any other country and relying only on ourselves. We had faith in our leader, our country and in ourselves. This gave us the strength that sustained us during our struggle for independence. If we had faith and self-confidence when to outward seeming we were powerless, then surely we are much better off today when we are a free people with the strength of a great country behind us. Why then should our faith and our confidence in ourselves weaken? It is true that we have tremendous economic and other difficulties to face; it is also true that while we have rehabilitated lakhs of refugees, large numbers still remain to be helped and rehabilitated. But we have faced even bigger problems in the past. Why should we not face these in the same way also? We must not let our minds get entangled in petty questions and difficulties and forget the main issues.

We belong to a great country, a country that is not only great physically but in things far more important. If we are to be worthy of our country, we must have big minds and big hearts, for small men cannot face big issues or accomplish big tasks. Let each one of us do his duty to his country and to his people and not dwell too much on the duty of others. Some people get into the habit of criticizing others without doing anything for themselves. Nothing good can come of that type of criticism. So, wherever you may be, whether you are in the Army or the Air Force or the Navy or in the civil employ of the Government, each one of you must do your duty efficiently and in a spirit of service to the nation. If the vast number of our countrymen apply themselves to their tasks in their innumerable capacities and co-operate with others, forgetting the petty things that divide them, we shall marvel at the speed with which India will progress.

I want you to think for a moment of the days when we fought the battle of India's freedom without arms and without much by way of resources. We had a great leader who inspired us. We had other leaders too, but it was the masses of this country who bore the brunt of the struggle. They had faith in their country and their leaders and they relied upon themselves. Today, we have more strength than we ever had. It is, therefore, surprising that some people should feel dejected, have no confidence in themselves and complain all the time.

Let us get back the purposefulness, the enthusiasm, the self-confidence and the faith which moved us at the time of our struggle for freedom. Let us put aside our petty quarrels and factions and think only of the great objective before us.

In our foreign policy, we have proclaimed that we shall join no power bloc and endeavour to co-operate and be friendly with all countries. Our position in the world ultimately depends on the unity and strength of the country, on how far we proceed in the solution of our economic and other problems and on how much we can raise the depressed masses of India. We may not be able to complete that task, for it is colossal. Even so, if we make some headway it will be easier for others to complete the task.

A nation's work never ends. Men may come and go, generations may pass but the life of a nation goes on. We must remember the basic fact that we can achieve little unless there is peace in the country, no matter what policy we pursue. There are some misguided people who indulge in violence and try to create disorder. I wonder how anybody with the least intelligence can think in terms of such anti-national activities. Bomb throwing, for instance, can do the country no good. On the contrary, it further aggravates our economic situation, which is a source of great anxiety to us. Therefore, it is the duty of everyone, no matter what his politics, to help in the maintenance of peace in the country.

The people have every right to change laws and even to change governments and they can exercise that right in a peaceful and democratic manner. But those who choose the path of violence have no faith in democracy. If their way were to prevail, there would be complete chaos in the country and the condition of the people would deteriorate even more. All progress would cease and the next few generations would have to carry a heavy burden.

I am still more distressed by those who, while condemning violence, join hands with those who indulge in violence. They think only in terms of winning an election and forget that the cause of the country and of the people is bigger than any party. If we forget India and her people while pursuing our smaller objectives, then we are indeed guilty of betraying our country. I wish to emphasize that all of us must understand that our most important objective is the safety and security of India and the prosperity and advancement of her people. That can only be achieved effectively if we stop quarrelling amongst ourselves and try to solve the great problems that confront us by democratic and peaceful methods.

We must look at our problems in a proper perspective. If we are preoccupied with petty problems, we shall fail to solve the larger and more important ones.

We must learn to depend on ourselves and not look to others for help every time we are in trouble. Certainly we want to make friends with the rest of the world. We also seek the goodwill and co-operation of all those who reside in this country, whatever their race or nationality. We welcome help and co-operation from every quarter but we must depend primarily on our own resources. We should not forget that those who lean too much on others tend to become weak and helpless themselves. A country's freedom can be preserved only by her own strength and self-reliance.

We are not hostile to any country and we do not want to meddle in other people's affairs. Every nation should be free to choose the path it considers best. We do not wish to interfere with the freedom of other nations and we expect them to feel the same about our freedom. That is why we have decided not to join any of the power blocs in the world. We will remain aloof and try to be friendly to all. We intend to progress according to our own ideas. We have decided to follow this policy, not only because it is essentially a sound one from our country's point of view but also because it seems to be the only way to serve the cause of world peace. Another world war will spell ruin and we shall not escape the general disaster. We are determined to make every possible effort in the cause of peace. That explains our present foreign policy. . . .

Each country should have the freedom to go the way it chooses. It is for its people to decide their future. Any attempt at outside interference or compulsion must necessarily lead to evil results. No country can impose freedom on any other. That is a contradiction in terms. The world has a great deal of variety and it should be no one's business to suppress this variety or to impose ways of thinking and acting on others. We should, therefore, survey world events in a spirit of understanding and friendship to all.

Our Constituent Assembly is busy framing a new constitution for India and soon we shall adopt a republican form of government. However, laws and constitution do not by themselves make a country great. It is the enthusiasm, energy and constant effort of a people that make it a great nation. Men of Law lay down constitutions but history is really made by great minds, large hearts and stout arms; by the sweat, tears and toil of a people.

Let us, therefore, learn to study our country's problems in the larger perspective of the world and let us not permit the minor questions of the day to overwhelm us. I have faith in India and her great destiny. A country must have military strength but armed power does not by itself constitute a country's real strength. Her real strength lies in the capacity
16*

of her people for disciplined work. Only hard work can produce wealth for us and rid us of our poverty. Each one of us, man or woman, young or old, must, therefore, toil and work. Rest is not for us. We did not win our freedom so that we might rest afterwards but in order to work harder to hold and strengthen that freedom. There is a great difference between the voluntary labour of a free man for an objective of his choice and the drudgery of a slave. Our labours as free men and women will lay the foundations for a great future and our labour of love for the cause of India and her people will endure; so will the fact that we are building, brick by brick, the great mansion of free India. There is joy in such work and even when we have departed that work will be there for future generations to see.[1]

[In August, 1949 Nehru became head of India's newly formed Atomic Energy Commission.]

4 | First Visit to United States of America

[Nehru made his first visit to the U.S.A. in October, 1949. He stopped in Cairo en route, to hold conferences with the Egyptian Prime Minister and King Farouk. While in the U.S., Nehru received an overwhelmingly warm reception throughout the country.]

["Voyage of Discovery"—From speech, House of Representatives and the Senate, Washington D.C., October 13, 1949.] I have come to this country to learn something of your great achievements. I have come also to convey the greetings of my people and in the hope that my visit may help to create a greater understanding between our respective peoples and those strong and sometimes invisible links, stronger even than physical links, that bind countries together.... [Your] President [Truman] referred the day before yesterday, in language of significance, to my visit as a voyage of discovery of America. The United States of America is not an unknown country even in far-off India and many of us have grown

[1] N.S., pp. 3-8.

up in admiration of the ideals and objectives which have made this country great. Yet, though we may know the history and something of the culture of our respective countries, what is required is a true under-standing and appreciation of each other even where we differ. Out of that understanding grows fruitful co-operation in the pursuit of common ideals. I have come here, therefore, on a voyage of discovery of the mind and heart of America and to place before you our own mind and heart. Already I have received a welcome here, the generous warmth of which has created a deep impression on my mind and, indeed, somewhat over-whelmed me.

During the last two days that I have been in Washington, I have paid visits to the memorials of the great builders of this nation. I have done so not for the sake of mere formality but because they have long been en-shrined in my heart and their example has inspired me as it has inspired innumerable countrymen of mine. These memorials are the real temples to which each generation must pay tribute and, in doing so, must catch something of the fire that burned in the hearts of those who were the torchbearers of freedom, not only for this country but for the world; for those who are truly great have a message that cannot be confined within a particular country but is for all the world.

In India, there came a man in our own generation who inspired us to great endeavour, even reminding us that thought and action should never be divorced from moral principle, that the true path of man is the path of truth and peace. Under his guidance, we laboured for the freedom of our country with ill will to none and achieved that freedom. We called him reverently and affectionately the Father of our Nation. Yet he was too great for the circumscribed borders of any one country and the message he gave may well help us in considering the wider problems of the world.

The United States of America has struggled to freedom and unparalleled prosperity during the past century and a half and today it is a great and powerful nation. It has an amazing record of growth in material well-being and scientific and technological advance. It could not have accom-plished this unless America had been anchored in the great principles laid down in the early days of its history, for material progress cannot go far or last long unless it has its foundations in moral principles and high ideals.

Those principles and ideals are enshrined in your Declaration of Independence, which lays down as a self-evident truth that all men are created equal, that they are endowed by their Creator with certain inalienable rights, that among these are life, liberty and the pursuit of happiness. It may interest you to know that, in drafting the Constitution of the Republic of India, we have been greatly influenced by your own Constitution. The preamble of our Constitution states:

We, the people of India, having solemnly resolved to constitute India into a Sovereign Democratic Republic and to secure to all its citizens:

Justice, social, economic and political;

Liberty of thought, expression, belief, faith and worship;

Equality of status and of opportunity, and to promote among them all Fraternity assuring the dignity of the individual and the unity of the Nation;

In our Constituent Assembly do hereby adopt, enact and give to ourselves this Constitution.

You will recognize in these words that I have quoted an echo of the great voices of the founders of your Republic. You will see that though India may speak to you in a voice that you may not immediately recognize or that may perhaps appear somewhat alien to you, yet that voice somewhat strongly resembles what you have often heard before.

Yet, it is true that India's voice is somewhat different; it is not the voice of the old world of Europe but of the older world of Asia. It is the voice of an ancient civilization, distinctive, vital, which at the same time has renewed itself and learned much from you and the other countries of the West. It is, therefore, both old and new. It has its roots deep in the past but it also has the dynamic urge of today.

But however the voices of India and the United States may appear to differ, there is much in common between them. Like you, we have achieved our freedom through a revolution, though our methods were different from yours. Like you we shall be a republic based on the federal principle, which is an outstanding contribution of the founders of this great Republic. We have placed in the forefront of our Constitution those fundamental human rights to which all men who love liberty, equality and progress aspire—the freedom of the individual, the equality of men and the rule of law. We enter, therefore, the community of free nations with the roots of democracy deeply embedded in our institutions as well as in the thoughts of our people.

We have achieved political freedom but our revolution is not yet complete and is still in progress, for political freedom without the assurance of the right to live and to pursue happiness, which economic progress alone can bring, can never satisfy a people. Therefore, our immediate task is to raise the living standards of our people, to remove all that comes in the way of the economic growth of the nation.

We realize that self-help is the first condition of success for a nation, no less than for an individual. We are conscious that ours must be the primary effort and we shall seek succour from none to escape from any part of our own responsibility. But though our economic potential is great, its conversion into finished wealth will need much mechanical and technological aid. We shall, therefore, gladly welcome such aid and co-operation on terms that are of mutual benefit. We believe that this may well help in the solution of the larger problems that confront the world. But we do not seek any material advantage in exchange for any part of our hard-won freedom.

The objectives of our foreign policy are the preservation of world peace and enlargement of human freedom. India may be new to world politics and her military strength insignificant in comparison with that of the giants of our epoch. But India is old in thought and experience and has travelled through trackless centuries in the adventure of life. Throughout her long history she has stood for peace and every prayer that an Indian raises, ends with an invocation to peace. It was out of this ancient and yet young India that Mahatma Gandhi arose and he taught us a technique of peaceful action. It was effective, and yielded results that led us not only to freedom but to friendship with those with whom we were, till yester-day, in conflict.

This is the basis and the goal of our foreign policy. We are neither blind to reality nor do we propose to acquiesce in any challenge to man's free-dom from whatever quarter it may come. Where freedom is menaced or justice threatened or where aggression takes palce, we cannot be and shall not be neutral. What we plead for and endeavour to practise in our own imperfect way is a binding faith in peace and an unfailing endeavour of thought and action to ensure it. The great democracy of the United States of America will, I feel sure, understand and appreciate our approach to life's problems because it could not have any other aim or a different ideal. Friendship and co-operation between our two countries are, therefore, natural. I stand here to offer both in the pursuit of justice, liberty and peace.[1]

[Address, Columbia University, New York, October 17, 1949, on being given Honorary Degree of Doctor of Laws.] If we seek to ensure peace, we must attack the root causes of war and not merely the symptoms. What are the underlying causes of war in the modern world?

[1] I.F.P., pp. 589-92.

One of the basic causes is the domination of one country by another or an attempt to dominate. Large parts of Asia were ruled till recently by foreign and chiefly European powers. We ourselves were part of the British Empire, as were also Pakistan, Ceylon, and Burma. France, Holland, Portugal still have territories over which they rule. But the rising tide of nationalism and the love of independence have submerged most of the Western Empires in Asia. In Indonesia I hope that there will soon be an independent sovereign state. We hope also that French Indo-China will achieve freedom and peace before long under a government of its own choice. Much of Africa, however, is subject to foreign powers, some of whom still attempt to enlarge their dominions. It is clear that all remaining vestiges of imperialism and colonialism will have to disappear.

Secondly, there is the problem of racial relations. The progress of some races in knowledge or in invention, their success in war and conquest, has tempted them to believe that they are racially superior and has led them to treat other nations with contempt. A recent example of this was the horrible attempt, so largely successful, to exterminate the Jews. In Asia and Africa, racial superiority has been most widely and most insolently exhibited. It is forgotten that nearly all the great religions of mankind arose in the East and that wonderful civilizations grew up there when Europe and America were still unknown to history. The West has too often despised the Asian and the African and still, in many places, denies them not only equality of rights but even common humanity and kindliness. This is one of the great danger points of our modern world; and, now that Asia and Africa are shaking off their torpor and arousing themselves, out of this evil may come a conflagration of which no man can see the range of consequences. One of your greatest men said that this country cannot exist half slave and half free. The world cannot long maintain peace if half of it is enslaved and despised. The problem is not always simple nor can it be solved by a resolution or a decree, but unless there is a firm and sincere determination to solve it, there will be no peace.

The third reason for war and revolution is the misery and want of millions of persons in many countries and, in particular, in Asia and Africa. In the West, though the war has brought much misery and many difficulties, the common man generally lives in some measure of comfort—he has food, clothes, shelter to some extent. The basic problem of the East, therefore, is to obtain these necessaries of life. If they are lacking, then there is the apathy of despair or the destructive rage of the revolutionary. Political subjection, racial inequality, economic inequality and misery—these are the evils that we have to remove if we would ensure peace. If we can offer no remedy, then other cries and slogans make an appeal to the minds of the people.

Many of the countries of Asia have entered the family of nations; others we hope will soon find a place in this circle. We have the same hopes for the countries of Africa. This process should proceed rapidly, and America and Europe should use their great influence and power to facilitate it. We see before us vast changes taking place not only in the political and economic spheres, but even more so in the minds of men. Asia is becoming dynamic again and is passionately eager to progress and raise the economic standards of her vast masses. This awakening of a giant continent is of the greatest importance to the future of mankind and requires imaginative statesmanship of a high order. The problems of this awakening will not be solved by looking at it with fear or in a spirit of isolationism by any of us. It requires a friendly and understanding approach, clear objectives, and a common effort to realize them. The colossal expenditure of energy and resource on armaments that is an outstanding feature of many national budgets today does not solve the problem of world peace. Perhaps even a fraction of that outlay, in other ways and for other purposes, will provide a more enduring basis for peace and happiness.

That is India's view, offered in all friendliness to all thinking men and women, to all persons of good will, in the name of our common humanity. That view is not based on wishful thinking, but on a deep consideration of the problems that afflict us all.[1]

[Speech, Overseas Press Club, New York, October 18, 1949.] You refer to me as the leader of India and a person who might influence events. That is true in a sense, but it is true not so much in the individual sense, but in another. Just as the United States, almost against her wishes or desires, has been thrust into a position of extreme importance in world affairs, and, whether she wishes it or not, has to assume leadership in world affairs, so in a different, entirely different context, India is inevitably drawn into the vortex of Asian and world affairs.

Our own desire was, and is, to be left in peace to develop ourselves. We have a hundred problems to face. We want to get going about them and we do not wish to interfere with anybody or to be interfered with. At the same time, we have the desire to co-operate with everybody, and to concentrate on the development of our own country. When you think of India or Asia, please remember always that the primary problems of Asia and India are problems that relate to the basic necessities of life—food,

[1] V.T.A., pp. 31–34.

clothing, housing, etc. There are many problems in Europe. There has been a great deal of destruction, a great deal of suffering. Nevertheless the primary problems are not so dominant as in Asia. So our outlook, not only in our domestic affairs, but our world outlook, is governed by that primary factor. It is important to remember this because once you see those primary cravings of humanity you have little leisure to look around and to play about on the chessboard of world politics. Other desires arise which sometimes may be described as love of power politics and the like, but those who want the primary cravings satisfied have no desire for anything else for the time being. That is our general outlook. . . .

The second thing I may point out is the fact that Asia, largely because of the progressive termination of colonial rule, is in a state of extraordinary upheaval and ferment. The upheaval need not necessarily take shape in actual revolutionary activities, but it is rapidly changing the continent. The change is coming in men's minds. Ultimately, of course, it takes shape elsewhere too.

The primary problem of Asia is probably the agrarian problem. As everywhere, where a country is undeveloped or not fully developed, that is a major problem. You may look upon it from any point of view. You may think of China as it is today under more-or-less Communist rule. The basic problem of China was the agrarian problem, and is the agrarian problem, and upon the measure in which that agrarian problem is solved or not solved will depend the future of China, whatever development takes place there. The same might apply to any country. It might apply to India with this difference, that in India something has been done in the past few years in regard to the agrarian problem and the semifeudal conditions that existed there. Pretty far-reaching changes are being made now. We are putting an end to the big landlord system, the zamindari system. This has been part of our program. We are doing it peacefully and more or less co-operatively, with compensation. It is rather a burden, the business of compensating landowners, but anyhow it avoids conflict and probably is cheaper in the end. And so one of the major upsetting features in Asia has been controlled in India because of this policy that we have pursued in regard to land.

The third point to remember is that these are really overlapping things —that still in Asia, nationalism is the primary urge, apart from the urge of hunger and starvation. Nationalism tends to fade away after political freedom to some extent, and economic problems come up. Nationalism is still strong because the memory of colonialism is near, but other problems come to the fore. Where actual freedom has not been obtained, nationalism is still the strongest feeling. Not only that, but it affects other countries. For instance, there is Indonesia. There has been a struggle against the Dutch there, which has powerfully affected the whole of Asia. You may remember that we had a conference on Indonesia last January in Delhi. I confess that when I invited various countries to that conference, I had no idea of the enthusiasm with which the invitation would be accepted. It was done rather in a hurry because the Dutch had just started what they called their police action—their second police action—and we gave just ten or twelve days' notice for this meeting. Every country of Asia was represented there—except Japan, and Japan was absent not because the Japanese didn't want to come, but because there were difficulties in the way of their coming.

It was astonishing; not only Asia, but also Australia was represented, and to some extent New Zealand. Why was this so? Because somehow or other not only was there a great deal of sympathy with the Indonesians in their fight for freedom, but first of all, every country in Asia immediately remembered its own recent colonial past, and secondly, each felt if a European imperialist power is still there, there is danger to Asia; there is danger to us. It hasn't quite gone away, this evil thing, imperialism. If France is functioning in Indo-China, quite regardless of other matters it excites people in Asia. There is an old colonialism still functioning, so that I don't think you can have a normal development in Asia till these traces of colonialism go. I have no doubt whatever that no colonial power, whatever it may be, can ever function in Asia with profit. It may, by military means, carry on for some time, for a few more years, but it cannot function there in peace or with profit. There would be trouble all the time. If that is so, then it seems to me the height of folly for any power to try to continue functioning thus because it simply means adding to its own burdens, creating ill will, and making a peaceful or compromise solution more difficult.

In the case of India, in spite of our long conflict with the British, a way out was found. For that, I think, certainly a great deal of credit was ours, meaning that the whole trend of our movement under Mahatma Gandhi was that we were always prepared for a peaceful settlement. And we strove to avoid ill will. But I should like to add that credit was also due to the present British government, which approached this question at last in a more friendly and a wiser way. It is astonishing how this settlement has resulted in a rapid elimination of the bitterness and ill will that prevailed previously. I hardly think you'll find any other example of that type. For that too, I think credit is due to both parties. But still, if the slightest thing happens that arouses the suspicion of the people, immediately old thoughts arise in their minds again. For instance, Mr Churchill may have no present authority or authoritative position in England, but Mr Churchill's past is ever before the Indian people, and if he says something —well, it is bound to be irritating. So you have to deal with Asia, which is emerging from its colonial status, which is highly sensitive, and which may make a mess of things here and there, but which realizes it is strong enough to make it frightfully difficult for anyone else to function. Even if it cannot function satisfactorily somewhere, it can make others, also, not function satisfactorily. All these primary nationalistic urges come in the way.

Now, look at this in the perspective of history. This is a very big thing that is happening in Asia. I am not prophet enough to say what will happen in the near future or the distant future, but one thing is perfectly clear to me, that after these painful years of transition which we are going through, Asia is going to play a fairly important part in world affairs. It must—the mere extent of it and the numbers of human beings involved are bound to play their part. You who are concerned with the press are naturally concerned a great deal with current events. You analyze them, you specialize in them, you know a lot about a particular problem, but I sometimes wonder if specialization doesn't come in the way of a wider outlook in perspective on things that are happening in the world today. There is a big problem, a general problem, in that so much knowledge has been gathered together. There is so much to learn that it has become impossible for persons to learn all of it. Persons specialize, they must, to be efficient in their particular branch of knowledge. The more they specialize in one thing and the more they know about it, the less they seem to know about anything else, with the result that the wide human outlook and understanding of events in perspective, which may be called a part of wisdom, somehow becomes less and less, while highly specialized knowledge becomes more and more. Possibly many of our difficulties in the world are due to that fact. Now that applies to the understanding of current events. Do you understand them in their narrow significance or do you see them as a part of a historic process in perspective? Unless you do the latter, it is a little difficult to understand the events. It is as if you saw a small part of a picture only, and not the whole.

What is happening in Asia is of tremendous significance to the world. I don't mean to belittle the problems of Europe or other parts of the world, but the fact is that Asia is in a growing, a dynamic phase. It will make many mistakes, no doubt, but it will grow because there is vitality behind it. Take India; we have made innumerable mistakes, but I am quite convinced that India is a country full of vitality today. Some of that vitality goes wrong occasionally, and does harm. Nevertheless, it is better to have vitality and go wrong occasionally than not to have it. So people talk and think in terms of immediate problems, immediate needs, immediate facts, immediate this, immediate that. That may be necessary, that may not be necessary, but I do suggest that you think from this long perspective of history and from the perspective, also, of vast masses on the move.

You hear about these things when there is a riot or a revolution, but the fact is that the movement takes place in the minds of people long before a riot or a revolution happens. This movement has taken place in the minds of the millions and millions of Asia, and that is a fact you cannot get over, that is a fact you cannot deal with by military means, except occasionally, except temporarily. It is a fact that has to be accepted, admitted, and dealt with accordingly.[1]

["Revolution in India"—Address, East and West Association, Foreign Policy Association, India League of America and Institute of Pacific Relations: New York, October 19, 1949.] I have been in the United States for exactly eight days today. It is not a very long time. Yet I was surprised when I suddenly realized that it was only eight days ago that I had come, because during these eight days so much of significance has happened in my life. Experience and emotion have so piled up, one on top of the other, that I have the feeling that I have been here for a long time. Sometimes, when there are no new experiences, time seems to stop. I have had this experience of time stopping for months and years in my life—a curious experience. And sometimes time seems to race on; rather, one feels as if it were racing on, although very little of it may have passed. So, during these eight days, much has happened to me which has not only powerfully affected me in the present but has left upon me its deep imprint, which I shall carry with me and remember for a very long time.

During these days, I have repeatedly had occasion to speak in public and my programme has often been a very full one. I knew that I was to come to this great banquet tonight. And I knew also that I had to speak here but I must apologize to you because I was expected, I am told, to prepare a written address, which I have not done. I have not done it, partly because I dislike very much this process of writing down speeches in advance, partly because I was not used to doing it in India. . . .

[1] Ibid., pp. 37–43.

But in the main, may I say that the real reason at the back of my mind, the sub-conscious reason, was a growing feeling of confidence, of being among my friends here in this country. I began to feel more and more at home and so I thought I could perhaps take the liberty of having a friendly talk with you rather than deliver a formal address.

If I may indulge in a bit of personal history, I might inform you that I began what is called public speaking at a fairly late stage in my life. I was at college in Cambridge. I joined a well-known debating society. But I never had the courage to speak there, in spite of the fact that they actually had a system of fining the members who did not speak every term. I paid the fine willingly.

It was many years later, through the force of circumstances rather than anything else, that I started addressing public audiences. I began with the peasantry of my province. They didn't think and I didn't think that I was delivering a public speech at all. But I used to meet them and talk to them and those talks gradually attracted more and more people. Yet they remained just personal talks. I didn't feel shy with them because they were very simple folk. And so, very slowly I got over this inhibition, this difficulty of speaking in public. But I retained that manner of speaking, that is to say, of speaking to friends as if we were having a quiet talk together, even when the audiences grew and became colossal in number. So, if I speak to you in a somewhat rambling fashion, you will forgive me. I need hardly say how overwhelmed I am by the magnificence of this occasion and by the very distinguished gathering that is present here. In spite of all that has been said about me by previous speakers, I am not a very aggressive person in public gatherings and I feel at times a little afraid of them. I am very grateful to the four host organizations for organizing this function. And may I say in this connection that I am grateful not only for this occasion but even more so to all the Americans who, in the course of the past many years, sent us their goodwill; and not only sent their goodwill but gave us their active support in the struggle for our freedom. I need not say anything to my own fellow countrymen here, because it was expected of them to give of their best. But it was very heartening to us in those days of struggle and conflict and ups and downs to hear the voices of goodwill and friendship and sympathy from America. I remember that on the last occasion, the beginning of my last term of imprisonment, a number of very distinguished citizens in America issued a manifesto—I think it was addressed to the President of the United States—appealing to him to take some action in regard to India. May I also say that all of us in India know very well, although it might not be so known in public, what great interest President Roosevelt had in our country's freedom and how he exercised his great influence to that end.

I have come to America for many reasons, personal and public. I have come after a long time of waiting because I have always wanted to come here ever since I was a student in England. But events took a different course soon after I went back to India and my travels and journeys were very limited. In the last two or three years, other limiting factors have come in and I could not come here earlier.

Originally, perhaps, it was curiosity that impelled me to come here. But in later years, more and more the thought came to me that it was necessary, it was desirable and, perhaps, inevitable that India and the United States should know each other more and co-operate with each other more. In a sense that co-operation in the past could hardly be called co-operation, because a subject country does not co-operate with a great and powerful nation. But since we have become independent, that idea took more definite shape. Though even now we may be a big country and we may have great potential resources, as we do have, nevertheless, we are new to these fields of international activity and in the terms that the world measures nations today, we are weak. We have no atom bomb at our disposal. We have no great forces at our command, military or other. Economically we are weak. And these are the standards—the yard measures—of a nation's importance today. We are strong in some ways— at least potentially so. Any person who can look ahead a little can say with a measure of confidence that India is bound to make good even in those material ways which count for so much in the world. All the factors are present there and the whole course of present-day history points to that. Anyhow, the time has come when we can look more towards the United States with some feeling of confidence which is necessary before we can really develop co-operative relations.

These relations cannot exist when one country is very weak and the other very strong. We are weak in some ways but there is one lesson we learned many years ago from our great leader, Mahatma Gandhi, in the days when we were still weaker. Our people, though they were unarmed, with no wealth or other outward symbol of strength at their command, faced a powerful and wealthy empire which had been in India for a large number of years.

It was a strange contest. I look back to that period just thirty years ago when Mahatma Gandhi, in a sense, burst upon the Indian scene. He was, of course, known before and loved and admired for his work in South Africa but he had not functioned on an all-India plane. He suddenly started functioning. And there was some magic about the message he gave. It was very simple. His analysis of the situation in India was essentially that we were suffering terribly from fear, especially the masses in India and even others. So he just went about telling us, "Don't be afraid. Why are you afraid? What can happen to you?" Of course, when he talked in these terms he was thinking of the political fear that we had. If we did something that the British Government did not like, well, we'd be punished. We'd be sent to prison. We might be shot. And so a general sense of fear pervaded the place. It would take hold of the poorest peasant, the lowliest of all our people, whose produce or nearly all of it went to his landlord and who hardly had enough food to eat. This poor man was kicked and cuffed by everybody—by his landlord, by his landlord's agent, by the police, by the moneylender. Everybody with whom he came into contact just pushed him about and he simply accepted it as something that fate had ordained for him. Whether there was something in the atmosphere or some magic in Gandhi's voice, I do not know. Anyhow, this very simple thing, "Don't be afraid," when he put it that way caught on and we realized, with a tremendous lifting of hearts, that there was nothing to fear. Even the poor peasant straightened his back a little and began to look people in the face and there was a ray of hope in his sunken eyes. In effect, a magical change had come over India.

There were many ups and downs. This teaching of his—"Do not be afraid"—kept us going and we found really that there was nothing to fear. Fear was something we had created. We went to prison in tens and hundreds of thousands. It was uncomfortable and many people endured a great deal of pain and suffering. But we found that it all depended on the way one looked at it. Obviously, if we had gone to prison for some high misdemeanour with disgrace attached to it, it would have been terribly painful. But because we felt we were serving a great cause, it became not a thing to be afraid of but something to be coveted. I put this to you, because, in the world today, we are again—compared with the great nations—weak. If there is an armed conflict, we are weak. As I said, we have no atom bomb. But, if I may say so, we rejoice in not having the atom bomb.

So while innumerable difficulties have surrounded us and sometimes tried to overwhelm us, we have never lost heart. The one thing that has really been painful and has hurt us has been our own inner weakness. We have lost all fear of external aggression. Not that we are impractical or idealistic, though it is good to be idealistic and we are that to some extent. After the last thirty years' experience, however, we shall not be afraid of external aggression, unless, of course, we ourselves go to pieces. That would be our fault. What has pained us is our own inner weakness, because that has sometimes made us doubt ourselves.

I mention this, because elsewhere I have talked about this fear complex that governs the world today. It is a curious thing. It is like the fear of a man who possesses a great deal of property and is continually afraid of losing it or of somebody stealing it; he lives in a state of constant apprehension. Possibly, he might lead a more comfortable and happier life if he didn't have it and didn't have this continual apprehension. However that may be, there is this fear complex all over. I do not say there is no justification for it. There is justification for it in this world. We have seen terrible things happen and terrible things may happen again. Any person in a place of responsibility cannot become totally irresponsible about the future. He has to guard against it. He must take steps to prevent the terrible things from happening. That is true. Nevertheless, this approach of fear is, from every point of view, the worst of all approaches. It is bad for one's self; it is bad for others. Some of you may be acquainted with wild animals. I have had some little acquaintance—not very much—and have found and am convinced that no animal attacks man, except very rarely, unless the animal is afraid. Sometimes, the fear in the man transfers itself psychologically to the animal. The man becomes afraid of the animal and then the animal becomes afraid of him and, between them, they make a mess of it. I know numerous cases of individuals who go into the jungles without a gun or arms and are never attacked by any animal, because they are not afraid of any animal and the wild animals come and they look them in the face and the animals pass by. Well, it is perhaps not fair to compare wild animals with men. Nevertheless, the analogy, I think, holds. One party gets afraid. One nation gets afraid, then the other gets afraid and so the fear rises to a crescendo and leads to deplorable consequences. I do not know if it is possible to divert this emotion to other channels. While one must take all steps to prevent an evil happening, one must also shed fear and act with a great deal of confidence, because that confidence itself brings confidence to the others who are afraid. And so we can gradually change the atmosphere in which we live.

India has been, for the last two years or more, an independent country. In another three months or so, we will formally inaugurate our Republic. That will be no addition to our freedom, except in the sense that it will be a confirmation of it and certain forms which exist now will go. Our purpose and our desire in the present is to be left in peace to work out our problems, not in isolation certainly, but in co-operation with others.

We have got enormous problems. Every country has problems, of course. But the fact of one hundred and fifty years of foreign rule, which resulted possibly in some good here and there, certainly resulted in stunting and arresting the growth of the people and of the country in many ways. Because it arrested the growth of the country, it arrested the solution of many problems that normally would have solved themselves—either by conflict or in peace; problems are solved and always a new equilibrium is established somehow or other. But because there was an overriding authority—that is, the British power in India—it prevented that natural equilibrium from being established in India from time to time and many things continued in India, which were completely out of date and out of place and which had no strength behind them, no roots in them. They were kept up, propped up, by an external authority. And so, problems accumulated—social, economic, political. As soon as the British left India, suddenly we had to face all those problems. We knew, of course, that we would have to face them. It was a big change. It was brought about co-operatively and peacefully and rather remarkably, for which credit is due to both the parties concerned, England and India. Nevertheless, however peacefully it was brought about, those arrested problems suddenly emerged. Not only did they emerge but all our people, who had been waiting for long years for political freedom, expected great things to come—great things in the sense of material betterment. Certainly, we wanted these great things to come. Certainly, we had told them that freedom confined to the political sphere would not be enough. It has no meaning to give a vote to a starving man.

We had talked to the people in economic terms also and they expected a tremendous change suddenly, rather unreasonably, because these magic changes cannot take place suddenly. Just at this moment came other things —came the partition of India. It came without our liking it. We were apprehensive of the consequences; therefore, we had resisted it. Ultimately, we came to the conclusion that Partition was probably a lesser evil than the continuation of an inner conflict which was delaying our freedom. We were anxious to have that freedom as quickly as possible. So we agreed to the partition. That Partition, as it turned out to be in its consequences, was far worse than even what we had anticipated. It was the cutting up of a living structure, of everything—all our Services, whether the Army or civil Services, transport and railways, communications, telephones, telegraphs and the postal system, irrigation and canals. Many families, domestic households, were suddenly cut in two. An extraordinary situation arose overnight. It created tremendous new problems, among which were upheavals, deplorable happenings and killings and then vast migrations. All our energies, that ought to have been devoted to constructive effort, to economic betterment, which we had planned for years previously, suddenly had to be applied to tackle these new problems. We had no time or leisure or resources left to deal with the other and more basic problems. Nevertheless, the world didn't stop. India could not stop. And we did try to deal with the basic problems to some extent.

Our basic problem is the land problem, as it is all over Asia. And we have gone pretty far in changing the whole antiquated and unfair land system in India. We are putting an end to the great landed estates and giving the land to the peasant, compensating the previous owner. This process is going on now. Some months ago, in my own province in India, that is, the United Provinces, which is the biggest province and has the enormous population of about sixty millions, we introduced a great reform in local self-government. In all the villages, a vast number of villages, every adult voted in what was probably one of the biggest elections that any country has had. We are going to have that all over India. That particular reform in local self-government, affecting all the villages, was really initiated some years ago when my sister, who is our Ambassador here, was the Minister for local self-government in that province. Now, this is an extraordinary and a most interesting experiment. Partly it is new. Partly it is going back to village self-government that existed before the British came. Anyhow, it is a tremendous experiment in democracy, important perhaps, because it is more basic than the Assembly that we may choose at the top. So, all these things have gone on. We are also proceeding with big river valley schemes which are basic for our development. All that has happened. But I want you to realize the background in which we have functioned. It has been made difficult by the after-effects of the war—and by all the other things that have happened. Still, I have little doubt that India is making good and going ahead.

There is a great deal of talk of Asia being a unit. Asia is in a sense a geographical unit, has been a unit in many other ways but in the main it was a unit in a negative sense. That is to say, practically all of Asia became the colonial domain of various European Powers. It was a unit in that sense; a colonial domain where various different peoples were struggling for freedom against European imperialists; it was a unit because of their struggles and a certain commonness of purpose. But there is, at the same time, a great deal of diversity. It is not quite correct to think of Asia as a compact unit. There is not very much in common between the Chinese and those who live in Western Asia; they represent entirely different cultural, historical and other backgrounds. So also, you can separate other regions of Asia. There is the Far Eastern region, the Middle Eastern, the Arab, the Iranian and the rest. Now whichever region you may take, India inevitably comes into the picture. . . .

I have said that we have no desire to play a leading role in the international sphere except when we are compelled by circumstances. People talk about India's desire for leadership in Asia. We have no desire for leadership anywhere. Our greatest anxiety and yearning today is to build up India and to solve somehow the problems that face us; and then, in so far as we can, to serve the other good causes we have at heart in Asia and in the rest of the world and to co-operate with other countries in the United Nations and elsewhere. Whether we want to or not, we realize that we simply cannot exist in isolation. No country can. Certainly we cannot. Our geography, our history, the present events, all drag us into a wider picture.

I have been asked whether it had struck me that there might be a certain parallel between the United States in the early years and India. It has, in the sense that a big country grew up here. Certain relatively smaller countries were around it—to the south especially—and economically and otherwise they were influenced greatly by the presence of this dominating country in the north. So, I was asked how the presence of a big country like India affected the surrounding smaller countries and whether it had the same type of effect. The parallel is not exact. Nevertheless, there is much in it. Whether we want to or not, in India we have to play an important role. It is not to our liking, because we have enough burdens of our own and we do not wish to add to them. But, as I said, we just can't choose in the matter. India, in Southern, Western and South-Eastern Asia, has to play a distinctive and important role. If she is not capable of playing it properly, then she will just fade out.

I am quite convinced that there is no question of India fading out. Therefore, only the other role remains. Because of that and also because the United States is playing a vital role in world affairs today—again hardly from choice but through the development of certain circumstances, through necessity almost—it seems natural for an Indian to think of closer relations with the American people and this great country. I think and I have been told that it is natural, in the present context, for many Americans to think of the importance of India in this respect. Therefore, the question of India and the United States understanding each other and developing closer relations is not only important from the point of view of these two countries but has a larger importance and significance.

Whether India has anything special to teach to the United States, I do not know. That is for you to judge. Certainly, I have not come to the United States to teach anybody anything. I have come here to improve my own education as far as possible, to learn something from America and to learn something about the world through American eyes, because both are important for me. I believe I still retain something of the spirit of a student and the curiosity of youth. It is not only this curiosity but rather a compelling necessity that makes me feel that I ought or rather that we in India ought to understand America better. Whether we agree with everything that the United States does or does not do is another matter.

This business of agreeing or not agreeing might be looked at in many ways. I think it is a wrong approach for any country or any people to expect complete agreement with another country or people about all things or to expect a duplication of their own ways and methods of thinking and action and life in the other country. The world naturally grows more uniform. Nevertheless, there is a great deal of variety in it, not only external variety in ways of life but a mental and emotional variety, too, because of different backgrounds and historical developments. If we seek to understand a people, we have to try to put ourselves, as far as we can, in that particular historical and cultural background. Normally, people do not make such an attempt at all. They feel rather irritated that the other person is so unlike them or does things in a different way. No attempt is made to understand, except rarely. I have an idea that many of our present problems—international troubles—are due to the fact that the emotional and cultural backgrounds of people differ so much. It is not easy for a person from one country to enter into the background of another country. So, there is great irritation, because a fact that seems obvious to us is not immediately accepted by the other party or doesn't seem obvious to him at all. Even when we understand the other party's background we may not be able to convince him or he may not be able to convince us. But that extreme irritation will go when we think, not that the other person is exceedingly stupid or exceedingly obstinate in not recognizing a patent fact as we see it but that he is just differently conditioned and simply can't get out of that condition. If you understand that, perhaps, your approach to him will be different from that blatant, direct approach which ends in this direct and blatant approach to you and which ultimately ends in the mutual use of strong language without the least understanding of each other's mind or function. One has to recognize that, whatever the future may hold, countries and people differ in their approach and their ways, in their approach to life and their ways of living and thinking. In order to understand them we have to understand their ways of life and approach. If we wish to convince them, we have to use their language as far as we can, not language in the narrow sense of the word but the language of the mind. That is one necessity. Something that goes even much further than that is not the appeal to logic and reason but some kind of emotional awareness of the other people.

If I may refer again to my personal experience during the eight days of my stay here, I have met many Americans. I had met distinguished Americans during the past years in India and in Europe. I have studied a good deal of American history. I have read a good many famous American periodicals. So, I have a fair knowledge, as far as a foreigner can have, of the American background. Nevertheless, the last eight days here have brought to me, although subconsciously—because I made my mind receptive to impressions and influences—some kind of an emotional awareness, apart from an intellectual understanding, of the American people. People tell me—and it is very likely—that I can't know what the United States of America is after just three days in Washington and a week in New York. Nevertheless, even my present experience has brought that emotional awareness to me, which helps me much more in understanding the American people and the United States than all my previous reading and intellectual effort. Therefore, this kind of personal contact and receptivity of mind is helpful and, indeed, desirable.

You will not expect me to say that I admire everything that I find here in the United States. I don't. The United States has got a reputation abroad . . . of being materialistic and of being tough in matters of money. Well, I could not imagine that any country could achieve greatness even in the material field without some basic moral and spiritual background. Also, Americans are supposed to be very hardheaded businessmen. I have found a very great deal of generosity and an enormous amount of hospitality and friendliness. Now, all this creates that emotional atmosphere that helps in the development of friendly relations and in the understanding of individuals as well as nations. I shall go back from here much richer than I came, richer in experience, richer in the fund of memories that I take back and richer in the intellectual and emotional understanding and appreciation of the people of this great country.

Someone referred to the part that the women of India played in our struggle for freedom. There is no doubt that the part the women of India played was not only significant but of paramount importance in that struggle; it made all the difference in the world. I am quite convinced that in India today progress can be and should be measured by the progress of the women of India. In a political and outward sense they had fewer barriers to face than the women of some European countries and, perhaps, even here; I mean in regard to the vote and other things. They had to face certain social barriers which you have not had. Our political movement swept away many of those social barriers and brought the women out. That shows that our political movement was something much more than a political movement, because it affected the lives of all classes of people. It touched those unfortunate people who had suffered so long, who are called the untouchables. They are not all untouchables; politically speaking, they are called untouchables. The movement affected them, affected the country's reaction to them. It affected women. It affected children. It affected the peasantry, the industrial workers and others. So, it was a vital movement which affected every class and every group in India. That is what a real movement should be. And in this movement the women of India, undoubtedly, played an exceedingly important part. Today, as perhaps you know, we have women in our Central cabinet and I believe in one or two provincial cabinets also. We had a woman governor in our biggest province. We have a woman among our ambassadors. In almost all fields of work our women take an active part.[1]

[From speech to National Foreign Trade Council and Far East–America Council of Commerce and Industry, New York, October 20, 1949.] There is the big land problem of Asia, the agrarian problem, the basic problem for a fundamentally agricultural country. Until these problems are solved, it will be difficult even to tackle other problems fully. In India, fortunately, we had paid attention to this agrarian problem some years back. We took steps that eased the situation. We hope to solve the problem, at any rate for the present. There are many aspects of it which will take some time. This has resulted, in spite of all our difficulties, in that fundamental stability that comes from the peasantry being more or less satisfied, especially in an agricultural country where seventy-five or eighty per cent of the people are dependent on agriculture. And that is the reason for the basic stability of India today, apart from any other reason.

But that is not enough. That is only a sort of clearing the ground. Ultimately we [must] advance industrially if we are to add to the wealth of the country. Even from the agricultural point of view, if we improve agriculture, make it more scientific, as we want to do, the result will probably be that quite a number of people who now totally depend upon

[1] N.S., pp. 107–20. (The date of this speech, noted incorrectly in N.S., has been accurately given above).

agriculture will be out of work and will have to be found other occupations.

Remember that one of the basic reasons for the poverty of India is the overburden on the land. Why? Don't think for the moment of the growth of population. That is important, but it is something apart. But the fact emerges that from the beginning of the nineteenth century or thereabouts, if you examine the figures of population in India, you find that progressively, the rural population has increased at the expense of the urban. Now that is very odd, because in the nineteenth century almost all over the world the urban population increased at the expense of the rural. In India it was the reverse. What did it signify? It signified that such manufactures or small industries as we had in India were gradually shrinking and, for lack of occupation, people were going to the land. But the land was not empty, it was full already. So the burden on the land increased and poverty grew. Obviously, that burden has to be relieved by people being taken away from the land and given other jobs in other productive activities. So from every point of view it became essential for us to think in terms of growing industry.

Some industry had developed in India in spite of all drawbacks and obstructions. India was relatively more highly industrialized than any other country in Asia except Japan. But as a whole India was agricultural, not industrialized. When we thought in terms of industrializing India, we thought in basic terms, not merely as had been done in the past, of putting up a textile factory here and there. Many textile factories had arisen— cotton, jute, and so forth. They could be added to. But in basic terms the aim was having more power, having more steel, having machine tool-making plants and factories, so that a basis of heavy industry should be laid down, out of which other industries could grow. Even previous to independence we had drawn up these plans. For years I sat as chairman of a national planning committee. The government of India also had many plans of its own. Our rooms and cupboards and archives are full of plans of various projects in India all over the country. There was no lack of thought although, perhaps, that thought was not co-ordinated. Today, also, we think in these basic terms. If India is to go ahead, we are prepared to do without comforts. We are prepared to do without the secondary things in life, in order to provide the primary things. First of all, obviously, we must have food, and enough food. Secondly, other necessaries. But apart from these, we want to concentrate on the growth of industry, the generation of more power, the production of more steel, of chemicals and such other things which are essential for the growth of industry. Unfortunately, financial difficulties have come in our way, and we have had to slow down somewhat. We have had to choose priorities and to delay something else. After all, we can't just plan or work on paper. We will only do as much as we can stand and support. We are not going to endanger our economy by schemes which we cannot carry out later. So we are picking and choosing the basic things.

Now, with this outlook in India, how far can co-operation with the United States be profitable, not only to India, but to the people of the United States? That is the problem before me. And this, I take it, is the problem before you. I think it is not only possible, but if I may put it more strongly, from a completely different point of view it is essential for you to co-operate with us. In the long run, though not in the immediate future, if a large part of the world is underdeveloped, economically backward, it is bound to pull down the rest. It affects the economy of the rest. The old idea according to which English economy developed in India by preventing the industrial growth of India, by considering India as a kind of agricultural colony of England, as a supplier of raw materials and a market for their finished goods, that idea no longer applies. And the idea that as Indian industry grows, its capacity to buy other goods will lessen, has been shown to be false, because the more any country's standards grow and the more it produces, the more it buys from outside. This kind of process supports world trade. If a country like India or China has no great capacity left for trade, that affects the rest of the world which produces. So it becomes essential from the point of view even of the rich and developed countries to see that other countries are in a position to absorb their goods, whether they are capital goods or other goods. It is not merely a question of looking at it from the point of view of doing good to India, though it would do good to India, but from the point of view of doing oneself good too in the bargain. And that is the right way of looking at it, because no satisfactory arrangement for co-operation can be based on any other consideration.

In regard to food, we would like to have wheat from America, not only to increase the supply for the market so that people may have more and prices may be favorably affected, but also to have a reserve and thereby also affect prices. In India wheat prices generally affect other prices. If wheat prices are low, the prices of other necessaries also go down. That is a controlling factor in regard to food prices and some other necessaries. We have given topmost priority to the matter of food. We are going as fast and as hard as possible in our grow-more-food campaign, and we are going to succeed. It will take two or three years or so. The other things are our major river-planning projects, which are going to give us water for new irrigation, stop floods, stop soil erosion, prevent malaria in various places, and produce a great deal of hydroelectric power. We want to go ahead with these schemes. We are going ahead with some, not with most of them, because for the moment our resources are limited. We want machinery for them, and much of the machinery can easily come from the United States. We also want technical assistance of the highest grade. We have got good engineers, but these are big undertakings and we want the best, not only in theoretical training, but in experience. We want to take no risks about these big jobs. The United States is one of the few countries which has people of such experience and training at its disposal.

Now, these are the main demands. As for other things—so many other things—we want to advance along all sectors of our national economy. We want to advance by our own efforts; we do not wish to rely needlessly on external help, not because it is not welcome, but because we want our people to feel that they can only progress, as any people must, by their own hard work. But there are certain essential things which, if we do not get them now, will delay our progress. Progress takes place anyhow, because ultimately it depends on the human being. If the human being is intent on going ahead, and has the will to do it, he will go ahead, in spite of all drawbacks. But it makes a difference whether he can go ahead fast or slow. And it makes a great difference in the present context when other events, totally unrelated to the peculiar problem before us, other events in India, in Asia, in the world, are somehow setting the pace. Therefore it becomes doubly necessary for us to make good on the economic front and the production front as rapidly as possible. I believe that that can be done principally by our own hard work and our own efforts, but certainly with the help of people in the United States.

For all the major undertakings, we have gone to the World Bank and the International Monetary Fund for loans, and we have received some loans and shall utilize them. Because we attach so much importance to our co-operation with the United States, we have sent here—in various capacities as ambassadors, as ministers, as consul generals—some of our best people. Young as we are in our foreign relations, we are not overflowing with an abundance of trained human material. But from such as we have, we have chosen our best people to send to the United States, because we attach importance to our work here and to our contacts and co-operation with the people of the United States. You are welcome to utilize them to the best advantage, and I am sure they will offer their services to the best of their abilities.

The question arises about private capital going to India. . . . [We already] have laid down what our policy is going to be. It is not meant for foreign countries alone. [In our general policy statement we] asserted that we would welcome foreign capital, and certain assurances were given. The matter is in some way continually under our consideration. But generally speaking, it is recognized that foreign capital can only come to India on a profitable basis, and with some assurance of safety. Otherwise the person who wants to send United States capital is hardly likely to do so. So far as any normal assurance is concerned, we have given it in these statements, whether in regard to the safety of capital there or to the removal of profits or even to the removal of capital later, subject to the state of the exchange market, because normally it has been a difficult one and, with devaluation of sterling and the rupee, has become even more difficult for us. Subject to these things that we cannot fully control, we give necessary assurances. We have further stated that there will be no differential treatment of foreign capital in India. Naturally, we are anxious and eager to encourage Indian industry, as any country would be, but in this larger context we think it is to the advantage of India to have foreign capital and to give it the necessary freedom to function.

I should like you to bear in mind the background of the situation in India. We have, as most countries have, a fairly difficult labor situation with which to deal. I think labor has on the whole acted well. But there are difficulties and one does not know exactly what is going to happen. Therefore, we have to think in terms of our labor, feeling that it is having a square deal. It is not merely a question of money; it is a question of making labor feel good. If it doesn't, even if there are no strikes, it just does not work as it ought to work. We want to increase labor's capacity and efficiency. We want to infuse it with some kind of idealism. We want our workers to feel that they are working for a cause from which they profit and the country profits. Keeping all this in view, we have framed our policy, which is not unchanging and which no doubt may be varied from time to time. But it does indicate the general lines of approach.

For the rest, I should only like to say that, since I spent a good deal of my life in one type of activity which was largely a struggle for India's freedom, when I speak about myself, please forget me as an individual and think of me rather as a symbol of a vast number of others who did likewise. Having won freedom, we were eager to reap the fruits of that freedom, not for ourselves, but for the country. Therefore we are bent and determined to see that those fruits come, and to work for them with all our might and energy.[1]

[1] V.T.A., pp. 70–77.

17+N. II

[From message to *New York Herald Tribune*, New York, October 26, 1949.] The interdependence of world problems expresses a truth which is evident to all thinking men and which we ignore at our peril. It is becoming increasingly difficult even to understand one problem unless we look at it in its world context. The interdependence of world problems means the interdependence of various parts of the world on one another. No country can isolate itself from the others and no country can solve the problems of war and peace by itself. The solution can only come by ever greater co-operation on a world scale. And so we advance necessarily to the realization of the world order and a world government.

There can be no doubt that a world government must come sometime or other. For the only alternative to it is world suicide. Instead of marching, however slowly, to this realization of a world order, we are faced by rivalry and tension all over the world. Which of these two powerful tendencies will triumph in the end, will decide the fate of the world for generations to come.

I have no doubt that ultimately a world order will be realized, though it may take a little time to do so because men's minds are not sufficiently attuned to it yet. In the economic sphere, this interdependence is patent today and, in spite of all the tension in the world, there is a strong tendency for mutual co-operation. We welcome, therefore, President Truman's Point Four, which will encourage the development of underdeveloped countries and thus relieve some of the economic tensions of today. It is difficult to say what the shape and form of this world order will be. We have to proceed firmly and yet cautiously. The greatest barrier to it is the psychological barrier and we must try to remove that. That means, first of all, putting an end to the psychology of fear that pervades the world, and encouraging the growth of good will among peoples.

India will help in this process to the best of her ability. Our nationalism has always been based on this conception of world order and international co-operation. I earnestly trust that the progressive forces of the world will co-operate together in this great task that confronts us.[1]

[From speech, University of California, October 31, 1949.] We live in an age of paradox and continuing crisis. We talk of peace and prepare for war. We discuss internationalism and one world, and yet narrow nationalisms govern our activities. There is said to be a conflict of ideologies, and this argument and the conflict that flows from it usually take place without much thought of the ideals and objectives that should govern us. We move

[1] Ibid., pp. 87–88.

from one temporary expedient to another, never catching up with the pace of events. Priding ourselves on shaping history, we function day to day as slaves of the events that inexorably unroll themselves before our eyes, and fear possesses us and hatred follows in its train.

None of us, and especially those who have to shoulder the burden of responsibility, can ignore the realities and dangers of the moment. We cannot live in an idealistic world of our own creation. Yet it may be that what we consider the immediate reality might only be a passing phase, and we have to look a little deeper in order to understand and control events. The world has made astonishing progress in technology and material advancement. That is all to the good and we must take full advantage of it. But the long course of history and human development shows us that there are certain basic truths and realities that do not change with the changing times, and unless we hold fast to them we are likely to go astray. The present generation has often gone astray in spite of all the wonderful accumulation of knowledge that we possess, and danger always looms ahead.

What, then, is lacking and how can we solve these crises in human affairs? I am no prophet, nor have I any magical remedy to suggest. I have tried to grope my way, to think straight and to co-ordinate, as far as possible, action to thought. I have often found it difficult to do so, for action on the political plane is not individual action but group and mass action. Nevertheless, I am convinced that any policy, any ideology, which ignores truth and character in human beings and which preaches hatred and violence, can only lead to evil results. However good our motives may be and however noble the objective we aim at, if the path we follow and the means we adopt are wrong and evil, we can never achieve that objective. If we seek peace we must labor for peace and not for war. If we seek harmony and good will among the various peoples of the world, we must not preach or practice hatred. It is true that there is plenty of violence and hatred in the world today and we cannot permit this to triumph, as we cannot submit to any aggression. We have to combat evil and aggression, but in doing so we have to remember not only our aims and objectives but also that the means we adopt should be in conformity with them.

The growth of modern civilization, with its magnificent achievements, has led more and more to the centralization of authority and power, and encroachments continue to be made on the freedom of the individual. Perhaps to some extent this is inevitable, as the modern world cannot function without considerable centralization. We see, however, this process of centralized authority being carried to such an extreme that individual freedom almost vanishes. The state becomes supreme in everything, or groups of individuals have so much concentrated power at their disposal that individual freedom tends to fade away. Different and sometimes hostile ideologies, from their respective points of view, encourage this concentration of power in the state or the group. This must ultimately result not only in human unhappiness but also in a lessening of that creative genius that is so essential for the growth of humanity. We have to find some balance between the centralized authority of the state and the assurance of freedom and opportunity to each individual.[1]

5 | Miscellany: End of 1949, Early 1950

[From speech, Joint Meeting of Vancouver Board of Trade, Canadian Club of City of Vancouver, and Vancouver Chamber of Commerce: Vancouver, Canada, November 3, 1949.] Asia is going to be dynamic and once you turn the mind of the Indian people in that direction, I have little doubt that they will produce very remarkable results, because the mind of India has been a very keen mind. One very remarkable discovery, perhaps one of the greatest in history, was made in India. That was the discovery of the zero symbol in numbers. Every child uses numbers today automatically, such a simple thing. Yet the old Romans and the old Greeks got entangled in a most complicated and cumbrous system of numerals, which sometimes we also write down in the letters of the alphabet today. Have you ever tried to add a sum written in Roman numerals? It is a very complicated process. It is extraordinary that with the tremendous creative genius of Rome and Greece and later Alexandria, even on the mechanical front, they just couldn't get out of the prison of their alphabetical numerals, which required an expert with a huge apparatus to do a simple sum in addition. How could the world progress when you couldn't even add numbers easily? Then the wonderful discovery took place in India, of the decimal system and the zero or the cypher sign. It seems simple to us, but

[1] Ibid., pp. 121–23.

it was an amazing discovery of the human mind, which opened the windows of progress. In fact, for a long time afterward India led in arithmetic and algebra. You call these symbols Arabic, just as the others are called Roman. You call them Arabic symbols, because they came to Europe by way of Arabia, from India. In Arabia, however, they are called Indian symbols, Indian numerals.

Now I am quite sure that Asia, and certainly India, has arrived at a stage of rapid change-over from its static condition. The American continent has tremendous responsibility cast upon it by circumstance, and a very great deal depends upon what this continent does in the future. Therefore, the relations of Asia to the American continent become important in every way. We should develop trade and commerce, but the more basic relationship comes from mutual awareness and mutual understanding of each other. If that comes, the rest follows fairly easily. . . .

About world co-operation. After this war the United Nations came into existence, above the ashes of the League of Nations. It is easy to criticize the League of Nations which, toward the end of its career, had become a rather feeble organization. It is easy also to criticize the United Nations, because it doesn't suddenly change the world, bring about peace all over the world. Yet, the fact remains that the United Nations continues to be the one big hopeful sign in the world. If it does not succeed as we would like it to succeed, it is not the fault of the United Nations, but the fault of us who are in the United Nations—or some of us. I think we should look upon the United Nations as laying the foundations of future world co-operation, a world order, one world, and making this one world strong.[1]

[From Press Conference—London, November 12, 1949.]

[Asked if he thought the Communist victory in China would lead to growth of Communism in India.] I will be quite frank with you. I think the Communist Party in India is the stupidest party there has ever been anywhere. It has done more damage to communist ideals than any opponents of Communism, because it has set itself out to fight every natural nationalist urge of the Indian people. It has set the whole of the nationalist movement against it. It has adopted methods which are completely violent and in the nature of rebellion because it has not the strength for a big one.

It has functioned in such a way as to irritate exceedingly all types of opinion in India except their own. My own information is that even within the Communist Party, people have disagreed with its policy and have expressed disapproval.[1]

[Questioned about a reported Indian barter deal for American wheat, Nehru was asked if it was not unfair for individual Commonwealth countries to make barter deals with countries outside, with the consequent loss of dollars to the sterling area dollar pool.] India [has] made no deal. It is true . . . that we are anxious to get wheat as cheaply as possible—if possible, free. [Or] on a deferred payment system, so that we can pay . . . later. . . .

[How soon [would] the Indian Government. . . recognise the Communist Chinese Government?] The Indian Government [will] take steps in accordance with reality. These steps would naturally be taken after consultation with other countries of the Commonwealth. We decide for ourselves [however].[2]

[Recognition of Government of People's Republic of China: Address to World Pacifists' Conference—Wardha, December 31, 1949.] The Government of India has recognized the new Government in China [on December 30, 1949] after satisfying itself that it had the support of the people and it intended to work for the good of the Chinese people. . . . We could not shut our eyes to the recent happenings in China. We do not want in any way to meddle with the Chinese people, either in their sentiments or any other matters. The Government is strong and we realize it and whether we prefer it or not, whether we like it or not, whether its fabric is like our own or otherwise we have to recognize it. We have to maintain our relations with it. It is not a matter of choice.[3]

["This Beautiful World of Ours"—For Children's Number, *Shankar's Weekly*: New Delhi, December 3, 1949.] Dear Children: I like being with children and talking to them and, even more, playing with them. For a moment I forget that I am terribly old and that it is a very long time ago since I was a child. But when I sit down to write to you, I cannot forget my age and the distance that separates you from me. Old people have a habit of delivering sermons and good advice to the young. I remember that I disliked this very much long, long ago when I was a boy. So, I suppose

[1] B.A.I., pp. 579–84.
[2] N.I.A., pp. 221–24.
[3] B.A.I., p. 587.

you do not like it very much either. Grown-ups have also a habit of appearing to be very wise, even though very few of them possess much wisdom. I have not quite made up my mind yet whether I am wise or not. Sometimes, listening to others, I feel I must be very wise and brilliant and important. Then, looking at myself, I begin to doubt this. In any event, people who are wise do not talk about their wisdom and do not behave as if they were very superior persons.

So, I must not give you a string of good advice as to what you should do and what you should not do. I suppose you have enough of this from your teachers and others. Nor must I presume to be a superior person. . . .

If you were with me, I would love to talk to you about this beautiful world of ours, about flowers and trees and birds and animals and stars and mountains and glaciers and all the other wonderful things that surround us in this world. We have all this beauty around us and yet we, who are grown-ups, often forget about it and lose ourselves in our offices and imagine that we are doing very important work.

I hope you will be more sensible and open your eyes and ears to this beauty and life that surround you. Can you recognize the flowers by their names and the birds by their singing? How easy it is to make friends with them and with everything in nature, if you go to them affectionately and with friendship. You must have read many fairy tales and stories of long ago. But the world itself is the greatest fairy tale and story of adventure that has ever been written. Only, we must have eyes to see and ears to hear and a mind that opens out to the life and beauty of the world.

Grown-ups have a strange way of putting themselves in compartments and groups. They build up barriers and then they think that those outside their particular barrier are strangers whom they must dislike. There are barriers of religion, of caste, of colour, of party, of nation, of province, of language, of custom and of wealth and poverty. Thus, they live in prisons of their own making. Fortunately, children do not know much about these barriers which separate. They play or work with one another and it is only when they grow up that they begin to learn about these barriers from their elders. I hope you will take a long time in growing up.

I have recently been to the United States of America, to Canada and to England. It was a long journey, right on the other side of the world. I found the children there very like the children here and so I easily made friends with them and, whenever I had the chance, I played with them a little. That was much more interesting than many of my talks with the grown-ups. For children everywhere are much the same; it is the grown-ups who imagine they are very different and deliberately make themselves so.

Some months ago, the children of Japan wrote to me and asked me to send them an elephant. I sent them a beautiful elephant on behalf of the children of India. This elephant came from Mysore and travelled all the way by sea to Japan. When it reached Tokyo, thousands and thousands of children came to see it. Many of them had never seen an elephant. This noble animal thus became a symbol of India to them and a link between them and the children of India. I was very happy that this gift of ours gave so much joy to so many children of Japan and made them think of our country. So, we must also think of their country and of the many other countries in the world and remember that everywhere there are children like you going to school and play, sometimes quarrelling but always making friends again. You can read about these countries in your books and when you grow up, many of you will visit them. Go there as friends and you will find friends to greet you.

You know that we had a very great man amongst us. He was called Mahatma Gandhi. But we used to call him affectionately Bapuji. He was very wise but he did not show off his wisdom. He was simple and childlike in many ways and he loved children. He was a friend of everybody, and everybody, peasant or worker, poor man or rich man, came to him and found a friendly welcome. He was a friend not only to all the people of India but also to all the people in the rest of the world. He taught us not to hate anybody, not to quarrel but to play with one another and to co-operate in the service of our country. He taught us also not to be afraid of anything and to face the world cheerfully and with laughter.

Our country is a very big country and there is a great deal to be done by all of us. If each one of us does his or her little bit, then all this mounts up and the country prospers and goes ahead fast.

I have tried to talk to you in this letter as if you were sitting near me.[1]

[From Address—University of Ceylon, Colombo, January 12, 1950.] One of the brighter features of this age is—and I attach a great deal of value to it—that the barriers that separated the so-called East from the so-called West are gradually disappearing. That is a good sign. But, at the same time, other barriers seem to be growing in the East and in the West. We meet repeatedly in conferences and talk about the problems that face us. Sometimes we solve a problem or two but for each problem that we solve, half a dozen fresh ones crop up.

I remember that somebody made a calculation of the number of international conferences that were held after the conclusion of the First World

[1] N.S., pp. 442–44.

War and before the commencement of the Second World War. It was a prodigious number. I do not quite know if we have exceeded that number since the Second World War ended.

This is an age of international conferences. A conference is always a good thing or almost always, because people, at any rate, meet round a table and discuss matters with good humour and, even if they do not always succeed in finding a solution, the effort is, nevertheless, always worthy of being made. That in itself results in something that is good. But I have often wondered why there has been this failure in the past to find solutions to our problems. Is it due to a lack of wit in statesmen or to a lack of understanding? I do not think it is either, because they have been able and earnest statesmen desiring peace and co-operation. Even so, somehow or other, solutions have escaped them. Why, then, is it so? I do not know; perhaps, we work too much on the superficial plane, finding solutions to the troubles of the moment and not looking to the deeper causes.

I put this to you for your consideration, because something does come in the way. With all the earnestness we may possess, sometimes we do not get over those old and new barriers that come in the way of mutual understanding. Then, I think that, in spite of our vaunted civilization, in spite of the advance of science and technology, we have lost our grip on some of the basic things of life, something that gives anchorage to life and some standard with which we could measure value.

We have advanced greatly in science—I am a great believer in science— and the scientific approach has changed the world completely. I think that if the world is to solve its problems, it will inevitably have to be through the means of science and not by discarding science. Nevertheless, I find that the sheer advance of science has often enough made people unscientific. That is an extraordinary thing to say but what I mean is that science has become so vast and all-pervading that scientists are unable to grasp things in their entirety and have become narrower and narrower in each individual subject. They may be very brilliant in some subjects but they seem to have no grip on life as a whole.

In the ancient civilizations of India and Greece that one reads about, one has or, at any rate, I have the sensation that people, though much more limited in the knowledge at their disposal, certainly had an integrated view of life. They were not so distracted; they could see life as a whole in spite of the fact that they did not know as much or nearly as much as the average undergraduate knows today. Because of this integrated view of life, they had a certain wisdom in their approach to life's problems.

Whether that is true or not I do not know, because one is apt to endow
17*

the past with a certain glamour. It may be that I am wrong but in any event one thing seems to me to be certain, namely, that we of today have no integrated view of life; that we, however clever we may be and however much of facts and knowledge we may have accumulated, are not very wise. We are narrower than the people of old, although every fact has gone to bring us together in this world. We travel swiftly, we have communications, we know more about one another and we have the radio and all kinds of things. In spite of all these widening influences, we are narrower in our minds. That is the extraordinary thing which I cannot understand.

I put this to this gathering of university men, because after all it is for the universities to tackle this problem more than for any other organization. If the universities do not teach some kind of basic wisdom, if they think in terms of producing people with degrees who want certain jobs, then the universities may have, perhaps, solved to a very minor extent the problem of unemployment or provided some technical help or other; but they will not have produced men who can understand or solve the problems of today.

You and I live in Asia. Perhaps, one of the biggest facts of today is this new and changing phase of Asia. What is happening in Asia is a fact of tremendous historical significance. It is difficult to grasp it entirely or to understand it but I think any person must see that something very big has happened and is happening all over Asia. There is a certain dynamism about it. We do not like much of what is happening and we may like something of what is happening but the fact remains that tremendous and powerful elemental forces are at play in Asia. For us just to sit in our ivory towers and look at them, with dislike or approval, is not good enough. If we wish to play any effective part in this world of ours we have to understand them. For some three or four hundred years, a good part of Asia was under a kind of eclipse and there was a basic urge for political freedom for a long time.

If you read the history of Asia—it is a long, long history—you will find that during the greater part of these thousands of years, Asia has played an important part in world affairs. It is only during the last three or four hundred years that Asia has become static, quiescent and rather stagnant in thought and in action in spite of all the virtues she might have possessed. Naturally and rightly, she fell under the domination of other more progressive, vigorous and dynamic countries. That is the way of the world and that is the right way. If you are static, you must suffer for it. And now, you see a change coming over Asia and because it is belated the change comes with a rush, upsetting many things and doing many things that one does not like. That this big change is coming over us, however, is a major fact. I do not know—I do not suppose any of you know—what ultimately this change will lead to in Asia.

You and I live in this changing Asia of today. Many of you will have the burden of facing these problems which are not of today or tomorrow but which may last for a generation or more than one generation. The burden is yours because many of us whom you honour are in the afternoon of our lives and have, perhaps, only a few more years to work and labour, which, I am sure, we will do to the best of our capacity and strength. And so, it is for you, young graduates of today, to prepare yourselves in mind and body and, as much as you can, in that deeper wisdom to understand these problems and to function actively and help in the solution of them. In the world of today, it is not enough for you to take up a distant and academic attitude and look on and just advise others or criticize others. Today, every man has to shoulder his burden. If he does not, well, he falls out; he simply does not count.

I have found many of our young men and women—I am talking more of India than of Ceylon because I do not know much about Ceylon—full of enthusiasm, full of energy, full of earnestness but, if you will permit me to say so, singularly academic or, if you like, singularly cut off from life's realities. During their student days, they often debated and passed resolutions on this subject or that but afterwards, when they went out into the world, they seemed to think that life itself was a continuous debating society where they could pass votes of censure or criticize others without doing much themselves.

Now, that is not a very helpful attitude. Perhaps it is due to the fact that for the past so many years, most of us did not have much chance of doing anything constructive. Our main job was to fight for the freedom of our country in a destructive way, in an oppositionist way and not in a creative way. The result is that we cannot get rid of this negative and destructive outlook. Instead of helping to build something, we just sit down and criticize others who may be, rightly or wrongly, trying to build. At least, they are trying to build. I think that mere criticism is a very unhelpful and bad attitude to adopt. In whatever country you may be, what is required today is a constructive and creative approach. Certainly there is always something to destroy, something that is bad; but mere destruction is not enough. You must also build.

One thing more. I take it that a university is essentially a place of culture, whatever "culture" might mean. But that takes me back to where I began. There is a great deal of culture all over the place and I, normally, find that those people who talk most loudly of culture, according to my judgment, possess no culture at all. Culture, first of all. is not loud; it is quiet, it is restrained, it is tolerant. You may judge the culture of a person by his silence, by a gesture, by a phrase or, more especially, by his life generally. The peculiar, narrow idea of culture that is spreading is that culture depends on the kind of headgear you wear or the kind of food you eat or on similar superficial things which, I do not deny, have a certain importance but which are very secondary in the larger context of life.

Each country has certain special cultural characteristics which have been developed through the ages. Similarly, each age has a culture and a certain way of its own. The cultural characteristics of a country are important and are certainly retained, unless, of course, they do not fit in with the spirit of the age. So, by all means, adhere to the special culture of your nation. But there is something that is deeper than national culture and that is human culture. If you do not have that human culture, that basic culture, then even that national culture of which you may be so proud has no real roots and will not do you much good. Today more especially, it has become essential for us to develop, in addition to such national culture as we may have, something that can only be called a world culture. There is much talk of One World and I believe that, at some time or other, that talk must bear fruit or else this world will go to pieces. It may be that we will not see that One World in our generation but if you want to prepare for that One World you must at least think about it. You have at least a culture to sustain you; and there is no reason why you should live your lives in narrow grooves, trying to think yourselves superior to the rest of the world.

We live surrounded by all kinds of dark fears in this new year. Probably, the prevailing feeling in the world of today is fear. Almost everybody is afraid of something; every country is afraid of some other country and, of course, fear is a thing which leads to all kinds of undesirable consequences. Fear is probably the most evil of sensations and we are living under the dominance of fear. If we could get rid of this fear to some extent, perhaps, it would be far easier for us to solve our problems.

Besides fear, we see in the world a great deal of hope and earnestness and a great deal of expectation of better things at the same time. We see creative and constructive as well as destructive and negative impulses at work. I do not know which will triumph in the near or the distant future, but obviously it will be impossible for me and impossible for you to function adequately if we do not believe in the ultimate triumph of the creative and unifying processes of the day.

However that may be, even the attempt to work for some great cause not only helps that cause but also helps us. We are not prophets and we do not know what the morrow may bring but it is rather satisfying to work for the morrow of your choice. It brings something into your life which makes it worth while. If you align yourself to some great purpose or to something elemental, it ennobles you. Whether the reward comes or not, the mere fact of working for it is a reward enough.

With all the evil that we see around us and with all its degradation, we have to live in this world. There is, nevertheless, plenty of good in the world and we have to see that there is plenty of what I as a Hindu would call the element of divinity in the individual as well as in the group. If we can have our feet firmly planted on the soil and do not lose ourselves in imaginary vagaries and at the same time have some of that divine fire in us, too, then, perhaps, we might be able to balance ourselves and develop some kind of an integrated life. . . . Whenever one thinks of the Buddha, one inevitably thinks of his great teaching; and I often feel that, perhaps, if we think more of that basic teaching of the avoidance of hatred and violence, we may be nearer the solution of our problems.[1]

[On the Commonwealth—January 13, 1950.] The Commonwealth nations freely exchange views and discuss problems of mutual interest and come as near as possible to each other. It is not a tribunal for deciding inter-Dominion disputes.

Each Commonwealth nation values co-operation with the rest but each of them values independence of action more.[2]

[Message to Asian Regional Conference of International Labor Organization—January 17, 1950.] It has become commonplace now to say that the outstanding event of the present day is the emergence of Asia. This emergence, coming after a long period of subjection and stunted growth has brought to us a large number of vital problems which incessantly call for solution. The problem of political freedom having been largely solved, we have now to face the more basic and intricate problems of economic advance.

We face an Asia, industrially and economically backward, but with a new social consciousness and with labour wide awake, insistent and sometimes turbulent. We may criticize this spirit of turbulence and regret it. But let us remember that for generations past this labour has seldom had a

[1] Ibid., pp. 429–35.
[2] B.A.I., p. 600.

square deal and if they are insistent in their demands today, are we to condemn them ? We can reason with them, we can appeal to them, we can explain to them the facts of the situation and, if we do so, I am sure they will understand and give their co-operation. But they will do so only if they are convinced of the social justice of our planning and our objectives. No plan and no approach is good enough if the burden of it falls chiefly on labour.

We want every group to progress. We mean ill to none. But, it must always be remembered that if anything comes in the way of the progress of the large masses of our people, then that obstruction has to be removed. The final test is: what is good for the people generally and not what is good for a particular section only.

We must always remember . . . that "poverty anywhere constitutes a danger to prosperity everywhere". Indeed it is not merely a danger to prosperity but a danger to peace in the world today.

South and South-East Asia demand development and much will depend on the speed with which this takes place.[1]

6 | Indo-Pakistan Relations

[From Press Conference, November 16, 1949.] One . . . misunderstanding . . . in other parts of the world [has been] that the partition of India [has been] viewed as if the Muslims and non-Muslims of India had been completely separated on a religious basis, that is to say, as an outcome of the old Muslim League's or Mr Jinnah's theory of two nations. So far as we are concerned we never accepted the theory; we repudiated it throughout.[2]

[Offer of No-War Pact to Pakistan.]

[From Draft of Joint Declaration suggested by Government of India to Pakistan High Commissioner in Delhi, December 22, 1949: "The

[1] Ibid., p. 606.
[2] K.F.S., p. 18.

Government of India and the Government of Pakistan, being desirous of promoting friendship and goodwill between their peoples who have many common ties, hereby declare that they condemn resort to war for the settlement of any existing or future disputes between them. They further agree that the settlement of such disputes between them shall always be sought through recognized peaceful methods such as negotiation, or by resort to mediation or arbitration by [a] special agency [to be] set up by mutual agreement for the purpose, or by agreed reference to some appropriate international body recognized by both of them. It is their earnest hope as well as their firm conviction that the implementation of this declaration in the spirit which lies behind it will serve to maintain good relations between the two countries and advance the cause of world peace."[1]

Continued efforts were made by Nehru to work out agreements between Pakistan and India for the greater protection of minorities. The following letter to the Prime Minister of Pakistan was written on January 18, 1950.]

I am writing to you about the proposed joint declaration by the Governments of India and Pakistan for the avoidance of war.

On the 16th January we received a copy of a statement which you were to make in the Pakistan Constituent Assembly in reply to a question regarding this proposed joint declaration by the Governments of India and Pakistan for the avoidance of war in the settlement of disputes. In this statement it is said that, in the view of the Government of Pakistan, the only way to promote peace is to resolve major disputes. Even if these disputes cannot themselves be settled before the declaration is made, at least the procedure for settling them can be laid down by agreement in precise terms in the declaration. Further that your Government urge the Government of India to agree to the concrete and precise suggestions of the Government of Pakistan already made regarding the procedure to be followed in the settlement of disputes.

I was not aware of any concrete and precise suggestions of the Government of Pakistan or its High Commissioner in Delhi in this respect. All that had happened previously was that your High Commissioner had mentioned various matters in dispute and referred to possible methods of settling them. No concrete or precise procedure had been suggested. We had dealt with the points raised by your High Commissioner whereupon it was agreed that a tentative draft of a declaration might be prepared. This draft was handed to your High Commissioner on the 22nd December 1949. The first reply to it that we received is the copy of your statement,

[1] S.D.A.A. (Vol. II), p. 324.

which reached us on the 16th January. We were surprised to find in this a reference to certain concrete and precise suggestions, which we had not thus far received. . . .

As you know, the Kashmir issue is before the United Nations and has therefore to be considered separately. . . .

The canal water issue has been the subject of correspondence between the two Governments and both are practically agreed that a joint technical commission should be set up for making a factual investigation. On the basis of the report of the commission, the two Governments will confer with a view to arriving at a settlement. If it is not found possible to reach a settlement, we are quite prepared to refer the matter to arbitration of some tribunal approved of by both Governments. You will appreciate that the manner of subsequent procedure as well as the forum can hardly be decided satisfactorily before we know what the results of the technical commission are and what the remaining points for decisions are.

We are prepared that the evacuee property dispute should be settled by arbitration, if negotiations and mediation fail.

So far as the division of the Reserve Bank's assets is concerned, the major portion of the assets claimed by Pakistan has already been transferred to the State Bank, and in regard to the remaining claims, disagreement has arisen on the question of the mode of payment. The question thus is one of the manner in which the claims have to be settled. This matter has already been discussed informally between the two Governments, and Pakistan themselves have suggested a conference to discuss it further. There are a number of other issues connected with this matter, all of which would have to be considered in arriving at a settlement.

The question of payment of sterling depends upon the amount that is due and of which type it is, that is, whether current or blocked. Both these matters are eminently fit for settlement by negotiation and indeed, as I have mentioned above, a conference is envisaged.

As you know, the Government of India have large claims of a financial nature on the Pakistan Government. These have been pending for a long time without any satisfactory settlement. This again should be dealt with by negotiation and, in the absence of any settlement, by other peaceful methods.

The whole object of the proposed joint declaration was to remove or lessen the unfortunate tension that exists between our two Governments and to produce an atmosphere which is more favourable to the consideration and settlement of particular disputes. If these disputes are satisfactorily settled separately, we would welcome it. But obviously there has been difficulty and delay in doing this. A joint declaration would, no doubt, be helpful in bringing us nearer to a settlement of all outstanding disputes between the two Governments, which the Government of India earnestly desire.

The procedure for settling disputes cannot be uniform in all cases. It is possible that one method may be appropriate for one dispute and another method for another dispute. Apart from negotiation and mediation, the only remaining peaceful methods are arbitration and reference to some international authority or tribunal. That is precise enough.

The proposal to make a joint declaration was made by the Government of India in all earnestness, so that we might take one effective step forward towards the resolution of existing disputes between the two Governments. Not to take this first step, because the other steps are not simultaneously taken, is to avoid taking any steps at all for the present at least. That is not a very helpful way of proceeding in this matter. For us to say that in no event are we going to war for a settlement of disputes is an important and significant contribution to peace between the two countries. The Government of India are prepared to say that, if the Government of Pakistan is also agreeable. Owing to geography and for many other reasons, it is inevitable that many issues arise between the two countries which require settlement. A firm declaration that we will in any event settle them by peaceful methods will itself be a great service to our two countries and the world, because it will remove fear of war from the minds of our peoples.

Any joint declaration that we might make must necessarily be in general terms to cover all cases that may arise now or hereafter. Apart from this joint declaration, and in pursuance of it, we can at once begin to consider specific . . . matters. . . .

I shall be glad to have an early reply from you.[1]

[In answer to Members of the Indian Parliament, including Congressmen, who suggested that an exchange of population between India and Pakistan would bring about a lasting solution of the Hindu-Muslim problem in the post-partition period.] It means acknowledging our inability to cope with any national problem in a civilized manner. This brutal and barbarous approach would be unique in the annals of history . . . such proposals shame us. . . . They [would] show that we are narrow, petty-minded, parochial bigots who talk of democracy and secularism but who,

[1] P.M.U.N., pp. 6–8.

in fact, are totally incapable of even thinking in terms of the world or of this great country. This is a proposition which, if it is followed, will mean the ruin of India and the annihilation of all that we stand for and have stood for. I repeat that we will resist such a proposition with all our strength; we will fight it in houses, in fields, and in market places. It will be fought in the Council Chambers and the streets, for we shall not let India be slaughtered at the altar of bigotry.[1]

7 | Sages of India

[Tagore and Gandhi—1949.] I have met many big people in various parts of the world, but I have no doubt in my mind that the two biggest I have had the privilege of meeting have been Gandhi and Tagore. I think they have been the two outstanding personalities in the world during the last quarter of a century. As time goes by, I am sure this will be recognized when all the field-marshals and dictators and shouting politicians are long dead and largely forgotten.

It amazes me that India in spite of her present condition—or is it because of it?—should produce these two mighty men in the course of one generation. And that also convinces me of the deep vitality of India and I am filled with hope, and the petty conflicts and troubles of the day seem very trivial and unimportant before this astonishing fact—the continuity of the idea that is India from long ages past to the present day. China affects me in the same way. India and China: how can they perish?

There is another aspect which continually surprises me. Both Gurudeva and Gandhiji took much from the west and from other countries, especially Gurudeva. Neither was narrowly national. Their message was for the world. And yet both were hundred per cent India's children, and inheritors, representatives and expositors of her age-long culture. How intensely Indian both have been, in spite of all their wide knowledge and culture. The surprising thing is that both of these men with so much in common and drawing inspiration from the same wells of wisdom and thought

[1] C.D.N., pp. 25–26.

and culture, should differ from each other so greatly. No two persons could probably differ so much as Gandhi and Tagore in their make-up or temperament.

It is interesting to compare and contrast them. Tagore, the aristocratic artist, turned democrat with proletarian sympathies, represented essentially the cultural tradition of India, the tradition of accepting life in the fullness thereof and going through it with song and dance. Gandhi, more a man of the people, almost the embodiment of the Indian peasant, represented the other ancient tradition of India, that of renunciation and asceticism. And yet Tagore was primarily a man of thought, and Gandhi of concentrated and ceaseless activity. Both, in their different ways, had a world outlook, and both were at the same time wholly Indian. They seemed to represent different but harmonious aspects of India and to complement one another.

Again I think of the richness of India's age-long cultural genius which can throw up in the same generation two such master types, typical of her in every way, yet representing different aspects of her many-sided personality.[1]

[Prophet and Politician—"Sri Ramakrishna as I understand him", New Delhi, 1949.] I do not know that I am particularly fitted to speak about the life and teachings of Sri Ramakrishna, because he was a man of God, and I am a man of earth, engaged in earthly activities which consume all my energy. But even a man of earth can admire, and perhaps be influenced by, a man of God. I admire godly men, and even though sometimes I do not altogether understand them, I have been influenced by what has been written about them by their disciples. These extraordinary personalities—Sri Ramakrishna and others like him—have powerfully influenced, not only their own generation, but succeeding generations. Not only so; they have also powerfully influenced great men and have changed the whole tenor of their lives.

Sri Ramakrishna was completely beyond the average run of men. He appears rather to belong to the tradition of the great rishis of India, who have come from time to time to turn our attention to the higher things of life and of the spirit. For, throughout her long history, and in spite of what has gone on elsewhere in the world, India has never ignored the spiritual values of life. She has always laid stress on the search for truth, and has always welcomed the searchers of truth in whatever guise they have come. Not only so; for, while India has built up this tradition of the

[1] V.B.Q. (1949), pp. 279–80.

search for truth and reality, she has also built up the tradition of the utmost tolerance toward all who strive for truth, no matter what path they may follow. Unfortunately, that tradition of tolerance has recently been shaken; we have at times fallen into evil ways, and have begun to think that we who walk in a certain narrow path alone are right, and others are wrong. This narrow-mindedness has never been the tradition of India. What made India great was her broad-mindedness, and her conviction that truth is many-sided and of infinite variety. How can any one man presume to say that he alone has grasped the entire truth. If he is earnest in his search, he may say that he has seen a particular facet of truth, but how can he say that no one else can do so unless he follows a similar path? India has always encouraged the pursuit of truth and of moral values, and this, perhaps, is the most distinctive feature of her culture. Thus, in spite of the many ups and downs of her history, the original impress still remains. . . .

I do not know how many of the younger generation read the speeches and the writings of Swami Vivekananda, but I can say that many of my generation were powerfully influenced by him, and I think it would be well worth while, and would do a great deal of good to the present generation, if they also were to study his works and teachings. They would learn much from them. They would, perhaps, catch a glimpse, as some of us did, of the fire that raged through Swami Vivekananda's mind and heart, and which ultimately consumed him at an early age. Because of this fire in his heart—the fire of a great personality expressing itself in eloquent and ennobling language—he spoke no idle words. He poured his heart and soul into the words he uttered . . . he spoke with a deep conviction and earnestness of spirit.

Much has happened since Swami Vivekananda's time, things which perhaps make some of us forget those who came before and shaped India in those early and difficult days. Curiously enough, if you read Swami Vivekananda's writings you will find that they are not old. They are as fresh today as when they were written, because what he wrote or spoke about dealt with certain fundamental aspects of the problems of the world today. He gave us something which brings us a certain pride in our inheritance. He did not spare us. He spoke of our weaknesses and our failings. He did not try to hide anything, and indeed he should not, because we have to correct those failings. Sometimes he strikes hard at us, while at other times he points out the great things for which India stood, and which, even in the days of her downfall, helped her to maintain—in some measure—her inherent greatness.

What Swamiji has written and said is still of interest and is likely to influence us for a long time to come. He was no politician in the ordinary sense of the word, yet he was, in my opinion, one of the great founders of the modern national movement of India, and a great number of people who took a more or less active part in that movement later on, drew their inspiration from Swami Vivekananda. Directly or indirectly, he has powerfully influenced the India of today, and it is my belief that our younger generation will take advantage of this fountain of wisdom, spirit, and fire that flowed through him.

In India and in the world we are faced with many problems, terribly difficult problems. How are we to deal with them? There are two ways: the way of the politician and the way of the prophet—I am not speaking of the opportunists. To some extent, unfortunately, the politician or states-man has to be an opportunist, in that he has to deal with things as they are, with the material he has. He cannot put across something which the people do not understand or cannot live up to. He has to face that difficulty always, especially in an age which calls itself democratic. Democracy, I believe, is fundamentally good—but democracy means that what you do must ultimately be understood and appreciated and acted upon by a large majority of the people. If this majority of the people do not understand or do not appreciate it, then even the truth that you possess cannot reach them. So it is that, very often, politicians and statesmen have to compro-mise, even with the truth, because the people's receptivity of truth is not sufficient. I do not know whether this is good or bad. But so it is, and, looking at it from a statesman's or politician's point of view, there appears to be no alternative, for, if he were to do anything else, he would soon be pushed aside, and another, with a clearer perception of the limitations of the people, would replace him. On the other hand, the prophet deals with truth in a different way. He adheres to truth, whatever the conse-quences; and often, because of this adherence, he is either stoned to death, or shot, or killed in some other way. That is the way of the prophet. That has been and always will be the way of the prophet. But though the prophet is slain, the truth does not die. Truth is greater than the prophet, and the prophet continues to live in that truth even more vividly than if he had not died.

Always there are these two approaches, the approach of the prophet and the approach of the political leader or statesman. Neither approach can be said to be, at least in terms of today, or in terms of a limited period, a wholly effective approach. In long-distance terms one might say perhaps that the prophet's approach is the better one; but one cannot carry on politics or the public affairs of a country in these days in long-distance terms, even though, generations later, the truth would be appreciated; if he attempted such a course, he would cease to have the opportunity to carry on. Though the prophet's way may be theoretically the better way, it does not seem difficult to believe that its effects would be seen or felt during his life time. Yet, on the other hand, however well meant, the politician's and statesman's way leads from compromise to compromise. It is a slippery path, and once one enters that path each succeeding compromise will lead him farther away from the truth. What he may wish to do may be ignored in the existing circumstances. Shall we then hold on to the truth as we see it, or shall we think so much about the existing circumstances as to forget the truth itself? That is the problem that humanity and those who are responsible for the ordering of the affairs of the world have continually to face, and it is indeed a difficult problem. All one can say is that insofar as it is possible the statesman should adhere to truth, or, at any rate, he should aim at truth, even though he may indulge in temporary compromises. Once he loses sight of truth, he may go very far astray. It is difficult to deal with day-to-day affairs without paying some heed to men's understanding of the truth and their receptivity to it. It is important to know how far the truth is understood and finds some kind of reception in men's minds. If the words of the politician are not understood, then even the words of the prophet would have no meaning. Therefore one has to interpret the truth, and even limit it to some extent, with reference to men's receptivity to it.

We are living in an age when scientific and technical progress has gone very far indeed, especially in the United States of America. Technically and industrially the Americans are a very advanced people, and have attained a high standard of material and physical life. I have no doubt that culturally also they are advancing in many ways. Nevertheless, it must be said of the whole world that man's mental and moral growth has not kept pace with this technical and scientific advance, and this is a very dangerous thing, because science and technology are weapons of tremendous power. We have these weapons, if you like, in the atomic power. When it is produced in simpler ways, atomic energy can be used for the tremendous benefit of mankind, or it can be used for destruction on a colossal scale. Science and technology in themselves are neither good nor bad; it is the user of them who is either good or bad. Therefore it is of the utmost importance that whoever holds these tremendous weapons should know how to use them properly. He should be sufficiently advanced, spiritually and morally, to know exactly how to use them to the best advantage. He should know exactly what his ultimate aim is. Unfortunately, humanity as a whole has not yet attained this standard despite all its religions, with all their churches, temples, and mosques. And this is the great misfortune of our age. We fight amongst ourselves for our petty dogmas and customs, and call ourselves religious even while we do not yet know how to behave decently toward our neighbors. And, all the while, the world hovers on the brink of repeated catastrophes.

Thus we find two types of forces in the world—the forces of destruction and the forces of construction. If at this time I say that I have faith in the forces of construction, I cannot justify that statement except by saying that it is simply an act of faith on my part; there is no particular logic behind it. It is just that I believe in it, even though I cannot justify it. Nevertheless, whether we believe in it or not, we should make up our minds definitely as to how we are going to strengthen the unifying and constructive forces, and oppose those forces which disrupt and destroy. And these things, I think, can be done only if we have a moral foundation, and certain moral concepts which will hold together our ideals and our life in general. If we have not these, then, I think, the disruptive forces are bound to gain the advantage.

Now . . . men like Swami Vivekananda, and men like Mahatma Gandhi are the great unifying forces, the great constructive geniuses of the world, not only in regard to their particular teachings, but also in their approach to the world, and their conscious and unconscious influence on it. This is of the most vital importance to us. You may or you may not accept some particular advice of Mahatmaji on economic or other grounds; but his fundamental approach to life, his constructive, unifying approach to the various problems—this is of vital importance. His approach—quite apart from the particular advice that he gave—was fundamentally the approach of India, of the Indian mind and of the Indian genius. And, if you are not able to accept that, then you really are on the side of destruction and disruption.

Sri Ramakrishna was a man of God, and had nothing to do with politics; it is his fundamental approach that counts. And while I am a man of politics, not dabbling much in, nor saying much about, other matters, spiritual and the like, nevertheless I do feel that our public affairs and our life in general would become much poorer in quality if that spiritual element and that moral standard were lacking.

India, like the rest of the world, faces difficult problems and questions, and all of us, whether as individuals, communities, groups, or nations, are being put to very severe tests. Because I have faith in India, I believe that she will not only survive these tests, but will make good, because there is a fundamental vitality which has enabled her to carry on through all these millennia of years—despite her weaknesses. But faith is not enough. We have to work for her success, and work always with a clear vision before us. And we must remember that while that clear vision may apply to India, it is essentially a larger vision to be applied to the whole world. It is not a narrowing vision, and our nationalism must not be a narrow nationalism. Swami Vivekananda, though a great nationalist, never preached narrowness. His nationalism was of the kind which automatically became a part of internationalism. And it is this broad approach that we must learn from these great men, and, if we learn it and act upon it to the best of our ability, we shall not only honor their memory, but we shall serve our country, and possibly serve humanity.[1]

8 | 1950—Republic Day, January 26

1950

[On January 26, 1950—precisely twenty years after India's first Independence pledge had been made—the free Republic of India was formally inaugurated.

Although Indo-Pakistan relations were by no means cordial—the Canal Waters dispute between the two countries remained unresolved, as did the settlement of financial claims, questions involving evacuee property, and the problem of Kashmir—Nehru and Liaquat Ali Khan, Prime Minister of Pakistan, succeeded in working out an agreement in connection with the two-way flow of refugees at the beginning of 1950.

During the same period a new self-confidence was to be discerned in India. Nehru's speeches of the period echo this development, despite the need to deal with the many difficult problems in realistic fashion, both at home and on the international scene.

Among the most alarming events of 1950 were the eruption of the Korean War in June and the fact that, in October, Chinese armed forces marched into Tibet. (Nehru's reactions to fresh developments in Sino-Tibetan-Indian and Sino-Indian relations, have been voiced in the period following Republic Day, 1950, and thus lie outside the scope of these volumes.)

[1] V.M.M., pp. 122–27.

Apartheid in South Africa, plus the fact that foreign footholds remained in India also continued to be disturbing, as did the situation in Indo-China, and related colonial problems.]

India Becomes a Republic : Message to the Nations, January 26, 1950

Events crowd in upon us and because of their quick succession we are apt to miss their significance. Some of us give messages on every occasion exhorting people to great endeavour and even these messages become stale [through] repetition.

Yet, undoubtedly, January 26, 1950, is a day of high significance for India and the Indian people. It does mean the consummation of one important phase of our national struggle. That journey is over, to give place to another and perhaps more arduous journey. A pledge is fulfilled and the fulfilment of every pledge gives satisfaction and strength for future endeavour.

There is a peculiar appropriateness about this January 26, for this day links up the past with the present and this present is seen to grow out of that past. Twenty years ago we took the first pledge of independence. During these twenty years we have known struggle and conflict and failure and achievement. The man who led us through apparent failure to achievement is no more with us, but the fruit of his labours is ours. What we do with this fruit depends upon many factors, the basic factors being those on which Gandhiji laid stress throughout his career—high character, integrity of mind and purpose, a spirit of tolerance and co-operation and hard work. I can only suggest to our people that we should found our republican freedom on these basic characteristics and shed fear and hatred from our minds and think always of the betterment of the millions of our people.

We are fortunate to witness the emergence of the Republic of India and our successors may well envy us this day; but fortune is a hostage which has to be zealously guarded by our own good work and which has a tendency to slip away if we slacken in our efforts or if we look in wrong directions.[1]

[1] N.S., p. 1.

9 | Postscript: "Changing India"

[A backward look at India's achievement of freedom, and a reaffirmation of her peaceful and democratic goals.]

August 1947 brought independence to India. In spite of the long-drawn-out struggle that preceded it, it came in peace and goodwill. Suddenly all bitterness of past conflict was forgotten and a new era of peace and friendship began. Our relations with Britain became friendly and we appeared to have no inherited problems and conflicts with any other country.

We had been conditioned for thirty years by Mahatma Gandhi and his gospel of peace which had left a powerful imprint not only on the minds of those actively interested in politics but also on the mass mind. Our success in attaining freedom through peaceful methods confirmed this way of thinking. Thus we entered the family of independent nations with a clean slate, without any inherited hatreds or enmities or territorial or other ambitions, determined to cultivate friendly and coöperative relations with all countries and to devote ourselves to the economic and social progress of India without getting entangled in national or international conflicts.

India had become free, but there were still some small parts of it under French and Portuguese control which were under colonial domination. Thus in our minds the freedom of India was not quite complete. We felt certain that France and Portugal would also follow the British example and that these enclaves of colonial territory would inevitably, and through peaceful methods, join independent India. We made the necessary approaches to the French and Portuguese Governments. The French enclaves became a part of the Union of India peacefully by agreement with France. Portugal proved much more intractable and gave a lot of trouble. . . .

August 1947 brought long-cherished freedom to our country. But in the wake of it came the Partition of India and, immediately after, mass killing on both sides of the new frontier and vast migrations. We had hoped that the Partition of India, which was brought about by agreement, would lead to the creation of two states which would be friendly neighbors and would coöperate with each other. That was natural, as not only geography but a common history and culture and the same language and many other factors common to both would, we thought, inevitably lead to friendly coöperation.

But this was not to be. The events after the Partition left a trail of great bitterness. We were trying to get over the immediate results of the Partition when the State of Kashmir was suddenly invaded from Pakistan and a new conflict arose. To us, trained and conditioned as we had been by Mahatma Gandhi, this came as a shock, for we had hoped that there would be no military conflicts with any other nation. After fourteen months, a cease-fire was agreed to and actual fighting stopped. Since then, although the Kashmir problem remained with us and gave a great deal of trouble, feelings in both countries gradually lost their bitterness and approached normality, in so far as the people were concerned.

We devoted ourselves to the major problem that confronted us—economic and social progress and the betterment of our people. Even before independence, we had given much thought to this matter and had come to the conclusion that we should proceed by the method of planning. Our resources were limited, and we wanted to utilize them to the best advantage to attain declared objectives. After independence, a Constituent Assembly was formed to draw up the new Constitution of India; this declared that India was to be a sovereign, democratic Republic which should secure for all its citizens: justice—social, economic and political; liberty of thought, expression, belief, faith and worship; equality of status and of opportunity. And among them all it was to promote fraternity, assuring the dignity of the individual and the unity of the nation.

On January 26, 1950, this new Republic came into existence and all our efforts were directed toward realizing the objectives laid down—political democracy and economic justice. We called the objective socialistic without adhering to any doctrinaire definition of the word. The system we evolved was consciously directed toward the welfare of the common man rather than to enrichment of the few; it is democratic because its processes are ultimately controlled by public discussion and by Parliament elected on the basis of universal adult franchise, and not by the secret purposes of a privileged minority.

While benefiting from foreign experiences—more especially, in the constitutional sense, from England and the United States—we did not wish to copy any foreign models. We believed that India had, by virtue of her long history and traditions, an individuality of her own and we should retain this without adhering to outworn ideas or traditions. We realized that the world was rapidly changing and we must keep pace with these changes without being swept away by them. We wanted to help, however modestly, in this developing pattern of international relations. We had no desire to interfere with other countries or impose our views on them. Thus, India started changes in her own life and institutions that are so decisive and far-reaching in their scope and intent that they may well be considered revolutionary, especially when viewed against the background of an ancient civilization and its ingrained conservatism. In foreign affairs, in a period when cataclysmic conflicts seem never too far below the horizon, she has invariably taken her stand with those who are striving for the maintenance of peace and for reconciliation and coöperation.

The twin policies which have guided us since independence are, broadly, democratic planning for development at home and, externally, a policy which has come to be named, rather inadequately, "non-alignment." Like the basic policies of most countries, these are not the product of any inspiration or arbitrary choice, but have their roots in our past history and way of thinking as well as in fundamental national exigencies. India's overriding and most urgent task is to raise the standard of living of her people and in order to achieve this, to carry out structural and organizational reforms not only as speedily as possible but with maximum popular support and participation. In foreign affairs, we had no interest other than to cultivate friendly coöperation with all countries and to help to keep world peace, as the sine qua non of everything else. In our approach to these problems, our attitude and ideas had inevitably been shaped by our own recent struggle for freedom, as well as by the accumulated experience of centuries, and above all by Mahatma Gandhi's teachings.

It is no sign of complacency to recognize that these policies have met with an encouraging measure of success. India, with a population of four hundred and forty six million and an electorate of over two hundred million, remains the largest functioning democracy in the world. Without deviating from democratic principles and procedures, she has launched upon extensive programs of modernization which are already bearing fruit. Far-reaching land reforms have taken place and our economy, still predominantly agricultural, is being steadily transformed by the spread of industrialization and the completion of vast new projects in the fields of power, transport and irrigation. Our Community Development schemes represent a rural reconstruction program which promises to transform the countryside and the vast population that live there. Recently, the Community Development movement has been extended to what is called *Panchayati Raj*; that is, there has been decentralization in favor of village-elected councils which have been given authority and resources to carry out schemes of development. Both industrial and agricultural production have increased substantially in volume as well as variety, and every effort is being made to ensure that the benefits of an expanding economy are shared equitably by all classes of the population. Education has spread remarkably at all stages and there are at present over fifty million boys and girls in schools and colleges. Special attention has been paid to scientific and technical education. The health conditions of the people have also made substantial progress. In the 1940s the expectation of life in India was thirty-two; now it is approaching fifty. Our planning, designed to equip the country with the technical skills and the productive facilities of a modern society, is essentially welfare-oriented. . . .

We have other positive aims also, such as the promotion of freedom from colonial rule, racial equality, peace and international coöperation, but "non-alignment" has become a summary description of this policy of friendship toward all nations, uncompromised by adherence to any military pacts. This was not due to any indifference to issues that arose, but rather to a desire to judge them for ourselves, in full freedom and without any preconceived partisan bias. It implied, basically, a conviction that good and evil are mixed up in this world, that the nations cannot be divided into sheep and goats, to be condemned or approved accordingly, and that if we were to join one military group rather than the other it was liable to increase and not diminish the risk of a major clash between them. Essentially, "non-alignment" is freedom of action which is a part of independence. This attitude no doubt displeased some people to begin with, but it has been of service to the cause of world peace at some critical moments in recent history. A large number of countries, including most of the newly independent states of Asia and Africa, have adopted a similar outlook on international affairs. It is possible that India has influenced their thinking to some extent in this matter; but, however that may be, "non-alignment" is now an integral part of the international pattern and is widely conceded to be a comprehensible and legitimate policy, particularly for the emergent Afro-Asian states. . . .

Consistent with our policy of promotion of peace and international coöperation, we welcomed the end of the civil war in our neighboring country China and the proclamation of the People's Republic of China in December 1949. We began developing friendly and coöperative relations with our northern neighbor. . . .[1]

We are far from being averse to change, we have embarked upon far-

[1] F.A. (Apr., 1963), pp. 453-57. © 1963 by the Council on Foreign Relations Inc., New York.

reaching changes and we propose to persevere with our plans and programs; but we are convinced that the methods by which changes are brought about are at least as important as the changes themselves. Means are more important than ends—this was the basic policy on which Mr Gandhi laid constant stress. We believe that any change should come through our own volition, as a result of our own experience, and that it should not be foisted on us through any kind of force or pressure. In the pursuit of change, we should seek to carry the mass of the people with us and win their support. This way of dealing with our problems may not result in as swift or spectacular transformation as we might wish, but at least the progress achieved will have a solid basis in the nation's consent and avoid a degree of dislocation and disorganization that we can ill afford.

It is in this spirit that we have set our hands to the task of developing, in this ancient land, a system combining political democracy and economic justice.

Can this enterprise survive the new strains and tensions? The question goes to the heart of the issues involved in the present conflict, and the answer lies only in part, though perhaps in large part, with us in India. I am confident in my own mind that we cannot let ourselves be panicked into abandoning either the goal or the methods of our policy as I have stated it. . . .

In India there are groups which may be called Right and others which may be called Left. But the antithesis between Right and Left is not so clear-cut as in some other parts of the world, or as widely permeating in its intellectual and political language. To the vast mass of our people, the reality is a deeply felt but undoctrinaire demand for better economic and social conditions. . . .

The defense of our freedom and the social progress to which we aspire can best be assured in our view by the flexible democratic structure that we have evolved for ourselves. This is not only in conformity with our larger interests, but also with the larger interests of the world.[1]

[1] Ibid., pp. 461–63.

Appendix

Nehru Family Circle

[Father and mother of Jawaharlal: Motilal and Swaruprani. (Motilal's career is referred to in the early chapters of these volumes.) Two younger sisters: the elder, Swarup; the younger, Krishna. Swarup married Ranjit Pandit; has become internationally famed as Vijaya Lakshmi Pandit, the first woman to be appointed a Provincial Minister in India before independence; subsequently has been Ambassador to the United States and the Union of Soviet Republics, High Commissioner to Great Britain, Indian Ambassador to the United Nations, President of the United Nations' General Assembly, etc., etc. Krishna married Raja Hutheesing. She is the author of several volumes that have been published.

Jawaharlal married Kamala Kaul on February 8, 1916, "the Vasanta Panchami day which heralds the coming of spring in India".[1] Their daughter, Indira, who was born on November 19, 1917 (according to the Gregorian Calendar), became the wife of Feroze Gandhi (not a relative of the Mahatma). Mrs Gandhi has been involved in Indian politics even as a child. Since India gained her independence, Mrs Gandhi served one term as Congress Party President. She acted as her father's hostess, and has consistently played a prominent role in conjunction with a number of political and social welfare activities in India. She is currently a member of the Indian Cabinet. (During the years preceding Indian independence the Nehru family, in general, was extremely active politically, many of its members having undergone prolonged and repeated imprisonments.)]

[As indicated in the Introduction, several documents that shed light upon various developments described in these volumes—but that would have interrupted the flow of the main text—follow. Unless otherwise indicated in headings and footnotes, subsequent passages are by Nehru.]

The Rise of Imperialism in the Nineteenth Century

As a result of the Mechanical Revolution, capitalist civilization spread all over the world and Europe was dominant everywhere. And capitalism led to imperialism. So that the century might also be called the century of

[1] T.F., p. 45.

imperialism. But this new Imperial Age was very different from the old imperialisms of Rome and China and India and the Arabs and Mongols. There was a new type of empire, hungry for raw materials and markets. The new imperialism was the child of the new industrialism. "Trade follows the flag", it was said, and often enough the flag followed the Bible. Religion, science, the love of one's own country, all were prostituted to one end—the exploitation of the weaker and industrially more backward peoples of the earth, so that the lords of the big machine, the princes of industrialism, might grow richer and richer. The Christian missionary, going in the name of truth and love, was often the outpost of empire, and if any harm befell him, his country made this an excuse to seize territory and extort concessions.

The capitalist organization of industry and civilization led inevitably to this imperialism. Capitalism also led to an intensification of the feeling of nationalism, so that you can also call this century the century of national- ism. This nationalism was not merely a love of one's own country, but a hatred of all others. From this glorification of one's own patch of land and contemptuous running down of others, trouble and friction between different countries were bound to result. Industrial rivalry and imperial rivalry between different European countries made matters worse. The map of Europe as settled by the Congress of Vienna in 1814–15 was another irritating factor. According to this, some nationalities had been suppressed and put forcibly under other people's rule. Poland had dis- appeared as a nation. Austria-Hungary became an ill-assorted empire containing all manner of people cordially disliking each other. The Turkish Empire in the south-east of Europe contained many non-Turkish peoples in the Balkans. Italy was split up into many States, and part of it was under Austria. Repeated attempts were made through war and revo- lution to change this map of Europe. In my last letter I mentioned some which followed soon after the Vienna settlement. In the second half of the century Italy managed to shake off the Austrians in the north and the Pope's domination in the centre, and became a united nation. This was followed soon afterwards by the unification of Germany under the leader- ship of Prussia. France was defeated and humiliated by Germany and deprived of two of her frontier provinces, Alsace and Lorraine, and from that day she dreamt of *revanche* (revenge). In less than fifty years there was a bloody and terrible revenge.

England, with her great lead, was the most fortunate of the European countries. She held all the prizes, and was well content with things as they were. India was the model of the new type of empire, a rich territory from the exploitation of which a river of gold flowed ceaselessly to England. All the other would-be empire-builders envied this possession of India by England. They sought to build empires elsewhere after this Indian model. The French succeeded in some measure; the Germans came rather late into the field, and there was little left for them. So there was political tension all over the world between these "Great Powers" of Europe, each trying to swallow more and more territory and coming up against another engaged in the same process. Between England and Russia especially there was continuous friction, for Russia seemed to threaten England's possession of India from central Asia. So England was always trying to checkmate Russia. When Russia, in the middle of the century, defeated Turkey and coveted Constantinople, England came down on the side of Turkey and drove Russia back. England did this not out of love for Turkey, but from fear of Russia and of losing India.

England's industrial lead gradually grew less and less as Germany and France and the United States crept up to her. By the end of the century matters were coming to a head. The world was too small for the vast ambitions of these European Powers. Each feared and hated and envied the other, and this fear and hatred made them increase their armies and their ships of war. There was a feverish competition in these engines of destruction. There were also alliances between different countries to fight others, and ultimately two systems of alliances faced each other in Europe—one was headed by France, to which England also privately adhered, and the other was headed by Germany. Europe became an armed camp. And there was ever fiercer competition in industry and trade and armaments. And a narrow spirit of nationalism was whipped up in each western country, so that the masses might be misled and made to hate their neighbours in other countries, and thus be kept ready for war.

A blind nationalism thus began to dominate [nineteenth-century] Europe. This was strange, for the speeding up of communications had brought different countries closer to each other and many more people travelled. One would have thought that as people grew to know their neighbours better, their prejudices would lessen and their narrow-mindedness give place to a broader outlook. To some extent this undoubtedly took place, but the whole structure of society under the new industrial capitalism was such that it bred friction between nation and nation, class and class, and man and man.

Nationalism also grew in the East. It took the shape of resistance to the foreigner, who was dominating and exploiting the country. At first the feudal relics in eastern countries resisted foreign domination, because they felt that their position was threatened. They failed, as they were bound to do. A new nationalism then arose tinged with a religious outlook. Gradually this religious colouring faded off and a nationalism of the western type emerged. In Japan, foreign domination was avoided, and an intense half-feudal nationalism was encouraged.

Asia began to resist European aggression from the earliest days, but the resistance became half-hearted when the power and efficiency of the new weapons which the European armies possessed were realized. The growth of science and the mechanical progress made in Europe had made these European armies far more powerful than anything the East had then. Eastern countries therefore felt powerless before them and bowed their heads in despair. Some people say that the East is spiritual and the West material. This kind of remark is very deceptive. The real difference between the East and the West at the time when Europe came as aggressor, in the eighteenth and nineteenth centuries, was the medievalism of the East and the industrial and mechanical progress of the West. India and other eastern countries were dazzled at first, not only by the military efficiency of the West, but also by their scientific and technical progress. All this combined to give them a feeling of inferiority in regard to military and technical matters. In spite of this, however, nationalism grew, and the desire to resist foreign aggression and turn out the foreigner. Early in the twentieth century an event occurred which had a great effect on the mind of Asia. This was the defeat of Tsarist Russia by Japan. For little Japan to defeat one of the greatest and most powerful of European Powers surprised most people; in Asia the surprise was a most pleasant one. Japan was looked upon as the representative of Asia battling against western aggression and, for the moment, became very popular all over the East. Of course Japan was no such representative of Asia, and she fought for her own land just like any Great Power of Europe. I remember well how excited I used to get when news came of the Japanese victories. . . .

So, as the imperialism of the West became more and more aggressive, nationalism grew in the East to counter it and fight it. All over Asia, from the Arab nations in the West to the Mongolian nations of the Far East, national movements took shape, advanced cautiously at first and moderately, and then become more and more extreme in their demands. India saw the beginnings and early years of the National Congress. The revolt of Asia had begun.[1]

A Fresh Look at the History of Indian Nationalism and British Rule in India

It was natural and inevitable that Indian nationalism should resent alien rule. And yet it was curious how large numbers of our intelligentsia, to the end of the nineteenth century, accepted, consciously or unconsciously, the British ideology of empire. They built their own arguments on this, and only ventured to criticize some of its outward manifestations. History and economics and other subjects that were taught in the schools and colleges were written entirely from the British imperial viewpoint, and laid stress on our numerous failings in the past and present, and the virtues and high destiny of the British. We accepted to some extent this distorted version, and, even when we resisted it instinctively, we were influenced by it. At first there was no intellectual escape from it, for we knew no other facts or arguments, and so we sought relief in religious nationalism, in the thought that at least in the sphere of religion and philosophy we were second to no other people. We comforted ourselves in our misfortune and degradation with the notion that though we did not possess the outward show and glitter of the West we had the real inner article, which was far more valuable and worth having. Vivekananda and others, as well as the interest of Western scholars in our old philosophies, gave us a measure of self-respect again and roused up our dormant pride in our past.

[1] G.W.H., pp. 399–401.

Gradually we began to suspect and examine critically British statements about our past and present conditions, but still we thought and worked within the framework of British ideology. If a thing was bad, it would be called "un-British"; if a Britisher in India misbehaved, the fault was his, not that of the system. But the collection of this critical material of British rule in India, in spite of the moderate outlook of the authors, served a revolutionary purpose and gave a political and economic foundation to our nationalism. Dadabhai Naoroji's *Poverty and Un-British Rule in India*, and books by Romesh Dutt and William Digby and others, thus played a revolutionary role in the development of our nationalist thought. Further researches in ancient Indian history revealed brilliant and highly civilized periods in the remote past, and we read of these with great satisfaction. We also discovered that the British record in India was very different from what we had been led to believe from their history books.

Our challenge to the British version of history, economics, and administration in India grew, and yet we continued to function within the orbit of their ideology. That was the position of Indian nationalism as a whole at the turn of the century. That is still the position of the Liberal group and other small groups as well as a number of moderate Congressmen, who go forward emotionally from time to time, but intellectually still live in the nineteenth century. Because of that the Liberal is unable to grasp the idea of Indian freedom, for the two are fundamentally irreconcilable. He imagines that step by step he will go up to higher offices and will deal with fatter and more important files. The machinery of government will go on smoothly as before, only he will be at the hub, and somewhere in the background, without intruding themselves too much, will be the British Army to give him protection in case of need. That is his idea of Dominion status within the Empire. It is a naïve notion impossible of achievement, for the price of British protection is Indian subjection. We cannot have it both ways, even if that was not degrading to the self-respect of a great country. . . .

It is not surprising that the Indian intelligentsia in the nineteenth century should have succumbed to British ideology; what is surprising is that some people should continue to suffer that delusion even after the stirring events and changes of the twentieth century. In the nineteenth century the British ruling classes were the aristocrats of the world, with a long record of wealth and success and power behind them. This long record and training gave them some of the virtues as well as failings of aristocracy. We in India can comfort ourselves with the thought that we helped substantially during the last century and three-quarters in providing the wherewithal and the training for this superior state. They began to think themselves—as so many races and nations have done—the chosen of God, and their Empire an earthly Kingdom of Heaven. If their special position was acknowledged and their superiority not challenged, they were gracious and obliging, provided that this did them no harm. But opposition to them became opposition to the divine order, and as such was a deadly sin which must be suppressed.

If this was the general British attitude to the rest of the world, it was most conspicuous in India. There was something fascinating about the British approach to the Indian problem, even though it was singularly irritating. The calm assurance of always being in the right and of having borne a great burden worthily, faith in their racial destiny and their own brand of imperialism, contempt and anger at the unbelievers and sinners who challenged the foundations of the true faith—there was something of the religious temper about this attitude. Like the Inquisitors of old, they were bent on saving us regardless of our desires in the matter. Incidentally they profited by this traffic in virtue, thus demonstrating the truth of the old proverb: "Honesty is the best policy." The progress of India became synonymous with the adaptation of the country to the imperial scheme and the fashioning of chosen Indians after the British mold. The more we accepted British ideals and objectives, the fitter we were for "self-government". Freedom would be ours as soon as we demonstrated and guaranteed that we would use it only in accordance with British wishes.

Indians and Englishmen are, I am afraid, likely to disagree about the record of British rule in India. That is perhaps natural, but it does come as a shock when high British officials, including Secretaries of State for India, draw fanciful pictures of India's past and present and make statements which have no basis in fact. It is quite extraordinary how ignorant English people, apart from some experts and others, are about India. If facts elude them, how much more is the spirit of India beyond their reach? They seized her body and possessed her, but it was the possession of violence. They did not know her or try to know her. They never looked into her eyes, for theirs were averted and hers downcast through shame and humiliation. After centuries of contact they face each other, strangers still, full of dislike for each other.

Yet India with all her poverty and degradation had enough of nobility and greatness about her; and, though she was overburdened with ancient tradition and present misery and her eyelids were a little weary, she had "a beauty wrought out from within upon the flesh, the deposit, little cell by cell, of strange thoughts and fantastic reveries and exquisite passions". Behind and within her battered body one could still glimpse a majesty of soul. Through long ages she had traveled and gathered much wisdom on the way, and trafficked with strangers and added them to her own big family, and witnessed days of glory and of decay, and suffered humiliation and terrible sorrow, and seen many a strange sight; but throughout her long journey she had clung to her immemorial culture, drawn strength and vitality from it, and shared it with other lands. Like a pendulum she had swung up and down; she had ventured with the daring of her thought to reach up to the heavens and unravel their mystery, and she had also had bitter experience of the pit of hell. Despite the woeful accumulations of superstition and degrading custom that had clung to her and borne her down, she had never wholly forgotten the inspiration that some of the wisest of her children, at the dawn of history, had given her in the *Upanishads*. Their keen minds, ever restless and ever striving and exploring, had not sought refuge in blind dogma or grown complacent in the routine observance of dead forms of ritual and creed. They had demanded not a personal relief from suffering in the present or a place in a paradise to come, but light and understanding: "Lead me from the unreal to the real, lead me from darkness to light, lead me from death to immortality." In the most famous of the prayers recited daily even today by millions, the *gayatri mantra*, the call is for knowledge, for enlightenment.

Though often broken up politically, her spirit always guarded a common heritage, and in her diversity there was ever an amazing unity. Like all ancient lands she was a curious mixture of the good and bad, but the good was hidden and had to be sought after, while the odor of decay was evident, and her hot, pitiless sun gave full publicity to the bad.

There is some similarity between Italy and India. Both are ancient countries with long traditions of culture behind them, though Italy is a newcomer compared to India, and India is a much vaster country. Both were split up politically, and yet the conception of Italia, like that of India, never died, and in all their diversity the unity was predominant. In Italy the unity was largely a Roman unity, for that great city had dominated the country and been the fount and symbol of unity. In India there was no such single center or dominant city, although Benares might well be called the Eternal City of the East, not only for India but also for Eastern Asia. But, unlike Rome, Benares never dabbled in empire or thought of temporal power. Indian culture was so widespread all over India that no part of the country could be called the heart of that culture. From Cape Comorin to Amaranath and Badrinath in the Himalayas, from Dwarka to Puri, the same ideas coursed; and, if there was a clash of ideas in one place, the noise of it soon reached distant parts of the country.

Just as Italy gave the gift of culture and religion to Western Europe, India did so to Eastern Asia, though China was as old and venerable as India. And, even when Italy was lying prostrate politically, her life coursed through the veins of Europe.

It was Metternich who called Italy a "geographical expression", and many a would-be Metternich has used that phrase for India; strangely enough, there is a similarity even in their geographical positions in the two continents. More interesting is the comparison of England with Austria, for has not England of the twentieth century been compared to Austria of the nineteenth, proud and haughty and imposing still, but with the roots that gave strength shriveling up and decay eating its way into the mighty fabric?

It is curious how one cannot resist the tendency to give an anthropomorphic form to a country. Such is the force of habit and early associations. India becomes *Bharat Mata*, Mother India, a beautiful lady, very old but ever youthful in appearance, sad-eyed and forlorn, cruelly treated by aliens and outsiders, and calling upon her children to protect her. Some such picture rouses the emotions of hundreds of thousands and drives them to action and sacrifice. And yet India is in the main the peasant and the worker, not beautiful to look at, for poverty is not beautiful. Does the beautiful lady of our imaginations represent the bare-bodied and bent workers in the fields and factories? Or the small group of those who have from ages past crushed the masses and exploited them, imposed cruel customs on them and made many of them even untouchable? We seek to cover truth by the creatures of our imaginations and endeavor to escape from reality to a world of dreams.

And yet, despite these different classes and their mutual conflicts, there was a common bond which united them in India, and one is amazed at its persistence and tenacity and enduring vitality. What was this strength due to? Not merely the passive strength and weight of inertia and tradition, great as these always are. There was an active sustaining principle, for it resisted successfully powerful outside influences and absorbed internal forces that rose to combat it. And yet with all its strength it could not preserve political freedom or endeavor to bring about political unity. These latter do not appear to have been considered worth much trouble; their importance was very foolishly ignored, and we have suffered for this neglect. Right through history the old Indian ideal did not glorify political and military triumph, and it looked down upon money and the professional money-making class. Honor and wealth did not go together, and honor was meant to go, at least in theory, to the men who served the community with little in the shape of financial reward.

The old culture managed to live through many a fierce storm and tempest, but, though it kept its outer form, it lost its real content. Today it is fighting silently and desperately against a new and all-powerful opponent —the *bania* civilization of the capitalist West. It will succumb to this newcomer, for the West brings science, and science brings food for the hungry millions. But the West also brings an antidote to the evils of this cutthroat civilization—the principles of socialism, of co-operation, and service to the community for the common good. This is not so unlike the old Brahman ideal of service, but it means the brahmanization (not in the religious sense, of course) of all classes and groups and the abolition of class distinctions. It may be that when India puts on her new garment, as she must, for the old is torn and tattered, she will have it cut in this fashion, so as to make it conform both to present conditions and her old thought. The ideas she adopts must become racy to her soil.[1]

The Record of British Rule in India

What has been the record of British rule in India? I doubt if it is possible for any Indian or Englishman to take an objective and dispassionate view of this long record. And, even if this were possible, it would be still more difficult to weigh and measure the psychological and other immaterial factors. We are told that British rule "has given to India that which throughout the centuries she never possessed, a government whose authority is unquestioned in any part of the sub-continent"; it has established the rule of law and a just and efficient administration; it has brought to India Western conceptions of parliamentary government and personal

[1] T.F., pp. 269–75.

liberties; and "by transforming British India into a single unitary state it has engendered amongst Indians a sense of political unity" and thus fostered the first beginnings of nationalism.[1] That is the British case, and there is much truth in it, though the rule of law and personal liberties have not been evident for many years.

The Indian survey of this period lays stress on many other factors, and points out the injury, material and spiritual, that foreign rule has brought us. The viewpoint is so different that sometimes the very thing that is commended by the British is condemned by Indians. As Dr Ananda Coomaraswamy writes: "One of the most remarkable features of British rule in India is that the greatest injuries inflicted upon the Indian people have the outward appearance of blessings."

As a matter of fact the changes that have taken place in India during the last century or more have been world changes common to most countries in the East and West. The growth of industrialism in western Europe, and later on in the rest of the world, brought nationalism and the strong unitary state in its train everywhere. The British can take credit for having first opened India's window to the West and brought her one aspect of Western industrialism and science. But having done so they throttled the further industrial growth of the country till circumstances forced their hands. India was already the meeting place of two cultures, the western Asiatic culture of Islam and the eastern, her own product, which spread to the Far East. And now a third and more powerful impulse came from further west, and India became a focal point and a battleground for various old and new ideas. There can be no doubt that this third impulse would have triumphed and thus solved many of India's old problems, but the British, who had themselves helped in bringing it, tried to stop its further progress. They prevented our industrial growth and thus delayed our political growth, and preserved all the out-of-date feudal and other relics they could find in the country. They even froze up our changing and to some extent progressing laws and customs at the stage they found them, and made it difficult for us to get out of their shackles. It was not with their good will or assistance that the *bourgeoisie* grew in India. But after introducing the railway and other products of industrialism they could not stop the wheel of change; they could only check it and slow it down, and this they did to their own manifest advantage.

"On this solid foundation the majestic structure of the Government of India rests, and it can be claimed with certainty that in the period which has elapsed since 1858 when the Crown assumed supremacy over all the territories of the East India Company, the educational and material progress of India has been greater than it was ever within her power to achieve during any other period of her long and checkered history." This statement is not so self-evident as it appears to be, and it has often been stated that literacy actually went down with the coming of British rule. But, even if the statement was wholly true, it amounts to a comparison of the modern

---

[1] Quotations from Report of the Joint Parliamentary Committee on Indian Constitutional Reform (1934). As cited in T.F., p. 275.

industrial age with past ages. In almost every country in the world the educational and material progress has been tremendous during the past century because of science and industrialism, and it may be said with assurance of any such country that progress of this kind "has been greater than was ever within her power to achieve during any other period of her long and checkered history"—though perhaps that country's history may not be a long one in comparison with Indian history. Are we needlessly cantankerous and perverse if we suggest that some such technical progress would have come to us anyhow in this industrial age, and even without British rule? And, indeed, if we compare our lot with many other countries, may we not hazard the guess that such progress might have been greater if we had not had to contend against a stifling of that progress by the British themselves? Railways, telegraphs, telephones, wireless, and the like are hardly tests of the goodness or beneficence of British rule. They were welcome and necessary, and, because the British happened to be the agents who brought them first, we should be grateful to them. But even these heralds of industrialism came to us primarily for the strengthening of British rule. They were the veins and arteries through which the nation's blood should have coursed, increasing its trade, carrying its produce, and bringing new life and wealth to its millions. It is true that in the long run some such result was likely, but they were designed and worked for another purpose—to strengthen the imperial hold and to capture markets for British goods—which they succeeded in achieving. I am all in favor of industrialization and the latest methods of transport, but sometimes, as I rushed across the Indian plains, the railway, that life-giver, has almost seemed to me like iron bands confining and imprisoning India.

The British conception of ruling India was the police conception of the State. Government's job was to protect the State and leave the rest to others. Their public finance dealt with military expenditure, police, civil administration, interest on debt. The economic needs of the citizens were not looked after, and were sacrificed to British interests. The cultural and other needs of the people, except for a tiny handful, were entirely neglected. The changing conceptions of public finance which brought free and universal education, improvement of public health, care of poor and feeble-minded, insurance of workers against illness, old age, unemployment, etc., in other countries, were almost entirely beyond the ken of the Government. It could not indulge in these spending activities, for its tax system was most regressive, taking a much larger proportion of small incomes than of the larger ones, and its expenditure on its protective and administrative functions was terribly heavy and swallowed up most of the revenue.

The outstanding feature of British rule was their concentration on everything that went to strengthen their political and economic hold on the country. Everything else was incidental. If they built up a powerful central government and an efficient police force, that was an achievement for which they can take credit, but the Indian people can hardly congratulate themselves on it. Unity is a good thing, but unity in subjection is hardly a thing to be proud of. The very strength of a despotic government may become a greater burden for a people; and a police force, no doubt useful in many ways, can be, and has been often enough, turned against the very people it is supposed to protect.

Britain's supremacy in India brought us peace, and India was certainly in need of peace after the troubles and misfortunes that followed the break-up of the Moghal empire. Peace is a precious commodity, necessary for any progress, and it was welcome to us when it came. But even peace can be purchased at too great a price, and we can have the perfect peace of the grave, and the absolute safety of a cage or of prison. Or peace may be the sodden despair of men unable to better themselves. The peace which is imposed by an alien conqueror has hardly the restful and soothing qualities of the real article.

It is a futile task to consider the "ifs" and possibilities of history. I feel sure that it was a good thing for India to come in contact with the scientific and industrial West. Science was the great gift of the West; India lacked this, and without it she was doomed to decay. The manner of our contacts was unfortunate, and yet, perhaps, only a succession of violent shocks could shake us out of our torpor. From this point of view the Protestant, individualistic, Anglo-Saxon English were suitable, for they were more different from us than most other Westerners, and could give us greater shocks.

They gave us political unity, and that was a desirable thing; but whether we had this unity or not, Indian nationalism would have grown and demanded that unity.

The political unity of India was achieved incidentally as a side product of the Empire's advance. In later years, when that unity allied itself to nationalism and challenged alien rule, we witnessed the deliberate promotion of disunity and sectarianism, formidable obstacles to our future progress.

What a long time it is since the British came here, a century and three-quarters since they became dominant! They had a free hand, as despotic governments have, and a magnificent opportunity to mold India according to their desire. During these years the world has changed out of all recognition—England, Europe, America, Japan. The insignificant American colonies bordering the Atlantic in the eighteenth century constitute today the wealthiest, the most powerful and technically the most advanced nation; the vast territories of the U.S.S.R., where till only yesterday the dead hand of the Tsar's government suppressed and stifled all growth, now pulsate with a new life and build a new world before our eyes. There have been big changes in India also, and the country is very different from what it was in the eighteenth century—railways, irrigation works, factories, schools and colleges, huge government offices, etc., etc.

And yet, in spite of these changes, what is India like today? A servile state, with its splendid strength caged up, hardly daring to breathe freely, governed by strangers from afar; her people poor beyond compare, short-lived and incapable of resisting disease and epidemic; illiteracy rampant; vast areas devoid of all sanitary or medical provision; unemployment on a

18*

prodigious scale, both among the middle classes and the masses. Freedom, democracy, socialism, communism, are, we are told, the slogans of impractical idealists, doctrinaires, or knaves; the test must be one of the well-being of the people as a whole. That is indeed a vital test, and by that test India makes a terribly poor show today. We read of great schemes of unemployment relief and the alleviation of distress in other countries; what of our scores of millions of unemployed and the distress that is widespread and permanent? We also read of housing schemes elsewhere; where are the houses of hundreds of millions of our people, who live in mud huts or have no shelter at all? May we not envy the lot of other countries where education, sanitation, medical relief, cultural facilities, and production advance rapidly ahead, while we remain where we were, or plod wearily along at the pace of a snail? Russia in a brief dozen years of wonderful effort has almost ended illiteracy in her vast territories and has evolved a fine and up-to-date system of education, in touch with the life of the masses. Backward Turkey, under the Ataturk, Mustapha Kemal's, leadership, has also made giant strides toward widespread literacy.

Indians have been accused of talking too much and doing little. It is a just charge. But may we not express our wonder at the inexhaustible capacity of the British for committees and commissions, each of which, after long labor, produces a learned report—"a great State document"— which is duly praised and pigeonholed? And so we get the sensation of moving ahead, of progress, and yet have the advantage of remaining where we were. Honor is satisfied, and vested interests remain untouched and secure. Other countries discuss how to get on; we discuss checks and brakes and safeguards lest we go too fast.

"The Imperial splendor became the measure of the people's poverty," so we are told (by the Joint Parliamentary Committee, 1934) of the Moghal times. It is a just observation, but may we not apply the same measure today? What of New Delhi today with its viceregal pomp and pageantry, and the provincial governors with all their ostentation? And all this with a background of abject and astonishing poverty. The contrast hurts, and it is a little difficult to imagine how sensitive men can put up with it. India today is a poor and dismal sight behind all the splendors of the imperial frontage. There is a great deal of patchwork and superficiality, and behind it the unhappy petty *bourgeoisie*, crushed more and more by modern conditions. Further back come the workers, living miserably in grinding poverty, and then the peasant, that symbol of India, whose lot it is to be "born to Endless Night".

It would be absurd to cast the blame for all India's ills on the British. That responsibility must be shouldered by us, and we may not shirk it; it is unseemly to blame others for the inevitable consequences of our own weaknesses. An authoritarian system of government, and especially one that is foreign, must encourage a psychology of subservience and try to limit the mental outlook and horizon of the people. It must crush much that is finest in youth—enterprise, spirit of adventure, originality, "pep" —and encourage sneakiness, rigid conformity, and a desire to cringe and please the bosses. Such a system does not bring out the real service mentality, the devotion to public service or to ideals; it picks out the least public-spirited persons whose sole objective is to get on in life. We see what a class the British attract to themselves in India! Some of them are intellectually keen and capable of good work. They drift to government service or semigovernment service because of lack of opportunity elsewhere, and gradually they tone down and become just parts of the big machine, their minds imprisoned by the dull routine of work. They develop the qualities of a bureaucracy—"a competent knowledge of clerkship and the diplomatic art of keeping office." At the highest they have a passive devotion to the public service. There is, or can be, no flaming enthusiasm. That is not possible under a foreign government.

But, apart from these, the majority of petty officials are not an admirable lot, for they have learned only to cringe to their superiors and bully their inferiors. The fault is not theirs. That is the training the system gives them. And if sycophancy and nepotism flourish, as they often do, is it to be wondered at? They have no ideals in service; the haunting fear of unemployment and consequent starvation pursues them, and their chief concern is to hold on to their jobs and get other jobs for their relatives and friends. Where the spy and that most odious of creatures, the informer, always hover in the background, it is not easy to develop the more desirable virtues in a people.

Recent developments have made it even more difficult for sensitive, public-spirited men to join government service. The Government does not want them, and they do not wish to associate with it too closely, unless compelled by economic circumstance.

But, as all the world knows, it is the white man who bears the burden of Empire, not the brown. We have various imperial services to carry on the imperial tradition, and a sufficiency of safeguards to protect their special privileges—all, we are told, in the interests of India. It is remarkable how the good of India seems to be tied up with the obvious interests and advancement of these services. If any privilege or prize post of the Indian Civil Service is taken away, we are told that inefficiency and corruption will result. If the reserved jobs for the Indian Medical Service are reduced, this becomes a "menace to India's health". And of course if the British element in the Army is touched, all manner of terrible perils confront us.

I think there is some truth in this: that if the superior officials suddenly went away and left their departments in charge of their subordinates, there would be a fall in efficiency. But that is because the whole system has been built this way, and the subordinates are not by any means the best men, nor have they ever been made to shoulder responsibility. I feel convinced that there is abundant good material in India, and it could be available within a fairly short period if proper steps were taken. But that means a complete change in our governmental and social outlook. It means a new State.

As it is, we are told that whatever changes in the constitutional apparatus may come our way, the rigid framework of the great services which guard and shelter us will continue as before. Hierophants of the sacred mysteries of government, they will guard the temple and prevent the vulgar from entering its holy precincts. Gradually, as we make ourselves worthy of the privilege, they will remove the veils one after another, till in some future age, even the holy of holies stands uncovered to our wondering and reverent eyes. . . .

The underlying assumption of the Indian Civil Service is that they discharge their duties most efficiently, and therefore they can lay every stress on their claims, which are many and varied. If India is poor, that is the fault of her social customs, her *banias* and moneylenders, and, above all, her enormous population. The greatest *bania* of all, the British Government in India, is conveniently ignored. And what they propose to do about this population I do not know, for in spite of a great deal of help received from famines, epidemics, and a high death rate generally, the population is still overwhelming. Birth control is proposed, and I, for one, am entirely in favor of the spread of the knowledge and methods of birth control. But the use of these methods itself requires a much higher standard of living for the masses, some measure of general education, and innumerable clinics all over the country. Under present conditions birth-control methods are completely out of reach for the masses. The middle classes can profit by them as, I believe, they are doing to a growing extent.

But this argument of overpopulation is deserving of further notice. The problem today all over the world is not one of lack of food or lack of other essentials, but lack of capacity to buy food, etc., for those who are in need. Even in India, the food supply has increased and can increase more than proportionately to the population.

Whenever India becomes free, and in a position to build her new life as she wants to, she will necessarily require the best of her sons and daughters for this purpose. Good human material is always rare, and in India it is rarer still because of our lack of opportunities under British rule. We shall want the help of many foreign experts in many departments of public activity, particularly in those which require special technical and scientific knowledge. Among those who have served in the Indian Civil Service or other imperial services there will be many, Indians or foreigners, who will be necessary and welcome to the new order. But of one thing I am quite sure: that no new order can be built up in India so long as the spirit of the Indian Civil Service pervades our administration and our public services. It will either succeed in crushing freedom or will be swept away itself. Only with one type of state is it likely to fit in, and that is the fascist type.

Even more mysterious and formidable are the so-called Defense Services. We may not criticize them, we may not say anything about them, for what do we know about such matters? We must only pay and pay heavily without murmuring.[1]

British Government—Congress Conflict

[The fundamental conflict between the Congress and the British Government has represented] something which did not depend on individuals

[1] T.F., pp. 275-84.

but arose from the very nature of our national struggle and the want of equilibrium [in] our agrarian economy, something that could not be liquidated or compromised away without a basic change. Our national movement had orginally begun because of the desire of our upper middle classes to find means of self-expression and self-growth, and behind it there was the political and economic urge. It spread to the lower middle classes and became a power in the land; and then it began to stir the rural masses, who were finding it more and more difficult to keep up, as a whole, even their miserable rock-bottom standard of living. The old self-sufficient village economy had long ceased to exist. Auxiliary cottage industries, ancillary to agriculture, which had relieved somewhat the burden on the land, had died off, partly because of State policy, but largely because they could not compete with the rising machine industry. The burden on land grew, and the growth of Indian industry was too slow to make much difference to this. Ill-equipped and almost unawares, the overburdened village was thrown into the world market and was tossed about hither and thither. It could not compete on even terms. It was backward in its methods of production, and its land system, resulting in a progressive fragmentation of holdings, made radical improvement impossible. So the agricultural classes, both landlords and tenants, went downhill, except during brief periods of boom. The landlords tried to pass on the burden to their tenantry, and the growing pauperization of the peasantry—both the petty landholders and the tenants—drew them to the national movement. The agricultural proletariat, the large numbers of landless laborers in rural areas, were also attracted; and for all these rural classes nationalism or *Swaraj* meant fundamental changes in the land system which would relieve or lessen their burdens and provide land for the landless.[1]

Brief Résumé of the Communal Problem in India

The communal problem, as it [is] called, was one of adjusting the claims of the minorities and giving them sufficient protection from majority action. Minorities in India, it must be remembered, are not racial or national minorities as in Europe; they are religious minorities. Racially India is a patchwork and a curious mixture, but no racial questions have arisen or can arise in India. Religion transcends these racial differences, which fade into one another and are often hard to distinguish. Religious barriers are obviously not permanent, as conversions can take place from one religion to another, and a person changing his religion does not thereby lose his racial background or his cultural and linguistic inheritance. Latterly religion, in any real sense of the word, has played little part in Indian political conflicts, though the word is often enough used and exploited. Religious differences, as such, do not come in the way, for there is a great deal of mutual tolerance for them. In political matters, religion has been displaced by what is called communalism, a narrow

[1] Ibid., p. 204.

group mentality basing itself on a religious community but in reality concerned with political power and patronage for the group concerned.

Repeated efforts were made by the Congress as well as other organizations to settle this communal problem with the consent of the various groups concerned. Some partial success was achieved, but there was always a basic difficulty—the presence and policy of the British government. Naturally the British did not favor any real settlement which would strengthen the political movement—now grown to mass proportions—against them. It was a triangle, with the government in a position to play off one side against the other by giving special privileges. If the other parties had been wise enough, they could have overcome even this obstacle; but they lacked wisdom and foresight. Whenever a settlement was almost reached, the government would take some step which upset the balance.

There was no dispute about the usual provisions for minority protection such as the League of Nations used to lay down. All these were agreed to and much more. Religion, culture, language, the fundamental rights of the individual and the group were all to be protected and assured by basic constitutional provisions in a democratic constitution applying equally to all. Apart from this the whole history of India was witness of the toleration and even encouragement of minorities and of different racial groups. There is nothing in Indian history to compare with the bitter religious feuds and persecutions that prevailed in Europe. So we did not have to go abroad for ideas of religious and cultural toleration; these were inherent in Indian life. In regard to individual and political rights and civil liberties, we were influenced by the ideas of the French and American revolutions, as also by the constitutional history of the British parliament. Socialistic ideas, and the influence of the Soviet revolution, came in later to give a powerful economic turn to our thoughts.

Apart from the full protection of all such rights of . . . the individual and the group, it was common ground that every effort should be made by the state as well as by private agencies to remove all invidious social and customary barriers which came in the way of the full development of the individual as well as any group, and that educationally and economically backward classes should be helped to get rid of their disabilities as rapidly as possible. This applied especially to the depressed classes. It was further laid down that women should share in every way with men in the privileges of citizenship.

What remained? Fear that bigger numbers might politically overwhelm a minority. Normally speaking, numbers meant the peasantry and the workers, the masses of all religious faiths, who had long been exploited not only by foreign rule but by their own upper classes. Having assured the protection of religion and culture, etc., the major problems that were bound to come up were economic ones which had nothing to do with a person's religion. Class conflicts there might well be, but not religious conflicts, except in so far as religion itself represented some vested interest. Nevertheless people had grown so accustomed to think along lines of religious cleavage, and were continually being encouraged to do so by communal religious organizations and government action, that the fear of the major religious community, that is the Hindus, swamping others continued to exercise the minds of many Moslems. It was not clear how even a majority could injure the interests of a huge minority like the Moslems, concentrated mostly in certain parts of the country which would be autonomous. But fear is not reasonable.

Separate electorates for Moslems (and later for other and smaller groups) were introduced and additional seats were given to them in excess of their population. But even excess in representation in a popular assembly could not convert a minority into a majority. Indeed separate electorates made matters a little worse for the protected group, for the majority electorate lost interest in it and there was little occasion for mutual consideration and adjustment which inevitably take place in a joint electorate when a candidate has to appeal to every group. The Congress went further and declared that if there was any disagreement between the majority and a religious minority on any issue touching the special interests of that minority, it should not be decided by majority votes but should be referred to an impartial judicial tribunal, or even an international tribunal, whose decision should be final.

It is difficult to conceive what greater protection could be given to any religious minority or group under any democratic system. It must be remembered also that in some provinces Moslems were actually in a majority, and as the provinces were autonomous, the Moslem majority was more or less free to function as it chose, subject only to certain all-India considerations. In the central government Moslems would also inevitably have an important share. In the Moslem majority provinces this communal-religious problem was reversed, for there protection was demanded by the other minority groups (such as Hindu and Sikh) as against the Moslem majority. Thus in the Punjab there was a Moslem-Hindu-Sikh triangle. If there was a separate electorate for Moslems, then others claimed special protection for themselves also. Separate electorates having once been introduced, there was no end to the ramifications and compartments and difficulties that arose from them. Obviously the granting of weightage in representation to one group could only be done at the cost of some other group, which had its representation reduced below its population figures. This produced a fantastic result, especially in Bengal, where, chiefly because of excessive European representation, the seats allotted to the general electorate were absurdly reduced. Thus the intelligentsia of Bengal, which had played a notable part in Indian politics and the struggle for freedom, suddenly realized that it had a very weak position in the provincial legislature, and this fixed and limited by statute.

The Congress made many mistakes, but these were in relatively minor questions of approach or tactics. It was obvious that even for purely political reasons the Congress was eager and anxious to bring about a communal solution and thus remove a barrier to progress. There was no such eagerness in the purely communal organizations, for their chief reason for existence was to emphasize the particular demands of their respective groups, and this had led to a certain vested interest in the status quo.

Though predominantly Hindu in membership, the Congress had large numbers of Moslems on its rolls, as well as all other religious groups— Sikhs, Christians, etc. It was thus forced to think in national terms. For it the dominating issue was national freedom and the establishment of an independent democratic state. It realized that in a vast and varied country like India, a simple type of democracy, giving full powers to a majority to curb or overrule minority groups in all matters, was not satisfactory or desirable, even if it could be established.[1]

From Letters to Nehru before Lucknow Session of Congress— 1936

[While in Europe in the mid-thirties Nehru received a series of letters from various leaders at home and abroad that shed revealing light upon the dominant role he was beginning to play in Indian affairs. Prasad's letter, in particular, indicates how sharply Nehru's position differed from that of most Congress leaders of the period.]

I. [From Rajendra Prasad—December 19, 1935.] "The chances are that you will be elected President of the next Congress. I know that there is a certain difference between your outlook and that of men like Vallabhbhai [Patel, etc.] and myself and it is even of a fundamental character. But I suppose that has been there all these years and yet we have worked together. Now that Bapu [Gandhi] has in a sense withdrawn himself and advises only when asked, it is possible that these differences may become more marked.

"You are undoubtedly dissatisfied with the present condition of things. Not one amongst us here is satisfied with them. But the difficulties are inherent in the situation and its seems to us that it is not possible to force the pace or cause any wholesale change. In all big struggles we have to come across such situations and however much we may chafe and fume we have to lie low and work and wait for better times. We are passing through one of such crises. But I see no reason to be disheartened. The spirit of freedom is not crushed nor is there anything like a spirit of resignation and helpless submission. I do not believe that any one has gone back to pre-non-cooperation mentality. I do not think we have gone back to 1923–28. We are in 1928–29 mentality and I have no doubt that better days will soon come. We have been carrying on to the best of our lights and ability and no one can do more. In any case you have certainly a free hand to shape things as you would like and to appoint any Working Committee of your choice, and you may rest assured that none of us will create any difficulty and even where we may not help we will never obstruct.

"It is not possible for me to explain in a letter the programme we have been trying to carry out. . . . But if it does not appeal to you no one is going to blindly stick to it, if a better programme can be evolved. We

[1] D.I., pp. 386–89.

have not made matters more complicated than they are and you can certainly write on a slate not disfigured by us.

"It has been wrongly and unfairly assumed that the Working Committee has been thinking of nothing except offices under the New Constitution. We have not as a matter of fact given to the matter any importance. On the other hand it is others who have been trying to force our hands to come to a decision. The first attempt was made . . . in April last and we felt it was too early to come to a decision on the question. We have stuck to that decision which was affirmed at Madras. At Lucknow the question will have to be tackled. It is not free from difficulties either way.

"As it strikes me it is not right to put it as if it were a question of acceptance or non-acceptance of offices. So far as I can judge no one wants to accept offices for their own sake. No one wants to work the constitution as the Government would like it to be worked. The questions for us are altogether different. What are we to do with this Constitution? Are we to ignore it altogether and go our way? Is it possible to do so? Are we to capture it and use it as we would like to use it and to the extent it lends itself to be used in that way? Are we to fight it from within or from without and in what way? It is really a question of laying down a positive programme for dealing with the situation created by the introduction of this Constitution in the light of circumstances as they exist. It is not a question to be answered *a priori* on the basis of pre-conceived notions of a so-called prochanger or nochanger, cooperator or obstructionist. There has been some amount of mudslinging but that is inevitable and we have to consider and decide the question irrespective of everything except the good of the country and the effect of our decision on the great objective we have in view. . . .

"We may keep ourselves in touch with foreign affairs through contacts formed by friends like you and we may spread authentic knowledge of the situation here through them, as we have been doing. More than this it is not possible to do. We are too keenly alive to the realities of the situation here to expect that they can make any impression on foreign countries. If we were strong and united we could compel even those countries not to ignore us, occupied as they are with their own baffling problems. . . .

"You will see that under the Constitution one has to be a member of the Congress for six months, to be a habitual wearer of Khadi and to do some manual labour as prescribed before one can be elected as a member of any elected committee or to any office."[1]

II. [From Subhas Chandra Bose, Badgastein (Autriche), March 4, 1936.]
"Among the front rank leaders of today—you are the only one to whom we can look up to for leading the Congress in a progressive direction. Moreover, your position is unique and I think that even Mahatma Gandhi will be more accommodating towards you than towards anybody else. I earnestly hope that you will fully utilise the strength of your public position in making decisions. Please do not consider your position to be

[1] B.O.L., pp. 159-61.

weaker than it really is. Gandhiji will never take a stand which will alienate you.

"As I was suggesting in our last talk, your immediate task will be a two-fold one—(1) to prevent office-acceptance by all possible means and (2) to enlarge and broaden the composition of the Cabinet. If you can do that, you will save the Congress from demoralisation and bring it out of a rut. Bigger problems may wait till tomorrow but the Congress has to be saved from demoralisation at once.

"I was extremely glad to hear that you were desirous of starting a *foreign department* of the Congress."[1]

III. [From H. N. Brailsford, London, March 8, 1936.]
"Don't undervalue yourself in this hour of misery. India has great need of you—especially, personally, of you. For I think I know, more or less, the other possible leaders. No one has your courage, your mental power and above all, your vision of a humane classless society. Try to draw strength from the belief that history has named you to lead."[2]

The Indian States and British Rule Before Independence

[Nehru was for long preoccupied with the fate of India's princely States before Independence. He wrote of these States and British Rule in *The Discovery of India*.] [The princely states of India] are unique of their kind in the world and they vary greatly in size and political and social conditions. Their number is six hundred and one. About fifteen of these may be considered major states, the biggest ... being Hyderabad, Kashmir, Mysore, Travancore, Baroda, Gwalior, Indore, Cochin, Jaipur, Jodhpur, Bikanir, Bhopal, and Patiala. Then follow a number of middling states, and lastly, several hundreds of very small areas, some not bigger than a pin's point on the map. Most of these tiny states are in Kathiawar, western India, and the Punjab.

These states not only vary in size from that of France to almost that of an average farmer's holding, but also differ in every other way. Mysore is industrially the most advanced; Mysore, Travancore, and Cochin are educationally far ahead of British India. Most of the states are, however, very backward, and some are completely feudal. All of them are auto-cracies, though some have started elected councils whose powers are strictly limited. Hyderabad, the premier state, still carries on with a typical feudal regime supported by an almost complete denial of civil liberties. So also most of the states in Rajputana and the Punjab. A lack of civil liberties is a common feature of the states.

These states do not form compact blocks; they are spread out all over India, islands surrounded by non-state areas. The vast majority of them

[1] Ibid., pp. 172–73.
[2] Ibid., p. 173.

are totally unable to support even a semi-independent economy; even the largest, situated as they are, can hardly hope to do so without full co-operation of the surrounding areas. If there was any economic conflict between a state and non-state India, the former could be easily reduced to submission by tariff barriers and other economic sanctions. It is manifest that both politically and economically these states, even the largest of them, cannot be separated and treated as independent entities. As such they would not survive and the rest of India would also suffer greatly. They would become hostile enclaves all over India, and if they relied on some external power for protection, this in itself would be a continuous and serious menace to a free India. Indeed they would not have survived till today but for the fact that politically and economically the whole of India, including the states, was under one dominant power which protected the states. Apart from the possible conflicts between a state and non-state India, it must be remembered that there is continuous pressure on the autocratic ruler of the state from his own people, who demand free institutions. Attempts to achieve this freedom are suppressed and kept back with the aid of the British power.

Even in the nineteenth century these states, as constituted, became anachronisms. Under modern conditions it is impossible to conceive of India being split up into scores of separate independent entities. Not only would there be perpetual conflict but all planned economic and cultural progress would become impossible. We must remember that when these states took shape and entered into treaties with the East India Company, at the beginning of the nineteenth century, Europe was divided up into numerous small principalities. Many wars and revolutions have changed the face of Europe since then and are changing it today; but the face of India was set and petrified by external pressure imposed upon it, and not allowed to change. It seems absurd to hold up some treaty drawn up a hundred and forty years ago, usually on the field of battle or immediately afterwards, between two rival commanders or their chiefs, and to say that this temporary settlement must last forever. The people of the state, of course, had no say in that settlement, and the other party at the time was a commercial corporation concerned only with its own interests and profits. This commercial corporation, the East India Company, acted not as the agent of the British crown or parliament but, in theory, as the agent of the Delhi emperor, from whom power and authority were supposed to flow, although he was himself quite powerless. The British crown or parliament had nothing whatever to do with these treaties. Parliament only considered Indian affairs when the charter of the East India Company came up for discussion from time to time. The fact that the East India Company was functioning in India under the authority conferred on it by the *diwani* grant of the Moghul emperor made it independent of any direct interference by the British crown or parliament. Indirectly Parliament could, if it so chose, cancel the charter or impose new conditions at the time of renewal. The idea that the English king or parliament should even in theory function as agents and therefore as subordinates of the shadow emperor at Delhi was not liked in England, and so they studiously kept aloof from the activities of the East India Company. The money spent in the Indian wars was Indian money raised and disposed of by the East India Company.

Subsequently, as the territory under the control of the East India Company increased in area and its rule was consolidated, the British parliament began to take greater interest in Indian affairs. In 1858, after the shock of the Indian mutiny and revolt, the company transferred its domain of India (for money paid by India) to the British crown. That transfer did not involve a separate transfer of the Indian states apart from the rest of India. The whole of India was treated as a unit, and the British parliament functioned in India through the Government of India which exercised a suzerainty over the states. The states had no separate relations with the British crown or parliament. They were part and parcel of the system of government, direct and indirect, represented by the Government of India. This government, in later years, ignored those old treaties whenever it suited its changing policy to do so, and exercised a very effective suzerainty over the states.

Thus the British crown was not in the picture at all so far as the Indian states were concerned. It is only in recent years that the claim to some kind of independence has been raised on behalf of the states, and it has been further claimed that they have some special relations with the British crown, apart from the Government of India. These treaties, it should be noted, are with very few of the states; there are only forty treaty states; the rest have "engagements and sanads." These forty states have three-fourths of the total Indian state population, and six of them have considerably more than one-third of this population [Hyderabad, Mysore, Travancore, Baroda, Kashmir, Gwalior].

In the Government of India Act of 1935, for the first time, some distinction was made between the relations of the states and the rest of India with the British parliament. The states were removed from the supervisory authority and direction of the Government of India and placed directly under the viceroy, who for this purpose was called the crown representative. The viceroy continued to be, at the same time, the head of the Government of India. The Political Department of the Government of India, which used to be responsible for the states, was now placed directly under the viceroy and was no longer under his executive council.

How did these states come into existence? Some are quite new, created by the British; others were the viceroyalties of the Moghul emperor, and they were permitted to continue as feudatory chiefs by the British; yet others, notably the Maratha chiefs, were defeated by British armies and then made into feudatories. Nearly all these can be traced back to the beginnings of British rule; they have no earlier history. If some of them functioned independently for a while, that independence was of brief duration and ended in defeat in war or threat of war. Only a few of the states, and these are chiefly in Rajputana, date back to pre-Moghul times. Travancore has an ancient, thousand-year-old historical continuity. Some of the proud Rajput clans trace back their genealogy to prehistoric times. The Maharana of Udaipur, of the Suryavansh or Race of the Sun, has a family tree comparable to that of the Mikado of Japan. But these Rajput chiefs became Moghul feudatories, and then submitted to the Marathas and finally to the British. The representatives of the East India Company, writes Edward Thompson, "now set the Princes in their positions, lifting them out of the chaos in which they were submerged. When thus picked up and re-established, 'the Princes' were as completely helpless and derelict as any power since the beginning of the world. Had the British Government not intervened, nothing but extinction lay before the Rajput States, and disintegration before the Maratha States. As for such States as Oudh and the Nizam's dominions, their very existence was bogus; they were kept in a semblance of life, only by means of the breath blown through them by the Protecting Power."

Hyderabad, the premier state today, was small in area to begin with. Its boundaries were extended twice, after Tipu Sultan's defeat by the British and the Maratha wars. These additions were at the instance of the British and on the express stipulation that the Nizam was to function in a subordinate capacity to them. Indeed, on Tipu's defeat the offer of part of his territory was first made to the Peshwa, the Maratha leader, but he refused to accept it on those conditions.

Kashmir, the next largest state, was sold by the East India Company after the Sikh wars to the great-grandfather of the present ruler. It was subsequently taken under direct British control on a plea of misgovernment. Later the ruler's powers were restored to him. The present state of Mysore was created by the British after Tipu's wars. It was also under direct British rule for a lengthy period.

The only truly independent kingdom in India is Nepal on the northeastern frontier, which occupies a position analogous to that of Afghanistan, though it is rather isolated. All the rest came within the scope of what was called the "subsidiary system", under which all real power lay with the British government, exercised through a resident or agent. Often even the ministers of the ruler were British officials imposed upon him. But the entire responsibility for good government and reform lay with the ruler, who with the best will in the world (and he usually lacked that will as well as competence) could do little in the circumstances.[1]

Documents Relating to Indo-Pakistan Kashmir Dispute

I. [Resolution Adopted by United Nations Commission for India and Pakistan, August 13, 1948—Karachi.]

[The United Nations Commission for India and Pakistan]: "Having given careful consideration to the points of view expressed by the Representatives of India and Pakistan regarding the situation in the State of Jammu and Kashmir, and

"Being of the opinion that the prompt cessation of hostilities and the correction of conditions the continuance of which is likely to endanger international peace and security are as essential to implementation of its

[1] D.I., pp. 306–10.

endeavours to assist the Governments of India and Pakistan in effecting a final settlement of the situation,

"Resolves to submit simultaneously to the Governments of India and Pakistan the following proposal:

PART I

Cease-fire order

"A. The Governments of India and Pakistan agree that their respective High Commands will issue separately and simultaneously a cease-fire order to apply to all forces under their control in the State of Jammu and Kashmir as of the earliest practicable date or dates to be mutually agreed upon within four days after these proposals have been accepted by both Governments.

"B. The High Commands of the Indian and Pakistan forces agree to refrain from taking any measures that might augment the military potential of the forces under their control in the State of Jammu and Kashmir.

"(For the purpose of these proposals 'forces under their control' shall be considered to include all forces, organised and unorganised, fighting or participating in hostilities on their respective sides).

"C. The Commanders-in-Chief of the forces of India and Pakistan shall promptly confer regarding any necessary local changes in present dispositions which may facilitate the cease-fire.

"D. In its discretion and as the Commission may find practicable, the Commission will appoint military observers who under the authority of the Commission and with the co-operation of both Commands will supervise the observance of the cease-fire order.

"E. The Government of India and the Government of Pakistan agree to appeal to their respective peoples to assist in creating and maintaining an atmosphere favourable to the promotion of further negotiations.

PART II

Truce Agreement

"Simultaneously with the acceptance of the proposal for the immediate cessation of hostilities as outlined in Part I, both Governments accept the following principles as a basis for the formulation of a truce agreement, the details of which shall be worked out in discussion between their Representatives and the Commission.

"A. 1. As the presence of troops of Pakistan in the territory of the State of Jammu and Kashmir constitutes a material change in the situation since it was represented by the Government of Pakistan before the Security Council, the Government of Pakistan agrees to withdraw its troops from that State.

2. The Government of Pakistan will use its best endeavour to secure the withdrawal from the State of Jammu and Kashmir of tribesmen and Pakistan nationals not normally resident therein who have entered the State for the purpose of fighting.

3. Pending a final solution, the territory evacuated by the Pakistan troops will be administered by the local authorities under the surveillance of the Commission.

"B. 1. When the Commission shall have notified the Government of India that the tribesmen and Pakistan nationals referred to in Part II A 2 hereof have withdrawn, thereby terminating the situation which was represented by the Government of India to the Security Council as having occasioned the presence of Indian forces in the State of Jammu and Kashmir, and further, that the Pakistan forces are being withdrawn from the State of Jammu and Kashmir, the Government of India agrees to begin to withdraw the bulk of their forces from that State in stages to be agreed upon with the Commission.

2. Pending the acceptance of the conditions for a final settlement of the situation in the State of Jammu and Kashmir, the Indian Government will maintain within the lines existing at the moment of the cease-fire those forces of its Army which in agreement with the Commission are considered necessary to assist local authorities in the observance of law and order. The Commission will have observers stationed where it deems necessary.

3. The Government of India will undertake to ensure that the Government of the State of Jammu and Kashmir will take all measures within their power to make it publicly known that peace, law and order will be safeguarded and that all human and political rights will be guaranteed.

"C. 1. Upon signature, the full text of the Truce Agreement or a communique containing the principles thereof as agreed upon between the two Governments and the Commission, will be made public.

"The Government of India and the Government of Pakistan reaffirm their wish that the future status of the State of Jammu and Kashmir shall be determined in accordance with the will of the people and to that end, upon acceptance of the Truce Agreement both Governments agree to enter into consultations with the Commission to determine fair and equitable conditions whereby such free expression will be assured."[1]

II.

[Although the Indian Government looked upon the August 13, 1948, U.N. Commission Resolution for India and Pakistan as "vague" and "far from satisfactory", it asserted on August 20, 1948 that, in its anxiety to restore peace at the earliest possible opportunity, it accepted the resolution. In doing so it made the following reservations, to which the Commission gave its unqualified acceptance.]

1. "The proposed administration by 'local authorities' of the territory

[1] G.I.I.S. (Aug., 1948), pp. 4–6.

evacuated by Pakistan troops could not question the sovereignty of the Jammu and Kashmir Government in that area nor afford any recognition to the 'Azad' Kashmir authorities. . . .

2. "The time when the withdrawal of Indian forces . . . is to begin, the stages in which it is to be carried out and the strength of Indian forces to be retained in the State would be decided by India and the Commission— to the absolute exclusion of Pakistan; further, the paramount need for security is recognized", i.e., the size of Indian forces which were to remain in Kashmir should be conditioned by the need to ensure its security against external aggression.

3. "Part III (of the resolution) does not in any way recognise the right of Pakistan to have any part in a plebiscite."

[Further, according to the Indian Government], "Pakistan made so many reservations that the Commission felt that [they were] tantamount to a *de facto* rejection.

"The Commission found the various provisos suggested by Pakistan 'beyond the compass of this resolution, thereby making impossible an immediate cease-fire and the beginning of fruitful negotiations between the two Governments and the Commission.'

"As a result of Pakistan's virtual rejection of the August 13 Resolution, complete deadlock [had] ensued. The Commission reported the matter to the Security Council. The Council, however, directed the Commission to continue its efforts for a solution. On December 11, 1948, the Commission formulated certain proposals in elaboration of Part III of August 13 Resolution. These proposals gave some recognition to the objections India had voiced at the time of adoption of April 21 Resolution. The Plebiscite Administrator under the new proposals was to be appointed by and to receive his powers from the lawful Government of the State of Jammu and Kashmir.

"As for Pakistan's *locus standi*, the Commission completely excluded it from having any role in the final disposal of Indian troops; and the Government of Kashmir was recognised as the Interim Government.

"The Prime Minister of India requested certain clarifications. The Commission set those out in two Aide Memoires dated December 20 and 22, 1948. These were:

1. that Pakistan must implement the first two parts of the August 13 Resolution before India could accept the proposals for a plebiscite, i.e., the Commission's proposals of December 11, 1948;

2. that the Plebiscite Administrator would have limited powers and would deal only with the organisation of the plebiscite itself;

3. that the term 'freedom of speech' during a plebiscite did not imply the right of Pakistan propagandists to play upon religious fanaticism; and

4. that there should be 'large-scale disarming' as well as disbanding of the Azad Kashmir forces.

"Pakistan", [according to India, next] "effected a complete *volte face* and accepted the Commission's proposals of December 11 which were, in all essential respects, based on the resolution of August 13.

"Exercising . . . self-restraint despite a favourable military position,

India brought about a Cease-Fire Agreement on January 1, 1949. On January 5, 1949, the Commission adopted a resolution which formally set forth the various steps to be taken before a plebiscite was to be held."[1]

[The Chairman of the U.N. Commission expressed concern to the Foreign Minister of Pakistan about Pakistan's refusal to accept the August 13 Resolution:] "The Commission observes with regret that the Government of Pakistan has been unable to accept the resolution without attaching certain conditions beyond the compass of this resolution, thereby making impossible an immediate cease-fire and the beginning of fruitful negotiations between the two Governments and the Commission to bring about a peaceful and final settlement of the situation in the State of Jammu and Kashmir."[2]

III. [Resolution Adopted by United Nations Commission for India and Pakistan—January 5, 1949.]

"The United Nations Commission for India and Pakistan, having received from the Governments of India and Pakistan, in communications dated December 23 and December 25, 1948, respectively, their acceptance of the following principles which are supplementary to the Commission's resolution of August 13, 1948:

"(1) The question of the accession of the State of Jammu and Kashmir to India or Pakistan will be decided through the democratic method of a free and impartial plebiscite.

"(2) A plebiscite will be held when it shall be found by the Commission that the cease-fire and truce arrangements set forth in Parts I and II of the Commission's resolution of August 13, 1948, have been carried out and arrangements for the plebiscite have been completed.

"(3) (a) The Secretary-General of the United Nations will, in agreement with the Commission, nominate a Plebiscite Administrator who shall be a personality of high international standing and commanding general confidence. He will be formally appointed to office by the Government of Jammu and Kashmir;

(b) The Plebiscite Administrator shall derive from the State of Jammu and Kashmir the powers he considers necessary for organizing and conducting the plebiscite and for ensuring the freedom and impartiality of the plebiscite;

(c) The Plebiscite Administrator shall have authority to appoint such staff of assistants and observers as he may require.

"(4) (a) After implementation of Parts I and II of the Commission's resolution of August 13, 1948, and when the Commission is satisfied that peaceful conditions have been restored in the State, the Commission and the Plebiscite Administrator will determine, in

[1] K.F.S., pp. 46–48.
[2] K.U.N., p. 7.

consultation with the Government of India, the final disposal of Indian and State armed forces, such disposal to be with due regard to the security of the State and the freedom of the plebiscite; (b) As regards the territory referred to in A (2) of Part II of the resolution of August 13, final disposal of the armed forces in that territory will be determined by the Commission and the Plebiscite Administrator in consultation with the local authorities.

"(5) All civil and military authorities within the State and the principal political elements of the State will be required to co-operate with the Plebiscite Administrator in the preparation for and the holding of the plebiscite.

"(6) (a) All citizens of the State who have left it on account of the disturbances will be invited and be free to return and to exercise all their rights as such citizens. For the purpose of facilitating repatriation there shall be appointed two Commissions, one composed of nominees of India and the other of nominees of Pakistan. The Commissions shall operate under the direction of the Plebiscite Administrator. The Governments of India and Pakistan and all authorities within the State of Jammu and Kashmir will collaborate with the Plebiscite Administrator in putting this provision into effect;

(b) All persons (other than citizens of the State) who on or since August 15, 1947, have entered it for other than lawful purpose, shall be required to leave the State.

"(7) All authorities within the State of Jammu and Kashmir will undertake to ensure, in collaboration with the Plebiscite Administrator, that:

(a) There is no threat, coercion or intimidation, bribery or other undue influence on the voters in the plebiscite;

(b) No restrictions are placed on legitimate political activity throughout the State. All subjects of the State, regardless of creed, caste or party, shall be safe and free in expressing their views and in voting on the question of the accession of the State to India or Pakistan. There shall be freedom of the press, speech and assembly and freedom of travel in the State, including freedom of lawful entry and exit;

(c) All political prisoners are released;

(d) Minorities in all parts of the State are accorded adequate protection; and

(e) There is no victimisation.

"(8) The Plebiscite Administrator may refer to the United Nations Commission for India and Pakistan problems on which he may require assistance, and the Commission may in its discretion call upon the Plebiscite Administrator to carry out on its behalf any of the responsibilities with which it has been entrusted.

"(9) At the conclusion of the plebiscite the Plebiscite Administrator shall report the result thereof to the Commission and to the Government of Jammu and Kashmir. The Commission shall then certify to the Security Council whether the plebiscite has or has not been free and impartial.

"(10) Upon the signature of the truce agreement the details of the foregoing proposals will be elaborated in the consultations envisaged in Part III of the Commission's resolution of August 13, 1948. The Plebiscite Administrator will be fully associated in these consultations;

"Commends the Governments of India and Pakistan for their prompt action in ordering a cease-fire to take effect from one minute before midnight of January 1, 1949, pursuant to the agreement arrived at as provided for by the Commission's resolution of August 13, 1948; and

"Resolves to return in the immediate future to the subcontinent to discharge the responsibilities imposed upon it by the resolution of August 13, 1948, and by the foregoing principles."[1]

A Few Salient Facts about India

Before partition, India was divided into two parts, the provinces, and approximately six hundred princely states. (It consisted of British India, in which the British Government, through its Governor-General, exercised virtually supreme authority. The Indian States and Agencies were governed by Indian rulers owing limited responsibility to the Viceroy, who was also Governor-General.) Among the provinces were: Ajmer-Merwara, Andaman and Nicobar Islands, Assam, Baluchistan, Bengal, Behar, Bombay, Central Provinces and Berar, Coorg, Delhi, Madras, Laccadive Islands, North-West Frontier Province, Orissa, Punjab, Sind, and United Provinces of Agra and Oudh. The largest of the Indian States and Agencies were Assam States, Baluchistan States, Central India Agency, Eastern States, Gujarat States and Baroda, Gwalior, Hyderabad, Jammu and Kashmir, Kolhapur and Deccan States, Madras States, Mysore, North-West Frontier Agencies, Punjab States, Rajputana, Sikkim, and Western India States.[2]

Prior to independence, nearly one-fourth of the total Indian population —92,973,000—were not British subjects. They lived in the Indian States, owing their allegiance to their respective rulers. 295,827,000 Indians, who were British subjects, resided in the provinces of British India.[3]

When India attained independence in 1947, it was welded into nine Part A States (former provinces), eight Part B States (units or groups of units formerly ruled by the princes), ten Part C States, and one Part D State.

---

[1] Ibid., pp. 19-20. (It may be noted that, whereas there have been periodic, free, democratic elections in India since the achievement of independence, similar elections have not been held in Pakistan.)

[2] Based on T.F., pp. 35-36; editor's footnote.

[3] T.A.Y. (Vol. XII-XIII), 1945; p. 333.

The Part A States were Andhra, Assam, Bihar, Bombay, Madhya Pradesh, Madras, Orissa, Punjab, Uttar Pradesh, West Bengal. The Part B States: Hyderabad, Jammu and Kashmir, Madhya Bharat, Mysore, Patiala and East Punjab, Rajasthan, Saurashtra, Travancore-Cochin. The Part C States: Ajmer, Bhopal, Coorg, Delhi, Himachal Pradesh, Kutch, Manipur, Tripura, Vindhya Pradesh. The Part D State was comprised of the Andaman and Nicobar Islands. (Since 1950 the states of India have been reorganised.)

India became a republic on January 26, 1950, retaining her membership in the Commonwealth. On the same date Rajendra Prasad was sworn in as the first President of India. Nehru, already Prime Minister since August 15, 1947, continued to hold that office. The Government of India Act of 1935 lapsed. New Delhi has remained the capital of India. Free India's new constitution became operative.

India is a democracy, in which free elections are held at regular intervals of five years. The Congress Party has remained the majority party. Opposition parties may and do function freely.

India's constitution, passed in November, 1949, guaranteed equality of status to both men and women. It abolished "untouchability", declaring its practice to be an offense punishable by law.

The fundamental rights secured under the Constitution included the right to freedom of speech, assembly and profession; the right to protection of life and personal liberty; the right to freedom of conscience and free profession, practice and propagation of religion; the right to private property; the cultural and educational rights of minorities.

The constitution further provided that a President was to be elected every five years as head of state. He was to be aided and advised within the administration by a Prime Minister, who must enjoy majority support in Parliament. (The President was, however, to be able to assume certain additional powers under certain circumstances.)

Parliament was to be composed of two Houses—the Council of States and the House of the People. Elections for the latter, as well as for State legislatures, were to be held every five years on the basis of adult franchise —without regard to color, caste, race, creed or sex—every man and woman in India being entitled to vote at the age of twenty-one.

The thirteen languages recognized by independent India's constitution, in addition to Hindi were: Assamese, Bengali, Gujerati, Kannada, Kashmiri, Malayalam, Marathi, Oriya, Punjabi, Sanskrit, Tamil, Telugu and Urdu.

Hindi was declared to be the official, national language for the Central Government by the Constituent Assembly. English was to be relinquished in favor of Hindi as the official national language after 1965. Hindi has not, however, actually been adopted as the official language in India, except in a few states. (English will continue to be the associate official language until 1975, at which time a further decision about the matter will be made.)

The population of India, as estimated by the Government of India, shortly after Independence Day, 1950, was 347,340,000. At this time there were approximately two hundred and fifty million Hindus in India, forty million Muslims, ten million Christians, forty-seven million of other denominations. The total area of India was then 1,221,880 square miles.[1]

Indian Planning Commission—1950

"The [Indian] Planning Commission was set up in March, 1950 by the Government of India, its terms of reference being to:
"(1) make an assessment of the material, capital and human resources of the country, including technical personnel, and investigate the possibilities of augmenting such of these resources as are found to be deficient in relation to the nation's requirements;
"(2) formulate a Plan for the most effective and balanced utilisation of the country's resources;
"(3) on a determination of priorities, define the stages in which the Plan should be carried out and propose the allocation of resources for the due completion of each stage;
"(4) indicate the factors which are tending to retard economic development, and determine the conditions which, in view of the current social and political situation, should be established for the successful execution of the Plan;
"(5) determine the nature of the machinery which will be necessary for securing the successful implementation of each stage of the Plan in all its aspects;
"(6) appraise from time to time the progress achieved in the execution of each stage of the Plan and recommend the adjustments of policy and measures that such appraisal may show to be necessary; and
"(7) make such interim or ancillary recommendations as appear to it to be appropriate either for facilitating the discharge of the duties assigned to it; or, on a consideration of the prevailing economic conditions, current policies, measures and development programmes; or on an examination of such specific problems as may be referred to it for advice by Central or State Governments".[2]

EXTRACTS FROM THE WILL AND TESTAMENT OF

JAWAHARLAL NEHRU

I have received so much love and affection from the Indian people that nothing that I can do can repay even a small fraction of it, and indeed there can be no repayment of so precious a thing as affection. Many have

---

[1] Facts and figures based on F.O.I., pp. 5-6. Additional data supplied by G.I.I.S., New York City.
[2] F.F.Y.P. (1952), Introduction, p. iii.

been admired, some have been revered, but the affection of all classes of the Indian people has come to me in such abundant measure that I have been overwhelmed by it. I can only express the hope that in the remaining years I may live, I shall not be unworthy of my people and their affection.

To my innumerable comrades and colleagues, I owe an even deeper debt of gratitude. We have been joint partners in great undertakings and have shared the triumphs and sorrows which inevitably accompany them.

                   *   *   *

I wish to declare with all earnestness that I do not want any religious ceremonies performed for me after my death. I do not believe in any such ceremonies and to submit to them, even as a matter of form, would be hypocrisy and an attempt to delude ourselves and others.

When I die, I should like my body to be cremated. If I die in a foreign country, my body should be cremated there and my ashes sent to Allahabad. A small handful of these ashes should be thrown into the Ganga and the major portion of them disposed of in the manner indicated below. No part of these ashes should be retained or preserved.

My desire to have a handful of my ashes thrown into the Ganga at Allahabad has no religious significance, so far as I am concerned. I have no religious sentiment in the matter. I have been attached to the Ganga and the Jumna rivers in Allahabad ever since my childhood and, as I have grown older, this attachment has also grown. I have watched their varying moods as the seasons changed, and have often thought of the history and myth and tradition and song and story that have become attached to them through the long ages and become part of their flowing waters. The Ganga, especially, is the river of India, beloved of her people, round which are intertwined her racial memories, her hopes and fears, her songs of triumph, her victories and her defeats. She has been a symbol of India's age-long culture and civilization, ever-changing, ever-flowing, and yet ever the same Ganga. She reminds me of the snow-covered peaks and deep valleys of the Himalayas, which I have loved so much, and of the rich and vast plains below, where my life and work have been cast. Smiling and dancing in the morning sunlight, and dark and gloomy and full of mystery as the evening shadows fall; a narrow, slow and graceful stream in winter, and a vast roaring thing during the monsoon, broad-bosomed almost as the sea, and with something of the sea's power to destroy, the Ganga has been to me a symbol and a memory of the past of India, running into the present, and flowing on to the great ocean of the future. And though I have discarded much of past tradition and custom, and am anxious that India should rid herself of all shackles that bind and constrain her and divide her people, and suppress vast numbers of them, and prevent the free development of the body and the spirit; though I seek all this, yet I do not wish to cut myself off from that past completely. I am proud of that great inheritance that has been, and is, ours, and I am conscious that I too, like all of us, am a link in that unbroken chain which goes back to the dawn of history in the immemorial past of India. That chain I would not break, for I treasure it and seek inspiration from it. And as witness of this desire of mine and as my last homage to India's cultural inheritance, I am making this request that a handful of my ashes be thrown into the Ganga at Allahabad to be carried to the great ocean that washes India's shore.

The major portion of my ashes should, however, be disposed of otherwise. I want these to be carried high up into the air in an aeroplane and scattered from that height over the fields where the peasants of India toil, so that they might mingle with the dust and soil of India and become an indistinguishable part of India.

Jawaharlal Nehru

21st June, 1954

Epilogue

In his last will and testament, Jawaharlal Nehru expressed the wish that there should be no religious ceremony in conjunction with his cremation. The force of the tide of tradition seems to have run stronger than did Nehru's desire. Yet is it not possible that it is precisely the freshness and courage of such a statement as Nehru's, that possesses a most subtle power to shock a custom-bound world into re-examining itself? Is it not by way of just such a lucid and shattering cry that the positive attributes of tradition may be restored to an entire people—renewed?

Nehru spoke eloquently, courageously, compassionately during his life-time about his dreams of a better world. He worked tirelessly, diligently to bring such a world into being. Yet again, although the tides of what we name "reality" in the everyday world seem to run stronger than did his dream, who is to say that his words—his vision—may not continue to serve as a measure—an abiding challenge—in the years to come?

Dorothy Norman

August 1, 1964

Glossary

Abhaya fearlessness

Adivasi old inhabitant, aborigine

Ahimsa literally non-violence

Ahrar a Muslim Party taking part in politics, sometimes rather militant

Ashram retreat or home for community living, hermitage, place for study and discipline of life

Azad Kashmir literally "free Kashmir". (The name given by Pakistan to Pakistan-held Kashmir)

Azan Muslim call to prayers

Bakr-Id Annual festival of Muslims, supposed to commemorate Abraham's sacrifice. The festival symbolizes the sacrifice through the killing of goats or certain other animals

Bande Mataram (at times spelled "Vande Mataram") a song which occurs in Bankim Chandra Chatterjee's Bengali novel. The song was quite popular during nationalist agitations in the early part of this century in Bengal. Subsequently it became a kind of unofficial National Anthem. (Some Muslims resented the song because of certain religious symbols it contained)

Bania trader, shopkeeper, merchant

Bapu Gujerati for father

Bhai brother

Bharat Mata Mother India

Chaprasi office messenger

Charkha spinning wheel

C.I.D. Criminal Investigation Department

Crore ten million, or one hundred lakhs

Darshan sight of venerated person or deity

Dharamshalas places where pilgrims rest or stay

Dharma righteousness, moral law, merit, virtue

Diwali (correctly spelled "Deepavali", but commonly called "Diwali") Hindu festival of lights

Gandhiji I have referred to Mr Gandhi or Mahatma Gandhi as "Gandhiji" . . . as he himself prefers this to the addition of "Mahatma"

to his name. But I have seen some extraordinary explanations of this "ji" in books and articles by English writers. Some have imagined that it is a term of endearment—Gandhiji meaning "dear little Gandhi"! This is perfectly absurd and shows colossal ignorance of Indian life. "Ji" is one of the commonest additions to a name in India, being applied [indiscriminately] to all kinds of people and to men, women, boys, girls and children. It conveys an idea of respect, something equivalent to Mr, Mrs, or Miss. Hindustani is rich in courtly phrases and prefixes and suffixes to names and honorific titles. "Ji" is the simplest of these and the least formal of them, though perfectly correct. I learn from my brother-in-law, Ranjit S. Pandit, that this "ji" has a long and honorable ancestry. It is derived from the Sanskrit *Arya*, meaning a gentleman or noble-born (not the Nazi meaning of Aryan!). This *arya* became in Prakit *ajja*, and this led to the simple "*ji*". (T.F., p. 40; Nehru's footnote)

Grouping   of geographically contiguous regional states to form one unit for the purpose of administration (or one administrative unit)

Guru   preceptor, teacher, spiritual guide

Gurudeva   reverend teacher

Harijan   literally "child of God", a name coined by Gandhi to describe the so-called untouchables

Hartal   strike, concerted cessation of work in the form of a protest (equivalent of a day of mourning on which businesses are closed)

Himsa   violence

Holi   Hindu spring festival

Id   Festival. (Usually applied to two of the principal festivals of Muslims, Id-ul-Fitr and Id-ul-Zuha or Bakr-Id). The first festival occurs at the time of the New Moon following the month of fasting. (See Bakr-Id)

Inquilab Zindabad   Long Live Revolution

Jagir   the holding of large areas of land with powers of revenue collection by the holder

Jagirdar   one who holds a jagir

Jai   victory

Jai Hind   victory to India

Jan   people

Jawahar   jewel

Jehad   religious crusade or war waged by Muslims against those they consider to be non-believers, or in behalf of a cause held by them to be religious

-ji   affix added to names denoting respect, e.g., Gandhiji. (See Gandhiji)

Jirga tribal meetings

Jugadharma (correctly spelled "Yugadharma") the duty appropriate to the time, or the spirit of the times

Juma Friday congregational prayers (Muslim)

Kafir (at times incorrectly spelled "Kafier") an infidel in the eyes of Muslims

Karma at one level, the theory of rebirth based on performance of actions in a past life. At another, the "name given to the creative force that brings beings into existence", the basis of created things being mutable nature. (Quotation from the Bhagavad-Gita, in *A Source Book In Indian Philosophy*, edited by Sarvepalli Radhakrishnan and Charles A. Moore)

Khadi hand-spun and hand-woven cloth

Khilafat the office, institution or dominion of a Kalif or Calif—the title of the successors of Mohammed both as temporal and spiritual rulers. Until the fall of the Ottoman Empire after the First World War, the Ottoman Emperors called themselves Khalifs

Kisan peasant

Kumbha Mela festival held every twelve years at confluence of banks of the sacred rivers Ganges and Jumna

Lakh one hundred thousand

Lathi (often spelled "lathee") long heavy stick used by police to disperse crowds

Lok Sabha House of the People, or Lower Chamber in India's Parliament

Lok Sevak Sangh association for service of humanity

Magh Mela fair in Hindu calendar month roughly corresponding to January

Maharajah (rajah) prince, or ruler

Maharani wife of a Maharajah, or ruler

Mahatma a great soul

Maidan open space, or esplanade

Mantram a ritualistic, devotional or sacred formula

Maulana title usually given to a learned Muslim or divine

Maulvi religious preacher, Muslim priest

Mela a fair that may be held in connection with a religious, or any other festival

Nabis prophets (Muslim)

Nasmyth hammer made in British foundry noted for excellence of its products

Nawab Muslim ruler of an Indian State, or a title conferred on descendants of former Muslim rulers or chieftains, or on important Muslim landlords

Newar broad tape

Panchayat village council consisting of five wise elders elected by the people; can be expanded to a larger, democratically elected council

Panchayat Raj administration through Panchayat, i.e. the people

Pandit prefix to name generally used to denote membership in Brahmin caste, e.g. Pandit Nehru; sometimes applied to Hindu teachers, learned men, Sanskrit scholars, irrespective of caste; a Brahmin versed in Hindu religion, science and laws

Panditji-Ki-Jai Victory to Pandit Nehru

Paramountcy the essence of the treaties of paramountcy that existed in India between the Princely States and Britain before independence involved the establishment of a relationship with the paramount power which gave the Indian Princes a status less than that of either independence or full national sovereignty. (Based on T.A.R., p. 169.)

Parity the identical number of legislative or cabinet posts to be made available to members of different faiths before Indian independence

Parsis Zoroastrians in India, who originally migrated from Persia

Patwaris village accountants who record assessments of land revenue and produce

Praja Mandal a People's assembly. (In effect, this term was used for popular associations in the autocratic Indian States, before Independence. The associations worked for democratic rule)

Prayashchit expiation, penance

Purda or purdah literally "curtain", custom of keeping women in seclusion, or under a veil

Purna Swaraj complete independence

Raj government, rule

Rajya Sabha Council of States. (Upper Chamber in India's Parliament)

Ramadan Muslim month of fasting. (Often spelled Ramazan)

Rashtrapati President

R.S.S.S. Rashtriya Swayam Sewak Sangh (a Right Wing group looking upon itself as saviour of the people)

Responsivists an offshoot of Swaraj Party

Rishi a seer

Ryot Indian peasant

Sabha organization

Sadhu one who has renounced; recluse, a mendicant

Sanad title, deed or other document conferring certain rights and privileges

Sangh organization

Sanyasi one who has renounced the worldly life, a recluse

Sardar leader or nobleman, an honorific term

Sarkar ruler, master. (Sarkar Salaam: obeisance or deference to the ruler; before Indian independence, to the British)

Sarvodaya universal good

Satyagraha adherence to truth. (In the Indian National Congress the word took on an added connotation, being utilized in conjunction with the practice of non-violent resistance)

Satyagrahi one who practises satyagraha

Sepoy an army private

Seva service

Seva Sangh service league

Sewak one who serves

Shri Mr

Shrimati Mrs

Sikhs adherents in India of sect founded by Guru Nanak

Sita-Ram invocation in memory of Sita, legendary idol of womanhood, and Rama, her husband, idol of manhood

Swadeshi literally "of one's own country". Home manufacture. In economics the doctrine of encouragement and preferential use of products of one's own country

Swaraj self-rule, political independence, self-government

Taluka an estate; applied to a tract of proprietary land usually smaller than a zamindari, although sometimes including several villages and not infrequently confused with a zamindari; a very large estate in the United Provinces (in Oudh)

Talukdar or taluqdar holder of a taluk, hereditary revenue collector appointed under early British rule in India

Tehsildar official revenue collector

Ulemas a body of scholars or divines trained in Muslim theology and law, and recognized as authorities in these and cognate fields

Viceroy representative of the Crown of England, and administrator of India. The term, prior to independence, comprised the dual but separate functions of Governor-General of British India with its eleven Provinces (Bombay, Madras, Bengal, United Provinces, Punjab, Central Provinces, Bihar, Orissa, Assam, Sind and North-West Frontier Province), and Crown Representative to nearly six hundred States (the

largest of which were Hyderabad, Kashmir and Mysore). The relationship between the Crown Representative and the Indian States was
governed by treaties which established Great Britain as the Paramount
Power and deprived the States of full sovereignty. The Paramount
Power, for example, reserved control over such central subjects as
defence, communications and foreign policy, as well as disciplinary
authority over the Princes in the event of misrule. The territories of
the Princes comprised roughly a third of India's territory and a quarter
of her population. The Crown Representative's relations with the
Indian States were administered up to the transfer of power to an
independent India by the Political Department. (Based on M.M.,
footnote, p. 46.)

Weightage   excess number of representatives, who could be expected to
be elected from a minority population, in order to increase the number
of minority representatives. (Not necessarily in order to equal majority
representation, but to approach it)

Yogi   one who practises yoga

Yogic   practice pertaining to yoga

Zamindar   landowner of large tract of land, sometimes including several
villages

Zamindari   land and privileges of a zamindar

Zindabad   Long Live

[Nehru approved this Glossary. Spelling, and definitions, of some specialised words
inevitably vary, however, both in general usage and in the course of these volumes.]

Bibliography

BOOKS

Azad, Maulana Abul Kalam. *India Wins Freedom*. New York: Longmans Green & Co., 1960.

Bolitho, Hector. *Jinnah*. London: John Murray, 1960.

Brailsford, H. N. *Subject India*. New York: The John Day Co., 1943.

Brecher, Michael. *Nehru: A Political Biography*. London: Oxford University Press, 1959.

Bright, J. S. *Before and After Independence*. New Delhi: The Indian Printing Works, 1950.

Bright, J. S. *Important Speeches of Jawaharlal Nehru* (1922 to 1946). Vol. I, 3rd Edition. Lahore: The Indian Printing Works. Vol. II, 1946–1957, 1st edition.

Bright, J. S. *The Life of Jawaharlal Nehru*. New Delhi: Indian Printing Works, 1958.

Bright, J. S. *Selected Writings of Jawaharlal Nehru* (1916–1950). New Delhi: The Indian Printing Works, 1950.

Brown, W. Norman. *India, Pakistan, Ceylon*. Ithaca, New York: Cornell University Press, 1951 (reprinted from *Encyclopedia Americana* articles by permission).

Campbell-Johnson, Alan. *Mission with Mountbatten*. London: Robert Hale Ltd., 1951.

Chablani and Chablani. *Motilal Nehru*. Delhi: S. Chand & Co., 1961.

Chakravarty, Amiya. *A Tagore Reader*. London: Macmillan & Co., 1961.

Connell, John. *Auchinleck—A Critical Biography*. London: Cassell & Co., 1959.

Fischer, Louis. *The Life of Mahatma Gandhi*. New York: Collier Books, 1962.

Goodrich, Leland M., ed. *Documents on American Foreign Relations* (Vol. IV). Boston: World Peace Foundation, 1942.

Gopal, Ram. *The Trials of Nehru*. Bombay: The Book Centre Private Ltd., 1962.

Gunther, John. *Inside Asia*. New York: Harper & Bros., 1939.

Gwyer, Sir Maurice, and A. Appadorai. *Speeches and Documents on the Indian Constitution 1921–47* (Vols. I and II). London: Oxford University Press, 1957.

Holborn, Louise W., ed. *War and Peace Aims of the United Nations*. Boston: World Peace Foundation, 1943.

Hutheesing, Krishna Nehru. *Nehru's Letters to His Sister*. London: Faber and Faber, 1963.

584   BIBLIOGRAPHY

India and The Aggressors. (The Trend of Indian Opinion between 1935-1940.) Delhi: Compiled by the Bureau of Public Information, Government of India.

Ismay, Lord. *The Memoirs of General Lord Ismay.* New York: The Viking Press, 1960.

Krishnamurti, Y. G. *Jawaharlal Nehru: The Man and His Ideas.* Bombay: The Popular Book Depot, 1945.

Lumby, E. W. R. *The Transfer of Power in India.* London: George Allen & Unwin Ltd., 1954.

Mende, Tibor. *Nehru: Conversations on India and World Affairs.* New York: George Braziller, Inc., 1956.

Menon, V. P. *The Transfer of Power in India.* Princeton, New Jersey: Princeton University Press, 1957.

Moon, Penderel. *Divide and Quit.* London: Chatto and Windus, 1962.

Moraes, Frank. *Jawaharlal Nehru.* New York: The Macmillan Co., 1956.

Murphy, Ray. *Last Viceroy.* London: Jarrolds Ltd.

Nanda, B. R. *The Nehrus—Motilal and Jawaharlal.* London: George Allen & Unwin Ltd., 1962.

Narasimhaiah, C. D. *Jawaharlal Nehru.* Mysore: Rao & Raghavan, 1959.

Nehru, Jawaharlal:

A Bunch of Old Letters. New York: Asia Publishing House, 1960.

An Autobiography. London: The Bodley Head, 1936.

China, Spain and the War. Allahabad and London: Kitabistan, 1940.

The Discovery of India. New York: The John Day Company, 1946.

Eighteen Months in India. Allahabad: Kitabistan, 1938.

Glimpses of World History. New York: The John Day Co., 1942.

Independence and After (1946-1949). Delhi: Publications Division, Government of India, 1949.

India and The World. London: George Allen & Unwin Ltd., 1936.

India's Foreign Policy. Delhi: Publications Division, Government of India, 1961.

Inside America—A Voyage of Discovery. New Delhi: National Book Stall, D. C. Malhotra, 1950.

Jawaharlal Nehru's Speeches, 1949-1953. Delhi: The Publications Division, Government of India, 1954. (Second Impression, 1957).

Nehru on Gandhi. New York: The John Day Co., 1948.

Prison Humours. Allahabad: New Literature, 1946.

Recent Essays and Writings. Allahabad: Kitabistan, 1934.

Soviet Russia. Bombay: Chetana, 1929.

The Unity of India. New York: The John Day Co., 1941.

Toward Freedom. New York: The John Day Co., 1941. [This edition includes sections not in the London edition of Nehru's *Autobiography* (1936), written in August, 1940, and October, 1940].

Visit to America. New York: The John Day Co., 1950.

Philips, C. H. *The Evolution of India and Pakistan* (Volume IV: 1858 to 1947). London: Oxford University Press, 1962.

Poplai, S. L. *Selected Documents on Asian Affairs* (India 1947–50). (Vol. II). London: Oxford University Press, 1959.

Pyarelal. *Mahatma Gandhi—The Last Phase*. Ahmedabad: Navajivan Publishing House. Vols. I & II: 1956, 1958.

Rabindranath Tagore (A Centenary Volume 1861–1961.) New Delhi: Sahitya Akademi, 1961.

Rao, M. V. Ramana. *A Short History of the Indian National Congress*. New Delhi: S. Chand & Co., 1959.

Sheean, Vincent. *Nehru: The Years of Power*. New York: Random House, 1960.

Singh, Anup. *Nehru The Rising Star of India*. London: George Allen & Unwin Ltd., 1940.

Sitaramayya, Dr. Pattabhi. *The History of the Indian National Congress, 1885–1935*. Bombay: Padma Publications, Ltd. (Second Edition, 1946; also first edition, 1935.) Unless otherwise specified, citations have been taken from the Second Edition.

Sitaramayya, Dr. Pattabhi. *The History of the Indian National Congress, 1935–1947*. Bombay: Padma Publications, Ltd., 1947.

Spear, Percival. *India—A Modern History*. Ann Arbor, Michigan: The University of Michigan Press, 1961.

Tendulkar, D. G. *Mahatma* (in eight volumes). New Delhi: The Publications Division, Government of India. (1951, ff.)

Zakaria, Rafiq, ed. *A Study of Nehru*. Bombay: Times of India, 1959 and 1960.

PAMPHLETS, ARTICLES, SPEECHES, ETC., BY JAWAHARLAL NEHRU

"A Cable from Pandit Nehru". *The New Republic*. August 4, 1947.

Can Indians Get Together? New York: The India League of America, Inc. (Reprinted from *New York Times*, July 19, 1942.)

"Changing India". *Foreign Affairs*. New York: Council on Foreign Relations. April, 1963, Vol. 41, No. 3.

"Colonialism Must Go". *The New York Times Magazine*, March 3, 1946.

"India Can Learn from China". *Asia and The Americas*, January, 1943.

Indian Writers in Council. Fort, Bombay: Ash Lane, International Book House, Ltd., 1945.

"India's Day of Reckoning". *Fortune Magazine*. April, 1942.

Isherwood, Christopher. *Vedanta for Modern Man*. New York: Harper & Bros., 1951. (*Sri Ramakrishna—As I Understand Him*, by Jawaharlal Nehru.) Permission to reprint granted by the copyright holder, the Vedanta Society of Southern California.

Jawaharlal Nehru on The Cripps Mission. London: The Ind a League, 1942.

Labour Monthly. London: August, 1938.

"Letter to a Young Chinese Journalist"—August 8, 1942. *Life Magazine*, March 1, 1943. ("India Speaks to China".)
Letter to African Leaders. Indian Information; Government of India, Washington, D.C. (Vol. 19, No. 194—October 15, 1946.)
Peace and India. London: The India League, 1938.
"Tagore and Gandhi." *Visva-Bharati Quarterly*, Santiniketan, 1949. (Gandhi Memorial Peace Number.)
"The Rashtrapati" by "Chanakya". Calcutta: *Modern Review*, November, 1937. (Written under above pseudonym by Jawaharlal Nehru.)

OFFICIAL RECORDS, REPORTS, PAMPHLETS, ARTICLES, DOCUMENTS

All India Congress Committee Report. August 7, 1942; August 8, 1942.
Congress Bulletin. New Delhi: No. 1, February, 1942; November, 1945. (Mss. sent to D. N. by J. N.)
Constituent Assembly Debates. Official Report (Vol. VIII). May 16, 1949.
Correspondence Between the Prime Ministers of Pakistan and India regarding Peaceful Settlements of Indo-Pakistan Disputes. New York: Pakistan Mission to the United Nations, 1950.
Facts on India. Washington, D.C.: Embassy of India, January 26, 1951.
Government of India Information Services. Washington, D.C.: October 8, 1947; October 22, 1947; February 20, 1948; June 11, 1948; July 30, 1948; August, 1948; October 18, 1948.
India News. Washington, D.C.: Indian Information Service, Embassy of India. February 22, 1963: "Roosevelt and India", by B. Shiva Rao.
India What Next? (Why the Talks Failed). London: The India League, 1942.
Indiagram. Washington, D.C.: Indian Information Service, Embassy of India. #27, February 10, 1959.
Indian Annual Register. New Delhi: Vol. II, 1933; Vol. II, 1937; Vol. II, 1946.
Indian Quarterly Register. New Delhi: Vol. I, 1927; Vol. II, 1929.
Kashmir—A Factual Survey. New Delhi: Information Service of India, 1956.
Kashmir and the United Nations. New Delhi: Ministry of External Affairs, Government of India Press, 1962.
Report of the 42nd Indian National Congress. Madras: 1927. (Ms. sent to D. N. by J. N.)
The First Five Year Plan. Government of India, Planning Commission, 1952.
White Paper on Jammu and Kashmir. Government of India, 1947.

JOURNALS AND NEWSPAPERS

Amrita Bazar Patrika (Calcutta). March 1, 1946; March 23, 1946; March 28, 1946.
Asia Magazine. February, May, 1939.

Far Eastern Survey. New York: American Council Institute of Pacific Relations, March 22, 1943. "Storm Over India", by Anup Singh.
India Today. New York: India League of America. October, 1948.
National Herald. Lucknow. May 31, 1939; June 1, 1939; January 19, 1940. (Mss. sent to D. N. by J. N.)
Pacific Affairs. March, 1940; "Indian Nationalism and the Far East", by Irving S. Friedman.
Sunday Amrita Bazar Patrika (Calcutta). March 10, 1946.
The Asiatic Review. London: East India Association. July, 1952.
The Leader. Allahabad. February 24, 1947.
The New York Times. September 3, 1944, p. 17.
Times of India. Bombay and New Delhi. October 3, 1953.
Twice A Year. A Book of Literature, The Arts and Civil Liberties. New York: Twice A Year Press. Vol. V–VI—1940–41; Vol. X–XI—1943; Vol. XII–XIII—1945.
Voice of India. Washington, D.C.: September, 1946; October, 1946; January, 1947.

Dates having to do with pre-World War II events, and World War II developments, have been gathered from various sources, in addition to those listed above, too numerous to mention. Special note must, however, be made of *History of World War II* by Francis Trevelyan Miller (The John C. Winston Company, Philadelphia, Toronto: 1945).

Index

Abdullah, Sheikh Saheb (Kashmiri leader), II: 233, 263, 347, 349, 350, 443
Abode of Happiness (Nehru's residence): see Anand Bhawan
Abyssinia
  Abyssinia Day, I: 418-19
  Britain and, II: 9
  Indian troops sent to, I: 125
  Italian occupation of, I: 213, 384, 387, 417, 447, 449, 566, 580, 587, 601, 608, 645, 657
Adams, G. F., I: 71
Afghan War (1919), I: 68
Afghanistan, I: 167
  delegation at Mussoorie, I: 68-72
  federation, I: 636
  India and, II: 266-7
  Indian Committee's pro-German propaganda in (during World War I), I: 30
  Indian troops sent to, I: 125
  and Russia, I: 135, 411
Aga Khan, I: 255-7, 302
age and youth, differing aims of, II: 183
Agrarian Movement, I: 55, 56, 62, 75, 258, 449, 453, 471, 692
agrarian problems in Asia, II: 496, 509
agriculture, Indian, II: 509-10
  increase in production after independence, II: 541
aggression, India's attitude toward, II: 99-100, 195
Ahmadnagar Fort prison, Nehru jailed in, II: 129
Ahmedabad, I: 50, 282
Ahrar (see Glossary), I: 517, 543
air raid precautions, I: 583
Albania, I: 628

Alexander, A. V., II: 205
Alexander, Horace, and the "Quit-India" movement, II: 117-18
Ali, Asaf, I: 677
Ali, Choudhury Rahmat, II: 224
Ali, M. Mohamad, I: 59
Alipore Central Jail, Nehru in, I: 343
Allahabad
  See Congress
  Earthquake Relief Committee, I: 339
  Hindu-Muslim riots in, I: 117
  Home Rule League in, I: 44
  Nehru arrested in, I: 77
  his boyhood in, II: 359
  as Congress Chairman of Municipality, I: 107
  imprisoned in, I: 98-9
  joins High Court Bar of, I: 17
  Unity Conference in, I: 540
All-Bengal Students Conference, I: 161-7
All-India Congress Committee: see Congress
All-India Federation, I: 238, 364, 422, 465-6, 489, 577, 593, 608-12, 618, 636
All-India Muslim League: see Muslim League
All-India Socialist Youth Congress (1928), I: 139
All-India Trade Union Congress, I: 147, 174-82, 192, 341, 455, 689
All-India Union, concept of, II: 226
All-Jammu and Kashmir National Conference, II: 347, 349
  See also Kashmir
All-Parties Conference, I: 141-2, 169-71, 198, 331, 511
All-Russia Congress of Soviets, I: 132-3

Almora Jail, Nehru imprisoned in, I: 357, 384
Amanullah, I: 166-7
America, South, I: 565
Amery, L. S. (Secretary of State for India), II: 55
Amritsar: see Congress
Amritsar massacre, I: 50-2
Anand Bhawan (Abode of Happiness: Nehru's residence), I: 79, 99, 357-8. See also Swaraj Bhawan
Andrews, C. F., his pamphlet on Indian independence, I: 73
Anglo-Polish mutual resistance agreement (1939), I: 634
Ansari, Dr M. A., I: 421
apartheid, Indian attitude toward, II: 537
Apollonius Tyanaeus, I: 5
appeasement, II: 29-30
Nehru's attitude toward, II: 46
of Japan, II: 106
Arabia, I: 59, 61, 304, 309, 569-70
and Brussels Congress, I: 120
Indian troops sent to, I: 125
Arms Act, I: 22
arti (Hindu religious custom), I: 113
Asia
agrarian problems in, II: 496, 509
attitude toward World War II, II: 137
colonialism in, II: 421-2
economic freedom of, II: 402-7
and imperialist aggression, II: 545
Inter-Asian Relations Conference, II: 310-15
nationalism in, II: 496-7
Nehru's concept of a federation of, II: 198
on future of, II: 97-8
on India's relationships in, II: 461-3
as new centre of world events, II: 214-16, 498
and the promise of freedom, II: 100
re-emergence of, II: 110-11
tremendous forces and changes in, II: 522-3
unitary character of, II: 222, 505
Western countries' lack of interest in problems of, II: 454

Asoka, I: 555
Asquith, H. H., I: 345-6
Assam, II: 323
Atlantic Charter, the, II: 54
Eastern nations and, II: 195
India's concern about, II: 136
Nehru on, II: 99
atomic bomb, Indian reactions to, II: 185, 264
Attlee, Clement, I: 371; II: 162
appoints Lord Mountbatten as Viceroy, II: 287
and Indian independence, II: 295, 303-5
and London Conference (1946), II: 275 ff.
and Nehru, at Prime Ministers Conference (1948), II: 414
Nehru's tribute to, II: 483
Auchinleck, General Sir Claude, and India's defence, II: 259
Australia, I: 144, 320, 406, 640
Austria, Nazi invasion of, I: 562
Autobiography, An (Nehru): see Toward Freedom
Azad, Maulana Abul Kalam, I: 667; II: 9-13, 126-7, 230, 239-41
on Gandhi's non-violence policy, II: 89
as official Congress spokesman, II: 166
See also India Wins Freedom

Bajaj, Jamnalal, I: 454-5
Bakr-id day, I: 113
Baldwin, Stanley, I: 180
Balkans, preparation for war in, I: 143
Baltic States, I: 661
Baluchistan, II: 267
Bande Mataram (see Glossary), I: 537, 541
banking system, British Government's control of, I: 35
Bankipore: see Congress
Bapu: see Gandhi, Mohandas K.
Barcelona: see Spain
beauty, Nehru on man's sense of, II: 519
Belgium, Nehru visits, I: 119

Bengal
  All-Bengal Students Conference, I: 161-7
  famine in (1943), II: 138-40
  Hindu and Muslim population figures, II: 95
  inability to resist Japanese aggression, II: 106
  and Pakistan, II: 170, 172
  partitioning of, I: 7-8, 11, 22, 24, 80, 109, 302
Bengali language, II: 188-9
Berle, A. A., Jr, II: 55
Berlin, Nehru visits, I: 119
Besant, Mrs Annie, I: 5, 6
  and Home Rule League, I: 44
  Independence Resolution supported by, I: 141, 183
  internment of, I: 36, 41
Bhagavad Gita (Indian Epic), I: 6
Bharat Mata (see Glossary), II: 362
Bhave, Vinoba, arrest of, II: 43
bhikkus (Buddhist monks), I: 278
Bhoodan (land-grant movement), II: 43
Bihar
  communal violence in, II: 271-2
  earthquake in, I: 337-40
birth control, Gandhi on, I: 373-5
Blanqui, Louis Auguste, I: 131
Blavatsky, Madame, I: 5, 6
Boer War, I: 4
Bohemia, I: 652
Bolshevism, I: 111, 130
Bombay
  See Congress
  Election Manifesto, I: 461-2, 467, 478, 482
  slum conditions in, I: 31
  violence and mutinies in, II: 201-5 passim
  Youth Conference (1928), I: 173
Bose, Sarat Chandra, I: 616-17
Bose, Subhas Chandra, I: 188, 213-214, 614-15, 617-22
  and Indian National Army, II: 173
  on Nehru's unique position as leader, II: 561
  sympathies with Japan, II: 111-12

bourgeoisie, in India, I: 20-21, 29, 35, 222, 302
boycotts
  of British goods, I: 9, 11, 14, 22-3, 127, 208, 224, 293, 312
  of foreign cloth, I: 90-9, 205, 208, 293
  of Japan, I: 251
  of the legislature, I: 210, 224, 312
Brahmin: see also Nehru Family
  Kashmiri Brahmins, I: 4-5, 40
  Nehru's background, I: 351
  and non-Brahmins, I: 414
Brailsford, H. N., II: 82
  on Nehru's role in Indian politics, II: 562
Brecher, Michael, I: 46, 688; II: 163
Britain, I: 33-5, 184-5
  and China, II: 29
  contrast in attitudes of Congress and communal bodies toward, II: 172
  imperialist expansion of, II: 544
  impossibility of Indian co-operation with, II: 67
  Indian hostility and distrust, II: 73-5, 88, 241-2
  and Indian support in World War II II: 5-6
  and India's Princely States, II: 562-5
  and Indonesia, II: 212
  influence on Indian institutions, II: 482
  on policy of, II: 7 ff., 9, 27, 66-7, 100
  record of her rule in India, II: 550-7
  wane of imperial power of, II: 195
British India, Indians resident in, before partition, II: 571
British and non-British subjects in India, pre-independence statistics, II: 571
Brooks, Ferdinand T., I: 5, 6
Brussels International Congress (1927), I: 119-28, 214
Bryce, James, I: 280
Buddha and Buddhism, I: 167, 277-8, 557; II: 525
Burma
  Indian troops sent to, I: 125
  Nehru envisages in Far East federation, I: 636
  visits, I: 489

Burma-China road, II: 29
Butler, Sir Harcourt (Governor of United Provinces), I: 69-73

Cabinet Mission to India (1946), II: 205, 223-6, 232-5
   Jinnah's rejection of Plan, II: 320
   Muslim League and, II: 275
   reactions to, II: 206 ff.
   See 1942 Plan, II: 79 ff.
Cairo Conference (1943), II: 135
Calcutta
   See Congress
   mutiny and communal riots in, II: 206, 252-4, 270-1
Cambridge University, Nehru at, I: 3, 11-17, 26, 550; II: 500
Campbell-Johnson, Alan, II: 325
   on the problem of the Princely States, II: 331
Canada, I: 245, 320, 406
   Nehru's first visit, II: 449
Canal Waters dispute (Indo-Pakistan), II: 528, 536
capitalism, I: 309-15, 697; II: 543-4
Casablanca Conference (1943), II: 135
Catholic Church: see Roman Catholicism
Cavour, Camillo Benso, Count di, I: 13
Central Volunteer Board, I: 78
Cervantes, Miguel de, I: 264, 562
Ceylon, II: 523
   Bernard Shaw's concept of, as cradle of human race, II: 417
   Nehru's concept of, in an eastern federation, I: 636
   message to youth of, II: 182
   rapprochement policy toward, II: 268-9
   visits, I: 119, 277
Chamberlain, Sir Austen, I: 45, 143-4
Chamberlain, Neville, I: 562-4, 568, 582-5, 599, 631, 653
Chambers of Commerce, I: 543
Chanakya (Nehru pseudonym), see "Rashtrapati"
charkha (see Glossary), I: 95, 230, 623; II: 178
Chauri Chaura, mob violence at, I: 82, 85

Chelmsford, Lord
   Montagu-Chelmsford reforms, I: 44-7
   and the Morley-Minto proposals, I: 24
   succeeded as Viceroy by Lord Reading, I: 77
Chiang Kai-shek, Generalissimo, I: 635, 636
   at Cairo Conference (1943), II: 135
   visit to India, and support for freedom movement, II: 75-8
Chiang Kai-shek, Madame
   sympathy for India's problems and independence, II: 78-9, 116
children, Nehru's attitude to, II: 518-20
China, I: 166, 180, 197, 309, 320, 400, 566, 571-4, 593, 596, 600, 608, 671, 684
   Britain and, II: 29
   and Brussels Conference (1927), I: 120
   continuity of, II: 530
   emancipation of, I: 122
   hostilities with Japan, I: 251, 262, 409, 449, 631-2, 645
   India sends medical unit to, I: 574, 633
   Indian troops sent to, I: 121, 125
   India's attitude toward Chinese Communist Party, II: 518
   India's desire for close contacts with, II: 76, 102, 196
   industrialization of, II: 112 ff.
   invades Tibet, II: 536
   nationalists in, I: 122, 125
   Nehru and interest in Industrial Co-operatives in, II, 112-13, 115
   on sufferings and staying power of, II: 52-3, 61, 111
   visits, I: 251, 634-6
   omitted in Clarence Streit's concept of union of democracies, I: 640
   problems of, II: 496
   Russia and, I: 135
   sends famine help to India, II: 140
   and thousand years' peace with India, II: 98
Chirol, Sir Valentine, I: 302
Christians in India, number of, II: 95
Church of England, I: 88

Churchill, Winston S., I: 57, 180, 245–6, 370, 407
becomes British Prime Minister, II: 21
at Casablanca and Cairo Conferences (1943), II: 135
and the Constituent Assembly, II: 287
displeased by U.S. attitude toward India, II: 137
fears Japanese threat to India, II: 71
and Indian public opinion, II: 498
his interpretation of Atlantic Charter, II: 54
requests considerate treatment of Nehru in prison, II: 43
C.I.D. (Indian Criminal Investigation Dept.), I: 24, 70, 72
Citrine, Walter, I: 175
Civil Disobedience Campaigns, I: 232, 236, 241, 244, 396, 413
after Declaration of Independence (1930), I: 217–24
after Delhi Pact, I: 247
decline of, I: 285, 291–5
Gandhi and, I: 217–21, 242; II: 40–5 passim
Gandhi's arrest for his part in, I: 268, 273, 275
Gandhi's withdrawal of, I: 346–9, 358
individual disobedience, II: 42
launched by Gandhi, I: 128
Nehru's statement on, at his trial, II: 44
suspension of, I: 81–5, 90
civil liberties
Civil Liberties Union (Indian) founded, I: 225
and Defence of India Ordinance, I: 641
Nehru's observations on, I: 225–7, 441
Civil Service, Indian, I: 12, 16, 105, 246
Clayton, Will (Acting Secretary of State, U.S.A.), Nehru appeals to, to hasten food permits for India, II: 269
cloth, foreign: see boycotts
"Cold War", the, II: 416
collective farms, I: 693; II: 169
collective security, I: 636–41
colonialism
in Asia, II: 421 ff.

colonialism—contd.
Nehru's insistence on ending, II: 208–13
pockets of, in India after independence, II: 538
See also I: 33–35; Appendix, II: 543–556; imperialism
Comintern (Communist International), termination of, II: 135
Commonwealth, the
Commonwealth Declaration (1949), II: 471–2
co-operation and independence in, II: 525
India as member of, II: 414–16
review of, and resolution for ratification of membership in, II: 474–86
Communal Award, I: 270–4, 538
communalism, I: 112–16, 160, 199, 257, 301–5, 328–31, 365, 391–2, 442, 479, 544, 612–13, 648, 667; II: 557–60
See also violence
communications, disruption of, following partition, II: 461
communism
Congress and, I: 281–3, 574
influence of, in mutinies, II: 201 ff.
Manifesto I: 131
Nehru's attitude toward, I: xiii, 56–8, 126, 129, 161, 165, 182, 300, 369; II: 183–4, 517–18
spread of, I: 280
Communist Party, British, I: 625
Communist Party, Indian, I: 370; II: 183–4
Nehru's opinion of, II: 517–18
communists, Indian
coercion and atrocities by, II: 413
effects of British attitude toward, II: 130–1
Community Development programmes, II: 540
Confucians, I: 309
Congress
acceptance of Cabinet responsibility, I: 483–7
and Agrarian Movement, I: 55–6

Congress—*contd.*

All-India Congress Committee, II: 25, 40-1, 65, 67, 71, 87, 294-5
and All-India Trade Union, I: 175
Allahabad session (1910), I: 38
and Amritsar massacre, I: 50
Amritsar session (1919-20), I: 59
Bankipore session (1912), I: 27
Bombay session (1934), I: 364-6, 542
British goods, boycott of, I: 11, 14, 22, 23, 127, 208, 224, 293, 312
and the Cabinet Mission (1946), II: 206, 224-5, 233-5; (1942), 79 ff.
Calcutta sessions (1906), I: 9, 10, 36, 38; (1920), I: 62, 101; (1928), I: 169, 170-1; (1933), I: 293-5
China, medical unit sent to, I: 574, 633
and Civil Disobedience, I: 219, 681
and communalism, I: 112-16; II: 558-60. *See also* communalism
and communism, I: 281-3
and concept of federation, II: 233-4
conflict with *Kisan* Movement, I: 578
Congress-League scheme, I: 37, 39
the Constitution and, I: 293, 364-5, 405, 538, 654
See also Constituent Assembly; and India
Lord Curzon and, I: 7
Delhi session (1923), I: 99-101
disapproval of Montagu-Chelmsford Report, I: 44
and disarmament, II: 23
and Dominion status, I: 184-5
effects of composition of, II: 560
elections: (1936), I: 477 ff.; (1937), I: 495-6. *See also* elections
Faizpur session (1936), I: 462-73
foundation of, I: 7, 21
Gandhi and, I: 58-68, 83, 109, 251-7, 280-1, 348, 356, 364, 396-7, 617, 620, 622
Gauhati session (1926), I: 119
Haripura session (1938), I: 503-4, 618
and independence, I: 145-6, 215-16, 233, 366, 463, 607
and an Interim Government, II: 242-3, 247

Congress—*contd.*

and International Peace Campaign, I: 571-4
Japanese goods, boycott of, I: 497
Jinnah and, I: 63, 112, 667-78; II: 218
Karachi session (1931), I: 241, 247-51, 293, 297, 413, 520
Lahore session (1929), I: 175, 185, 187-91, 214-16
and League Against Imperialism, I: 128
Lucknow sessions: (1916), I: 37-9, 41; (1936), I: 371, 416, 420, 424-9, 451-60
Madras session (1927), I: 140-6, 187
as majority party, II: 572
ministers resign, I: 663-4, 678-9, 686-7, 695
and Montagu Declaration, I: 44
and Muslim League, I: 170, 490, 505-49, 663, 667-78, 687-8; II: 224 ff., 242-3, 254, 273-4, 287
Nagpur session (1920), I: 59
National Planning Committee, I: 656, 688-98
and nationalism, I: 637
Nehru as member of, and offices held by, I: 26, 44, 99-101, 108, 118, 142, 175, 187-210, 326, 424, 448, 451, 457, 463, 498-501; II: 21-6, 163, 292-3
his review of policy of, II: 22-6
political objectives of, I: 360
and political prisoners, I: 493-5
policy of defiance, I: 295
and post-war reforms, II: 169-70
protests on use of Indian troops in China, I: 121
regards Pakistan's formation as a disaster, II: 291, 320
relations with British Government, I: 66, 77, 183-6, 252-7, 295, 353, 663; II: 556-7
and representation and rights of minorities, I: 67, 101, 496-7, 660, 663
and 1st Simla Conference (1945), II: 165-6; 2nd Simla Conference (1946), II: 225-6

Congress—*contd.*
and Simon Commission, I: 140
and State rulers, I: 611
terrorism condemned by, I: 62
Tripuri session (1939), I: 614–15
as a true political body, II: 171
and World War I, I: 32
and World War II, I: 142–5, 502–4, 586, 641–8, 656, 657–9, 679–86, 688–98; II: 100
and Lord Zetland, I: 665–6, 668, 682
See also Congress Socialist Party *under* Socialism
Congress Working Committee
arrest of members, I: 223
and Cripps Mission, II: 82–5
and independence, II: 73–4
and "Quit India" movement, II: 118–23
suspension of, I: 326–7
and Wavell's proposals for reconstruction of Executive Council, II: 163
Congress of Oppressed Nationalities: *see* League Against Imperialism
Conservative Party, British, I: 256, 270
Constituent Assembly
Churchill and, II: 287
conception of, II: 130
Congress adopts proposal for, I: 364–5, 405
continuing need for, II: 18–20, 246
creation and functions of, II: 278 ff.
definition of function of, I: 405, 669–70
Gandhi and, I: 598
Jinnah's directive on, II: 273
members' pledge on granting of independence, II: 337
and the Mountbatten Plan, II: 322–4
Nehru addresses, on the Draft Constitution, II: 424–32
addresses, on Kashmir question, II: 389–98, 439–43
his policy for, II: 251, 252
no compulsion under, II: 304
renewed demand for, I: 424, 436–7, 447, 462, 468, 481, 538, 612, 618–19, 663, 664, 668–70, 688
and rulers of the Indian States, II: 92–3

Constitution (under British rule), I: 142, 169, 207, 608
Joint Committee on Indian Constitutional Reform, I: 363, 367
provisional draft by British, I: 293, 363
suspension of, I: 686
Constitution for a Free India: *see* India
Coomaraswamy, Dr Ananda K., II: 551
cottage industries, II: 169
councils, village, II: 540. *See Panchayat*
cow sacrifice, I: 113, 537, 540
Craddock, Sir Reginald, I: 44–5
Crimea Conference (Yalta), II: 162
Criminal Law Amendment Act, I: 42
Criminal Procedure Code, I: 106
Cripps, Sir Stafford
Nehru on, II: 95
wartime visit to India, II: 71
Cripps Mission to India, II: 79 ff., 20 ff.
culture, II: 523–4
Curzon, Lord
attitude toward Congress, I: 7
and the Official Secrets Act, I: 8
and partitioning of Bengal, I: 7, 8, 11, 22
Czechoslovakia
Britain and, II: 9
dissolution of Republic of, I: 562, 627
Nazi occupation of, I: 143, 213, 545, 569, 580, 583, 603, 615, 624, 643, 652, 653, 657, 684
Nehru visits, I: 564

Dacca, Muslim League founded at, I: 38
Daladier, Edouard, I: 562, 584–5
Damascus, French destruction in, I: 162
Daridranarayan ("Lord of the Poor"), I: 85
Debating Society (Cambridge University), Nehru and, II: 500
Declaration of London (1948), II: 414–15
defence of Asia, India's role in, II: 212 ff., 217
Defence Council and Second World War, II: 32
Defence of India Act, I: 29, 47
Defence of India Ordinance, I: 641
"Defence in Political Cases", Nehru's directive on, I: 223

Dehra Dun Jail, Nehru imprisoned in, I: 350; II: 48
Delhi, I: 24, 50, 51
as centre of Indo-Persian culture, I: 40
Unity Conference at, I: 117
See also Congress
Delhi Pact (1931), I: 241-7
Desai, Mahadev, I: 677
Dev, Narendra, I: 485 *n.*
Dev, S. D., I: 454-5
Devanagari script, I: 522-3
Dhammapada (Buddhist Scriptures), I: 5
dictatorship, Nehru on, II: 195
Direct Action (Muslim call for violence), II: 242-3
disarmament, Nehru on, II: 64
Discovery of India, The (Nehru), II: 129, 562
Disraeli, Benjamin, I: 264
Divine Right of Kings, II: 297
Dollfuss, Engelbert (Austrian Chancellor), I: 345
domestic programme, II: 250, 509-13
Dominion Status, I: 115, 128, 139, 142, 169-72, 189, 192, 199, 201, 202, 245, 306, 318, 328-9, 331, 353, 660; II: 35, 65, 319, 320
and the Commonwealth decision, II: 486
old idea of, inapplicable to India, II: 104
Doulatram, Jairamdas, I: 454-5
Dublin: *see* Ireland
Dutch East Indies, I: 144
Dyer, General Reginald, and the Amritsar massacre, I: 47, 51

East Africa, I: 209, 387
East Bengal, violence in, II: 271
East India Company, II: 563-4
East-West barriers and contrasts, II: 520-1, 545
Eastern Federation, Nehru on the need for an, II: 51-3
economic policy, II: 379-80
Eden, Anthony, I: 411; II: 90, 137
Edinburgh Review, Aga Khan's article in, on Hindu-Muslim problems, I: 302

education, I: 695
statistics, II: 541
Edward, Prince of Wales, visit to India by, I: 77
Egypt, I: 197, 306-7
Anglo-Egyptian treaty, I: 180
British victories in, in World War II, II: 135
Indian troops sent to, I: 29, 125
National Movement in, I: 312
Nehru visits, I: 561
Eighteen Nations Conference on Indonesia, II: 449-53, 458, 497
Eire: *see* Ireland
Election Manifesto (Bombay, 1936), I: 461-2, 467, 478, 482
elections, I: 436 ff., 461
first post-World War II general election, II: 169-70
regulations, II: 572
Employers' Associations, I: 543
Engels, Friedrich, I: 131
England: *see* Britain
English language
influence of, in India, II: 482
as associate official language, II: 572
equal rights, Gandhi on, II: 172, 181
Ethiopia, Italian invasion of, I: 384, 424, 433, 445, 447
Europe
results of Congress of Vienna, II: 544
rivalry of imperialist powers in, II: 544-5
underground movements in, II: 204
Executive Council
Britain's attitude toward convening of, II: 172
Britain's expansion of, II: 32
disagreements on composition of, II: 245
Wavell's proposals for reconstitution of, II: 163, 169

Fabian Socialism: *see* Socialism
Faizpur: *see* Congress
Family Circle, Nehru's, II: 543
family unit, Nehru on importance of the, II: 60
famine, II: 138-40, 196

Fascism, I: 108, 111, 167, 213, 313, 345, 389, 398, 427-8, 445, 473, 565-7, 606, 617, 620, 624-5, 628-9, 637, 640, 643
as an intensification of imperialism, II: 103
and the Muslim League, II: 344-5
Nehru's attitude toward, II: 47, 106, 358
fear, II: 503, 524
Federal Court
and Cabinet Delegation's plan, II: 277
and I.N.A. prisoners, II: 335
and the Interim Government, II: 257
and interpretations of provincial constitutions, II: 245-6
Federal Union: see Clarence Streit
federation, Congress and concept of, I: 465; II: 233-4
Fiji, I: 209
indenture system in, I: 26, 28
Finland, Russian invasion of, I: 634; II: 5, 9-10, 15-16
Fischer, Louis, II: 54, 239
Five-Year-Plans (Indian), I: xiii, 688
flag, India's national, I: 542-3
food, India's need of, II: 510, 511, 518
foreign policy, II: 353 ff., 380-6, 460-71, 493
Forward Bloc, I: 614
four freedoms, unfulfilled promise of, II: 99
Fourteen Points (Jinnah's), I: 534-45
France, I: 166
colonial territory of, in India, II: 538
degradation of Vichy regime, II: 99, 135
and Indo-China, II: 53
Nehru on, II: 11
visits, I: 119, 384, 561
reactionary policy of, II: 27
and World War I, I: 649, 651
and World War II, II: 21
Franco, General Francisco, I: 448, 581, 627, 671
freedom
as aim of subjugated peoples, II: 99 ff.
India's fight for, I: 554-60; II: 184-5
Nehru regards as a common heritage, II: 270

French Revolution, I: 13, 134, 564, 636
Freud, Sigmund, I: 6
fundamental rights
under the Constitution, II: 572
Karachi resolution on (1931), II: 169

Gandhi, Indira Nehru (see also Nehru, Indira), II: 543
Gandhi, Mohandas K., I: vii-viii, x ff., 3, 7, 28, 37, 41, 111, 140-1, 153
abhorrence of Untouchability, I: 270-1
and aims for new India, II: 177-9
ashes immersed in the Ganges, II: 366
assassination of, II: 363-6
attitude toward aggression, II: 105
and Bihar earthquake, I: 340
on birth control, I: 373-5
and Chiang Kai-shek, I: 636; II: 105
and Chinese nationalists, I: 122
and Civil Disobedience, I: 242, 268, 271, 285-7, 346-9, 358
and the Communal Award, I: 270-1
and communalism, I: 114
condemnation of secret activities, I: 268, 285
and Congress, I: 58-68, 109, 141, 251-7, 280-1, 348, 356, 396-7, 443, 490, 616, 620; II: 22
and Congress leaders, I: 186-7
and Congress leadership and Civil Disobedience, II: 40-1, 43
as Congress representative in London, I: 255
and Constituent Assembly, I: 598
and Declaration of Independence, I: 217
his definition of a democrat, I: 252
designates Nehru as his successor, II: 71
and Dominion Status, I: 185-6
on equal rights, II: 172, 181
essence of his teaching, I: 42
and Hind Swaraj, II: 177-8
and Hinduism, I: 65
imprisonment of, I: 82, 223, 228, 238, 240, 272-3, 294-5; II: 135
and independence, I: 297, 446
on industrialization, II: 50

Gandhi—*contd.*
and the intelligentsia, I: 117
interpretations of, in U.S.A., II: 106
and Lord Irwin, I: 241–5
and Kashmir's accession to India, II: 347
and the *khadi* movement, I: 186, 379, 623–4
and language question, I: 530
and the League Against Imperialism, I: 127–8
and Madras Congress session, I: 141
meeting with the Viceroy (1939), I: 668–70, 673
and Motilal Nehru Report, I: 169
and Nazi occupation of Czechoslovakia, I: 603
and Nazism, I: 646
Nehru-Gandhi relationship, I: x ff., 41–3, 129, 299, 346–9, 358–63, 371–3, 453–60, 615; II: 42, 62, 67, 177–80, 561–2
Nehru's praise for character and leadership of, II: 64, 293, 370–5, 443–6, 501–2
Nehru's speech at funeral of, II: 366–70
on Nehru's presidency of Congress, I: 187–91, 371, 421
non-violent non-co-operation campaign, I: 47–50, 52, 75, 80–5, 114, 229, 271, 396–9; II: 62, 67, 89–90
and No-Rent campaign, I: 258
and pacifism, I: 63, 401–2
personality of, I: 220
and pietism, I: 64
and the police as an armed force, I: 23
popularity with the masses, I: 116, 220, 347, 468
protest-fast, II: 135–6
religious outlook, I: 85–7
retires from Congress, I: 364, 371, 622
and resistance to Japan, II: 105–6, 116
and the Resolution of Remembrance, I: 238
and the Salt March, I: 218–20
and Satyagraha, I: 20, 74
and the Seva Sangh, I: 561

Gandhi—*contd.*
and Simla Conference (1945), II: 166
social theories of, I: 371–83
and socialism, I: 213, 375–6, 378
in South Africa, I: 375
and Subhas Bose, I: 615
and *Swaraj*, I: 76
and Tagore, II: 56–9, 530–1
tours India, I: 186
and the underprivileged, I: 76, 79, 375
and village industries, II: 113
and World War II, I: 641–2, 687
and zamindari system, I: 327
Gandhi-Irwin Pact: *see* Delhi Pact
Gandhiji: *see* Glossary
Ganga (river Ganges), Nehru on significance and symbolism of, II: 574–5
Garibaldi, Giuseppe, I: 11, 13
Gauhati: *see* Congress
Gaulle, General Charles de, II: 135
Geneva Disarmament Conferences, I: 143
Germany
Indian revolutionaries in, I: 30
India's changed attitude toward, in World War I, I: 29, 32
invades France, I: 649, 651
Poland, I: 634, 641, 646, 657
Russia, II: 53
Nehru's distrust of, II: 70
he visits, I: 119, 384
no submission to, II: 72, 75
occupies Czechoslovakia, I: 213, 545, 569, 580, 583
Russia's relations with, I: 650–2, 661
surrender of, II: 162
and World War II, I: 649, 651, 661
See also Nazism
Glimpses of World History (Nehru), I: 260–7, 595
Gokhale, Gopal Krishna, I: 8, 9, 23, 24, 25, 27, 28, 44
Gorakhpur, Nehru in prison at, II: 44, 48
Government of India Acts, I: 46, 363–8, 391, 393, 395, 405, 422–3, 424, 435–6, 461–2, 465, 481, 608, 613–14, 654–5, 659–60; II: 72

Government of India Acts—*contd.*
Nehru on Britain's amendment of, II: 7
and the Princely States, II: 564
Gradualists: *see* Liberals
Grand National Consolidated Trade Union, I: 131
"Great Calcutta Killing", the, II: 243, 271
Greece, I: 61
Guadalcanal, Japanese abandon area of, II: 135
Gunther, John, I: 169

Haldane, Viscount, I: 16
Halifax, Lord, I: 385; II: 55, 128
hand-weaving and spinning: *see khadi*
Hardinge, Lord, I: 26
Harijan (Child of God): *see* Untouchables
Harijan (periodical), Gandhi's writing in, I: 460
Haripura: *see* Congress
Harriman, Averell, II: 78
Harrison, Agatha, I: 453–4
Harrow, Nehru at, I: 3, 9–11
Hatta, Mohammad (Vice-President of Indonesian Republic), II: 181
health, in India's domestic policy, II: 541
Himalayas, power and resources of, II: 406
Hind Swaraj (Gandhi booklet on Civil Disobedience), II: 177–8, 180
Hindi language and literature, I: 518–31; II: 188, 190, 572
Hindu Mahasabha: *see* Mahasabha
Hindu-Muslim coalition governments, II: 95
Hindus, I: 5, 19, 20, 22, 48, 199, 256, 309, 370, 377, 665
economic differences with Muslims, I: 408–9, 479
Gandhi and, I: 65, 300
ideological fusion with other groups, I: 328
join in repelling invaders in Kashmir, II: 350
and nationalism, I: 75
political differences with Muslims, I: 37–9, 62, 75, 112–18, 160, 301–4, 479, 604–5, 658, 670, 674

Hindus—*contd.*
population figures, II: 95
religion and politics, I: 86
and results of partition and independence, II: 342, 345
Hindustani language, I: 518–31
as national language, I: 304–5, 392
basic, I: 528–30
characteristics of Hindustani-speaking peoples, I: 323
See also Hindi; Urdu
Hiroshima, atomic bomb dropped on, II: 186
History of Nationalism in the East (Kohn) I: 302
Hitler, Adolf
death of, II: 162
no sympathy for, II: 72
his theories' appeal to Muslim League, II: 344
world domination as aim of, II: 63
See also Germany; Nazism
Hoare, Sir Samuel, I: 275, 647, 668
Holland: *see* Netherlands
Holmes Smith, J. (Methodist Minister), II: 4–5
Home Rule Leagues, I: 36, 52
Nehru as secretary of, I: 44
Hong Kong, vested interests in, II: 103
Hopkins, Harry, II: 90
Hull, Cordell, II: 55
and Indian freedom, II: 128
Hunter Commission, I: 52
Hutheesing, Krishna, II: 543
Nehru's letters to, I: 266, 350; II: 48–9, 59–60, 131–2, 142–3, 157–61
Hyderabad, II: 353
accession negotiations, II: 433–9
Nizam of, II: 433, 436
hydroelectric power, II: 512

"imperial preference", I: 35
imperialism
Nazism and Fascism as intensifications of, II: 103
Nehru's impatience with, II: 195

imperialism—*contd.*
  his view of World War II as an ad-
    venture in, II: 5–6
  nineteenth century spread of, II: 543 ff.
  See also colonialism
Imperialism, League Against: *see* League
    Against Imperialism
Imphal, battle of, II: 173
I.N.A.: *see* Indian National Army
Independence Day, I: 215, 217–18, 237,
    337–8, 605; II: 486–90
independence, Indian, I: 73, 139–42,
    145–6, 153–67, 201–10, 306, 317–
    18, 336, 442, 452, 463; II: 66, 457
  accelerated desire for, after World War
    II, II: 195, 199
  attainment of, II: 291, 335
  and communalism, I: 257, 331
  Declaration of Independence, I: 215–16
  and Dominion Status, I: 169–72, 353
  role of Constituent Assembly in attain-
    ing, II: 19–20
  U.S.A.'s concern for, II: 136–7
Independence—the Immediate Need (C. F.
    Andrews' pamphlet), I: 73
Independence League
  foundation of, I: 183
  Nehru as Secretary of, I: 192
Independence Leagues (Japanese-spon-
    sored), II: 173
Independent, the (Allahabad newspaper),
    I: 51–2
India
  Constitution, and question of allegiance
    to British Sovereign, II: 473
  Jinnah and, I: 535
  Nehru and debate on draft Con-
    stitution, II: 424–32
  need for democratic instrument, to
    be framed by Indians, I: 389–90,
    654
  preamble to, II: 492
  rights under, II, 572
  and democracy, II: 400 ff.
  discovery of zero, decimal system and
    further mathematical contributions
    of, II: 516–17
  emergence of, in world affairs, II: 453 ff.

India—*contd.*
  Nehru on potential, and handicaps of,
    II: 98–101
  and Pakistan and Kashmir, II: 345 ff.
  peaceful and democratic goals of India
    after independence, II: 538–42
  problems of unity in, II: 108–11
  Republic of, its founding (1950), I: ix;
    II: 449, 536 ff.
  war penetrates, II: 62
India Bill: *see* Government of India
    Act
India League of America, II: 499
India League of London, I: 564
  Nehru speaks at meeting of, II: 418
India Office (London), I: 12, 241; II: 290
India Wins Freedom (Azad), II: 239, 322 *n*.
Indian Annual Register, I: 294–5, 297; II:
    236, 239, 274
Indian Army
  enlargement of, II: 22, 135
  must become national, not mercenary
    army, II: 104
  problems relating to, II: 136
Indian Atomic Energy Commission,
    Nehru becomes head of the, II:
    490
Indian Councils Act: *see* Morley-Minto
    Reforms
Indian Independence Act (1947), II: 329–
    31
Indian literature, development of, II:
    186–92
Indian National Army
  disaffection and punishment of, II:
    174–7
  origins of, II: 169, 173
  problem of prisoners, and indepen-
    dence, II: 335
Indian National Congress: *see* Congress
Indian Ocean region, concept of a union
    of countries in, II: 212
Indian Planning Commission (1950), II:
    573
Indian Unrest (Chirol), I: 302
Indian Council of World Affairs, Nehru's
    speech on foreign policy at meet-
    ing of, II: 460–71

"Indianization" as a misleading term, II: 65
Indians abroad, Nehru's policy on conduct of, I: 168
Indo-Aryan languages, I: 392
Indo-China
and Brussels Congress, I: 120
Chinese troops invade, II: 162
France and, II: 53
India and, II: 537
Japan and, II: 53
Indonesia
Asian concern over, II: 449 ff.
as a dominated country, II: 469
Eighteen Nations Conference on, II: 449–53, 458, 497
European and U.S.A. concern over, II: 464–5
imperialism and, II: 211–12
nationalism in, II: 497
Nehru's concern for independence of, II: 222
Netherlands' military attack upon, II: 334
"Indusco", II: 112
Industrial Co-operatives in China, II: 112–13, 115
industrialization, II: 50
of China, II: 112–13, 115
essential to India's economy, II: 113 ff.
India's handicaps in development of, II: 98–101 passim
industry, I: 31, 32, 48
agricultural workers and, I: 300, 622, 627
British attitude toward Indian, I: 33–5
development and increased production, II: 510, 540–1
economic programme, I: 204–6
and National Planning Committee, I: 690
Resolution on Fundamental Rights, I: 249–50
spread of industrialism, I: 156–7, 559
in World War I, I: 310
Inner Temple, London, Nehru at the, I: 17, 245
Inter-Asian Relations Conference (1947), II: 270, 310–15

interdependence of world problems, II: 514
Interim Government, II: 242–5, 248–51
formation of, II: 247
Nehru's offices in, II: 247
International Monetary Fund makes loans to India, II: 512
International Peace Campaign (1938), I: 571–4
international relations, India's aim in development of, II: 540
International, Second and Third, I: 181–2
international understanding, factors in, II: 506–8
internationalism, Nehru on, II: 198
Iqbal, Sir Muhammed, I: 214
Iran, and Russian aggression, II: 216
Iraq, I: 162
Ireland, I: 12, 640, 649; II: 140
the Irish Free State, I: 202
irrigation projects, II: 512
Irwin, Lord, I: 117, 128, 140, 183–6, 225, 241–6
Islam: see Muslims
Italy, I: 166, 652
Nehru visits, I: 119, 561
occupation of Abyssinia, I: 213, 384, 387, 433, 601
opportunism of, in World War II, II: 26
preparation for war, I: 143

Jala-Usha, S.S., launching of, II: 387–8
Jallianwala Bagh: see Amritsar massacre
Jamiat-ul-Ulema (Muslim organization), I: 517, 543
Jammu: see Kashmir
Japan, I: 309, 409
abandons Guadalcanal area, II: 135
as ally of Germany, I: 652
atomic bombs dropped on, II: 168
Churchill fears threat to India, II: 71
and disaffection of Indian National Army, II: 175
Gandhi's attitude toward, II: 105
India boycotts goods from, I: 251, 497

Japan—*contd.*
India's dilemma about, in World War II,
II: 105, 106–8
India's policy of no surrender to, II:
72, 75, 86
invades Manchuria, I: 251, 262, 318
Nehru's advice to, after World War II,
II: 196–7
his attitude toward guerilla warfare
against, II: 96
his distrust of, II: 70, 88–9
relations with U.S.A., I: 410
Russo-Japanese War, I: 6, 22
spectacular victories in East, II: 72
surrender of, II: 169
U.S.A. and China fear threat to India,
II: 77–8
Java, I: 120; II: 181
Jayakar, M. R., I: 228
Jesus Christ, I: 167, 278, 377
Jews
India as asylum for, I: 619
Jinnah, Mohammed Ali, I: 38, 39; II: 130
as arbiter of Muslim League aims, II:
170
character of, I: 547–9
Congress and, I: 63, 112, 667–8; II:
306–8
and the Constituent Assembly, II: 275
death of, II: 336
demands corridor linking East and
West Parkistan, II: 320
his Direct Action call, II: 242–3
disagreements with Wavell and Nehru,
II: 242
his Fourteen Points, I: 534–45
as Governor-General of Pakistan, II:
336
growing influence of, II: 129
as Muslim League leader, I: 64, 505–49
Nehru's correspondence with, I: 530–
45, 671–8, 687–8
policy concerning partition, II: 111
and proposals for an Interim Government, II: 244–5, 254 ff. *passim*
rejects the Cabinet Mission Plan, II: 320
and 1st Simla Conference (1945), II:
166; 2nd Simla Conference (1946),
II: 225

Jinnah—*contd.*
talks with Nehru on an umpire to settle
differences, II: 225
Johnson, Colonel Louis (Roosevelt's
envoy in New Delhi), II: 92
on the Cripps Mission, II: 90
Junagadh, II: 330–2, 433

Kabir (Muslim poet), I: 558
Kamal Pasha, I: 156, 166–7
Karachi
See Congress
mutiny in, II: 206
Resolution on Fundamental Rights, I:
248–51; II: 169
Kashmir
accedes to India, II: 347
documents in Indo-Pakistan dispute
over, II: 565–71
freedom movement in, II: 233
and Jammu, after independence, II:
345–6
Maharajah of, II: 233, 347, 349
Nehru defies order to leave, II: 263–4
his journey to, and arrest, II: 232–3
on problem of, II: 439–43
Pakistan's role in invasion of, and encouragement of violence, II:
346 ff., 376–8, 389 ff., 407–9
problem of, counterbalances joy over
independence, II: 292
U.N. and, II: 528
Kaul, Kamala: *see* Nehru, Kamala Kaul
Keane, M. (Chief Secretary to United
Provinces Government) signs order
barring Nehru from Dehra Dun, I:
71
Kellogg-Briand Pact, I: 318
Keynes, John Maynard, I: 13
khadi (*see* Glossary), I: 62, 85, 186–7, 293,
348, 379, 434, 443, 486, 622–4;
(*khaddar*), I: 95
Khan, Liaquat Ali, I: 670
and Interim Government, II: 259–60
as Prime Minister of Pakistan, II: 336
visits Punjab with Nehru, II: 341–2
Khilafat Movement (*see* Glossary), I: 47,
59–62; II: 11

Kisan movement (*see* Glossary), I: 53–6, 70, 259, 423, 493, 543, 577, 627
Kohn, Hans, I: 302 *n.*
Korea
  Korean War, II: 536
  promise of freedom for, II: 101
Kripalani, J. B., I: 454–5
Kripalani, Krishna, I: 696
Kultur, I: 166
Kuomintang, and the Brussels Conference, I: 120

labour, attitude toward, II: 513
Labour Commission, I: 179–81
Labour Party (British), I: 126, 177–82, 292, 346, 367, 492, 594, 625
  and Indian problems, II: 165
  See Attlee, for granting of India's Independence
Lahore
  See Congress
  demonstration against Simon Commission, I: 147
  Press Conference in (1947), II: 308–9
  violence in, following independence, II: 342–3
Lala Lajpat Rai, I: 147–9
land
  as India's basic problem, II: 505
  land reforms, II: 169, 496, 505, 540
  relation of poverty to burden on the, II: 510, 557
languages
  and the Constitution, II: 572
  development of, in India, II: 186–92
lathee charges (*see* Glossary), I: xiv, 149–53, 224, 229
Leader, the (Allahabad newspaper), I: 51
League Against Imperialism, I: 119–28
  Nehru's final break with, I: 128
  Socialist character of, I: 127
League of Nations, I: 143–4, 164, 318, 384, 386, 407–8, 615, 638–9, 665
legislatures, I: 436 ff., 467, 477 ff.
  See also Congress, elections
Lenin, Vladimir Ilyich, I: 57, 111, 128, 132, 134, 136, 137
Liberals (English), I: 345–6, 625

Liberals (Indian), I: 117, 255, 291, 292, 355–7, 367, 398, 513, 637
Lincoln, Abraham, I: 394
Linlithgow, Lord, I: 399, 641, 659–64, 667–70
  extension of term as Viceroy, II: 129
  his statement on British policy (August, 1940), II: 35–6
  reactions to statement, II: 37–41
Lithuania, preparations for war in, I: 143
Lloyd George, David, I: 180, 399
loans to India, II: 512
local government, II: 505
Lokamanya: *see* Tilak
London Conference (December, 1946), II: 275, 277
  Congress attitude toward, II: 278
London, Declaration of (1948), II: 414–15
London Federation of Peace Councils, I: 564
London Round Table Conferences: *see* Round Table Conferences
"Lord of the Poor", I: 85
Lothian, Lord, I: 384–98
Lucknow
  See Congress
  as centre of Indo-Persian culture, I: 40
  Nehru imprisoned in District Jail, I: 78, 90
  Simon Commission at, I: 149, 151
Lucknow Pact, I: 39, 46, 112
Lytton, Lord, I: 370

MacDonald, Ramsay, I: 180, 184, 238, 271
machinery, India's need of, II: 512
Madras
  See Congress
  and rumour of Japanese invasion, II: 106
Madras Mail, the, I: 327
Mahabharata (Indian Epic), I: 324
Maharashtra, aggressive nationalism in, I: 23
Mahasabha (Hindu right-wing organization), I: 39, 662, 669, 674
  and communalism, II: 200
  and Muslim League, I: 329, 516

Mahatma (Tendulkar), I: vii
Mahmud, Dr Syed, I: 117; II: 129
Majlis, I: 12, 13, 26
malaria, prevention of, II: 512
Malaya, I: 631
    Nehru visits, I: 489
    triumphal reception for Nehru and
    Mountbatten in, II: 219–21
Manchester Guardian, the, I: 293, 345, 580
Manchuria
    Britain and, II: 9
    Japanese invasion of, I: 251, 262, 318,
        433, 447, 580, 587, 601, 643, 657
Mao Tse-tung, I: 633
Marx, Karl, I: 131, 266, 369, 388
Marxism, I: 57, 129, 139, 278, 375, 625, 626
Marxist Socialism, I: xiii, 129
Mazzini, Giuseppe, I: 13, 280
Meerut trial, I: 174–5, 181, 194
Mende, Tibor, I: 56–8
Menon, V. P., I: 688; II: 332
    and Dominion Status for India,
      II: 319
Mesopotamia, I: 407
    Indian troops sent to, I: 125, 633
    rebellion against British, I: 162
middle classes, I: 430–1
Middle East, II: 265–6
    Indian co-operation with leaders in, II:
      195, 198, 199
    R.A.F. mutiny in, II: 201
migrations of Hindus, Muslims, and
    Sikhs following partition, II: 345
militarism
    dangers of, II: 167–8
    Nehru's impatience with, II: 195
military disaffection in Indian National
    Army, II: 174–7
Mill, John Stuart, I: 171
minority groups, I: 496–7, 660; II: 527
Minto, Lord, I: 302
    See also Morley-Minto Reforms
Mississippi Valley Committee, I: 550
Modern Review (periodical), I: 368, 498
Moghal period, I: 523
Mohammed, I: 167
monarchical system as a disappearing
    institution, II: 283

money-making, II: 60
Mongolia, I: 309, 433, 447
monks (Buddhist), I: 278
Montagu, Edwin, I: 44
Montagu-Chelmsford Reforms, I: 44–7
Montagu Declaration, I: 44–6
Moon, Penderel, on migrations following
    partition, II: 345
Moors: *see* Spanish Morocco
Moravia, I: 652
Morley, Lord, I: 280, 346. *See also*
    Morley-Minto Reforms
Morley-Minto Reforms, I: 24–6, 27, 44
Moscow Declaration (1943), II: 162
Motilal Nehru Report: *see* Nehru, Motilal
Moulvies: *see* Glossary
    and Gandhi's non-violence policy
    I: 60
Mountbatten, Lord
    becomes Viceroy, II: 287–8, 291, 294–
      5, 303
    his first impressions of Nehru and other
      leaders, II: 316
    first meeting with Nehru, II: 219–20
    and the Japanese surrender, II: 169
    Nehru's friendship with, and tribute on
      his leaving India, II: 410–12, 416
    triumphal reception in Malaya with
      Nehru, II: 219–21
Mountbatten Plan, II: 321–4
    acceptance of, II: 325
    Mountbatten's amendment of, II: 320
    Nehru's view of, II: 318–19
Munich I: 563–4
    pre-World War II crisis, appeasement
      and Pact, I: 420, 562, 585, 589–92,
      630, 647
Murphy, Ray, on Nehru and Mount-
    batten in Malaya, II: 219–21
Muslims, I: xiv, 5, 19–20, 22, 25, 48, 155,
    198, 199, 256, 370, 377, 395, 665;
    II: 110
    and Civil Disobedience, I: 223
    ideological fusion with other groups, I:
      328
    in Java, II: 181
    join in repelling invaders in Kashmir,
      II: 350

Muslims—*contd.*
and nationalism, I: 75
origins of, in India, I: 523, 558
and partition of India, II: 111
political and economic differences with
Hindus, I: 37–9, 62, 75, 112–18,
160, 301–4, 328–31, 408–9, 479,
604–5, 658, 670, 674
population figures, II: 95
religion and politics, I: 86
and results of partition, II: 345
of same stock as Hindus, II: 110
and talk of a separate Northwest state,
II: 102
See also Muslim League; Pan-Islamism
Muslim League, I: 25, 37–9, 46, 59–
62, 662, 665, 669; II: 345
adoption of Fourteen Points, I: 542
amendments to Motilal Nehru Report,
I: 169
anti-British development of, I: 61–2
calls for Direct Action, II: 242–3
and communal rule, II: 200
condoning of violence by, I: 546
and the Cripps Mission, II: 81, 85
decision to join Interim Government,
II: 259 ff.
and Fascism and Nazism, II: 344–5
and first post-war general election, II:
170
and Government of India Act, I: 364
and Hindu Mahasabha, I: 329
increasing power of, II: 129
Jinnah's leadership in, I: 64, 505–49
Liaquat Ali Khan and, I: 670
and Muslim members of the Executive
Council, II: 165–6
and Nehru's Objectives Resolution,
II: 302
non-participation in Constituent
Assembly, II: 321
and Pakistan, I: 64, 214, 515–16, 560,
670
and proposals for the Interim Government, II: 254–7
religious and medieval character of, II:
171
resolution on war aims of, I: 647

Muslims—*contd.*
rift with Congress, I: 170, 490, 505–49,
667–78, 687–8; II: 273–4, 287
See also Simla Conferences
Mussolini, Benito, I: 108, 111, 387, 417–
18, 562, 585, 587, 651
execution of, II: 162
See also Abyssinia, Italian occupation
of; Fascism; Italy
Mussoorie, and order of externment
issued against Nehru, I: 68–73, 106
Nehru's visit with family, I: 68
mutinies, II: 201–6

Nabha Jail, Nehru imprisoned in, I:
101–6
Nagasaki, atomic bomb dropped on, II:
168–9
Nagpur: *see* Congress
Nagri script, I: 541
Naini Prison, Nehru imprisoned in, I:
224, 229, 343, 357
Nanak, Guru (founder of Sikh religion),
I: 558
Naoroji, Dadabhai, I: 9
Narayan, Jaya Prakash, I: 423
National Academy of Sciences, I: 551
national freedom for all countries, Nehru's
ideal of, II: 164
National Government
Nehru on composition of, II: 111
proposals for, II: 103–4
Rajagopalachari's proposals to Britain
for, II: 34
National Planning Committee, I: 656,
688–98
Nehru and, II: 49–50
National Publications Society, I: 485 *n.*
National Week, I: 52, 219
nationalism, I: 4, 19, 22–3, 27, 176, 212
262, 282, 287, 308, 313, 398, 428,
600
anti-British feeling, I: 75
in Bengal, I: 22, 28
Congress and, I: 637
dominating political ideology, I: 280
as a force in Asia, I: 314–18; II: 496–7
Gandhi and, I: 52, 58, 575

nationalism—*contd.*
 growth of, in Eastern countries, II:
  545-6
 hatred as a result of, II: 544
 history of, in India, II: 546-50
 and Indian Communist Party, II: 517
 middle classes and peasantry and, I: 257
 Muslim *bourgeoisie* and, I: 302
 ordinances against, I: 258
 and political unity, I: 560
 revival of Nationalist Movement, I:
  35-6, 40-41, 173
 Simon Commission and, I: 140
 summary of, I: 574-80
 Tagore and, I: 251
nationalization of industries, II: 186
Naval Disarmament Conference, I: 143
Nazism, I: 213, 279, 289, 345, 428, 445,
  546, 562, 615, 617, 620, 637, 643,
  646, 650-2; II: 20, 28-9, 103, 358
 Muslim League and, II: 344-5
Nehru Family, I: 45; II: 543
 Kashmiri Brahmins, I: 4-5
 and background, I: 351
Nehru, Indira (*see also* Gandhi, Indira
 Nehru), I: 69, 384, 419, 501, 561; II:
  57, 543
 Nehru's letters to, I: 260 ff., 595
Nehru, Kamala Kaul, I: 41, 68-73, 118,
  213, 228, 230, 236, 260, 337, 357,
  383-4, 417, 419
Nehru, Motilal, I: xv, 3-13, 17, 25-6, 36,
  38-41, 49-52, 69-73, 77-9, 82,
  85-6, 90, 98-100, 102, 105, 127,
  140-1, 151, 183, 190-2, 194, 213,
  224, 228-30, 235, 239-41, 357-8;
  II: 543
 heads committee on constitution question, I: 169-70
 Jawaharlal's early relationship with, I:
  14-16
 on his son's proposed Presidency of
  Congress, I: 187-90
 Motilal Nehru Report (1928), I: 168-
  70, 189
Nehru, Swaruprani, I: 3, 68-71, 195, 213,
  240, 260, 295-6, 337, 384, 419,
  561; II: 543

Nepal, II: 269
nepotism, I: 107
Nestorians (Christian sect), I: 558
Netaji (the Leader): *see* Bose, Subhas
Netherlands (Holland)
 and Indonesia, II: 334, 465
 Nehru visits, I: 119
 See also Eighteen Nations Conference
Netherlands East Indies, I: 144
 See also Indonesia
New Times (periodical), I: 534
New York Times, Nehru article on India,
  II: 108-11
New Zealand, I: 320, 640
newar weaving (*see* Glossary) as one of
 Nehru's occupations in prison, I:
  230
News Chronicle, Nehru cables to, on World
 War II, I: 657
Noakhali, violence in, II: 271
non-alignment, India's policy of, II: 302
  540, 541
Non-Co-operation Movement, I: 359, 627
 beginning of, I: 49, 68, 487
 and Delhi Congress, I: 100-1
 gains impetus, I: 73-7, 413
 Gandhi and, I: 47-50, 100, 114, 229,
  271, 396
 and independence, I: 159
 and World War II, I: 681
 See also Civil Disobedience
non-violence, I: 75, 683
 confusion in India on, II: 205
 and India's armed forces, II: 22-3, 105
 Nehru on, I: 81; II: 26
No-Rent Campaign, I: 258
Norman, Dorothy, I: vii, 129 *n.*, 564 *n.*
 II: 62 *n.*, 221 *n.*, 575
North-West Frontier Province, II: 323-4
 and invasion of Kashmir, II: 346, 348-9
Norway, I: 640
No-Tax Campaign, I: 231-3

Oakes, M. L. (Superintendent of Police,
 Mussoorie), Nehru and, I: 70-2
Objectives Resolution, Nehru's, II: 294-
  302, 424-8
Officers' Training Corps, I: 16

Official Secrets Act, I: 8
Oppressed Nationalities, Congress of: *see*
League Against Imperialism
Overseas Press Club, New York, Nehru's
speech at, II: 495-9
Owen, Robert (British social reformer), I:
131

pacifists, Nehru's views on, I: 401
Pakistan
accused of organizing raids on Kashmir,
II: 351, 376-8
Congress regards creation as a disaster,
II: 291
creation of, II: 333-40
developments leading to creation of, II:
291, 345
hate propaganda in, II: 445
India's relations with, II: 526
joint declaration for avoidance of war,
II: 527-9
and Kashmir problem, II: 346-7
and Kashmir Standstill Agreement, II:
346
Muslim League's election policy, II: 170
Nehru's attitude toward formation of,
II: 171
population exchange proposals, II: 529
as proposed autonomous Muslim area,
I: 64, 214, 515-16, 560, 670
protests about Indian action in Kashmir, II: 351-2
psychological problem of India and, II:
461
suggested connotations of the name, II:
224
See also partition
Palestine, I: 120, 180, 407, 449, 569-70,
580, 591, 596, 606
Pan-Islamism, rebirth of, II: 11
Panchayat and *Panchayati Raj* (*see*
Glossary), I: 56, 133, 481; II: 540
Pandit, Vijaya Lakshmi, II: 543
Pant, Pandit G. B., II: 166
Parliament, composition of, II: 572
Partabgarh, peasants' march from, I: 53,55
partition
bitterness and violence as aftermath to,
II: 538-9

partition—*contd.*
Jinnah as champion of, II: 111
and the Mountbatten Plan, II: 321 ff.
the Muslim League and, II: 129
Nehru's attitude toward, II: 345, 413
and 2nd Simla Conference, II: 225-8
tremendous problems of, II: 504-5
See also Pakistan
Patel, Sardar (Vallabhbhai), I: 189-90,
247, 421, 454-5; II: 194, 261, 261 *n.*
Gandhi and, I: 371
and the mutinies, II: 206
Nehru's tribute to, II: 375
his offices under Independence, II: 291
and the Princely States, II: 292, 331-2
Pathan, I: 322-3
Pearl Harbor, Japanese attack on, II: 62
peasant movement: *see Kisan*
Peasant Unions, I: 543
P.E.N., Nehru as Vice-President of
Indian Centre of the, II: 186
Persia, I: 197, 304, 407
Indian troops sent to, I: 125, 633
Persian as a Court language in India, I:
523
role of Persian language in Indian
literature, II: 187
and Russia, I: 165
Pethick-Lawrence, Lord, II: 194, 205,
225, 231
Phillips, William (Roosevelt's envoy to
New Delhi), II: 128
anxiety over India's situation in World
War II, II: 136-8
conveys Roosevelt's concern over
Gandhi's fast, II: 136
pietism, Gandhi's influence on, I: 64
Pioneer, the (Indian periodical), I: 15
Pius XI, Pope, I: 377
Plato, I: 553
Poland, I: 649-51, 653, 661, 678
Anglo-Polish mutual assistance agreement (1939), I: 634
invaded by Germany, I: 634, 641, 646,
657
preparations for war in, I: 143
invaded by Russia, I: 634
Police Force, International, II: 164-5

Poona Pact, I: 273-4
population exchange (India and Pakistan),
    Nehru on proposals for, II: 529-30
population figures, II: 95
    before and after Independence, II:
    571-3
    rural increases against urban, II: 510
Portugal and colonial territory in India,
    II: 538
poverty in India, I: 53-6, 154, 163-4, 178,
    231, 261, 310, 449
    as a danger to prosperity and world
    peace, II: 526
    industrialization as a cure for, II: 101
    Nehru on conditions and causes of, II:
    183, 250-1
    over-burden on land as basic reason
    for, II: 510
Prasad, Rajendra, I: 46, 421, 424, 454-7,
    537, 668, 687; II: 21, 560
    becomes first President of India, II: 572
Prayashchit (see Glossary), I: 4
Press Laws, I: 24
Prime Ministers Conference (London,
    1948-9), II: 414, 471 ff.
Princely States, the
    attitude toward independence, II: 228-9
    Britain and, II: 562-5
    description and history of, II: 562-5,
    571
    problem of, after independence, II:
    331-2
    proposals for role of, under indepen-
    dence, II: 92-3
    and Nehru's Objectives Resolution,
    II: 297
    Sardar Patel and, II: 292
    and transfer of power, II: 331-2
prison sentences, Nehru's: initial refer-
    ences, I: first, 77; second, 91; third,
    101; fourth, 224; fifth, 230; sixth,
    258; seventh, 340. II: eighth, 42;
    ninth, 127
Proja Party (Muslim organization), I: 543
property tax, II: 7
prophets and sages, II: 530-6
prostitutes, segregation of, I: 107
provinces, list of, II: 571

Provincial autonomy: see Government of
    India Act
Provincial Governments
    their problems and independence, II:
    342
    proposals for, II: 245
Provisional Government: see Interim
    Government
Public Safety Ordinance, I: 181
public speaking, Nehru's early attitude
    toward, II: 500
Punjab
    approach of partition causes communal
    conflict in, II: 331
    martial law in, I: 47, 50-2
    and the Mountbatten Plan, II: 322-3
    Muslim and Hindu population figures,
    II: 95
    Nehru speaks at Provincial Conference
    in (1928), I: 155-61
    and Pakistan, II: 172
    proposals to divide, II: 306-9
    Provincial Government's crisis and inde-
    pendence, II: 342-4
    violence in, II: 308-9
Purna Swaraj (see Glossary), I: 210, 216;
    II: 473
Pyarelal, C.
    on Inter-Asian Relations Conference
    (1947), II: 309
    the Interim Government, II: 244
    the "Quit India" movement, II: 117
Pythagoras, I: 5

Question of Language, The (Nehru's
    article), I: 518-30, 531, 541
"Quit India" movement, II: 117-27
    Nehru on the Resolution, II: 123-7
    prison sentences follow, II: 127

racial discrimination, II: 103, 195, 222,
    264-5, 415, 537, 557
Rajagopalachari, C. R., I: 454-5
    on Nehru's opposition to Nazism and
    Fascism, II: 105-6
    on proposals for a Provisional National
    Government, II: 34
Ramakrishna, Sri, II: 531-6

Ramayana (Indian Epic), I: 324
"Rashtrapati, The" (Nehru anonymous article, opposing his re-election to Congress), I: 498 (*see Chanakya*)
Razakars, II: 434 (*see* Hyderabad)
Reading, Lord, I: 77, 117
refugee problems, II: 449
following independence and partition, II: 342-3
Rekhta (Persianized form of Hindi language), I: 523
religion
Nehru on organized, I: 87-9
on I: 349-50, 450; II: 182, 544
Republic as Nehru's aim for India, II: 278-87
Resolution of Remembrance, I: 237, 238
Responsivists, I: 292
Reuters Agency, I: 631
Revolt of 1857, I: 22, 123, 301
R.I.A.F.: *see* Royal Indian Air Force
Right *v.* Left groups, II: 542
R.I.N.: *see* Royal Indian Navy
Rolland, Romain, I: 129, 267
Roman Catholicism, I: 88-9, 374
Roosevelt, Franklin D., I: 583; II: 71, 128, 135-7
and the Atlantic Charter, II: 54
at Casablanca and Cairo Conferences (1943), II: 135
concern for results of Gandhi's fast, II: 136
and the Cripps Mission, II: 90-2
and Indian independence, II: 78-9, 501
Round Table Conferences, I: 422, 428
First (1930), I: 210, 236-7, 241, 242
Second (1931), I: 253-7, 258, 270
Third (1932), I: 274-5, 293, 298, 363, 395
Rowlatt Acts, I: 47-8, 52, 162,
Royal Agricultural Commission, I: 222
Royal Air Force, mutiny in India in the, II: 201
Royal Indian Air Force, hunger strikes in, II: 201
Royal Indian Navy, I: 144
grievances and indiscipline in, II: 201 ff.

Ruskin, John, II: 183
Russell, Bertrand, I: 13, 41
Russia, I: 34, 45, 80, 108, 139, 156, 166, 182, 197, 320, 332, 409-10, 516, 585, 637
All-Russia Congress of Soviets, I: 132-3
and the Anti-Comintern Pact, I: 650
as a bulwark against Fascism, I: 624, 630
and Communist Party of India, II: 183-4
"Dictatorship of the Proletariat", I: 133
foreign policy, I: 624, 630
Germany invades, II: 53
growth of Soviet Republic, I: 629-30
India's desire for close contact with, II: 102, 167-8
invades Poland, I: 634, 650
Kerensky period, I: 57, 132
and Nazism, II: 28-9
Nehru's attitude toward, I: 128-37, 161, 369, 450
first visit to, I: 58, 119, 128-37,
his view of invasion of Finland, II: 9-10, 15-16
post-World War II policies of, II: 216
preparations for war, I: 143
relations with Britain, I: 410, 630
with Germany, I: 650-2, 661
with U.S.A., I: 135, 587, 630
revolution's effect on India, I: 56-8, 311
termination of Comintern, II: 135
Union of Peasant Labourers, I: 134
village soviets, I: 133-4
in World War II, I: 649-50, 661; II: 14-17
Young People's League, and other youth movements, I: 134
Russo-German ten-year non-aggression pact (1939), I: 634; II: 9
as an example of opportunism, II: 15
Russo-Japanese War, I: 6, 22
effect on morale in Asia, II: 546

St John Ambulance Brigade, I: 28

Salt March, the (Gandhi's resistance to the salt tax), I: 218–20, 223, 412
Samurai (Japanese warrior class), I: 309
Sanskrit language, role of, in Indian literature, II: 187–92
Sapru, Sir Tej Bahadur, I: 228, 238
Sapru-Jayakar proposals, I: 228–9, 238
Sarkar Salaam (*see* Glossary), I: 344
Saturday Review, the, on Indian self-government, I: 16
Satyagraha (*see* Glossary), I: 49–50, 87, 236, 296, 347, 612
  its value in strengthening the Indian people, II: 65
  views of Gandhi and Nehru on, II: 20, 21
science, II: 553
  effects of advances in, II: 521
  Indian Science Congresses, I: 549, 551
  Nehru as a devotee of, II: 357
  political implications of, I: 549–53
Sea Customs Act, I: 368
Second International, I: 181
Sedition Bill (British), I: 293
self-government: see *Swaraj*
self-help, as first condition of a nation's success, II: 493
Sen Gupta, J. M., I: 188–9
separate electorates, I: 25, 46–7
  See also communalism, Congress, Muslim League
separatism, Muslims' proposal of, for North-West India, II: 102
Sepoy Mutiny: see Revolt of 1857
Servants of India Society, I: 27
Shah, K. T., I: 485 *n.*
Shanghai, British troops sent to, I: 180
Shankaracharya, I: 557
Shaw, George Bernard
  Nehru's interest in, I: 13; II: 416–18
  on Stalin and Hitler, I: 651
Sheikh Saheb: *see* Abdullah
Short History of the Indian People, The (Green), I: 171
Siberia, I: 309
Sikhs
  ideological fusion with other groups, I: 328

Sikhs—*contd.*
  join in repelling invaders in Kashmir, II: 350
  population figures, II: 95
  results of partition, II: 342, 345
  and Simla Conference (1945), II: 166
Simla Conferences
  (1945), II: 165–6
  (1946), II: 225–8
Simon, Sir John: see Simon Commission
Simon Commission, I: 140, 141, 147, 149, 151, 168, 180, 183, 236, 422
Sind and the Muslim League, II: 170
Singapore
  British naval base at, I: 144
  mutiny in, I: 30
  vested interests in, II: 103
Singh, Sardar Baldev (Sikh leader), II: 176–7
Sinn Fein, I: 12
Sitaramayya, Dr P., on the Untouchables, I: 274
Smith, James (British trade unionist), as probable initial outliner of Soviet idea, I: 131
social reform, I: 287–8
social services, I: 690
Socialism, I: 13, 79, 117, 129, 212, 283, 299–300, 336, 346, 401, 516, 697
  Congress Socialist Party, I: 370–1, 421–2, 574–6
  freedom of the individual under I: 626; II: 164
  Gandhi and, I: 213, 375–6, 378
  Nehru's interest in, and advocacy of, I: 139–140, 153 ff., 203, 213
  on role of, in India, II: 413
  spread of ideas, I: 280
  and world federation, I: 318
Society of Friends (Dublin), Tagore and the, I: 369
Socrates, I: 266
soil erosion as a problem in India, II: 512
South Africa, I: 27, 28, 202, 209
  Nehru on racial policy in, II: 222, 267–8, 270, 415
  on U.N. policy in, II: 222, 267–8

South Africa—*contd.*
treatment of Indians as a world issue, II: 469
South America, I: 565
South-East Asia
India and, II: 215
Nehru's visit to, II: 218
South-West Africa, Nehru's opposition to South Africa's proposed annexation of, II: 268
Soviet Russia (Nehru), I: 129–137
Soviet Russia: *see* Russia
Spain
Britain and, II: 9
Civil War in, I: 420, 448–9, 562–3, 624, 627
Fascism in, I: 345, 448, 472–3, 566, 569, 571–4, 580, 587, 593, 596, 600, 606, 608, 615, 628, 643, 645
Liberalism in, I: 345
Nehru visits, I: 562–3
Spanish Morocco, Fascist regime's treatment of, I: 571
speeches, Nehru criticizes misleading reports of his, II: 44
Spinners Association, I: 444
Nehru as Secretary of, I: 118
spinning as one of Nehru's occupations in prison, I: 99, 230
spinning wheel in India's economy, I: 95, 623
Spinoza, Benedict, I: 383
Stalin, Josef, I: 650, 651
Stalingrad, battle of, II: 135
States and Agencies (Indian), list of the, II: 571
Statesman, the (newspaper), Indian leaders statements in, I: 347, 534
Stilwell, General Joseph (U.S. Army), II: 136
Streit, Clarence, and his concept of Federal Union, I: 640
strikes, II: 201
Nehru's attitude toward, II: 413
student demonstrations, II: 201
Sudetenland Germans, comparison of with Indian Muslims, I: 546

Sun Yat-sen, Madame, Nehru's meetings with, I: 129
Swadeshi (*see* Glossary), I: 11, 23, 282, 291, 310, 373
Swaraj (*see* Glossary), I: 9, 11, 14, 52, 55, 76, 87, 97, 100, 109, 115, 140–1, 158–9, 229, 248, 286, 306, 312, 362, 486
Purna Swaraj (*see* Glossary), I: 210, 216; II: 473
Swaraj Bhawan (Abode of Freedom), I: 337, 357–8, 362
Swaraj Bhawan Trust, I: 357, 361
Switzerland, I: 143, 640
Nehru visits, I: 119, 384
Sylhet, II: 323
Syria
and Brussels Congress, I: 120
independence of, II: 101
rebellion against the French, I: 162

Tagore, Sir Rabindranath, I: 251, 290–1, 353, 368–9, 384, 420, 636
Nehru on, II: 56–9, 530–1
talukdars (*see* Glossary), I: xiv, 55, 281–3, 327, 382, 692
Tamil, impress of India on the, I: 322–3
Tao (The Way or Path), I: 89
Taxila, University of, I: 323
Teheran, Allied leaders (in World War II) meet at, II: 135
Thailand, France cedes Indo-Chinese territory to, II: 53
Theosophical Society, I: 6
theosophy, I: 5, 6
Third International, I: 181–2
Thompson, Edward (writer on Indian history), II: 4 *n.*
Thoreau, Henry David, I: 289
Tibet
Indian troops sent to, I: 125
Chinese invasion of, II: 536
Tilak, Bal Gangadhar, I: 8, 11, 14–15, 23–4, 27, 35–6, 44, 59, 68, 487
Toller, Ernst, I: 129
Toward Freedom (Nehru's autobiography), I: 372, 416, 458

trade, international II: 511
Trades Disputes Act, I: 181
trade unions, right to form, II: 170
    See also All-India Trade Union Con-
        gress
Tranquillity Acts, I: 368
Trevelyan, G. M., I: 11
Trincomalee, Royal Indian Naval base at,
    I: 144
Tripuri: see Congress
Truman, Harry, and Point Four, II: 514
Turkey, I: 61, 156, 167, 197, 304
    Britain at war with, I: 37, 407
    dismemberment of the Ottoman Em-
        pire, I: 59
    Indian troops sent to, I: 29, 125
    and Russian aggression, II: 216

Uganda, Nehru on conduct of Indians in,
    I: 168
Ulemas (see Glossary), Gandhi and the,
    I: 60
underground organizations in Europe in
    World War II, II: 204
Union Now (Clarence Streit), I: 640
Union of Peasant Labourers (Russia), I:
    134
United Nations, II: 464, 517
    and equity in world's resources, II:
        216
    first Indian delegation to, II: 354
    and the Kashmir question, II: 376,
        377-8, 569-71
    Nehru's address to General Assembly
        (Paris, 1948), II: 419-24
    his attitude toward, II: 197-8
    on India's association with, II: 267,
        457
    signing of the Charter, II: 162
United Provinces Agrarian Movement: see
    Agrarian Movement
United Provinces Political Conference
    (1923), Nehru as President of, I:
    108-12
United States of America, I: 158, 166,
    279, 320, 516, 662; II: 103,
    416

United States of America—contd.
    compelled to join war after Japanese
        attack, II: 167
    and 1929 depression, I: 313
    exchange of representatives with India,
        II: 54
    important future role of, II: 97
    and Indian independence, II: 77-8
    India's desire for close contacts and
        co-operation with, II: 102-3, 168,
        501, 506, 508
    and lend-lease, II: 53
    Nehru addresses American audience,
        on freedom, I: 554-60
    he analyzes, II: 508
    his first visit to, and speeches in, II:
        490-516
    receives honorary degree in, II: 493-5
    non-recognition of Soviet Russia, I: 135
    relations with Japan, I: 410
    responsibility of, toward India, II: 105
    on strategic importance of India in
        World War II, II: 55
    and understanding of India's problems,
        II: 3-4
    and its Western allies, I: 652
    and wheat for India, II: 511, 518
unity
    Nehru on Indian unity, I: 555-7; II:
        400-1
    see also Unity Conference
Unity Conference (Allahabad), I: 540
universities, II: 356-60
U.N.: see United Nations
Untouchables, I: 20, 268, 270-4, 285-6,
    300, 340, 435, 499
    Nehru on the, II: 250, 509
    proposal to abolish Untouchability, II:
        169
    and Simla Conference (1945), II: 166
Upanishads (philosophical dialogues), I: 6;
    II: 548
Urdu language, I: 518-31; II: 188, 190

Vedic Age, I: 155-6
Viceroys: see Glossary
    Nehru on, I: 246

Viceroys—*contd.*
Initial references to Viceroys cited, beginning 1899, *see* Lords: I: Curzon (1899–1905), 7; Minto (1905–10), 25; Hardinge (1910–16), 26; Chelmsford (1916–21), 44; Reading (1921–26), 77; Irwin (1926–31), 117; Willingdon (1931–36), 246; Linlithgow (1936–43), 399. II: Wavell (1943–47), 137; Mountbatten (1947); Governor General of Independent India, 1947–48), 287
village-elected councils: *see Panchayat*
village industries, II: 112–14
Gandhi and, II: 113
Village Industries Association, I: 444, 689
village life, Gandhi and Nehru on, II: 178, 179
violence
intensified by independence, II: 291
widespread communal, II: 252–4, 270–2, 308
See also communalism
Vivekananda, Swami, II: 532–3, 535–6
Vyapar Mandal (Association to Boycott Foreign Cloth), I: 94
See also boycotts

war, proposed Indo-Pakistan declaration on, II: 527–9
Wavell, Lord,
and 1946 Cabinet Mission, II: 231–3
differences with Nehru and Jinnah, II: 242, 245
and India's strategical importance in World War II, II: 162
and Nehru, on formation of the Interim Government, II: 247–63
and proposals for reconstitution of the Executive Council, II: 163
seeks fresh solution to "Indian problem", II: 169
and the Simla Conference (1945), II: 166

Wavell, Lord—*contd.*
succeeds Lord Linlithgow as Viceroy, II: 137
Wedderburn, Sir William (President of Allahabad Congress), and Hindu-Muslim Conference, I: 38
Wedgwood Benn and Dominion Status, I: 200, 201
"weightage" (*see* Glossary), I: 169
wheat
effect of wheat prices on cost of other commodities, II: 511
for India, from U.S.A., II: 511, 518
"white man's burden" of Empire, II: 555
will and testament of Nehru, extracts from, II: 573–5
Willingdon, Lord, I: 246
Wilson, Woodrow, and his Fourteen Points, I: 46
Winant, John G. (American Ambassador to Britain)
on Indian freedom, II: 77–8
on strategic importance of India as a war-base, II: 55
women
contribution of Indian, I: 412–13, II: 508–9
equality advocated for, I: 66, 183
mistreatment of, I: 275–6
Wood, Dr Joseph (Headmaster of Harrow), on Nehru as a pupil, I: 10
Workers' and Peasants' Party (1926), I: 139
World Bank and loans to India, II: 512
world issues, II: 63, 514
world organization, Nehru on, I: 636–41; II: 51–2, 168, 399–400, 470, 524
World War I
changes following, I: 427, 595
effect of, on Indian industry, I: 310, 312
India's situation, on eve of, I: 19–24
Nehru's views on, I: 161–2
reactionary attitudes following, I: 637
World War II
Congress statement on, II: 100
Congress Working Committee Resolution on, I: 641–8
developments in, II: 28–32, 135, 162

World War II—*contd.*
Nehru on India's political faith on eve of, I: 624–34
on war, I: 648–59, 679–86; II: 3 ff.
war resistance policy, I: 628–9, 633; II: 459, 467–9

Yalta Conference, II: 162

Young People's League (Russian organization), I: 134

zamindar (*see* Glossary), I: 30, 54, 160, 231, 281–3, 295, 298, 307, 327, 352, 382, 490, 543, 692; II: 496
Zetland, Lord, I: 647 *n.*, 665–6, 668, 682